DAVIESS COUNTY COURT HOUSE AND FAMOUS OLD ELM.

HISTORY OF DAVIESS COUNTY INDIANA

Its People, Industries and Institutions

A. O. Fulkerson

HERITAGE BOOKS
2013

HERITAGE BOOKS
AN IMPRINT OF HERITAGE BOOKS, INC.

Books, CDs, and more—Worldwide

For our listing of thousands of titles see our website
at
www.HeritageBooks.com

A Facsimile Reprint
Published 2013 by
HERITAGE BOOKS, INC.
Publishing Division
5810 Ruatan Street
Berwyn Heights, Md. 20740

Copyright © 2001 Heritage Books, Inc.

Copyright © 1915 B. F. Bowen & Company, Inc.

— Publisher's Notice —

In reprints such as this, it is often not possible to remove blemishes from the original. We feel the contents of this book warrant its reissue despite these blemishes and hope you will agree and read it with pleasure.

This single volume was previously published as a two volume set.

International Standard Book Numbers
Paperbound: 978-0-7884-1840-2
Clothbound: 978-0-7884-6810-0

DEDICATION.

This work is respectfully dedicated to

THE PIONEERS,

long since departed. May the memory of those who laid down their burdens by the wayside ever be fragrant as the breath of summer flowers, for their toils and sacrifices have made Daviess County a garden of sunshine and delights.

PREFACE

All life and achievement is evolution; present wisdom comes from past experience, and present commercial prosperity has come only from past exertion and suffering. The deeds and motives of the men who have gone before have been instrumental in shaping the destinies of later communities and states. The development of a new country was at once a task and a privilege. It required great courage, sacrifice and privation. Compare the present conditions of the people of Daviess county, Indiana, with what they were one hundred years ago. From a trackless wilderness and virgin land, it has come to be a center of prosperity and civilization, with millions of wealth, systems of railways, grand educational institutions, splendid industries and immense agricultural and mineral productions. Can any thinking person be insensible to the fascination of the study which discloses the aspirations and efforts of the early pioneers who so strongly laid the foundation upon which has been reared the magnificent prosperity of later days? To perpetuate the story of these people and to trace and record the social, political and industrial progress of the community from its first inception is the function of the local historian. A sincere purpose to preserve facts and personal memoirs that are deserving of perpetuation, and which unite the present to the past, is the motive for the present publication. A specially valuable and interesting department is that one devoted to the sketches of representative citizens of these counties whose records deserve preservation because of their worth, effort and accomplishment. The publishers desire to extend their thanks to the gentlemen who have so faithfully labored to this end. Thanks are also due to the citizens of Daviess county for the uniform kindness with which they have regarded this undertaking, and for their many services rendered in the gaining of necessary information.

In placing the "History of Daviess County, Indiana," before the citizens, the publishers can conscientiously claim that they have carried out the plan as outlined in the prospectus. Every biographical sketch in the work has been submitted to the party interested, for correction, and therefore any error of fact, if there be any, is solely due to the person for whom the sketch was prepared. Confident that our effort to please will fully meet the approbation of the public, we are,

Respectfully,

THE PUBLISHERS.

CONTENTS

CHAPTER I—RELATED STATE HISTORY 33
First White Man in Northwest Territory—English and French Claims—Three Successive Sovereign Flags Over Present Indiana Territory—Passing of the Indians—Battle of Fallen Timbers—Northwest Territory—Early Settlements—Activities of the Traders—French and Indian War—Pontiac's Conspiracy—Northwest Territory and Quebec Act—Revolutionary Period—George Rogers Clark and His Campaign—First Surveys and Early Settlers—Ordinance of 1787—First Stage of Government Under the Ordinance—Second Stage—Organization of the Northwest Territory—Representative Stage of Government—First Counties Organized—First Territorial Legislature of Northwest Territory—Division of 1800—Census of Northwest Territory in 1800—Settlements in Indiana Territory in 1800—First Stage of Territorial Government—Changes in Boundary Lines of Indiana—Second Stage of Territorial Government—The Legislative Council—The First General Assemblies—Congressional Delegates of Indiana Territory—Efforts to Establish Slavery in Indiana—The Indian Lands—Organization of Counties—Changes in the Constitution of Indiana—Capitals of Northwest Territory and of Indiana—Military History of State—Political History—Governors of Indiana—A Century of Growth—Natural Resources.

CHAPTER II—PHYSICAL AND GEOLOGICAL FEATURES 63
Location and Area of County—Topography—Elevation—Coal Discoveries—Cannel Coal.

CHAPTER III—EARLY SETTLEMENT OF DAVIESS COUNTY 65
The First Actual Settler—Other Early Settlers—Congressional Donations of Land to Early Settlers—Land Titles—Emigration Receives a Setback—Indian Troubles—Measures for Protection—Forts and Block Houses—Encounter with Indians—Killing of Thomas Eagle—Occupations of Early Settlers—First Mills—Early Clothing Material—Pioneer Farm Implements and Machinery.

CHAPTER IV—CREATION AND ORGANIZATION OF THE COUNTY ... 81
Naming of the County—Legislative Act Creating Daviess County—Organization—The County Seat—First Court House—Second Court House—Present Court House—County Jails—The County Infirmary.

CONTENTS.

CHAPTER V—COUNTY GOVERNMENT _____ 91
Commissioner System—The County Council—Early Business Proceedings—Interesting Sidelights—Sundry Orders of the Board—Rates of Tavern Keepers—Order for a Court House—First Settlement with County Treasurer—Criminals Branded—Debtors' Room—Completion of Court House—Completion of First Jail—County Deficit—Board of County Justices—New Form of Government—Return to Board of Justices System—Board of Commissioners Again.

CHAPTER VI—POLITICAL HISTORY _____ 108
Board of County Commissioners—Auditor—Clerk of the Circuit Court—Sheriff—Treasurer—Recorder—Surveyor—Coroner—Prosecuting Attorney—State Senators—Representatives in the Legislature—Presidential Electors, 1844 to 1912.

CHAPTER VII—THE WABASH AND ERIE CANAL _____ 122
Competition with Eastern States as to Internal Improvements—Congressional Act Authorizing Wabash and Erie Canal—Financial Crash of 1847—Incidents of Canal Days—Whiskey as Free as Water—Cholera Epidemic—Traveling on a Canal Boat.

CHAPTER VIII—AGRICULTURE AND STATISTICS _____ 130
Reclaiming Waste Lands—Modern Methods Applied in Farming—Statistical Items of Interest—Daviess County Productions—Valuations—County Auditor's Report—Social Statistics—Local Option Elections—Rise and Fall of the Daviess County Fair.

CHAPTER IX—THE "UNDERGROUND RAILROAD" _____ 137
The Fugitive Slave Law—Great Risks in the Operation of the "Underground Railroad"—Slavery in Daviess County—An Early Kidnapping Case—Route of the "Underground Railroad"—Its Operations in Daviess County—Officers Outwitted—A Washington Kidnapping Case.

CHAPTER X—DAVIESS COUNTY IN WAR _____ 148
War with Mexico—War Between the States—Daviess County's Patriotic Resolution—First Company of Volunteers—The Sixth Regiment—"Copperheads"—Various Commands in Which Daviess County Soldiers Served—Losses—Scattering Military Events—Home Guards—Daviess County Escapes Draft—Recruits and Veterans—Soldiers' and Sailors' Monument—The Oldest Veteran.

CHAPTER XI—DAVIESS COUNTY NEWSPAPERS _____ 177
First Journalistic Ventures—Washington Papers—Mayor Knocks Editor Down—"Press Day" in Olden Times—Other Newspapers of the County.

CHAPTER XII—CHURCH HISTORY OF DAVIESS COUNTY _____ 184
Presbyterian Churches—Methodist Episcopal Churches—Christian Churches—The Baptist Church—United Brethren Church—Catholic Churches—Interesting Reminiscences—Summary of Church History.

CONTENTS.

CHAPTER XIII—EDUCATIONAL HISTORY 207
Early Schools—First School Houses—Early Teachers—Curriculum of Pioneer Schools—Locking the Teacher Out—School Examiners—School Laws Changed—Views of an Examiner—The County Institute—County Superintendents—A Strenuous Election Contest—A Resume of the Work of the County Superintendents—County Teachers' Association—County Institutes—Rural Elementary Schools—Early Washington Schools—Superintendents and Principals—School Buildings—Elnora Schools—Odon Schools—Catholic Schools—County Seminary.

CHAPTER XIV—THE BENCH AND BAR 246
Establishment of the Circuit Court—First Judges and First Grand Jury—First Murder Case—Attorneys Admitted to Practice in the Early Courts—Circuit Court Judges—Prominent Attorneys Who Have Practiced in the Daviess Courts—Present Members of the Bar.

CHAPTER XV—PHYSICIANS AND SURGEONS 253
Registration of Physicians by Years—Optometrists—Dentists.

CHAPTER XVI—SECRET SOCIETIES 257
Free and Accepted Masons—Allied Organizations—Independent Order of Odd Fellows—Knights of Pythias—Ancient Order of Hibernians—Knights of Columbus.

CHAPTER XVII—PATRIOTIC ORDERS OF DAVIESS COUNTY 263
Grand Army of the Republic—Ladies of the Grand Army—Society of the Daughters of the American Revolution—Lineage of Members.

CHAPTER XVIII—TOWNSHIPS OF DAVIESS COUNTY 272
Veale Township—First Distillery—Washington Township—Reeve Township—Barr Township—Amusements of the Pioneers—Bogard Township—Elmore township—Madison Township—Steele Township—Harrison Township—Van Buren Township.

CHAPTER XIX—TOWNS AND VILLAGES 281
Alfordsville — Albright — Black Oak — Cannelburg — Chelsea — Cornettsville—Corbytown—Cosby — Corning—Cumback — Eldon—Elnora—Epsom—Farlen—Glen Dale—Graham—Hyatt — Hudsonville—Jacob—Jordan—Lasca—Lettsville—Liverpool—Marsh—Maysville—Montgomery—Odon—Plainville—Raglesville—Sandy Hook—Smiley—South Washington—Thomas—Trainor—Tom's Hill—Waco—Postoffices in Daviess County Outside of Washington.

CHAPTER XX—CITY OF WASHINGTON 299
First Called Liverpool—Original Plat—Additions—First Buildings and Stores—Early Business Interests—Professional Interests—Slow Growth—Incorporation of the Town—Organization Under a City Charter—Banks—City Finances—Public Utilities—Railroad Shops—Postoffice—Public Library.

HISTORICAL INDEX

A

Agricultural Societies _____ 134
Agriculture _____ 130
Albright _____ 282
Alfordsville _____268, 282, 296
Altitudes _____ 63
Amusements of Pioneers_____ 275
Ancient Order of Hibernians_____ 261
Asiatic Cholera _____ 127
Attorneys _____ 246
Attorneys, Prominent _____ 249
Auditor's Report, County_____ 133
Auditors, County _____ 110

B

Baptist Church _____ 190
Barr Township—
   Area _____ 275
   Churches _____196, 205
   Name _____ 274
   Natural Resources _____ 275
   Organization of _____ 274
   Population _____ 275
   Settlement _____ 274
Battle of Fallen Timbers_____34, 41
Bench and Bar _____ 246
Benevolent Institutions, State____ 61
Black Oak _____282, 296
Block Houses _____ 69
Board of County Justices_____104, 106
Bogard Township—
   Churches _____ 205
   First Settlers _____ 276
   Land Entries _____ 276
   Name _____ 276
   Organization of _____ 276
   Population _____ 276
   Settlement _____ 276
Boundaries of Indiana, Changes in_ 47
Business Proceedings of County____ 93

C

Canal-boat Experiences _____ 128
Canal Days _____ 125
Canal History _____ 122
Cannel Coal _____ 64
Cannelburg _____282, 296
Capitals of Indiana _____ 54
Capitals of Northwest Territory___ 54
Capture of Vincennes _____ 37
Catholic Churches _____ 195
Catholic Schools _____ 242
Census of Northwest Territory ____ 44
Changes in State Constitution_____ 52
Chelsea _____ 283
Cholera Epidemics _____ 127
Christian Churches _____188, 192
Church History _____ 184
Circuit Court Judges _____ 248
Civil War _____55, 148
Claims of English Colonies _____ 33
Claims of Northwest Territory_____ 34
Clerks of the Courts _____ 110
Clothing Material, Early _____ 77
Coal Discoveries _____ 64
Columbus, Knights of _____ 261
Commissioner System _____ 91
Commissioners' Acts, Early_____ 93
Commissioners, Board of_____94, 108
Congressional Land Donations_____ 66
Constitution, Changes in _____ 52
Constitutional Convention, 1850___ 53
"Copperheads" in Daviess County_ 154
Corbytown _____ 284
Cornettsville _____283, 296
Corning _____ 284
Coroners _____ 112
Cosby _____ 284
Counties, Organization of_____43, 51
County Auditors _____ 110
County Commissioners _____94, 108
County Council _____ 91

HISTORICAL INDEX.

County Fair ----------------------- 134
County Government -------------- 91
County Infirmary ------------------ 89
County Institute ------------- 217, 226
County Justices, Board of-------- 104
County Political History --------- 108
County Recorders ---------------- 112
County Seat Located ------------- 83
County Seminary ----------------- 244
County Superintendents ---------- 217
County Surveyors ---------------- 112
County Teachers' Association------ 225
County Treasurers ---------------- 111
Court House, First --------------- 84
Court House History--------84, 98, 101
Courts and Lawyers -------------- 246
Creation of Daviess County ------ 81
Criminals Branded --------------- 100
Cumback ------------------------- 284

D

Daughters of the American Revolution -------------------------- 269
Daviess County in War ----------- 148
Daviess County Newspapers ------ 177
Debtors' Room ------------------- 110
Dentists ------------------------- 256
Distillery, First in County--------- 272
Doctors ------------------------- 253
Draft, Daviess County Escapes----- 168
Drainage ------------------------ 63

E

Eagle, Thomas, Killing of--------72, 247
Early Clothing Material ---------- 77
Early Farm Implements --------- 78
Early Lawyers ------------------ 248
Early Settlement ---------------- 65
Early Teachers ----------------- 209
Eastern Star, Order of --------- 259
Educational History ------------ 207
Educational System of State----- 61
Eldon -------------------------- 285
Election, First Territorial -------- 48
Elections, Local Option --------- 134
Elections, Presidential ---------- 114
Elementary Schools, Rural------- 230

Elmore Township—
  Character of Settlers ---------- 277
  Churches ---------------------- 205
  First Settlers ----------------- 276
  Land Entries ------------------ 277
  Name ------------------------- 276
  Organization ------------------ 276
  Population -------------------- 277
  Teachers, Early --------------- 210
Elnora—
  Bank -------------------------- 286
  Beginnings -------------------- 285
  Business Interests ------------- 283
  Churches ------------------188, 286
  Incorporation ----------------- 285
  Lodges ------------------------ 268
  Name Changed ---------------- 285
  Officers, First ---------------- 285
  Population -------------------- 287
  Postoffice -------------------- 297
  Public Utilities --------------- 286
  Schools ---------------------- 236
Encounter with Indians ----------- 70
English Colonies, Claims of------- 33
Epidemic of Cholera ------------- 127
Epsom -------------------------- 287

F

Fair, County -------------------- 134
Fallen Timbers, Battle of-----34, 41
Farlen -------------------------- 287
Farm Implements, Early --------- 78
Farm Statistics ----------------- 132
Farming Industry --------------- 130
Fifty-eighth Regiment ----------- 163
Fifty-second Regiment ---------- 161
First Court House --------------- 84
First General Assemblies -------- 49
First Saw-mill ------------------ 76
First Schools ------------------ 207
First Settler in County---------- 65
First Territorial Legislature ------ 43
First Territorial Surveys---------- 39
First White Men in Territory----- 33
Forts -------------------------- 69
Forty-second Regiment --------- 159
Fraternal Orders --------------- 257
Free and Accepted Masons-------- 257
French and Indian War --------- 35

HISTORICAL INDEX.

G

General Assemblies, First	49
Glen Dale	287
Governors of Indiana	58
Graham	288
Grain Mills, First	77
Grand Army of the Republic	263
Grand Jury, First	246

H

Harrison Township—
Churches	205
Creation of	106
First Settlers	279
Land Entries	280
Population	280
Hibernians, Ancient Order of	261
Home Guards	161
Hudsonville	288, 297
Hyatt	288, 297

I

Incidents of Canal Days	125
Independent Order of Odd Fellows	259
Indian Lands	50
Indian Struggles	41
Indian Troubles	67
Indian Wars	33
Indiana, Capitals of	54
Indiana, Changes in Boundaries	47
Indiana, Governors of	58
Indiana, Growth in Population	59
Indiana, Natural Resources	60
Indiana Political History	57
Indiana Territory, Settlement in	45
Indiana, Wealth of	60
Infirmary, County	89
Internal Improvements, State	37

J

Jacob	288
Jail History	87, 102
Jordan	288
Judges, Early	246
Judges of Circuit Court	248
Jury, First Grand	246
Justices of the Peace	94

K

Kidnapping Cases	139, 143
Killing of Thomas Eagle	72, 247
Knights of Columbus	261
Knights of Pythias	260
Knights Templar	259

L

Ladies of the G. A. R.	268
Land Donations by Congress	66
Land Titles, Early	66
Lands Purchased from Indians	51
Lasca	288
Lawyers Now at the Bar	251
Legislative Act Creating County	81
Legislative Council, First	48
Legislators	113
Legislature, First Territorial	43
Lettsville	289
Liverpool	84, 273, 289, 299
Local Option Elections	134
Locating the County Seat	83
Location of Daviess County	63
Lodges	257
Log School Houses	207
Loyalty of Daviess County in War	150

Madison Township—
Churches	206
Land Entries	277
Name Changed	106, 277
Organization of	277
Population	278
Settlement	277

M

Marsh	289
Masonic Order	257
Maysville	289
Medical History	253
Memorial to Capt. Joseph H. Daviess	83
Methodist Episcopal Churches	186
Mexican War	148
Military Events	160
Military History of County	148
Military History of Indiana	55
Mills	76, 291

HISTORICAL INDEX.

Montgomery—
Banks ---------------------- 291
Business Interests ---------- 291
Churches ---------------198, 291
First Events ---------------- 290
Growth --------------------- 290
Industries ------------------ 291
Location ------------------- 290
Marriage, An Early --------- 290
Mill ------------------------ 291
Postoffice ------------------ 297
Schools ----------------243, 290
Monument to Soldiers and Sailors-- 170

N

Natural Features ------------- 63
Natural Resources of State---- 60
Newspapers of the County ---- 177
Ninety-first Regiment -------- 167
Northwest Territory ---------- 34
Northwest Territory, Capitals of-- 54
Northwest Territory, Census of--- 44
Northwest Territory, Organization of -------------------------- 42

O

Occupations, Early ----------- 75
Odd Fellows ----------------- 259
Odon—
Banks ---------------------- 292
Business Interests, First----- 292
Churches -----------188, 194, 293
Incorporation --------------- 292
Lodges --------------------- 267
Name Changed -------------- 292
Officers, First -------------- 292
Population ------------------ 293
Postoffice ------------------ 298
Public Utilities ------------- 293
Schools --------------------- 239
Settlers, First -------------- 292
Optometrists ---------------- 256
Order of the Eastern Star ---- 259
Ordinance of 1787 ----------- 39
Organization of Counties----43, 51
Organization of Northwest Territory -------------------------- 42
Owl Prairie ----------------- 296

P

Panic of 1847 --------------- 123
Patriotic Orders ------------- 263
Patriotic Resolutions -------- 150
Perkins Store --------------- 298
Perry Township -----------94, 95
Physicians and Surgeons ----- 253
Plainville—
Bank ----------------------- 294
Business Interests ---------- 293
Churches ---------------193, 294
Decline of ------------------ 293
Location -------------------- 279
Lodges --------------------- 268
Postoffice ------------------ 298
Recent Growth ------------- 293
Schools --------------------- 294
Political History of County---- 108
Political History of Indiana --- 57
Pontiac's Conspiracy --------- 36
Poor Farm ---------------89, 106
Population of Indiana by Decades-- 59
Population, Territorial ------- 45
Postoffices in Daviess County-- 296
Presbyterian Churches ------- 184
Present Court House --------- 86
Presidential Elections ------- 114
Press, The ------------------ 177
Primitive School House ------ 208
Prosecuting Attorneys ------- 113

Q

Quebec Act ------------------ 36

R

Raglesville ------------------ 294
Rates of Tavern Keepers ----- 97
Reclamation of Waste Lands-- 130
Recorders, County ---------- 112
Reeve Township—
Boundaries ----------------- 274
Churches ------------------- 205
Creation of ----------------- 94
First Settler ---------------- 274
Land Entries --------------- 274
Lister of Property ---------- 94
Name ---------------------- 274
Overseers of Poor ---------- 95

HISTORICAL INDEX.

Reeve Township—
  Population 274
  Settlement 274
  Teachers, Early 210
Registration of Physicians 253
Related State History 33
Reminiscences 200
Representative Stage of Government 42
Representatives 113
Revolutionary Period 36
Royal Arch Masons 259
Rural Elementary Schools 230

S

St. Clair's Defeat 34
Sandy Hook 294
Saw-mill, The First 76
School Examiners 213
School History 207
School Laws, Changes in 214
School, Early 207
Second Court House 85
Secret Societies 257
Seminary, County 244
Senators, State 113
Settlement in Indiana Territory.. 45
Settlement of County 65
Settlers, Occupations of 75
Sixth Regiment 153
Sixty-Fifth Regiment 165
Slavery Days 137
Slavery, Efforts to Establish ... 50
Slavery in Daviess County 138
Smiley 294
Social Statistics 134
Soldiers from Daviess County 151
Soldiers Monument 170
South Washington 295
Spanish-American War 56
State Benevolent Institutions ... 61
State Educational System 61
State History 33
State Military History 55
State Political History 57
State Senators 113
Statistics, General 132
Steele Township—
  Churches 206
  Land Entries 279

Steele Township—
  Location 278
  Organization of 278
  Population 279
Summary of Churches 204
Surveyors, County 112
Surveyors, First Territorial 39

T

Tavern Tax 95
Teachers' Association 225
Teachers, Early 209
Territorial Congressional Delegates 49
Territorial Election, First 48
Territorial Government 46
Territorial Legislature, First .. 43
Territorial Surveys, First 39
Territory Northwest of Ohio 34
Thomas 295
Tom's Hill 295
Topography of County 63
Towns and Villages 281
Townships of Daviess County 272
Trainor 295
Treasury, County 111
Treasurer, County, Settlements..99, 103
Troubles with Indians 567
Twenty-fourth Regiment 156
Twenty-seventh Regiment 157

U

Underground Railroad 137
United Brethren Church 194

V

Van Buren Township—
  Churches 206
  Creation of 107
  Early Industries 280
  Land Entries 280
  Organization of 280
  Population of 280
  Settlement 280
  Teachers, Early 210
Veale Township—
  Boundaries 272
  Churches 206
  Creation of 94

HISTORICAL INDEX.

Veale Township—
  Distillery _____ 272
  Infirmary _____ 89
  Listers of Property _____ 94
  Location _____ 272
  Named, How _____ 272
  Natural Features _____ 272
  Organization of _____ 272
  Overseers of Poor _____ 95
  Schools _____ 210
  Settlers, Early _____ 272
  Soil _____ 272
  Teachers, Early _____ 210
Veteran, the Oldest _____ 176
Villages _____ 281
Vincennes, Capture of _____ 37
Vincennes, Oldest Settlement in Indiana _____ 38
Volunteers for the Civil War___ 151
Votes for Constitutional Convention 52

W

Wabash & Erie Canal _____ 122
Waco _____ 295
Wallace Township _____106, 277
War with Mexico _____ 148
Wars, Indiana's Part in_____ 55
Wars with Indians _____ 33
Washington—
  Additions to _____ 300
  Banks _____ 304
  Business Interests, Early ____ 301

Washington—
  Carnegie Library _____ 311
  Churches _____184, 201, 206
  City Finances _____ 307
  Financial Statement _____ 307
  First Buildings _____ 300
  Growth _____ 301
  Incorporation as a Town_____ 302
  Lodges _____ 257
  Mayors _____ 304
  Officers, First Town _____ 303
  Organization Under City Charter 303
  Plat, Original _____ 299
  Postoffice _____ 309
  Public Library _____ 310
  Public Utilities _____ 308
  Railroad Shops _____ 308
  Schools _____ 232
  Survey of _____ 93
  Town Officers, First _____ 303
Washington Township—
  Boundaries _____ 273
  Churches _____ 206
  Creation of _____ 94
  Lister of Property _____ 94
  Organization of _____ 273
  Overseers of Poor _____ 95
  Population _____ 273
  Schools _____ 210
Waste Lands Reclaimed _____ 130
Wayne, Gen. Anthony _____ 41
Wealth of Indiana _____ 60
White Men, First in Territory___ 33

BIOGRAPHICAL INDEX

A

Alberty, Henry --- 580
Allen, Prof. Hamlet --- 336
Allen, Josiah G. --- 705
Allen, Milton L. --- 482
Allison, Isaac --- 507
Amick, Clyde T. --- 701
Auterburn, William C. --- 445

B

Backes, Henry --- 512
Bacon, William J. --- 436
Banta, Charles A. --- 452
Barber, Lew W. --- 541
Barber, Stanton --- 590
Barkley, Nicholas F. --- 600
Barley, Thomas F. --- 489
Barnett, William W. --- 710
Barr, Robert J. --- 383
Batchelor, Stephen H. --- 535
Bean, Edward W. --- 697
Bechtel, Aaron D. --- 660
Beeker, Louda --- 473
Bennett, Michael J. --- 623
Berens, Peter --- 622
Biddinger, Andrew J. --- 342
Billings, John W. --- 525
Bonham, Martin L. --- 400
Bowman, Ira E., M. D. --- 610
Bowman, Willard --- 670
Boyd, Samuel B. --- 339
Brett, Matthew L. --- 539
Buchanan, Rev. Charles H. --- 329
Burrell, James A. --- 379
Bussard, Porter --- 598
Buzan, Albert --- 467
Buzan, Elmer --- 353

C

Cadden, Daniel --- 511
Callahan, Stearer Y. --- 447
Camp, William C. --- 557
Caress, John --- 500
Carnahan, Magness J. --- 315
Cavanaugh, John P. --- 388
Clark, A. Lawrence --- 563
Clark, John L. --- 327
Conlin, James M. --- 572
Correll, George W. --- 372
Courtney, William H. --- 699
Covalt, Edgar L. --- 579
Crooke, Harry H. --- 552

D

Dearmin, Walter T. --- 613
Dearmin, William --- 571
DeMotte, Jerome, M. D. --- 359
Dillard, John W. --- 398
Dillon, Franklin D. --- 605
Doolin, George W. --- 412
Dyke, George W. --- 340

E

Eads, John --- 694
Edwards, Joseph --- 407
Emmerling, George --- 587
Englehart, Raymond --- 716

F

Faith, Edward C. --- 658
Faith, George Alvin --- 530
Farris, Clifford --- 643
Fitzpatrick, John --- 521
Forsythe, Ernest E. --- 323

BIOGRAPHICAL INDEX.

Foust, William C. ---------------- 414
Franklin, Joseph D. --------------- 532
Freshley, Frederick J., M. D. ------ 497
Fulkerson, Alva O. --------------- 368
Fyffe, George W. ----------------- 637

G

Garten, James H. ---------------- 357
Gill, James A. ------------------- 419
Gillaspie, James W. -------------- 615
Gilley, James E. ----------------- 498
Gilliatt, Ollie ------------------- 449
Godwin, George ----------------- 366
Golliher, Paul ------------------- 608
Greenwood, Arthur H. ----------- 523
Gregory, Franklin S. -------------- 426
Gross, Lawrence C. -------------- 569

H

Haag, Andrew ------------------- 625
Ham, William ------------------- 651
Haney, Oscar ------------------- 518
Harris, Lew -------------------- 502
Hastings, Elmer E. --------------- 332
Hastings, John ------------------ 640
Hastings, Milton S. -------------- 347
Hastings, Paris A. ---------------- 351
Hayes, Courtland E. ------------- 568
Hayes, Daniel W. ---------------- 371
Hollingsworth, Dr. Ernest --------- 712
Horrall, Leonidas S. -------------- 349
Horrall, Thomas G. -------------- 538
Hyatt, Elisha ------------------- 381
Hyatt, Hiram ------------------- 364

I

Isenogle, Willard E. -------------- 479

J

Jackman, David S. --------------- 618
Jepson, Nathaniel H. ------------- 656
Johnson, Alfred E. --------------- 374
Johnson, Luther ----------------- 397
Johnson, Marion M. ------------- 681

K

Keith, Charles W. --------------- 529
Keith, George J. ---------------- 390
Keith, Louis W. ---------------- 633
Ketchem, Silas M. --------------- 692
Kettery, Joseph E. --------------- 456
Kiefer, William H. -------------- 344
Killion, Albert ------------------ 432
Killion, Ernest E. ---------------- 411
Killion, William A. -------------- 441
Killion, Nathan E. --------------- 355
Koller, John ------------------- 577
Kramer, Frank ----------------- 556
Kramer, Henry J. --------------- 628

L

Lane, Alonzo A. ---------------- 549
Laughlin, Edgar T. -------------- 361
LaVelle, William A. ------------- 653
Lawyer, John A. ---------------- 443
Ledgerwood, Milton B. ---------- 647
Lee, Lester -------------------- 554
Lett, Emery -------------------- 495
Littell, Charles A. --------------- 405
Lockwood, Aaron W. ----------- 547
Loughmiller, William E. --------- 421

Mc

McCall, Andrew ---------------- 481
McCarter, William H. ----------- 661
McMullen, Frank A. ------------ 593

M

Mackell, James F. --------------- 559
Malone, Albert ----------------- 672
Mangin, Frank ----------------- 574
Mason, Robert W. -------------- 607
Mattingly, Hon. Ezra ------------ 316
Meade, Alfred D. --------------- 626
Meads, James M. --------------- 534
Meads, Joseph H. --------------- 509
Merriman, Prof. Eugene D. ------ 318
Meurer, George W. ------------- 678
Mitchell, Ringgold S., M. D. ----- 377
Montgomery, John D. ----------- 450

BIOGRAPHICAL INDEX.

Morgan, Hugh _____ 486
Myers, Daniel I. _____ 477
Myers, Stephen E. _____ 707
Myers, Thomas C. _____ 428

N

Neal, William H. _____ 582

O

O'Bryan, Thomas _____ 409
O'Connor, Edward T. _____ 565
Osmon, Austin B. _____ 475

P

Peek, Charles E. _____ 588
Peek, John M. _____ 584
Poindexter, Henry _____ 472
Poindexter, Huette _____ 602
Porter, Hon. James _____ 334
Pownall, Clarence _____ 677
Pownall, George W. _____ 663
Pownall, Theodore C. _____ 664

R

Ragle, Peter _____ 492
Read, Nathan G. _____ 416
Reed, William W. _____ 491
Resler, Thomas E. _____ 665
Riester, George _____ 714
Ritter, Benjamin H. _____ 466
Ritterskamp, Ernest G. _____ 395
Roberts, Rett A. _____ 631
Rosenbury, Wirtsel V. _____ 469
Rust, James W. _____ 642

S

Scudder, Charles P., M. D.__ 320
Scudder, William C. _____ 542
Sefrit, Charles G. _____ 464
Shanks, John G. _____ 638
Shanks, William J. _____ 519
Shirley, Mary C. _____ 438

Sims, Alfred _____ 513
Sims, John A. _____ 487
Singleton, Thomas C. _____ 596
Small, Joseph _____ 575
Smiley, Roland M., D. D. S. _ 430
Smiley, Wilson S. _____ 457
Smith, Cecil S. _____ 461
Smith, Edward B. _____ 433
Smith, John T. _____ 703
Spencer, John H. _____ 566
Stalcup, Stephen _____ 684
Standiford, A. L. _____ 462
Stillwell, Jacob C. _____ 595
Stuckey, Charles L. _____ 536
Sutherland, William M. _____ 592
Swann, Silvester _____ 504
Swinda, William H. _____ 709

T

Taylor, James P. _____ 645
Taylor, Louis G. _____ 544
Taylor, Oliver A. _____ 655
Thias, William _____ 680
Thomas, John _____ 417
Todd, George F. _____ 689

U

Ulrich, William E. _____ 560

V

Vance, Oliver M. _____ 635
Van Trees, Warren _____ 393
Veale, Zadock D. _____ 505

W

Wadsworth, Thomas G. _____ 484
Walker, Oliver _____ 454
Waller, William S. _____ 385
Wallick, Oscar M. _____ 648
Walls, John W. _____ 620
Weaver, Jacob C. _____ 675
Weaver, John W. _____ 686
Weaver, Levi W. _____ 668

Whisman, Sylvester A. _____ 325
White, Florian B. _____ 629
Wichman, John _____ 402
Willey, Joseph _____ 545
Williams, Adolphus G. _____ 459
Williams, John Willis _____ 527

Williams, William H. _____ 562
Witsman, James _____ 403
Woodling, Haman _____ 470

Y

Yenne, Charles H., M. D. _____ 423

HISTORICAL

CHAPTER I.

RELATED STATE HISTORY.

The first white men to set foot upon the Northwest Territory were French traders and missionaries under the leadership of La Salle. This was about the year 1670 and subsequent discoveries and explorations in this region by the French gave that nation practically undisputed possession of all the territory organized in 1787 as the Northwest Territory. It is true that the English colonies of Virginia, Connecticut and Massachusetts claimed that their charters extended their grants westward to the Mississippi river. However, France claimed this territory and successfully maintained possession of it until the close of the French and Indian War in 1763. At that time the treaty of Paris transferred all of the French claims east of the Mississippi river to England, as well as all claims of France to territory on the mainland of North America. For the next twenty years the Northwest Territory was under the undisputed control of England, but became a part of the United States by the treaty which terminated the Revolutionary War in 1783. Thus the flags of three nations have floated over the territory now comprehended within the present state of Indiana—the tri-color of France, the union jack of England and the stars and stripes of the United States.

History will record the fact that there was another nation, however, which claimed possession of this territory and, while the Indians can hardly be called a nation, yet they made a gallant fight to retain their hunting grounds. The real owners of this territory struggled against heavy odds to maintain their supremacy and it was not until the battle of Tippecanoe, in the fall of 1811, that the Indians gave up the unequal struggle. Tecumseh, the Washington of his race, fought fiercely to save this territory for his people, but the white man finally overwhelmed him, and "Lo, the poor Indian" was pushed westward across the Mississippi. The history of the Northwest

Territory is full of the bitter fights which the Indians waged in trying to drive the white man out and the defeat which the Indians inflicted on general St. Clair on November 4, 1792, will go down in the annals of American history as the worst defeat which an American army ever suffered at the hands of the Indians. The greatest battle which has ever been fought in the United States against the Indians occurred in the state of Ohio. This was the battle of Fallen Timbers and occurred August 20, 1794, the scene of the battle being within the present county of Defiance. After the close of the Revolutionary War the Indians, urged on by the British, caused the settlers in the Northwest Territory continued trouble and defeated every detachment sent against them previous to their defeat by Gen. Anthony Wayne at the battle of Fallen Timbers in 1794. Although there was some trouble with the Indians after this time, they never offered serious resistance after this memorable defeat until the fall of 1811, when Gen. William Henry Harrison completely routed them at the battle of Tippecanoe.

TERRITORY NORTHWEST OF THE OHIO (1670-1754).

Ohio was the first state created out of the old Northwest Territory, although Indiana had been previously organized as a territory. When the land comprehended within the Northwest Territory was discovered by the French under La Salle about 1670, it was a battle ground of various Indian tribes, although the Eries, who were located along the shores of Lake Erie, were the only ones with a more or less definite territory. From 1670 to 1763, the close of the French and Indian War, the French were in possession of this territory and established their claims in a positive manner by extensive exploration and scattered settlements. The chief centers of French settlement were at Detroit, Vincennes, Kaskaskia, Cahokia, Fort Crevecour and at several missionary stations around the shores of the great lakes. The French did not succeed in doing this without incurring the hostility of the Iroquois Indians, a bitter enmity which was brought about chiefly because the French helped the Shawnees, Wyandots and Miamis to drive the Iroquois out of the territory west of the Muskingum river in Ohio

It must not be forgotten that the English also laid claim to the Northwest Territory, basing their claim on the discoveries of the Cabots and the subsequent charters of Virginia, Massachusetts and Connecticut. These charters extended the limits of these three colonies westward to the Pacific ocean, although, as a matter of fact, none of the three colonies made a settlement west of the Alleghanies until after the Revolutionary War. New York sought to strengthen her claim to territory west of the Alleghanies in 1701, by getting from the Iroquois, the bitter enemies of the French, a grant to the territory from which the French and their Indian allies had previously expelled them. Although this grant was renewed in 1726 and again confirmed in 1744, it gave New York only a nominal claim and one which was never recognized by the French in any way.

English traders from Pennsylvania and Virginia began in 1730 to pay more attention to the claims of their country west of the Alleghanies and north of the Ohio river. When their activities reached the ears of the French the governor of French Canada sent Céleron de Bienville up and down the Ohio and the rivers and streams running into it from the north and took formal possession of the territory by planting lead plates at the mouth of every river and stream of any importance. This peculiar method of the French in seeking to establish their claims occurred in the year 1749 and opened the eyes of England to the necessity of taking some immediate action. George II, the king of England at the time, at once granted a charter for the first Ohio Company (there were two others by the same name later organized), composed of London merchants and enterprising Virginians, and the company at once proceeded to formulate plans to secure possession of the territory north of the Ohio and west of the Mississippi. Christopher Gist was sent down the Ohio river in 1750 to explore the country as far west as the mouth of the Scioto river, and made several treaties with the Indians. Things were now rapidly approaching a crisis and it was soon evident that there would be a struggle of arms between England and France for the disputed region. In 1754 the English started to build a fort at the confluence of the Monongahela and Allegheny rivers, on the site of the present city of Pittsburgh, but before the fort was completed the French appeared on the scene, drove the English away and finished the fort which had been begun.

FRENCH AND INDIAN WAR (1754-63).

The crisis had finally come. The struggle which followed between the two nations ultimately resulted in the expulsion of the French from the mainland of America as well as from the immediate territory in dispute. The war is known in America as the French and Indian War and in the history of the world as the Seven Years' War, the latter designation being due to the fact that it lasted that length of time. The struggle developed into a world-wide conflict and the two nations fought over three continents, America, Europe and Asia. It it not within the province of this resume of the history of Indiana to go into the details of this memorable struggle. It is sufficient for the purpose at hand to state that the treaty of Paris, which terminated the war in 1763, left France without any of her former possessions on the mainland of America.

PONTIAC'S CONSPIRACY (1763-64).

With the English in control of America east of the Mississippi river and the French regime forever ended, the Indians next command the attention of the historian who deals with the Northwest Territory. The French were undoubtedly responsible for stirring up their former Indian allies and Pontiac's conspiracy must be credited to the influence of that nation. This formidable uprising was successfully overthrown by Henry Bouquet, who led an expedition in 1764 into the present state of Ohio and compelled the Wyandots, Delawares and Shawnees to sue for peace.

NORTHWEST TERRITORY AND QUEBEC ACT.

From 1764 to 1774, no events of particular importance occurred within the territory north of the Ohio river, but in the latter year (June 22, 1774), England, then at the breaking point with the colonies, passed the Quebec act, which attached this territory to the province of Quebec for administrative purposes. This intensified the feeling of resentment which the colonies bore against their mother country and is given specific mention in their list of grievances which they enumerated in their Declaration of Independence. The Revolutionary War came on at once and this act, of course, was never put into execution.

REVOLUTIONARY PERIOD (1775-83).

During the War for Independence (1775-1783), the various states with claims to western lands agreed with the Continental Congress to surrender their claims to the national government. In fact, the Articles of Confederation were not signed until all of the states had agreed to do this and Maryland withheld her assent to the articles until March 1, 1780, on this account. In accordance with this agreement New York ceded her claim to the United States in 1780, Virginia in 1784, Massachusetts in 1785 and Connecticut in 1786, although the latter state excepted a one-hundred-and-twenty-mile strip of three million five hundred thousand acres bordering on Lake Erie. This strip was formally relinquished in 1800, with the understanding that the United States would guarantee the titles already issued by that state. Virginia was also allowed a reservation, known as the Virginia Military District, which lay between the Little Miami and Scioto rivers, the same being for distribution among her Revolutionary veterans. There is one other fact which should be mentioned in connection with the territory north of the Ohio in the Revolutionary period. This was the memorable conquest of the territory by Gen. George Rogers Clark. During the years 1778 and 1779, this redoubtable leader captured Kaskaskia, Cahokia and Vincennes and thereby drove the English out of the Northwest Territory. It is probable that this notable campaign secured this territory for the Americans and that without it we would not have had it included in our possessions in the treaty which closed the Revolutionary War.

CAPTURE OF VINCENNES.

One of the most interesting pages of Indiana history is concerned with the capture of Vincennes by Gen. George Rogers Clark in the spring of 1779. The expedition of this intrepid leader with its successful results marked him as a man of more than usual ability. Prompted by a desire to secure the territory northwest of the Ohio river for the Americans, he sought and obtained permission from the governor of Virginia the right to raise a body of troops for this purpose. Early in the spring of 1778 Clark began collecting his men for the proposed expedition. Within a short time he collected about one hundred and fifty men at Fort Pitt and floated down the Ohio to the falls near Jeffersonville. He picked up a few recruits at this place and in June floated on down the river to the mouth of the Tennessee river. His original intention was to make a descent on Vincennes first, but, having received erroneous reports as to the strength of the garrison located there, he decided to commence active operations at Kaskaskia. After landing his troops near the mouth of the Tennessee in the latter part of June, 1778, he marched them across southern Illinois to Kaskaskia, arriving there on the evening of July 4. The inhabitants were terror stricken at first, but upon being assured by General Clark that they were in no danger and that all he wanted was for them to give their support to the American cause, their fears were soon quieted. Being so far from the scene of the war, the French along the Mississippi knew little or nothing about its progress. One of the most important factors in establishing a friendly relation between the Americans and the French inhabitants was the hearty willingness of Father Gibault, the Catholic priest stationed at Kaskaskia, in making his people see that their best interests would be served by aligning themselves with the Americans. Father Gibault not only was of invaluable assistance to General Clark at Kaskaskia, but he also offered to make the overland trip to Vincennes and win over the French in that place to the American side. This he successfully did and returned to Kaskaskia in August with the welcome news that the inhabitants of Vincennes were willing to give their allegiance to the Americans.

However, before Clark got his troops together for the trip to Vincennes, General Hamilton, the lieutenant-governor of Detroit, descended the Wabash and captured Vincennes (December 15, 1778). At that time Clark had only two men stationed there, Leonard Helm, who was in command of the fort, and a private by the name of Henry. As soon as Clark heard that the British had captured Vincennes, he began to make plans for retaking it. The terms of enlistment of many of his men had expired and he had difficulty in getting enough of them to re-enlist to make a body large enough to make a successful attack. A number of young Frenchmen joined his command and finally, in January, 1779, Clark set out from Kaskaskia for Vincennes with one hundred and seventy men. This trip of one hundred sixty miles was made at a time when traveling overland was at its worst. The prairies were wet, the streams were swollen and the rivers overflowing their banks. Notwithstanding the difficulties which confronted him and his men, Clark advanced rapidly as possible and by February 23, 1779, he was in front of Vincennes. Two days later, after considerable parleying and after the fort had suffered from a murderous fire from the Americans, General Hamilton agreed to surrender. This marked the end of British dominion in Indiana and ever since that day the territory now comprehended in the state has been American soil.

VINCENNES, THE OLDEST SETTLEMENT OF INDIANA.

Historians have never agreed as to the date of the founding of Vincennes. The local historians of that city have always claimed that the settlement of the town dates from 1702, although those who have examined all the facts and documents have come to the conclusion that 1732 comes nearer to being the correct date. It was in the latter year that George Washington was born, a fact which impresses upon the reader something of the age of the city. Vincennes was an old town and had seen several generations pass away when the Declaration of Independence was signed. It was in Vincennes and vicinity that the best blood of the Northwest Territory was found at the time of the Revolutionary War. It was made the seat of justice of Knox county when it was organized in 1790 and consequently it is by many years the oldest county seat in the state. It became the first capital of Indiana Territory in 1800 and saw it removed to Corydon in 1813 for the reason, so the Legislature said, that it was too near the outskirts of civilization. In this oldest city of the Mississippi valley still stands the house into which Governor Harrison moved in 1804, and the house in which the Territorial Legislature held its sessions in 1805 is still in an excellent state of preservation.

Today Vincennes is a thriving city of fifteen thousand, with paved streets, street cars, fine public buildings and public utility plants equal to any in the state. It is the seat of a university which dates back more than a century.

FIRST SURVEYS AND EARLY SETTLERS.

The next period in the history of the territory north of the Ohio begins with the passage of a congressional act (May 20, 1785), which provided for the present system of land surveys into townships six miles square. As soon as this was put into operation, settlers—and mostly Revolutionary soldiers—began to pour into the newly surveyed territory. A second Ohio Company was organized in the spring of 1786, made up chiefly of Revolutionary officers and soldiers from New England, and this company proposed to establish a state somewhere between Lake Erie and the Ohio river. At this juncture Congress realized that definite steps should be made at once for some kind of government over this extensive territory, a territory which now includes the present states of Ohio, Indiana, Illinois, Michigan, Wisconsin and about a third of Minnesota. Various plans were proposed in Congress and most of the sessions of 1786 and the first half of 1787 were consumed in trying to formulate a suitable form of government for the extensive territory. The result of all these deliberations resulted in the famous Ordinance of 1787, which was finally passed on July 13, 1787.

ORDINANCE OF 1787.

There have been many volumes written about this instrument of government and to this day there is a difference of opinion as to who was its author. The present article can do no more than merely sketch its outline and set forth the main provisions. It was intended to provide only a temporary government and to serve until such a time as the population of the territory would warrant the creation of states with the same rights and privileges which the thirteen original states enjoyed. It stipulated that not less than three nor more than five states should ever be created out of the whole territory and the maximum number was finally organized, although it was not until 1848 that the last state, Wisconsin, was admitted to the Union. The third article, "Religion, morality and knowledge being necessary to good government and the happiness of mankind, schools and the means of education shall forever be encouraged," has given these five states the basis for their excellent system of public schools, state normals, colleges and universities. Probably the most widely discussed article was the sixth, which provided that slavery and involuntary servitude should never be permitted within the territory and by the use of the word "forever" made the territory free for all time. It is interesting to note in this connection that both Indiana and Illinois before their admission to the Union sought to have this provision set aside, but every petition from the two states was refused by Congress in accordance with the provision of the Ordinance.

FIRST STAGE OF GOVERNMENT UNDER THE ORDINANCE.

The ordinance contemplated two grades of territorial government. During the operation of the first grade of government the governor, his secretary and the three judges provided by the ordinance were to be appointed by Congress and the governor in turn was to appoint "such magistrates and other civil officers in each county and township as he shall deem necessary for the preservation of the peace and good will of the same." After the federal government was organized a statutory provision took the appointment of these officers out of the hands of Congress and placed it in the hands of the President of the United States. All executive authority was given to the governor, all judicial authority to the three judges, while the governor and judges, in joint session, constituted the legislative body. This means that during the first stage of territorial government the people had absolutely no voice in the affairs of government and this state of affairs lasted until 1799, a period of twelve years.

SECOND STAGE OF GOVERNMENT UNDER THE ORDINANCE.

The second stage of government in the territory was to begin whenever the governor was satisfied that there were at least five thousand free male inhabitants of the age of twenty-one and above. The main difference between the first and second stages of territorial government lay in the fact that the legislative functions were taken from the governor and judges and given to a "general assembly or legislature." The ordinance provided for the election of one representative for each five hundred free male inhabitants, the tenure of the office to be two years. While the members of the lower house were to be elected by the qualified voters of the territory, the upper house, to consist of five members, were to be appointed by Congress in a somewhat complicated manner. The house of representatives was to select ten men and these ten names were to be sent to Congress and out of this number five were to be selected by Congress. This provision, like the appointment of the governor, was later changed so as to make the upper house the appointees of the President of the United States. The five men so selected were called councilors and held office for five years.

INDIAN STRUGGLES (1787-1803).

The period from 1787 to 1803 in the Northwest Territory was marked by several bitter conflicts with the Indians. Just as at the close of the French and Indian War had the French stirred up the Indians against the Americans, so at the close of the Revolutionary War did the English do the same. In fact the War of 1812 was undoubtedly hastened by the depredations of the Indians, who were urged to make forays upon the frontier settlements in the Northwest Territory by the British. The various uprisings of the Indians during this critical period greatly retarded the influx of settlers in the new territory, and were a constant menace to those hardy pioneers who did venture to establish homes north of the Ohio river. Three distinct campaigns were waged against the savages before they were finally subdued. The first campaign was under the command of Gen. Josiah Harmar (1790) and resulted in a decisive defeat for the whites. The second expedition was under the leadership of Gen. Arthur St. Clair (1791), the governor of the Territory, and was marked by one of the worst defeats ever suffered by an American army at the hands of the Indians. A lack of knowledge of Indian methods of warfare, combined with reckless mismanagement, sufficiently accounts for both disasters. It remained for Gen. Anthony Wayne, the "Mad Anthony" of Revolutionary fame, to bring the Indians to terms. The battle of Fallen Timbers, which closed his campaign against the Indians, was fought August 20, 1794, on the Maumee river within the present county of Defiance county, Ohio. This crushing defeat of the Indians, a rout in which they lost twelve out of thirteen chiefs, was so complete that the Indians were glad to sue for peace. On June 10, 1795, delegates from the various Indian tribes, headed by their respective chiefs, met at Greenville, Ohio, to formulate a treaty. A treaty was finally consummated on August 3, and was signed by General Wayne on behalf of the United States and by ninety chiefs and delegates of twelve interested tribes. This treaty was faithfully kept by the Indians and ever afterwards Little Turtle, the real leader of the Indians at that time, was a true friend of the whites. While there were several sporadic forays on the part of the Indians up to 1811, there was no battle of any importance with them until the battle of Tippecanoe in the fall of 1811.

ORGANIZATION OF THE NORTHWEST TERRITORY.

The first governor of the newly organized territory was Gen. Arthur St. Clair, a gallant soldier of the Revolution, who was appointed on October 5, 1787, and ordered to report for duty on the first of the following February. He held the office until November 22, 1802, when he was dismissed by President Jefferson "for the disorganizing spirit, and tendency of every example, violating the rules of conduct enjoined by his public station, as displayed in his address to the convention." The governor's duties were performed by his secretary, Charles W. Byrd, until March 1, 1803, when the state officials took their office. The first judges appointed were Samuel Holden Parsons, James Mitchell Varnum and John Armstrong. Before the time came for the judges to qualify, Armstrong resigned and John Cleves Symmes was appointed in his place. The first secretary was Winthrop Sargent, who held the position until he was appointed governor of Mississippi Territory by the President on May 2, 1798. Sargent was succeeded by William Henry Harrison, who was appointed by the President on June 26, 1798, and confined by the Senate two days later. Harrison was later elected as the first delegate of the organized Northwest Territory to Congress and the President then appointed Charles Willing Byrd as secretary of the Territory, Byrd's appointment being confirmed by the Senate on December 31, 1799.

REPRESENTATIVE STAGE OF GOVERNMENT (1799-1803).

The Northwest Territory remained under the government of the first stage until September 16, 1799, when it formally advanced to the second or representative stage. In the summer of 1798 Governor St. Clair had ascertained that the territory had a population of at least five thousand free male inhabitants and, in accordance with the provisions of the Ordinance of 1787, was ready to make the change in its form of government. On October 29, 1798, the governor issued a proclamation to the qualified voters of the territory directing them to choose members for the lower house of the territorial Legislature at an election to be held on the third Monday of the following December. The twenty-two members so elected met on January 16, 1799, and, pursuant to the provisions of the ordinance, selected the ten men from whom the President of the United States later chose five for the Legislative Council. They then adjourned to meet on September 16, 1799, but since there was not a quorum on that day they held adjourned sessions until the 23rd, at which time a quorum was present.

At the time the change in the form of government went into effect there were only nine counties in the whole territory. These counties had been organized either by the governor or his secretary. The following table gives the nine counties organized before 1799 with the dates of their organization and the number of legislators proportioned to each by the governor:

County.	Date of Organization.	Number of representatives.
Washington	July 27, 1788	2
Hamilton	January 4, 1790	7
St. Clair	April 27, 1790	1
Knox	June 20, 1790	1
Randolph	October 5, 1795	1
Wayne	August 6, 1796	3
Adams	July 10, 1797	2
Jefferson	July 29, 1797	1
Ross	August 20, 1798	4

FIRST TERRITORIAL LEGISLATURE OF NORTHWEST TERRITORY.

The twenty-two representatives and five councilors were the first representative body to meet in the Northwest Territory and they represented a constituency scattered over a territory of more than two hundred and sixty-five thousand square miles, an area greater than Germany or France, or even Austria-Hungary. It would be interesting to tell something of the deliberations of these twenty-seven sterling pioneers, but the limit of the present article forbids. It is necessary, however, to make mention of one important thing which they did in view of the fact that it throws much light on the subsequent history of the Northwest Territory.

DIVISION OF 1800.

The Legislature was authorized to elect a delegate to Congress and two candidates for the honor presented their names to the Legislature, William Henry Harrison and Arthur St. Clair, Jr., the son of the governor. The Legislature, by a joint ballot on October 3, 1799, elected Harrison by a vote of eleven to ten. The defeat of his son undoubtedly had considerable to do with the subsequent estrangement which arose between the governor and his legislature and incidentally hastened the division of the Northwest Territory. Within two years from the time the territory had advanced to the second stage of government the division had taken place. On May 7, 1800, Congress passed an act dividing the Northwest Territory by a line drawn from the mouth of the Kentucky river to Fort Recovery, in Mercer county, Ohio, and thence due north to the boundary line between the United States and Canada. Governor St. Clair favored the division because he thought it would delay the organization of a state and thus give him a longer lease on his position, but he did not favor the division as finally determined. He was constantly growing in disfavor with the people on account of his overbearing manner and he felt that he would get rid of some of his bitterest enemies if the western inhabitants were set off into a new territory. However, the most of the credit for the division must be given to Harrison, who, as a delegate to Congress, was in a position to have the most influence. Harrison also was satisfied that in case a new territory should be formed he would be appointed its first governor and he was not disappointed. The territory west of the line above mentioned was immediately organized and designated as Indiana Territory, while the eastern portion retained the existing government and the old name—Northwest Territory. It is frequently overlooked that the Northwest Territory existed in fact and in name up until March 1, 1803.

CENSUS OF NORTHWEST TERRITORY IN 1800.

The division of 1800 left the Northwest Territory with only about one-third of its original area. The census of the territory taken by the United States government in 1800 showed it to have a total population of forty-five thousand three hundred and sixty-five, which fell short by about fifteen thousand of being sufficient for the creation of a state as provided by the Ordinance of 1787, which fixed the minimum population at sixty-thousand. The counties left in the Northwest Territory, with their respective population are set forth in the appended table, all of which were within the present state of Ohio, except Wayne:

Adams	3,432
Hamilton	14,632
Jefferson	8,766
Ross	8,540
Trumbull	1,302
Washington	5,427
Wayne	3,206
Total	45,365

The population as classified by the census with respect to age and sex is interesting and particularly so in showing that considerably more than one-third of the total population were children under ten years of age.

	Males.	Females.
Whites up to ten years of age	9,362	8,644
Whites from ten to sixteen	3,647	3,353
Whites from sixteen to twenty-six	4,636	3,861
Whites from twenty-six to forty-five	4,833	3,342
Whites forty-five and upward	1,955	1,395
Total	24,433	20,595
Total of both sexes		45,028
Total of other persons, not Indians		337
Grand total		45,365

The above table shows in detail the character and distribution of the population of the Northwest Territory after the division of 1800. It is at this point that the history of Indiana properly begins and it is pertinent to set forth with as much detail as possible the population of Indiana Territory at that time. The population of 5,641 was grouped about a dozen or more settlements scattered at wide intervals throughout the territory. The following table gives the settlements in Indiana Territory in 1800 with their respective number of inhabitants:

Mackinaw, in northern Michigan -------------------- 251
Green Bay, Wisconsin ---------------------------- 50
Prairie du Chien, Wisconsin ---------------------- 65
Cahokia, Monroe county, Illinois ------------------- 719
Belle Fontaine, Monroe county, Illinois -------------- 286
L'Aigle, St. Clair county, Illinois -------------------- 250
Kaskaskia, Randolph county, Illinois ---------------- 467
Prairie du Rocher, Randolph county, Illinois ---------- 212
Settlement in Mitchel township, Randolph county, Ill.----- 334
Fort Massac, southern Illinois --------------------- 90
Clark's Grant, Clark county, Indiana ---------------- 929
Vincennes, Knox county, Indiana -------------------- 714
Vicinity of Vincennes (traders and trappers) ---------- 819
Traders and trappers at Ouitenon and Fort Wayne ----- 155
Fur traders, scattered along the lakes --------------- 300

Of this total population of nearly six thousand, it was about equally divided between what is now Indiana and Illinois. There were one hundred and sixty-three free negroes reported, while there were one hundred and thirty-five slaves of color. Undoubtedly, this census of 1800 failed to give all of the slave population, and it is interesting to note that there were efforts to enslave the Indian as well as the negro.

All of these settlements with the exception of the one in Clark's Grant were largely French. The settlement at Jeffersonville was made in large part by soldiers of the Revolutionary War and was the only real American settlement in the Indiana Territory when it was organized in 1800.

FIRST STAGE OF TERRITORIAL GOVERNMENT.

The government of Indiana Territory was formally organized July 4, 1800, and in a large book kept in the secretary of state's office at Indianapolis, there appears in the large legible hand of John Gibson the account of the first meeting of the officials of the Territory. It reads as follows:

"St. Vincennes, July 4, 1800. This day the government of the Indiana Territory commenced, William Henry Harrison having been appointed governor, John Gibson, secretary, William Clarke, Henry Vanderburgh & John Griffin Judges in and over said Territory."

Until Governor Harrison appeared at Vincennes, his secretary, John Gibson, acted as governor. The first territorial court met March 3, 1801, the first meeting of the governor and judges having begun on the 12th of the preceding January. The governor and judges, in accordance with the provisions of the Ordinance of 1787, continued to perform all legislative and judicial functions of the territory until it was advanced to the representative stage of government in 1805. The governor had sole executive power and appointed all officials, territorial and county.

CHANGES IN BOUNDARY LIMITS OF INDIANA.

During this period from 1800 to 1805, the territory of Indiana was considerably augmented as result of the organization of the state of Ohio in 1803. At that date Ohio was given its present territorial limits, and all of the rest of the Northwest Territory was included within Indiana Territory from this date until 1805. During this interim Louisiana was divided and the northern part was attached to Indiana Territory for purposes of civil and criminal jurisdiction. This was, however, only a temporary arrangement, which lasted only about a year after the purchase of Louisiana from France. The next change in the limits of Indiana Territory occurred in 1805, in which year the territory of Michigan was set off. The southern line of Michigan was made tangent to the southern extreme of Lake Michigan, and it so remained until Indiana was admitted to the Union in 1816. From 1805 to 1809 Indiana included all of the present states of Indiana, Illinois, Wisconsin and about one-third of Minnesota. In the latter year Illinois was set off as a territory and Indiana was left with its present limits with the exception of a ten-mile strip along the northern boundary. This strip was detached from Michigan and this subsequently led to friction between the two states, which was not settled until the United States government gave Michigan a large tract of land west of Lake Michigan. Thus it is seen how Indiana has received its present boundary limits as the result of the successive changes in 1803, 1805, 1809 and 1816.

SECOND STAGE OF TERRITORIAL GOVERNMENT (1805-1816.)

The Ordinance of 1787 provided that whenever the population of the territory reached five thousand free male inhabitants it should pass upon the question of advancing to the second or representative stage. Governor Harrison issued a proclamation August 4, 1804, directing an election to be held in the various counties of Indiana territory on the 11th of the following month. In the entire territory, then comprehending six counties, there were only three hundred and ninety-one votes cast. The following table gives the result of this election:

County.	For Advance.	Against Advance.	Total.
Clark	35	13	48
Dearborn	0	26	26
Knox	163	12	175
Randolph	40	21	61
St. Clair	22	59	81
Wayne	0	0	0
Total	260	131	391

It will be noticed that there is no vote returned from Wayne and this is accounted for by the fact that the proclamation notifying the sheriff was not received in time to give it the proper advertisement. Wayne county at that time included practically all of the present state of Michigan and is not to be confused with the Wayne county later formed within the present limits of Indiana. As result of this election and its majority of one hundred and twenty-nine in favor of advancing to the second stage of government, the governor issued a proclamation calling for an election on January 3, 1805, of nine representatives, the same being proportioned to the counties as follows: Wayne, three; Knox, two; Dearborn, Clark, Randolph and St. Clair, one each. The members of the first territorial legislature of Indiana convened at Vincennes on July 29, 1805. The members of the house were as follows: Dr. George Fisher, of Randolph; William Biggs and Shadrach Bond, of St. Clair; Benjamin Parke and John Johnson, of Knox; Davis Floyd, of Clark, and Jesse B. Thomas, of Dearborn. This gives, however, only seven representatives, Wayne county having been set off as the territory of Michigan in the spring of this same year. A re-apportionment was made by the governor in order to bring the quota of representatives up to the required number.

The Legislative Council consisted of five men as provided by the Ordinance of 1787, namely: Benjamin Chambers, of Dearborn; Samuel Gwathmey, of Clark; John Rice Jones, of Knox; Pierre Menard, of Randolph, and John Hay, of St. Clair. It is not possible in this connection to give a detailed history of the territory of Indiana from 1805 until its admission to the Union in 1816. Readers who wish to make a study of our state's history can find volumes which will treat the history of the state in a much better manner

DAVIESS COUNTY, INDIANA. 49

than is possible in a volume of this character. It may be noted that there were five general assemblies of the Territorial Legislature during this period of eleven years. Each one of the five general assemblies was divided into two sessions, which, with the dates, are given in the appended table:

First General Assembly—First session, July 29, 1805; second session, November 3, 1806.

Second General Assembly—First session, August 12, 1807; second session, September 26, 1808.

Third General Assembly—First session, November 12, 1810; second session, November 12, 1811.

Fourth General Assembly—First session, February 1, 1813; second session, December 6, 1813.

Fifth General Assembly—First session, August 15, 1814; second session, December 4, 1815.

CONGRESSIONAL DELEGATES OF INDIANA TERRITORY.

Indiana Territory was allowed a delegate in Congress from 1805 until the close of the territorial period. The first three delegates were elected by the Territorial Legislature, while the last four were elected by the qualified voters of the territory. The first delegate was Benjamin Parke, who was elected to succeed himself in 1807 over John Rice Jones, Waller Taylor and Shadrach Bond. Parke resigned March 1, 1808, to accept a seat on the supreme judiciary of Indiana Territory, and remained on the supreme bench of Indiana after it was admitted to the Union, holding the position until his death at Salem, Indiana, July 12, 1835. Jesse B. Thomas was elected October 22, 1808, to succeed Parke as delegate to Congress. It is this same Thomas who came to Brookville in 1808 with Amos Butler. He was a tricky, shifty, and, so his enemies said, an unscrupulous politician. He was later elected to Congress in Illinois and became the author of the Missouri Compromise. In the spring of 1809 the inhabitants of the territory were permitted to cast their first vote for the delegate to Congress. Three candidates presented themselves for the consideration of the voters, Jonathan Jennings, Thomas Randolph and John Johnson. There were only four counties in the state at this time, Knox, Harrison, Clark and Dearborn. Two counties, St. Clair and Randolph, were a part of the new territory of Illinois, which was cut off from Indiana in the spring of 1809. The one newspaper of the territory waged a losing fight against Jennings, the latter appealing for support on the ground of his anti-slavery views. The result of the election was as follows: Jennings, 428; Randolph, 402; Johnson, 81. Jonathan Jennings may be said to be the first successful politician produced in Indiana. His congressional career began in 1809 and he was elected to Congress four successive terms before 1816. He was president of the constitution convention of 1816, first governor of the state and was elected a second time, but resigned to go to Congress, where he was sent for *four more terms* by the voters of his district.

EFFORTS TO ESTABLISH SLAVERY IN INDIANA.

The Ordinance of 1787 specifically provided that neither slavery nor any voluntary servitude should ever exist in the Northwest Territory. Notwithstanding this prohibition, slavery actually did exist, not only in the Northwest Territory, but in the sixteen years while Indiana was a territory as well. The constitution of Indiana in 1816 expressly forbade slavery and yet the census of 1820 reported one hundred and ninety slaves in Indiana, which was only forty-seven less than there was in 1810. Most of these slaves were held in the southwestern counties of the state, there being one hundred and eighteen in Knox, thirty in Gibson, eleven in Posey, ten in Vanderburg and the remainder widely scattered throughout the state. As late as 1817 Franklin county scheduled slaves for taxation, listing them at three dollars each. The tax schedule for 1813 says that the property tax on "horses, town lots, servants of color and free males of color shall be the same as in 1814." Franklin county did not return slaves at the census of 1810 or 1820, but the above extract from the commissioners' record of Franklin county proved conclusively that slaves were held there. Congress was petitioned on more than one occasion during the territorial period to set aside the prohibition against slavery, but on each occasion refused to assent to the appeal of the slavery advocates. While the constitution convention of 1816 was in session, there was an attempt made to introduce slavery, but it failed to accomplish anything.

THE INDIAN LANDS.

The United States government bought from the Indians all of the land within the present state of Indiana with the exception of a small tract around Vincennes, which was given by the Indians to the inhabitants of the town about the middle of the eighteenth century. The first purchase of land was made in 1795, at which time a triangular strip in the southeastern part of the state was secured by the treaty of Greenville. By the time Indiana was admitted to the Union in 1816, the following tracts had been purchased: Vincennes tract, June 7, 1803; Vincennes treaty tract, August 18 and 27, 1804; Grouseland tract, August 21, 1805; Harrison's purchase, September 30, 1809; Twelve-mile purchase, September 30, 1809.

No more purchases were made from the Indians until the fall of 1818, at which time a large tract of land in the central part of the state was purchased from the Indians. This tract included all of the land north of the Indian boundary lines of 1805 and 1809, and south of the Wabash river with the exception of what was known as the Miami reservation. This treaty, known as St. Mary's, was finally signed on October 6, 1818, and the next Legislature proceeded to divide it into two counties, Wabash and Delaware.

ORGANIZATION OF COUNTIES.

As fast as the population would warrant, new counties were established in this New Purchase and Hamilton county was the tenth to be so organized. This county was created by the legislative act of January 8, 1823, and began its formal career as an independent county on the 7th of the following April. For purposes of reference, a list of the counties organized up until 1823, when Hamilton county was established, is here appended. The dates given represent the time when the organization of the county became effective, since in many instances it was from a few months to as much as seven years after the act establishing the county was passed before it became effective.

1. Knox _____June 20, 1790
2. Clark _____Feb. 3, 1801
3. Dearborn _____Mch. 7, 1803
4. Harrison _____Dec. 1, 1808
5. Jefferson _____Feb. 1, 1811
6. Franklin _____Feb. 1, 1811
7. Wayne _____Feb. 1, 1811
8. Warrick _____Apr. 1, 1813
9. Gibson _____Apr. 1, 1813
10. Washington ____Jan. 17, 1814
11. Switzerland ____Oct. 1, 1814
12. Posey _____Nov. 1, 1814
13. Perry _____Nov. 1, 1814
14. Jackson _____Jan. 1, 1816
15. Orange _____Feb. 1, 1816
16. Sullivan _____Jan. 15, 1817
17. Jennings _____Feb. 1, 1817
18. Pike _____Feb. 1, 1817
19. Daviess _____Feb. 15, 1817
20. Dubois _____Feb. 1, 1818
21. Spencer _____Feb. 1, 1818
22. Vanderburgh ___Feb. 1, 1818
23. Vigo _____Feb. 15, 1818
24. Crawford _____Mch. 1, 1818
25. Lawrence _____Mch. 1, 1818
26. Monroe _____Apr. 10, 1818
27. Ripley _____Apr. 10, 1818
28. Randolph _____Aug. 10, 1818

29.	Owen	Jan.	1, 1819	38.	Morgan	Feb.	15, 1822
30.	Fayette	Jan.	1, 1819	39.	Decatur	Mch.	4, 1822
31.	Floyd	Feb.	2, 1819	40.	Shelby	Apr.	1, 1822
32.	Scott	Feb.	1, 1820	41.	Rush	Apr.	1, 1822
33.	Martin	Feb.	1, 1820	42.	Marion	Apr.	1, 1822
34.	Union	Feb.	1, 1821	43.	Putnam	Apr.	1, 1822
35.	Greene	Feb.	5, 1821	44.	Henry	June	1, 1822
36.	Bartholomew	Feb.	12, 1821	45.	Montgomery	Mch.	1, 1823
37.	Parke	Apr.	2, 1821	46.	Hamilton	Apr.	7, 1823

The first thirteen counties in the above list were all that were organized when the territory of Indiana petitioned Congress for an enabling act in 1815. They were in the southern part of the state and had a total population of sixty-three thousand eight hundred and ninety-seven. At that time the total state tax was only about five thousand dollars, while the assessment of the whole state in 1816 amounted to only six thousand forty-three dollars and thirty-six cents.

CHANGES IN THE CONSTITUTION OF INDIANA.

The Constitution of 1816 was framed by forty-three delegates who met at Corydon from June 10 to June 29 of that year. It was provided in the Constitution of 1816 that a vote might be taken every twelve years on the question of amending, revising or writing a wholly new instrument of government. Although several efforts were made to hold constitution conventions between 1816 and 1850, the vote failed each time until 1848. Elections were held in 1823, 1828, 1840 and 1846, but each time there was returned an adverse vote against the calling of a constitutional convention. There were no amendments to the 1816 Constitution, although the revision of 1824, by Benjamin Parke and others was so thorough that it was said that the revision committee had done as much as a constitution convention could have done.

It was not until 1848 that a successful vote on the question of calling a constitution convention was carried. There were many reasons which induced the people of the state to favor a convention. Among these may be mentioned the following: The old Constitution provided that all the state officers except the governor and lieutenant-governor should be elected by the legislature. Many of the county and township officers were appointed by the county commissioners. Again, the old Constitution attempted to handle too many matters of local concern. All divorces from 1816 to 1851 were granted by the Legislature. Special laws were passed which would apply to particular counties and even to particular townships in the county. If Noblesville wanted an alley vacated or a street closed, it had to appeal to the Legislature for permission to do so. If a man wanted to ferry people across a stream in Posey county, his representative presented a bill to the Legislature asking that the proposed ferryman be given permission to ferry people across the stream. The agitation for free schools attracted the support of the educated people of the state, and most of the newspapers were outspoken in their advocacy of better educational privileges. The desire for better schools, for freer representation in the selection of officials, for less interference by the Legislature in local affairs, led to a desire on the part of majority of the people of the state for a new Constitution.

The second constitutional convention of Indiana met at Indianapolis, October 7, 1850, and continued in session for four months. The one hundred and fifty delegates labored faithfully to give the state a Constitution fully abreast of the times and in accordance with the best ideas of the day. More power was given the people by allowing them to select not only all of the state officials, but also their county officers as well. The convention of 1850 took a decided stand against the negro and proposed a referendum on the question of prohibiting the further emigration of negroes into the state of Indiana. The subsequent vote on this question showed that the people were not disposed to tolerate the colored race. As a matter of fact no negro or mulatto could legally come into Indiana from 1852 until 1881, when the restriction was removed by an amendment of the Constitution. Another important feature of the new Constitution was the provision for free schools. What we now know as a public school supported at the expense of the state, was unknown under the 1816 Constitution. The new Constitution established a system of free public schools, and subsequent statutory legislation strengthened the constitutional provision so that the state now ranks among the leaders in educational matters throughout the nation. The people of the state had voted on the question of free schools in 1848 and had decided that they should be established, but there was such a strong majority opposed to free schools that nothing was done. Orange county gave only an eight per cent vote in favor of free schools, while Putnam and Monroe, containing DePauw and Indiana Universities, respectively, voted adversely by large majorities. But, with the backing of the Constitution, the advocates of free schools began to push the fight for their establishment, and as a result of the legislative acts of 1855, 1857 and 1867, the public schools were placed upon a sound basis.

Such in brief were the most important features of the 1852 Constitution. It has remained substantially to this day as it was written sixty-five years ago. It is true there have been some amendments, but the changes of 1878 and 1881 did not alter the Constitution in any important particular. There was no concerted effort toward calling a constitutional convention until the Legislature of 1913 provided for a referendum on the question at the polls, November 4, 1914. Despite the fact that all the political parites had declared in favor of a constitutional convention in their platforms, the question was voted down by a large majority. An effort was made to have the question submitted by the Legislature of 1915, but the Legislature refused to submit the question to the voters of the state.

CAPITALS OF NORTHWEST TERRITORY AND INDIANA.

The present state of Indiana was comprehended within the Northwest Territory from 1787 to 1800, and during that time the capital was located within the present state of Ohio. When the Ordinance of 1787 was put in operation on July 17, 1788, the capital was established at Marietta, the name being chosen by the directors of the Ohio Company on July 2, of the same year. The name Marietta was selected in honor of the French Queen, Marie Antoinette, compounded by curious combination of the first and last syllables of her name.

When Indiana was set off by the act of May 7, 1800, the same act located the capital at Vincennes where it remained for nearly thirteen years. The old building in which the Territorial Assembly first met in 1805 is still standing in Vincennes. In the spring of 1813 the capital of the territory was removed to Corydon and it was in that quaint little village that Indiana began its career as a state. It remained there until November, 1824, when Samuel Merrill loaded up all of the state's effects in three large wagons and hauled them overland to the new capital—Indianapolis. Indianapolis had been chosen as the seat of government by a committee of ten men, appointed in 1820 by the Legislature. It was not until 1824, however, that a building was erected in the new capital which would accommodate the state officials and the General Assembly. The first court house in Marion county was built on the site of the present building, and was erected with a view of utilizing it as a state house until a suitable capitol building could be erected. The state continued to use the Marion county court house until 1835, by which time an imposing state house had been erected. This building was in use until 1877, when it was razed to make way for the present beautiful building.

MILITARY HISTORY.

Indiana has had some of its citizens in four wars in which United States has engaged since 1800: The War of 1812, the Mexican War, the Civil War, and the Spanish-American War. One of the most important engagements ever fought against the Indians in the United States was that of the battle of Tippecanoe, November 7, 1811. For the two or three years preceding, Tecumseh and his brother, the Prophet, had been getting the Indians ready for an insurrection. Tecumseh made a long trip throughout the western and southern part of the United States for the purpose of getting the Indians all over the country to rise up and drive out the white man. While he was still in the South, Governor Harrison descended upon the Indians at Tippecanoe and dealt them a blow from which they never recovered. The British had been urging the Indians to rise up against the settlers along the frontier, and the repeated depredations of the savages but increased the hostility of the United States toward England. General Harrison had about seven hundred fighting men, while the Indians numbered over a thousand. The Americans lost thirty-seven by death on the battlefield, twenty-five mortally wounded and one hundred and twenty-six more or less seriously wounded. The savages carried most of their dead away, but it is known that about forty were actually killed in the battle and a proportionately large number wounded. In addition to the men who fought at Tippecanoe, the pioneers of the territory sent their quota to the front during the War of 1812. Unfortunately, records are not available to show the enlistments by counties.

During the administration of Governor Whitcomb (1846-49) the United States was engaged in a war with Mexico. Indiana contributed five regiments to the government during this struggle, and her troops performed with a spirit of singular promptness and patriotism during all the time they were at the front.

No Northern state had a more patriotic governor during the Civil War than Indiana, and had every governor in the North done his duty as conscientiously as did Governor Morton that terrible struggle would undoubtedly have been materially shortened. When President Lincoln issued his call on April 15, 1861, for 75,000 volunteers, Indiana was asked to furnish 4,683 men as its quota. A week later there were no less than 12,000 volunteers at Camp Morton at Indianapolis. This loyal uprising was a tribute to the patriotism of the people, and accounts for the fact that Indiana sent more than 200,000 men to the front during the war. Indiana furnished practically seventy-five per cent of its total population capable of bearing arms, and on this basis Delaware was the only state in the Union which exceeded Indiana. Of the troops sent from Indiana, 7,243 were killed or mortally wounded, and 19,429 died from other causes, making a total death loss of over thirteen per cent for all the troops furnished.

During the summer of 1863 Indiana was thrown into a frenzy of excitement when it was learned that General Morgan had crossed the Ohio with 2,000 cavalrymen under his command. Probably Indiana never experienced a more exciting month than July of that year. Morgan entered the state in Harrison county and advanced northward through Corydon to Salem in Washington county. As his men went along they robbed orchards, looted farm houses, stole all the horses which they could find and burned considerable property. From Salem, Morgan turned with his men to the east, having been deterred from his threatened advance on Indianapolis by the knowledge that the local militia of the state would soon be too strong for him. He hurried with his men toward the Ohio line, stopping at Versailles long enough to loot the county treasury. Morgan passed through Dearborn county over into Ohio, near Harrison, and a few days later, Morgan and most of his band were captured.

During the latter part of the war there was considerable opposition to its prosecution on the part of the Democrats of this state. An organization known as the Knights of the Golden Circle at first, and later as the Sons of Liberty, was instrumental in stirring up much trouble throughout the state. Probably historians will never be able to agree as to the degree of their culpability in thwarting the government authorities in the conduct of the war. That they did many overt acts cannot be questioned and that they collected fire arms for traitorous designs cannot be denied. Governor Morton and General Carrington, by a system of close espionage, were able to know at all times just what was transpiring in the councils of these orders. In the campaign of 1864 there was an open denunciation through the Republican press of the Sons of Liberty. On October 8 of that year the Republican newspapers carried these startling headlines: "You can rebuke this treason. The traitors intend to bring war to your home. Meet them at the ballot box while Grant and Sherman meet them on the battle field." A number of the leaders were arrested, convicted in a military court and sentenced to be shot. However, they were later pardoned.

The Spanish-American War of 1898 has been the last one in which troops from Indiana have borne a part. When President McKinley issued his call for 75,000 volunteers on April 25, 1898, Indiana was called upon to furnish three regiments. War was officially declared April 25, and formally came to an end by the signing of a protocol on August 12 of the same year. The main engagements of importance were the sea battles of Manila and Santiago and the land engagements of El Caney and San Juan Hill. According to the treaty of Paris, signed December 12, 1898, Spain relinquished her sovereignty over Cuba, ceded to the United States Porto Rico and her other West India Island possessions, as well as the island of Guam in the Pacific. Spain also transferred her rights in the Philippines for the sum of twenty million dollars paid to her for public work and improvements constructed by the Spanish government.

POLITICAL HISTORY.

It is not possible to trace in detail the political history of Indiana for the past century and in this connection an attempt is made only to survey briefly the political history of the state. For more than half a century Indiana has been known as a pivotal state in politics. In 1816 there was only one political party and Jennings, Noble, Taylor, Hendricks and all of the politicians of that day were grouped into this one—the Democratic party. Whatever differences in views they might have had were due to local issues and not to any questions of national portent. Questions concerning the improvements of rivers, the building of canals, the removal of court houses and similar questions of state importance only divided the politicians in the early history of Indiana into groups. There was one group known as the White Water faction, another called the Vincennes crowd, and still another designated as the White river delegation. From 1816 until as late as 1832, Indiana was the scene of personal politics, and during the years Adams, Clay and Jackson were candidates for the presidency on the same ticket, men were known politically as Adams men, Clay men or Jackson men. The election returns in the twenties and thirties disclose no tickets labeled Democrat, Whig or Republican, but the words "Adams," "Clay," or Jackson."

The question of internal improvements which arose in the Legislature of 1836 was a large contributing factor in the division of the politicians of the state. The Whig party may be dated from 1832, although it was not until four years later that it came into national prominence. The Democrats elected the state officials, including the governor, down to 1831, but in that year the opposition party, later called the Whigs, elected Noah Noble governor. For the next twelve years the Whigs, with their cry of internal improvements, controlled the state. The Whigs went out of power with Samuel Bigger in 1843, and when they came into power again they appeared under the name of Republicans in 1861. Since the Civil War the two parties have practically divided the leadership between them, there having been seven Republicans and six Democrats elected governor of the state. The following table gives a list of the governors of the Northwest Territory, Indiana Territory and the state of Indiana. The Federalists were in control up to 1800 and Harrison and his followers may be classed as Democratic-Republicans. The politics of the governors of the state are indicated in the table.

GOVERNORS OF INDIANA.

Of the Territory Northwest of the Ohio—
    Arthur St. Clair _____1787-1800

Of the Territory of Indiana—
    John Gibson (acting) _____July 4, 1800-1801
    William H. Harrison _____1801-1812
    Thomas Posey _____1812-1816

Of the State of Indiana—
    Jonathan Jennings, Dem. _____1816-1822
    Ratliff Boon, Dem. _____September 12 to December 5, 1822
    William Hendricks, Dem. _____1822-1825
    James B. Ray (acting), Dem. _____Feb. 12 to Dec. 11, 1825
    James B. Ray, Dem. _____1825-1831
    Noah Noble, Whig _____1831-1837
    David Wallace, Whig _____1837-1840
    Samuel Bigger, Whig _____1840-1843
    James Whitcomb, Dem. _____1843-1848
    Paris C. Dunning (acting), Dem. _____1848-1849
    Joseph A. Wright, Dem. _____1849-1857
    Ashbel P. Willard, Dem. _____1857-1860
    Abram A. Hammond (acting), Dem. _____1860-1861
    Henry S. Lane, Rep. _____January 14 to January 16, 1861
    Oliver P. Morton (acting), Rep. _____1861-1865
    Oliver P. Morton, Rep. _____1865-1867
    Conrad Baker (acting), Rep. _____1867-1869
    Conrad Baker, Rep. _____1869-1873
    Thomas A. Hendricks, Dem. _____1873-1877
    James D. Williams, Dem. _____1877-1880
    Isaac P. Gray (acting), Dem. _____1880-1881
    Albert G. Porter, Rep. _____1881-1885

Isaac P. Gray, Dem. ----------------------------1885-1889
Alvin P. Hovey, Rep. ----------------------------1889-1891
Ira J. Chase (acting), Rep.-----Nov. 24, 1891 to Jan. 9, 1893
Claude Matthews, Dem. -------------------------1893-1897
James A. Mount, Rep. --------------------------1897-1901
Winfield T. Durbin, Rep. -----------------------1901-1905
J. Frank Hanley, Rep. --------------------------1905-1909
Thomas R. Marshall, Dem. ---------------------1909-1913
Samuel R. Ralston, Dem. ------------------------1913-

A CENTURY OF GROWTH.

Indiana was the first territory created out of the old Northwest Territory and the second state to be formed. It is now on the eve of its one hundredth anniversary, and it becomes the purpose of the historian in this connection to give a brief survey of what these one hundred years have done for the state. There has been no change in territory limits, but the original territory has been subdivided into counties year by year, as the population warranted, until from thirteen counties in 1816 the state grew to ninety-two counties by 1859. From 1816 to 1840 new counties were organized every year with the exception of one year. Starting in with a population of 5,641 in 1800, Indiana has increased by leaps and bounds until it now has a population of two million seven hundred thousand eight hundred and seventy-six. The appended table is interesting in showing the growth of population by decades since 1800:

Census Decades.	Population.	Increase.	Per Cent of Increase.
1800	5,641		
1810	24,520	18,879	334.7
1820	147,178	122,658	500.2
1830	343,031	195,853	133.1
1840	685,866	342,835	99.9
1850	988,416	302,550	44.1
1860	1,350,428	362,012	36.6
1870	1,680,637	330,209	24.5
1880	1,978,301	297,664	17.7
1890	2,192,404	214,103	10.8
1900	2,516,462	324,058	14.8
1910	2,700,876	184,414	7.3

Statistics are usually very dry and uninteresting, but there are a few figures which are at least instructive if not interesting. For instance, in 1910, 1,143,835 people of Indiana lived in towns and cities of more than 2,500. There were 822,434 voters, and 580,557 men between the ages of eighteen and forty-four were eligible for military service. An interesting book of statistics from which these figures are taken covering every phase of the growth of the state is found in the biennial report of the state statistician.

The state has increased in wealth as well as population and the total state tax of six thousand forty-three dollars and thirty-six cents of 1816 increased in 1915 to more than six million. In 1816 the only factories in the state were grist or saw mills; all of the clothing, furniture and most of the farming tools were made by the pioneers themselves. At that time the farmer was his own doctor, his own blacksmith, his own lawyer, his own dentist and, if he had divine services, he had to be the preacher. But now it is changed. The spinning wheel finds its resting place in the attic; a score of occupations have arisen to satisfy the manifold wants of the farmer. Millions of dollars are now invested in factories, other millions are invested in steam and electric roads, still other millions in public utility plants of all kinds. The governor now receives a larger salary than did all the state officials put together in 1861, while the county sheriff has a salary which is more than double the compensation first allowed the governor of the state.

Indiana is rich in natural resources. It not only has millions of acres of good farming land, but it has had fine forests in the past. From the timber of its woods have been built the homes for the past one hundred years and, if rightly conserved there is timber for many years yet to come. The state has beds of coal and quarries of stone which are not surpassed in any state in the Union. For many years natural gas was a boon to Indiana manufacturing, but it was used so extravagently that it soon became exhausted. Some of the largest factories of their kind in the country are to be found in the Hoosier state. The steel works at Gary employs tens of thousands of men and are constantly increasing in importance. At Elwood is the largest tin plate factory in the world, while Evansville boasts of the largest cigar factory in the world. At South end the Studebaker and Oliver manufacturing plants turn out millions of dollars worth of goods every year. When it is known that over half of the population of the state is now living in towns and cities, it must be readily seen that farming is no longer the sole occupation. A system of railroads has been built which brings every corner of the state in close touch with Indianapolis. In fact, every county seat but four is in railroad connection with the capital of the state. Every county has its local telephone systems, its rural free deliveries and its good roads unifying the various parts of the county. All of this makes for better civilization and a happier and more contented people.

Indiana prides herself on her educational system. With sixteen thousand public and parochial school teachers, with three state institutions of learning, a score of church schools of all kinds as well as private institutions of learning, Indiana stands high in educational circles. The state maintains universities at Bloomington and Lafayette and a normal school at Terre Haute. Many of the churches have schools supported in part by their denominations. The Catholics have the largest Catholic university in the United States at Notre Dame, while St. Mary's of the Woods at Terre Haute is known all over the world. Academies under Catholic supervision are maintained at Indianapolis, Terre Haute, Fort Wayne, Rensselaer, Jasper and Oldenburg. The Methodists have institutions at DePauw, Moore's Hill and Upland. The Presbyterian schools are Wabash and Hanover Colleges. The Christian church is in control of Butler and Merom Colleges. Concordia at Fort Wayne is one of the largest Lutheran schools in the United States. The Quakers support Earlham College, as well as the academies at Fairmount, Bloomingdale, Plainfield and Spiceland. The Baptists are in charge of Franklin College, while the United Brethren give their allegiance to Indiana Central University at Indianapolis. The Seventh-Day Adventists have a school at Boggstown. The Dunkards at North Manchester and the Mennonites at Goshen maintain schools for their respective churches.

The state seeks to take care of all of its unfortunates. Its charitable, benevolent and correctional institutions rank high among similar institutions in the country. Insane asylums are located at Indianapolis, Richmond, Logansport, Evansville and Madison. The State Soldiers' Home is at Lafayette, while the National Soldiers' Home is at Marion.

The Soldiers and Sailors' Orphans' Home at Knightstown, is maintained for the care and education of the orphan children of Union soldiers and sailors. The state educates and keeps them until they are sixteen years of age if they have not been given homes in families before they reach that age. Institutions for the education of the blind and also the deaf and dumb are located at Indianapolis. The state educates all children so afflicted and teaches them some useful trade which will enable them to make their own way in the world. The School for Feeble Minded at Fort Wayne has had more than one thousand children in attendance annually for several years. Within the past few years an epileptic village has been established at New Castle, Indiana, for the care of those so afflicted. A prison is located at

Michigan City for the incarceration of male criminals convicted by any of the courts of the state of treason, murder in the first or second degree, and of all persons convicted of any felony who at the time of conviction are thirty years of age and over. The Reformatory at Jeffersonville takes care of male criminals between the ages of sixteen and thirty, who are guilty of crimes other than those just mentioned. The female criminals from the ages of fifteen upwards are kept in the women's prison at Indianapolis. A school for incorrigible boys is maintained at Plainfield. It receives boys between the ages of seven and eighteen, although no boy can be kept after he reaches the age of twenty-one. Each county provides for its own poor and practically every county in the state has a poor farm and many of them have homes for orphaned or indigent children. Each county in the state also maintains a correctional institution known as the jail, in which prisoners are committed while waiting for trial or as punishment for convicted crime.

But Indiana is great not alone in its material prosperity, but also in those things which make for a better appreciation of life. Within the limits of our state have been born men who were destined to become known throughout the nation. Statesmen, ministers, diplomats, educators, artists and literary men of Hoosier birth have given the state a reputation which is envied by our sister states. Indiana has furnished Presidents and Vice-Presidents, distinguished members of the cabinet and diplomats of world wide fame; her literary men have spread the fame of Indiana from coast to coast. Who has not heard of Wallace, Thompson, Nicholson, Tarkington, McCutcheon, Bolton, Ade, Major, Stratton-Porter, Riley and hundreds of others who have courted the muses?

And we would like to be living one hundred years from today and see whether as much progress will have been made in the growth of the state as in the first one hundred years of its history. In 2015 poverty and crime will be reduced to a minimum. Poor houses will be unknown, orphanages will have vanished and society will have reached the stage where happiness and contentment reign supreme. Every loyal Hoosier should feel as our poetess, Sarah T. Bolton, has said:

> "The heavens never spanned,
> The breezes never fanned,
> A fairer, brighter land
> Than our Indiana."

CHAPTER II.

PHYSICAL AND GEOLOGICAL FEATURES.

Daviess county lies about half way in a line from the center of the state to the southwestern corner. It is south of Greene county, west of Martin, north of Dubois and Pike and east of Knox.

The county has an extreme length from north to south of twenty-eight miles and a width of twenty miles. It includes practically all of township 5 north, ranges 5 and 6 west; township 4 north, range 6 west; township 3 north; ranges 6 and 7 west; township 2 north, ranges 6 and 7 west; all but the eastern row of sections of townships 2, 3 and 4 north, range 5 west, most of township 4 north, range west, and parts of townships 1 north, ranges 5, 6 and 7 west; townships 3 and 4 north, range 8 west, and township 5 north, range 7 west. It has an area of 432 square miles.

The county has ten civic townships, as follow: Steele, Washington, Veale, Elmore, Bogard, Barr, Harrison, Madison, Van Buren and Reeve.

TOPOGRAPHY.

In the northeastern corner of the county the surface is rather hilly, but going west, southwest and south this quickly changes to a rolling country and that in turn to a very level surface. Most of Elmore, Bogard, Steele, Washington and Barr townships are of this level character, with some rolling land. Northeast of Washington a conspicuous group of hills exists. The southern part of this county, as White river is approached, again becomes quite hilly. Many prairies exist along Smothers creek and Prairie creek and their tributaries, which drain the northern central part of the county. Indian Pond and First creeks drain the extreme northern part, while Veale's, Aikman's, Mud and Sugar creeks drain the extreme southern part. The west fork of White river flows along the western side, the east fork along the south side.

The country appears to range in elevation from three hundred and ninety-six feet above tide in the southwestern corner to over six hundred feet east of Raglesville and just northeast of Washington. Washington has an elevation of four hundred and eighty-four feet and low water near the same place is about four hundred and twenty-four feet above tide.

Coal has been found in abundance in many sections of the county; at Washington, Montgomery, Epsom, Odon, Raglesville, Cannelburg and other places. The towns mentioned all have mines in operation, which furnish the market a splendid article of fuel and make Daviess county well known as a coal producing territory. It has been estimated by a former state geologist that an aggregate of eight feet of coal, in the average, extended over the entire county, two hundred and seventy thousand acres. At Washington is mined some of the best coking coal found in the western coal field.

COAL GIVES IMPETUS TO WASHINGTON.

The discovery of coal on the eastern confines of the deserted village of Greenup in a great measure started Washington on her first movement toward enlargement of territory and an increased activity in business pursuits and returns; this also meant a decided growth in population, and when workmen on the grade of the Ohio & Mississippi railroad cut into a rich vein of bituminous coal at Washington, the fact that the county seat had been located upon vast coal deposits first became apparent. This was in 1857, and that year noted a further advance in growth and prosperity of the chief city of the county. The discovery of the precious commodity was immediately followed by the opening of coal mines, which called into active life an industry that put Washington more prominently on the map than was ever anticipated; and from the years 1858 to 1860, miners flocked into Washington from near and far. Many of the men brought families; the scale of wages being remunerative, they prospered, built homes and in many cases became permanent and valued citizens of the community. The Ohio & Mississippi railroad officials had the coal thoroughly tested to determine its steam-producing qualities and in a short time the wood-burning locomotives, then in general use, were converted into coal burners.

At Cannelburg a remarkable vein of cannel coal was discovered and soon the mines of the Buckeye Cannel-Coal Company were distributing an article that has no superior anywhere. Many millions of tons of coal have been mined in Daviess county, but the supply still lying in the ground will not be exhausted for many years to come. Mines are in active operation in various parts of the county, giving employment to a small army of men.

CHAPTER III.

EARLY SETTLEMENT OF DAVIESS COUNTY.

There is a difference of opinion as to who was the first actual settler in Daviess county, but most authorities give this distinction to William Ballow, who settled in the Sugar Creek hills, sixteen miles southeast of the present city of Washington, in 1801. Some claim this distinction for Eli Hawkins, who came from South Carolina, in 1806, and settled near the present site of Maysville. But this can hardly be correct, for Mr. John Thompson, who wrote a series of papers for one of the local publications, several years ago, and who is recognized as good authority on early historic matters, mentions seven others who came to this region before Eli Hawkins arrived. One of these seven, mentioned by Mr. Thompson, was David Flora, who lived in a log cabin, nearly opposite the present site of the Meredith House, in Washington. According to this authority, David Flora was the second settler, admitting William Ballow to have been the first. The next settler, in order, according to Mr. Thompson, was Thomas Ruggles; followed in succession by Doctor Harris, Richard Palmer, William Hawkins, and finally, Eli Hawkins, mentioned above, in 1806.

That Eli Hawkins did arrive in what is now Daviess county as early as 1806, is not a matter of doubt, as the county records contain a copy of the deed made to him on November 8, 1806, by John Rice Jones and Mary Jones, his wife. The land deeded lay in the vicinity of Maysville, consisting of four hundred acres, for which Mr. Hawkins paid four hundred dollars. This land was a portion of section 6, township 2, range 7. This deed to Eli Hawkins was not, however, the earliest deed made to land in Daviess county, but it was probably the first purchase of land on which an actual settlement was made.

EARLY SETTLERS.

An article compiled by John Wooldridge, A. M., published in a county history about thirty years ago, contains some interesting information regarding early deeds and early settlers of Daviess county. Liberal excerpts

(5)

are taken from Professor Wooldridge's article in the preparation of this chapter.

In order to give an idea of the rapidity with which settlement was made in Daviess county, after the advent of the adventurous first settlers, a number of the first land entries are given, as shown by the county deed records. This will not only show the location, but also the names of some of the first settlers, the most authentic record that can be obtained.

In 1783 Congress made numerous donations of land to the early French settlers about Vincennes, and, in 1807, the Congress made what has since been called French locations. These donations are mostly in Knox county, but a considerable portion are in Daviess county. The boundary lines of the locations run east and west, and north and south, while those of the donations run at an angle of nearly forty-five degrees from the true meridian. Eli Hawkins settled on location No. 62, and his brother, William, on location No. 63, recently the property of Joseph M. Taylor. William McIntosh settled on location No. 67; William Morrison, on location No. 134; David Flora, on No. 159; Touissant Dubois, on No. 300; Emanuel Van Trees, on No. 304; Samuel Baird, on No. 144; Jesse Purcell, on No. 185; Elijah Purcell, on No. 192; John Allen, on No. 258; William Flint, on No. 189; William Baker, on No. 193; John Aikman, on No. 192; James Barr, on No. 210; Amable Godall, on No. 202, and John McDonald, the old government surveyor, on No. 242. It is not easy to determine the exact dates of the above mentioned settlements, but it is sufficient to know that most of them were made prior to the War of 1812.

Others to obtain land titles prior to 1814 were the following: In 1808, Daniel Comer, Richard Steen, Josiah Culbertson, Simon Nicholas, Amos Rogers, William Ballow, John Wallace, Clayton Rogers, Daniel Gregory, Thomas Aikman, William Horrall, Thomas Horrall, Hezekiah Ragsdale, Ebenezer Jones, Vance Jones, John Aikman. There was no land entry in 1812, and only one in 1813, indicating an unsettled, or a disturbed state of society, which made it questionable whether Daviess county was the proper place to locate. The one land entry made in 1813 was made by Jeremiah Lucas.

EMIGRATION RECEIVES A SETBACK.

All of the above named individuals entered lands and settled within the present limits of Washington township, except Clayton Rogers, whose land lay in what is now Veale township. Rogers, therefore, was somewhat isolated from his neighbors. During the period which elapsed while these entries were being made, additions were constantly coming into the settlement and the population was increasing rapidly. The pioneers were prosperous, making steady progress in clearing up their claims and in improving and adding to the comforts of their homes, until the latter part of 1811, in which year the troubles with the Indians began, inaugurating a period of unrest which continued for a number of years. The Indian troubles and the War of 1812 caused a sudden cessation in the movement of new settlers to Daviess county. This is indicated by the fact that no land entries were made in 1812, and only one in 1813, as has already been noted.

The victory of General Harrison's army in the battle of Tippecanoe gave assurance of more peaceful conditions regarding the Indians, and the promise of a settlement of the controversy involved in the War of 1812 gave further assurance of a settled condition in the affairs of the pioneers. As an indication of this, the activities in land entries were resumed, as shown by the records. In 1814 deeds were recorded by the individuals named below, for lands entered in Daviess county: Joseph Case, Thrice Stafford, Robert Hays, John Tranter, John Case and Elias Stone. In 1815 the following persons entered lands: Jonathan Morgan, Daniel Clift, George Clift, William Ballow, William Williams and Jacob Reeder. In 1816: Joseph Hays, Edward Adams, John Davidson, Benjamin Hawkins, George Gregory, Caleb Brock, Henry Foster, William Patterson, Nicholas Hutson, James Montgomery and John Johnson. In 1817: Robert Burris, Alexander Stephenson, James Henry, Dennis Clark, George Keith, Jesse Morgan, Alexander Bruce, Samuel Comer and Thomas Patten.

THE INDIAN TROUBLES.

According to a history of the time compiled by John Wooldridge, A. M., referred to above, the difficulties experienced by the early settlers with the Indians in Indiana were incidental to the efforts of Governor William Henry Harrison to break up the Indian confederacy, at the head of which was the noted chief, Tecumseh, and his brother, the Shawnee prophet, the headquarters of whom were at Prophetstown, now quite an important village situated in Whiteside county, state of Illinois. The general history of these efforts of Governor Harrison, resulting in the battle of Tippecanoe, November 7, 1811, is so sufficiently detailed in all histories of the United States as not to require recital in this connection. But the incidents with which the early settlers of Daviess county were immediately connected, and in which some of them were personally engaged are, necessarily, here introduced.

William McGowen, one of the earliest settlers, lived near the present site of Mt. Pleasant, in Martin county, and kept a farm across the east fork of White river, near his home.

One evening, early in the spring of 1812, just after Mr. McGowen had retired, an Indian put his gun through the opening, about a foot square, in the wall of his log cabin and fired at him as he lay in bed, lodging several buckshot under his left arm, from the effects of which he almost instantly expired. This Indian was not pursued. Not long after this first tragic incident, John and William Smith and a Mr. Perry, while carrying provisions from the "settlement," as Washington was then called, to the men at McGowen's farm, were discovered by three Indians while crossing a small prairie. The Indians waylaid them at what was then called "the narrows," near the farm afterward known as the Houghton farm. They fired upon the white men, lodging two balls in Perry's back, and sending one ball through John Smith's thigh and two through William Smith's hat. After thus emptying their guns they rushed upon the white men, who, by throwing the loads off their shoulders, were enabled to outrun their enemies and escape to the farm without further injury.

MEASURES FOR PROTECTION.

The occurrence of such difficulties as these clearly demonstrated to our early pioneers the necessity of devising measures for mutual protection and defense against the common enemy, hence the erection of suitable forts, conveniently located. The entire number of these forts erected in Daviess county was ten, but only five of the number were erected in 1812. These five were as follow, with their location: Hawkins fort, located on the Hawkins farm, on the southeast quarter of section 32, township 3, range 7; Conner fort, on the southeast quarter of section 4, township 2, range 7; Coleman fort, some distance south of Conner; Purcell fort, in the Purcell neighborhood, and Ballow fort, on the northwest quarter of section 9, township 2, range 7. The other five follow: Richard Palmer, David Flora, built across Main street in the town of Washington, from, and almost directly opposite the Meredith House; Ebenezer Jones, about one and one-quarter miles south of Washington; John Aikman, on the southwest quarter of section 10, township 2, range 7, and one on Prairie creek, on the present site of Lettsville.

PIONEERS WHO OCCUPIED THE FORTS.

The following is a list of the heads of families that assembled in each of the first-named five forts: Hawkins fort, Cornelius Bogard, Eli Hawkins and a Mr. Curry, the young men being Charles, Eli, Joseph and William Hawkins; Conner fort, Friend Spears, James and Thomas Aikman, Ebenezer Jones, Alexander Stevens, Chris Gregory, John Stringer, William White, John Wallace, the Widow Wallace and two sons, the Widow Ellis, Vance Jones, Ephraim Thompson, G. Ragsdale, Thrice Stafford and Alexander Stephenson, beside a large number of young men, among them Wiley R. Jones, Jesse Hallem, William Phillips, John and Jacob Stafford, Samuel Aikman, John and Josiah Wallace, John, David and William Ellis, Coleman Morgan and Wesley Wallace, John Ragsdale and John Thompson; Coleman fort, Joshua Reeves, Henry Edwards, Samuel Comer, John Smith, Mr. Perry, Alexander Hays, J. Waters, J. Freeland, Amos Rogers, Simon Nicholas, Abraham Dodamel and Robert Hays, the young men being John, Hugh and three other Edwards boys and William Percy; Purcell fort, Robert Bratton, Andrew Little, Daniel Gregory, Josiah Culbertson, John Forden, "Obe" and William Flint, Richard Palmer, Henry Mattingly and a Mr. Carland, the young men being John Bratton, John, Joseph, Samuel and Josiah Culbertson; Ballow fort, John, Thomas and William Horrall, Jeremiah Lucas, Charles Sinks, Richard Steen, Thomas Scaler and Nathan Davis, the young men and boys being George Mason, Fleming Ballow, John, James and Samuel Steen and Samuel Sinks. These names comprise a list of nearly, if not quite, all the male inhabitants of Daviess county at the breaking out of troubles with the Indians.

A BLOCK HOUSE DESCRIBED.

It will now be appropriate to record such other Indian difficulties as occurred within the limits of the country, or in which inhabitants of Daviess county were especially interested by participation. These Indian troubles will, however, be preceded by a brief description of the forts and blockhouses, used as places of refuge. The fort was usually about one hundred and fifty feet square. A trench about twenty inches wide and three feet deep was dug, into which were set timbers, twelve feet long, with sharpened tops, some round, others split. The earth was then firmly packed on either side of the timbers. Near the middle of the thick wall was a gateway for wagons. Within the enclosure was a hewed log house, twenty-seven by eighteen feet in dimensions. It was a two-story building, the upper story being reached by means of a ladder. At the northeast and southwest corners were block houses, in which lived some of the inhabitants, while others built huts of various sizes and forms, according to their taste and means. The block houses were two stories in height, the lower story being about eighteen feet square, and the upper about twenty feet square, the projection of two feet being on the two outer sides of the fort. If, however, a block house were built independent of a fort, it had a projection on each side. The manner of life in the forts was simple, the food consisting of corn bread, a little meat, a few potatoes, turnips, cabbages, pumpkins and hominy. No wheat was raised at that early day.

ENCOUNTER WITH INDIANS.

Not long after the erection of the earliest forts a serious affair occurred on Steele's prairie. A few families, having built some cabins there, were moving in their household goods. While unloading their second load they were attacked by Indians, and two of them killed, the elder Mr. Hathaway being killed outright, and W. Bogard after a protracted struggle in defense of his life. Old Mr. Sinks was shot in the left shoulder, and Richard Hathaway through the neck. The two latter were in the wagon handing out goods, the younger Hathaway falling unconscious in the wagon when shot. Upon the firing of the guns, with the attendant war cries of the Indians, the four horses attached to the wagon became frightened and ran to the lower end of the prairie. By this time young Hathaway had recovered from his faint, and he and Mr. Sinks, having detached the horses from the wagon by cutting the harness, attempted to ride two of the animals back to the fort, but the rough gait of the horses irritated the wounds of the two men to such a degree that they were obliged to walk. A Miss Case, who had been left at some stables, a short distance from where the killing of Bogard and Hathaway occurred, haltered a two-year-old colt and rode nine miles to the nearest fort to give the alarm. The attack having been made about sundown, most of her journey was accomplished by night, a feat requiring no small degree of courage. Upon her arrival at Hawkins fort, runners were despatched to Forts Conner, Purcell and Ballow. As many as could procure horses collected at Hawkins fort and about three o'clock the next morning set out for Steele's prairie, where the murders had been committed. On their way up, the party unknowingly passed the two wounded men, Sinks and Hathaway, who, upon hearing them approach and supposing them to be Indians, retired from the path in order to escape notice. The horsemen having passed on, the two wounded men returned to the trail and proceeded to the fort, arriving there some time before noon. Here they first heard of Miss Case's heroism.

Upon arriving at the place where Bogard and Hathaway lay dead upon the ground, a portion of the little band of settlers made arrangements to carry the bodies back to the fort, and in due time, assisted by those remaining deposited the mangled corpses in the Maysville cemetery, the first interment to occur in that resting place for the dead. Investigation made at the scene of the murders led to the conclusion that seven Indians had taken part in the attack, this conclusion being based on the finding of seven beds, or nests, each evidently having been occupied by one person, so artfully constructed as to conceal its occupant from view. Those of the horsemen who did not return with the two bodies attempted to find the Indian trail, this, however, proving a very difficult task. From what could be discovered, it was concluded that the Indians were making for the mouth of the Eel river. The pursuers, after crossing Smothers creek, skirting along the edge of the river bottom, passing through English Prairie, through the timber and on through Owl prairie and, having lost what feeble traces of a trail they thought they had occasionally discerned, came to a halt at sundown. A portion of the company built camp-fires and the remainder went on a few miles still farther up the country, but failing to find any new traces of the red men's footsteps, they returned to the camp. During the night it was concluded useless to further pursue the Indians, as, from all that could be observed, they had crossed to the west side of the river, and so made good their escape. The baffled pursuers, therefore, returned to the forts.

ONE LONE INDIAN LAID LOW.

In 1813 another incident occurred, in which, instead of a white man being slain, an Indian lost his life. Palmer fort was built early in the spring of that year. One rainy night three Indians walked around this fort and in the morning their footprints were discovered. A very large dog, owned by a man named Baker, living in the fort scented the Indians and started on the trail. The men, armed and on horseback, immediately followed them to Prairie creek. The Indians had crossed the creek on a drift opposite the site of the block house, built that spring by Captain Patterson, but at that time abandoned. They evidently had occupied the blockhouse during the latter part of the night, and had baked a johnny-cake on a board before the fire, out of some corn-meal left by Patterson. Mr. Baker's dog and some of the men easily followed the Indians across the creek on the drift, but it was found necessary to swim the animals across, which caused considerable delay. Meanwhile, two Indians came out of a house and darted off at full speed. When the last horse had been swum across, a third and very large Indian came out of the house and followed his companions. The white men, seven in number, and all well mounted, started in full pursuit, preceded by the dog. The country between Prairie creek and Smothers creek then consisted of sandy ridges, covered with oak bushes, marshes and ponds, through which the Indians kept straight on. It was impossible for the mounted men to follow directly, for their horses would have stuck fast in the mire; hence, considerable time was lost by making more or less wide detours. Time also was lost in crossing Smothers creek, which, like Prarie creek, was too high for fording. Upon reaching the upper ground of White river bottom, however, the white men, guided by the dog, discovered that they had so well kept the trail as nearly to have overtaken the Indians, and began firing upon the latter. The large Indian who had, during the entire chase, which was very exciting, kept in the rear, at length received a slight wound in the right knee, whereupon he climbed a large hackberry tree and made two attempts to shoot his pursuers, but each time the powder flashed in the pan. Being defenseless, he was overpowered and slain, after, however, giving his companions time to escape. This was the only Indian killed hereabout during the troublous times.

KILLING OF THOMAS EAGLE.

Some four or five years after the events related above, a number of friendly Indians were collected on what is now called Owl prairie. Hearing of their presence, a number of settlers from Washington and vicinity went up to trade with them, taking along lead, powder, tobacco and whiskey. Among those who went up was Obed Flint, a Mr. Frost and Thomas Eagle. Mr. Eagle, a veritable giant of a man, was desirous of exhibiting his strength and to this end bantered one of the smaller Indians to let him throw him over the fire. With the Indian's consent, Eagle made the attempt and succeeded only in throwing him half way over the fire, the Indian falling upon the coals and being quite severely burned. An Indian named "Big File," observing the occurrence, and not understanding the reason of the attempt by Eagle, rushed upon him and stabbed him to death with a large knife. "Big File" was indicted by the grand jury, but succeeded in escaping the penalty of his crime.

It is related that William Smothers, of Kentucky, whose father had been killed in that state by the Indians, had taken a vow of vengeance, and had come to Indiana for the purpose of executing that sanguinary vow. He had formerly lived near Owensboro, Kentucky, and is said to have taken as much pleasure in hunting Indians as in hunting bears, or other wild animals. Four or five dead Indians are said to have been found on his hunting grounds, two of whom he is said to have confessed to have killed by the accidental discharge of his gun. He saw one fall through a hole cut in the ice to catch fish, went to the place, but could see nothing but blood, which he supposed to have flowed from a wound accidentally inflicted upon himself by the Indian with his tomahawk, and that he had fainted, fallen through the ice into deep water, and had thus been drowned. On another occasion his gun was accidentally discharged while he was passing down the creek, immediately after which he heard a noise in the water. Upon going to see what occasioned the noise he saw a log with blood on it, but no Indian; so supposed the Indian had fallen into the water and, becoming entangled, was unable to extricate himself and was thus drowned. Such "accidents" became altogether too common, and Mr. Smothers left for some other happy hunting ground.

The killing of the four white men, McGowen, Hathaway, Eagle and Bogard, and of the one Indian, comprises the list of casualties within the limits of Daviess county during, and in consequence of, the Indian troubles; but, simultaneously with these difficulties, were other causes of excitement which seemed to prevent the inhabitants of the county from entertaining any proper sense of security. On one occasion Fort Harrison, then held by Capt. Zachary Taylor, was besieged by a large body of Indians, and all who could procure horses were required to repair to its relief. This fort was completed in October, 1811, and was located on the east bank of the Wabash, above the present site of Terre Haute. Probably not over twenty men went, but the hurry and bustle of preparation, the mending of bridles and saddles, the gathering together of the horses, the grinding of corn in the little hand-mill, the baking of quantities of bread, and other preparations for departure, caused as much anxiety and wakefulness, perhaps, as would the preparation for the march of an entire regiment. After the farewell, full of forebodings, had been bidden, for none knew how many would fail to return alive, nothing was heard of the little band of warriors for sixteen days, at the end of which time news came that all had returned safely to Vincennes, and two days afterward they marched home.

RANGERS TO FIGHT INDIANS.

Early in the spring of 1812, when it was confidently anticipated that a war would soon break out between Great Britain and the United States, a call was made among the residents of Daviess county for volunteers to fight the Indians. From fifteen to twenty answered the call, none of them heads of families, but all of mature age. They were to serve for one year, furnish their own horses and horse feed, one good rifle each, with shot-bag, powder-horn and ammunition; one leather belt, one tomahawk, one large butcher knife and a small knife, from four to five inches long; and were to receive as wages one dollar per day. Thus mounted and accoutered, they were named "rangers." During the time for which they were enlisted they were called out many times, but reference is here made to only one of these expeditions, mainly to record the killing of two more of the early citizens of Daviess county and, incidentally, to illustrate the superior skill and cunning of the Indian in desultory warfare. In the latter part of September, 1812, General Samuel Hopkins was in Vincennes in command of about two thousand volunteers. The duty assigned to his command was that of breaking up and destroying the settlements of Indians along the Wabash and Illinois rivers. The destruction of one Kickapoo town at the head of Lake Peoria was accomplished, and the mounted forces returned to Vincennes, most of them being discharged on account of refusing to obey their commander. General Hopkins immediately organized another force, chiefly infantry, to operate against the Indians in the vicinity of Prophetstown. Accompanying this expedition was a number of Daviess county rangers. The Winnebago town, lying on Wild Cat creek, one mile from the Wabash river, had been surrounded and found deserted, and General Hopkins's command, to use his own language, was "embarked in the complete destruction of the prophet's town, which had about forty cabins and huts, and the large Kickapoo village adjoining it on the east side of the river. . . . Seven miles east of us a party of Indians was discovered on Ponce Passu (Wild Cat creek). They had fired on a party of ours on the 21st (September) and killed a man by the name of Dunn, a gallant soldier in Captain Duval's company. On the 22nd, upward of sixty horsemen, under command of Lieutenant-Colonels Miller and Wilcox, anxious to bury their comrade, as well as to gain a more complete knowledge of the ground, went on to a point near the Indian encampment, fell into an ambush, and eighteen of the party were killed, wounded and missing." Two of those killed in this ambuscade,

Samuel Culbertson and Jesse Jones, were from the settlement at the forks of the White river. The former was the son of Josiah Culbertson, a worthy citizen of Daviess county and a soldier of the Revolutionary War, and the latter a son of Ebenezer Jones, who lived in Daviess county from 1811 to 1863.

BURIAL PARTY AMBUSHED.

The country immediately around the encampment, a short distance above the present site of LaFayette, was finely timbered and to all appearances a body of rich land. Some of the men strayed off from the main body for the purpose, as they said, of looking at the country. While one of these parties, consisting of three, was out some distance from the main body, they were fired on by the Indians and one of their number was killed. His name was Dunn. Upon the return of the two survivors to camp, sixty men were detailed to bury their dead comrade, and the men from this part of the country were part of this detail. Approaching the spot where the slain man lay, they discovered an Indian mounted on quite a fine horse. Dropping their burial tools, they, in a very tumultuous manner, started in pursuit. The Indian at first kept a northeast course, but gradually inclined to the north until he arrived at the head of a ravine running directly west to the Wabash river. He entered the ravine, which was quite steep at the sides, and covered with timber and thick underbrush. When his pursuers had proceeded about three hundred yards down the hollow, they received a very heavy fire on both flanks, which added much to their disorder and confusion. A general rout ensued, and every man who could, made the best of his way back to camp. Those who effected an escape had to cut their way through the enemy's lines. The next day almost the whole army went out to bury the dead. who were found much mutilated, and some that were reported missing never were found.

OCCUPATIONS OF EARLY SETTLERS.

The early settlers of Daviess county were largely from Southern states. It is estimated that about one-half of the first settlers were from South Carolina and one-fourth from Kentucky and Tennessee. The principal inducement that brought these people was that they might obtain cheap lands and establish homes for their families. Finding a desirable location in the primitive prairie or the unbroken forest was the first concern of these pioneers; the next concern, and the most important, was to find means of subsistence for the family. In the accomplishment of this purpose it was necessary to use all the ingenuity and all the means nature had placed within their reach. Timber must be cleared and the prairie lands must be broken and all brought to a state of cultivation. In that period of Daviess county history implements of industry for this kind of work were few, and of a very crude sort. The cabins, which served for domiciles were built of round logs. These logs usually were not hewn. The roof was made of clapboards held in place by poles. The spaces between the logs in the side of the cabin were filled with sticks and clay. The fireplace at one end of the cabin was, of course, indispensable, serving both heating and cooking purposes. Square openings for the one door, and probably two windows, were cut in the side of the cabin. Greased paper, instead of glass, was the material used for windows in the primitive cabin, and skins of animals were used for the door openings. Some of the more pretentious cabins had glass windows and doors made of sawed lumber; the doors hanging on hinges of rawhide, with a rawhide latch-string hanging outside. The synonym for genuine hospitality, "the latch-string is out," had its origin from this kind of a door in the pioneer cabin. The floor of the primitive cabin generally was of clay, hard packed, though some cabins had floors made of puncheon, hewn with the broad-axe and laid on sleepers.

THE FIRST SAW-MILL.

The first lumber was made with the whip-saw. This kind of a saw continued in use for some time after saw-mills had been introduced. It is generally conceded that James C. Veale built the first saw-mill in Daviess county, some time between 1808 and 1810. This mill was located on Veale's creek, but did not make enough lumber to supply the demand. Slabs from this mill were in great demand for the flooring of cabins, being more desirable for that purpose than the roughly-hewn puncheon. Veale's mill was carried away by a freshet, in the spring of 1812, and after a considerable time was rebuilt. The second mill of this kind was built, also on Veale's creek, by Eli Chapman, in 1815. It was of greater capacity than Veale's mill, furnished more lumber, and continued in operation for a longer time. The third mill was a different design than either of the two mentioned. The motive power, instead of being water, consisted of two or three yoke of oxen haltered within a tread-mill. This ox-mill was located in the town of Washington, and was erected by William McCormick. The next saw-mill of the pioneer period was erected in Washington by B. Duncan, Wil-

EVIDENCE OF WASHINGTON COUNTY PROSPERITY.

MOONLIGHT ON WHITE RIVER.

liam and R. Graham, and J. Thompson. This was the first mill to manufacture lumber for export, considerable quantities being shipped down the river to a mountain market. In the course of a few years steam saw-mills began to be erected and superseded, to a large extent, mills operated by other motive power. In the time further back than is within the memory of anyone now living, the lumber business was one of the important industries of Daviess county.

THE FIRST GRAIN MILLS.

The first mills to grind both corn and wheat were turned by hand. Richard Palmer is credited with having been the pioneer in the erection and operation of a mill of this kind in Daviess county. His mill was built on Palmers creek, on land afterward owned by William McCluskey. This mill was equipped with a bolting apparatus and other facilities for the manufacture of a fairly good article of flour, for those times. Another mill was built on this same creek, on the Hawkins farm, by William Hawkins. Both of these mills were built, it is said, in 1816. The Palmer mill was built of round logs, without chinking, which made it a rather uncomfortable place in which to do business in cold weather. The Hawkins mill was neatly built of hewed logs and was much more convenient and comfortable. The old-fashioned tub wheel was used in both these mills, the tub wheel embodying substantially the same principle as the turbine wheel of modern times. The capacity of each of these mills was about two and one-half bushels the hour. While they were both equipped for the manufacture of flour and corn-meal, the latter product was most in demand. Very little flour was used by the pioneer families. Wheat bread was regarded as a luxury, only to be indulged in, if at all, on special occasions. Corn-meal was the staff of life; corn bread, the corn-dodger, the hoe-cake, the johnny-cake, as made by the thrifty housewife of those times, being the food that furnished the brawn and muscle for the men who cleared the forest and cultivated the fields in the early days of Daviess county.

EARLY CLOTHING MATERIAL.

The question of securing houses in which to live, and the food necessary to sustain life, was not the most perplexing problem of the pioneers. Houses easily could be built, sufficiently stable to afford shelter for the family, from material with which the forest abounded. Food for the family was produced with slight labor from the fertile soil, supplemented by the abundance of wild game in the forest. But the material from which the necessary clothing could be made was not so easily obtained. Flax was the principal dependence at first, and its cultivation and manufacture into fabrics was attended with no little exertion and anxiety. The cultivation of cotton was attempted. As most of the pioneers had come from states where cotton raising was the chief agricultural industry, cotton being then the principal fabric from which clothing was made, they, very naturally, tried the experiment of cotton cultivation in their northern homes. But the experiment was a failure. The seasons were too short, the facilities of separating the seed from the cotton were too meager, and this line of industrial effort was abandoned after a few years. Wool was found to be the main dependence for clothing. But the raising of sheep in sufficient numbers to supply the demand for wool had its difficulties, on account of the abounding wolves, with an inherited appetite for fresh mutton. The protection of sheep, however, was an absolute necessity in order to secure the necessary wool, and this protection was afforded. In time a combined warfare on the wolves resulted in a decrease of these pests, and in an increase of the necessary sheep. As the production of wool increased, carding, spinning and weaving, became an almost daily industry in every house. At first all this was done by hand, but, in 1815, Eli Chapman put up a carding machine, in connect with his saw-mill, on Veale's creek, and did a large and profitable business in wool-carding. Deer skins, bear skins, and the skins of other animals were largely used in the manufacture of clothing for the men. Clothing from such material had the quality of being cheap, warm and durable, and especially adapted to the rugged work required of the pioneer.

All the fabric for clothing, from the material from which the fabric was made, was made by the women. Linsey-woolsey, as it was called, was the common cloth from which women's dresses were made. The chain of this cloth was of coarse cotton, and the filling of wool. Blue, turkey-red and copperas, were the favorite colors of this rather fantastic cloth. The loom was a necessary article of furniture; as necessary as were the bed and dining-table. The loom and the spinning wheel of that day filled the place of the piano and phonograph of the present day.

EARLY FARM IMPLEMENTS AND MACHINERY.

Another difficulty experienced by the pioneer farmer was in the preparation of the ground for seed; as the plow, harrow, and other farm implements were neither so common nor so perfect as they are at present. Plow-irons, hoes, mattocks and similar implements were brought here from their original homes by the settlers, and by dint of ingenuity and hard work the latter managed to stock them, or furnish the necessary wooden parts to fit them for the uses intended. The wooden parts were made from green timber, worked into the desired shape by the broad-axe and draw-knife, the dependable tools of the mechanic of those times. The implements thus made were unwieldy and unshapely, but service rather than shape was the point aimed at.

The first and only thrashing-machine made in Daviess county, according to an old historical authority, was invented and built by James and William Thompson, in what was known as the McTaggart barn, a building thirty by forty feet in size. Thirty feet of the west end of the barn was used for the horse-power. This horse-power was a large driving-wheel, sixteen feet in diameter, with gearing and belting, by which the thrasher and cleaner were propelled. The cylinder of the thrashing part of this machine was a wooden shaft, three feet long, moving on an iron axle. From each end of this wooden shaft projected eight arms, to the outer ends of which eight ribs were fastened. The ribs were faced with heavy hoop-iron, and as this cylinder, or reel, revolved, the sheaves of wheat were fed into it through rollers, and thus the grain was beaten out of the straw. The grain was separated from the straw by passing into a hopper, through a wire grating, three feet wide and six feet long, fixed in the floor, the straw being passed out of an upper window in the barn. From the hopper, the grain was fed to the cleaner as fast as thrashed. Two horses were required to run this machine, and it required six hands—three men and three boys—to perform the necessary labor. The thrashing of one hundred bushels of wheat was considered a good day's work for this outfit. The first portable thrashing-machine was introduced by a Mr. Parsons. This was a four-horse-power machine, with a center gearing-wheel, driving a shaft which operated an iron cylinder by which the grain was thrashed out. To the center driving-wheel were attached four arms, or shafts; to the outer end of each of these arms one of the four horses was hitched; these horses, moving in a circle, the wheel was made to go around. A driver stood on a platform over the driving-wheel in the center, and it was his duty to see that the horses kept moving. This machine only thrashed the wheat; the sheaves being fed into the cylinder, the grain, straw and chaff all coming out in a pile together. The man with the rake separated the straw from the wheat and the chaff, as it came from the machine, and the fanning-mill, operated by hand, did the rest. Because of the manner of its operation, this machine was known as the "straw-piler," by the people of that period. Some of the citizens of Daviess county can measure a memory of thrashing-machines from the "straw-piler" age, to that of the "cyclone" thresher, operated by steam power. The improvement in farming implements, farm machinery and methods of farming, has kept pace with the improved facilities in every other industrial vocation, for the past seventy-five years; and the farmers of Daviess county have kept fully abreast of the times.

CHAPTER IV.

CREATION AND ORGANIZATION OF DAVIESS COUNTY.

Knox county, out of which Daviess county was created, as a civic organization antedates both the territorial and state governments of Indiana. It was laid off and organized in the spring of 1790, by Winthrop Sargent, secretary of the Northwest Territory, acting under special instructions from Governor Arthur St. Clair, who was then at Kaskaskia, organizing St. Clair county. The county was named in honor of Gen. Henry Knox, then secretary of war of the United States, and originally embraced all the territory now constituting the states of Indiana and Michigan. Daviess county was created out of territory belonging to Knox by "an act for the formation of a new county out of the county of Knox," approved on December 24, 1816. The measure creating the new county came under the category of special laws, and is of sufficient value and interest to deserve preservation in these pages.

AN ACT FOR THE FORMATION OF A NEW COUNTY.

Section 1. Be it enacted by the General Assembly of the State of Indiana, That from and after the 15th day of February next all that part of the county of Knox which is contained within the following boundary shall constitute and form a new county, viz: Beginning at the forks of White river, running thence with the east fork of White river to the mouth of Lick creek; thence with said creek to the line of Orange county; thence north with the said line to where it strikes the west branch of White river, thence down the said west fork to the place of beginning.

Section 2. That said new county shall be known and designated by the name and style of the County of Daviess, and shall enjoy all the rights and privileges and jurisdictions which to a separate county do or may properly appertain or belong: Provided, always, That all suits, pleas, plaints, actions and proceedings in law or equity which may have been commenced or instituted before the 15th day of February next, and are now pending within the said county of Knox, shall be prosecuted and determined in the same manner as if this act had not been passed: Provided, That all taxes of whatever nature or kind assessed or which may be assessed previous to the said 15th day of February, or now due, or which may become due before that time within the bounds of the said new county, shall be collected in the same manner and by the same officers as if the aforesaid new county had never been enacted.

Section 3. That William Bruce and Henry Ruble, of the county of Knox; David Robb and William Barker, of the county of Gibson, and Thomas Fulton, of the county of Orange, be, and they are hereby appointed commissioners to fix the seat of justice for said county of Daviess; and the several sheriffs of the counties of Knox, Gibson and Orange shall notify the said commissioners of their said appointments; and the said sheriffs shall receive from the said county of Daviess so much as the county court of said county of Daviess shall decree just and reasonable, who are hereby authorized to allow the same out of any moneys in the county treasury, not otherwise appropriated; and the said commissioners shall on the first Monday of March, next, meet at the house of Alexander Bruce, of said county, and shall immediately proceed to establish the seat of justice for said county of Daviess; and until suitable public buildings be erected, so as to accommodate the courts aforesaid, the said courts shall meet at the house of said Alexander Bruce, and shall then adjourn the said court to the courthouse, after which time the said courts for the county of Daviess shall be holden at the county seat as aforesaid established: Provided, that the agent or person appointed by law to lay off the town and sell the lots at the seat of justice of the county of Daviess, shall reserve ten per centum out of the proceeds of the sale of the town lots, and shall pay the same over to such person as shall be appointed to receive it by law, for the use of the public library for said county, in such installments, and at such times, as shall be prescribed by law.

Section 4. Refers to Knox county.

Section 5. That the said county of Daviess shall constitute and form a part of the representative and senatorial district for the county of Knox.

Isaac Blackford,
Speaker of the House of Representatives.
Christopher Harrison,
President of the Senate.

Approved: December 24, 1816.
Jonathan Jennings.

MEMORIAL TO CAPTAIN DAVIESS.

This county was named in honor of Captain Joseph H. Daviess, who was a brave and intrepid soldier. He was killed early on the morning of November 7, 1811, while leading his men in a desperate charge in the battle of Tippecanoe. The state of Illinois also named one of its counties after this pioneer hero-warrior, this latter county appearing on the map as Jo Daviess county.

Daviess county, Indiana, when first formed, contained all of its present territory and also all of Martin county, except that portion lying south of Lick creek; all of Greene county, east of the west fork of White river, and all of Owen county, east of the west fork of White river. At the time of its enaction Daviess county was about fifty-seven miles in length and in its greatest width about thirty-one miles. It is now twenty-eight miles in length, from north to south, and in width eighteen miles.

The organizing sheriff of Daviess county was Obed Flint, who was commissioned by the governor of the state and authorized to call an election for the selection of county officials. The sheriff performed his duty by selecting the day and pasting notices for the first election held in this county. On the appointed day, which was in February, 1817, the electors of the county met at their several polling places and elected William Ballow, John Aikman and Ephraim Thompson, county commissioners; William H. Routt, James G. Read, associate judges; Emanuel VanTrees, clerk of the board of commissioners and ex-officio clerk of the circuit court.

THE COUNTY SEAT.

Two persons from Knox county, two from Gibson county and one from Orange county were mentioned by name in the act enacting the county, to serve as commissioners to select a site for the county seat. Only two of them, however, laid a claim for their services in this capacity, namely: William Bruce and Henry Ruble. If the others performed the office assigned them, no record is extant to that effect. Be that as it may, Emanuel VanTrees and Peter Wilkins donated to the newly-formed county thirty-seven and one-half acres of land for a county seat, and on the 17th day of March, 1817, the board of commissioners ordered that Emanuel VanTrees "shall survey the land given as a donation for the county seat." On the 18th, the board "proceeded to lay out the town and ordered the survey, and called the name thereof Washington. And the survey was performed by Emanuel VanTrees until finished."

The foregoing quotations were taken from the minutes of the board of commissioners, the original entries being in the handwriting of Emanuel VanTrees, and it is of record that when the seat of justice was laid off and platted it was given the name it always has borne. Previous to this event, however, the town of Liverpool was laid out and platted in the fall of 1815, by Isaac Galland, David Flora and George Curtis, the same being a tract of land containing forty-nine and sixteen hundredths acres. The plat of the town is thus described in the Knox county records, the land then being part and parcel of that county:

"A plan of the town of Liverpool, in Indiana Territory, as laid out in the forks of White river, in Knox county, by Isaac Galland, George Curtis and David Flora. It contains one hundred and eighty-six lots, each one being sixty feet in width and one hundred twenty feet in length, each street sixty feet wide, to remain open and common highways forever. Lots 61, 62, 63, 64, 97, 98 and 99 to form a public square, to remain for the benefit of the public forever." Adjoining this strip of lots on the north the town of Washington was laid out; immediately Liverpool lost its identity and was henceforth known and designated as Washington.

FIRST COURT HOUSE.

The first building in which court was held in Daviess county and which by courtesy became known as "the court house," was a log structure, the home of Alexander Bruce. This primitive and temporary temple of justice stood on the southeast corner of Main and Second streets and was used by the county for court purposes from April 21, 1817, until 1825, when the first court house built by the county was finished.

In May, 1818, the board of county commissioners asked for plans to be submitted for a court house, which was designed to be two stories in height, thirty-five by forty-five feet, ground dimension, of brick construction. (For full details of plans see chapter on Political History, under early proceedings of the board of commissioners.) James G. Read, an associate judge and prominently identified with the county's early history, was awarded the contract for the sum of two thousand nine hundred seventy-nine dollars, but did not turn the finished work over to the county until several years had elapsed.

The foundations for the court house were laid in the fall of 1818 and the building was partially completed a year later. But, by reason of various causes and excuses, this much-needed official building was not ready for occupancy when the year 1824 rolled around, six years after the laying of the foundation. One reason for the delay was probably the extremely low condition of the county treasury and the public credit. In the year last mentioned, a contract was let to the lowest bidder for furnishing the court house and in the following year the building was occupied. But in order to complete the work the board of commissioners permitted a subscription paper to be circulated, by which means a small amount of money was secured for the purpose. The inducement held out to subscribers to the court house building fund was the promised remission of taxes equal to the amount of each individual subscription. The structure stood on the "public square," donated for the purpose, as has each of its successors.

SECOND COURT HOUSE, BUILT IN 1841.

The county's initial attempt at building a court house did not prove a very flattering success. There always seemed to be something wrong with the structure and the roof had a chronic habit of leaking. It was an inconvenient, uncomfortable, cheerless box of a concern, to say the least; and not many years after its occupancy the need of a better and more commodious place for the county's offices, safe receptacles for the county records and actions, and a light, airy and habitable courtroom, became apparent. In January, 1835, John Murphy, George Roddick, Daniel McDonald, George A. Waller, Barton Peck, James Whitehead and John VanTrees, were appointed a committee to report on the advisability of building a new court house. This committee was practically unanimous in favor of the proposition and so reported its deliberations to the board. Thereupon, John VanTrees, Barton Peck and James Braza, in May, appointed a committee to superintend the work of constructing the new court house in contemplation. Advertisements appeared in the newspaper, calling for bids for the contract, to follow plans and specifications already prepared, but the actual work was delayed. In September, 1837, the *Washington Philanthropist* contained a call for bids for constructing the buildings and in November of that year the committee was instructed by the board to proceed without further delay, and was authorized to borrow one thousand dollars or one thousand five hundred dollars for the purpose. Contracts were let, Lewis Jones taking the brick and stone work, and the firm of Whitehead & Berry, the woodwork. Jones complied with his contract and turned over the finished product in November, 1838, for which he was paid the sum of three thousand seven hundred seventy-six dollars and twenty-five cents. Not so with Whitehead & Berry, who failed to meet their obligations. Their sureties were finally called upon to "make good," but the county was not able to occupy the building until late in the year 1841. Even then the officials were not properly supplied with office furniture and apparatus, and most of what they did have was borrowed from the Methodist church, in which latter edifice the county officials had found shelter while the new court house was in the course of construction.

PRESENT COURT HOUSE.

As early as the year 1868, the board of commissioners, having in view the construction of a modern and expensive building for county offices and the courts, began to levy a small tax as the nucleus of a building fund. On the first day of June, 1869, this fund amounted to $3,642.82; June 1, 1870, $9,130.57; June 1, 1871, $10,678.41; June 1, 1872, $14,580.88; June 1, 1876, $56,471.52.

In the month of September, 1873, by a concerted movement of citizens, the need and desirability of a new court house were brought to the attention of the board of county commissioners, which led to the appointment by that body of Matthew L. Brett, Richard N. Read and Joseph G. Thompson, as a committee to mature plans for a building that would meet the requirements of the county and also harmonize with the wishes and tastes of the community generally; at the same time keeping in mind the financial capacity of the county, and the state of the treasury. A small appropriation was made to defray expenses of the committee in visiting various localities and inspecting court houses in the state, but the contract for the building was not awarded until early in the year 1877, the contracting firm of McCormick & Sweeney being the successful bidders G. N. Bunting was selected as the architect and superintendent of the work.

As soon as the weather became favorable, in the spring of 1878, excavation for the building commenced and by the end of the year the structure was under roof and nearing completion. To meet the financial needs of contractor and superintendent and to pay for material, the county was forced to place bonds to the amount of fifteen thousand dollars on the market, but before the year had begun to grow old the court house was finished and occupied. In the spring of 1878 a two-thousand-pound bell was placed in the tower of the building, at a cost of one thousand five hundred and twenty-five dollars, the present, beautiful and substantial temple of justice standing as a splendid monument to the excellent business capacity and judgment of the county's public officials. Taking the material of which it is constructed and the workmanship employed, the building could not today be put up in the same workmanlike manner for double the cost, which was eighty-eight thousand twenty-one dollars and fifteen cents, not including the bell.

COUNTY JAILS.

A detailed description of the plans for the first county jail erected in Washington in 1819, is set out in one of the succeeding chapters of this volume. The first move by the board of commissioners in the relation was made in May, 1819, when plans, specifications and bids were asked for by the board for a jail building. The structure was to be built of logs, to be eighteen by twenty-eight feet in dimensions, two stories high, walls one foot thick and to contain a criminals' room and a debtors' room. The contract was let to Aaron Freeland and Jesse Purcell for one thousand and ten dollars, and according to agreement the jail was turned over to the board in a finished condition in December, 1819. It stood on the northeast corner of the tract of land now occupied by the court house, which was early known as the public square.

SECOND COUNTY JAIL BUILT IN 1830.

The records do not state how the county jail happened to get in the way of fire and was destroyed. But that is neither here nor there. The building was leveled to the ground by fire in 1829 and for some time thereafter the clerk of the board, in making up his minutes, often mentioned the bastile as "the late county jail."

The loss of this public institution was quite serious. Although the citizens of Washington and the county generally were law-abiding and peace-loving, still the same could not be said of all. There were unruly ones. Whisky was only worth about twenty cents a gallon and a good many people made daily use of the stuff that both cheers and inebriates. Horse-racing, bull-baiting, cock-fighting, gambling and other intensive amusements were quite rife in those callow days of Daviess county, and now and then hilarity degenerated into misdemeanors and sometimes crime. The need of a place to incarcerate the unruly and law-defying citizens, therefore, went without serious question and the county found itself absolutely compelled to furnish a successor to "the late jail." This necessarily found expression in the action of the board of justices when, in January, 1830, that august body let and awarded a contract to James Whitehead, for the building of a jail, same style as "the late jail" and to cost three hundred ninety-eight dollars eighty-seven and one-half cents. The building, as completed in November, 1830, was of logs and was eighteen by twenty-eight feet in dimensions.

THIRD COUNTY JAIL COMPLETED IN 1860.

Daviess county built, at different periods, two log jails, small affairs, one of which was destroyed by fire and the other, as the county increased its population and malefactors became more numerous, was found inadequate and obsolete. Each building was provided with a room for that class of debtors who either were unable or unwilling to meet their obligations and, by reason thereof, were liable to imprisonment until their debts were canceled or compromised. Happily, the law under which unfortunates of this class were deprived of their liberty long since has been abolished and no "debtor's room" figures in modern plans for county jails in the great commonwealth of Indiana.

The county bastile, built of logs in 1830, which lasted until the year 1859, stood on the northwest corner of the public square. The question of replacing this crude structure with one of greater dimensions and more substantial material was considered by the board in the year last mentioned above. Matthew L. Brett and Andrew Martin were appointed by the board as a committee to prepare plans and perform other pertinent duties, among which was the letting of the contract for the proposed improvement. Following instruction, this committee presented designs for the jail and awarded the building contract to the firm of Richards & Harris, for the sum of five thousand two hundred twenty-nine dollars. To finance the undertaking the board appropriated the sum of seven thousand dollars. Thomas F. Baker put in the iron work for the cells and when the structure was turned over to the board in its finished state, December 2, 1860, the appropriation had been consumed.

FOURTH JAIL ERECTED IN 1884.

In the year 1883, the board of county commissioners issued twenty-five thousand dollars in bonds, to secure the means wherewith to erect a combined jail and turnkey's residence that would meet the requirements of that period and several future generations. These bonds were arranged in series and of different denominations. They sold at a premium, which indicates the splendid financial condition of the county at that time. Brentwood Tolan, of Fort Wayne, was selected as the architect and, although not the lowest bidder, the contract was let to J. G. Miller, for the sum of twenty-five thousand five hundred dollars. The old jail building was sold and removed from its site. In 1881 a lot was purchased of Alexander Leslie, situated on the southeast corner of Walnut and Third streets, for which one thousand two hundred dollars was paid, and here the present substantial brick county jail and sheriff's residence combined, was constructed, the same being completed in 1884, at a total cost of twenty-eight thousand eight hundred and thirty-six dollars.

THE COUNTY INFIRMARY.

In all communities under civil government it is necessary and obligatory to provide ways and means for the care and comfort of the unfortunate citizens, who are incapacitated by disease, physical or mental deformities or the ravages of time. Some time had elapsed after Daviess county had gathered well along on its way in growth and prosperity, before the authorities were called upon for assistance by a helpless or indigent person. When the time came in which it was apparent that public assistance to the needy was inevitable, certain persons in the community, willing and trustworthy, were empowered by the trustees of the townships to render assistance to worthy mendicants, in the way of food and shelter. For the first three years of the county's existence the expense in this relation was negligible. In 1835, the amount of money expended throughout the county in public charities only reached the sum of two hundred and fifty dollars. But the system of providing for the poor was inconvenient and unsatisfactory, so that, in March, 1841, the board of justices issued bids for the sale to the county of a tract of land, to contain either forty or eighty acres of land. A committee made up of Joseph Warner, Samuel Kelso and Abner Davis, was appointed in June, 1842, to examine several tracts of land offered for sale and after consideration, the board purchased eighty acres, three and one-half miles south of Washington, in section 14, Veale township, the price being two hundred and eighty dollars. Half of the farm was secured of David Hogshead and the other "forty" of Lewis Jones.

On the county farm when purchased were a small house and barn. William T. Wallace and John Bishop were selected as a committee to superintend the construction of other necessary buildings, but if any were put up no record of the fact has been made. William Harlin was appointed superintendent of the infirmary and, in 1843, he managed the farm and the two inmates of the newly-erected eleemosynary institution. Hamlet Sanford and Joseph Allison were selected as the "visitors," or inspectors and, while in the performance of their onerous duties, the "visitors" found three inmates on the farm in 1845. The superintendent reported for the fiscal year 1846-7 that the institution's expenses amounted to four hundred ninety-two dollars and six cents. In 1848 Dr. Samuel W. Peck was appointed county physician.

John Jones was the superintendent in 1853 and was under contract to maintain the inmates at one dollar and thirty-five cents each per week and have the use of the farm. There is nothing to show what profit Mr. Jones made out of this contract or whether any of the inmates were able to walk at the end of the year. However, the old farm, by the year 1864, proved a failure in serving its purpose and was sold to Thomas Cunningham for one thousand dollars. Another place, containing one hundred acres, situated in section 12, Washington township, was bought of John McCarey, for which three thousand five hundred dollars was paid. Later, different tracts of land were added to the farm which now contains two hundred and forty-four acres, a part of which lies in section 13, and valued at forty thousand dollars.

On this county farm was built, in 1866, under the superintendency of a building committee composed of John Hyatt, Dr. G. G. Barton and R. A. Clements, a large brick building, in which were dormitories, sitting-rooms, dining-rooms, kitchen, and living-rooms for the superintendent and his family.

That structure stands today and is performing the duties for which it originally was intended, although sadly out of date in its arrangement and appointments. Some minor improvements have been made to the farm in recent years, but nothing over which the county particularly exults.

Quill White, the present superintendent of the Daviess county infirmary, in his report for the year 1914, stated that the farm's receipts for that year amounted to two thousand five hundred sixty-nine dollars and thirty-three cents, and the amount disbursed was three thousand five hundred twenty-four dollars and fifty-three cents.

CHAPTER V.

COUNTY GOVERNMENT.

It will have been noticed, that, when the county was organized, a board of commissioners was elected, whose office was to transact the county's business affairs. Under this commissioners' system, some of the most important details, pertinent to the starting of the county's governmental machinery, were inaugurated and carried into effect. This system was continued until the fall of 1824, when, by reason of complaints and grievances set up by certain of the taxpayers, the office was abolished and in its stead was created, by the Legislature, a somewhat similar body, clothed with the same duties, authority and responsibilities as its predecessor, and named the board of county justices, which was made up of the oldest justice (in point of service) from each township, whose members elected a presiding officer with the title of president of the board. This ruling body remained under the law until September 1831, when the board of commissioners again was placed at the head of the county's affairs, only to be superseded once more, in 1836, by a board of justices, which performed its functions until September, 1842, when three commissioners took their seats and conducted the business of the county under the system first adopted.

THE COUNTY COUNCIL.

From 1842 to 1899, a period covering fifty-seven years, the board of county commissioners held full sway and carried on the county business in its own way, being deterred in its methods only through fear of each member's constituency. From time to time members of the board displayed qualities and performed official acts that were quite reprehensible and, it is said, more than one left the county without warning or ceremony. The taxpayers, as a rule, were long-suffering and patient, but the time came when patience ceased to be a virtue and the Legislature finally was prevailed on to pass a measure restricting the power of the board of commissioners. This "happy consummation" reached fruition when the General Assembly passed an act entitled "an act concerning county business," approved March 3, 1899. The first section reads as follows:

"Be it enacted by the General Assembly of the state of Indiana, That there is hereby enacted in the several counties of this state a body to be known as a county council and styled according to the name of the county, etc."

Under this law the board of county commissioners was commanded to meet within twenty days after the act went into effect and divide the county into four districts, from each of which a member should be returned by election to the newly-created council and, in addition thereto, three councilmen at large, to be elected by the voters of the whole county. The salary for each councilman is placed at ten dollars per annum and the time for opening the session of the council is designated as the first Tuesday after the first Monday of September, of every year, "for the purpose of fixing the rate of the tax levy and making appropriations." Section 15 of the act, a very important one, is as follows:

"The power of fixing the rate of taxation for county purposes, and for all purposes where the rate not fixed by law is required to be uniform throughout the county, shall be vested exclusively in the county council; and neither the board of county commissioners, nor any county officer or officers, shall have power to fix the rate for any purpose whatever. The power of making appropriations of money to be paid out of the county treasury shall be vested exclusively in such council, and, except as in this act otherwise expressly provided, no money shall be drawn from such treasury but in pursuance of appropriations so made."

Section 32 of the act declares that "the county council shall have the exclusive power to authorize the borrowing of money for the county"; and, in section 29, the language is plain and unequivocal in defining the reason for the measure as follows: "The intent of this act is to place limits and checks upon payments out of such treasury and not to extend or increase them."

On Monday, August 7, 1899, the county council of Daviess county, Indiana, by order of the board of commissioners of said county, met in the circuit court room in the court house, in the city of Washington, Indiana, the following members being present: John G. Leming, George W. Smith, James W. Cain, Andrew T. Myers, Frank B. Arford, John Downey, Anderson Veale. The council then adjourned to meet in regular session on the first Tuesday, after the first Monday in September, 1899. The following, in the relation, is taken from the council's record of proceedings:

"Come now the members of the Daviess county council, this the 5th day of September, 1899. The meeting is called to order by John Downey, president, in the chair, with Robert Russell, clerk of the council, present upon call of the roll, the following members are present and answer to their names, towit: John Downey, James W. Cain, John Leming, Anderson Veale, George W. Smith, Frank Arford, Andrew T. Myers." The members of the council all being present, that body immediately began the business for which it was created.

EARLY BUSINESS PROCEEDINGS.

Below are presented some interesting details of the proceedings of the county's business agents during its formation period, the following being excerpts from the early proceedings of the board of commissioners. Under date of March 15, 1817, there is the following entry:

"State of Indiana,
"Daviess County.

"At a meeting of the county commissioners of said county, the commissioners being present, William Ballow, John Aikman and Ephraim Thompson, and they received the report from the sheriff respecting the county seat of Daviess county, and made the same publicly known, then adjourned to Monday next, nine o'clock. Accordingly they met on the 19th instant, and ordered that Emanuel VanTrees shall survey the land given as a donation for the county seat of Daviess county, given by Emanuel VanTrees and Peter Wilkins, and found the same to be thirty-seven acres and one-half and thirty-two [the latter figures probably that many one-hundredths]. The commissioners then proceeded to appoint an agent for said county and unanimously agreed that John Allen, senior, shall be the agent, who, accordingly, came forward and gave his bond for twenty thousand dollars, and his security were James ————, Samuel J. Kelso, and Peter Wilkins; and then adjourned to the 18th instant at 9 o'clock. Accordingly met to [by] appointment and proceeded to lay out the town and ordered the survey and called the name thereof, Washington. And the survey was performed by Emanuel VanTrees until finished.

"The commissioners appointed the public square to be between Main street and Walnut street and between the lots numbered 44 and 45 and 64 and 65."

"Monday, the 12th day of May, the commissioners met agreeable to act of the Legislature, at the court house, in our said county of Daviess, and proceeded to business. Ordered that a township be laid off, towit: Beginning at the range line of ranges 7 and 8, township 2, sections 7 and 8; thence east running with the section line to the corner between sections 10 and 11; thence north with the section line, including all the inhabitance north of the beginning line and to be called the township of Washington.

"Further ordered that a township be laid off, towit: Beginning at range 7, thence down the west fork of White river to the injunction [junction]; thence up the east fork to the mouth of Aikmans creek; thence up said creek to the head; thence to the corner between sections 10 and 11. To be called Veel's [Veale] township."

"Further ordered that a township be laid off, beginning at the mouth of Aikman creek and running up said creek to the head; thence on a direct line to the mouth of Lick creek; thence down White river to the [place of] beginning. To be called Reeves [Reeve] township."

"Further ordered that a township be laid off, towit: To commence at the section line between sections 10 and 11; thence north with the said line; thence east to range [Orange county, now] line, and with said line to Lick creek; thence down said creek to the mouth; thence on a direct line to the beginning. To be called Perry township."

[This subdivision of the county extended into what subsequently became Orange county, which was part and parcel of Daviess at that time.]

"Further ordered that the following be the number of justices of the peace to be elected in each township in said county, towit:

"For the township of Washington, three justices of the peace; township of Reeves, two; township of Veele [Veale], two; township of Perry, two.

"And further ordered that elections be held in the different townships of said county of the first Saturday in June, next, 1817; and be it further ordered that the sheriff be [ordered] to advertize the election at the following places, towit: Which are hereby established: For the township of Washington, at the court house in Liverpool; Veele [Veale] township, at the house of James Veele, junior, now John Colemans; Reeves township, at the house of Martin Palmar; Perry township, at the house of Henry Hall.

"And be it further ordered that William Palmar and Aaron Freelan be and they are hereby appointed constables for the township of Washington; and for the constables of Veele township, William Veele is hereby appointed; for the township of Reeve, John Davison is hereby appointed constable; for the township of Perry, William Hays."

"The commissioners met on the 13th of May, agreeable to adjournment, and proceeds to appoint listers of taxable property in the several townships, towit: for the township of Washington, Vance Jones; Veele, James C. Veele, junior; Reeve, Mason Ballow; Perry, George Mitcheltree. Ordered that

Thomas Bradford be and he is hereby appointed inspector for Washington township, on the first Monday in June, next election; Joel Halbert, inspector for Perry township; Henry Edwards for Veele township; William Ballow for Reeves township.

"Further ordered that overseers of the poor be appointed in each township, as follows: Washington township, William Hawkins and Ebenezer Jones; Veele, John Coleman and John Evans; Reeves, James Aikman and Joshua Reeves; Perry, Joel Halbert and Frederick Shaltz.

"Ordered that the clerk shall alter the number of justices of the peace in Washington township from two to three."

SOME INTERESTING SIDELIGHTS.

Then follows a list of appointments for road supervisors in the various townships, also agents for the same. At this session of the commissioners' court an important measure was passed in the appointment of Ebenezer Jones, treasurer for the county, "for the time being by law." It should here be stated that G. L. VanTrees was the first clerk of the board of commissioners and the foregoing extracts from the minute book of that important body were recorded by him. To proceed with the records:

"June, the 28th, 1817. The county commissioners met and proceeded to lay a tax on the taverns in said county, that is to say: The taverns in Liverpool shall pay twelve dollars annually, except Miss Ogden; she and the tavern keepers in all other places in this county shall pay ten dollars, that is, for the present year, and each tavern keeper shall sell for no more than the following rates, that is to say: For whiskey, per half pint, twelve and one-half cents; rum, brandy or wine, per half pint, fifty cents; twenty-five cents per meal for breakfast, dinner or supper; for lodging, or bed, twelve and one-half cents; a horse to hay or feed per night, thirty-seven and one-half cents."

The prices quoted above seem ridiculously low to the present-day reader, especially the rates set for ardent drinks, but these were the days before "Uncle Sam" took over the control of the manufacture of spirituous, vinous and malt liquors. Before the inauguration of the tax, good whisky could be obtained for twenty cents a gallon, so that the prices laid down by the board of county commissioners were quite liberal for the dealer. The rates determined for the guidance of tavern keepers in providing food and provender for man and beast would seem, at this day, to have been a little arbitrary.

However, the traveling public of the twentieth century would hail with glee legislation somewhat on the same line.

The time and attention of the board for some time after its organization were employed in hearing and granting petitions for appointing viewers and hearing reports in relation to these primitive but needed improvements. As a matter of fact, road building is about the first thing to be considered in a new settlement and the authorities in all new communities legislate liberally for roads and bridges.

SUNDRY ORDERS OF THE BOARD.

At a sitting of the board on the 11th of August, 1817, it was ordered that a "ferry be established across the east fork of White river by Frederick Sholtz, or his agent, provided he shall comply with the laws of the state in that case made and provided." At this same session it was ordered that "the following rates of taxes shall be collected for the year of 1817 for the county tax. On land, for one-half the rates that are payable to the state and on negroes the same; horses, thirty-seven and a half cents per head, as the law directs. Hall and Sholtz shall pay each for the said year fifteen dollars. And their rates shall be as follows, and they shall charge no more than the following rates for ferrying: For a loaded wagon and team, $1.00; stages or two-horse wagon, 62½ cents; man and horse, 12½ cents; footmen, per head, 6¼ cents.

"Ordered, that Judge James G. Read be appointed to judge all moneys that may be shown him by the county treasurer or sheriff, to be by him adjudged whether it be passable or not."

At the session of the board held on August 13, 1817, it was ordered that "a writ of *ad quad damnum* do issue to the sheriff to summon a jury and to meet and view a mill seat, the property of Simon Adams and James Gilley." This formidable legal writ was to be issued to "the agent of section No. 16, in township 1, range 5, if applied for."

"The commissioners met according to adjournment on the 14th day of August, 1817, and proceeded to examine all listers' books of taxable property of the several townships. The commissioners proceeded to settle with the sheriff, Daniel Comer, and by viewing the law and his accounts the said sheriff is hereby allowed the sum of fifty-two dollars. Ordered that the clerk do advertise the sale of the court house to the lowest bidder on the last Saturday of September next."

"November 10, 1817. The county commissioners met according to law and ordered that the clearing off of the public square in Washington town shall be sold to the lowest bidder."

"November the 15th, 1817. Ordered that six acres of land be offered for sale to the highest bidder on Thursday next, with Ephraim Thompson donated to the county, to be sold in two-acre lots." It was also ordered that Emanuel VanTrees "receive an order on the county treasurer for fifty dollars, for twenty-five days services done to said commissioners," which was accordingly done.

"Ordered that William Bruce and Peter Ruble do receive an order on the county treasurer for such lawful demands as they may claim for establishing the county seat when demanded."

"In vacation of the commissioners," records Clerk VanTrees, some time in January, 1818, "the six acres of land were sold, which were given by Ephraim Thompson to the county, which were sold to James G. Read, on the first Monday of January, 1818, for one hundred and eighty-three dollars, payable in eighteen months from the day of sale."

Tuesday, February 10, 1818. Among matters adjusted it was "ordered that Ebenezer Jones be and he is hereby appointed treasurer for the county of Daviess for one year from the date hereof. Whereupon he took the oath of office according to law, administered by Parmenes Palmer, Esqr.

"Ordered that James G. Read receive from the county treasurer one thousand eighty-seven dollars, and twenty-two and three quarters cents, for building a jail in the town of Washington, in our said county, out of any money in the treasury received from the sale of lots in said town.

"Ordered that Alexander Bruce receive from the treasury of our said county thirteen dollars, for the use of a house for the county commissioners in the year 1817."

RATES OF TAVERN KEEPERS CHANGED.

At its sitting of May 13, 1818, the commissioners' court changed the tariff devised for tavern keepers to correspond with the following schedule: Supper or breakfast, 25 cents; dinner, 37½ cents; whisky, one-half pint, 12½ cents; gin, one-half pint, 25 cents; French brandy or rum, 50 cents; lodging, 12½ cents; horse, per night, to hay and corn or oats, 75 cents; single feed, 25 cents; hay only, per night, 25 cents.

The rates for ferrying also were revised, and the per diem of jurors was certainly no bait to entice the settler from any business pursuit in which he happened to be engaged, as the following indicates: "Ordered, that each grand juror do receive an order on the county treasurer for seventy-five cents per day for sitting on the grand jury at the circuit court at last March session; where they may apply for the same."

ORDER FOR A COURT HOUSE.

"May the 11th, 1818. It is ordered that a court house shall be built of good brick, thirty-five feet by forty-five feet long, two storys high, the first story to be twelve feet high between floors. The foundation to be dug eighteen inches in the ground, to be well walled with good, hard-burnt brick, such as will not decay by wet, at least two and one-half feet high, all the brick to be eight inches long and the width and thickness in proper proportions. The outside of the walls shall all be good hard brick. The thickness of the walls of the first story shall be sixteen inches, or the length of two bricks, all of which shall be laid on with good sand and lime and to be one-third of the mortar lime and two-thirds thereof sand, well sifted and mixed. All such work to be done in a complete, workmanlike manner. And there shall be two fire-place chimneys, each of which shall have a fireplace, above each of which shall be two and one-half feet in the back part thereof, the lower floor to be well laid of brick, the two chimneys to be on the east end of the house. There shall be one double door, each three feet wide, so as to shut and meet each other in the middle and make a door six feet wide and seven feet high, besides an oval arch above that, with sash and glass. Said door to be lined and paneled, and with good hinges and lock. There shall be a good stone sill under said door, fastened in the wall of the house. There shall be eight windows in the lower story and eight in the upper story, each window to contain sash and glass eight by ten inches and each window to contain thirty-six lights, with good panel window-shutters to each window. The timber for the floor between the first and second storys there shall be a girder the short way through the middle of the house, 4x18 inches, thirty-two joists, 3½x12 inches, with two columns under the girder at proper distances; and for the upper floor shall be a girder length ways through the house forty-five feet, 9x12 inches thick and forty joists 3x9 inches, with one column; all to be done in a nice and good workmanlike manner.

"There shall be good, full-trimmed window frames and a door frame, with their proper molding, to be of black walnut, as wide as the wall is by four inches thick. There shall be sixteen pair of rafters, which shall be of good sound wood, four inches the one way by five inches the other way, good sheeting seven-eighths of an inch thick; there shall be good, yellow poplar shingles, thirteen inches long and five-eighths of an inch thick at the butt, four inches wide, and the roof well put on with good nails, all of which to be done in a good, workmanlike manner. All the above work to be done against next Christmas, three years. One-third of the payments shall be paid in eighteen months from the day of the contract and the other payments in three years from next Christmas."

The first liquor license granted by the board, as shown by the clerk's record, was issued to William Bowen, on the 7th of November, 1818, the same to be in effect until the 27th of August, 1819.

"Monday the 8th day of February, 1819. County commissioners met in court house. Adjourned to meet at the house of Judge J. G. Read, where the sheriff opened the session by proclamation."

FIRST RECORDED SETTLEMENT WITH COUNTY TREASURER.

"The commissioners met on the 10th of February, 1819, according to adjournment. The commissioners settled with the treasurer, E. Jones. It appears as follows:

"Money received by the treasurer	$1,126.43¼
"Money paid out by him	1,064.63¾
"The balance	61.74½
"Percentage as compensation	56.30
"Money left in the treasury	5.44

"Likewise settled with said treasurer for the money received and paid out, arising from the sale of town lots; whereas this day the county is indebted to said Jones in the sum of thirty-two dollars twelve and one-half cents. The said Jones agrees to take an order on the treasury for twenty dollars only; which order is given in full."

"Ordered that James G. Read and Henry Cruse do receive an order on the county treasurer for the sum of eight hundred dollars out of any money arising from the sale of lots, as part pay of building the court house.

"Ordered, that Emanuel VanTrees [clerk] receive the kee [key] of the court house and to take charge of said house."

"Ordered, that Solomon Suplee and John R. Beard do receive an order on the treasury for eight dollars and twenty-five cents for preparing a house for a jail."

CRIMINALS WERE BRANDED.

"Ordered, that Jake Lynch be allowed 3 dollars 50 cents for hinges and branding iron."

"May 12, 1819. Ordered, that the building of a jail in the town of Washington will be sold to the lowest bidder, on the first Saturday of June, next, when the description will be made known by the agent.

"Ordered, that Henry Cruse be allowed four dollars for the rent of his house at last court.

"Ordered, that the court house be built in the center of the public square."

"June the 5th, 1819. The commissioners, William Ballow, Ephraim Jones and John Aikman, met at the court house [so named by courtesy], for the purpose of forming a plan for the building of a jail house, for the county of Daviess, in Washington.

"Ordered, that a jail be built eighteen feet wide and twenty-eight feet long, two storys high, the first story to be nine and one-half feet between the first floor and the lower part of the jail and the second story to be eight feet between the second and the under part of the second tier of joists. Two rooms and an entry above, in the second story; a criminal room nine by sixteen feet in the clear and an entry of four feet in the clear.

ROOM FOR DEBTORS.

"And debtors room nearly twelve by sixteen feet in the clear. The one partition next the criminals room to be of twelve inch square timber, laid close, and the partition between the entry and the debtor's room to be of two-inch oak. The upper floor above the criminal room to be of timber, two inches thick, laid tuching each other, and the floor of the criminal room to be the same as the upper; logs of ten inches thick, the edges to be squared. To be twelve good, oak sleepers for the first floor and the said first floor to be laid of one and one-fourth inch of well seasoned boards and well laid and nailed with sufficient nails; two nails in each plank on each sleeper. Said floor to be of quarter plank. The second floor or the lower floor, of the criminals' and debtors' room, to be well laid and tunged and grooved and two spikes in each plank; each joist of two-inch seasoned oak plank, the joists of the floor of the debtors' room to be four inches thick by ten inches deep, and the joists above the said debtors' room to be the same as the criminals' room, with squared timber; all said joists for said floors and entry to be no more than two feet apart from center to center. The floor above the criminals' room to be sealed with inch oak plank well nailed fast, tunged and grooved, and the upper part of the entry to be sealed the same way, also the upper floor of the debtors' room the same sealing. The logs for the walls of the house to be of good oak timber, twelve inches thick, well squared and laid close to each other, notched with a half duf tale [dove tail]; to have good rafters and good sheeting and a good joist shingle roof, with the gavel [gable] ends well finished, two common sice [size] doors in the lower, or jailor's room, well checked and cased with plank; common bottom doors, two twelve-lite [light] windows well finished and glass put in them. To have a plain pair of stairs to go up in the entry and two doors, the one to go out into the debtors' room and the other in the criminals' room, two feet wide and five feet high, to be made of two-inch oak plank and doubled crossways and sufficiently spiked as the agent (John Allen) may direct, and hung; and the grates to be put in, the county to find the grates and the hinges. All said work to be done in a complete, workmanlike manner, and to be finished against the first day of March next, the county to pay to the builders one hundred dollars when the walls are raised and two hundred dollars when this is finished and the rest in six months from that time."

On August 4, 1819, the board met and created the township of Barr, taking its territory from the east part of Washington township. John Perkins was appointed inspector of elections, and an election was ordered to be held on the first Saturday in September, 1819, for two justices of the peace.

"Ordered, that the jail be built on the west end of the public square, adjoining the cross street, beginning twenty feet south of the stray pen."

"Ordered, that John Allen, agent for Daviess county, do receive the same precent [per cent] on all moneys collected and paid as is allowed to the county treasurer by law; and also that he, the said Allen, do receive reasonable and full payment for his services, done in laying off the town of Washington and selling the same [lots], and for all public duties done by him respecting his agency."

THE COURT HOUSE IS FINISHED.

The board of commissioners met in adjourned session on November 10, 1819, and made settlement with James G. Read, whose contract for building the court house was for the sum of two thousand nine hundred and seventy-nine dollars. He had received three hundred dollars on the contract, and the board, after deducting one hundred dollars, which had been left undone by the contractor, and allowing him one hundred and forty-nine dollars for extra work, he was given an order on the treasury for two thousand two hundred twenty-five dollars and fifty cents, to be paid out of any money in the treasury derived from the sale of lots of the town of Washington.

"The commissioners agreed with Samuel VanTrees for him to paint the roof of the court house and to paint the walls on the outside and pencil the same; all the said painting to be done with a sufficiency of Spanish brown and oils, and to be done in a good and workmanlike manner; for which work the said VanTrees is to receive one hundred dollars, so soon as said work shall be finished."

FIRST JAIL COMPLETED.

"December 4, 1819. The commissioners being notified that the jail of this county is completed, met on the present instant. Present, Ehpraim Thompson, William Ballou. Having examined said jail, find it complete and receive the same. Ordered, that Aaron Freeland receive an order on the county treasurer for the sum of one hundred dollars, to be paid out of any money arising from the sale of lots in the town of Washington.

"N. B. Jesse Purcell received in the fall of 1819, the sum of thirty dollars, as part pay for the building of the jail."

"February the tenth, 1820. Ordered, that Abner Cosby do receive an order on the county treasury for four dollars and fifty cents, for making hooks, hasps and steeples [staples], and repairing hinges, etc., for the jail.

"Ordered, that Jesse Purcell, Aaron Freeland and William Quigley do receive an order on the county treasury for two hundred dollars, out of any money arising out of the sale of the town lots, as part pay for building the jail in Washington. An order given to William Quigley for fifty dollars out of the above two hundred dollars."

"February the 16th, 1820. William Ballou received an order on the treasury for forty-four dollars, as his pay for being in session as a commissioner in 1818 and 1819. John Aikman and Ephraim Thompson had heretofore received their orders."

DEFICIT IN THE COUNTY TREASURY.

"February the 16th, 1820. The commissioners proceeded to settle with Ebenezer Jones, when it appears that the treasurer has received for the revenue the sum of_____$808.46½
"Paid out on orders _____ 767.97½

                                                                    30.49
"His percentage _____ 40.40

"Therefore he overpaid _____$ 9.91

"Also settled with the said treasurer for the money arising from the sale of the town lots, where it appears there is due him $62.50."

"Tuesday, May 9, 1820. Ordered, that a new township be laid off; that is to say, all that part of Daviess county laying north of Prairie Creek, and to be known as Bogard township. The election to be held at the house of Michael Robeson, on the second Saturday in June next."

The following order of the commissioners' court suggests the idea that the jail was destroyed: "Ordered, that Jesse Purcell receive an order on the county treasury arising from the sale of the town lots, the sum of sixty dollars as part pay for building the late jail in Washington. The order given immediately."

"August 11, 1820. Ordered, that Jesse Purcell, Aaron Freeland and William Quigley, receive an order, or orders, on the county treasury for six hundred and fifty dollars, which with the orders given heretofore, will amount to one thousand and ten dollars, the full amount for building the late jail, to be paid out of any money arising from the sale of town lots."

SETTLEMENT WITH THE COUNTY TREASURER.

"Tuesday the 13th, February, 1821. The commissioners proceeded to settle with the treasurer, where it appears as follows:

"Received _____$632.85
"Paid out _____ 627.06
"His percentage _____ 30.55

"And the treasurer throwing away a balance agrees to be even to this date."

It will be seen by the above figures that the board found a balance in the treasury of five dollars and seventy-nine cents. The treasurer's fees for collecting the taxes amounted to thirty dollars and fifty-five cents, so that the county found itself short of funds to meet its obligations to the treasurer in the amount of twenty-four dollars and seventy-six cents. This sum of money the treasurer very generously donated to the county, as shown by the ingenuous statement of the clerk of the board, Emanuel VanTrees.

"May the tenth, 1821. Ordered, that a county tax be laid for the year 1821 and rated as follows, to wit: On town lots at the rate of 50 cents per 100 dollars; horse, 37½ cents; on all white males over 21 years of age, 50 cents; on pleasure carriages, 4 wheels, $1.25; 2 wheels, $1.00; on each silver watch, 25 cents; gold watch, 50 cents."

By petition the township of Elmore was enacted out of the north part of Bogard township, by the board of county commissioners at its session of the 13th of August, 1821. An election was ordered to be held at the house of James Robeson, on the next succeeding Saturday in September. Samuel Doty was appointed inspector of elections for the township.

COUNTY SEEKS AID OF CITIZENS.

"May the 16th, 1822. Ordered that a subscription paper be circulated among the citizens of Daviess county, to raise a fund for the purpose of repairing the new court house in Washington, so far as to accommodate the courts at their sittings and if the sum of two hundred and fifty dollars or more be subscribed by responsible citizens the same shall be appropriated to the repairing of said house; and if at any time hereafter a tax shall be laid for the purpose of completing the public building in Daviess county, the amount which any individual or company shall voluntarily subscribe and pay by virtue of said subscription shall be deducted from the amount which may be levied on him by such tax, and if the sum subscribed and paid shall exceed the amount of any tax which may be laid for the purpose above said then the amount of such excess shall be refunded at any time after two years from the first day of January next."

BOARD OF COUNTY JUSTICES.

The last meeting of the board of county commissioners was held in August, 1824, when the governing body of the county was changed by an act of the Legislature, not only in the number of its members but also in name, as the following extract from the records show:

"At a meeting of the board of county justices of the county of Daviess and state of Indiana, on Monday the sixth day of September, one thousand eight hundred and twenty-four, agreeable to law in such case made and provided: Present, the Honorable Samuel Smith, Stephen Maston, George H. Routt, Joseph Hays, Joseph Brown, Thomas Morgan, Charles F. Wells, John Shircliff, Thomas Howell, and Amos Rogers, justices of the peace, who proceeded to organize themselves into a board and proceeded to elect a president for said board by joint ballot. Whereupon it appears that George H. Routt was duly elected president of the said board."

"January term, 1830. Ordered that the clerk advertise, at least twenty days before the next sitting of this board, that sealed proposals will be received at the clerk's office for the building of a county jail, the jail to be built after the plan of the late county jail that was destroyed by fire, etc."

At the March term of the justices' court the contract for a county jail was awarded to James Whitehead, his bid being for the sum of three hundred ninety-eight dollars eighty-seven and one-half cents; one-third to be paid upon commencement of the work of construction, and the balance upon acceptance of the complete building. At the January term, 1831, James Whitehead reported the completion of the jail and the board of justices accepted it.

In May, 1831, George H. Routt, who had been president of the board of justices since its organization, died; and at the session of the board held that month George H. Routt was elected successor to the deceased chairman.

"March term, 1832. Ordered that the board 'will receive sealed proposals for weather-boarding the jail in the following manner, to wit: To be lathed with oak lath one- and-a-quarter inch thick, to be placed three feet apart and pinned with one pin in each log, with inch pins well fastened, upon which the weather-boarding is to be nailed with sufficiently large nails; the weather-boarding to be planed and to show only five inches to the weather."

"May term, 1832. Ordered, that the Right Honorable George Allen Waller, Esquire, sheriff of said county of Daviess, be and he is hereby allowed one dollar for a bucket by him magnanimously furnished for the use of the courts of said county."

NEW FORM OF GOVERNMENT.

Pursuant to an act of the General Assembly entitled "An act to regulate the mode of doing county business, etc.," approved January 19, 1831, the board of justices divided the county into three districts, from each of which later was elected a county commissioner, to form a board of commissioners under the law. Accordingly, three commissioners were elected on the first Monday in August, 1831, and on the 5th of September, 1831, this new board of commissioners, composed of Samuel I. Kelso, from the first district, and Jacob D. Crabs, from the second district, met at the court house, organized the board of county commissioners and proceeded to transact the business affairs of the county, and superseded the nondescript board of justices. On the second day of the term Alexander English, member from the third district, appeared and took his seat.

"May term, 1835. Ordered, that James Calhoun be allowed the sum of five dollars and fifty cents for recording the indentures of Angeline Taylor, Samuel C. Taylor, Cemantha Taylor, Cyrus Taylor, Joseph Abel, and Martha

Abel, and for transcribing the indentures of R. Walker, H. Brandus, B. N. Helphinstine, Will H. Helphinstine and N. H. Taylor, bound by overseers of the poor."

Wallace township was established in 1823 and at the September (1835) term of the commissioners court, on petition of certain of the citizens of the township, the name was changed to Madison.

At the September term of the board of commissioners the township of Steele was made a separate subdivision of the county. John McCormick was appointed inspector of elections, Joseph H. McCloskey and William Lester overseers of the poor.

At the May term of the board, in the year 1836, John Vantrees, Barton Peck and James Breeze were appointed a commission to superintend the construction of a new court house.

At the November session, 1838, Lewis Jones was paid one thousand one hundred dollars, the last installment on his contract for the brick and stone work.

RETURNS TO BOARD OF JUSTICES SYSTEM.

The board of commissioners adjourned *sine die* in June, 1836, and in pursuance of an act passed by the General Assembly and approved on February 8, 1836, entitled "An act regulating the mode of doing county business in the counties of Daviess and Martin," a meeting was held on September 1, 1836, of the several justices holding the oldest commissions in the several townships. They appeared as follow: from Washington, William G. Cole; Barr, Charles D. Morgan; Bogard, Franklin Milhite; Steele, John Cawood; Madison, Joseph B. Van Matre, all of whom proceeded to organize the board by the election of a presiding officer in the person of John Cawood.

On the second day of the January term, 1840, the firm of Berry & Whitehead was paid seven hundred dollars, per order on the treasury, the last installment, on contract, for woodwork on the court house.

At the March term, 1841, the board ordered the submission of sealed proposals for the sale to the county "of 40, 80 or more acres of land in Daviess county, suitable to be converted into a farm for the support of the paupers of said county."

During the June (1841) session of the board of justices, the township of Harrison was created out of parts of Veale and Reeve townships. The elections were ordered held at the house of Jeremiah Allen, and that person was appointed inspector of elections for the newly-created township.

At the September term (1841) of the board of justices, on petition of citizens of Madison and Barr township, namely: Henry O'Neal, Pleasant Franklin, James M. O'Neal, Charles Ledgerwood, Thomas W. Hughes, William Roach, Charles Kilgore, Hezekiah Blevins, William D. Farrell, James B. Wood, John Adams, Wesley D. Kaggs, Stephen Kilgore and others, a new township was laid off, out of territory within the confines of the townships named, and was called Van Buren.

THE BOARD OF COMMISSIONERS AGAIN.

A special session of the board of justices was held on the 5th of August, 1842, and after certain important affairs of the county were given proper attention the board ceased its functions and adjourned *sine die*. On the 5th of September, following, the newly-elected board of commissioners organized and took up the duties of its office. The personnel of the board follows: Hiram Palmer, first district; James P. McGaughey, second; Charles D. Morgan, third.

CHAPTER VI.

POLITICAL HISTORY.

In this chapter there is presented a list of the county officials of Daviess county from the year 1816 to the year 1915, together with a list of state senators and representatives in the Legislature from the beginning of the county government to the present date, closing with a statement of the official vote of the county in all presidential campaigns from the year 1844, the first year in which the records of such vote are available.

BOARD OF COUNTY COMMISSIONERS.

From 1817 to 1820—William Ballow, John Aikman, Ephraim Thompson; 1821—William Ballow, John Aikman, James C. Veale; 1822—William Ballow, James C. Veale, William Wallace; 1823-24—James C. Veale, William Wallace, Joseph Brown. From September, 1824, to September, 1831, a board of justices was the governing body of the county. At the date last mentioned the county again elected a board of commissioners, whose names follow: 1831—Samuel J. Kelso, David Crabs, Alexander English; 1832-33—Samuel J. Kelso, David Crabs, Joseph Brown; 1834—Joseph Brown, David Crabs, Benjamin Godwin; 1835—David Crabs, Alexander English, David Crabs. In the month of August, 1835, Jacob D. Crabs resigned and John M. Horrall was appointed by the circuit court to fill vacancy. In 1836 the board of justices was re-established and performed its functions as the business agent of the county until in September, 1842, when the board of county commissioners once more came into its own. 1842-43—Hiram Palmer, James P. McGaughey, Charles D. Morgan; 1844—Hiram Palmer, Charles D. Morgan, John D. McCluskey; 1845—Charles D. Morgan, John D. McCluskey, Hamlet Sanford; McCluskey resigned and J. P. McGaughey was appointed to fill the vacancy; 1846—Hamlet Sanford, William H. Houghton, John Lester; 1847—H. Houghton, Hamlet Sanford, Henry Taylor; Sanford resigned before the expiration of his term and John English was appointed to fill the vacancy; 1848-49—H. Houghton, Henry Taylor, David M. Hixson; 1850—David M. Hixson, H. Houghton W. H. Wells; 1851—H.

DAVIESS COUNTY, INDIANA.   109

Houghton, W. H. Wells, William McCormick; 1852—W. H. Wells, William McCormick, J. C. Steen; 1853-56—William McCormick, J. C. Steen, H. K. Brown; 1857—J. C. Steen, William McCormick, Bazzel Liles, vice Brown, removed; Richard B. Dobbyn, vice McCormick, Bazzel Liles, vice Brown, B. Dobbyn, Thomas McCracken; 1859—Richard B. Dobbyn, Thomas Mc-Cracken, Owen O'Donald; Jacob C. Dillon, vice O'Donald; 1860-62—Thomas McCracken, Richard B. Dobbyn, David Solomon; 1863—John C. Dillon, Thomas McCracken, John McCory; 1864—John McCory, John C. Dillon, William Seals; 1865—William Seals, John McCory, William T. Dickinson, Stephen D. Wright to fill vacancy created by the removal from the county of McCory; 1866—same; 1867—Stephen D. Wright, William T. Dickinson, William Kline; 1868-69—William Kline, Stephen D. Wright, John Ferguson; 1870-72—John Ferguson, Elliott Chappell, Peter Honey; 1873—Peter Honey, John Ferguson, William Kline; 1874-75—William Kline, Peter Honey, William Boyd; 1876—John Ferguson, John F. Franklin, John R. Wedding; 1877-78—John F. Franklin, John R. Wedding, J. M. Boyd; 1879—J. M. Boyd, Peter Honey, William Kline; 1880-81—Peter Honey, William Kline, John Clark; 1882-85—John Clark, John Fanning, Francis Zinkans; 1886-87—John Fanning, Francis Zinkans, Thomas J. Payne; 1887-88—John Fanning, Thomas J. Payne, Joseph C. Allison; 1888-89—Joseph C. Allison, Thomas J. Payne, William Kline; 1889-90—Joseph C. Allison, Thomas Bennington, William Kline; 1890-91—William Kline, Thomas Bennington, Andrew Lillie; 1891-92—Thomas Bennington, Andrew Lillie, Frank Lamb; 1892-93—Andrew Lillie, Frank Lamb, Peter McArtor; 1893-94—Frank Lamb, Peter McArtor, James Porter; 1894-95—Peter McArtor, James Porter, James R. Steen; 1895-96—James Porter, James R. Steen, James H. Daugherty; 1896-97—James R. Steen, James H. Daugherty, Hugh McKernan; 1897-98—James H. Daugherty, Hugh McKernan, George W. Wilson; 1898-99—Hugh McKernan, George W. Wilson, John W. Daugherty; 1899—Hugh McKernan, George W. Wilson, W. H. McCarter; 1899-1900—George W. Wilson, William C. McCarter, O. M. Vance; 1900-01 —W. H. McCarter, O. M. Vance, R. D. Smith; 1901-02—O. M. Vance, R. D. Smith, W. H. McCarter; 1902-03—J. G. Shanks, R. D. Smith, W. H. McCarter; 1903-04—W. H. McCarter, J. G. Shanks, H. H. Sefrit; 1904-05 —John G. Shanks, Henry H. Sefrit, W. H. McCarter; 1905-06—John G. Shanks, H. H. Sefrit, William F. Killion; 1906-07—H. H. Sefrit, William F. Killion, John G. Shanks; 1907-08—William F. Killion, John G. Shanks, H. H. Sefrit; 1908-09—John G. Shanks, H. H. Sefrit, William F. Killion; 1909-10—H. H. Sefrit, William F. Killion, Robert J. Barr; 1910-11—William F. Killion, Robert J. Barr, Richard McDonald; 1911-12—Robert J. Barr, Richard McDonald, James T. Sause; 1912-13—Richard McDonald, James T. Sause, James M. Meads; 1913-14—James T. Sause, James M. Meads, Thomas H. Arvin; 1914-15—James M. Meads, Thomas H. Arvin, James T. Sause; 1915—Thomas H. Arvin, James T. Sause, L. S. Horrall.

AUDITOR.

The office of county auditor, as such, was not established in Daviess county until after several years of its history had been made. The clerk of the county board was, however, to all intents and purposes the county auditor, and the first person to hold this position in this bailiwick was Emanuel VanTrees, a very versatile and capable public servant, notwithstanding his evident lack of a college education. Emanuel VanTrees was a community builder. He knew what he wanted and was alive to the interests of Daviess county, for which he gave the best that was in him in his official capacity. While not familiar with the rules of orthography nor the "art of speaking the English properly," yet the early records of the proceedings of the board of commissioners, in his handwriting, show plainly that he knew how to make himself understood. This valued pioneer frontiersman and town-builder kept the records of the board from 1817 to 1824, in which latter year John VanTrees began his ministration of the office and continued the same until 1845. In the latter year Matthew L. Brett was elected county auditor and remained in the office four years. His successors follow, namely: 1859-67—R. N. Read; 1867-74—N. G. Read; 1874-82—T. J. Lavelle; 1882-90—James C. Lavelle; 1890-94—Elijah H. Tomey; 1894-98—Robert Russell; 1898-1902—Robert Russell; 1902-06—Thomas Nugent; 1906-12—Thomas Nugent; 1912-16—Lew S. Core, the present incumbent; 1916, Jacob G. Clark.

CLERK OF THE CIRCUIT COURT.

The clerk of the county board also acted as clerk of the circuit court. Emanuel VanTrees first performed the duties of this office and was succeeded by John VanTrees about the year 1824. The latter was succeeded in 1857 by John S. Berkshire, whose incumbency terminated in 1863. Then followed, in 1863-70, Mike Murphy; 1870-78—George Walters; 1878-82—Joseph Wilson; 1882-90—Joseph J. Lacy; 1890-98—Thomas D. Slimp; 1898-1902—Thomas Harris; 1902-12—William A. Wallace; 1912-16—William H. Kiefer; 1916—Edwin E. Meade.

SHERIFF.

1816-17—Ovid Flint, appointed by the governor of the state to organize the county; 1818-24—Daniel Comer; 1824-26—George A. Waller; 1826-31—Richard Palmer; 1831-35—George A. Waller; 1835-38—Robert Raper; 1838-40—Andrew Martin; 1840-43—F. Wilhite; 1843-47—B. Goodwin; 1847-51—R. B. Sutton; 1851-54—B. Goodwin; 1854-56—Isaac W. McCormack; 1856-60—B. Goodwin; 1860-62—Joseph Brown; 1862-64—Michael Nash; 1864-68—Isaac W. McCormack; 1868-72—James M. Graves; 1872-76—Isaac W. McCormack; 1876-78—N. G. Read; 1878-80—Zachariah Jones; 1880-84—Francis A. Ward; 1884-88—John A. Bair; 1888-1892—Charles Colbert; 1892-96—John G. Leming; 1896-98—William Bowman; 1898-1900—Jabez A. McCord; 1900-04—John D. Morgan; 1904-08—Milton Fitzgerald; 1908-12—Fielding Colbert; 1912-16—George W. Harmon; 1916—Christopher D. Guthrie.

TREASURER.

Most of the county officials were appointed by the county governing body and for many of the first years of the county's existence this custom obtained in the selection of the county treasurer.

Ebenezer Jones was appointed by the board of county commissioners, in 1817, to the office of county treasurer for one year, and was regularly reappointed for the term of one year until 1821, in which year Hezekiah Ragdill became treasurer. Then again came Jones, who remained in charge of the county's strong (?) box until 1831. In the year last mentioned, John W. Waller was appointed, succeeding himself in 1832. George Roddick was the incumbent in 1833, William Brutton in 1834 and John W. Waller in 1835. The latter resigned the office in September, 1836, at which time Emanuel VanTrees was appointed, remaining in the office a number of years. From 1852, during which period Abraham Perkins was the treasurer, the following named persons have served the county in this responsible position: 1854-56—John Thompson; 1856-60—William Sanford; 1860-64—B. Goodwin; 1864-67—William Sanford; 1867-70—George W. McCafferty; 1870-74—William Kennedy; 1874-78—John B. Spaulding; 1878-82—H. C. Brown; 1882-86—R. H. Greenwood; 1886-90—Joseph B. Smith; 1890-92—Robert J. Barr; 1892-96—Henry Aikman; 1896-98—John Wadsworth; 1898-1900—Albion Horrall; 1900-02—George B. McWilliams; 1902-06—Hilary C. Truelove; 1906-10—George Godwin; 1910-12—Theodore T.

Jones, who died in 1811, John Clark being appointed to fill the vacancy; 1912-14—John Clark; 1916—Elmer Buzan.

RECORDER.

1824-29—J. H. McDonald; 1829-36—J. Calhoun; 1836-40—John M. Waller; 1840-47—John Hyatt; 1847-1854—John S. Berkshire; 1854-62—William R. Berkshire; 1862-70—Enoch Barton; 1870-78—A. J. Smiley; 1878-82—Solomon Williams; 1882-90—John H. Kidwell; 1890-94—John Dosch; 1894-1900—Francis G. Lutes; 1900-1904—Friend B. Colbert; 1904-08—William P. Smoot; 1908-12—Henry H. McCracken; 1912-16—Harry P. VanTrees; 1916—Thomas C. Singleton.

SURVEYOR.

1824-52—W. H. Root; 1852-56—John P. Agan; 1856-60—John Cassidy; 1860-62—J. C. Spink; 1862-66—W. P. Boyden; 1866-68—William Shanks; 1868-72—D. H. Kennedy; 1872-76—William Shanks; 1876-88—T. J. Smiley; 1888-92—Grant Faith; 1892-94—Thomas Nugent; 1894-96—Edward C. Faith; 1896-98—Alexander C. Swickard; 1898-1900—Nelson C. Adkins; 1900-02—Thomas J. Smiley; 1902-04—Franklin L. Snider; 1904-06—George L. Harris; 1906-08—George A. Faith; 1908-10—Albert F. Annen; 1910-14—Michael T. Madden; 1914—William J. Shanks.

CORONER.

1818-26—Joseph Daugherty; 1826-31—P. Blackburn; 1831-39—Joseph Daugherty; 1839-41—Samuel A. Rodarmel; 1841-45—Thomas Brown; 1845-49—Joseph Daugherty; 1849-51—J. D. Tremor; 1851-52—James Martin; 1852-54—B. F. Meredith; 1854-56—T. P. VanTrees; 1856-57—A. G. Williams; 1857-60—Thomas Brown; 1860-62—James Solomon; 1862-64—W. T. Morgan; 1864-66—W. E. Hopkins; 1866-68—August Kauffman; 1868-70—John Stevens; 1870-74—D. R. Agan; 1874-76—Warren Hart; 1876-80—Elias Grace; 1880-84—Jesse Winterbottom; 1884-86—W. C. Slater; 1886-88—James F. Parks; 1888-90—Charles P. Scudder; 1890-96—Charles C. McCown; 1896-98—Milton P. Tolliver; 1898-1900—Chauncey E. Trainor; 1900-02—Ora K. McKittrick; 1902-08—Clifford O. Bonham; 1908-10—Union H. Holder; 1910-12—Tie between Holder and Orris E. Lett; on a recount Holder being declared re-elected. 1912-14—Orris E. Lett; 1914—Huette Poindexter.

PROSECUTING ATTORNEY.

1886-88—James D. Laughlin; 1880-90—Lewis Stephens; 1890-92—William Heffernan; 1892-94—James M. Huff; 1894-96—Peter R. Wadsworth; 1896-98—James B. Marshall; 1898-1904—Alvin Padgett; 1904-08—Edgar T. Laughlin; 1908-10—Elmer E. Hastings; 1910-14—Flavian A. Seal; 1914—Charles M. Mears.

STATE SENATORS.

William Polke, 1817-21, with Knox and Sullivan counties; Frederick Sholtz, 1821-25, with Knox, Sullivan and Greene; John Ewing, 1825-33; William Wallace, 1833-34, with Knox, Sullivan, Vigo and Owen; Henry M. Shaw, 1835-36; Thomas C. Moore, 1836-39; Robert M. Carman, 1839-41, with Knox and Martin; Abner M. Davis, 1841-44; Elijah Chapman, 1844-46; Richard A. Clements, 1846-47; Aaron Houghton, 1847-50; William E. Niblack, 1850-51, with Martin; William E. Niblack, 1851-52; G. G. Barton, 1853-55; John P. Freeland, 1855-57, with Knox and Martin; James D. Williams, 1859-67 and 1871-73; W. S. Turner, 1867-69, with Knox; Andrew Humphreys, 1875-77; David J. Hefron, 1877-83; J. P. McIntosh, 1883-87, with Greene; George W. Alford, 1887-91, with Martin; William Kennedy, 1891-95, with Martin; H. Q. Houghton, 1895-99, with Martin; Eph Inman, 1899-1903, with Knox; Richard Milburn, 1903-07, with Dubois; Ezra Mattingly, 1907-11, Henry Gers, 1911-15, James Porter, 1915, with Pike.

REPRESENTATIVES IN THE LEGISLATURE.

From 1821 to 1852 Daviess county had a joint representative with Martin county. Following are the names of representatives for that period, and the year in which each served:

James G. Reed, 1821; William H. Routt, 1822-23; James G. Reed, 1823-24; William Wallace, 1825-26; James G. Reed, 1826-31; William Wallace, 1831-32-33; Erasmus McJunkin, 1832; David McDonald, 1833-34; Patrick M. Brett, 1834-35; Josiah Culbertson, 1834-35; Lewis Jones, 1835-36; James Breeze, 1836-37; Abner M. Davis, 1837-38; John Flint, 1838-40; Samuel H. Smyth, 1840-41; Richard A. Clements, 1841-43; Silas T. Halbert, 1843-44; James P. McGawhey, 1844-45; Richard A. Clements, 1845-46; Zachariah Walker, 1846-47; Elias S. Terry, 1847-48; Benjamin Goodwin, 1848-51;

John Scudder, 1851-52; Rowland Sutton, 1853; James McConnell, 1855; T. A. Slicer, 1857; Richard A. Clements, Jr., 1859; Mathew L. Brett, 1861; Noah E. Given, 1863; Howard Crooke, 1865; John H. O'Neal, 1867; John Hyatt, 1869; Robert Haynes, 1871; Mathew L. Brett, 1873; Harvey Taylor, 1875; Patrick H. McCarty, 1877; Samuel H. Taylor, 1879; Clement Lee, 1881; Haman Woodling, 1883; Samuel H. Taylor, 1885; Oliver H. McKittrick, 1889; Henry Aikman, 1891; Josiah G. Allen, 1893-95; Sanford Patterson, 1897; James M. Hough, 1899; James F. Parks, 1901; Aikman Carnahan, elected in 1902, died before the meeting of the Legislature; Paris A. Hastings, elected at a special election to fill the vacancy, served in the Legislature of 1903; Harry H. Crooke, 1905; Thomas D. Slimp, 1907; Charles A. Banta, 1909; Solomon L. McPherson, 1911; John Hoddinott, 1913; George L. Harris, 1915.

PRESIDENTIAL ELECTIONS, 1844 TO 1912.

The early elections returns of presidential elections, prior to 1844, in which Daviess county participated are missing from the county records, but the following will be sufficient to show the political drift in the county since that date, and also the general result in some of the most important and most exciting political contests in national history.

It is said that no election ever caused more disappointment, both to the victors and the vanquished, than that of 1840. General Harrison had been elected by the Whig party, over Martin Van Buren, the Democratic candidate, by an overwhelming vote. This result was a surprise to both parties. The Whigs were greatly elated and the Democrats were correspondingly depressed; they were puzzled, they were grieved, they were angry. The disappointment of the Whigs came afterward and was of a different character. One month after General Harrison was inaugurated he died, and John Tyler, the vice-president, became president. The death of Harrison was a sad disappointment to the Whigs, but the succession of Tyler, and his adoption of a diverse administration policy, was regarded as a party calamity.

In 1844 the Democrats failed in their effort to re-nominate Van Buren, after an exciting convention contest, and, for the first time in political convention history, a "dark horse," in the person of James K. Polk, of Tennessee, was made the party candidate. Henry Clay was the candidate of the Whig party. The Daviess county vote on these two candidates, at the election held in November, 1844, was: Clay, 807; Polk, 764. Indiana gave its twelve electoral votes for Polk, with a popular vote of 70,181 for Polk, and 67,867 for Clay. In the national electoral vote, Polk received 170, and Clay 105.

THE ELECTION OF 1848.

The candidates for president in 1848 were, Zachary Taylor, Whig; Lewis Cass, Democrat, and Martin Van Buren, the candidate of what was known as the "Free Soil" party. In this contest the Whig party was again successful, electing its candidate by a total electoral vote of 163 to 127 for the opposing candidate. Indiana gave its twelve electoral votes to Cass, the popular vote being 74,745 for Cass; 69,907 for Taylor. Van Buren, the Free Soil candidate, received 8,100 votes in the state. In this election, Daviess county gave 735 votes for Taylor, 708 for Cass and 2 for Van Buren.

THE ELECTION OF 1852.

The death of Taylor, soon after his accession to the presidency, was the second disappointment of the kind experienced by the Whig party. The agitation of the slavery question, and policies for the extension or restriction of slave territory, had become a prominent political issue. On this question the Whig party was divided, the northern wing being anti-slavery, or, at least, opposed to the extension of that institution into the free territories; the southern wing of the party holding to opposite views on this question. Though General Taylor was a Southerner, and a slaveholder, he was supported by the northern contingent of the party, although with some misgivings. Taylor lived long enough to make it evident that slavery, as a political power, could not rely on him to assist it in its struggle with Northern sentiment. His death was a grievous disappointment of these hopes. Fillmore, the vice-president, who succeeded Taylor, became an active agent in promoting the compromise measures, which the anti-slavery contingent of the Whig party abhorred.

In 1852 the Whigs nominated General Winfield Scott, as their candidate for president, but the convention that nominated Scott was not characterized by political harmony. The advocates of the respective sides of the dominant issue, the slavery question, were much in evidence. The Democrats nominated Franklin Pierce as their candidate. John P. Hale was the candidate of the anti-slavery faction of the Democratic party, known as the Free Soil Democrats. Of the total electoral vote, Pierce received 254, and Scott, 42. Indiana gave its 13 electoral votes to Pierce; the popular vote for the several candidates was: Pierce, 95,340; Scott, 80,901; Hale, 6,929. The Daviess county vote was: Pierce, 720; Scott, 826; Hale, 6.

THE ELECTION OF 1856.

The election of 1852 gave the death-blow to the Whig party. It had served its purpose, if it had any, and had outlived its usefulness. It was unable to cope with the one vital issue of the day, that of slavery in the territories. A remnant of the Whig party formed a combination with the American, or "Know-Nothing" party, under the name of American-Whig party, and presented Millard Fillmore as its candidate for president, in 1856. The Democratic candidate was James Buchanan. The new Republican party made its first appearance in this year with John C. Fremont as candidate for president. The result of the election was 174 electoral votes for Buchanan, 114 for Fremont and 8 for Fillmore. Buchanan received the thirteen electoral votes of Indiana. The popular vote was: Buchanan, 118,670; Fremont, 94,375; Fillmore, 22,386. The Daviess county vote was: Buchanan, 1,115; Fillmore, 939; Fremont, 26.

THE ELECTION OF 1860.

In this election it was the Democratic party that was affected by dissension and division, due to the efforts of contending factions to control the convention, and dictate the party policy regarding the slavery question. The result of this dissension was the nomination of Stephen A. Douglas, by the northern wing of the party; and John C. Breckinridge, by the southern faction. The Republican party, which had now become a strong, aggressive organization, presented Abraham Lincoln as its candidate. The Constitutional Union party, composed of remnants of the American and Whig parties, had John Bell as their candidate. All these candidates received a share of the electoral vote in the general election, as follow: Lincoln, 180; Breckinridge, 72; Douglas, 12; Bell, 39. Indiana's thirteen electoral votes were counted for Lincoln. Of the popular vote of the state, Lincoln received 139,033; Douglas, 115,509; Breckenridge, 12,295; Bell, 5,306. In Daviess county Lincoln received 934; Douglas, 749; Breckenridge, 529; Bell, 133.

THE ELECTION OF 1864.

The secession of several of the Southern slavery states, and the resulting Civil War, following the election of Lincoln, form a chapter in American history that is beyond the scope of a work of this character. There was a new alignment of political parties in consequence of the rebellious action of the Southern states. Many of the leading Democrats of the North came to the support of Lincoln. Among the first, and most prominent of these, was Stephen A. Douglas, Democratic candidate in opposition to Lincoln in the election. The death of Douglas, soon after the inauguration of Lincoln, was a serious loss to the latter's administration and the cause of the Union. Political lines, however, were not wholly obliterated on account of distractions of the Civil War. While the Democratic party was seriously disrupted, because of the large Southern element that had left it, yet it still was an aggressive, militant party, a party to be reckoned with in the election of 1864. In that year the Democrats had for their candidate General George B. McClellan, a brilliant soldier, and very popular. The Republican party renominated Lincoln. A fraction of the Republican party, who were dissatisfied with Lincoln's administraton, nominated John C. Fremont, but he afterward withdrew from the canvass, and left the contest between Lincoln and McClellan. The result of the election was a decided endorsement of Lincoln's administration. Of the total electoral vote, Lincoln received 212, McClellan, 21. The thirteen electoral votes of Indiana were given to Lincoln. The popular vote was: 150,422 for Lincoln; 130,233 for McClellan. Daviess county gave Lincoln, 1,227, and McClellan 1,299.

THE ELECTION OF 1868.

General Ulysses S. Grant was the Republican candidate for president in 1868; Horatio Seymour was the Democratic candidate. The military achievements of Grant, and his great popularity, especially among the soldiers who served in his command, made his election a foregone conclusion. The voting was a mere formality. Of the electoral vote Grant received 214; Seymour, 80. Indiana gave thirteen electoral votes to Grant, and a popular vote of 176,552. Seymour's Indiana vote was 166,980. Daviess county gave Grant 1,682, Seymour, 1,732.

THE ELECTION OF 1872.

The campaign for the presidency in 1872 was characterized by something in the nature of political freaks. General Grant was the necessary and logical candidate of the Republican party, but there was a considerable disaffection in that party. Several leading Republicans had been in disagreement with certain features of Grant's administration policies, and refused to support him for re-election. Among the leaders of the opposition was

Horace Greeley, who was actively identified with the organization of the Republican party. The disaffected element held a convention and organized the Liberal-Republican party, and nominated Horace Greeley for candidate for President. By action of the Democratic convention, Greeley was endorsed as the Democratic candidate. Greeley had been most bitter in his denunciation of the Democratic party and it was regarded as a political freak for that party to adopt Greeley as a party leader. A straight Democratic candidate, in the person of Charles O'Conor, was brought out by an element of the party who declined to follow the Greeley leadership. The Prohibition party made its first appearance in this campaign, with a presidential candidate in the person of James Black. Greeley died a few days after the election, and before the electoral votes were counted. In the election Grant received 286 of the 349 electoral votes. Indiana's fifteen electoral votes were counted for Grant. Indiana's popular vote: Grant, 186,147; Greeley, 163,632; O'Conor, 1,417. Daviess county vote: Grant, 1,914; Greeley, 1,618; O'Conor, 17.

THE ELECTION OF 1876.

The candidates for the presidency in 1876 were: Rutherford B. Hayes, Republican; Samuel J. Tilden, Democrat; Green Clay Smith, Prohibition; Peter Cooper, Greenback. The contest was exciting and the result of the election close, and in dispute. An election commission finally settled the matter by giving Hayes 185, and Tilden 184 electoral votes. The popular vote of Indiana in that election was, Tilden, 213,526; Hayes, 208,011; Cooper, 17,233; Smith, 141. Daviess county: Tilden, 2,350; Hayes, 2,026; Cooper, 25.

THE ELECTION OF 1880.

The presidential candidates were, James A. Garfield, Republican; Winfield S. Hancock, Democrat; James B. Weaver, Greenback; Neal Dow, Prohibition. The electoral vote was divided between Garfield and Hancock, Garfield receiving 214, and Hancock 155. The fifteen electoral votes of Indiana were cast for Garfield, and the popular vote of each candidate was: Garfield, 232,164; Hancock, 225,522; Weaver, 12,986. Daviess county gave Hancock 2,387; Garfield, 2,320; Weaver, 85.

THE ELECTION OF 1884.

The candidates in 1884 were James G. Blaine, Republican; Grover Cleveland, Democrat; Benjamin F. Butler, Populist; John P. St. John, Prohibition. The electoral vote was divided between Cleveland and Blaine, Cleveland receiving 219, and Blaine, 182. Cleveland received Indiana's fifteen electoral votes. The popular vote was: Cleveland, 244,990; Blaine, 238,463; Butler, 8,293; St. John, 3,028. The vote of Daviess county was 2,480 for Cleveland; 2,278 for Blaine; 113 for Butler; 2 votes for St. John, in Van Buren township.

THE ELECTION OF 1888.

General Benjamin Harrison, of Indiana, was the Republican candidate for President, in 1888; Grover Cleveland, the Democratic candidate for re-election; Clinton B. Fisk, Prohibition; A. J. Streeter, Greenback. Harrison received 233 electoral votes; Cleveland, 168. Indiana's popular vote: Harrison, 263,361; Cleveland, 261,013; Fisk, 9,881; Streeter, 2,694. Daviess county voted, Harrison, 2,694; Cleveland, 2,689; Fisk, 6; Streeter, 39.

THE ELECTION OF 1892.

General Harrison was a candidate for re-election on the Republican ticket, in 1892; Grover Cleveland was again the candidate of the Democratic party. The candidate of the Prohibition party was John Bidwell; James B. Weaver was the People's party candidate. Of the electoral vote Cleveland received 277, Harrison, 145; Indiana's fifteen electoral votes were counted in the Cleveland column. The popular vote of Indiana for the several candidates was: Cleveland, 262,740; Harrison, 255,615; Weaver, 22,208; Bidwell, 25,807. The contribution of Daviess county to this vote was, 2,498 for Cleveland; 2,610 for Harrison; 908 for Weaver; 55 for Bidwell.

THE ELECTION OF 1896.

William McKinley was the Republican candidate for President in 1896; W. J. Bryan was the candidate of the Democratic party, on a free-silver platform; John M. Palmer was the candidate of the faction of the Democratic party that was not in accord with Bryan's free-silver ideas; Joshua Levering was the Prohibition candidate. Of the electoral vote, McKinley received 271, Bryan, 176. Indiana distributed its popular vote among the several candidates, giving McKinley 323,754; Bryan, 305,573; Palmer, 2,145; Levering, 3,192. Daviess county vote: McKinley, 3,120; Bryan, 3,378; Levering, 19.

THE ELECTION OF 1900.

The election of 1900 was practically a renewal of the contest of 1896. William McKinley was the Republican candidate for re-election to the presidency, and William Jennings Bryan made his second race as the candidate of the Democratic party. John G. Woolley was the candidate of the Prohibition party, and Eugene Debs, candidate of the Socialist party. McKinley was again elected, Indiana's fifteen electoral votes contributing to that result. The following is the popular vote of Indiana in this election: McKinley, 336,063; Bryan, 305,584; Woolley, 13,718; Debs 2,374. The vote of Daviess county was: McKinley, 3,298; Bryan, 3,424; Woolley, 175; Debs, 168.

THE ELECTION OF 1904.

The death of McKinley within a year after the beginning of his second term made Theodore Roosevelt, who had been elected as vice-president, successor to the presidency. Roosevelt was the candidate of the Republican party for President, in 1904; Alton B. Parker, the Democratic candidate; Swallow, the Prohibition candidate, and Debs, the Socialist candidate. Roosevelt received a majority of the electoral vote, including the fifteen from Indiana. Of the popular vote of Indiana, Roosevelt received 368,289; Parker, 274,345; Swallow, 23,496; Debs, 12,013. Daviess county divided its vote as follow: Roosevelt, 3,682; Parker, 2,802; Swallow, 169; Debs, 148.

THE ELECTION OF 1908.

William Jennings Bryan made his third race as candidate of the Democratic party for the presidency in 1908. William Howard Taft was the candidate of the Republican party; Chafin of the Prohibition party; Debs of the Socialist party, and Watson, of Georgia, was the candidate of the Populist party. Indiana's fifteen electoral votes were given to Taft. The popular vote of the state for the several candidates was: Taft, 348,993; Bryan, 338,262; Chafin, 18,045; Debs, 13,476; Watson, 1,193. Daviess county's vote: Taft, 3,424; Bryan, 3,253; Chafin, 134; Debs, 204; Watson, 53.

THE ELECTION OF 1912.

The Republican convention of 1912, like that of the Democratic party in 1860, resulted in a split. William H. Taft was nominated for re-election by the regular Republican organization. The dissenting faction, at a subsequent convention, organized the Progressive party and nominated Theodore Roosevelt for President. Woodrow Wilson was the nominee of the Democratic party, and Chafin and Debs were the candidates of the Prohibition and Socialist parties, respectively. In the following election Wilson received Indiana's fifteen electoral votes, and a safe majority of the electoral votes. The popular vote of Indiana was: Wilson, 281,890; Roosevelt, 162,007; Taft, 151,267; Debs, 36,931; Chafin, 19,249. Daviess county voted 2,759 for Wilson; 2,005 for Taft; 1,061 for Roosevelt; 150 for Chafin; 327 for Debs.

CHAPTER VII.

THE WABASH AND ERIE CANAL.

In the early thirties the people of Indiana went wild in their efforts to compete with some of the older Eastern states in the location and construction of internal improvements. Railroad projects which had been promoted in some of the Eastern states, were still in the experimental stage. For land transportation the old stage coach was considered the most dependable, and for the greater convenience and comfort of this means of travel the public enterprise was enlisted in the construction of plank roads. Taxes were laid and large expenditures were made in this method of improvement of some of the main thoroughfares traveled by the stage coach. The larger handling of public traffic and the more extensive travel of those times was by boats, and the location of early settlements and towns at points, either on a river or easily accessible to a navigable watercourse, was considered an important advantage. As the physical formation of the country did not provide for navigable watercourses sufficient to meet the demand, public enterprise turned to the construction of canals to supply the deficiency. The construction of canals was not a new project. Most of the ancient nations had canals. The Egyptians very early made a canal connecting the Nile with the Red Sea. The great canal of China was constructed about the seventh century. The Erie canal, so important to New York city, was begun in 1817 and completed in 1825. Many of the older Eastern states had constructed canals, and they had been in successful operation for several years before the canal idea struck the people of Indiana.

The act of Congress making the first land grants for the construction of the Wabash & Erie canal was passed in 1827. The act of the Indiana Legislature, authorizing the commencement of the work, was passed at the session of 1830-31. A second grant of lands for the continuation of the canal from the mouth of the Tippecanoe river to Terre Haute was passed by Congress in 1831. A third grant of half of the unsold lands in the Vincennes land district, for the continuation of the canal from Terre Haute to the Ohio river at Evansville, was made by Congress in 1845. The work on the canal was begun at Fort Wayne in 1832, finished from Toledo, Ohio, to Lafayette in 1841, to Terre Haute in 1849, and to Evansville in 1852.

FINANCIAL CRASH OF 1847.

In the meantime Indiana was going to the limit in the promotion of plank roads, railroads, and other internal improvements. During these years so much work in the way of public improvements was in progress in the state that wages were high, and all kinds of produce and provisions were bringing good prices. The great amount of money that was paid out for labor and produce, apparently, made good times in all parts of Indiana where this work was being done. But this was fictitious prosperity. The prosperity was only apparent. The people had gone wild in extravagance; they engaged in much speculation for which promissory notes were given, with little regard for the future pay-day. The retail merchants contracted debts with the wholesale merchants. They sold quantities of goods on credit to their customers, who were wholly dependent on these works for the money with which to pay their store accounts. The crash came in 1847, and there was a general suspension of every sort of business. The state was involved in the financial disaster; thousands of men who were on the road to fortune could do nothing but stand idly by and see their fond hopes disappear. Col. W. M. Cockrum, of Oakland City, Indiana, author of the "Pioneer History of Indiana," relating the condition of financial distress prevailing at that time, says:

"So wide was the disaster in the country bordering on these undertakings of the state that it was very distressing. In 1838 there were so many individuals involved in that ruin that it was very embarrassing to all the people. At the meeting of the Legislature, in 1838, Governor Wallace, in his message said: 'Never before—I speak advisedly—never before have you witnessed a period in our local history which more urgently calls for the exercising of all the soundest and best attributes of grave and patriotic legislation than the present.'

"In 1839 work was suspended on most of the state improvements and the contracts surrendered. It became evident that the state could not finish all these works. The Legislature of 1841 passed an act authorizing any private company to take charge of and complete any of the work, except the Wabash & Erie canal. It was thought that by the aid of the government the state could finish the canal in the next few years. The state made several attempts in this direction without success. Everything lay quiet until 1846, when Charles Butler, who represented the bondholders, offered to take the state's interest in the canal for one-half the debts, and for the lands granted for its construction. He proposed to finish the canal on this condition, and the further condition that the state would issue new certificates for the other half, and pay interest at four per cent. per annum, the state reserving the right of redemption."

The state accepted this proposition and the canal was finished under this management. It was completed and began operation from Terre Haute to Evansville in 1852. The entire length of the canal in Indiana was three hundred and ninety-five miles; in Ohio, eighty-four miles. making its entire length four hundred and seventy-nine miles.

PROMISING INVESTMENTS GO GLIMMERING.

The construction of the Wabash & Erie canal, and the hopes and ambitions the enterprise aroused, the failures and disappointments experienced, is all a part of the history of Daviess county. Along the meandering course of the canal, through the county, several towns were located, and there was quite a demand for town lots, the price of real estate in the vicinity of the canal route materially increasing. Some of these towns were laid out on a large scale; several houses were built, including stores, and small industries of various kinds were established. During the short time the canal was in operation, some of the towns became extensive shipping points for grain and produce. and the merchants located there enjoyed a large trade from the surrounding country. But all the bright prospects and promising financial investments went glimmering when the canal failed. The site of these flourishing towns is now but a memory. The thousands of dollars expended by Daviess county in the canal project was compensated, in some measure, however, by the bringing in of a large immigration and the consequent development of the material resources of the county.

The amount of labor and patient energy expended in the digging of the canal is a wonder to the present age. That was before the day of the steam shovel and other modern machinery for such work, all work of excavating being laboriously done by pick and shovel. Irish laborers were mostly employed for this work. as they were the most expert in handling the implements used. The dirt was loaded into a wheelbarrow, or a dump cart drawn by a mule, and carried to the place of dumping. The plow and scraper were used to some extent by a few of the contractors; but most of the work in the construction of that great ditch was the slow process above stated. The trace of the old canal can still be followed in its course through Daviess county. In many places deep excavations are seen, giving some idea of the immense cost, and the great amount of time and labor required in the removal of all the dirt with shovel and wheelbarrow.

INCIDENTS OF CANAL DAYS.

There are still a few of the citizens of Daviess county living who were employed in the digging of the canal in this county, and those who have had that experience, and a memory reaching back to that time, can relate many interesting incidents connected with that great enterprise. Among those who have had this experience, and a memory to relate it, is Warren ("Dodge") Hart. Mr. Hart lives at Maysville, one of the flourishing towns in canal days; now a deserted village. Mr. Hart is the authority for the following statements relating to the digging of the canal through this county:

Mr. Hart introduces himself as the "jigger" boy, a very important and necessary function, second only to the paymaster with the canal diggers. The "jigger" was about two swallows of whiskey, and the number of "jiggers" that a contractor would give a day to his employees was as important a consideration as the amount of money he would give for labor. One dollar per day was the usual money consideration, and the number of "jiggers" was fixed by agreement, five to ten a day being the usual allowance. It was not unusual for a contractor who was short of hands to increase the number of daily "jiggers" over the allowance by other contractors. This proposed increase brought the contractor all the hands he needed. It was the duty of Mr. Hart, as "jigger" boy, to see that the agreed number and specified amount was delivered on time. Contractors bought whiskey by the barrel, at about twenty cents per gallon, so the "jigger" was not an expensive luxury in those times.

Some of the contractors who had contracts for work in this county were "Doo" Munson, Coffee and Burns. Most of their employees were Irish. After the canal was finished many of these had saved up enough money to buy land and locate in the county, settling mostly in Barr and Washington townships. Many of these families became prominent in county affairs, and have contributed no small part to the development of the county.

Laborers lived in rude shanties, sometimes cooking their own meals. Others obtained meals from boarding houses that were established at every "dump." The rations usually consisted of bread, potatoes, and plenty of black coffee, sweetened with molasses. Meat was on the bill of fare about once a week. The laborers received their wages every three months. Pay-day was the occasion for a holiday, in which drunks and fights were the principal amusement.

In most cases the contractors had one section each, and these sections, as a rule, were a mile long. Where the sections required heavy work they were made shorter, in order that the work might all be completed about the same time. The embankments were made by hauling the dirt in one-horse carts. The usual outfit for a crew of men, where the haul was not over two hundred yards, was four carts and four men to each cart to shovel in the dirt. The work was so timed that the loaded cart was ready to pull out as soon as an empty cart was returned to be loaded. Over each squad of forty men there was a boss; usually the most important man on the works, the boss let no opportunity escape to magnify his office.

WHISKEY AS FREE AS WATER.

There were no restrictions then on the sale of intoxicating liquor. Whiskey was as free as water, and often more easily obtained than water. There was great opportunity for profitable business in setting up a "grocery" or "doggery," as drinking places were called, in the vicinity of the canal works. A board shanty and a barrel of whiskey was all the preparation necessary to equip a business place of this kind. As a rule, contractors objected to establishments of this kind because of the demoralizing effects among their employees, and they would not permit whiskey joints to remain within their jurisdiction.

The canal followed the water-level of rivers as far as practicable. In many places the fall was so great that it was necessary to build locks in order to secure a new water-level. The locks were made of sufficient length to accommodate the largest boats, and were about eighteen feet wide. The material used was heavy hewn timber, with very heavy double gates at each level. Several locks of this kind were built on the canal in Daviess county by Contractor Munson. One of these was about two miles below Elnora, called the "Patterson Lock." There was one at Plainville, one at Jordan station, one at Thomas station and one at Sandy Hook. American laborers were exclusively employed in the building of locks, culverts and constructive work where timber was required. Irish skill was better adapted to the handling of a shovel than the broadaxe.

An aqueduct was built across the east fork of White river, just east of the junction of the east and west forks of that stream. This was quite

an extensive and expensive structure, and an important link connecting the
canal in Daviess county with its southern extremity. During the Civil War,
when southern Indiana was in a state of terror on account of the Morgan
raid, Governor Morton ordered a battery to be sent, on request of citizens
of Daviess county, to defend this aqueduct against a possible attempt of
the ruthless raider to destroy it. If Morgan ever had any such designs,
or had ever heard of the aqueduct, he was too busy finding a way of escape
from the invincible "Home Guards" to give the matter any special attention.
The aqueduct was burned by ferry-boat men about the close of the Civil
War, but the canal had ceased operations prior to that time and the loss
was not material.

The canal was tested in 1852 by letting in the water to discover if
there were any leaks. Boats began running in the early part of 1853 and
continued until 1860, when navigation was suspended and the canal was
practically abandoned on account of railroad competition. The motive
power was mules, two or more mules being hitched tandem for the heavy
freighters.

CHOLERA EPIDEMIC.

The Asiatic cholera, which had been prevalent throughout Ohio, Indiana
and Illinois during the years 1849 to 1851, made its appearance in Daviess
county in the summer of 1852. The disease was most prevalent among the
laborers on the canal. Their manner of living, with little regard for sanitary
conditions or cleanliness of habit, offered a special invitation to this
disease, and the attack was almost universally fatal. Within a few days
after the appearance of the disease a number of deaths occurred. These
were mostly in the camps located in the vicinity of Plainville and Sandy Hook.
Following the first attack a number of men fled from the camps. Some of
these had already the poison of the disease in their systems and this soon
became virulent, resulting in death within a few hours. It was not an unusual
occurrence for men fleeing from the afflicted camps to be attacked with the
disease and die on the roadside. Victims of the disease in camp were often
left lying for days before being given burial, few able persons being left
to attend to this duty. Some were buried in the little shanties where they
died. Other bodies were buried in long trenches by friends who braved
danger and remained to care for the sick and dying. A number of graves
of cholera victims were located in the vicinity of Sandy Hook, but all traces
of these have disappeared. There is no record of the number of deaths
resulting from this epidemic.

TRAVELING ON A CANAL BOAT.

In 1850, an English gentleman, named Beste, and his family, came over from England, and, like all visitors to America before the Civil War, they had to make a tour of the West. They reached Indianapolis, traveling by river and rail, and after remaining at that place for some time, bought a team of horses and a spring wagon and proceeded by the National road to Terre Haute. They were detained there for several months on account of sickness. They then decided to abandon their contemplated trip to St. Louis in the wagon and return by the Wabash & Erie canal, which was then in operation. The following extract from a sketch written by Mr. Beste relating his experience on this trip, and describing the appointments and accommodations of a canal boat, is reproduced from "Readings in Indiana History," published by Indiana University:

"At five o'clock in the afternoon, we stepped from the little quay at Terre Haute on board the Indiana canal boat. Three horses were harnessed to a rope, about fifty yards ahead of the boat; they started at a moderte trot, and the town where we had tarried so long was soon lost to our sight. No other passengers were on board, and we wandered over the vessel well pleased with the promise it gave us of tolerable accommodation. The captain, a very young man, was civil and attentive to our wants, and told us that tea would be served at seven o'clock, which there, on that day, was the precise hour of sunset.

"The construction of the canal boat was, in miniature, much the same as that of the river and lake steamers. There was no hold or under deck, but on the deck at the stern were raised the kitchen, steward's room and offices; in the center of the boat was the large saloon—the sitting room of all by day, the sleeping room of male passengers by night. Adjoining it was the ladies' saloon; beyond which, again, was a small cabin containing only four berths. This cabin was separated by a doorway and curtain from the ladies' saloon, and the other side opened upon the bow of the vessel. In it was a looking glass, a hand basin, two towels, a comb and a brush for the use of the ladies.

"It was a rule in the boats that no gentleman should go into the ladies' saloon without express invitation from the ladies. Consequently the third little room was sacred to the female sex, unless entered from the bow, in which case a male occupant would cut off the ladies from their wash house. Doctor Read had, however, declared that it was necessary that I should have this small room, in order that I might be secure from the draughts and the night air that would be let into the men's saloon at night; and the canal boat agents at Terre Haute had contracted to secure the same for me throughout the length of the passage. Doctor Read had particularly insisted on this, fearing that the slightest chill would produce a return of the illness from which I was, in truth, scarcely convalescent.

"A flat roof spread over the whole of the saloons, and on it was piled the luggage; and here passengers walked up and down or sat to enjoy the view.

"The view, however, 'was nought,' as yet. The banks were low, and thick woods, in which were only partial clearings, shut us in on both sides.

"Our children wondered where they were to sleep, as there were no visible berths amid the red moreen curtains that hung around the ladies' saloon, to give it an air of comfort in this August weather. They dreaded to have to pass four nights on the floor, as they had done at Mrs. Long's hotel; but they said they were more used to hardships than they had then been; and they also drew comparative comfort from seeing a wash-hand basin and two towels, instead of that amiable woman's small, tin pie-dish. The steward, however, soon solved their doubts by hooking up some shelves to the wall, and laying mattresses and sheets upon them.

"We were summoned to tea, but after the good living at the Prairie House (Terre Haute), all complained of the bad tea and coffee, of the hot, heavy corn-bread, and of the raw beefsteak.

"After tea we all began a most murderous attack upon the mosquitoes that swarmed on the windows and inside our berths, in expectation of feasting upon us as soon as we should go to bed. But those on whom we made war were soon replaced by others, and the more we killed the more they seemed to come to be killed, like Mrs. Bond's ducks; it was as though they would defy us to exterminate them. At last we gave up the task as hopeless and resigned ourselves, as well as we could, to pass a sleepless night."

CHAPTER VIII.

AGRICULTURE AND STATISTICS.

In the various lines of industrial pursuits there is none that has claimed the attention of the larger portion of the people to a greater degree than has that of agriculture. Upon this line of industry every other industrial activity is dependent. The success of the farmer contributes to the success of the merchant, the manufacturer, the mechanic, the capitalist, and the man without capital, depending upon his daily labor for a living. The race could exist for but a brief period, were it not for that which the soil brings forth, and this must be largely produced by the diligent and industrious husbandman. Some sections of the state of Indiana, as well as of many other states, have other resources which furnish wealth in abundance, but the great wealth comes from the soil and the abundant harvests which the soil produces. Of the many excellent farming communities in this state there are few, if any, that can produce better crops, one year with another, than does the county of Daviess.

RECLAIMING WASTE LANDS.

Nearly all the land in Daviess county is tillable and capable of producing abundant crops. With the exception of a section in the southeastern part of the county, the land is generally level. For the most part, this comparatively level land was originally covered with a heavy growth of fine timber, with an interspersion of prairie land. All this has been brought into a high state of cultivation by the industry of the land owners and the application of modern farm methods.

Until a few years ago there were sections of land in the western and southwestern part of the county that were covered with swamps and considered of little value. No attempts were made by the owners to improve this land and it was not salable at any price. The land was covered with water the greater part of the year, the water standing from one to five or six feet deep, the habitation of frogs, turtles, and amphibious creatures of various sorts. There were also large sections in the western part of the county of deep sandy land, with a growth of small shrubbery and wild weeds, which was a favorite resort for rabbits and other small game. This land was also considered of little value. As an illustration of the estimated value of this land, only a few years ago, a gentleman related to the writer his experience in a real estate deal within the last five years. He said he held a mortgage for seven hundred and fifty dollars on one hundred and sixty acres of this sandy land and the mortgagor urged him to take the land and release the mortgage. He declined to do this, preferring the seven hundred and fifty dollars, which was finally paid. He says this same tract of land can not be bought now for less than one hundred dollars per acre. Another real estate experience related by this same gentleman: At an auction held on the street, in Washington, this county, one busy Saturday afternoon, a few years ago, he bid off two quarter sections of this apparently worthless land, paying five dollars an acre for the same. Before the deeds were executed, and before the purchase price had been actually paid, the purchaser was offered an advance of one dollar an acre for his bargain and he accepted the offer, realizing something like three hundred dollars profit on the afternoon transaction. This looked like "easy money" and he congratulated himself on his lucky deal. But looking at the matter from the present standpoint, he is confirmed in the opinion that the man who paid him one dollar per acre for his bargain is the one to whom congratulations are due. That same land is now worth from forty thousand to fifty thousand dollars.

MODERN METHODS APPLIED.

All this increase in the value of these lands has been due to the application of modern methods of farming, and the science, skill and industry of the educated farmer. The swamp lands have been dredged and drained and brought into a high state of cultivation, producing from fifty to one hundred bushels of corn per acre. The sandy lands have been cleared of the useless growth of wild weeds and brush, and, figuratively, made to "blossom as the rose." This is not altogether a figurative expression, either, for on these sand lands are produced some of the choicest cantaloupes and the juciest watermelons to be found. The development of the melon industry within the last few years has been a boon to the owners of sandy lands in Daviess county, as well as in other counties in this section of the state. Some have sold their land at what would have been considered a fabulous price a few years ago, others have engaged in the melon industry with profit, where intelligence and business principles were employed in the industry.

Daviess county is well adapted to the raising of all the staple products common to other counties in this section of the state. The productions are so varied as to warrant the assertion that drouth, or excessive rains, or overflowing of the lowlands, or other unusual occurrence of any season, or any year, can not so seriously affect conditions that the husbandman will be completely disappointed in his expectations of a fair return for his labor. While Daviess county will not rank as high as some of the adjoining counties in the production of wheat, it stands well toward the head of the list in the production of corn, a yield of one hundred bushels per acre being not an unusual production for this cereal. There is also a good deal of attention being given to stock-raising, the eastern part of the county being especially well adapted for that industry.

STATISTICAL ITEMS OF INTEREST.

From the biennial report, 1913 and 1914, of the Indiana state bureau of statistics, the following items are gleaned:

Number of square miles in Daviess county, 433. Number of farms, 2,587. Number of acres, 269,678; valuation, $6,569,045. Average valuation per acre, $24.36. Number of families in Daviess county, 6,231; number of dwellings, 6,144.

Population of Daviess county in each decade since the organization of the county, as shown by the United States census report:

1810 (estimated)	300	1870	16,747
1820	3,432	1880	21,552
1830	4,543	1890	26,227
1840	6,720	1900	29,914
1850	10,352	1910	27,747
1860	13,325		

DAVIESS COUNTY PRODUCTIONS.

From the state statistical report for 1912 the following items are gleaned regarding the principal productions of Daviess county farms:

	Acres.	Bushels.	Average per Acre.
Wheat	34,892	473,957	13.58
Corn	50,956	1,455,742	28.55
Oats	10,118	136,608	13.50
Rye	1,107	17,813	
Buckwheat	10	500	

	Acres.	Bushels.
Barley	11	110
Potatoes	48	1,103
Tomatoes	378	*2,160 tons.
Timothy	16,036	13,285 tons.
Alfalfa	91	85 tons.
Clover	4,091	4,140 tons hay, 1,316 bu. seed.

* Not excelled by any county in this section of the state.

Value of cattle sold in 1912, $137,956. Value of cattle on hand, January 1, 1913, $219,483.

Value of hogs sold in 1913, $309,715. Value of hogs on hand, January 1, 1914, $148,452. Hogs died of disease in 1913, 2,326.

Value of sheep sold in 1913, $13,379. Value of sheep on hand, January 1, 1914, $10,265. Wool clip, 19,190 pounds; selling value, $3,983.

Value of horses and colts sold in 1912, $70,110. Value of horses and colts on hand, January 1, 1913, $545,646.

Value of mules sold in 1912, $55,617. Value of mules on hand, January 1, 1913, $181,898.

FROM THE COUNTY AUDITOR'S REPORT.

The following items of interest are taken from the annual report of the county auditor, for the year ending, December 31, 1914:

Number of miles of gravel and macadam roads in Daviess county, completed and under repair, about three hundred and twenty-five miles. Average cost, per mile, $3,037. Total amount of bonds sold for the construction of gravel roads, $987,176.55. Total cost of repair of gravel roads in all the townships for 1914, about $31,174.01. The total amount of outstanding indebtedness for the construction of free gravel roads in the county, which is against the townships that are constructing the roads, was, on the 31st day of December, 1914, $427,389.24.

The total valuation of the real estate and personal property in Daviess county, less the mortgage exemption, is $14,430,160.

The total amount of current taxes charged in 1912 was $435,673.66; in 1913, $427,290.91; in 1914, $419,131.03.

Expenditures, 1914: For poor expense, $4,438.84; for orphans, $872.34; for bridges, $16,990.85.

SOCIAL STATISTICS.

A glance at the statistics relating to matrimonial alliances in Daviess county discloses the fact that a considerable number do not prove to be satisfactory to the contracting parties. Covering a period of six years, the number of divorces granted averages about ten per cent of the number of licenses issued, as appears in the following exhibit:

	Licenses Issued.	Divorces Granted.		Licenses Issued.	Divorces Granted.
1906	254	24	1909	242	14
1907	231	24	1910	236	22
1908	265	26	1911	234	34

LOCAL OPTION ELECTIONS.

The question of the regulation of the liquor traffic, and of the prohibition of the sale of intoxicating liquor, by vote and remonstrance, has been agitated by the people of Daviess county, as it has by the people of about every other county in the state. Under the provisions of the county option law, enacted by the Legislature in 1908, the question was submitted to a vote of the people of Daviess county, at an election held on May 26, 1909. The result of this election was a vote of 1,456 against, and 683 in favor of the sale of intoxicants, a "dry" majority of 773. By virtue of this action, Daviess county was without a licensed saloon for two years. In the meantime a succeeding Legislature repealed the county option law and enacted what is known as the Proctor law, which gave to cities, incorporated towns and townships the exclusive right to vote upon this question. Under this law an election was held in the city of Washington, this county, March 29, 1911, resulting in a "wet" majority of 328. On the same date Elmore township voted "dry" by 160 majority. On March 28, Barr township voted "dry" by 33 majority; and Madison township gave the same expression by a majority of 123. A "dry" majority of eighty was given by Barr township at another election held on March 28, 1913.

RISE AND FALL OF THE DAVIESS COUNTY FAIR.

As early as the year 1855, an agricultural society was organized in Daviess county, the first annual fair being held in that year. For several years thereafter annual fairs were held and were quite generally patronized by the farmers, among whom there was a spirited rivalry as to which one could produce the biggest corn, the best wheat, oats, potatoes and the biggest pumpkins. Among the stock raisers there was an effort to excel in the exhibit of cattle, horses and hogs; those who could show imported and fancy breeds of stock being most conspicuous in these annual exhibits. That was the time when the manufacture of wagons, buggies, plows and other farm implements was strictly a home industry. These were all strictly "home made," and the maker took especial pride in the exhibition of his skill and workmanship at the annual county fair. And the ladies, who were adept in the art of cooking, needle work, painting and the domestic arts generally, exhibited that in which each was most proficient and interested. The result was that the exhibits and displays, at the annual fairs for several years, were attractive and instructive, and the fair was popular and a financial success.

Eventually the Civil War came on, and the diversion of the public interest and attention, incident thereto, affected the Daviess county fair, as it did all other county fairs in the state. The patronage of the fair was not sufficient to meet the expenses of the associatiton. In order to cover this deficiency, the association had recourse to means of raising money by the introduction of horse-racing, cheap shows and the like. Concessions were secured by fakirs, mountebanks and nondescripts, with various gambling devices, all of whom sought the nimble coin of the unwary, reaping rich harvests from the pockets of their dupes. All these things militated against the annual county fair, as such things always do. The attendance became less each year until, finally, the fair was discontinued for want of financial support.

AMBITIOUS ASSOCIATION TOILS.

In May, 1884, the Daviess County Agricultural, Mineral, Mechanical and Industrial Association was organized. The objects of this association, as set forth in the articles of the association, were, "the encouragement, promotion and improvement of the agricultural, horticultural, mechanical, mining, manufacturing and industrial interests of Daviess county." It might appear that the name of this association was rather top-heavy, and somewhat expansive, but the objects of the association were also expansive, worthy of the name, and of the highest ambition of the enterprising promoters.

The capital stock of the association was fixed at ten thousand dollars, in ten-dollar shares, and thirty directors constituted the board of control. The first meeting of the stockholders was held, June 14, 1884, for the purpose of electing officers of the association. Zack Jones was elected president; Henry Walter, vice-president; Charles W. Thomas, treasurer, and Ed F. Meredith, secretary. The first fair was held on the grounds of the association, west of Washington, from October 6 to 11, inclusive. The grounds consisted of forty acres of land, on which was a beautiful grove, an abundance of water and a fine half-mile race track. The fair had an auspicious beginning and the annual meets continued for several years, with gratifying success. But interest in the exhibits, after a time, grew less; the racing and other attractions began to decline, because of the competition of larger attractions elsewhere, and the enterprise was finally abandoned. The association went out of existence several years ago, and the fair grounds went to another ownership.

CHAPTER IX.

THE "UNDERGROUND RAILROAD" IN DAVIESS COUNTY.

One of the interesting topics of the early history of Daviess county, and other counties adjoining, is that of an organization known as the "underground railroad." This was a secret system by which slaves, endeavoring to escape from their masters in the slave states, were afforded protection and transportation on their way to Canada. There was a line of "stations," extending from several points on the Ohio river, and the escaping slave was transported from one station to another, under the protection of friends enlisted in the cause. Those who engaged in this business incurred great risks, and many narrow brushes with death, in their desire to assist and protect the escaping bondman. Not only from the slaveholders, in pursuit, did the "station masters," and those assisting the runaways, have cause to fear; but there were men in all the border counties ready and willing to aid the cause of the slaveowner in the apprehension of his "property," for the liberal reward that was offered. These men acted as spies and were of great service in giving information to the slaveowner, being ever ready to assist in the apprehension of the runaway.

The fugitive-slave law, that was enacted by Congress, in 1850, gave the slaveowners, or those hunting their runaway slaves, the power to organize a posse in any place in the United States to aid them in the reclamation of their slaves. Under this law, a great impetus was given to the hunting of fugitive slaves in all the free states bordering on the slaves states, and in no section was there greater activity in this line of industry than in the counties of southwestern Indiana. This law was taken advantage of by many men who never owned a slave, or who had never lived in a slave state. The kidnapping of free negroes was a common occurrence in those days. It was no trouble for a man, well advanced in moral degeneracy, and inclined to take another step in that direction, to seize upon a free negro, take him before a compliant justice of the peace, present a description of the alleged runaway—a description that had been previously obtained by co-conspirators—and the rights of the alleged slave owner were fully established. By a decision of the highest court, a negro had no rights that a white man was bound to respect.

GREAT RISKS WERE INCURRED.

Those who were engaged in the operation of this "underground railroad" system not only incurred great risks in the personal danger to life and property, but also subjected themselves to the severe penalty prescribed by the fugitive-slave act. That law imposed a fine of one thousand dollars and imprisonment on any one harboring, or in any way aiding fugitives in escaping. As the courts were constituted in that period, a very small incident was easily construed as "aiding and harboring" fugitives.

In Daviess county, as in the other counties in this part of the state, the greater porton of the early settlers came from slave states. Some had come in order to get away from slavery and its blighting influence, and they had strong convictions as to the evils of that institution. Others, who found a home in this county, brought with them the views of the community from which they came, as to the slavery question. The prevalent opinion was that slavery was right, and that the slaveowner's right to his slave was as legitimate as was his right to any other of his chattels. Slavery had existed in all the settled sections of the Northwest Territory for several years after Indiana Territory was organized, and at the time of the passage of the fugitive slave law, in 1850, there was but little open opposition to slavery. This was true of Daviess county, especially. But when the obnoxious fugitive-slave law came in force so many brutal and unjust acts were committed by conscienceless kidnappers, that a great change in sentiment resulted. There was a rapid growth of anti-slavery sentiment in Daviess county, and the activities of the "underground railroad" system were greatly enlarged.

SLAVERY IN DAVIESS COUNTY.

Before entering upon a further review of the underground railroad, and some of the exciting incidents connected therewith, it will be of interest to give some of the experiences of early settlers who brought their slaves with them to Daviess county, and for some time held them in slavery. An old history of the county is authority for the following statements:

So far as it can be established, Eli Hawkins, who came from South Carolina, in 1806, was the first to bring slaves to what is now Daviess county. He had two slaves, Jake and Ann. James C. Veale had one slave, named Sam; and William Ballow brought four to the county, namely: Buck, Isaac, Ralph and Mary. John Coleman had one, known as Cornelius Simms. William Hawkins had four: Peggy and her three children, David, Henry and

Judy; and there was a boy by the name of Dish, residing with J. Forden, but belonging to the Flint family. William Ballow sold Isaac to Eli Hawkins, who thus became the owner of three slaves. All these, with one exception, remained in servitude until after the death of Mr. Hawkins.

Mrs. Catherine Hawkins, widow of Eli, married a Mr. Merril, who had some difficulty with Isaac and Jake, a part of his matrimonial inheritance, and Jake and Isaac proceeded to "start something" that was probably in the nature of a surprise. They instituted proceedings to determine the legality of their being held as slaves in a free territory. They had for their attorney Amory C. Kinney, one of the first lawyers in the county, and the case was tried before the associate judges of the county, Philip Burton and Ephraim Thompson. The decision of the court was that the slaves, by law, were free, and from this decision there was no appeal. No other action of this kind was taken by any of the other slaves, and there was no need of such action. By this decision slavery in Daviess county was automatically abolished. The freed slaves remained in the county and some of them acquired property and established homes of their own. The success of Lawyer Kinney in obtaining freedom for these two colored men aroused a considerable amount of prejudice against that race, among a number of the white people. Numerous threats and suggestions of violence were made against the negroes and the lawyer who had been instrumental in securing their freedom; but none of these threats was ever carried into execution, and the bitter feeling and vindictive abuse gradually died away.

AN EARLY KIDNAPPING CASE.

The first case of kidnapping that occurred in Daviess county, of which there is any record, occurred in 1824. That this was more than twenty-five years before the enactment of the fugitive-slave law is evidence that kidnapping did not have its origin in the enactment of that obnoxious law. The victim of this kidnapping affair was a colored man by the name of Sam, who was claimed as the property of a family living near Vincennes, by the name of McClure. The affair occurred on a Sunday, in the summer of the year mentioned, when most of the people of Washington were out of town, some engaged in hunting or fishing, and a large number attending a camp-meeting south of the village. The McClures were anxious to get possession of their alleged property, but did not dare to come to Washington, themselves, to accomplish their purpose; thence they engaged Richard Palmer to deliver Sam to them, the place of delivery to be on the west bank of White river, in

Knox county. Palmer met with considerable opposition in attempting to carry out his part of the scheme, but he finally succeeded in delivering the "goods" at the place agreed and the McClures were there ready to receive the same. They straightway bound Sam securely with a stout rope and started with him on their way to St. Louis. On the second night of their journey Sam managed to free himself from the rope that bound him and got away. When his captors discovered his absence, Sam was far on his way towards Indiana, and he was getting farther in that direction very fast. He managed to elude his pursuers, one of their horses, which Sam had appropriated for this occasion, aiding in his rapid progress. A few days after his unwilling departure, Sam came riding into Washington, swinging his old hat and making such demonstrations of joy as he was justified in feeling. Palmer was prosecuted and fined for his part in the affair, and he attempted no more kidnapping after that experience.

ROUTE OF THE "UNDERGROUND RAILROAD."

There were many places where runaway negroes might cross the Ohio river from Kentucky into Indiana, and there were several routes of the "underground railroad," each connected with a definite place of crossing the river. One of the crossing-places was near the city of Evansville. This was a very popular place of crossing, for the reason that there were many free negroes in that vicinity. It was necessary to have assistance in getting across the Ohio, and it was necessary to have a safe place for hiding after getting across. Both of these advantages were afforded at the crossing in the vicinity of Evansville. The assistance in crossing the river was afforded by friendly white people, and a safe hiding place was found among the free negroes on the Indiana side.

There were several routes of the "underground railroad" from this favorite crossing-place, and several well known "stations" on each route. One route that was familiar and much traveled was through the counties of Vanderburg, Warrick, Gibson, Pike and Daviess, and on to the north. Among the well known places of rendezvous, or stations, along this route, where the runaway could always find shelter and protection, were the following: In Gibson county, the home of Reuben Walters, living near Fort Branch; David Stormont, living northwest, and John Carithers, living east of Princeton; Mace Kirk, at Wheeling; Dr. John W. Posey, Petersburg, and Peter Stephenson, living in the southwestern part of Daviess county. There were many other places where the fugitive negro found friendly shelter. All these stations were known to those operating the "system," and to the fleeing fugitive, as well. They were also known to the slaveholders, through information furnished by the local spies, and the harboring-places were honored with frequent visits by slaveowners and accompanying constables, in the hunt for missing human property. But it was an exception when they found what they were looking for. This was before the days of wireless telegraphy, but these "underground railroad" stations had a system that enabled them to operate their lines by a code of signals equal to any of the modern methods of communication. By some secret sign, or code, which was well understood by the runaway slave and those aiding him, he was passed along from one station to another until he reached Canada, the land of freedom.

OPERATIONS IN DAVIESS COUNTY.

During the days of slavery, Daviess county contained a number of men who were actively engaged in what they called "human freedom," which was another name for the "underground railroad" enterprise. Among the number who were most zealous in the cause were the following: Peter Stephenson, Friend Spears, Elijah Johnson, John Thompson and Frederic Myers. Peter Stephenson was the most active of them all. His home was known, from the Ohio river to the state of Pennsylvania, as one of the most important and the most reliable "stations" of the entire route. He was a good man, and as true as steel to any cause that he espoused. He was trusted as a neighbor and respected by everyone, including his political opponents. Alfred E. Johnson, a veteran of the Civil War, now a resident of Washington, relates some interesting incidents pertaining to the life of Peter Stephenson, and his activities in behalf of "human freedom." Mr. Johnson says:

"For forty years I lived within a mile and a half of the home of 'Uncle Peter,' as he was familiarly called. I well remember his calls at my father's house, in the 'wee sma' hours of the night,' and we knew something about the business to be transacted before daylight. Uncle Peter was always provided with a carriage, fitted with curtains that would securely conceal what was on the inside. No move was made, save only on dark nights, and then the fugitive was only taken on short trips.

"There was a 'station' in Washington, but I never knew by whom it was kept. I have always believed it was on the John Thompson farm, just south of the city. There was another important stopping place in Martin county, said to be near old Hindostan, a town now extinct.

OUTWITTED THE OFFICERS.

"Stephenson was often bold to the extreme. On one occasion he had secreted at his home two blacks, while the officers searched likely places for them without success. Uncle Peter was more than a match for them all, as the fugitives wanted were, at the time of the officers' visit, and for two days afterward, snugly secreted under the floor of Stephenson's cooper shop. After the hunt was over and the officers had gone, he and his assistants brought the fugitives out from their hiding place and ran them safely through to the next 'station,' which was in Martin county. On another occasion he kept three men and one woman for three weeks, before an opportunity offered to send them to the next 'station.' During those three weeks the runaway slaves were secreted in a ravine, south of where the Scudder school house now stands. At that time the country was heavily timbered, an almost impenetrable forest covering the section of county in which this ravine was located. While these fugitives were in hiding, Mr. Stephenson supplied them food and blankets for their sustenance and comfort.

"After the close of the Civil War, when there was no longer need for secrecy, 'Uncle Peter,' in a public address, related what he had done for the downtrodden race, whose members were valued as we value horses and cattle on the farm.

"Peter Stephenson was a very conscientious man, a loved neighbor and a Christian. He was one of the early pioneers, having come to Daviess county from Ohio. He was born, I think, in 1800; his death occurred in the seventies. But few persons are now living who knew him personally. To me, the memory of Peter Stephenson is one that I shall always cherish. He outlived all his co-workers of the 'underground railroad.' He lived to see his cherished desire accomplished—the freedom of the slave. He was of the John Brown type in character, but more considerate in conduct that was John Brown."

"UNCLE PETER'S" RESOURCEFULNESS.

Professor Hamlet Allen relates a little incident that occurred at the home of Peter Stephenson, during that exciting period, which aptly illustrates the resourcefulness of Stephenson, and the skillfulness of his methods in the protection of his charges. Mr. Allen says:

"At one time there came to the home of Peter Stephenson a colored woman and her small babe. The woman had struggled thus far in her efforts to get to the land of freedom; not so much on her own account, as on account of her child. It was a case something like that of Eliza Harris, in 'Uncle Tom's Cabin.' Her child was about to be taken from her and sold and the mother had hurriedly decided to save her child by flight. Almost exhausted, the fleeing mother reached the home of Stephenson, with her master and a few other human hounds not far behind in pursuit. It was a time for quickness of thought, on the part of Stephenson, but he was equal to the occasion. There was a dry cistern on his premises and he hurriedly placed the woman and child therein. Then he placed a cover over the cistern and went about his ordinary business, in which he was complacently engaged when the human hounds arrived. The premises were diligently searched, every possible place where a fugitive might be concealed was inspected, but the cistern was overlooked, on the reasonable presumption that it was full of water. Finally they went away and Stephenson availed himself of the opportunity to provide more comfortable quarters for his guests. That they were well fed and properly clothed, and in due time sent along on the way to freedom, is the rest of the story. In relating this incident, Mr. Stephenson said, 'If I ever uttered a fervent and sincere prayer in my life, it was that the baby in the cistern would not cry while these men were searching the premises; and my prayer was answered.'"

A WASHINGTON KIDNAPPING CASE.

Not infrequently kidnappers were frustrated in their efforts to get away with their victims, especially if the victim was captured some distance from the Ohio river. There were determined men in all the counties in southern Indiana who were vigilant and watchful; and it required the utmost caution in their movements and skillful handling of their captive, for the kidnappers to get by these watchful waiters. It also required courage to meet the opposition likely to arise on the way. Courage was one moral quality in which the kidnapper was wholly deficient, as a rule, these kidnappers being as cowardly as they were contemptible. The men who opposed their nefarious business were men of courage and conviction and ready at all times to defend the rights of man to life and liberty, regardless of race or color.

In Colonel W. M. Cockrum's "Pioneer History of Indiana" is the story of a kidnapping case that occurred in Washington, along in the fifties, which had an unpleasant ending for the kidnappers. This story will serve as a sample illustration of many other experiences of like character.

Along in the early fifties two negro men, who lived in Kentucky, but had been for some time in Indiana, working on the Wabash and Erie canal, between Washington and Terre Haute, had determined to go to their homes. They had got as far as Washington on their way when they fell in with a man who seemed very friendly. He asked them where they were going and when he learned their destination, he told them that he and a friend of his were going in the same direction, nearly to the Ohio river; that they were going in a wagon, and if the colored men wanted to they could go along in the wagon and it would not cost them anything for the ride; that the accommodating strangers would have provisions with them for the trip, and all that would be required of the colored men was to assist in the preparation of the food. They said they would not be ready to start before three or four o'clock in the afternoon of that day. This offer seemed very favorable to the two colored men and they very gladly accepted it. They promised to be at an agreed point on the south side of Washington at the agreed time. Here the two men with the wagon found them and they all started on their way.

CIRCUMSTANCE AROUSED SUSPICION.

They took the Petersburg road and it was late in the evening when they crossed White river at the ferry. John Stucky, who crossed the river at the same time, knew one of the white men and at once suspected what he was up to; but he could not draw him into a conversation, and could get no chance to talk to the colored men. Stucky heard the white men tell the ferryman that they would stay all night in a wagon-yard at Petersburg. Stucky took notice that, after the party was over the river, they traveled at a pretty swift gait, and he could not keep up with them. He reached Petersburg some time after the wagon had put up at the wagon-yard. He took notice of the situation and then called on Dr. John W. Posey, to whom he related the circumstances, and his suspicions regarding the party stopping at the wagon-yard. Doctor Posey at once understood the situation and sent a spy to the wagon-yard to get all the information possible as to designs of the white men. The spy soon returned and reported that he found the party eating supper, except one of the white men who was some distance away engaged in earnest conversation with a noted hotel-keeper, a slavery sympathizer. The spy said he had talked with the negroes, who said that their homes were in Kentucky; that they were on their way home, and that the white men were letting them ride in their wagon most of the way.

While circumstances looked suspicious, there was no positive evidence of anything wrong. But Doctor Posey decided to have a watch kept on their movements and to wait for further developments. About two hours before daylight, the following morning, the man who had been on watch came hurriedly to Posey's home and reported that the party were getting ready to start; that they had their team hitched to a three-seated express wagon; that the noted hotel man was with them, and two other men whom the watchman did not know. The doctor at once got busy. He had three horses saddled and sent for a neighbor to ride one; one of his hired hands was called to ride another, and the doctor rode the third, all three being well armed. In the meantime it was learned that the express wagon had gone. Posey and his party hurried on after the wagon, which had taken the road to Winslow, expecting to overtake the wagon party at that place. It was evident that the party was traveling at a rapid pace, as it was learned the travelers had passed through Winslow about dawn, a half hour before the arrival of the pursuing party. Following on after them, the Posey party met a man a few miles out of Winslow, who reported that he had met the express wagon about a mile ahead; that there were two runaway negroes, tied together in the wagon, and that the party was driving very fast. Later the pursuing party met Rev. Eldridge Hopkins, who had also met the express wagon with its occupants. Hopkins consented to join the Posey party in pursuit. As Hopkins was well acquainted with the country roads he proposed a plan to get in ahead of the express wagon and intercept the kidnappers at a designated point. In this he was successful. In the meantime the pursuing party found a justice of the peace; a warrant was obtained, and a constable was secured to execute the same. When the kidnappers arrived at a point beyond the line in Warrick county they were met by a constable with a warrant for their arrest. The kidnappers put up a bold front, and made a good many threats; but they were taken to a justice's court, at which quite a crowd of people had gathered who were very much in sympathy with the captive negroes.

JUSTICE RENDERS UNPOPULAR DECISION.

The man who claimed to own the negroes showed a handbill, giving a perfect description of the two men in custody, and an offer of a reward of two hundred dollars for their return to his plantation in Tennessee. This handbill was, no doubt, printed in Washington the day before, while the negroes were waiting for their new-found friends. Hopkins, who was a ready talker, volunteered to defend the negroes and made a strong speech in their behalf. But the sympathy of the justice was against them; he believed that all negroes were slaves, or ought to be, and that those who claimed their homes in a slave state were certainly slaves. As the man who claimed to own these negroes had shown a notice giving an exact description of them, the justice decided to let him go with his property.

The decision of the justice infuriated Hopkins and he declared that he would see that this man did not get on the other side of the Ohio river with his alleged property. As a means of hindering the progress of the kidnappers, Hopkins found an opportunity of removing one of the linchpins that held in place a wheel of their express wagon, putting the pin in his pocket. He told Doctor Posey and his two men that they might return home, as he could secure enough men out of the crowd assembled to assist him in the proposed undertaking. In the meantime the kidnappers had started off on the road leading to Boonville. They had not proceeded far on the way until the wheel from which the linchpin had been removed came off. While they were hunting for the missing pin the rescuing party came up, having in the meantime disguised themselves by blacking their faces. Leveling their guns at the kidnappers they demanded an explanation as to why they had the two negroes tied. The explanation not being satisfactory, Hopkins demanded that the negroes be released, and then directed the negroes to bind the white men who had them in charge. Then Hopkins organized a stump court-martial to try the kidnappers. The pretended owner produced the hand bills that had been used effectively in the justice court. Hopkins told him that these bills had been printed in Washington, an assertion which the pretended owner did not deny. After hearing all the evidence, the court decided the kidnapping party were all guilty and that all of them should be hanged. However, the court decided that leniency would be shown to any of the gang who would tell the whole truth. At this one of the party began to weaken, and Hopkins took the fellow aside and obtained from him the whole story. He said that the pretended owner of the negroes lived in Washington, and that it was the intention to take the negroes to Mississippi and sell them; that it was the agreement to pay the man making the confession, and another man whom they had engaged in Petersburg, one hundred dollars, each, to go with them and watch the two negroes, until they were sold. He further stated that the team which the kidnappers used belonged to the leader, the pretended owner of the negroes.

NEGROES EXECUTE "COURT'S" ORDER.

After hearing this confession Hopkins held another consultation with his "court" and it was decided to modify the first decree. He informed the conspirators of the decision, which was that they were not to be hung, but a sound thrashing would be administered, instead, and that the two negroes were to execute the sentence. Accordingly, two stout hickory gads were procured, the "convicts" were securely tied to a tree and the two negroes did the rest. After the sentence of the "court" had been fully carried out to the satisfaction of all parties, with the possible exception of the kidnappers, the latter were told to move off in different directions, and not to look back, under penalty of being shot. And they went.

A few weeks after the events above recorded, Mr. Hopkins had occasion to visit Doctor Posey, at Petersburg. While there he sent a man to Washington to learn what he could about the two men who were engaged in the kidnapping. He learned that they had returned to Washington, the next day after they were so soundly thrashed, and reported that they had fallen in with a band of horse thieves, who had beaten them fearfully, and had taken their team and everything else that they had. Whether this story found ready credence among the citizens of Washington is not a matter of record. But it is certain that this kidnapping experience was sufficient to last the men engaged in it for the rest of their lives.

These kidnapping stories might be multiplied by the score, not only in Daviess county, but in almost every other county in the state. It is probable that there were fewer outrages of this kind committed in this than there were in some of the counties nearer the border, because of the greater distance, and the greater difficulty in getting the captives safely landed in Kentucky. But Daviess county was the scene of many such outrages, a record which no citizen of the present day will point to with pride. Under the decision of the highest court a negro had no rights that a white man was bound to respect, not even the right of personal possession of himself after he had paid the price. The crimes that were committed under the operation of the fugitive-slave law—crimes against justice and humanity, and sanctioned by courts, high and low—are a stain upon the pages of the nation's history, a stain that required the blood of multiplied thousands of her best citizens to erase, in the resulting Civil War. As before stated, some of these crimes were committed in Daviess county, and, in some measure, her citizens were ready to give consent and encouragement to them. In a much larger measure was demanded the blood of some of the best of her sons, as a requital for the sins of the fathers.

CHAPTER X.

DAVIESS COUNTY IN WAR.

There were white men in this part of the country long before the establishment of the great Northwest Territory and many of them had sanguinary conflicts with the aborigines who were the original possessors of the land. In the wars with France the Indians became the hirelings of England, and were also made the catspaws of the "mother country" during the strenuous years of the struggle for liberty by the colonists, and later on in the War of 1812. But no record of the names and service of these early frontiersmen is extant. After the War of 1812, militia organizations were kept intact until the general fear of danger from the red men was past, and then were allowed to fall into gradual desuetude.

THE WAR WITH MEXICO.

A small contingent of Daviess county men served in the Mexican War, and in 1846 were enlisted for the struggle with that turbulent people. Among those enlisting were Charles Childs, Thomas Coulter, Gabriel Moats, Nelson Bolton, Patrick Carley and Jacob Leap, all of whom served in Company H, Second Indiana Regiment, Capt. Joseph W. Briggs commanding. These patriots served one year and fought in the battle of Buena Vista. In 1847 Captain Ford, Third United States Dragoons, recruited in this county Alexander H. Dougharty, Thomas Coneter, William Samples, John Samples, Jacob Leap, William Sanders, William Smith, William Hubbard and Nelson Jackson. He got his men as far as the barracks in St. Louis, but no farther, peace having been declared between the belligerents before he could proceed to the front.

WAR BETWEEN THE STATES.

The causes leading up to the Civil War need no explanation in these pages, as thousands of volumes have been written and published on that subject. The bitterness of the people of the Southern states engendered by the stand of the North against the extension of the system of slavery into the territories and new states was intensified when the great champion of equal rights, Abraham Lincoln, became President of the United States on the 4th day of March, 1861. To emphasize the determination of the Southern extremists to carry their ends and disrupt the Union, a bold attempt to prevent the inauguration of Lincoln by assassination had been frustrated. The next disloyal move was the firing on Fort Sumter, in the outer harbor of Charleston, on the 12th of April, 1861.

The insult offered the flag at Fort Sumter and the secession of several of the Southern states from the Union could only be interpreted in one way. War had been declared by one section of the country against the other, and Abraham Lincoln, true to his determination to preserve republican institutions at all hazards, issued a call for seventy-five thousand volunteers to put down the rebellion.

How the people of Washington and the county at large stood in this dark hour of the country's travail may be best illustrated by an editorial of the time, written and published by S. F. Horrall, in his issue of the *Telegraph*, of date February 1, 1861. A short time before active hostilities commenced he wrote:

"That the action of South Carolina and other seceding states is treason against the general government is true; and yet, strange as it may seem, we find men in the free states who try to justify this treason, as if there could be any justification of a crime so heinous and damnable. However, we never find one who is not willing to admit that secessionists have acted hastily, that they have been guilty of treason; but for all this they are disposed to say: 'Let the seceders alone! If you disturb them, if you execute the laws, they will fight, and down goes the fabric of the government.' Are they not bent on doing violence to the laws of the government, setting the powers that be at defiance, regardless of any consequences? Has one word been uttered by any one of the seceding states that in case of a satisfactory compromise, giving them all they have ever asked, that goes to prove that they would accept the compromise and come back into the Union? We can hardly believe that they will ever willingly come back until, by experience, they have learned the sad lesson of secession. As to war, God knows we hope we may never see the day that the first blow is struck; for then we may not guess at the end. We hope that the virtue of forbearance will be clung to till the last ray of hope shall have vanished, then, if it comes to the worst, let us prepare to meet the issue."

DIRE PROPHECIES REALIZED.

The editor of the *Telegraph* was, like many of his compatriots, far-seeing, and his dire prophecies were fully realized. Others thought the rebellion could be terminated within a few weeks and this feeling seemed to have prevailed at Washington, as indicated by the call of the President for less than one hundred thousand men. But events proved that the pessimist had the better of the argument and in a very short time calls for troops by the hundreds of regiments became the order of the day, and every loyal state in the Union vied with the others in an effort to recruit its quota and get to the front before its neighboring commonwealth. In this regard, Indiana was supremely loyal and active. The excitement caused by the fall of Fort Sumter created the utmost excitement throughout the land and in Washington, this county, men, women and children could think and talk of nothing but the outrage offered the flag and the call to arms. All felt instinctively that the crisis had come; that an awful calamity had overtaken the country.

On the 19th of April, Editor Horrall again gave way to his patriotism in the following pertinent paragraph: "Friends, the national flag, the glorious stars and stripes, which you have so long looked upon with patriotic pride, has been dishonored! The colors have been struck to the traitors, and what will you? Will you who love the honor of your country stand idly by and see that emblem of our liberty torn asunder? Never! Never!! Never!!! We know that patriotism is at no discount in Indiana, and honestly believe that one hundred thousand can be raised in ten days to fight for the flag, the Union, the Constitution and the enforcement of the laws. And since it has come to the worst, since nothing will appease the wrath of the traitors, we say, in God's name, let us, one and all, fight for our flag, our country and our God. We are sadly mistaken if Indiana shall be last in rank; but we are not mistaken. The war now commenced, every patriot will do his duty; and, if we have traitors in our midst, we very much mistake the feeling of this state, if it will not soon become so hot that it will not hold those who rejoice at the hoisting of the hateful traitor flag."

DAVIESS COUNTY'S PATRIOTIC RESOLUTION.

On the 17th day of April, five days after the Union flag had been lowered at Fort Sumter, a monster mass meeting was held at the court house, attended by the leading men of all political parties. Noah S. Given was the chairman of this most notable gathering, and John Van Trees, secretary. The Saxe band was there and its rendering of patriotic airs added to the enthusiasm, if that were possible. The chairman, in accepting the honor conferred, declared himself in favor of putting down the rebellion no matter at what cost of life and treasure. His speech rang loud and true throughout the old court house and every word uttered stirred within the hearts of his auditors the resolution to do and dare all for their country. A committee, composed of S. F. Horrall, editor of the *Telegraph;* W. R. Gardiner (now nestor of the Daviess county bar), John Hyatt, Edward McCrisaken, O. F. Rodarmel and Joseph Peck, appointed by the chair, presented the following resolutions, which met the approbation of practically every one present:

"Whereas, With sorrow and deep regret, we lament the condition of our beloved country, and with feelings of pain we have learned that the flag of our country has been lowered to a hostile foe; therefore be it

"Resolved, That with our utmost energy and power we will sustain the Union, the Constitution and the laws of the United States of America, and that we will protect, with our lives, our fortunes and our sacred honors, the flag of our country from insult, whether from foreign or domestic foe."

Chairman Given was not the only one to declaim in patriotic tone on this occasion. Several short speeches, abounding in expression of love and loyalty and replete with maledictions on all traitors, were received with hearty approval and acclaim. To everyone who would speak, the audience gave willing ear. The people could not get enough of it, so that the meeting adjourned, with the understanding that it should be reconvened on the following evening at the same place. All who desired could not secure admittance at this second assemblage, which was presided over by J. W. Burton, with S. F. Horrall as secretary. Judge Burton, patriot and eloquent orator, delivered "a brilliant, stirring, fiery speech, incisive with patriotism and logic, and full of searching blows of keen invective." Matthew L. Brett, S. F. Horrall and others also shone in this gathering as loyal citizens and as eloquent mouthpieces for their country, and it should be related, that men and women came from all parts of the country to attend these meetings, showing by voice and action they were with the government heart and soul. Throughout the country, by day and night, union meetings were held at school house or church, and in the county seat and villages men and women blocked the streets, all eager to learn the trend of events and express their views upon what already had taken place.

FIRST COMPANY OF VOLUNTEERS.

The people of this community did not expend all their energies in street-corner harangues and mass-meetings. They were too full of eagerness to meet insult and wrong in a substantial way for that. So it came about that on the 18th of April, 1861, through the activity of partisans, over one hundred men had enrolled for three months' service. This was the first company of volunteers formed in the county, the members of which elected Charles Childs, captain; Richard W. Meredith, first lieutenant, and Alanson Solomon, second lieutenant. On the 19th the organization offered its services, by wire, to the governor, which were immediately accepted, with orders to report at Indianapolis for active service without delay. It is related that "at this time the town of Washington was a sight the oldest inhabitant had never before witnessed. The Saxe horn band was scarcely off duty day or night, but paraded the streets at the head of militia companies, firing the hearts of all with the grand strains of 'Hail Columbia,' 'The Red, White and Blue,' 'Yankee Doodle' and other national airs. In every direction the stars and stripes were flung to the breezes, until the wonder was where all the banners came from. All business, except that of making 'war to the knife and knife to the hilt,' was abandoned. America never before had seen such a popular uprising."

The premier military company of Daviess county, organized for the Civil War, prepared to start for Indianapolis on Saturday, the 20th of April, and just before it entrained a silk flag, hastily made by the ladies, was presented to the "boys," a short address in this behalf being made by Mrs. P. Cruse. The banner was received by Captain Childs and accepted for the company by Citizen Cook, who eloquently pledged the lives of the recipients to the maintenance of its honor and safe keeping; and the reader may rest in the assurance that all of the people of Washington and a large part of the county were at the depot of the Ohio & Mississippi railroad to see the soldiers off to a war, from which, mayhap, they never were to return. Finally, the "boys" were on board the cars and as the train pulled out the scene was one never to be forgotten. Many of those left behind were in tears, others were shouting their throats into fragments bidding the company goodbye and Godspeed, while the band kept in unison with the occasion, as it rendered patriotic selections.

Upon reaching camp at the state capital, Captain Childs' command was assigned to the Sixth Regiment and became Company C; it was mustered into the United States service for the period of three months, April 24, 1861, six days after it was organized. Upon the expiration of its term of service Company C returned home and the regiment went into the three-years service. In September and October, 1861, a company was organized at Washington which became Company E, Sixth Regiment Indiana Volunteer Infantry, and during its term of service had the following officers: Captains, Charles R. Van Trees and Oscar F. Rodarmel; first lieutenants, Henry C. Hall, Sr.,

Alanson Solomon, O. F. Rodarmel and Henry E. Van Trees; second lieutenants, Alanson Solomon, O. F. Rodarmel and H. E. Van Trees.

THE SIXTH REGIMENT.

Thomas T. Crittenden was colonel of the Sixth Indiana while in the three-months service. The regiment left camp at Indianapolis on May 30, 1861, fully armed and equipped, and proceeded to West Virginia. On the 2nd of June, Webster, West Virginia, was reached and that night the men marched, in a downpour of rain, to Phillipi, where a battle took place the following morning, in which the Sixth was engaged. Returning to Grafton, the regiment was brigaded under General Morris and, marching to Laurel Hill, was in the engagement with Garrett at Carrick's ford on July 12. The latter part of July found the organization back in camp at Indianapolis and on the 2nd of August it was mustered out of the service. This regiment was reorganized for the three-years service on September 20, 1861, and on the same day Colonel Crittenden took five hundred of the men and moved into Kentucky to oppose General Buckner. This portion of the regiment moved from Louisville to Muldraugh's Hill and from there to Nolan creek where, in October, it was strengthened by the arrival of three hundred recruits under Lieutenant-Colonel Prather. Becoming a part of Rosseau's brigade, of McCook's division, it was marched with Buell's army to Mumfordsville, Woodsonville and Bowling Green. In March, 1862, the command marched to Nashville and there went into camp, remaining a few weeks, after which time the regiment again was on the march, this time to Savannah, Tennessee, and thence to Shiloh. On the day of its arrival at Shiloh the regiment performed service in saving one of the Federal batteries from capture and in charging the enemy. After participating in the siege of Corinth the regiment marched with Buell's army through Alabama, to Stevenson, then on after Bragg, arriving in Louisville on the 1st of October. The month of November saw the regiment again back in Tennessee, where later it took part in the battle of Stone's River. In the spring and summer of 1863, the Sixth campaigned in Tennessee and fought in the battle of Chickamauga, on the 19th and 20th of September, where Colonel Baldwin was killed. After this sanguinary battle the regiment took part in the engagements at Browns Ferry and Mission Ridge and then marched to the relief of Knoxville, remaining in east Tennessee until the spring of 1864. Taking an active part in the Atlanta campaign, the Sixth fought at Tunnel Hill, Rocky-Face Ridge, Resaca, Buzzard Roost, Dallas, New Hope, Allatoona Ridge, Kenesaw Mountain, Marietta and before Atlanta, from the latter place returning to Chattanooga, in August, where the non-veterans were mustered out. Those remaining were transferred to the Sixty-eighth Regiment, and when this organization was mustered out, nineteen men still remaining of the old Sixth were transferred to the Forty-fourth Regiment, which was mustered out of the service on September 14, 1865.

Company C, during its three months' service in the war was free from casualties of any serious importance, with the exception of the death of private Joseph G. Scott, who died while on his way home. Company E, of the Sixth, enlisted for three years, was not so fortunate, as it lost several men, both by disease and death in battle. Wayne Alford died of disease at Corinth, in June, 1862; Isaac Alexander, disease, at Knoxville, in April, 1864; Abram W. Carnahan died in Andersonville prison, in August, 1864; Benton McCafferty was wounded at Mission Ridge; Lafayette Alford died at home, of disease, in May, 1862; John Azbell died at Chattanooga of wounds, in November, 1864; Josiah Farley was killed at Mission Ridge in November, 1863; Josiah Graham was killed at Chickamauga, in September, 1863; Napoleon Hubard was killed at Mission Ridge; John Hill died of disease at Woodsonville, Kentucky, in February, 1862; John Killion died of disease at Woodsonville; James Lambert died of disease at Iuka, in June, 1862; Joshua McLuin died of disease at Nashville, in January, 1863; Charles Palmer was killed at Chickamauga, in September, 1863; William H. Wilson died of disease at Louisville, in April, 1863; Aaron Hunter, a recruit, was killed at Shiloh, April 7, 1862; Robert Warner, recruit, died of disease at Louisville, in 1862; Lieut. Alanson Solomon died of exposure at his home in Washington, Indiana, in May, 1862.

THERE WERE SOME "COPPERHEADS" HERE.

A very large majority of the Democratic party in the North was opposed to secession and gave its support to the Union cause, but there were some men within that party's ranks who were traitors. Among these were statesmen, able lawyers, capitalists and a contingent made up of the riff-raff of society. Some of the spokesmen for the Confederacy, by reason of violence of speech or reprehensible acts, were caught red-handed and deported into the rebel lines, where they belonged. The less important, though more brazen and blatant ones, kept up a continual yelping at home, until the patience of their neighbors reached a limit and the "copperheads" were squelched. There was a sprinkling of this class of citizens in Daviess county, who early began to show their colors, as the following article, taken from the *Telegraph's* issue of April 19, 1861, shows: "We have a few secessionists, it appears, in our town, who seem to glory that the flag of our country has been torn from Fort Sumter, and the Federal troops been obliged to surrender. In the days of Christ, there was one whose heart was so damnably corrupt that, for thirty pieces of silver, he betrayed his Master. In the Revolution there were those who fought under the enemy's flag; therefore, it is not astonishing to us that we find some who are willing to join an army of traitors. If they prefer to do so let them go; God knows we are better off without than with them." A flag pole, one hundred feet in height, with Old Glory floating from its topmost point, was early erected in Washington. The flag, so proudly waving in the breeze, called forth sentiments of loyalty and love for the Union from the many and irritated a few disloyal ones to utterances that often placed their lives in danger. To the west, a short distance from the county seat, was Maysville, to which place a man named Rice journeyed from Washington and cut the flag rope. While in the act of desecrating the flag he was arrested and fined by Justice Cloud. His arrest was fortunate, for had it not occurred the infuriated citizens of Maysville, most probably, would have made short work of him.

LINCOLN CALLS FOR MORE MEN.

The government and its advisers were not long in reaching the conclusion that the acts of the Southern rebels meant more than a three-months' application of the rod to the recalcitrants, and in July, 1862, the call for five hundred thousand men to put down the rebellion went forth over the land and met with instant response. Nelson M. Bolton at once led the movement for recruiting a company of volunteers at Washington and before the end of July, had named sufficient men, who enlisted, to form Company D, Twenty-fourth Regiment, Indiana Volunteer Infantry. The officers of this organization, during the war were: Nelson M. Bolton and Samuel F. ————, captains; Jacob Covert, S. M. Smith, Henry H. Hyatt, first lieutenants; S. M. Smith and Henry H. Hyatt, second lieutenants. Company K, of the same regiment, had for its captain, Thomas Johnson, of Washington, and T. M. Gibson, second lieutenant. When the regiment was re-organized, Samuel M. Smith became captain of Company C, and Anthony Johnson, second lieutenant, with Henry H. Hyatt, adjutant of the regiment; W. S. Waller, second lieutenant of Company E.

HISTORY OF THE TWENTY-FOURTH (SIXTH) REGIMENT.

With Alvin P. Hovey as colonel, the Sixth Regiment was mustered into United States service at Vincennes, July 3, 1861. It moved to St. Louis on the 19th of August and thence into the interior of Missouri; there remaining until February, 1862, when it was sent to assist in the reduction of Fort Donelson, but arrived there too late.

The regiment was hotly engaged at Shiloh, losing, among many others, Major Gerber. It was at the siege of Corinth and then went to Memphis. The month of July found the Sixth at Helena, Arkansas, where it wintered, in the meantime engaging in several expeditions. In the spring of 1863 the regiment was in Hovey's division, in the Vicksburg campaign, fighting at Port Gibson, Champion's Hill and elsewhere, distinguishing itself at Champion's Hill by a terrific charge on the enemy. After the fall of Vicksburg, the Twenty-fourth went to New Orleans, and, during the fall of 1863, was at New Iberia and Algiers, close by. It was veteranized in January, 1864, and was given a furlough home. In December it was consolidated with the Sixty-seventh Regiment under its old name and, in January, 1865, moved to Florida, in April participating in the investment of Mobile. It then moved to Selma, Alabama, and soon thereafter transferred to Galveston, Texas. The regiment again was transferred, in July, 1865, by being organized as a battalion with five companies. The other companies were mustered out, their terms having expired. The casualties of the regiment were: Captain S. M. Smith, wounded at Shiloh and Champion's Hill; James P. Cruse, died of disease after reaching home, January, 1862; Milton Jackson, died of disease at St. Louis; Asbury D. Alexander, died of disease at St. Louis, in January, 1865; John Balthus, died of disease in 1861; William Bradbury, died of disease in 1862, at Jefferson City, Missouri; William Brown, died at St. Louis, in November, 1862; William Edwards, died of disease in 1862 at Helena, Arkansas; Jackson Edwards, killed at Magnolia Hills; William Graham, killed in May, 1863, at Champion's Hill; Thomas Hardin, died of disease at home in 1862; Peter Hawkins, died of disease at home in 1862; George Hawkins, died of disease at Tipton, Missouri, in 1862; George Messer died of disease at Tipton, Missouri, in December, 1861; John Montgomery, died at Vicksburg, in July 1863; Harvey Peck, accidentally killed at Milliken's Bend, Louisiana, in April, 1863; Henry Rhodes, died at Helena, Arkansas, in September, 1862; Francis A. Shepard, died of wounds, in May, 1863; James Tisdal, died of disease at St. Louis, in 1862; Daniel Fee, a recruit, died in May, 1864, at New Orleans; W. S. Helms, recruit, died in May, 1865; James Mallory, recruit, died in Louisiana in 1864; Enoch Nash, recruit, died in Louisiana in 1864; E. M. Thomas, recruit, died in Louisiana in 1864.

COMPANIES B AND E, TWENTY-SEVENTH INFANTRY.

In July, 1861, a company was organized at Raglesville and in August, of the same year, one at Washington, both being assigned to the Twenty-seventh Regiment. Company B, of Raglesville, was officered during the war as follows: Captains, Jackson L. Moore, William E. Davis and John W. Thornburgh; first lieutenants, J. N. Thornburgh, W. S. Davis and Thomas W. Casey; second lieutenants; Thomas W. Casey, J. W. Thornburgh and William Hubbard. The officers of Company E were: George W. Burgh, George L. Fesler and James Stevens, captains; John A. Cassidy, James Stevens and Bethuel Clark, first lieutenants; James Stevens and George W. Roddick, second lieutenants. In 1862 George W. Burge was made a major of the Twenty-seventh.

The Twenty-seventh Regiment was mustered into the service of "Uncle Sam" at Indianapolis, September 12, 1861, and then entrained for Washington City, at which point it was transferred to Banks' army of the Shenandoah, passing the winter near Frederick City, Maryland. In March the regiment took position across the Potomac; pursued Jackson's army, after the battle of Winchester Heights, and on May 12, fought at Front Royal. On the 25th of May it fought gallantly at Winchester, its brigade (Gordon's) withstanding the assaults of twenty-eight Confederate regiments for three and one-half hours, repulsing them. But the odds were too great, so that the Federal forces were compelled to fall back into the town, where, in the streets, the fight was hotly continued. The retreat was continued and the regiment re-crossed the Potomac on May 26. The regiment fought at Cedar Mountain, in August, and at Antietam lost heavily on September 17. Until the following year the Twenty-seventh did guard duty, after which it participated in the battle of Chancellorsville, fighting bravely, but losing heavily. Moving north in pursuit of Lee's army, it gave a splendid account of itself in resisting the headlong charges of the enemy and was the loser of many men. In September the regiment was transferred to the west, with the Twelfth Corps, and, during the fall and winter of 1863-4, was assigned to the Twentieth Corps, and was stationed at Tullahoma. Returning from a furlough, after part of the regiment had veteranized, the regiment fought at Resaca

May 15, 1864, defeating the Thirty-second and Thirty-eighth Alabama regiments and taking one hundred prisoners, including the colonel and the battle flag of the Thirty-eighth Alabama. The regiment then participated in the Atlanta campaign. The non-veterans were mustered out in November, 1864, and those remaining were transferred to the Seventieth Regiment and served throughout the Carolina campaign, at the end of which they were transferred to the Thirty-third Regiment. The final muster-out took place at Louisville, Kentucky, July 21, 1865.

The casualties in Company B follow: William Hubbard, wounded and discharged in December, 1863; Ira C. Brashears, discharged in June, 1863, with loss of right arm; Elisha Guthrie, killed in July, 1863; Stephen Boardman, died of disease in November, 1863; Alonzo C. Burgher, died at Darnestown in November, 1861; W. J. Flinn, died at New Hope Church, Georgia, in May, 1864; W. R. Carson, killed at Cedar Mountain; Joshua Gough, died at Philadelphia in May, 1862; Willis Hubbard, died at Belle Isle; William Hanna, died at Chattanooga, in June, 1864; G. W. Herrondon, died in September, 1864; Anderson Dickert, killed at Resaca in May, 1864; John Correll, died at Chattanooga in July, 1864; W. B. Matthews, killed at Chancellorsville in May, 1863; George W. Stout, died at Atlanta in August, 1864; Pierson Wagley, died at Darnestown, Maryland, December, 1861.

Casualties in Company E: William C. Boyd, died in Libby prison; Joseph Carrall, killed at Chancellorsville in May, 1863; James M. Chapman, killed at Gettysburg in July, 1863; Thomas W. Hill, killed at Cedar Mountain; Patrick Curley, died at home in November, 1862; Lewis Clark, died at Alexandria, Virginia, in December, 1863; B. T. Gregory, died at home in December, 1862; Thomas Gregory, killed at Dallas, Georgia, in May, 1864; William Gaines, died at Frederick City, Maryland, in December, 1861; James Herinshaw, died at Williamsport, Maryland, in December, 1862; G. W. Honey, died at Atlanta, Georgia, in August, 1864; Henry Huskes, died at Washington, in September, 1862; John Jones, died of wounds at Alexandria, Virginia, in 1862; John R. Kellar, killed at Dallas, Georgia, in May, 1864; Thomas Layton, died in January, 1862; Nathan Logan, killed at Antietam in September, 1862; James Lashley, died in June, 1864; Philip Ross, killed at Cedar Mountain in August, 1862; Daniel S. Sparks, killed at Cedar Mountain; Franklin Smith, killed at Antietam; John J. Williams, died at Darnestown, Maryland, in 1861; John Weber, killed at Peach Tree Creek, in August, 1864; W. H. Wilson, killed at Gettysburg in July, 1863.

COMPANY G, FORTY-SECOND REGIMENT.

Eli McCarty, Isaac W. McCormack, S. F. Horrall and others organized a company for the Forty-second Regiment, Indiana Volunteer Infantry, in September, 1861, which was familiarly known as McCarty's Company. On the 27th of September the men entrained for Evansville and upon arrival there went into camp, and were designated as Company G, of the Forty-second. It had for its officers, during the war, Eli McCarty, Isaac W. McCormack, Spillard F. Horrall and Joshua A. Palmer, captains; I. W. McCormack, S. F. Horrall, J. A. Palmer and W. H. Faris, first lieutenants; S. F. Horrall, J. A. Palmer, W. H. Faris and William A. Myers, second lieutenants. When the war was drawing to a close, J. G. Stubblefield became adjutant and Rev. Henry O. Chapman, chaplain of the regiment; and Harrison Peachee, captain of Company D. The regiment was organized at Evansville, with James G. Jones as colonel, and early in October found its way to Henderson, Kentucky, thence to Calhoun, Owensboro and, on the 25th of February, 1862, Nashville, Tennessee. The regiment then moved into the interior of the state and then to Huntsville, Alabama, where it remained until the latter part of September. It went with Buell's army and pursued Braxton Bragg and participated in the battle of Perryville, October 8, 1862, losing one hundred and sixty-six in killed, wounded and missing. Returning to Nashville, the regiment later took part in the battle of Stone's River, losing seventeen killed and eighty-seven wounded. It remained in camp near Murfreesboro until June 24, then moved with Rosecrans' army to Tullahoma, thence to Chattanooga and, on September 19 and 20, fought at Chickamauga, losing eight killed and eighty-five wounded and missing. The regiment assisted in the storming of Lookout Mountain and fought at Mission Ridge, losing forty-three killed and wounded. It was veteranized on January 1, 1864, and then was furloughed home. Returning, the unit joined General Sherman at Chattanooga, and on May 7, started on the Atlanta campaign, in which it sustained a loss of one hundred and three men and officers, killed and wounded. After the fall of Atlanta it pursued Hood's battered army to Kingston, Rome, Resaca, thence to Gaylesville, Alabama, and then returned to Atlanta. It was with Sherman on his famous march to the sea and participated in the Carolina campaign, losing ten men, killed and wounded, at Bentonville.

The regiment arrived in Washington City, took part in the Grand Review, then went to Louisville, Kentucky, where it was mustered out on July 21, 1865. The regiment, during its term of service, lost in killed, wounded and missing, six hundred and twenty-nine, of which eighty-six were killed on the field and four hundred and forty-three wounded. It was in the following battles and skirmishes: Wartrace, Perryville, Stone's River, Elk River, Chickamauga, Lookout Mountain, Chattahoochie River, Peachtree Creek, Atlanta, Jonesboro, Savannah, Charleston, Black River and Bentonville.

LOSSES OF COMPANY G.

Casualties of Company G: Henry Baker, died at Vining's Station, Georgia, in August, 1864; Robert S. Walker, killed at Perryville in October, 1862; Andrew J. Brown, same as last mentioned; W. B. Burrows, died of wounds in February, 1863; James M. Campbell, died in March, 1862; Henry Craft, died in July, 1863; John S. Gregory, died at Murfreesboro in July, 1863; Isaac S. Haller, mortally wounded at Chickamauga in September, 1863; George W. Horrall, died at Nashville in July, 1863; Samuel Havens, died at Wartrace, Tennessee, in April, 1862; Henry S. Hunter, killed at Perryville, in 1862; Reuben Hunter, died of wounds in 1864; William P. Jones, died of disease at Evansville, in March, 1862; John McCarty, died at Wartrace of disease in April, 1863; Charles McCracken, wounded and discharged in January, 1864; Richard McGeeher, died of wounds at Murfreesboro in January, 1863; A. R. Newberry, wounded and discharged in March, 1863; E. W. Pride, died of disease at Evansville in January, 1862; Hubbard Pride, killed at Stone's River on December 31, 1862; J. T. Pride, wounded and discharged; Samuel Rattan, died of wounds received at Lookout Mountain in November, 1863; Harrison Risley, killed at Resaca in May, 1864; John Russell, wounded and discharged in December, 1862; William Sullivan, died at Evansville in January, 1862; Oscar Owanigen, died, cause and date not stated; W. E. Wells, wounded and discharged in February, 1863; B. F. Walker, mortally wounded at Stone's River in December, 1862; Nicholas F. Wallace, mortally wounded at Stone's River; D. C. Wallace, wounded and discharged in March, 1864; J. P. Wallace, same; Stephen H. Williams, died of wounds at Perryville in October, 1862; James H. McCafferty, recruit, died at David Island, New York, in May, 1865.

SCATTERING MILITARY EVENTS.

The military history of regiments with which Daviess county patriots were identified, appears in this chapter, as shown by the records in the office of the adjutant-general of the state, and, as a whole, may be considered reliable. A full roster of all the men who served in the Civil War from this county also has been published, from the adjutant-general's office; but to give the long list of names would take too much space. However, one gathers a definite general knowldge of the county's valiant service in the great conflict in what has herein been written and before this chapter is brought to a close events and personages deserving special mention, and not heretofore touched upon, will have received their just dues. To continue, B. F. Burlingame, of Daviess county, who went out in September, 1861, as second lieutenant of Company A, Seventh Regiment, rose to the rank of quartermaster, and Richard J. Graham became regimental adjutant of the Thirteenth, and was promoted to captain, major and lieutenant-colonel on the reorganization of that regiment. In September, 1861, Samuel W. Peck became surgeon, with rank of major, of the Eighteenth, and S. A. Wadsworth arose from the rank of second lieutenant to that of captain of Company E, Eighteenth Regiment. John A. Cassidy, captain of Company D, Twenty-seventh Regiment, was killed at Chancellorsville in May, 1863. James Neal, active in the enlistment of men in the summer of 1861, was commissioned adjutant of the Frst Cavalry, Twenty-eighth Regiment.

THE HOME GUARDS.

Companies of home guards were often organized during the troublous time of the "late unpleasantness," during the Civil War. From the outbreak of hostilities in 1861, and all during the year, there were constant calls for men to join the various organizations forming by enthusiasts. Among those taking a prominent part in forming companies of home guards were Captains Bradley, Childs, Wigmore and H. S. Bingham. Among the notable events was the leasing of the *Telegraph* by S. F. Horrall to E. A. Lewis and the enlistment of the patriotic editor. On New Year's day, 1862, Capt. C. R. Van Trees was the recipient of a valuable sash, presented by admiring citizens; and in February, upon the receipt of news that Fort Donelson had fallen into the hands of the Federals, a great jollification took place at Washington. Upon this occasion W. R. Gardiner delivered a speech and G. W. Walters found it a good opportunity to call for recruits.

HISTORY OF THE FIFTY-SECOND REGIMENT.

Twenty-two men were secured by William A. Bodkin, late in 1861, for Company A, Fifty-second Regiment, Indiana Volunteer Infantry, and eighteen for Company E, same regiment, by David J. Temple and R. W. Meredith, all of whom were mustered into the service on February 1, 1862. David J. Temple began his service as second lieutenant and later, being promoted to a captaincy, was transferred to Company I. R. W. Meredith was first lieutenant of his company, but resigned before the expiration of 1862. William A. Bodkin was first lieutenant of Company A and later attained the rank of captain.

The Fifty-second Regiment was partly formed at Rushville and was consolidated with the Fifty-sixth at Indianapolis. It broke camp on February 7, 1862, and moved to Fort Henry and thence to Fort Donelson, where it participated in the memorable siege of that fort; later performing duty at Fort Henry and Fort Heinman until April 18, when it moved to Pittsburg Landing and took part in the siege of Corinth. The regiment was at Memphis, Fort Pillow, Columbus, and other points of engagement, and fought Faulkner's guerrillas near Durhamsville on September 17. Following this it did garrison duty at and near Fort Pillow until January, 1864, skirmishing and engaging in numerous expeditions; then moved with Sherman against Meridian in January, 1864, fought at Jackson, and veteranized at Canton, Mississippi, on February 27, after which it took a veteran furlough. The regiment returned to Columbus, Kentucky, and in May returned to Vicksburg, from which point it pursued and fought General Forrest's forces at Tupelo, Mississippi. The regiment was engaged at Hurricane Creek on August 13 and at Franklin, Missouri, on October 1, in which latter engagement it drove Price out of the state. The Fifty-second then moved to Nashville, where it fought on December 15-16, and joined in pursuit of Hood. It then moved to Eastport, thence to New Orleans, Dauphin Island and to Spanish Fort, helping reduce the latter; fought at Blakely on April 9, 1865, the day of Lee's surrender, and then moved to Montgomery, Alabama, performing garrison duty there and in other parts of the state, until mustered out, September 10, 1865. The casualties of the regiment follow: Reuben Johnson, died at Vicksburg in March, 1864; Philip Dermosly, veteran, died in September, 1864; Michael Gatlet, died in May, 1862; Charles H. Flanders, veteran, died in March, 1864, all of Company A; Preston T. Linville, died at Corinth in May, 1862; Thomas C. Duffy, veteran, died at Memphis in October, 1864; William Moley, died at Fort Pillow in May, 1863; Robert Ormsby, died at Memphis in August, 1862.

THE FIFTY-EIGHTH REGIMENT.

In the fall of 1861, through the efforts of Green McDonald, James A. Dale and J. S. Canfield, about fifty men were raised to fill the ranks of Company H and other companies of the Fifty-eighth Regiment, Indiana Volunteer Infantry. The officers of Company H, during the war, were James A. Dale and Green McDonald, captains; G. McDonald, John S. Canfield and Zachariah Jones, first lieutenants; J. S. Canfield, Z. Jones and Peter Honey, second lieutenants. The regiment was organized at Princeton in October, 1861, Col. Henry M. Carr, commanding officer. In December the regiment went to Louisville, joined Buell's army and spent the winter in Kentucky. On the first of March, 1862, it reached Nashville. After remaining at Nashville for about a month the regiment moved with Buell's army in a hurried march to join Grant's army at Pittsburg Landing, arriving there at the close of the second day of the battle of Shiloh. Following the army in its movement on Corinth, the regiment participated in the siege resulting in the evacuation of that place, and then moved with Buell's command through northern Alabama, repairing and guarding the railroad, through Tuscumbia and Huntsville, and thence to Decherd, Tennessee. The regiment had several minor engagements with the enemy in the vicinity of McMinnville during the summer of 1862. About the first of September of that year the regiment participated in the retrograde movement of Buell's concentrated army after Bragg, moving through Nashville and Bowling Green, finally reaching Louisville, about the first of October. After a rest of two days the regiment moved with the army to Bardstown, driving Bragg from that place and following his retreat to Perryville, where a severe battle was fought. Following Bragg's retreating forces for some days after that engagement the Fifty-eighth then turned again in the direction of Nashville, arriving there in the latter part of November. The regiment then moved with Rosecrans's army, in the Murfreesboro campaign, and in December charged the enemy at Lavergne, driving him from that place and on to Murfreesboro; was engaged in the battle of Stone's River, December 31 and on the 1st and 2d of January following, losing in that engagement one hundred and ten in killed, wounded and missing, out of about four hundred engaged. The Fifty-eighth Regiment remained in the vicinity of Murfreesboro until June 24, 1863, and then moved with the army toward Chattanooga; participated in the bloody battle of Chickamauga, losing one hundred and seventy in killed wounded and missing; also participated in the charge and severe battle of Mission Ridge, November 25, and then moved with the army sent to the relief of Knoxville, spending the winter in the vicinity of Knoxville, where it suffered greatly for want of provisions and clothing.

RE-ENLISTED AS VETERANS.

It was under these conditions that the Fifty-eighth Regiment re-enlisted as veterans, January 24, 1864, and was returned to Indiana on veteran furlough, arriving at Indianapolis, March 4. At the expiration of their furlough the veterans returned to the field, in April, and the regiment was then put in charge of the pontoon train of Sherman's army, preparing to advance on Atlanta. In this service the regiment bridged all the streams from Chattanooga to Atlanta, often under a galling fire from the enemy in position to dispute the crossing.

In October, one hundred and seventy men of the Tenth Regiment were consolidated with the Fifty-eighth Regiment. After the fall of Atlanta, the Fifty-eighth moved with the army of Georgia, under General Slocum, and bridged the streams from Atlanta to Savannah. The non-veterans were mustered out in December. In the Carolina campaign the Fifty-eighth bridged the streams for the army of Georgia. In this campaign alone it made over sixteen thousand feet of bridges. Later, on the way to Washington, D. C., it bridged all the streams with the exception of the James. On July 25, 1865, the organization was mustered out at Louisville, Kentucky. It lost during its term of service, in battle and disease, two hundred and sixty-five men.

Casualties of Company H: Capt. James H. Dale, November 25, 1863, wounded at Mission Ridge, resigned; W. H. Lyndall, died at Lebanon, Kentucky, in February, 1862; John H. Groves, died in January, 1863, of wounds received at Stone's River; John G. Auld, died at Nashville in April, 1862; John H. Barr, died at Bardstown, Kentucky, in January, 1862; William Brown, died at Louisville in January, 1862; Andrew Cunningham, killed at Stone's River in December, 1862; David Dickerson, died at Lebanon, Kentucky, in March, 1862; Zeddeck Dickerson, died at Nashville in August, 1862; George D. Kendall, died at Bardstown, Kentucky, in January, 1862; Franklin Lavely, died at Nashville in April, 1862; John Lavely, died at Bardstown in December, 1861; John Shaley, died at Corinth in May, 1862; Jesse Worrell, died at home in June, 1862.

HEAVY CALLS FOR TROOPS IN 1862.

In the months of July and August, 1862, after a lull in recruiting, the government issued calls for large bodies of men, which prompted certain of Daviess county's citizens to lend their aid in augmenting the forces of the Northern armies. To this end, Captain Childs, Captain Johnson and Lieutenant Hall called for men to form companies, and to create enthusiasm and success in these efforts, war meetings were held in various sections of the county, at which leading men with gifts of oratory used every persuasion of speech to induce able-bodied men to enlist. In this they were quite successful. In the latter part of July over one thousand men had responded to the urgent call of their country and were ready at Washington, under Captain Johnson, to repel invaders, the word having reached here that rebels had crossed the Ohio and were headed in this direction. This "scare" made enlistment in township militia companies quite brisk, each township organizing its own company, fully officered. In August recruits for the Fifty-eighth Regiment were sought by W. H. Kendall, who, while in the performance of his undertaking, was forced to shoot a rebel sympathizer. Captain Cassidy and Lieutenant McCormack gathered together sixty recruits for their commander. The men recruited by the officers mentioned were assigned to Company I, of the Sixty-fifth Regiment, and were mustered into the service on the 20th of August. The officers of the company, during the war, were Charles Childs, S. K. Leavitt, Harvey Taylor and Samuel H. Mulholland, captains; James Neal, H. Taylor, S. H. Mulholland and Saulsbury Lloyd, first lieutenants; James P. C. Prewitt, S. H. Mulholland and Elam Ritchey, second lieutenants.

SIXTY-FIFTH REGIMENT.

This organization, formed at Princeton, was mustered in at Evansville, with John W. Foster as colonel, and was then sent to Henderson, Kentucky, to protect the place from guerrillas, being moved to Asbury in August. After an all-night march it attacked Adam Johnson's regiment and took possession of Madisonville. Having been mounted in April, the regiment did duty on the Nashville railroad and elsewhere until August, 1863; was moved to eastern Tennessee in September and, on a raiding expedition up the valley, captured trains, locomotives and other property. It engaged the enemy near Zollicoffer and on the 22d of September lost fifteen men at Blountsville. On October 11 it fought at Rheatown; on the 14th again at Blountsville, and the next day at Bristol. The regiment fought at Walker's Ford all day on November 17, losing twelve men. Company K performed excellent service at Mulberry Gap. On December 14 the regiment lost seventeen men in a skirmish at Bean's Station and the next day lost fourteen men at Powder Springs Gap, later in the day the list of casualties being increased by the loss of three men at Skagg's Mills. The regiment skirmished at Dandridge on January 17, 1864. Being dismounted in April, the Sixty-fifth joined Sherman in the Atlanta campaign and was in all engagements of that march, losing an aggregate of twenty-nine men. It pursued Hood, fighting at Columbia, Franklin and Nashville; was transferred to the Atlantic coast in February, 1865; sustained a heavy attack at Fort Anderson, skirmished at Town Creek, and on June 22, 1865, was mustered out at Greensboro. During its term of service the regiment lost twenty-six killed, eighty-six wounded and sixty-one captured.

Casualties in Company I: Capt. Charles Childs died at home in December, 1863, of chronic diarrhoea; James Bruce, died at Knoxville in February, 1864; Henry Block, killed on picket near Atlanta in August, 1864; James Bolin, died at Knoxville in December, 1863; Charles R. Chapman, died at Henderson, Kentucky, in March, 1863; W. T. Cunningham, died at Madisonville, Kentucky, in December, 1862; Henry S. Davis, died at Camp Nelson in January, 1864; Jacob Davis, died at Knoxville in January, 1864; George Goodwin, drowned near Owensboro, Kentucky in July, 1863; Turman Halcolm, died in November, 1864; Elias P. Hulon, died at Chattanooga in June, 1864; Manoah Humphreys, died at Henderson, Kentucky, in February, 1863; Albert C. Johnson, killed at Resaca in May, 1864; Penanas Lamb, died in Libby prison in February, 1864; John W. Moore, died at Madison, Indiana, in September, 1863; George W. Owen, died at home in April, 1864; William O'Marry, killed at Resaca in May, 1864; Caleb Reynolds, died in a Confederate prison in April, 1864; David Sears, died at Knoxville in February, 1864; John M. Sears, died in a Confederate prison in April, 1864; John C. Smelser, died at Knoxville in May, 1864; E. W. T. Walker died in a Confederate prison in January, 1864; Isaac Watson, died in a Confederate prison in February, 1864; Lewis Wise, died at home in August, 1863; Solomon Williams, died at Evansville in September, 1864.

Recruits: H. H. Brown, died in a Confederate prison in April, 1864; Warren A. Cramer, killed near Atlanta in August, 1864; Gabriel Moots, killed at Resaca in May, 1864; John Mode, died at Louisville in February, 1865; Alfred Spears, died at Knoxville in December, 1863; Emanuel Smith, died at Camp Nelson, Kentucky, in January, 1864; W. T. Smiley, died in a Confederate prison in March, 1864.

NINETY-FIRST REGIMENT.

A small squad of men became a part of Company B, of the Eighteenth Regiment, in August, 1862, and in July and August, through the efforts of Z. V. Garten, Thomas Wadsworth and Starling Sims, a full company was raised for the Ninety-first Regiment, the company being given the initial letter C. The men mainly came from around Raglesville and Odon. The officers of Company C, during the war, follow, namely: J. H. Garten, Z. V. Garten and R. B. Dunlap, captains; Thomas Wadsworth, R. B. Dunlap and William F. Wirts, first lieutenants; Starling Sims and James H. Garten, second lieutenants. The regiment rendezvoused at Evansville on October 10. A battalion of seven of its companies performed guard duty in Kentucky until June 15, 1863, when it marched to Rushville, Bowling Green and Burksville, in pursuit of Morgan. The battalion was joined by three companies in the late summer and in September moved to Nashville, thence, in November, to Russellville, Camp Nelson and Point Burnsides, moving thence in January, 1864, to Cumberland Gap, where part of the command had a skirmish. The regiment fought at Pine Mountain, New Hope Church, Decatur, Peachtree Creek, siege of Atlanta, Utoy Creek and elsewhere; joined the pursuit of Hood, on November 3 fought at Franklin and on December 15 and 16 fought at Nashville, soon thereafter being transferred to Washington City. It participated in the capture of Wilmington, North Carolina, then moved to Goldsboro, thence to Raleigh and on May 8, 1865, to Salisbury, where it was mustered out of the service on June 26. The regiment lost eighty-one men killed and wounded.

Casualties in Company C: Capt. Z. V. Garten, wounded and discharged in September, 1864; Capt. J. H. Garten, wounded and discharged in December, 1864; W. H. Taylor, died at Madisonville, Kentucky, in February, 1863; David B. Keyser, died at Hopkinsville, Kentucky, in July, 1863; R. Fietner, died in Kentucky in September, 1863; Luke Adkins, died at Knoxville in July, 1864; Nelson Adkins, died at Nashville in July, 1864; James Critchlow, died at Washington, D. C., in April, 1865; W. H. Carter, died at Marietta, Georgia, in August; Benjamin Eaton, died at New Albany in February, 1865; Elias Gough, died at Henderson, Kentucky, in December, 1862; William Hastings, died at Evansville; Joshua T. Hastings, died at Henderson, Kentucky, in November, 1862; John T. ———, died at Knoxville in July, 1864; Jacob T. Tilburn, died at Cumberland Gap in January, 1864; John L. Morrison, died at Madisonville, Kentucky, in February, 1863; Carroll Nash, died at Evansville in January, 1864; Charles Osman, died at Henderson, Kentucky, in December, 1862; Thornton C. Pearce, died at Madisonville in February, 1863; Julius Smith, died at Henderson in November, 1862; William Stanley, died at Cumberland Gap in March, 1864; George Heimer, cause and date of death not stated.

DAVIESS COUNTY ESCAPES DRAFT.

The draft was put into operation in Indiana in October, 1862; but Daviess county entirely escaped any indignity of that kind, as she had the high mark of distinction of having furnished her full quota, being one of only fifteen counties in the state to be so "forehanded."

The call for six-months men had been issued in June, 1863, to which a full company responded in the county. This company was assigned to the One Hundred and Seventeenth Regiment, Indiana Volunteer Infantry, as Company K, and was officered, during the war, as follow: James R. Bryant and John B. Wirts, captains; John B. Wirts and John S. Canfield, first lieutenants; John S. Canfield and James A. Carnahan, second lieutenants. With a beautiful flag, the gift of Washington ladies, the company left the county seat for Indianapolis on August 11, 1863, where the regiment was organized. This regiment left for Kentucky on the 17th of September and later moved to Nicholasville, Cumberland Gap, and thence into eastern Tennessee, remaining near Greenville until November; then moved to Bean's Station and later to Clinch Mountain Gap. Here it was nearly captured by the enemy. The regiment then moved to Cumberland Gap, thence to Tazewell and on to Knoxville; in December, 1863, to Strawberry Plains, thence to Maynardsville; then back to Cumberland Gap, from which place it returned home, the term of enlistment having expired.

Casualties in Company K: William J. Alford, died in Andersonville prison in September, 1864; John Blough, died at Knoxville in January, 1864; John Burriss, died at Tazewell in January, 1864; Alonzo Cunningham, died at Knoxville in November, 1863; Harvey H. Dickinson, died at Indianapolis; Thomas J. Helpenstein, died of disease at Greenville in October, 1863; Alonzo C. McGaughey, died at Camp Nelson in December, 1863; Zachariah Moody, died in Andersonville prison in March, 1864; William Potts, died at Knoxville in December, 1863; David Snider, died in Andersonville prison in August, 1864; William R. Strickland, died at Tazewell in January, 1864; William Winn, died at Camp Nelson in January, 1864.

RECRUITS AND VETERANS.

Under the call of October, 1863, Daviess county's quota was one hundren and forty-three men, and efforts at once were put forth to meet the government's requirements. To this end C. R. VanTrees called for volunteers and the number desired was soon forthcoming. Of this contingent, and those secured under calls of February and March, twenty men were assigned to Company D, Twenty-fourth Regiment; twelve to Company E, Twenty-seventh Regiment; forty-five to Company G, Forty-second Regiment; about twelve joined Company H, of the Fifty-eighth Regiment; twenty joined Company I, of the Sixty-fifth Regiment; eighteen were taken to Company C, of the Seventieth Regiment; thirty went to Company K, of the Seventieth Regiment; and six to Company C, of the Ninety-first Regiment. During the winter of 1863-64 large numbers of recruits and veterans left for the field. The veterans re-enlisting, remained with their regiments and the recruits were assigned to the older organizations. No draft took place in the county in 1864, this being avoided by the general acceptance of a bounty of four hundred dollars offered by the board of commissioners. In January, 1865, the bounty was increased to six hundred dollars. In all, beginning with a fifty-dollar bounty in 1863, Daviess county paid in bounties the sum of fifty-nine thousand three hundred and fifty dollars, and considered the money well spent, as it avoided trouble always consequent on the exercise of the draft and made it possible for the county to present a good appearance on the war records of the state.

By the 19th of September, 1862, the county was credited with furnishing one thousand two hundred and thirty-seven volunteers. Under the call of June, 1863, a full company of one hundred men was supplied; the quota of the October call, numbering one hundred and forty-three, was furnished. Under the calls of February, March and July, 1864, the county was credited with seven hundred and thirty-five men and under the last call, December 19, 1864, the official credit for the county was one hundred and six men; but at this time the county was short of men. In addition, there were three companies of minute-men in the state service, one hundred and eighty men, beside eleven companies mustered into the "Legion," with about fifty men in each company, or a total of five hundred and fifty in the "Legions." The grand total of men enlisting for the Civil War from Daviess county, as shown by the adjutant general's report and the county records, is three thousand and forty-two men, a splendid showing, and one of which Daviess county shall always be proud.

DAVIESS COUNTY SOLDIERS' AND SAILORS' MONUMENT.

When the Children of Israel, after their forty years of wilderness wandering, had finally reached the Jordan and were about to enter the Promised Land, a chosen man from each tribe was directed to take up a stone from the bed of the river that was made dry for their passage. These stones were carried to the place of their first encampment, and there piled into a heap, to remain as a memorial. "And Joshua spake unto the Children of Israel, saying: When your children shall ask their fathers in days to come, What mean these stones; then ye shall say, Israel came over this Jordan on dry land. That all the people of the earth may know, the hand of the Lord it is mighty; and that ye may fear the Lord forever."

Monuments and memorials characterize every age and every people in sacred and profane history. From the time of the proud and rebellious Absalom, who sought to perpetuate his memory by the erection of a monument in his name in the king's dale, down to the latest time; wherever heaves the turf or rises the lettered stone, in every receptacle of the dead in all ages; by the towering monuments of granite, by the mighty pyramids of the desert, in all the ways known to art and science since the beginning of time, we hear man's voice protesting against death and crying for immortality.

"WHAT MEAN THESE STONES?"

There are some events in the history of individuals, and of nations and communities, that may well be and should be perpetuated by the erection of monuments. To this end the stones were gathered from the bed of the river Jordan, that historical inquiry might be excited among the children of generations to come. To this end monuments and memorials have been established in towns and cities all over our land, as a testimony of the heroism and sacrifice of those who offered their lives to save the flag from dishonor, and to preserve a nation threatened with destruction. To this end the citizens of Daviess county have contributed of their means for the erection of a monument to preserve and perpetuate the memory and achievements of those from this county who responded to their country's call; who, in the days of the Civil War, gave the supreme test of patriotism. Daviess county has honored herself in dedicating this monument in honor of her sons who

SOLDIERS' MONUMENT, WASHINGTON.

have fought her country's battles. Its value is not to be reckoned by the cost of material and construction, but rather for the purpose it will serve the generations to come who shall make inquiry as to its meaning. As in the case of the rude pile of stones by the river Jordan, it will serve as an answer to the inquiry of children of future generations, when they shall ask, "What mean these stones?"

PRELIMINARY STEPS FOR THE ERECTION OF A MONUMENT.

The initiatory steps for the erection of a soldiers' monument were taken by the local Grand Army post in the early part of 1911. In order to secure an appropriation from the county for that purpose it was necessary to have a petition signed by a majority of the legal voters of the county, in accordance with the provisions of an act of the Legislature. This petition, duly signed and verified, being presented to the county commissioners, that body could ask the county council for an appropriation for the specified amount for the specified purpose. A committee was appointed by U. S. Grant Post No. 72, Grand Army of the Republic, to make a canvass of the county to secure the required number of signers to the petition. This committee was composed of the following persons: P. H. Ragsdale, Philip Hart, W. S. Waller, James Wykoff, John M. Jackman, John Russell, George W. Fyffe, Abner Colbert, D. J. Murphy and Benjamin Folson. By the latter part of October, 1911, a sufficient number of signatures to this petition had been obtained and, on November 7, 1911, the petition was presented to the board of county commissioners. The following from the official proceedings of the commissioners show the further progress of the work:

"November 7, 1911. Comes now U. S. Grant Post No. 72, Grand Army of the Republic, and through its committee presents a petition requesting an appropriation of $40,000 for the purpose of erecting a soldiers' monument, the petition being presented, on behalf of the committee, by P. H. Ragsdale, W. P. Gardiner, Mayor John W. McCarty, J. Earl Thompson and Elmer E. Harstings. After fully examining said petition the board finds the petition is signed by more than a majority of the legal voters of the county, and therefore refers the same to the county council and recommends an appropriation of $40,000 for the purpose of erecting a soldiers' monument."

It seems the county council was not inclined to grant the full amount of the appropriation requested. That body made an appropriation of thirty thousand dollars, as is indicated by the next action of the commissioners, at their January meeting, 1912. At that meeting they gave notice that they would receive designs and plans for a soldiers' monument, with samples of granite to be used, including walks and approaches, the cost not to exceed thirty thousand dollars. Bids to be submitted March 6, 1912.

On March 6, 1912, in connection with the Grand Army committee, the commissioners examined designs and plans submitted and after due consideration accepted the plans submitted by the Washington Monumental Works, and the auditor was directed to advertise for bids for the erection of a monument according to these plans.

At their meeting on May 9, 1912, the commissioners ordered the issuance of bonds to secure funds for the erection of the monument, said bonds to be in the amount of eighteen thousand dollars, and to bear four per cent. interest; bonds to be in series of one thousand dollars each, payable on the 15th of May and the 15th of November, each year.

On June 4, 1912, the contract and bond of Wey & Backus, of Terre Haute, for the construction of the monument were accepted and approved by the commissioners.

On October 7, 1912, the work of construction of the base of the monument, done by Noah Bogard, sub-contractor, was accepted and Wey & Backus, contractors, were directed to settle for the same.

On November 4, 1912, the bid of the Washington National Bank for bonds to the amount of eighteen thousand dollars was accepted.

On November 14, 1912, George W. Correll, of Odon, was appointed to inspect the sample of Barre granite, submitted by Wey & Backus. Correll reported on November 16, stating that he had inspected the material in the sample submitted and found it to be first quality, fine-grained, light Barre granite.

On January 6, 1913, at the joint meeting of the commissioners and the Grand Army committee, Wey & Backus submitted photographs of statuary for the monument, and the same were approved.

On July 2, 1913, the auditor presented to the commissioners the written acceptance of work done by George Correll, superintendent of construction. The Grand Army committee also filed a statement of its entire satisfaction with the work done and the material used.

DESCRIPTION OF MONUMENT.

The material used in the construction of this monument is Barre granite, of fine grain and whitish gray color. The design of the monument is a massive, rather than a stately structure. The base is about thirty feet, and the dies of the shaft are massive blocks of granite about six feet square. On the top of the shaft is the figure of a soldier, representing a color-bearer, holding a flag. On the pedestal on the east side of the shaft is the figure of a soldier representing an infantry sentinel with martial equipment. On the west side is the figure of an artilleryman. All this statuary is carved from Barre granite and is a most artistic production of the sculptor's skill. From the base to the top of the figure surmounting the shaft the height is about forty feet. The monument stands in front of the south entrance to the court-house lawn, facing Walnut street. The approach to the monument is by wide stone steps from the street sidewalk. Around the base of the monument is a wide space paved with concrete, and on either side is a settee made of granite. On the face of the lower die fronting the street is this inscription:

"This Memorial is the Tribute of the People of Daviess County to the Memory of her brave Soldiers who endured the hardships and fought the battles of 1861 to 1865, that the Union might be preserved."

On the opposite side of the monument, facing the north, is a panel bearing this inscription:

"This panel is dedicated to the memory of the Pioneers who blazed the way and cleared the fields. To the brave hearted Soldiers of the Indian Wars who fought the battles of Civilization upon Indiana's soil, and to all who answered the call of Patriotism upon the Nation's battlefields."

On the face of a granite block standing at the edge of the pavement, on each side of the approach to the monument, is a bronze tablet on which is inscribed the names of those who had official direction of the construction. On one of these tablets are the following names of the monument committee:

P. H. Ragsdale, chairman; Philip Hart, secretary; William S. Waller, John Russell, Benjamin J. Tolson, John W. Kellams, Abner D. Colbert, John W. Jackman, James W. Wykoff, George W. Snider.

On the other tablet are the names of the board of commissioners and of the county council, who were officially connected with the monument construction, as follow:

Board of Commissioners: Robert J. Barr, Richard McDonald, James T. Sause, John M. Meads.

County Council: Hugh McKernan, Haman Woodling, John H. Arvin, James Porter, William G. Scudder, Simeon Martin, Arthur H. Trueblood.

The total cost of the monument was about eighteen thousand dollars.

DEDICATION OF THE MONUMENT.

The dedication of the monument took place on Wednesday, October 8, 1913, an occasion long to be remembered by all who participated in the event. To the veterans of the Civil War, especially, it was a memorable day, not only because it marked the consummation of a long-desired wish, in the completion of a soldiers' monument, but also, by some who participated in the dedication ceremonies it was recalled that this date was the anniversary of the battle of Perryville, one of the bloodiest battles of the Civil War. Daviess county soldiers bore a conspicuous part in that battle, and many fond hearts of friends at home were broken with grief because of sons, brothers and husbands who fell in that battle.

The following account of the dedicatory ceremonies is reproduced from the *Daviess County Democrat*, of October 11, 1913:

"The beautiful soldiers' and sailors' monument on the south lawn of the court house, Daviess county's tribute to the love and memory of her representatives, both living and dead, in past wars, was dedicated today with imposing ceremonies. It was the biggest day in years for the old soldiers. They were here from all parts of Daviess county and many attended from adjoining counties.

"The Grand Army post room, in the basement of the court house, and the lawn in front, was the scene of the greatest activity, from early in the morning. The veterans gathered in groups, chatting over present and past times, and the feeling in their hearts seemed to be one of thankfulness that they had been allowed to live and enjoy the pleasures of this day. Around these groups of veterans were large crowds of spectators, among whom were many children who for the first time, and probably the last time, had the opportunity of hearing the story of the war as told by these veterans, and to hear the music of the fife and drum as played by those whose hearts were stirred by the thrilling music.

"The stores along Main street were handsomely decorated, as were many private houses. The big parade was the feature of the morning exercises. Undoubtedly it was the greatest patriotic pageant ever seen in the city. About two thousand children took part in the parade and made one of the prettiest sights in the entire parade, with their flags waving and the sounds of happy cheers.

"The parade was headed by the city officials, followed by the fire department with decorated wagons. Following them came the county officials and the two thousand children of the public and parochial schools, each carrying a flag. Company D, Indiana National Guard, with the flag it used in the Spanish-American War in 1898, came next and they were followed by the pupils of the high school, two hundred and fifty strong. The Grand Army post, headed by Kiefer's band, was next. Some of the veterans had the uniforms that they had worn in the service and this gave the age-broken veterans a more patriotic appearance. There was a large turnout of veterans and they marched the entire distance, though with halting step. Following the Grand Army, came the Ladies Circle of the Grand Army of the Republic, and then the Eagles, led by "Uncle Sam" and his banner and a drum corps. The Independent Order of Odd Fellows brought up the rear, with a large delegation. The line of march was from the court house east on Walnut to Seventh, south to Main, west to Meridian, north to Walnut, east to the court house. The streets were lined with spectators along the way.

"The parade disbanded at the court house, at the base of the new monument, which the school children and lodges saluted with three cheers. After the crowd had assembled, the school children sang 'The Battle Cry of Freedom.' Rev. J. W. Darby, pastor of the Christian church, gave the invocation, followed by music by Kiefer's band. The presentation of the monument to the Grand Army post was then made by Mayor John W. McCarty in a very appropriate speech. The veterans accepted the monument and then proceeded with its dedication, according to the prescribed ritual of the order, which was very beautiful and impressive. Following the dedication, the school children sang 'The Star Spangled Banner,' and then the Ladies of the Circle gave their flag drill, a very pretty and patriotic exercise. The morning exercises closed with the singing of 'America' by the audience.

"The exercises of the afternoon were held in the First Christian church, which was well filled with those eager to hear the addresses of Hon. Ezra Mattingly and Judge W. R. Gardiner. After a selection by a mixed double-quartet, Mr. Mattingly made a short address, reciting the part that Indiana had in the Civil War. Mr. Mattingly is thoroughly familiar with the war history of Indiana and his remarks were listened to with great interest.

"Hon. W. R. Gardiner was the principal speaker of the afternoon. His speech was a gem, both in thought and in rhetoric, and is classed as one of the finest patriotic addresses that the local Grand Army ever listened to. He paid a fine tribute to the veterans of '61 to '65, extolling them for their valor and praising them for their pluck in enduring the hardships which they had to face during the war. The afternoon program ended with the benediction by A. E. Johnson, chaplain of the post.

THE OLDEST VETERAN.

"John Harris, a member of Company D, Eightieth Indiana, was the oldest veteran in attendance at the reunion and dedication. He is past eighty-eight, but is still spry. He marched with the rest of the veterans in the parade. His home is near Alfordsville and he lives on the same farm on which he lived before he enlisted in the army. He has made that place his home ever since he returned from the war. Frank A. Evans, of McCormick avenue, this city, was the youngest veteran to register. He served in Company B, One Hundred and Thirty-seventh Indiana. James Sinclair, aged sixty-six, of Company D, Eightieth Indiana, and R. H. Bell, sixty-five years old, of Company I, Tenth New York Artillery, were other young veterans in attendance."

CHAPTER XI.

DAVIESS COUNTY NEWSPAPERS.

The first journalistic venture made in Daviess county was by William C. Berry & Son, who started a paper called *The Philanthropist* in 1836. Either because of its high-sounding name, or for some other reason, this paper did not long survive. It ceased to exist within a year and the same parties afterward made another attempt to establish a newspaper under the more modest name of *The Chronicle*. This latter paper continued until 1840. This was the year of intense political excitement, when the Whig party was much in evidence, and there was a demand for a paper advocating that political faith. This demand was supplied by Terry & Smith, who established *The Harrisonian*, supporting Gen. William Henry Harrison for president. Definite data is lacking as to the length of existence of this paper, but it certainly lived to celebrate the election of its favorite candidate.

The Harrisonian, however, did not have a monopoly of the political discussion incident to that campaign. Another paper, called *The Jacksonian Democrat*, published by Jeremiah Young, came into the field in advocacy of the opposition party. *The Jacksonian Democrat* made a vigorous fight for the principles of the party it espoused, but the success of the Whig party accomplished its quietus.

The Hoosier was published during the year 1842 by James J. Marts. *The Pilot* was established in 1843 by Charles G. Berry, but it only lasted for a few months. It was succeeded in the same year, first by *The Saturday Morning Expositor*, published by Jones & Trowbridge, and this by *The Literary Journal*, published by John Brayfield & Co. This last newspaper venture was the first to approach anything like success. It was continued until 1853, when, on account of the death of Mr. Brayfield, it was sold and the name changed to the *Washington Telegraph,* with J. M. Mason as editor. Mr. Mason continued the paper until 1855, when it was again sold to James Stell, who published it in support of the Know-Nothing, or American, party until 1858. In that year the *Telegraph* passed into the hands of S. F. Horrall, who continued as editor and publisher until 1861, when the paper was sold to Lewis & Gardner.

NUMEROUS FUTILE VENTURES.

In the meantime some other efforts had been made in the attempt to establish a newspaper in Washington, and these efforts generally resulted in failure. Rev. Hamilton Robb, a Baptist minister, started a Democratic paper called *The Sun,* but this paper with luminous title had scarcely begun to shed its rays upon the community when James Wilkins obtained possession of the plant and changed the name of the paper to *The Bee,* whereupon *The Sun* went into an eclipse. But *The Bee* soon followed its predecessors. In 1856 it came into the hands of Oliver P. Baird, who changed the name to the *Washington Democrat.* Lewis & Gardner came into possession of the *Democrat,* in 1861, and consolidated that paper with the *Telegraph,* changing the name to the *Washington Conservator,* on an independent policy. This consolidated independent paper died a natural death inside of six months.

The *Washington Telegraph* was revived in the early part of 1862, by Dr. W. A. Horrall and William Chapman. Horrall disposed of his interest to Jacob Covert in 1863; Chapman did likewise a few months later, and Covert continued the paper alone for about a year, at the end of which time he retired. Finally, the plant came into the hands of J. M. Griffin, who, in 1865, removed it to Mitchell, Indiana, and the *Washington Telegraph* ceased to be.

Jasper H. Keys & Co. published *The True Union Spirit* for about ten weeks, in 1865; in 1873 *The Age* was published for a few months by Samuel Sawyer; *The Enterprise,* published by John Geeting; *The National Ventilator,* published by Parks & Sanford, in favor of the Greenback party; the *Washington Commercial,* published a few months in 1881, by S. F. Horrall, and the *Washington Republican,* by Dr. W. A. Horrall, in 1883, were all started to fill a long-felt want. Generally, the want was the most distressingly felt by the venturesome publishers.

THE WASHINGTON HERALD AND GAZETTE.

By Charles G. Sefrit.

The *Washington Herald* (daily) and the *Washington Gazette* (weekly) are published in Washington by the Gazette and Herald Company, a corporation that was organized with a capital stock of twelve thousand dollars in 1905, which organization was effected to promote the consolidation of the *Herald* and the *Gazette,* at that time separate publications, the *Herald* being owned by a stock company, of which Charles G. Sefrit was the manager, and the *Gazette* by Paris A. Hastings. When the consolidation was made, the name *Gazette and Herald* was adopted for the new paper, but in a short time this was discarded and the daily edition was printed as the *Herald* and the weekly edition as the *Gazette,* thus retaining both the original names. Mr. Sefrit became the managing editor of the new paper and Mr. Hastings the business manager. Seven years later, in August, 1912, there was a reorganization of the company. Mr. Hastings sold his interest to Mr. Sefrit; the capital stock was increased to sixteen thousand dollars, and Mr. Sefrit became the general manager and editor, with John T. Harris as general foreman and advertising agent, which organization of the office has continued since 1912. The *Herald* now is one of the most influential of the country newspapers of the state, and its editorial expressions are generally quoted over Indiana.

The *Gazette* was established in February, 1865, a weekly paper published by two printers, Jacob Covert and George W. Colbert. Its publication has been continuous since that time. The first office of the *Gazette* was in a small frame building on Fourth street, owned by Col. John Van Trees, which stood on the opposite side of the street from the present office of the Gazette and Herald Company. Covert sold his interests to John A. Rodarmel in 1868. Both Rodarmel and Colbert were scarcely out of their 'teens, and the editorial work of the paper was done by John Evans and William Thompson, lawyers, and Dr. W. A. Horrall, all of whom, with the first proprietors and Mr. Rodarmel, long have been dead. Spillard Fletcher Horrall, a Union army captain who had done much correspondence while at the front for the old *Evansville Journal* under the pen name of "Q. K. Juniper Wiggins," bought the *Gazette* in 1870 and published and edited it until 1876, when he sold out to Malachi Krebs, who kept the paper for some eighteen months. Krebs was a vitriolic writer; kept himself in hot water most of the time because of his caustic criticisms of his political adversaries, and had two or three personal encounters, one of them with Col. Samuel H. Taylor, when a cane and an ink-well were used by the belligerents as weapons, without particular damage to either of the gladiators, however.

MAYOR KNOCKS EDITOR DOWN.

Fist fights were not uncommon among the politicians in those days. While Captain Horrall had the paper, William D. Bynum, now of Indianapolis, then mayor of Washington, incensed at some sulphuric editorial comments on him, met the editor one Saturday evening and knocked him down a time or two in order to even up. Malachi Krebs was a firebrand. He did not get along well with many of his own partisans. Nevertheless, the Republicans, while Krebs was editor of the *Gazette,* elected, in 1878, the greater part of their county ticket for the first time after the war. The county campaign of 1878 was conspicuous for extreme bitterness and acrid exhibitions of political animosities. Most all of the leading spirits of that savagely-contested campaign have been returned to the mother dust. Col. Sam Taylor, John Henry O'Neall, David J. Hefron, Col. Steve Belding, Capt. Samuel H. Mulholland, Samuel E. Kercheval, Capt. Green McDonald, Henry C. Brown, Malachi Krebs, Joseph Wilson, Edward F. Meredith, all have passed among the shades. A few of their contemporaries, yet waiting at green old ages, are Judge William R. Gardiner, Col. N. H. Jepson, Capt. Zack Jones, who was elected sheriff on the Republican ticket, and William Kennedy, the Democratic nominee for county clerk, who was defeated by Joseph Wilson.

Malachi Krebs retired from the *Gazette* after the election of 1878, and the paper became the property of his sureties, Moses L. B. Sefrit, Henry C. Brown, Oliver H. Brann, Henry H. Hyatt, N. H. Jepson and William Armstrong, who continued its publication, with John A. Rodarmel as manager, until 1880, when it was bought by Rodarmel, William Martin and Henry C. Brown. Later Frank A. Myers bought Martin's interest and became the editor. Then Elisha Hyatt purchased Brown's share, and this finally fell into the hands of Heber H. Allen, who owned it for a short time. After the death of Rodarmel, the paper passed to Moses L. B. Sefrit and Charles G. Sefrit, in 1887. Mr. Sefrit, the elder, died in 1892, and the *Gazette* for several years was published by Charles G. Sefrit and his brother, Frank I. Sefrit. Charles G. Sefrit left the paper in 1896, and for some two or three years it was owned by Frank I. Sefrit and Paris A. Hastings. Frank I. Sefrit was appointed postmaster in 1897, and two years later sold out to Mr. Hastings, who was the owner of the paper from that time until its consolidation with the *Herald* in 1905.

The *Herald* was founded by Duncan Smith, now a noted Chicago writer of humorous paragraphs. Then, in 1895, it was bought by Graham Sanford, who later took for his partner his brother, George L. Sanford. At first it was printed on a big job press in the second story of the building at Third and Main streets, now occupied by the State Bank of Washington. Later a cylinder press was bought, and the office was moved to the building at Fourth and Van Trees streets now occupied by the Gazette and Herald

Company. Graham and George Sanford sold out in 1904 to a company which changed the political complexion of the *Herald* from independent Democrat to Republican, and chose Charles G. Sefrit for the paper's editor. A year later the *Herald* and the *Gazette* were merged.

"PRESS DAY" IN OLDEN TIMES.

When the old *Gazette* was founded, and for more than fifteen years thereafter, the paper was printed on a "Washington" hand-press. It was a nerve-racking and muscle-tiring job to get out the weekly edition with the slow hand-press, and on print day, which was Friday, everybody worked at the office until long after midnight, getting the sheets printed, folded and ready for mailing. All the papers that went into the postoffice had to be addressed by hand, as there was no mailing machine, and one of the duties of the "local" editor was to write the addresses on the big bunch of "single-wraps." Printing was tedious work, but it was well done, on rag paper that cost from seven to ten cents, or more, the pound. It was good paper, though, as the files of nearly half a century ago prove. Early in the 'eighties the proprietors discarded the old "Washington" and bought a second-hand Babcock cylinder-press, which had to be turned by hand and was a regular man-killer. It required a powerful man to turn the crank single-handed. After Hugh McKernan opened his planing-mill at the rear of the Hyatt building on Third street, power was secured from the mill, the day of hand-press work for the *Gazette* ended and a daily edition was begun. In 1912 the Cranston cylinder-press, which was put in by the Sanfords, was replaced by a Goss "Comet," a web perfecting power-press that prints and folds the editions of the *Herald* and the *Gazette* at one operation from a continuous roll. The *Herald's* is the first perfecting press to be installed in Daviess county. Likewise the *Herald* was the first newspaper in the county to put in a Merganthaler linotype, which does away with type-setting by hand. This machine was purchased by the *Herald* in 1905.

FOUND SUCCESS IN WIDER FIELDS.

The *Gazette* and the *Herald,* in the fifty years of their combined existence, have turned out many newspaper men, some of whom have gained prominence in the profession. Jacob Covert, one of the original founders of the *Gazette,* went from Washington to Evansville and from there to Washington City, where he obtained a situation in the government printing office, that he held until his death. Duncan Smith went from the *Herald* to Chicago to become one of the celebrated paragraphers of the second city of the Union. Frank I. Sefrit went from the Gazette to Salt Lake, where for years he was the manager of the *Salt Lake Tribune,* one of the leading newspapers of the inter-mountain states. He now is the editor and general manager of the *American Reveille,* at Bellingham, an influential Republican paper of the state of Washington. Graham, George L. and Leigh Sanford, brothers, all of whom started with the *Herald,* now are prospering in the newspaper and printing business in Nevada. Louis B. Sefrit went from the *Gazette* to Seattle, Washington, where he held a responsible place with the *Seattle Times* until his sudden death from pneumonia in 1909. Jack Mattingly, who learned to be a good reporter on the *Herald,* and Jack McCafferty, who had his training in the *Gazette* office, went to Salt Lake to work on the *Tribune.* Each of these bright young men died at Salt Lake. Walter McCarty, now with the *Indianapolis News,* was a "cub" reporter on the *Herald.* Carl C. Brayfield, a versatile Indiana writer who died a few years ago at Charlestown, was associated with the *Gazette* for many years.

THE DEMOCRAT.

The *Daviess County Democrat* was established on December 12, 1863, by T. R. Palmer and Stephen Belding, as a six-column folio, with the subscription price at two dollars per year, and with the motto: "The Union, the Constitution and the Enforcement of the Laws." On June 4, 1868, the paper was enlarged to a seven-column quarto, a patent inside being adopted, and the motto dropped. On October 17, 1868, Colonel Palmer sold out to Mr. Belding, who was the sole proprietor until October 23, 1869, when Elias F. Widner was admitted to partnership, and the firm became S. Belding & Company. The office of the publication, which had up to this time been on Van Trees street, in the rear of the postoffice, was removed, June 10, 1870, to the Gallagher block, on Main street. At this time Mr. Widner sold out to Mr. Belding. The patent-inside feature was discarded on November 13, 1869, and on April 8, the subscription price was reduced to one dollar and fifty cents per year. On July 1, 1876, the paper was enlarged to an eight-column folio. In 1873 a power press was set up and the paper took on a more prosperous appearance. On February 20, 1881, the establishment was moved to larger quarters on Third street, just south of where now stands the Neal & Eskridge store, and in 1885 a half interest in the newspaper was sold to Samuel B. Boyd, the firm name becoming Belding &

Boyd. In June, 1886, the publication of a daily paper was started, the paper being named the *Washington Democrat*. From the start, this publication proved a success, and today it is considered one of the best small-city newspapers in Indiana. On October 1, 1887, Mr. Belding sold his half interest in the *Democrat* to B. F. Strasser, who remained a partner of Samuel B. Boyd until October 7, 1891, when Mr. Boyd became the sole owner. On May 25, 1889, the newspaper plant was moved into the new Democrat building, erected on East Third street, between Van Trees and Walnut streets. On January 1, 1906, Mr. Boyd sold a half interest in the newspaper to Henry Backes, who at that time was city editor of the *Democrat;* Simultaneous with the formation of the new partnership of Boyd & Backes, a Mergenthaler linotype machine was installed. About a year later an addition was built to the Democrat building, almost doubling the floor space, and, as the business rapidly grew, a vast amount of new machinery was added, including a more rapid newspaper press. In January, 1915, the *Washington Democrat* secured the franchise of the United Press Association, with a leased wire running direct into the office, placing the *Democrat* in a class with the metropolitan newspapers for quick handling of the world's news. The partnership formed in 1906 continues at this time, with Mr. Boyd as editor and Mr. Backes as business manager. Both the *Washington Democrat* and the *Daviess County Democrat* contain eight pages, six columns to the page, the subscription price of the daily being ten cents per week and the weekly one dollar per year.

OTHER NEWSPAPERS IN COUNTY.

There have been other newspapers started in some of the smaller towns of the county during its history, but these journalistic enterprises were usually of brief existence. The exception to this newspaper experience is the *Odon Journal*, published at the flourishing little town of that name in Daviess county. This paper was established in 1873, and is still being published, with a good list of subscribers and a fair advertising patronage. The present editor and publisher is John B. Stott.

CHAPTER XII.

CHURCH HISTORY OF DAVIESS COUNTY.

In the history of the world, church history has gone hand in hand with the material development of nations that have arisen. But, unlike the history of nations, the church has not only continued to exist, but has continued to increase in power and influence. It has gone from continent to continent, and from hamlet to hamlet, until every town and city today boasts of its coterie of churches. Washington, like all other cities, has within its borders representatives of several of the prominent religious bodies of the world, each with an active, progressive membership and shepherded by an efficient pastor.

WESTMINSTER PRESBYTERIAN CHURCH.

The Westminster Presbyterian church claims to be the oldest church organization in Daviess county, and the claim seems to be well established. Its origin dates back to 1810, when missionaries of the Presbyterian faith visited this part of what was then the Territory of Indiana, preaching and teaching in the humble homes of the pioneers who had settled in this section. In August, 1814, Rev. George T. Scott, of Vincennes, organized a church, with a membership of seventeen. In the same year a young man was ordained for the ministry by the Muhlenburg presbytery, and in May of the following year Rev. John M. Dickey came to serve this newly-organized church, as the first regular pastor. Rev. Dickey came on horseback, with his wife and all his earthly possessions carried on the horse behind him. The library of Mr. Dickey consisted of a Bible, Bunyan's "Pilgrim's Progress," a theological dictionary and Fisher's catechism. For four years he ministered to the needs of the small congregation, which was scattered over an area of ten by sixteen miles. During his pastorate his wife died, and he afterward married the daughter of Ninien Steele, one of his elders. It may be interesting to know that Rev. John M. Dickey was the grandfather of Rev. Sol. C. Dickey, D. D., of Winona, Indiana.

The first church home of this congregation was located on the north side of Palmers creek, two and one-half miles south of the village, now the

CHRISTIAN CHURCH, WASHINGTON.

PRESBYTERIAN CHURCH, WASHINGTON.

city of Washington, just across the road from the present home of David Kribs. The church was built of unhewn logs, with clapboard roof, held in place by poles, a dirt floor and seats of split logs planed with the broad axe. It had no chimney, nor any method of heating, and consequently could only be used during the warm season. This was the third Presbyterian church in Indiana Territory, and, humble and crude as it may seem, it was quite as pretentious as the homes of the people who assembled there for worship. How long this house was used as a place of worship is not definitely known, but after Daviess county was organized, and the town of Washington was laid out, there is recorded a deed, dated on August 7, 1819, conveying to the trustees of the Presbyterian society lot No. 89, of the original town of Washington, as laid out by Peter Wilkins and Emanuel Vantrees. Thirty-five dollars was the price paid for this lot, which is the location on the corner of what is now East Sixth and Hefron streets. A small frame building was erected on this lot, soon after the purchase was made. This building served for a church, a school house and a court house, in the early period of Washington's history. In 1832 this building was replaced by a brick structure. The work required in the erection of this latter building was arduous and long, the labor, for the most part, being performed by the members of the congregation. The clay from which the bricks were made was tramped by bare feet, and the women took their turn in cooking for the men while they worked.

In 1868 the congregation had grown to such numbers that a new church was imperative. The old building was sold to the Christian denomination, and in the same year the work of erecting a larger house of worship was begun, on lots donated by Philip and Sarah Cruse. In 1890 this church was remodeled, at an expense of several thousand dollars, and in 1896 Mrs. W. L. Jackson gave five hundred dollars as a nucleus for a fund for a pipe-organ for the church. The second melodeon used in the church is still in the possession of David Kribs.

The present church building was erected in 1910-11, and was formally dedicated on February 12, 1912. It is a beautiful structure, built of smooth Bedford stone, in the classic order of architecture, commodious, convenient and artistic, standing as a monument to the untiring zeal and liberality of the Westminster Presbyterian church, and its faithful pastor, Dr. William P. Hosken.

The following have served as pastors of the Westminster Presbyterian church since its organization: Rev. John M. Dickey, 1810; Rev. Ransom Hawley, 1823-34; Rev. Calvin Butler, 1834-38; Reverend Adams; Reverend

Wall, 1846-48; Rev. H. L. McGuire, 1848-52; Rev. S. Taylor, 1853-54; Rev. J. C. Martin, 1855-57; Rev. H. B. Scott, 1858-60; Rev. Francis Lynn, 1860-62; Rev. O. M. McKee; (supply) Rev. C. McCain, 1863-66; Rev. A. Taylor, 1866-68; Rev. John Carson; Rev. A. Sterritt, 1871; Rev. E. C. Trimble, 1872-76; Rev. E. A. Burnett, 1876-77; Rev. John Gerish, 1878-80; Rev. R. E. Hawley, 1880-86; Rev. James Omelvena, 1887-95; Rev. Alexander Urquhart, 1895-97; Rev. I. I. Gorby, D. D., 1898-; Rev. James A. Douglass, 1905-10; Rev. William P. Hosken, D. D., 1910 to the present time.

On January 20, 1909, a union of the Cumberland Presbyterian and the Westminster Presbyterian churches was consummated, this united body taking the name of the Westminster Presbyterian church of Washington.

In November, 1914, the centennial of the Westminster Presbyterian church was celebrated. On this occasion an extended history of the congregation was given, relating many interesting facts and incidents of the hundred years of its existence. It is from this historical sketch that this article has been compiled.

FIRST METHODIST EPISCOPAL CHURCH, WASHINGTON.

The First Methodist Episcopal church of Washington had its origin in 1816. The first sermon preached here by a minister of that denomination was in the private house of Samuel Miller. The house of Thomas Meredith also was used for that purpose. Rev. John Shrader had charge of the circuit that included Washington at that time, preaching here once each month. The worship was conducted in private residences, and sometimes in the school house or court house, until 1827, when a small brick church was erected at the corner of Hefron and First streets. It seems that the contractor who erected this building slighted his job. The structure was considered unsafe and was used only about two years, when it was abandoned, and for eight years the congregation again resorted to private residences for worship. The congregation purchased a lot at the corner of Third and Flora streets, upon which stood a small dwelling. This was remodeled by Lewis Jones, John Fryer and William Bratton and converted into a house of worship, the modest little church being formally dedicated by Rev. John Wood, in 1837. The membership of the church at that time was one hundred and twenty-five.

In 1858 another church building was erected, at a cost of about two thousand dollars, and was dedicated by Rev. Calvin Kingsley, a prominent Methodist divine, who afterward became bishop. There was a continued

FIRST METHODIST EPISCOPAL CHURCH, WASHINGTON.

increase in the membership of the congregation each year until the necessity of a larger building became apparent. Accordingly, the leading spirits of the congregation began to devise plans for the erection of a church to meet the demands. A location was purchased on the corner of Meridian and Van Trees streets, where a modern and conveniently-arranged church was erected and formally dedicated in 1890. This is the church in which the congregation at present worships. Rev. W. S. Rader has been the pastor in charge since 1913. The present membership of the church is eight hundred and fifty, with a Sunday school enrollment of eight hundred. A. O. Fulkerson has been the efficient superintendent of the Sunday school for fifteen years. Dr. R. M. Smiley is director of the large choir, one of the best in the conference. Doctor Smiley has served this church as chorister for about twenty-five years.

During the more than one hundred years of history of the Washington Methodist church, about sixty-two ministers have served the church as pastors. Among these are the names of men who have been prominently identified with the larger work of the denomination, men of recognized ability throughout the church and in the state. The pastorate of the larger number of these ministers was for a period of only one year. Until the pastorate of Rev. John Tolbert, in 1841, no minister has a record of more than one year's service. After Rev. Tolbert the following served for two year each: James R. Williams, from 1843; J. W. Julian, from 1849; T. S. Whited, from 1854; J. F. McCan, from 1856; Charles Cross, from 1860; Stephen Bowers, from 1864; W. F. Harned, from 1866; Aaron Turner, from 1869; Hayden Hayes, from 1871; John Walls, from 1874; F. A. Friedly, from 1876; Walter Underwood, from 1881; W. F. Sheridan, from 1891; E. A. Campbell, from 1899. The following served for a period longer than two years: T. C. Danks, 1883 to 1886; M. S. Heavenridge, 1886 to 1891; C. E. Asbury, 1893 to 1898; Samuel Reid, 1901 to 1904; J. W. Baker, 1904 to 1908; H. H. Allen, 1910 to 1913, the beginning of the present pastorate.

OTHER METHODIST CHURCHES IN THE COUNTY.

There are about twenty other churches of the Methodist denomination in Daviess county. The most of these are small country churches, where there is no settled pastor and preaching services are irregular. On account of this condition, some of the country churches that once were prosperous and gave promise of permanency have suffered a decline. In some instances the larger part of the membership has been transferred to some other church; only a faithful few remaining to give the church "a name to live."

The Elnora Methodist church is the most prosperous one of the denomination outside of Washington. They have a fine new brick church, costing twelve thousand dollars; a parsonage costing one thousand dollars, and a membership of four hundred and fifty. They have a large Sunday school enrollment, an active Epworth League, and are well equipped in every way for aggressive work.

The Odon Methodist church was organized in 1858. It has a comfortable frame building and an active membership of three hundred.

FIRST CHRISTIAN CHURCH OF WASHINGTON.

In September, 1864, a call was sent out over the community, asking that every person who at any time had been identified with the religious movement known in history as the Reformation Movement, to meet on a certain day to devise means for the organization and establishment of a congregation advocating that faith in this community. About forty persons responded to that call, but only thirteen had the courage to face the bitter struggles that were to confront them in the establishment of such a congregation. But these thirteen, like the people of the thirteen original colonies, believed in the mission they were called to fulfill; and they went forth as true disciples consecrated to the service of the Master. The following are the original charter members, and no list of names would be a fair representation of the people to be honored by this community if these were omitted in the record of county history:

Mr. and Mrs. James Ragsdale, Mr. and Mrs. Nelson Cunningham, Mrs. Hannah S. Thomas, Miss Mattie Thomas, Mr. and Mrs. Thomas Jones, Mr. and Mrs. David McDonald Wilson, Mrs. Laycock, David Nixon and George Waller. Of these thirteen original members, Mrs. Nelson Cunningham and Miss Mattie Thomas are the only two now living.

For one year this little congregation met regularly for worship, in a little dingy room in the old court house, always with a faith and confidence that, somehow, God would lead them to a solution of the problem of securing a place of worship that would be suitable and inviting to those whom they sought as members of their little band. At the end of the first year the opportunity came to purchase the little brick church on Sixth and Hefron streets. Here they continued to worship until 1897, all the time growing in faith and numbers. Among those who were added to the roll of membership, during the early years of the church history, were many whose names should have an equal place of honor with the original thirteen, because they contributed a full share of the toil and struggle incident to the establishment of the church. Space forbids the mention of all these names here, but they should be inscribed in bronze upon the walls of the church and written upon the tablets of memory, as a testimonial of their service in making this congregation what it is today.

Rev. John Mathes was the first regular pastor of the congregation. Though his service was only for half time, his work will ever stand as a monument to him, as well as to the little flock that stood so nobly by him. To David Hixon, the first elder of the congregation, must be ascribed much of the credit for the success of the cause. Faithful in rain or sun, and under all circumstances, he met with his people, advised, counseled, prayed and toiled until the very day of his death. The memory of David Hixon is held in sacred reverence by this congregation.

From the very first the congregation has been served by some whose names have become prominent in history, many of these names being household words among the men of their faith. Among these are the following: Rev. Charles Robertson, who served as pastor for two years; Rev. Henry Pritchert, who served three years; Rev. Jacob Wright, one year; Rev. J. L. Griffin, two years; Rev. J. C. Holloway, three years; Rev. B. C. Sherman, one year; Rev. Holloway was again called to the pastorate and served another year, followed by Rev. Peter J. Martin, who served for two years.

In 1887 the congregation had grown strong enough to support a pastor for full time, and Rev. George G. Alford was called to the pastorate that year. He served four years, doing splendid work during his entire pastorate. In 1892 he was followed by Rev. A. B. Cunningham, who soon became one of the best-loved men who ever preached in Washington. Rev. W. P. Waldren followed Mr. Cunningham, served as pastor for six months, and Rev. C. W. Brickert was next in succession. It was during the latter's pastorate that the church-building project came to be considered seriously, for the little brick church had long since become inadequate to meet the growing needs of the Bible-school and congregation.

Accordingly a building committee was appointed to look into the matter of a better location and also the matter of a new church building. On that committee were Hugh Barr, E. L. Hatfield, T. D. Slimp, C. E. Mattingly and James H. Wilson. After some consideration of various locations and plans, the present location was decided upon, Hugh Barr making the proposition that he would give five thousand dollars to the enterprise, the congregation to raise the rest. Mr. Barr afterward gave an additional five hundred dollars on the day of dedication. The lot cost the congregation three thousand dollars. The committee accepted the building plans submitted by W. S. Kaufman, of Richmond, Indiana, and awarded the contract for its construction to J. F. Brown & Brother, of this city. The contract called for a ten-thousand-dollar building, but when it was completed such changes had been made that the total cost had been increased to sixteen thousand dollars. The building was dedicated on February 21, 1897, and continued to be the home of the congregation until January 6, 1911, when it was completely destroyed by fire. Every piece of furniture, pipe-organ, hymn books, tables and dishes, were completely destroyed.

Undaunted by their misfortune, the congregation met and decided to rebuild. A building committee was appointed, consisting of M. S. Hastings, T. D. Slimp, Elkanah Allen, George J. Keith, P. A. Hastings and Lester Routt. The building was completed and formally dedicated on May 19, 1912, Hon. M. S. Hastings, of the building committee, delivering the dedicatory address. This church building is one of the most beautiful in architectural design, the most complete in modern equipment, that could be desired. The congregation, after all their struggles, now have a home of which they may be justly proud. With a membership of more than one thousand, the congregation exerts a wide and beneficent influence. It supports the home work in the city of Washington at an expense of about three thousand dollars, annually, and gives to missions and charity about one thousand dollars, annually.

In addition to those named, who have served as pastors of this congregation, are the following: Rev. E. O. Tilburn, G. W. Thompson, Rev. E. A. Cantrell, Rev. J. F. Floyd, Rev. H. W. Laye, Rev. Kyle Brooks, Rev. E. E. Davidson, Rev. J. B. Cleaver, and Rev. J. W. Darby, the latter's service beginning on January 1, 1912.

FIRST BAPTIST CHURCH OF WASHINGTON.

The First Baptist church, of Washington, was organized on February 4, 1840. The meeting for the organization of this congregation was held in the Presbyterian church, the little organization band being composed of Revs. William Reese and John Graham and four members from the Veale Creek church. Rev. William Reese was chosen moderator of this meeting and James Johnston, clerk. Articles of faith were adopted and the following persons subscribed to the same: William Stansil, Celia Stansil, W. G.

BAPTIST CHURCH, WASHINGTON.

Cole, Margaret Cole, Reason W. Brand, Frances Brand, Mary S. Clapp, Louisa McDonald and Eunice W. Packard. The new church was named the Washington Baptist church and Elder William Stansil was chosen pastor. Mr. Stansil continued as pastor of the church for a period of ten years. A writer says: "He was a strong man physically; a fine voice; a deep thinker; he was uneducated, except the teaching of the three R's by his wife, after they were married."

Among the other pastors of the church were: Revs. G. W. Harpole, John Graham, B. B. Arnold, Hamilton Robb, T. N. Robinson, J. R. Philips, T. R. Palmer, R. M. Parks, Hillory Head, W. L. Boston, E. R. Pierce, William McNutt, Charles R. Garten and J. B. Cheirs. Rev. Palmer was a printer as well as a preacher, and, associated with Stephen Belding, founded the *Daviess County Democrat*, in 1867.

During the early history of the church the meetings were held in private houses, in school houses and in the court house. It was not until April, 1859, that definite steps were taken to build a house of worship. A contract was made with John Richards to erect a building, at a cost of four thousand dollars. This building was occupied in June, 1860, though not entirely completed at that time. However, it is said, that after their "twenty years wandering," worshipping from place to place, the congregation was happy to get into a home of their own. From this time dates the beginning of the larger work of the congregation.

Under the influence of energetic and efficient ministry, the congregation had a steady growth for many years. There was a large increase in the membership, including many people of wealth and influence. The old church had been enlarged and remodeled from time to time to meet the requirements of the increased membership, but the time came when a building of larger capacity was required to accommodate the congregation. The question of the erection of a larger building suitable to their needs, with modern appointments, began to be agitated about 1902. Liberal subscriptions for this purpose were readily obtained and the matter took definite shape by the employment of Architect Osterhage, of Vincennes, to make plans for the desired building. The plans were accepted and a contract was made with Patterson & Reister, of Washington, for the construction work. The work was completed and the building formally dedicated on Sunday, May 3, 1914. The new church is modern in every particular. In the architectural design the building is faultless, while the interior finish and convenience of appointments leave nothing to be desired. It is one of the most beautiful and attractive public buildings in the city.

BETHANY CHRISTIAN CHURCH.

The Bethany Christian church was organized on the first Sunday in June, 1830, with the following charter members: John Davis, George Morgan, Benjamin Fitzgerald, William Faith, David M. Hixon and Sarah Bogard. The early history of the church is incomplete and it is not possible to get an accurate statement of many interesting incidents concerning its early years. It is known that David M. Hixon was one of the three first elders of the congregation, but it is uncertain as to the names of the other two. Some time after the organization of this church, Mr. Hixon moved to Washington and was one of the charter members of the Christian church in that place.

Bethany Christian church may claim the distinction of being the mother church of the Christian denomination in Daviess county. When Bethany was organized, the nearest congregation of that faith was about forty miles distant, on the banks of White river, in Lawrence county. Since the organization of Bethany, something near twelve hundred and sixty names have been enrolled as members of the congregation. In this list are found the names of men and women who were prominent in the early religious history of Daviess county, and who contributed largely to the early development of the county. The founders of this church were people of small means and it was some time before the little congregation was able to provide a house in which to hold services. For about twelve years after organization the faithful band held regular services in the homes of the members, manifesting a commendable zeal and devotion in the cause of the Master. In 1842 their numbers had increased and conditions were such that they were able to build a modest little frame house of worship. This was built on a tract of ground donated by a Mrs. Roderick. This house served them as a place of worship for over forty years. In 1888 the present brick building was erected. During its history this congregation has had the service of some of the ablest ministers in the denomination, among whom the following have served as pastors in later years:

John Mathis, James Mathis, ——— Noyes, Dan Collins, 1878 to 1880; William Krutsinger, 1881 to 1887; E. G. Denny, 1888 to 1889; H. H. Adamson, 1895 to 1900; B. L. Martin, 1901 to 1902; W. M. Davis, 1902 to 1904; Shannon Baker, 1907 to 1908; Everett Stivers, 1910; R. W. Alexander, 1911 to 1915; J. H. Moore, the present pastor. A notable event in 1859 was a visit made to this church by Alexander Campbell and Barton W. Stone. Ministers ordained by this church: Joseph A. Murray, May

14, 1865; Bruce W. Fields, Dimmit Jarvis, George W. Harpold, Nathaniel Peachee, Cornelius Burke, dates not known.

The following have served as elders: David Hixon, George T. Hays, A. T. Banta, Thomas Cunningham, William H. Allison, Elmer Grow and James Williams. The present officers are: Elders, W. H. Allison, W. H. Clarke, I. A. Bailey, Thomas J. Hays and Lew Harris; deacons, Joseph Meads, W. G. Banta and W. A. Hunter; trustee, T. J. Hays, Joseph Williams, Mort Billings, W. H. Allison and Lew Harris.

The present membership is about one hundred and seventy-five. The congregation also maintains a well-regulated cemetery.

PLAINVILLE CHRISTIAN CHURCH.

The Plainville Christian church was reorganized in 1888, by Evangelist Barrows and Rev. Ed McCormick. There were about fifty original members, among whom were the following: S. H. Dyer, James Wiltsman, John G. Littlell, O. H. McKittrick, Mrs. Lou McKittrick, Parnetta Rankin, Mary Killian, Ransom Law, Ann Bennington, Rachel Williams, Alice Crosley, Paul Golliher, W. O. Littell, T. E. Littell, B. F. Corlett, D. B. Burks, Margaret Cox, Lucy Marlatt, Lafayette Marlatt, Lizzie O'Mabey, Gallatin England, Linda England, Alice Crosby.

The first evangelist to hold a meeting was A. L. Crim, of Clark county, Indiana. At this series of meetings more persons were received into fellowship than were received by any other of the ministers who have held such meetings there.

The house in which the congregation worships was built in 1892, and was dedicated in that year, by Rev. L. L. Carpenter. It has served the purpose for which it was erected since that time, but it will soon have to be replaced by a new church of large capacity, on account of the enlarged membership. A nice lot in the central part of the town has been selected as a location for the new church building, and plans for its erection are being considered.

Ministers and evangelists who have served this church since its organization: S. H. Dyer, A. L. Crim, Ed McCormick, F. T. Porter, G. P. Crawford, W. M. Gard, Rev. J. Tomlinson, T. Vance, Wit Littell, G. M. Shutts, G. Halleck Rowe, A. W. Crabb, R. W. Alexander, Charles H. Buchanan, the latter having served longer than any other minister, except Elder Dyer. Rev. Claris Yuell is the present pastor.

(13)

The present membership of the church is two hundred and twenty. Charles Dyer is superintendent of the Sunday school, which has an enrollment of one hundred and twenty-five, and an average attendance of one hundred. The other church auxiliary societies are the Young People's Society of Christian Endeavor, the Ladies' Aid Society, and the Woman's Christian Temperance Union.

CHRISTIAN CHURCH OF ODON.

The Christian church of Odon was established in 1852, and was reorganized by Wayne Alford in 1870. The first place of worship was in a school house. In 1853 a church building was erected which served the congregation until 1892, when the present building was erected, at a cost of three thousand dollars. This church was dedicated in 1892, by Dr. L. L. Carpenter. The present membership of the church is three hundred; Sunday school enrollment, three hundred and eight. The congregation has an active Christian Endeavor Society, as an auxiliary in church work, and the church is out of debt.

The governing board of the church is composed of nine elders and fifteen deacons. The present officers are: C. L. Mount, president of the board; A. A. Lane, treasurer; C. A. Pickett, secretary. Joe Callahan is superintendent of the Sunday school; Paul Sears, president of the Christian Endeavor Society.

The following have served as pastors of the congregation: John Mathis, Thomas Littell, M. Cummings, William Littell, Charles R. Scoville, J. S. Denny, C. H. Buchanan, H. A. Turney, W. B. Morris, C. M. Day, and A. C. Trusty, the present pastor.

THE ODON UNITED BRETHREN CHURCH.

The Odon United Brethren church was organized by Rev. Joseph Stubblefield, during the conference year of 1862-63. The first church building was begun during the pastorate of Rev. John Granger, in the year 1868. The church was dedicated on May 28, 1870, during the pastorate of Rev. Ephriam Thomas, by Bishop Jonathan Weaver.

The present building, a beautiful brick edifice, standing among large maple trees, on one of the finest locations in Odon, was erected in 1904, while Dr. J. T. Hobson was pastor. It was completed and dedicated, April 30, 1905, by Dr. C. M. Brooke, Rev. S. Z. Todd being the pastor at that time. The Ladies' Aid Society completed the basement of the church, at a cost of about three hundred dollars. This church is one of the best-organized churches in the county. While the membership is not the largest, it comprises a band of active and devoted workers in the cause of the Master.

The following are the names of those who have served as pastors of this church since its organization:

Joseph Stubblefield, 1862-63; William Wheeler, 1863-64; Z. B. Ellege, 1864-66; John Granger, 1866-69; Ephriam Thomas, 1869-71; Thomas Butler, 1872-73; I. K. Haskins, 1873-75; J. D. Current, 1875-77; H. C. Funkhouser, 1877-78; J. Riley, 1878-79; W. A. Richardson, 1879-82; D. Arbaugh and A. Myers, 1882-83; D. Arbaugh, 1883-84; John Breden, 1884-87; W. J. Johnson, 1887-88; A. B. Condo, 1888 to June, 1890; A. C. Scott, June, 1890, to September, 1890; A. W. Arford, 1890-91; A. C. Scott, 1891-92; L. L. Schoonover, 1892-93; J. A. Bell, 1893-96; H. W. Lashbrook, 1896-97; A. W. Arford, 1897-98; J. C. Mills, 1898-1900; J. T. Hobson, 1900-01; J. W. Gilley, 1901-03; J. T. Hobson, 1903-04; L. T. Todd, 1904-05; W. E. Snyder, 1905-09; D. P. McCoy, 1909-11; L. L. Schoonover, 1911-12; T. A. Garriott, 1912-14; D. P. McCoy, 1914-15.

CATHOLIC CHURCHES IN DAVIESS COUNTY.

It is, perhaps, idle today to go back earlier than 1819 to find any Catholics in Daviess county. True, priests and bishops passed through, en route from Louisville and Vincennes and back, but to dwell on these would be no more fruitful of satisfactory results than to claim that a certain old converted Indian chief, who was camped with his tribe on the bank of White river about 1795, and who used to attend mass at Vincennes, was the first Catholic in the county. To leave the merely hypothetical and come down to the authentic, and not to narrow the honors too much, the Murphys and the Spinks at Washington, and the Montgomerys at Black Oak Ridge, were the first Catholic settlers in Daviess county,

The first church in either county was the rude log one put up at Black Oak Ridge; the second was the log one at St. Mary's; the third was at St. Simon's, Washington; the fourth at St. Rose, Mt. Pleasant; the fifth, St. Patrick, at Glencoe; the sixth, the one at Miles settlement; the seventh, St. Patrick's, at the present site; the eighth, St. John's at Loogootee; the ninth, St. Martin's, at Haw Creek; the tenth, St. Louis, at Shoals; the twelfth. St. Joseph's; the thirteenth, St. Michael's. Several churches were built at some of these points, for instance, four at St. Peter's, two at St. Simon's, four at St. Mary's and two at Loogootee. Three of the above, those at Mt. Pleasant, Miles's settlement and Glencoe, have been abandoned for other sites, the last named only partially, however, so we have at present ten parishes proper—four in Martin and six in Daviess county. The great majority of the Catholic population are those who came from Kentucky or Ireland. The Germans stand next as to number, though they are quite modern as to date of settlement. There are and have been a few French families; a few other families came direct from Maryland and a few from North Carolina, Tennessee, Pennsylvania and Ohio. The first settlers were attracted to these counties because of the rich land for sale at a very low price. This "land craze," as it may be called, gave rise entirely to St. Joseph's, St. Peter's and St. Mary's parishes and largely to that of Mt. Pleasant. The Wabash & Erie canal gave rise to St. Patrick's parish, and added materially to St. Simon's, St. Peter's and St. Mary's. The Ohio & Mississippi railroad gave rise to St. John's at Loogootee and added to all convenient to its line. The opening of the coal mines at Washington, Cannelburg and Montgomery added many new names to the lists of St. Simon's and St. Peter's, benefiting the former much more substantially than the latter, and largely gave rise to the church of the Immaculate Conception. The piking of the state road from New Albany to Vincennes, which work was never finished, benefited chiefly the Mt. Pleasant or present Haw Creek parish. The last, and also most important, influx of Catholics was occasioned by the concentration of the Baltimore & Ohio Southwestern Railroad shops at Washington, Indiana.

ST. MARY'S CHURCH.

St. Mary's, Daviess county, located in Barr township, was visited in 1828 by the Rev. Simon P. Lalumiere, who celebrated the august mysteries in the house of Nathaniel Spalding. The house still exists and is pointed out to the stranger as the beginning of St. Mary's. Divine services continued to be held at this house for about five years. Bishop Brute writes: "A few days after (November 6, 1834) I went with the Reverend Mr. Lalumiere who visited his two missions—first St. Peter's and then to St. Mary's. The last was not quite completed and I was requested to name it. It was a great happiness to me to put the first church which I was called upon to bless in my new diocese, under the patronage of the Blessed Mother of God, so l named it St. Mary's, and promised to return again in two weeks and bless it when it was finished."

The Reverend M. de St. Palais was appointed the first resident pastor of St. Mary's, and remained from 1836, the year of his arrival in this country, until 1839, when he was removed to Chicago. The log church becoming too small for the congregation, Father de St. Palais built a new church.

The Rev. John Guerguen became the second pastor, and had charge of St. Mary's and the neighboring missions until 1848, when he was succeeded by the Rev. P. J. R. Murphy. Father Murphy had charge also of Mt. Pleasant, and built a church there. The town and church are now both extinct. Bishop Flaget, accompanied by Father Abell, in August, 1823, confirmed thirty-four persons at Mt. Pleasant; in 1829 Bishop Flaget again visited the place, and found about forty Catholic families there.

The Rev. John Mougin resided at St. Mary's from 1858 to 1860, when he built a church at Loogootee, and resided there until 1866, visiting St. Mary's from Loogootee. Reverend J. Lablanc was pastor of St. Mary's, residing at St. Mary's, until February, 1873, attending also Miles's settlement, eight miles from St. Mary's. For six months St. Mary's was then attended alternately by the pastors of St. Peter's and of Loogootee. The Rev. G. M. Ginnsz came next, and was pastor from November, 1873, until September, 1875. The Rev. John W. Doyle succeeded him and was the pastor for three years. During the pastorate of Father Doyle the first steps were taken for the erection of a new church, the one so long occupied having become too small for the congregation. Plans were made and the work of construction was begun in 1879, the church being completed in the spring of 1881. This is the third church built by St. Mary's congregation and is their present place of worship.

ST. PATRICK'S CHURCH.

One of the old record books at St. Simon's contains the following names as being those confirmed at St. Patrick's by Bishop de la Hailandiere on November 24, 1845: James Taylor, Stephen Pennington, Michael Delaney, William Kane, George Major, John Delaney, John Brewer and Thomas Agan. Land was first secured about 1837 at old St. Patrick's, or Glencoe, as it was usually called, by Father Lalumiere, who bought eighty acres with the intention, it is said, of laying off and founding a town, to be known as O'Cownettsville, but this project fell through and the land was sold. Soon the place was attended from St. Peter's and in 1840 the Reverend J. Delaune built the first and only church, which was of logs.

Part of the land on which the church stands was devoted to burying purposes for those convenient to it and is known as the new cemetery, though the old cemetery was continued in use for the benefit of the cluster of families living in that locality. The present St. Patrick's church was built in 1860 by Reverend B. Piers, who was then attending the parish from Montgomery.

In 1880 Father Doyle resigned on account of ill health, and he was soon after succeeded by the Rev. G. M. Ginnsz, who showed considerable spirit in his efforts for the betterment of the parish and people. As one means to this end he organized St. Patrick's Total Abstinence Society, with a membership of sixty. This did much good for sobriety, charity and benevolence, and is still in existence. In 1883 he made some improvements and added the finishing touches to the priest's house, which was built by Father Doyle. But his most important and, of course, most arduous work was the building of the chapel and school house on the site of old St. Patrick's. He began this work in August, 1887, and completed it in November of the same year. This building is of brick and contains two well-furnished schoolrooms, each twenty-two by twenty-eight feet, and prettily arranged chapel that contains twenty-four pews. The total cost was four thousand dollars and not a cent of debt remains on it. The chapel is used only for the celebration of mass when persons are brought there for burial in the old burying ground. The building is quite a handsome and showy one and the people of that locality are proud of it..

ST. PETER'S CHURCH AT MONTGOMERY.

St. Peter's is the oldest parish in either Daviess or Martin county, and was built about 1818, by Catholics from Kentucky, a church-loving people, who had not been here long before they were sought out by Fathers Blanc and Champonier, of Vincennes. The first settlers were the Montgomerys, the Kidwells, and the Dants, and it was at the house of Mr. Montgomery that mass was first said. Very soon—perhaps in 1820—these men, under the direction of Father Blanc, built a rude log church, scarcely sixteen by twenty feet. When Father Blanc was recalled to New Orleans in 1820, he was succeeded in his visitations by Reverend Championer, who visited the place monthly for about two years. He was succeeded by Reverend Lalumiere, who visited the settlement from Vincennes for a time, and afterward became its first resident pastor. He is credited, as early as 1823, with building a hewed-log church, twenty-four by thirty feet, and a frame one, forty by sixty feet, which was completed in 1827, and blessed by Bishop Flaget in 1829, assisted by the young Father Abel, on which occasion forty-seven persons were confirmed. The third church was of brick. Part of these bricks were intended for college buildings, but, with the removal of Father Sorin to the northern part of the state, these buildings were lost sight of. The church was built by French carpenters from Vincennes under the direction of Right Reverend Bishop de la Hailandiere, and Father Ducoudray, who was later its pastor. It is said by some that these carpenters were brought over especially to do the bishop's work. Certain it is, that much of their work was very faulty and this church did not last long. One of the subscriptions later on was for strengthening its walls, to render it safe. This was soon after Father Piers took charge in 1847, and it could not have been built longer than five years, as Father Sorin left in 1842. It was then decided to erect a new church, and to exchange the old site to the proposed site, Montgomery. The church was completed in 1869, at a cost of eight thousand dollars, a great part of the work being done by the parishioners. Father Piers had all the features of the building planned before he began the work, and carved out with a pen knife a perfect model of the contemplated structure. The church was blessed on July 18, 1865, and August Farrell and Sarah Healey were the first couple married in it. The substantial two-story frame school building Father Piers put up soon after, and in 1885 the present school building was completed. The belltower and steeple were put on the church in 1887, and a fine new bell was purchased. John Byrne taught here, or in the parish, during war-times, and left behind him some creditable work in the way of well-trained minds—several of his pupils subsequently figuring conspicuously in the affairs of Daviess county. Miss Byrne, a niece of Father Piers, also conducted the school creditably a number of years, and afterward Frank Walker. The school is not now maintained.

The succession of clergy, as gleaned from records and traditions, is as follows, with no uncertainty, unless as to exactness of two or three dates: Rev. Napoleon Blanc, previous to 1820; Rev. M. Championer, 1820 to the time when Rev. S. P. Lalumiere took charge, and remained until 1837; Rev. M. de St. Palais until 1839; Rev. J. Delaune until 1841; Reverend Granedir only transiently; Rev. E. Sorin until 1843; Reverends Chartier, Courjault, Francois Parret, transiently during 1843, after the departure of Father Sorin; Father Ducoudray, 1842 (end of year) until 1847; then Father Barthol Piers until 1895, when Father P. Rowan took charge.

INTERESTING REMINISCENCES.

In connection with Reverend Father Sorin's stay in this parish the following will be of interest: In August, 1888, on the occasion of the celebration of Father Sorin's jubilee, at Notre Dame, John Breen and a Mr. Kelley were the only ones present from the locality of St. Peter's. During their stay Mr. Breen, in a conversation with Father Sorin, referred to the tradition among the people here as to his intending to found a college at St. Peter's, and he told this incident of his stay here:

"Yes; I, with some of the brothers, was temporarily at St. Peter's. We were upon very close rations, too. One day a neighbor named Hayes came to see me and asked how I was. I told him that I was not feeling well; that I had not had anything for dinner that day. He at once requested me to send some of the brothers with him and he would see that I was not without my dinner another day. I did so, and soon we had several sacks of meal, meat, and other desirable provisions."

On the same occasion he related to Mr. Breen the circumstances of his leaving the southern for the northern part of the state as follows:

"Bishop de la Hailandiere sent for me and told me of the extensive lands near the lakes in the north, and offered them to me on the condition that I would found a college there; I did not want to go, but he insisted, and proffered me his horse to ride; I went, and the trip took me a week. I was pleased with the place and at once made arrangements to establish ourselves." One of the brothers who left St. Peter's with Father Sorin, Brother Vincent, lived to be more than ninety-three years of age.

In the sermon at the golden jubilee of Father Sorin, at Notre Dame, in August, 1888, Bishop Ireland spoke of six brothers who came with Father Sorin from France; 1841 as the year of his coming and 1842 as the year he first set foot on the banks of the St. Joe river. This agrees with existing records and traditions, and the names of these six brothers are well remembered by several. The following were named by Miss Lizzie O'Dell, who went to school to these brothers; Anselm, Gashien, Joachim, Lawrence Vincent, Francis and Marien; one, who was known as Brother Joseph, was teaching at St. Peter's when the above mentioned arrived. He had been connected with the Trappist order of Europe, but could not endure the severities of their rule and left. About ten others joined them, but when they left for the north, these latter, who were young men of the surrounding neighborhood, did not go along, not having taken their obligations. When

ST. SIMON'S CATHOLIC CHURCH, WASHINGTON.

they left St. Peter's they had the land they were on nearly all in wheat, having leased much of it in order to have it cleared. There were no Sisters of the Holy Cross with Father Sorin.

Father Lalumiere had introduced the Sisters of Charity at an earlier date, but they remained but a short time; later Father Ducoudray induced the Sisters to establish a school here, but they only remained about three years.

St. Peter's cemetery is the most historic of all the parochial burying grounds in Daviess county, because it contains the remains of early settlers from other parishes, or at least many of them.

With the beginning of Father Rowan's pastorate of St. Peter's parish marked improvements were projected and perfected, in church, school and parish. The prominent improvements which were made during his pastorate are the interior decorations, the covering of the church with a slate roof, and new oaken seats of superior workmanship. The parochial school, under the charge of the Sisters of Providence, also was established. The elegant home of the priest, erected of brick and stone of the most modern style of architecture, with modern conveniences, stands adjacent to the church on the north side. The whole amount of improvements made by Father Rowan aggregate more than twelve thousand dollars in value. The value of Roman Catholic property, in Montgomery, and the appendix at Cannelburg, including the quarter-section of coal land, one mile west of the village, is estimated at fifty-five thousand dollars, which indicates a marvelous growth since its establishment in 1818. The parish is in a very healthy state, St. Peter's being the second oldest parish in the state of Indiana.

ST. SIMON'S CHURCH AT WASHINGTON.

This parish is noted as one of the oldest, strongest and wealthiest Catholic organizations in the state. This influential society had its inception near the beginning of the century, when, in the year 1819, a few Catholic families, who had settled in the vicinity, were visited by Bishop Flaget and united in a body for divine worship. The parish was sparse and scattered, and religious services intermittent and irregular. Ten years later, in 1829, the spiritual impulses of the scattered members of the Catholic society were accentuated and given a new vigor by the visit of Father John Abell, from the diocese of Bradstown, Kentucky, now Louisville, who, in June of that year, preached the jubilee in Washington. During this time and until 1837 the Catholics of this vicinity attended services at St. Peter's, at Montgomery.

In this latter year the society was placed under the spiritual control of Rev. Simon P. Lalumiere, and the next year, 1838, a house of worship was built. This old church was in use for nearly half a century and was torn down about 1895 to give place for the present magnificent church edifice at Washington. The early years of this church were years of struggle. In 1840 twelve pews accommodated the worshipers. The growth of the church was slow, but constant, and was swelled year by year by the addition of new families, until today the congregation of St. Simon's numbers more than three hundred families, among whom are many representatives of the wealth, culture and refinement of the city. The church is not only very strong financially, but is a power for good in the community, exerting a great and constantly-increasing influence in the society of that city.

Following faithfully in the footsteps of the pioneer missionary, Father Lalumiere, the following pastors have served this congregation: Reverends Anthony Parrott, H. Dupontavice, John McDermott, P. Hyland, J. B. Chasse, John Guerguen, Hugo Peythieu, John W. Doyle and W. V. Boland.

St. Simon's church is situated on the northwest corner of Hefron and Third streets, its main facade and entrance being on the former street. Near the front, on Third street, is a side entrance. In point of architecture the edifice is a pleasing combination of the Gothic and the Circle, the roof having the distinct lines of the former and the windows and arches a graceful blending of the two, constructed from plans by James J. Egan, of Chicago. The ground space of the church is one hundred and thirty feet and four inches by fifty-five feet and ten inches. On the southeast corner is the massive tower, with an elevation of one hundred and fifteen feet, surmounted by a golden cross. On the east side is the vestry, eighteen by twenty-two feet, and on the west the chapel of the Blessed Virgin Mary, eighteen by thirty-four feet. The sanctuary is twenty-five by eighteen feet. The interior of the church presents a noble and harmonious appearance, and the plan is such as to create the impression of greater size than a view of the exterior would suggest. The first appearance upon entering is one of much effectiveness, and the eye is charmed and soothed by the noble perspective, which is beautifully strengthened and softened by the subdued light from the magnificent windows. The harmonious effect of these windows is particularly striking, creating at once upon the beholder a feeling of proper reverence for the holy spot. The first windows noticeable upon entering the vestibule are dedicated to St. Joseph and the Blessed Virgin. On the right side of the hall the first window is a gift of William M. Hayes; second, memorial of Mrs. Anna Cabel; third, gift of James McMullen; fourth, gift of Alice Maher; fifth, gift of the Sodality of the Blessed Virgin

Mary; sixth, gift of Miss Alice Foster; seventh, gift of Mrs. Harriett Murphy; eighth, gift of Anna Donita Wells. Lighting the altar, and rendering especially conspicuous the rear of the church, is a magnificent window, seven by sixteen feet, the gift of Rev. Hugo Peythieu, a former pastor of St. Simon's. On the left, the windows are inscribed as follows: Jacob Zinkan, Hugh McKernan, Ernest A. Crosson, Altar Society, memorial to William McTegart, Sr.; memorial to William McTegart, Jr.; St. Simon's Total Abstinence Society, William Brady. The tower windows were donated by M. F. Burke, Mrs. Thomas Dean, Michael Doyle, Mollie Flynn, Rev. Thomas McLaughlin, Rev. Patrick Rower, Joseph B. Graham and Robert C. Graham. Over the principal entrance are two large windows, memorials to the late James Campbell and Sarah Campbell. Father Doyle furnished the windows for the vestry and the chapel.

St. Simon's church contains one hundred and sixty pews and has a seating capacity of seven hundred. The building was completed in 1886 at a cost of twenty-five thousand dollars. The dedicatory services were presided over by Bishop Chatard and attended by clergy from all parts of the state, and instructive letters were delivered by Chancellor Dennis O'Donaghue and others. The parish owns considerable valuable property adjacent to the church, comprising the pastor's residence, the parochial school and the school of the Sisters of Providence.

ST. MARY'S CHURCH.

St. Mary's church (or the German church of the Immaculate Conception), at Washington, dates its formation from about the year 1874. For several years prior to that year it had been evident that the German Catholics of the town required a church building of their own, but it was not until the year named that active steps were taken for the erection of such an edifice. Forty German families then formed themselves into a congregation and raised a suitable structure of brick, at a cost of thirteen thousand dollars. The erection began in the spring, and, although unfinished, was used for divine services the following December. In January, 1872, the congregation was fully organized by Rev. John P. Sassel, who also started a German school. He labored with heroic self-denial for the welfare of his little flock until his death, on August 10, 1879, and to his earnest work the church is indebted for its permanent prosperity.

Father Sassel was succeeded by the Rev. L. M. S. Burkhardt, in September, 1879, and this worthy priest erected the school building in 1881, at a cost of four thousand dollars, and a parsonage, in 1885-86, at a cost of three thousand dollars. This building is of brick, is two stories high, and contains eight rooms. Father Burkhardt was followed, in October, 1889, by Rev. William Bultmann, in whose time the interior of the church was frescoed, and a new organ introduced. Father Bultmann expired on February 14, 1893, and on April 3, of the same year, the present worthy incumbent, Reverend Torbeck, was appointed to the pastorate. Father Torbeck has also labored effectively for the good of the congregation and has placed a furnace in the church and parsonage, and inclosed the grounds with an iron-rail fence. He has also enlarged the school to three rooms, which are in charge of three Sisters of Providence, who give instructions to about one hundred and sixty pupils. The congregation of the church numbers at present about one hundred and sixty families, and the church is practically out of debt.

St. John's cemetery, one mile north of the city of Washington, owned jointly by the congregations of St. Mary and St. Simon, comprises forty acres, ten of which were dedicated by Bishop Chatard on September 15, 1895, and is free from debt.

SUMMARY OF CHURCH HISTORY.

It will be a matter of surprise to the people of Daviess county to know that there have been more than one hundred churches established within the limits of the county during its history of nearly one hundred years. No less than ten different denominations have erected buildings at various places in the county, and half a dozen other sects have held services in school houses, or other buildings. A study of the religious history of the county reveals some very interesting facts. Many of the churches that were organized and gave promise of permanency, became divided on questions of church policy and disorganization resulted. One of the disturbing elements that caused dissension was secret societies. Another was the question of instrumental music in church worship, and various other questions which would seem trivial and non-essential to most of the church members of the present age. Tenacity of opinion was a marked characteristic of the early settlers, and this disposition was especially manifested in their inherited religious belief.

In consequence of these church dissensions scores of churches established in the county, with once flourishing congregations, have long ago ceased to exist, their existence and location being known only to a few of the oldest inhabitants. For the information of readers of this work and the preservation of these historical facts, a list of all the churches established in Daviess county is here given. This list is as complete as it is possible to make, and in order to assist in the location of the churches they are arranged by townships and sections.

BARR TOWNSHIP.

Section 9, Amish, Christian (Antioch); section 33, Christian (Bethany); section 16, Methodist, Catholic (St. Peter's); section 10, Catholic (St. Mary's); section 31, Baptist (Mt. Olive, No. 1); section 1, Church of God; section 15, Methodist (Morris Chapel); Cannelburg, Christian, Catholic (All Saints).

BOGARD TOWNSHIP.

Section 10, United Brethren (Fairview); section 5; Methodist (Pleasant Valley); section 11, Christian (Concord); section 12, Methodist (Pleasant Union); section 15, Methodist (Talbert's Chapel); section 17, Methodist (Pleasant Grove); section 21, United Brethren (New Bethel); section 30, Methodist (Mt. Zion), Epsom Methodist, Epsom Christian, Cornettsville Methodist, Cornettsville Baptist, Catholic (St. Michael's), Amish.

ELMORE TOWNSHIP.

Section 1, United Brethren (Mud Pike); section 4, Christian; section 22, United Brethren; section 13, Baptist (Friendship); section 26, Methodist, Elnora Methodist, Elnora Christian (Owl Prairie), Elnora Holiness.

HARRISON TOWNSHIP.

Section 32, Cumberland Presbyterian (Union), Hudsonville Methodist, Hudsonville Christian, Waco Christian; section 6, Baptist (Aikman Creek), Glendale Methodist.

Section 5, Methodist (Ebenezer); section 22, Catholic (St. Patrick's); section 22, Glencoe Chapel, Mission of St. Patrick's.

REEVE TOWNSHIP.

Section 3, Methodist (Union); section 15, Methodist (Mt. Nebo); section 18, Methodist (High Rock); section 31, Methodist (Oak Grove),

Alfordsville Methodist, Alfordsville Christian; section 2, United Brethren (McCord); section 30, Catholic (St. Patrick's), Baptist (Sugar Creek).

WASHINGTON TOWNSHIP.

Section 1, Baptist (Veale's Creek); section 6, United Brethren (Friendship); section 10, Christian, Maysville Methodist, Lettsville Methodist.

WASHINGTON CITY.

Methodist (First), Methodist (Second), Methodist (colored), Presbyterian, Presbyterian (Cumberland), Russellites, Baptist, Congregational, Baptist (colored), United Brethren, Christian, Christian Science; Catholic (St. Mary's), Catholic (St. Simon), Catholic (Immaculate Conception), Episcopal.

MADISON TOWNSHIP.

Section 7, United Brethren (Pleasant Hill); section 13, United Brethren; section 16, Methodist (Wesley Chapel); section 26, Baptist (Mt. Olive); section 20, Methodist (Good Hope), Odon Methodist, Odon United Brethren, Odon Christian.

STEELE TOWNSHIP.

Section 25, United Brethren (Otterbein); section 25, Lutheran; section 29, United Brethren, Plainville Methodist, Plainville Christian, Plainville United Brethren; section 7, Baptist (Bocum).

VAN BUREN TOWNSHIP.

Section 5, Church of God (Shiloh); section 9, Methodist (Macedonia); section 29, Christian (Liberty); section 16, Baptist; section 31, United Brethren, Raglesville Methodist, Raglesville United Brethren, Center Methodist; section 8, Cumberland Presbyterian.

VEALE TOWNSHIP.

Section 15, Methodist (Bethel); section 21, Cumberland Presbyterian (Mt. Olive); section 23, Methodist (Pleasant Hill); section 35, Methodist (Cumback).

UNITED BRETHREN CHURCH, WASHINGTON.

CHAPTER XIII.

EDUCATIONAL HISTORY—EARLY SCHOOLS.

The compiler of the history of the early schools of Daviess county is greatly handicapped, because few records of them have been preserved. The historian must depend largely upon the memory of the older inhabitants who were born and reared in the county. Some of this educational history has been collected and recorded in "An Educational History of Daviess County, Indiana, by William K. Penrod, with sketches of the townships by members of the World's Fair educational committee." This little book of eighty-two pages was published in 1893. Some valuable information has been obtained from the files of the *Daviess County Democrat* and from the records of the Daviess county commissioners.

The first school houses were built where they would accommodate the children of the largest number of settlers. There was no sanitary school house law, laying down rules to be followed in selecting the sites and erecting the buildings and furnishing the same.

In 1846, a log school house was built in Bogard township, within the limits of what is now Epsom. As early as 1820 a school house was built in Elmore township, about three-fourths of a mile northeast of the point where now stands the Hastings school. In 1830 two school houses were built in Harrison township. One was located near where the church at Aikman's Creek now stands and the other was situated near Hudsonville. No school house was built in Madison township until 1840. It was probably in the forties that the first school house was built in Reeve township. It was near what is now known as the McCord school. It was about 1834, in the west central part of Steele township, that its first school house was erected. The first house erected for school purposes in Van Buren township was situated about one mile east of Raglesville; it was probably built sometime between 1830 and 1840. The first school taught in Veale township was in a vacated log church in 1819, while the first school house built in this township was in 1828. As early as 1820, a log school house was erected within three-fourths of a mile of where the Sugarland consolidated school of Washington township now is, and it was in this year that a similar building was erected near what is now the Prairie school house.

THE PRIMITIVE SCHOOL HOUSE.

These old-time school houses were of the same type. The following descriptions of some of these buildings are calculated to give an adequate idea of them. "These were small in size and of poor architecture. The only thing commendable was the huge fireplace, which took up nearly one end of the school house." "They were constructed of round logs, with the bark remaining on them, and sheltered with clumsy clapboards, which were weighted down to the roof. The greater portion of one end of the buildings was used for a fireplace, while at the other end was a door which was constructed of boards and hung on wooden hinges." "It was built of logs, with a clapboard roof and a puncheon floor. The seats that the children of pioneer parents sat upon, while getting their dearly-bought education, were clumsy affairs, made by splitting saplings and inserting legs on the round side." "The buildings erected upon these lots were all log, and part of them unhewn. The manner of lighting and heating was of the rudest type—the principal, and almost the only, reception for light being the door, while the fireplaces, with a width of six or seven feet and built of clay and sticks, furnished a limited amount of heat." "It was a very low house, made of partly-hewn logs, covered with clapboards and heated by an immense fireplace which occupied almost one end of the house. The furniture was prepared from saplings obtained from the forest which surrounded the building, with the ax and auger as the only tools. There were but two benches in the house, and these stood along the entire length of the opposite walls with a clumsy, high desk made of rough boards, in front, to serve as a receptacle for a few books." "It was built of logs slightly hewn on one side and put together so that large openings were left between them. The cracks, partially closed by mud and sticks, served as ventilators—letting in an abundance of the outer atmosphere. The floor was made of split logs which were laid with the flat side upwards. Clapboards, pinned together, formed the door. The house was covered with boards which were held in their proper place by poles placed across them and fastened to the rafters. It was partially warmed by a huge fireplace, eight or ten feet in width, placed at one end of the building."

The laws of harmony were not violated in the equipment of these pioneer school houses. The seats were made from the timber taken from the nearby forests. Trees or saplings, from six to ten inches in diameter, were cut into the required lengths and halved. The flat sides of these halves were smoothed somewhat imperfectly with a common chopping ax or, better still, with a broad ax. Legs were inserted in the round side, and there were no backs to these rude seats. These home-made seats required that certain portions of the home-made trousers, worn by the boys of those days, be patched frequently. Along one side of the room, wooden pegs were inserted into the wall and a plank placed thereon; this served as the writing desk for the entire school. Maps, charts, globes, and blackboards were unknown to both teacher and pupil of these first Daviess county school houses.

As one writer has said, "They had little money and less time to devote to the work. Much as they believed in education, they found it impossible to educate their children as they wished. As a result, there was far more ignorance in the second generation of Indianians than in the first. The parents simply did the best they could. This applies to teachers, books, buildings and clothing. Hard necessity will explain nearly all their shortcomings. That they believed in education, is shown by the laws which they enacted and the letters they wrote. There is no more pathetic feature of our early history, than this struggle to establish schools. The woods, the roads, the streams, and even the wild animals, seemed to oppose, and were banded together to prevent the children from having school."

It was for the settlers of the different communities to determine, without the intervention of township, county or state officials, the kind and character of school buildings to be erected. The following sections from the school law of 1843, compared with the school law of three-quarters of a century later, show that the authority in regard to the schools is being centralized. The voters at school meetings possessed the power "to direct the building, the hiring, or the purchase of a school house, or site for the same, and to fix the sum to be expended therefor, or for the furniture and appendages thereto, or for a school library or apparatus, and for the keeping the same in repair," and "to determine the amount of work to be done by each able-bodied white male resident of the district, between the ages of twenty-one and fifty years, towards building a school house, not to exceed two days' work each."

THE EARLY TEACHERS.

The biggest element in the success of any school or system of schools, is its teacher or teachers. The early teachers of Daviess county would compare favorably with the teachers of any other county in the state. Even this being true, their knowledge of what are today known as the common branches, was quite limited. Their knowledge, in most cases, did not extend beyond reading, writing and arithmetic. Some half dozen of these early schoolmasters of Daviess county, who knew a little of Latin and less of algebra and geometry, as one has put it, "enjoyed an enviable reputation for scholarship." The following, from George Cary Eggleston, in regard to one of his teachers, applies to these: "For one thing, the 'rule of three' had set no bounds to his mathematical acquirements. It was wonderingly said of him that 'he knew the whole arithmetic,' and it was darkly whispered that, in addition to that, he possessed certain occult knowledge which in our time would be described as an acquaintance with elementary algebra and the rudiments of geometry. I think I do not wrong the good man's memory or betray any confidence by saying that I met him many years afterward, when he was an old man and I a college student, and that he then confessed to me that even at the time of my earliest school days he had been able to find out the value of 'x' in a simple 'equation."

Tradition tells us that James C. Veale taught the first school taught in Daviess county. This was before Indiana became a state, and in 1811, the year of the battle of Tippecanoe. It is said that he taught a subscription school near Maysville, in that year. In 1815, John Aikman began a school, in what is now Washington.

It is claimed for Cyrus McCormick that he is entitled to the distinction of being the first Latin teacher in the county. Contemporary with Aikman and McCormick, is the eccentric Thomas Howard, who first agitated changing the name of Liverpool to Washington.

Other early teachers in what is now Washington and Washington township, were: W. G. Cole, Rev. Robert J. Davis, Isaac Heaton, Dudley Johnson, W. D. Shepherd and Rev. Hiram Hunter. Some of the pioneer teachers outside of Washington township, are, Mrs. Emily Hum and Wesley Skaggs, of Elmore township; Jabez Art, of Reeve township; John M. Strange and Henry Gore, of Van Buren township, and Daniel Jackson, John Stephens and Aaron Godwin, of Veale township.

The methods and devices used by these early teachers have changed, as have the buildings in which they taught, and as have the books and apparatus which they used. Some of these teachers taught "loud schools." In the "loud schools" the pupils were required to study their lessons "out loud." The thought was that the teacher could tell whether the pupils were studying or not. As a prominent writer has said, "The idler who was roaming at one word, or over one line of poetry, or trumpeting through his nose, was, for aught the teacher knew, committing his lesson."

Spelling occupied a prominent place in the curriculum of early times. Eggleston, in writing on this subject, says, that both he and his brother "could read before we entered our first school. Neither of us, indeed, could ever remember a time when we could not read or ride a horse, and neither ever knew when or how he learned either art. But at school no account whatever was taken of our ability to read, nor were we permitted to practice that art. It was the fixed rule of the master that each scholar should 'go through the spelling book three times, twice on the book and once off the book,' before beginning to read. 'On the book,' meant spelling and pronouncing the words with the book before the eyes. 'Off the book,' meant spelling from memory, as the words were given out." "In addition to the regular spelling lesson of the day, the whole school was required, as a final exercise, each afternoon, to stand in one long row, called 'the big spelling class,' for competitive examination in the art. If a word was misspelled by one, it was passed to the next below, and so on until some one succeeded in spelling it correctly. The successful speller was said to have 'turned down' all who had failed, and was entitled to take his place above them in the line. At the close of the exercise, the scholar who stood at the head of the class, was assigned to the foot of it for the next day, and a record was kept of the number of times each had 'gone foot.' Some small distinction was supposed to have been achieved by the scholar whose record, at the end of the term, showed the greatest number of goings to the foot or 'head marks.' This was about the only use made of the principle of rewards in the country schools at that time. No other word of praise was ever spoken by the teacher. Indeed, he would have put himself in serious danger of losing his place, had he indulged in any impulse he might have had to commend a pupil. It was, at that time, held that commendation was sure to spoil a child and breed vanity and conceit in his mind."

Discipline in those days nearly always took the form of whipping. The schoolmaster on his way to school each morning cut enough "switches" to supply him for the day. These switches were usually of goodly size and of sufficient heft to enable the master to apply them to the calves of the culprit, without much exertion, in a way that would make the pupil cry for mercy. It was something to be remembered, when a day passed without some one getting a whipping. Dr. R. S. Mitchell, a prominent and highly respected physician of Washington, in telling of some of his boyhood experiences in school, said that one of his teachers gave him four whippings a day, one for each quarter of the school period. But one of his playmates, the son of the teacher, received as many; which, from one standpoint, left little cause for grievance.

Here and there was a schoolmaster who sought to govern his school by the use of less severe forms of punishment. These resorted to the use of fools' caps, dunces' stools, and the like. Sometimes, an offender was made to stand on the floor on one foot, until he could stand no longer. The boys were apt to conclude that such a master was "afeard" to whip them, and insolently revolted.

"LOCKING OUT" THE TEACHER.

William K. Penrod, in his "Educational History of Daviess County," says that the custom of treating was inaugurated in this county by William Heaton in the winter of 1824. Be that true or not, it is one of the primitive customs that has survived. There are some teachers in the county who yet treat, but they should be given no credit for so doing. Frequently, teachers had to be "locked out" before they would treat, and, sometimes, severer methods were resorted to, before he would capitulate. Now and then, there would be a teacher who did not consider it a joke to be "locked out" and resisted with all his might. Such a teacher scared the pupils into letting him in, if there were not too many "big scholars," by threatening to batter the door down and flogging all who had taken part in locking him out. Sometimes, he would smoke the pupils out by climbing on the roof to the chimney and stopping it up. In most cases, however, the pupils came off with victory. The "treat" usually consisted in apples or candy. "Just why a bushel of apples should have been so placative, in a country in which everybody had unlimited apples at home, it is difficult to conjecture."

Then, as now, it was sometimes difficult for the teachers of the country schools to secure boarding places. In the pioneer days of Daviess county, and even later, the teachers sometimes "boarded around." In fact, they were paid in part, by the patrons boarding the teachers. By this system, each patron was "to board" the teacher his proportionate share of the time the school was in session. The system of "boarding around" had some features to commend it. The teachers had the opportunity of becoming really acquainted with both his pupils and patrons. He knew the home-life of his pupils, and this knowledge is always worth much to any teacher.

SCHOOL EXAMINERS.

An advance educational step was made in 1853, when the state Legislature enacted the law which provided for school examiners. Some of the provisions of this law are: "The board of county commissioners of each county of this state are hereby authorized to appoint at least one and not more than three school examiners, whose term of office shall expire on the first Monday in March of each year. . . . It shall be the duty of said school examiner to examine all applicants for license, and if found qualified, license them as common school teachers for three, six, twelve, eighteen, or twenty-four months, at the discretion of the examiner. . . . But the school examiner shall be entitled to an advance fee of fifty cents from every applicant for examination. . . . No person shall be declared qualified to receive a license as common school teacher, unless he or she may possess a knowledge of orthography, reading, writing, arithmetic, geography, and English grammar."

No qualification whatever was required of one to fill the office of school examiner—the official who was to decide whether applicants possessed the requisite knowledge to be common school teachers. The great majority of those who were appointed to this office were among the leading teachers of the county.

The first school examiner of Daviess county was William T. Ballow, a teacher of Washington township. He received his appointment on June 13, 1853. He was reappointed for another year on March 8, 1854. The law provided that one, two, or three could be appointed. On March 10, 1855, the commissioners for some reason appointed two persons as examiners. It certainly was not because the work was so heavy that one person could not do it. It may have been for the convenience of the teachers. It was not as easy then to get from the northern part of the county to Washington, as now. Ballow and John T. Hastings, a teacher of Madison township, received the appointments for this year.

The southern part of the county had a representative when the appointments were made on March 5, 1856. Thomas H. Kyle, of Reeve township, was named as the third examiner, Ballow and Hastings being reappointed. Kyle was a farmer and never had taught. For some reason, but two examiners were appointed on March 7, 1857. For the fourth time, Ballow was appointed. William Gaffney, a young teacher of Washington township, who had been a student at Indiana University, was selected as Ballow's co-worker.

Three examiners were again appointed on March 5, 1858. Gaffney was reappointed and, to assist him, John Spalding and Arthur Connelly were selected. Spalding was a Van Buren township teacher. It is said that he was the first teacher to use the word "method" in this township. Connelly was a wielder of the birchen rod in Harrison township. Gaffney and Spalding were reappointed on March 10, 1859, for another term, and to assist them Joseph McClesky was added. On March 10, 1860, Gaffney and Spalding were again appointed. For the third examiner, William C. Lemmon, a doctor, was named.

SCHOOL LAWS CHANGED.

In 1861, the school law was materially amended. Some of the more important amendments are noted below. The boards of county commissioners of the several counties of the state at their June session, 1861, and every three years thereafter, were authorized to appoint a school examiner. It was left to the will of the examiner, whether he should examine applicants for a teacher's license orally or by written examinations. The standard for a license was fixed by the examiner. It was made the duty of examiners to visit the schools of their counties. It was provided that the examiners should receive, "such remuneration per diem as shall be reasonable and just." As to what the legislators thought was "reasonable and just," is expressed in the provision that the examiner shall receive in the aggregate not more than one hundred dollars per annum, for his services, and a fee of one dollar for each male, and fifty cents for each female applicant, for a teacher's license.

In accord with this law, the county commissioners on June 6, 1861, appointed William S. Gaffney, the "Irish poet," who had served four terms under the old law. On September 4, 1861, the appointment of Gaffney was rescinded. The following record of the commissioners, gives the reason for their drastic action: "Whereas, William S. Gaffney, who was appointed school examiner of Daviess county, Indiana, by an order of this board at its June term, 1861, for the term of three years, from the date of said order, has rendered himself wholly incompetent to discharge the duties of said office, by misconduct and incompetency, the order is hereby rescinded." Noah S. Given, a lawyer, was appointed for the unexpired term. The term ended on the first Monday in June, 1864.

Samuel H. Taylor, a young lawyer who had but recently emigrated from Maryland, succeeded Given, being appointed on June 4, 1864. The law in regard to the appointment of school examiners was amended in 1865, so that they were to be appointed at the June session of the county commissioners and every three years thereafter. Taylor was re-appointed on June 5, 1865.

THE FEE FOR EXAMINERS.

The law of 1865 provided, "That the examiner should receive three dollars per day for each day actually employed." The following entry in the record of the county commissioners, seems to indicate that they thought much time was not needed by the examiner to visit schools and examine applicants for a teacher's license: "And that in the discharge of the duties of said office of examiner, that he be limited to a term not exceeding seventy-five days in any one year."

Taylor's law practice had increased to such an extent that he resigned as examiner in December, 1866. It was on December 3, of that year, that John R. Phillips, a Baptist minister, was appointed to serve for the unexpired term. That the commissioners thought that the duties of the examiner were not of much importance, and did not require much time in their performance, is indicated by the following: "Ordered by the board, that John R. Phillips, school examiner of Daviess county, be allowed twenty days to visit the various townships of said county for the purpose of advancing the educational interests of the county." Phillips was reappointed to serve "three years from and after the 9th day of June, 1868, and until his successor is appointed and qualified and that in the discharge of the duties of said office of examiner that he be limited to a time not exceeding seventy-five days in any one year."

Phillips resigned, and George A. Dyer, a doctor and the prosecuting attorney for the town of Washington, was appointed to the vacancy on December 9, 1868. Dyer was appointed to a full term on June 9, 1871. He was limited by the county commissioners to ninety-five days of service per year. Dyer was the last school examiner of Daviess county.

The school examiners did little toward influencing the educational life of the county. Their only legal duty from 1853 to 1861, was to license teachers. The examiners could place the standard of qualifications for teachers as high as they pleased, in so far as the law was concerned, but as a matter of fact, the standard was very low. Frequently an applicant would be asked but a few oral questions and then be granted a license; the standard had to be low in order that there be enough teachers. The salary of the examiners was not sufficient to secure efficient service.

VIEWS OF AN EXAMINER.

During the twenty years from 1853 to 1873, the time during which there was such an official as school examiner in Daviess county, twelve different persons served in that capacity. Of this number, William S. Gaffney, John R. Phillips and George A. Dyer really made themselves felt, in matters pertaining to education. Gaffney made commendable efforts to arouse interest in their work, among the teachers of the county, and to secure uniformity of text-books. In a letter, "To the Teachers of the County," among other things, he says, "Were it the deep interest alone which I have always manifested in regard to the glorious cause of human education, I should be pleased to address you; but in the relation which I at present bear towards the teachers of this county, I conceive it my province to advance any such information as may prove auxiliary to their noble and laborious duties. And as we have (I am pained to say) no organized association for the purpose of consulting with each other, I take advantage of the avenue of communication offered through *The Bee*, by courtesy of its gentlemanly editor, in sending you this, our first greeting.

"The province of the teacher is to educate—educate rightly—and in order to do this, he must become acquainted with the duties of his vocation, for his responsibility is manifold.

"I shall take occasion to recur to this subject at some future period, advising for the present that all would-be practical teachers procure a copy of 'Page's Theory and Practice of Teaching,' a most excellent work of the kind, and which contains more solid information and instruction on the subject than time or space would admit of us advancing.

"It has often occurred to my mind that the procuring of good, sound, reliable text-books is only second to the right mode of teaching; and to this particular I chiefly devote the substance of this letter, hoping that it may aid the teacher in making good selections. Our correspondence with publishers is more extensive, perhaps, than that of any other teacher in the county, and as we are posted up in relation to school books, we shall take pleasure in recommending such as we may have occasion to notice, after first having given them a careful examination." Following this, he names several books and gives reasons why he thinks they are good text-books.

In *The Bee* of April 30, 1858, he addresses a letter "To Teachers and Friends of Education in Daviess County." From this follows a paragraph or two: "Could the teachers of this county be convinced of the great importance of periodical meetings among themselves, I think they would not prove so lukewarm in regard to the matter, nor would the cause of education languish for want of soul. Points of controversy in regard to select discipline, salary of teachers, text-books, etc., are continually arising, and an interchange of opinion among teachers, in reference to these matters, would prove very satisfactory. My province, however, is to qualify common school teachers; yet, having a decided interest in the cause of education in this county, I should be pleased to see parent, teacher and pupil mutually related.

"The salary of teachers, I am aware, is merely nominal, and until this particular is officially rectified, we can not expect to have good instructors. The majority of applicants as teachers of our common schools are young and inexperienced, and therefore unqualified to assume the awful responsibility of training immortal minds."

THE COUNTY INSTITUTE.

School-examiner John R. Phillips probably held the first county institute in Daviess county. The statement has been made that the first county institute in Daviess county was held in 1868. This is incorrect, as the *Daviess County Democrat*, of August 20, 1868, in writing of the institute of that year, refers to preceding institutes. Phillips presided over the one held that year and he was appointed examiner in 1866. He had become prominent enough in the educational affairs of the state, to be nominated by the Democrats that year for state superintendent.

George A. Dyer, the last of Daviess county's school examiners, thought that all teachers should attend the county institute, judging from a notice he put in the county newspapers. It reads, "All teachers in Daviess county are hereby notified to attend, and on failure so to do, unless a satisfactory excuse therefor be given, may expect to have their licenses revoked."

COUNTY SUPERINTENDENTS.

In 1873 the state Legislature created the office of county superintendent by these words, "The township trustees of the several townships shall meet at the office of the county auditor of their respective counties, on the first Monday in June, 1873, and biennially thereafter, and appoint a county superintendent, who shall be a citizen of such county. . . ." The only qualification required by this law for this important official was, that the person appointed be a citizen of the county for which such citizen was to serve.

On June 2, 1873, the township trustees of the county, consisting of Henderson McCafferty, of Barr township; Joseph Hastings, of Bogard township; Joseph M. Boyd, of Elmore township; Benjamin W. Steen, of Harrison township; Andrew Shaffer, of Madison township; Joseph A. McCord, of Reeve township; Leonard Connell, of Steele township; George M. Harrod, of Veale township; Jesse Trueblood, of Van Buren township, and Samuel H. Mulholland, of Washington township, met at the office of Nathan G. Read, county auditor, to elect the first county superintendent of Daviess county.

George A. Dyer, the county school examiner; James A. Pritchard, a lawyer; Henry B. Kohr, a prominent teacher of the county, and Edward Wise, were voted for and, on the third ballot, Pritchard and Wise each received five votes. By the law when there was a tie the county auditor was to cast the deciding vote. Nathan G. Read, the auditor, voted for Wise, thereby electing him. On the first and on the second ballots Dyer received one vote. Kohr received but one vote and that was on the second ballot. On each of the three ballots, Pritchard received five votes. Wise received three votes on the first ballot, three on the second and five on the third. Wise was re-elected in June, 1875, and resigned in September, 1876, to accept a position in the South.

On September 23, 1876, E. C. Trimble, a Presbyterian preacher, was elected to the vacancy. Henderson McCafferty, his opponent, received three votes and Trimble received five. Two of the trustees were not present. On June 1, 1877, Trimble was elected for a full term; he was opposed by F. M. Walker, a Barr township teacher. Trimble received six votes on the first ballot and Walker received four.

There were five candidates to succeed Superintendent Trimble. When the trustees met on June 2, 1879, to select his successor, the interest was intense and considerable feeling was manifested by some of the supporters of the candidates. David M. Geeting, a teacher, of Washington township; F. M. Walker, a teacher, of Barr township; Caleb O'Dell, the trustee of Madison township; Henderson McCafferty, who had been trustee of Barr township, and Hamlet Allen, the principal of the Washington high school, were candidates. On the fourth ballot, David M. Geeting, who was afterwards elected state superintendent, received six votes and was elected. On the second ballot, O'Dell received five votes. Walker received four votes on three different ballots. McCafferty and Allen never received more than one vote.

On June 6, 1881, Geeting was re-elected on the first ballot, receiving six votes, and Levi Reeves received four votes. Much was said in the newspapers and among the politicians about this election, as Geeting, who was a Republican, was elected by a Democratic vote. All of the Democratic trustees denied having voting for Geeting. This denial was the principal cause of the talk. Geeting's supervision of the schools of the county justified his re-election.

Samuel B. Boyd, a Steele township teacher, was first elected county superintendent on June 4, 1883, he having received six votes on the first ballot and Francis A. Myers received four votes. James M. Boyd was put in nomination, but did not secure further support. On June 1, 1885, Boyd was re-elected. He had made such an efficient official that he received the vote of each of the trustees.

Peter R. Wadsworth, the trustee of Van Buren township, was elected on June 6, 1887, to succeed Boyd. This was the first time in the history of the county that the trustees promoted one of their number to be county superintendent. Wadsworth received the unanimous vote of the trustees, although he had met with much opposition in the caucus of his party associates. On June 3, 1889, Wadsworth was re-elected, receiving the votes of nine of the ten trustees.

Wadsworth was elected for the third time on June 1, 1891. Politics entered into this election, as politics had figured in most of the preceding elections. On the first ballot, Wadsworth received five votes, Christopher J. Cooney obtained two votes, and Elisha A. Riggins secured three votes. On the second ballot, Wadsworth received six votes. Each of the candidates was from Van Buren township.

A STRENUOUS ELECTION CONTEST.

The election of June 5, 1893, was the most hotly contested, in some ways, in the history of the election of county superintendents in Daviess county. On the one hundred and twenty-ninth ballot, Wadsworth was elected for the fourth time. In their caucus, the Republicans had selected William A. Wallace, a Veale township teacher, as their candidate. The Populist trustees, of whom there were three, supported Joseph A. Alexander, the superintendent of the Odon schools. The two Democratic trustees voted for A. O. Fulkerson, a teacher of Van Buren township, just about to graduate from the State Normal. It was evident that the Populist and the Democratic trustees would not vote for Wallace. In order to break the deadlock, the Republicans decided to vote for Wadsworth, hoping that some of the Populist or the Democratic trustees would support Wadsworth. Some one of them did, thereby electing him.

Wadsworth was elected prosecutor at the November election, in 1894, and he at once resigned as county superintendent. William A. Wallace was elected to succeed him, on November 12, 1894, on the twenty-seventh ballot. William K. Penrod, Joseph M. Porter, F. M. McConnell and William Sanford were the other candidates voted for. Penrod, a young and energetic teacher, from Madison township, was close to Wallace as a competitor.

There was no election of a county superintendent in June, 1895, as the Legislature had passed a law which provided for the election of county superintendents in September, instead of June. As a result of this law, and on its being declared unconstitutional, Wallace held over until June, 1899. The Legislature had changed the term from two to four years. Wallace was elected for the second time on June 5, 1899. He met with much opposition in his own party. It took twenty-three ballots to decide the contest. Solomon W. Satterfield, a teacher, of Van Buren township and a graduate of the Indiana State Normal and of the State University, and Alanson C. Wise, teacher of Washington township, Republicans, and Sanford Patterson, a teacher of Barr township and a Democrat, were his opponents. On the first ballot Wallace received five votes, Wise secured two, and Satterfield also obtained two. On the twenty-third ballot Wallace received six votes, Wise secured two, while Satterfield and Patterson had each to be content with one.

DEMOCRAT ELECTED IN 1903.

The majority of the trustees in 1903 were Democrats, and in the election held on June 1 of that year Philander McHenry, a Steele township teacher and a Democrat, was elected. Seventeen ballots were taken before he received the nomination. A. O. Fulkerson, John Doyle, W. L. Stuckey, F. L. McCafferty, W. T. Brown and Frank Dixon were McHenry's opponents.

The Republicans had a majority of the trustees in 1907. Four Republican teachers were candidates to succeed McHenry. B. J. Burris, principal of the Plainville schools; J. M. Vance, teacher of English in Washington high school; J. K. McCarter, a Madison township teacher, and Grant Callahan, a teacher of the Odon high school, sought the Republican nomination. Burris received the nomination on the second ballot. In the election he received seven votes and McHenry three.

Burris resigned in January, 1911, and on the 7th of that month Alva O. Fulkerson, teacher of history in the Washington high school, a graduate of the Indiana State Normal and of Indiana University, was elected to the vacancy. Philander McHenry, who had served one term, sought the nomination. At the election Fulkerson received seven votes and J. M. Vance received three. Fulkerson was re-elected for a full term of four years on June 5, 1911, receiving the vote of all of the trustees. The Legislature of 1913 extended the term of office to August 16, 1917.

A RESUME OF THE WORK OF THE COUNTY SUPERINTENDENTS.

Edward Wise, the first county superintendent of Daviess county, had attended college and in many ways was well qualified for the duties of this important office. He did much to arouse interest in the schools, secure uniformity of text-books, and raise the qualification of teachers. It is interesting and instructive to read some of the comments he made upon teachers and their work after he had visited them in their schoolrooms. On October 7, 1873, he visited William H. Allen, the present county attendance officer, who was teaching school No. 8 in Bogard township, and in the record of his visits he states that Allen had an unabridged dictionary and that he was teaching spelling by having the pupils sound every vowel. Wise states that this is not correct, and it would appear that Allen must have been using a form of the phonetic method. Wise remarks in another place that "Henry B. Kohr is the best teacher in Daviess county," and in another that a certain teacher "drinks a little too much." This teacher's license was later revoked. After visiting one school he reports, "No wood; burn bark."

At a meeting of the county board of education on August 6, 1873, teachers' salaries were fixed at one dollar and fifty cents per day for teachers holding a six months' license, one dollar and seventy-five cents for a twelve months' license, and two dollars for eighteen and twenty-four months' licenses, respectively. Mitchell's Geography, Harvey's Grammar, Brown's Physiology, Butler's Speller and Ray's Arithmetic were adopted as the textbooks to be used.

In commenting upon the township institutes, he says of the Van Buren township institute that there were ten teachers present and thirteen enrolled, and that the "teachers appear lively and in earnest; made a few remarks upon Theory and Practice." In speaking of the institutes in another township he says, "It has done no good this winter."

E. C. Trimble, the second county superintendent, was a Presbyterian preacher and well educated. He worked along the lines started by his predecessor and made special efforts towards grading the schools. At its September meeting in 1878 the county board of education adopted a resolution "declaring it to be the sense of the board that the county schools be graded at the earliest practicable time." The following rule of the county board of education adopted in May, 1878, indicates that the idea of the purpose and manner of holding examinations of pupils has materially changed. The rule reads: "Every teacher, before the close of his school term, shall hold a public examination of the pupils of his school, and shall notify the county superintendent and trustee of the same." Different inferences may be drawn from the following record, made on August 8, 1878: "After grading the papers of the July examination and finding evidence of fraud, decided to reject all the papers and to hold another examination on August 17."

SUPERINTENDENT'S STRICTURES ON TEACHERS.

David M. Geeting was the first teacher elected to the county superintendency of Daviess county. He was considered one of the best teachers of the county at the time of his election. Under his supervision the schools of the county made rapid progress. Geeting required his teachers to make monthly reports to him; in this way he kept in closer touch with what they were doing. He did not hesitate to record uncomplimentary things about his teachers, as the following record will show: He visited a school in Barr township and "found the teacher had dismissed school 'to go to mill.' Saw the teacher and recommended that he do such work on Saturday or hire it done." In speaking of a Veale township institute, he says, "A good interest was manifested, but some of the most ludicrous blunders were made by 'the oldest teacher in the township,' among them being the admission of the fact that he never read anything but the Bible—all other books were novels." On January 22, 1881, he records, "Attended Steele township teachers' institute at Plainville. In this township are four good live teachers and four 'sore-heads,' and the result is the institutes are almost a failure." In his report to the county board of education in May, 1881, among other things he says, "You have among your teachers, too, a few, a very few, whose only relief is railing at the trustee, county superintendent, state board of education, our Legislature, and the governor. They oppose school visiting, and I am fully convinced that, should I keep as untidy school premises, as poor discipline over my pupils, and such little interest in my recitations, I should not court school visiting from any one, if I did not oppose it."

This report shows that Superintendent Geeting was abreast of the times. He says that he noted the following points when he visited a school: "First, inspection of the school and school grounds. Second, inspection of the teacher before his class." Under the second head, he notes the following points: "Does he require the pupil to do the work of the recitation? Does he give his undivided attention to the class? Are the pupils interested in the recitation? Are all the pupils reciting the entire lesson? Are the dull pupils called upon, as well as the bright ones? Are the pupils reciting thoughts or mere words? Does the teacher make his work practical? Does he require the work to be done neatly? Are the questions such as will stimulate the pupil to think? Is he energetic and enthusiastic in his work?"

Geeting was succeeded by Samuel B. Boyd. Boyd was a successful teacher of the county, and he was equally as successful as county superintendent. He sought to raise the character of the work of the teachers, by visiting them in their schools and in the township institutes, and suggesting better methods to be used. Closer gradation of the pupils was accomplished under his supervision. On September 1, 1883, the following text-books were adopted for six years: McGuffey's Revised Reader, McGuffey's Revised Spelling Book, Ray's Revised Arithmetic, Harvey's Grammar, Eclectic Geography, Eclectic System of Penmanship, Steele's Physiology, and the Eclectic United States History.

Peter Ragle Wadsworth came to the office of county superintendent, with the experience both of a teacher and a trustee. His social disposition enabled him to make many acquaintances among teachers, patrons, and pupils. He was a popular superintendent, but no records of his work are to be found in the office of the county superintendent.

William Alfred Wallace succeeded Wadsworth as county superintendent of Daviess county. Previously, he was a teacher of Veale township. Although no new lines of work were instituted by him, yet he made especial efforts to keep the boys and girls in school, until they at least graduated from the grades. He sought to get them to remain in school until they had completed the common school course, by holding commencement exercises for the graduates and offering medals to those who made the highest grades in the different townships. He urged the trustees and the teachers to do what they could to furnish their pupils with the young people's reading circle books. The following, from the "Daviess County Common School Manual," published by Superintendent Wallace in 1899, in regard to grading and classifying pupils, is of interest: "The teacher is the proper person to grade and classify the pupils. The patrons and the pupils have no right to dictate in the matter. The teachers should know where the pupils belong and then have the courage to place them there. Patrons and pupils have been dictating the grading long enough. The teacher must do it from this time on. Pupils are crowded through the school too rapidly, especially in the primary grades. It is not the grade or the year that a pupil is in or the book that he is studying, that makes the scholar; not by any means. What he knows of the subject matter contained in the book and his actual standing in the grade, is the only true test. Better, a good third-year pupil than a poor sixth-year one."

Wallace, who had served over eight years, was succeeded by Philander McHenry, a teacher who had had varied experience as an instructor. McHenry was a man of force and brooked no opposition to his plans. Some of the teachers, it seems, did not pay the county institute fee. In order to compel each teacher to pay this fee, McHenry had the following resolution passed by the county board of education: "No person shall be employed as a teacher, principal, assistant principal, or superintendent, who does not possess at the time of his employment a receipt for his or her county institute fee for the county institute immediately preceding the term of employment." He made earnest efforts to get music taught in the rural schools.

Benjamin J. Burris, a teacher of the Plainville schools and a Spanish-American War veteran, succeeded McHenry. He put a great deal of energy into his work and succeeded in getting the course of study organized, as it had never been before. The work of consolidation was begun. Trustee W. L. Brown, of Washington township, ably assisted by Burris, built the Longfellow consolidated school, the first in the county. High school work made great advances under the supervision of the new county superintendent. Burris frequently issued bulletins to his teachers making suggestions for improvement and offering plans that had been tried out by successful teachers. These bulletins were of great value to teachers. Burris discontinued the plan of holding commencement exercises for eighth-grade graduates on the ground that it tended to cause them to discontinue their school work by not entering the high school.

OLD HIGH SCHOOL BUILDING, WASHINGTON.

NEW HIGH SCHOOL BUILDING, WASHINGTON.

AN ENERGETIC SUPERINTENDENT.

Burris resigned a short time before the expiration of his term of office, to take up the study of law. Alva O. Fulkerson, who was at the head of the department of history of the Washington high school, a graduate of the Indiana State Normal School and of Indiana University, and who had taught in country, village, town and city schools, was elected to succeed him. Fulkerson holds that the greatest need of the rural schools is closer supervision. He has this in mind in planning and directing the work of the teachers under his supervision. This is a difficult task, with so many teachers scattered over such a wide territory. To accomplish as much as possible along this line, he prepares each week, while the schools are in session, a column for the newspapers of the county in which he makes suggestions for the improvement of the work, gives plans and devices, discusses the course of study, and points out mistakes being made. Monthly reports are required from the teachers. He visits as many township institutes as possible, to discuss with the teachers their difficulties and to keep in personal touch with them. Consolidation is being pushed. The Montgomery, the Cannelburg, and the Sugarland, are consolidated schools in whole or in part. George B. Drew, who was trustee of Barr township, built the Montgomery and the Cannelburg buildings, and Grant Keith, the ex-trustee of Washington township, built the Sugarland, the most up-to-date building in the county. Fulkerson, in order to consolidate and centralize the work, holds a county-township institute. This plan is a time-saver for the superintendent and creates enthusiasm in the teachers. He has held four eighth-grade county commencements. Charles A. Greathouse, state superintendent, made the address at the first; President George R. Grose, of DePauw University, delivered the address at the second; Supt. J. G. Collicott, of the Indianapolis schools, made the address at the third; and Louis J. Rettger, of the Indiana State Normal, spoke at the fourth institute. His idea is to make the county the school unit, as nearly as possible. The efficiency of the township high schools has been greatly increased under Fulkerson's supervision.

COUNTY TEACHERS' ASSOCIATION.

The first Daviess County Teachers' Association was organized in September, 1870. The plan and purpose of this association was good, but it failed to accomplish much. The first president of this association was

County School Examiner George A. Dyer. The secretary was Benjamin S. Henderson. The members of the committee that formulated the constitution and by-laws were, Elbert Bogart, Lizzie Hogshead, W. H. Johnson and Howard Williams. Meetings were held during the school year of 1870-1871. These were not generally attended. Because of this lack of interest, the association was soon abandoned.

In 1895, another county teachers' association was organized. Beginning with that year, fifteen sessions were held before the meetings were abandoned. The sessions were held on Friday and Saturday following Thanksgiving, of each year. These associations did much in directing the educational thought of the county. The association was abandoned in 1909 for two years, and in 1911 it was reorganized, to be again abandoned in 1914.

County Supt. W. A. Wallace was the president of the first association, which was held in November, 1895. Succeeding him as presiding officer were the following prominent teachers of the county: A. C. Wise, F. B. Colbert, J. M. Vance, J. S. Westhafer, Philander McHenry, W. F. Axtell, A. O. Fulkerson, Robert Core, F. M. McConnell, Hamlet Allen, Lew S. Core, William Young, William T. Brown and Charles McMullen. After the intermission of two years, John Doyle was president for the session of 1911, and Rett A. Roberts, O. M. Shekell and C. T. Amick were his successors in order.

The State Teachers' Association had changed its time of meeting from the Christmas holidays to October. Because of this and as so many other educational meetings were being held, it was felt that the County Teachers' Association had served its purpose and should be abandoned.

COUNTY INSTITUTES.

Among the important school laws passed by the Legislature of 1865, was the one providing for a county teachers' institute. This law provided that one county institute should be held each year in each county and when there was an average attendance of twenty-five teachers, the county should pay thirty-five dollars for its maintenance, and when there was an average attendance of forty or more teachers, the county should pay fifty dollars for its upkeep.

There is no record of the first institute held under this law, but from the best information it was held in 1866, the year following the passage of the law. An institute was held the week beginning August 17, 1868. The late Judge David J. Hefron, then a Barr township teacher, is reported as giving a lecture and also a Reverend Mr. Fisk, of Petersburg. There was an attendance of between forty-five and fifty. Those enrolled were G. W. Morin, J. A. Murray, Aikman Carnahan, Hamlet Allen, M. E. Barton, J. Carnahan, Susan Cosby, Fred Agan, B. Agan, O. Cosby, M. T. Connaughton, L. Clark, J. Beckett, J. C. Allison, Weston Wise, F. Arford, A. Connolly, H. B. Kohr, H. Williams, J. Laverty, William Kennedy, J. C. Porter, S. Loveless, John McIntire, N. J. Goshorn, Thomas Kilgore, J. C. Lavelle, F. M. Walker, Levi Reeves, G. Robinson, Anna Kennedy, R. Graham, L. Wilson, L. Wells, M. Stubblefield, L. Ryan, Ophelia Roddick, M. Feagans, J. Feagans, L. Hogshead, M. E. Flinn, Emma Baldwin, M. Perkins, M. Dyer, J. Morgan, E. Connaughton, Thomas Lavelle, A. W. Arford, W. H. Allison, J. Nichols, E. S. Pershing, Thomas Wade, A. W. Smith, J. Mahoney, Frank Myers, J. Winklepleck, L. Cosby, M. Gallagher and D. H. Morgan.

The following resolutions, passed by the teachers' county institute of 1869, are significant:

"Resolved, First, That this institute as a body request the county school examiner to use his influence to the farthest extent with the town and township trustees, and request them to increase the salary of teachers. And also that he request the town and township trustees to purchase with the special school fund, the necessary school books and stationery to be used in the town or township, in order that a uniform system may be adopted.

"Second, That we, as members of the Daviess County Teachers' Institute, will not agree to teach for less than two dollars per day, and ask as much more as the grade of certificate may call for; and also request the trustees to give extra compensation to those teachers who have attended the county institute for 1869."

Howard Williams, George W. Morin and Hamlet Allen composed the committee that formulated these resolutions. The ideas in these resolutions are now a part of the school laws of the state.

A. W. Smith, who was the secretary of the institute, gave lessons on penmanship. He was asked by the institute to formulate his rules for writing in verse. The following is the result:

> While writing be erect and free,
> With nature for your guide;
> Incline your heft upon your left,
> The right arm near the side.

So lightly then you hold the pen,
 'Twill almost from you slip;
Let both points press with equal stress,
 In sight your knuckles keep.

While fingers bend let arm attend,
 And on the muscles play;
As rolling rest; while nails light pressed,
 Slide freely every way.

With equal height and slope now write,
 With equal space now combine;
Trace with dry pen your copy then,
 And keep it next your line.

As the number of teachers in the county has increased the attendance and the interest at the county institutes have increased. Now, instead of local talent furnishing the instruction and discussions, some of the best educators of the country are employed. As an incentive for teachers attending the county institutes two per cent. is added to the general average of those teachers who attend the entire institute. This means an increase in the wages of the teachers of from six dollars to about fifteen dollars per year. These institutes have served to create a better attitude among teachers toward their work, to advance the standards, to increase the professional interest, to keep teachers in touch with advanced thought along educational lines, and to cause others to have a higher regard for the profession.

Edgar James Swift, of St. Louis; Rosa M. R. Mikels, of Indianapolis; Z. M. Smith, of Lafayette, Indiana; Roberta McNeil, of Lafayette, Indiana; and May Robinson, of Washington, Indiana, were the instructors for the 1914 institute. O. L. Warren, of Elmira, New York; Anna H. Morse, of Charleston, Illinois, and Richard Park, of Sullivan, Indiana, are the instructors for 1915.

The following teachers were enrolled at the 1914 institute: Hamlet Allen, Norma Allen, Ottie L. Allen, Thomas E. Arvin, William Arterburn, C. T. Amick, Inez Bonham, Maggie Bradley, Ernest Burch, Margaret Brewer, Edith Brother, Helen Brother, Mabel Burris, Mannie Burris, Bessie Brown, Jessie Brown, Eunice Brown, Oscar Booker, Etta Berry, Flossie Barley, Ray Cunningham, Helen Cochran, Edith Cottingham, Harriet E.

Cook, Susie Colbert, Amanda Colbert, Minnie Cox, Hazel A. Chinn, Murl Cunningham, G. A. Cunningham, Leo Clements, Lewis Clements, A. L. Chestnut, Floyd Carpenter, Owen Crecelius, A. Lawrence Clark, Blanche Collins, Hazel Clinton, Flora Clinton, N. H. Chattin, Sidney Carnahan, Minnie Carnahan, T. E. Colbert, V. E. Dillard, Elbert Dougherty, Helen Downs, J. A. Deal, James D. Dwyer, Omer Dages, Corrien Dages, Ella Donahue, Ada Evans, Omer Edwards, Bernice Elmore, Gladys Edwards, Blanche Fish, Dennie Ford, Kell Ferguson, Roy Flint, Edith Flick, Don C. Faith, Walter Funcannon, Hazel Feagans, Earl Freed, Bertha Gamble, Carrie Greenwood, Rookh Greenwood, Ephraim Gregory, Grant Giltner, Lena Goss, Rebecca Graves, W. A. Grannan, J. W. Gillaspie, Margaret Grannan, Harvey Gilliatt, James E. Gilley, Eulala Guthrie, Cora Hunter, Mary Hasting, Harry Herman, Hazel Hoopingarner, Hilda Hoopingarner, Albert Heithecker, Harry Hunter, Mary Harard, Dully Harrod, Bernadette Hopkins, Hazel Johnson, Elsie Jones, J. S. Ketcham, Britta Ketcham, Margaret Kauffman, Bessie Keller, Mary Long, W. A. Lavelle, Ethel Littell, Hazel Lett, John Ledgerwood, J. C. Lemmon, Paris Laughlin, Stella McCafferty, Grace McCafferty, Rollie Morin, Ruth McCown, Ermel McCafferty, T. R. McCafferty, Lucy McGehee, W. L. McCormick, O. M. McCracken, O. P. McCoy, Dello McWilliams, Carl McWilliams, Clarence McCoy, Albert Malone, Ellis Malone, Hugh Morgan, Mary Mattingly, E. E. Meade, Roscoe Myers, E. H. Myers, C. Will Myers, Grace Myers, Carrie Myers, G. E. Nicholson, Mayme Nicholson, Gladys Norman, Cora Nugent, Stella O'Donald, Beryl O'Donald, John O'Connor, Joanna O'Connor, Nora O'Connor, James O'Neal, Maggie O'Donaghue, Arlie O'Brian, Famie O'Dell, F. F. Osmon, Alice Pate, Agnes Pate, Louis Pate, Edna Pickett, Luther Potts, Lola Parsons, Helen Palmer, Lora Pershing, Albert Pershing, Benjamin Ritter, Rett A. Roberts, May E. Robinson, Clara Shaffer, Irene Spitz, Estella Spitz, Josephine Sanford, Eula Sanford, Pauline Sanford, Mary C. Shirley, Flossy Smiley, Minnie Standley, H. A. Sass, Shellie Simuel, Ray Stuckey, Cecil Smith, Henry Sipes, S. P. Sears, Sherman Stickles, Nimrod Slaven, Martha Sommers, Anna Belle Smeltzer, Grant Scales, O. M. Shekell, Pearl Taylor, Jeannette Ward, A. P. Westhafer, Lottie Westhafer, Elsie Wadsworth, Forrest Wadsworth, Bert White, Charles L. White, Edith Wood, Harry Winklepleck, E. O. Winklepleck, Walter White, Claude Ward, Mary Wright, Katharine Wilson, Dorothy Winston, Luke Young, Madge Yenne, Elmer York, Dora York, Ernest Zimmerman.

THE RURAL ELEMENTARY SCHOOLS.

The following article on "The Rural Elementary Schools of Daviess County," by County Superintendent A. O. Fulkerson, appeared in State Superintendent Charles A. Greathouse's report for 1914:

"During the past two decades there has been quite a change in elementary rural schools of Daviess county. This change has taken place in the school buildings, in their equipment, in the personnel and preparation of the teachers, and in the attitude of the patrons toward the schools.

"The type of school building of twenty years ago was a frame, about a third longer than wide, with three windows on each side and a door in one end. The majority of the buildings in the county are of this type, but they are being rapidly replaced by more modern structures.

"It was difficult for pupils to see to study their lessons in these old-style buildings on cloudy days, and it was almost impossible to read written assignments on the poor blackboards, because of the cross rays of light. In some of these old buildings, in order to have more light, two additional windows were placed in the door end. This made matters worse instead of better.

"At first, a great majority of these buildings were heated by large wood stoves placed in the center of the room. On cold days, it kept one person almost constantly busy carrying in the wood and building the fires. The wood stoves have been replaced by coal stoves. This method of heating was bad. Those seated near the stove would get too warm, while those seated in the remote parts of the room would almost freeze.

"The question of ventilation was never thought of when these school houses were being built. There was no great scarcity of fresh air, though, for after these buildings had been used two or three years, the openings about the doors, windows and in the floors permitted ample ventilation.

"These school houses were built in the main in the centers of the most populous districts, in order to accommodate the greatest number. For different reasons the centers of population have changed. This has caused the abandonment of some schools and the erection of others.

"The equipment of the schools of twenty years ago has changed as much as anything else. The double seat has been replaced by the single seat. Then the adjustable seat was unknown. More charts, globes and maps were purchased then than now, but much of this equipment was of little value. The accounting law has made trustees more careful in their purchas-

SUGARLAND CONSOLIDATED SCHOOL

ing. Many good pictures are seen on the walls of the school rooms today. This was not true twenty years ago.

"In Daviess county there is a greater per cent. of the enumeration enrolled in the public schools than ever before. This is not true, though, of the rural elementary schools. The reasons for this are, that there was but one high school in the county twenty years ago, while today there is a high school in nine of the ten townships of the county. Pupils complete the work in the grades much younger and then enter high school or quit school.

"Not only is the per cent. of the enumeration enrolled greater today, but the per cent. of attendance of the enrollment is much greater than formerly. This is due in a great part to the compulsory attendance law. Parents, too, realize more than ever the importance of educating their children.

"In twenty years the personnel of the teaching corps of the rural schools has almost entirely changed. Of the one hundred twenty-five teachers in the rural schools of Daviess county then, seven are of the teaching force this year. Of this number, one is teaching in the same district in which he taught twenty years ago, but a new building has been erected since that time. This teacher has not taught in this district all these twenty years, although he has taught there several terms. On an average, the teaching force in the rural schools of the county changes every four or five years. Many quit teaching, and the great majority of the better teachers get more desirable positions. The rural schools are teachers' training schools for consolidated, town, and city schools. The beginning teacher of today is much better qualified than the beginning teacher of a score of years ago.

"In nearly every way, the elementary rural schools of the county are better than they were two decades ago. This has been brought about in the main by helpful school legislation. The compulsory attendance law is and has been a large element in this advancement. Attendance officers, many times, are not as efficient as they might be because they receive nothing for travelling expenses. The operation of the minimum term law has been an element in increasing the efficiency of the teachers. The law raising the qualifications for teachers has been a great help to the rural schools, although many for whom it did the most good, at first opposed it. The sanitary school house law has revolutionized the character of the school buildings that are erected in the rural districts. It has meant much to the physical welfare of the children. The medical inspection law and the uniform text-book law have each contributed to the uplift of the rural school.

"Today there are ninety-four rural elementary schools in Daviess county. This does not include the consolidated schools. Twenty years ago there were one hundred twenty-one. Six of the ninety-four school buildings have two rooms. There are an even hundred teachers employed to teach in these buildings. Twenty-seven of these are teaching for the first time. As required by law, these beginners are high school graduates and have had a term or more of professional training. Only forty of the remaining sixty have taught more than three years. Many of this forty who have had four or more years of experience make teaching a secondary matter. As a result the children under their instruction do not get their best efforts.

"The township trustees, in nearly every instance, give more attention to the town, consolidated, and high schools in their townships than to the 'little red school house.' They equip the town, consolidated, and high schools better and appoint the best teachers to them. This course of action is causing many opponents of consolidation to favor it.

"The greatest need of the rural elementary schools is closer supervision. Yet great advancement has been made along this line in the last half dozen years, because of the trustees, county superintendent, and state superintendent. The trustees have made the principals of their consolidated and high schools the heads of all the schools of their townships. While these principals can give no direct supervision, their efforts in this direction in the township institutes are very helpful. The state course of study and bulletins sent out by the state superintendent have very materially aided in unifying the work of the district schools.

"Some of the teachers are making commendable efforts to present the subjects of agriculture and domestic science in a way that will be interesting and helpful to their pupils. The very great majority of the patrons are pleased that these subjects are being taught.

"Some of the things that are detrimental to the progress of the district schools are the practice of employing home teachers, irrespective of their qualifications; those holding the lowest grade of license, and personal and political friends."

EARLY WASHINGTON SCHOOLS.

It was a century ago that John Aikman taught the first school in Washington. This was a "pay" school. This was the year before Indiana became a state. Aikman taught another school the next year, 1816. Thomas Howard, a Yankee schoolmaster, succeeded Aikman. The text-books then were not as varied as now. The most used book was the American Spelling Book. Some of the advanced pupils studied the English Reader and Pike's Arithmetic.

Col. John Allen, with his large family, settled near Washington in December, 1816. Dudley Johnson, his son-in-law and an especially fine penman, was one of the hamlet's early teachers. About this time Cyrus McCormick taught a school in what was then the Presbyterian church. He is entitled to the distinction of being the first Latin teacher in Daviess county. This building stood just across the Bedford road from where the new high school building now stands. William G. Cole, Charles McIntyre and Isaac Heaton were other early teachers. To encourage his pupils, Heaton gave rewards of merit for especially good work. Some of his "Rewards of Merit," in water colors, are still kept as heirlooms in the families of some of his pupils.

Heaton's immediate successors were W. D. Shepard, a Scotchman by the name of Damerel, David McDonald, afterwards a judge of the United States Court for Indiana; Hiram A. Hunter, a Cumberland Presbyterian minister, and Emanuel Van Trees. Miss Mary Cowardin assisted Hunter. Van Trees became one of the county's first clerks of the circuit court and his records as such are models of neatness. Succeeding these were Patrick M. Brett, in 1831, Rev. John Graham and Rev. Calvin Butler. Brett was a great believer in the injunction, "Spare the rod and spoil the child." Graham was a Scotchman and a Baptist minister. He was an expert with the pen and a fine linguist. Butler was assisted in directing the boys and girls in the paths of knowledge during the year 1835 by Eliza McCoy. A Miss Bruner taught in 1836 and Mary S. Clapp in 1837.

From 1839 to 1850, a Miss Cummings, Sarah A. Osgood, Thomas Ballow, a Miss Fisk, Josiah Peck, Mary Ann Bascom, Alice Belding and Michael Burke were the teachers.

During the next ten years the teachers were: Rev. F. Snell, an Episcopal minister; William Chase, Samuel Gee, a Miss Cressy, Delight Weber and Sarah M. Jackson.

In 1861, C. P. Parsons, later of the Evansville high school, attempted to establish a young ladies' academy, but this resulted in a failure. Not long after this the women of the town made another attempt to found a secondary school, with Samuel Loveless as the principal. The result was the same as in the first instance.

Other teachers after this date were Rev. Charles Cross, a Methodist minister; Mrs. J. Blair Carnahan, Rev. James M. Berry, a Baptist minister; a Mr. and Mrs. Howe, Rev. McCain, a Presbyterian; Howard Williams, Laura E. Agan and Mrs. Laura Clark.

In 1864, Rev. John R. Phillips, a Welshman and a Baptist minister, was in charge. The following year he and Mrs. T. R. Palmer taught in a two-story building situated on northeast Fifth street. For the next few years Phillips had charge at the seminary. Rebecca Wirt and Anna S. Kennedy were his assistants.

Succeeding these up to 1874 were Edward Wise, the first county superintendent; Tolbert Bartl, E. P. Cole and wife.

The year 1874 marks the beginning of Washington's graded school system. At that time John H. O'Neall, John Hyatt and Philip A. Spink were the school trustees. They appointed W. T. Fry as superintendent of the schools and Hamlet Allen, principal of the high school. Fry served as superintendent for three years. During this time there were seven separate school buildings, situated in different parts of the city. The old brick seminary, on East Walnut street, was the principal building. The grade teachers during these three years were George W. Morin, W. Hays Johnson, Mary E. Barton, Laura E. Agan, Ophelia H. Roddick, D. M. Geeting, T. T. Pringle, John A. Geeting, Mrs. Anna C. McGuire, Laura F. Ladd, Sarah Agan, Emma Trimble and Wilson S. Davis.

SUPERINTENDENTS AND PRINCIPALS.

W. T. Fry, the first superintendent, who served from 1874 until 1877, began the work of grading the schools. He was succeeded by D. Eckley Hunter, who served from 1877 until 1885. He was one of the prominent educators of the state and did much to advance the schools of Washington. Hunter was succeeded by William F. Hoffmann, who was the principal of the high school at the time of his promotion to the superintendency. The schools continued to advance under the superintendency of Hoffmann. W. F. Axtell, an Indiana University graduate and principal of the high school, succeeded Hoffmann in 1894. Axtell directed the educational affairs of the city until 1913, when he was succeeded by Eugene D. Merriman, who is the superintendent at this writing.

Hamlet Allen, the first principal of the high school, is sometimes called "The Father of the Washington High School," and he well deserves this title. He organized it and has served as its principal twenty-six years. He was principal from 1874 until 1879. He was succeeded by T. G. Alford, who served during the year 1879-1880. Robert C. Duncan and William J. Vickery were Alford's successors. They served but a year each. In 1882 William F. Hoffmann was elected to the principalship. He served until

1885, when he was promoted to the superintendency. William F. Axtell succeeded Hoffmann and served until 1894, when he again succeeded Hoffmann, but this time as superintendent. Hamlet Allen was again elected to the principalship in 1894. He served continuously in this position from that date until 1915.

SCHOOL BUILDINGS.

The advance from Washington's log school building in 1815 to her splendid modern high school building of 1915 marks her progress not only in the educational field, but along other lines as well. During this century of progress Washington has used nearly all kinds of buildings for school purposes. Sometimes it was a log building, sometimes a frame, sometimes a brick. Sometimes the building was erected to be used for school purposes, sometimes it was intended to be used as a place of worship, sometimes for a dwelling place, and sometimes for a place of business. Until the erection of the high school and grade building on Walnut street in 1876-77, the old seminary building, which stood on the same site, was the most pretentious structure for school purposes that Washington had ever had. This graded school building was a splendid brick structure, three stories in height and a basement. It was built in 1876, at a cost of forty thousand dollars. Such a building now would cost more than twice that amount. This building was destroyed by fire in 1897.

At once the trustees began planning and erecting what is now known as the Junior High School building. This building is on the site of the seminary building, which was torn down, and the high school and grade building, which burned in 1897. It is located at the northwest corner of Walnut and Northeast Seventh street.

To better provide for the needs of the high school, the present commodious and modern high school building, at the corner of Walnut and Sixth streets, was erected in 1912-1913, at a cost of about sixty-five thousand dollars.

The Southside grade building was erected in 1896, at a cost of about twenty-five thousand dollars. It is a brick building, two stories high, with a basement, and has nine rooms. It is a handsome structure, located on Southeast Third street and Southside avenue.

The West End grade building was greatly damaged by fire in 1890. It was remodeled and repaired to meet modern requirements. It is a brick structure of two stories and contains nine rooms and a basement. It is located at the southwest corner of Van Trees and Northeast Eighth streets.

The colored school building is located on West Walnut and Ninth streets. It is a brick building, two stories high, with two rooms. It is not a modern structure.

PROGRESS OF THE SCHOOLS.

As has been stated above, the Washington schools have made great progress in so far as the buildings are concerned. In other ways they have made equal advancement.

In 1874 there were eight hundred and twenty-seven pupils enrolled, with an average attendance of three hundred and fifty-seven. In 1914, forty years later, there was an enrollment of one thousand four hundred and seventy-seven, with an average attendance of one thousand two hundred and forty-two. In the high school in 1874, there were forty-five enrolled and forty years later there were two hundred and eighty enrolled. There were seven in the first graduating class and fifty-four in the class of 1915. Seven hundred ninety-two have graduated from the high school. In 1874 there was one high school teacher and in 1914 there were fifteen.

The course of study has been extended until it includes the regular classical course, which prepares its students for entrance into the best universities, and a department of manual training, domestic science, music, art, and a business course.

The school has made an enviable record in athletics as well as along literary lines. Its football team has won the state championship twice and its track team has done equally as well.

In 1874, Hamlet Allen constituted the high school faculty. In 1914 it consisted of Hamlet Allen, geometry; Edith Wood, Latin; C. C. Rhodes, German and chemistry; H. A. Sass, history; Wiley Hitchcock, science; Leland Burroughs, English; Madge Yenne, English; Grace Rust, algebra; Ethel Reeve, cooking; L. H. Moorman, manual training; Mrs. Elizabeth Merriman, sewing; Mary Wright, commercial course; May E. Robinson, art; V. E. Dillard, music; Carl McWilliams, agriculture.

THE ELNORA SCHOOLS.

Elnora is one of the newest towns of the county. The development of its school system is, therefore, a thing of recent years. "Owl Town" had never had a school. The few pupils who lived here were distributed among the nearby schools of Elmore township, the Nugent district taking the most of them. There was no school in what is now the town of Elnora until 1887.

In the latter year Harvey Manning, trustee of Elmore township, established district No. 9, and built a one-room frame building, and appointed R. W. Wadsworth as teacher. This building still stands and is being used as a boarding house. The enrollment the first year was seventy-two, and the average daily attendance was forty-two. The following year the building was enlarged and Lee Wadsworth and Emma Allen were appointed teachers.

Albert Malone and Ella Crosby were the teachers for the year 1889-90. The enrollment for this term was one hundred and one, with an average daily attendance of sixty-one. In the autumn of 1890, J. Sherman Westhafer took charge of the school. Westhafer was appointed principal for the following year. The enrollment for the year 1891-92 was one hundred and thirty-two, and the average daily attendance was eighty-five. Two teachers were employed.

At the beginning of the school year 1892-93 the town took over the school. Westhafer was retained as principal by the town school board for one year, when he was succeeded by Hiram I. Williams, of Raglesville, who was principal for one year, and he was succeeded by J. S. Westhafer. During the year 1894-95 three teachers were employed.

In the year 1895 the south half of the present school building was erected. Ida Campbell was the first principal in the new building, serving from 1895 to 1898. Up to this time the school work done here was similar to that done in the district schools. Under Miss Campbell's administration a more systematic classification of pupils was made and the beginning of a high school course was introduced. Pupils were required to form lines and march into the building in an orderly manner; this was a new departure in school management, and met with objections on the part of patrons. Under the charge of Principal A. O. Fulkerson in 1898-99, the organization work of Miss Campbell was extended and the course of study was augmented by additional high school work.

Roland D. Winklepleck was elected principal in 1899 and served one year. The teaching force was at this time increased from four to five teachers. Elementary Latin, civil government, general history, physical geography, English and algebra were the only high school subjects taught at this time.

Fenton B. Williams was principal from 1900 to 1902, and little change was made by him in the high school work. The enrollment was increasing rapidly at this time, and six teachers were employed for the year of 1901-2. Robert J. Core was appointed assistant principal in 1901, remaining in that capacity for three years. The principal and assistant had charge of the high school work and the eighth grade.

In 1902 J. E. Garten became principal for a term of two years. The high school work was extended by Garten until it included three years of work; the length of the school term now was one hundred and twenty days, and the annual salary of the principal was three hundred and sixty dollars.

Robert C. Harris, now of the manual training high school, Indianapolis, was principal for the year of 1904-05, and Wiley Hitchcock, now of the Washington high school, was assistant principal. For the first time pupils were graduated from the high school in 1905, the graduates being Milton B. Nugent and Ada Bair. Dean M. Inman was chosen principal in 1905 and Wiley Hitchcock assistant principal; the period of school attendance at this time was lengthened to one hundred and forty-five days.

In 1906 the teaching force was increased to seven teachers. Dean M. Inman was employed as superintendent and Charles McMullen as principal of the high school. The high school course was made to conform to the requirements of the state board of education for commissioned high schools. For the first time two teachers devoted their entire time to the high school, the enrollment in the high school at this being twenty-three pupils, while the length of the term was extended to one hundred and sixty days. Inman and McMullen were in charge until 1909. In 1908 the high school was certified by the state board of education.

For the year 1909-10 Clyde T. Amick, of Scipio, Indiana, was employed as superintendent and Charles McMullen as principal. At this time music and drawing were added to the course and the high school was commissioned.

In 1913 a new steam-heating system was installed and a basement room fitted up for a manual training shop, the work in manual training being confined to the seventh and eighth grades. In 1914 an additional room was built to be used by the domestic science classes. The enrollment in the high school for the year 1914-15 was fifty-six pupils, a gain of one hundred and forty-three per cent. since 1906. The year 1915 completed the sixth year of Amick's services as superintendent of the Elnora schools. Charles McMullen retired from the schools in 1915 after serving nine years as principal.

THE ODON SCHOOLS.

The following sketch of the Odon schools was prepared for the most part by James E. Garten for *The Odonian*, the annual issued by the graduating class of 1915 of the Odon high school:

"A frame school house was built in the year 1850 on the south side of what is now East Main street, Odon. It was not very large, as every stick of timber that went into it was hauled from the saw-mill at one load. The first teacher was a knight of the birch named Shelby.

"At that time the McGuffey readers and spelling books and the Ray arithmetics were just beginning to come into use. Then it was necessary for a teacher to know how to make goose-quill pens. History and physiology were yet to appear in a course of study. The three R's were commonly massaged into the pupil's system, with a liberal anointing of hickory oil. The youth of that day was taught to read in a loud declamatory tone of voice, and to spell huge words without batting an eye or gaining the faintest glimmering of their meaning. But it was in practical life that he gained his real education. He found that plowing in stumpy ground strengthened and increased his vocabulary; that playing marbles and seven-up developed the mathematical faculty; and that nothing is such a stimulant to English composition as writing letters to a fellow's best girl.

"It was still more than two generations to the nearest concrete sidewalk. Odon was not Odon at all, but Clarksburg, and the postoffice was not even Clarksburg, but Clark's Prairie. A single street, now Main street, with a few houses and one modest store comprised the entire town. The nearest railroad was at Bedford. The first buggy was yet to be made. Young couples went joy-riding in ox-carts. Clothing was homespun; books were few, and too much respected to be widely read; there were deer and wild turkeys in abundance on the prairie south and west of the town.

"After one brief term of service the school house was destroyed by fire, and it was not until 1856 that a building was erected to replace it. The second school house was built on the hill north of Main street and a short distance west of the first. It was a larger and more ambitious structure than its predecessor. Capt. Z. V. Garten and the late Howard Crooke, who were then in business in Clarksburg, contributed all the material for the building, and Miles Reynolds and Captain Garten did the carpenter work. The school house was to be used for religious services and all public gatherings, as well as for all educational work. It witnessed the advent of Spencerian steel pens, desks made to seat two pupils each, maps and globes.

"In 1873 a two-story brick building was built. It stood beside and east of the old frame structure. This building had but two rooms at first, which were much longer than they were wide. It took a hefty kid to throw a paper wad from one end of his school room to the other. The door was in the south end of the building opening into a small hallway. Henry B. Kohr was the first teacher to preside 'up-stairs,' while Alexander O'Dell was in charge on the first floor. There was no effort made to grade the schools except by the readers used. Harvey's English Grammar, Ray's Third Part Arithmetic and Anderson's History of the United States were being used about this time.

"It was early in the eighties that the school building underwent some modifications. The door in the south end was closed up, the lower room was divided by a partition, and two doors were placed on the west side. One of these admitted into what afterward came to be known as the intermediate room and the other opened into the primary room and gave admission to the stairway."

As near as can be ascertained, the first group of teachers was S. B. Boyd, now editor of the *Daviess County Democrat,* principal; Mary Campbell, intermediate, and Clarinda Wilson, primary. Among the early principals were Caleb O'Dell, Hugh Funkhouser, J. W. Stotts, Joel Danner and W. J. Johnson. Johnson was succeeded by Ezra Mattingly. It was Mattingly who decided to hold some commencement exercises. The common branches, algebra, physical geography, civil government and bookkeeping comprised the first high school course. It was but one short year in length. The text-books used were Ray's Higher Arithmetic, Schuyler's Algebra, Anderson's Manual of Civil Government, Bryant and Stratton's High School Bookkeeping, Holbrook's Grammar and Heuston's Physical Geography.

"The First Annual Commencement of the Odon Public Schools," as the program reads, was held at "Stoy's Opera House, Saturday evening, March 31, 1888." This was the biggest educational event that Odon had ever seen. A commencement speaker was not employed, but each candidate for a diploma recited an original essay, called a "final." The teachers that year were Ezra Mattingly, principal; John B. Crooke, intermediate, and Clarinda Wilson, primary. Mattingly remained as principal until 1890, when he was succeeded by William Tipton. Tipton served as principal but one year. His successor was Thomas Benton George. George was the last principal of the old building on the hill.

It was in the summer of 1892 that the present school building was begun. When the time came for the fall term to begin the new building was not yet complete and the old one had been disposed of. The various teachers were quartered in different parts of town. The high school, with J. A. Alexander as principal, occupied the opera house. Alexander revived the high school work and, to a great degree, started the Odon schools in the direction of their present efficiency.

After the Christmas holidays the schools were assembled in the new building. In the spring a commencement was held by Alexander for the graduates in the common branches; this was the first commencement ever held in Madison township for eighth-grade graduates.

For the year 1893-94 Charles Williams was principal. He dropped some of the high school subjects taught by Alexander, but still offered a mixed eighth-grade and high school course. Williams was followed by Howard Clark, who remained principal until the close of the school year of 1896-97. During the last two years of his service his wife, Mrs. Lenora Clark, taught a part of the common branches and a few high school subjects, her husband being the first principal to devote his entire time to high school work. The Clarks extended the high school course of study to two years' work.

S. W. Satterfield became the principal in the fall of 1897 and held the position two years. During his second year he added a third year's work to the course of study.

William Abel became the head of the schools in the fall of 1899. On the contract he is called a "supervising principal." The following year the course of study received its fourth year of high school work. Abel was given the title of superintendent the next year. John Satterfield was the principal. During the winter of 1901 Satterfield resigned on account of ill health, and the vacancy was filled by Edward W. Bennett.

The 1901 term began with Abel as superintendent and Bennett as principal. About the middle of the school year Abel resigned and Bennett was promoted to the superintendency, with Edgar A. O'Dell as the principal. A high school commission was secured late in the year.

No change was made in the superintendency or principalship for the year 1902-03. The next year F. M. McConnell became superintendent and Arthur Mayfield was principal. This arrangement remained until the early part of the year 1905-06, when McConnell resigned to accept a situation in Montana. Mayfield became superintendent, with Grant Callahan as the

(16)

principal. In 1906 an addition was built to the school building. This gave three new rooms, one of which is used as the assembly room. Mayfield resigned the superintendency in the spring of 1908 and Lawrence Maher was elected to the vacancy. He served for two years.

J. W. Gillaspie, the present superintendent, was elected in 1910. Under his efficient supervision the schools have made commendable progress.

CATHOLIC SCHOOLS.

ST. SIMON'S SCHOOL, WASHINGTON.

About 1819, a few Catholic families had settled in the vicinity of Washington. In 1837 they were united into a body under the care of Father Simon Lalumiere, for whom the church and school were named. Father Lalumiere built a church in 1838, which stood a little farther north on the lot where the church now stands.

The first Catholic school was held in the basement of the church and was attended by both boys and girls, the girls sitting on one side and the boys on the other. It was taught by the Brothers.

On September 26, 1857, St. Simon's Academy for girls was founded by the Sisters of Providence from St. Mary's of the Woods. Father Chasse was pastor at this time. The Sisters occupied a small brick house belonging to the Father, which stood on Hefron street between the school and the church and faced the east. At first the Sisters taught in an old frame house which sood on the corner of Second and Hefron streets. There were four Sisters employed; one taught the boys on the first floor, one taught the girls on the second floor, one taught music and one was the housekeeper, who assisted in teaching. The present academy was built in 1875 by the Sisters and the old frame building was moved back and it was replaced in 1910 by the new wing.

In 1868, a boys' school was conducted on East Hefron street. It was a small frame structure and school was held here until 1875. The teachers in this building were Hugh M. Quigley, 1868 to 1870; George D. Kelley, 1870 to 1874; Matthew F. Burke, 1874 to 1875; John J. Gleason, 1875 to 1878. While Gleason was teaching, the new school, facing north on Hefron street, between First and Second streets, was finished. The following teachers taught here: John J. Gleason, F. M. Walker, Thomas Crosson, the Brothers, John D. Kelly and John J. Barrett. In 1893, the Sisters took complete charge and continued to teach the boys until they reached the eighth grade.

Under Barrett three boys graduated. They were John Jordan, in 1892; Thomas Bowler and Frank Fitzpatrick, in 1893.

The first commencement of St. Simon's Academy was held in 1890. Mayme Doyle, Julia Riley and Tillie Gers were the graduates. One or more have finished the course every year since.

The old school for boys was torn down in 1913 and replaced by the modern commodious building which now stands at the corner of Second and Hefron streets. This building was dedicated by Father Boland on December 6, 1914.

(This article was prepared by Miss Katharine Wilson, a teacher in the public schools.)

ST. MARY'S GERMAN SCHOOL, WASHINGTON.

In 1873, about thirty German families withdrew from St. Simon's church and formed a separate congregation. They bought a site upon which to erect a church, school and parsonage at the corner of Van Trees and West Second streets. The first German school was held in 1873, in the Keller house, a little two-room frame house across from the church. Sister Blondina was the teacher.

In 1874 and 1875, the school was in the back part of the church where the choir steps now are. A board petition was erected between the church and the school room, which had only a few benches. Later, probably in 1876, the school was moved to a little frame house, west of the church. This had been the pastor's residence; it had two small rooms, so the partition was taken out to make one larger room.

Father Sassel taught the school himself for a time. Later, the congregation built a new room at the back, and Miss Mary Miller taught the lower grades for a year or two.

In 1881, the present brick school east of the church was erected. This building had two rooms, one up stairs and one down. It has been remodeled since and modern improvements added. The school is now in the care of the Sisters of Providence.

ST. PETER'S SCHOOL, MONTGOMERY.

The exact period when the first parochial school was taught at St. Peter's, Montgomery, has not been determined, but it is certain that a log school building was located near the present cemetery of the church. School was held in this building before 1850.

It was during the spring of 1853 and 1854 that Mary A. O'Kavanaugh, afterwards Mrs. Raphael Wathen, a young Irish lass from Enniscorthy, County Wexford, Ireland, who had graduated from a young ladies' seminary of that town, taught a subscription school here for Father Piers.

About 1875, a two-room brick school house was built on the site of the present parochial school building. The brick from the old church which stood on the church farm, and which is but a short distance west beyond the limits of the town of Montgomery, were used in the construction of this two-room building. Father Pierce erected this building.

The present commodious school building was erected about 1905 by Father Matthews. The Sisters of Providence taught in this building three or four years. At present a parochial school is not maintained.

THE COUNTY SEMINARY.

It was the idea of the early educators of the state that the county seminaries were to furnish opportunities for the boys and girls to get what would now be termed a high school education. In order to provide for these, fines before justices of the peace, circuit courts, forfeitures, etc., were to be used to found and maintain a county seminary.

As soon as the county was organized, funds began to accumulate. These funds were placed in charge of a trustee to manage. Robert Oliver was one of the first trustees in Daviess county. He served over ten years. He was succeeded by Lewis Jones. In January, 1832, Oliver reported the total amount of the fund to be $504.74¼, of which $386.11¾ was cash on hand, and $118.62½ in the form of notes drawing interest. On September 1, 1841, the fund had increased until it amounted to $2,584.97. A lot was bought in Washington in 1838, upon which to erect a seminary building. A two-story brick building was begun probably in 1839, but was not finished until 1841. At that time the trustees, Samuel J. Kelso and William G. Cole, made the following report: Total fund received to September, 1841, $2,584.97; paid to contractors, $2,584.97, leaving yet due the contractors, $729.01; total cost of seminary, grounds, etc., $3,313.98.

Trouble arose over the management of the funds. Jephtha Routt, in 1844, obtained a judgment in the circuit court for two hundred dollars and sixty-two cents. He proceeded to levy upon the seminary building to satisfy the judgment. He was paid part of the judgment and given assurance that the remainder would be forthcoming. The property was yet heavily encumbered. A sheriff's sale in some manner was ordered and Graham bought certain rights. In September, 1846, he was paid four hundred and twenty dollars and eighty cents for all his claims. At the April term of court in

OLD SEMINARY BUILDING, WASHINGTON.

1844, "The State on the relation of Alfred Davis *vs.* Thomas Graham, John B. Coleman and Charles F. Wells" was filed. A judgment of five hundred dollars was rendered against the defendants, but the Legislature in some manner annulled it.

Under the constitution of 1852, county seminaries were sold and the proceeds were placed in the common school fund. The Daviess County Seminary was sold at auction on December 12, 1853, to James S. Morgan for one thousand one hundred and eighty dollars. He failed to pay and in April, 1855, the property was sold to the town of Washington for five hundred dollars. It was used by the town for a public school building.

CHAPTER XIV.

THE BENCH AND BAR.

The Daviess county circuit court was established in 1817. On April 21, of that year, court convened for the first time, in the house of Alexander Bruce, located on the southeast corner of Main and Second streets. The president judge was William Prince, then a resident of Princeton, Gibson county. Judge Prince was a man prominent in affairs connected with the early settlement of Indiana territory. With the commission of captain, he served on the staff of General Harrison at the battle of Tippecanoe, and was afterward appointed as Indian agent by Harrison, with headquarters at Vincennes, then the capital of Indiana territory. Judge Prince was also land agent and had much to do with the organization of several of the counties in the southwestern part of the state, and the location of county seats. He was one of the commissioners appointed to locate the county seat of Gibson county, and was honored in having the town (Princeton) named after him.

In the organization of the early court, the bench was composed of a president judge and two associate judges. The two associate judges of the first Daviess county court were William H. Routt and James G. Read. Emanuel Van Trees was appointed clerk, George R. C. Sullivan, prosecuting attorney, and Obed Flint, sheriff. The first grand jury was composed of seventeen "good, true and lawful men," whose names are as follows: John Aikman, Alexander Bruce, Joseph Bruce, Joseph Bradford, Samuel Channis, Dennis Clark, Jacob Freeland, David Flora, Samuel Kelso, George Lashley, John McClure, Joseph Miller, John Stringer, James Warnock, Archibald Williams, John Walker and Peter Wilkins.

It does not seem that this grand jury wasted much time in hearing witnesses testify as to misdemeanors; nor did the jury waste time in argument as to the guilt or innocence of persons accused. They assumed that their business was to return an indictment; it was the business of the lawyers and the court to determine whether the person indicted was guilty. The record shows that on the next day after the first grand jury was convened, they returned twelve indictments, all for assault and battery. One of these cases was against Andrew Hilton, and another against Thomas Meredith. Hilton's case was continued to the next term of court, and, when called, resulted in his acquittal. Regarding the Merideth case, the record says: "And Mr. Merideth being called appeared in proper person and for plea said that he could not say but that he was guilty in manner and form as he stood charged in the indictment, therefore it is considered by the court, that he make his fine to the state of Indiana, for the use of the county of Daviess for county seminary, three dollars." So, if this fine was paid, Mr. Merideth's name is entitled to a conspicuous place on the scroll of fame for having made the first contribution to an educational institution in Daviess county. The next contribution to the educational fund, as appears on record, was at the next term of court, when Joseph Whitney paid a fine of ten dollars for that purpose.

It appears that most of the trials in this court, during the years 1817 and 1818, were for assault and battery. It also appears that the defendants in these cases were frequently the same individuals. A man by the name of John Colbert was before the court as a defendant in an assault and battery case no less than ten times during these years; each time, he was called on to contribute from two to five dollars for the benefit of the county seminary.

The first murder case that appears on the court docket was at the June term of court, 1818. The defendant in the case was a Delaware Indian, named "Big File," who had been indicted for the murder of Thomas Eagle, several months previous. It seems that Eagle, and some other white men, were visiting a friendly band of Indians in Owl Prairie, and that Eagle, who was a very strong man, made a banter that he could throw one of the smaller Indians across a fire, as an exhibition of his strength. In attempting this feat, with the Indian's consent, Eagle succeeded in throwing the Indian only half way. The Indian fell into the fire and was severely burned. Thinking that this was done purposely, Big File attacked Eagle with a big knife and stabbed him to death. At the June term of court the record says, "the accused being solemnly called, came not, and an *alias capias* was issued for said Big File, returnable to the next term." In following the history of this case it appears that court procedure in criminal cases in the early times was about as slow and uncertain as is too frequently the practice in these later days. At the following September term of the Daviess circuit court, the Big File murder case was called and, for some reason, continued. The case was still on the docket at the October term, 1819, at which time it was finally disposed of by a *nolle prosequi* being entered in the case.

At the June term of court, 1818, John Law was admitted to practice in this court. Attorneys who had been admitted to practice in the court about a year previous to this were, William P. Bennett, Jacob Call, Nathaniel Huntington and George R. C. Sullivan. At this same term of court, Thomas H. Blake succeeded William Prince as president judge. Blake was succeeded by G. W. Johnston at the following September term. At the June term, 1819, Johnston was succeeded as president judge by Jonathan Doty, with William H. Routt and James G. Read as associate judges. These associate judges continued until September, 1821, when they were succeeded by Ephraim Thompson and Philip Barton. There were no further changes in the associate judges until 1825, when Philip Barton was succeeded by Rawley Scott, who served until 1829 and then gave place to Michael Murphy. Jacob Call, one of the first attorneys admitted to practice at the Daviess county bar, succeeded Judge Doty, as president judge, at the April term, 1822; Call was succeeded by John R. Porter at the September term, 1824. It seems there were no other changes in the personnel of the court until 1830, when John Law was commissioned president judge, serving from January until August 10, of that year, when G. W. Johnston again appears as the presiding officer of the court. In December, 1831, Amory Kinney succeeded Judge Johnston and served as president judge until January, 1837. Elisha M. Huntington succeeded Judge Kinney in 1837. Huntington served until the April term, 1839, when he was succeeded by David McDonald, whose term as president judge was continued until 1853, when the new constitution became effective, providing for one circuit judge, instead of the associate bench. Those who served as associate judges, in addition to those named, were John L. Caldwell, Elijah Chapman, Cornelius Berkshire, Kenneth Dye and Erasmus H. McJunkin. Mr. McJunkin was a prominent attorney. He died in 1834 and the court records show that the local bar passed suitable resolutions extolling his merits and expressing profound sorrow at his death.

THE CIRCUIT COURT JUDGES.

The first circuit court judge under the new constitution was Alvin P. Hovey, who began his term in February, 1853, and served until the February term, 1854. He served with distiction as a soldier in the Civil War, which came on a few years later, rising to the rank of major-general. General Hovey was elected as representative in Congress, for the first congressional district, in 1886; was elected governor of the state, in 1888, and died during his term of office.

General Hovey was succeeded as circuit judge by William E. Niblack,.

who took his office in 1854 and served four years. Judge Niblack was also a man distinguished in public affairs. He served several terms in Congress as representative of the Vincennes district, and was a member of the state supreme court. He was regarded as one of the leading jurists of the state.

In February, 1858, Ballard Smith succeeded Judge Niblack on the bench and served one year. Michael F. Burke was commissioned judge of this circuit by Gov. A. P. Willard, in February, 1859. Judge Burke continued in this service until his death, which occurred May 22, 1864. The vacancy caused by Judge Burke's death was filled by Judge James C. Denny, who received his appointment from Governor Morton. At the following election Judge John Baker was the successful candidate for the circuit judgeship. Judge Baker continued in office until the February term, 1871, when he was succeeded by Judge Newton F. Malott, who had been elected in the fall of 1870. Judge Malott continued as judge of this circuit until the fall of 1884, when there was a change in the judicial districts, by which his resident county (Knox) became part of another circuit. By this change Daviess county became a part of the forty-ninth judicial circuit. David J. Hefron was appointed by Gov. Isaac P. Gray as judge of this new circuit. At the following election Judge Hefron was elected as his own successor and continued in office until November, 1898. H. Q. Houghton, who had been elected as circuit judge, succeeding Judge Hefron on the bench and served for a period of twelve years, his term ending November 1, 1910, when James W. Ogdon, the present judge, assumed the duties of the office.

PROMINENT ATTORNEYS WHO HAVE PRACTICED IN THIS COURT.

From the earliest times the bar of the Daviess circuit court has ranked with the highest in character and legal attainment. Among the prominent resident attorneys who were early in the practice here were: Charles R. Brown and Amory C. Kinney, who were the first resident lawyers in Washington; soon after them came Erasmus H. McJunkin, David McDonald, Capt. W. Warner, E. S. Terry, Samuel Howe Smydth, R. A. Clements, John N. Evans, Michael F. Burke, John Baker and others. In addition to these, there is a long list of distinguished attorneys from other parts of this state, and some from other states, who have practiced in this court. Among these are the following: Lovell H. Rousseau, Richard H. Rousseau, John R. Porter, John H. Dowden, John S. Watts, Thomas H. Carson, Richard W. Thompson, George G. Dunn, Samuel B. Gookins, John Payne, James Hughes, Tilghman A. Howard, P. M. Brett, Elijah Bell, Delana R. Eckles,

B. M. Thomas, Albert S. White, Edward A. Hennegan, A. G. Caldwell, E. B. Talcott, D. K. Weis, Charles Dewey, Elisha M. Huntington, Moses Tabb, John Law, Samuel Judah, Joseph Warner, Willis A. Gorman, Francis P. Bradley, William G. Quick, George Proffit, Craven P. Hester, John C. Graham, Joseph Dunn, William E. Niblack, Henry S. Lane, Hugh L. Livingston, G. W. Johnston, Paris C. Dunning, G. R. H. Moore, Samuel H. Buskirk, L. Q. DeBruler, A. B. Carlton, Nathaniel P. Usher, John Baker, J. W. Burton, Cyrus M, Allen, William Jones, L. B. Parsons, and many others of later time.

It is related that Abraham Lincoln at one time visited this court in the interest of a client and was admitted to practice at this bar, the oath required of a practicing attorney being administered by Col. John Van Trees, who was at that time clerk of the court. It is also stated that Lincoln made a speech on the tariff question in the court house at the time of his visit. The story of Lincoln's visit and practice in this court may be of a traditional character, but it is not improbable. At that time it was customary for lawyers to travel the "circuit," as it was called, and it was not unusual for noted attorneys to go a long distance outside of their circuit. It is certain that Abraham Lincoln, after he had established a reputation as a lawyer in his Illinois home, was frequently called as counsel in cases in Indiana courts. That there is no special mention in the court record that Abraham Lincoln, of Illinois, was present as counsel for plaintiff, or for defendant, is not a matter of wonder, since he was not so attractive a personage as some of the other visiting lawyers of that time. To the court attendants, and the crowd that usually gathered from miles around in those days, to hear the lawyers "plead," the appearance in town of Joshua Spraggins, who had recently killed a bear up on Wolf creek, would attract more attention than would Abe Lincoln.

It will be of interest to note several others in the foregoing list of attorneys, in practice at the Daviess county bar, who were afterward distinguished in state and national affairs.

Lovell H. Rousseau was admitted to the bar at Bloomfield, Indiana; served in the Indiana Legislature, and in the Mexican War. Settling in Louisville after the Mexican War, he took high rank as a lawyer. He took a decided stand for the government and against secession, and at the outbreak of the Civil War tendered his services in behalf of the Union. He rose to the rank of major-general in the army and his command bore a conspicuous part in some of the most important engagements of the war.

Gen. Tilghman A. Howard achieved distinction in military service in the Mexican War; was United States senator from Indiana, and filled other high public positions. Albert S. White and Henry S. Lane also represented Indiana in the United States Senate. George G. Dunn and Richard W. Thompson were both members of Congress, and both held high rank as lawyers and public speakers. David McDonald was judge of the United States district court, as was Elisha M. Huntington. Charles Dewey was distinguished as a member of the supreme court. Paris C. Dunning became governor, James Hughes was judge and member of Congress, and a major-general of the Indiana Legion during the Rebellion. George H. Proffit gained great renown as an orator. As a political campaign speaker he had few if any equals. He stumped the state for Harrison, in 1840, was sent to Congress, and afterwards was minister to Brazil. These are some, but not all, of the distinguished men whose names are recorded as members of the Daviess county bar in the earlier period of the county's history. Among the attorneys and legal firms in the practice here about a generation later were the following: Col. Samuel H. Taylor, J. W. Burton, G. G. Barton, John C. Billheimer, John M. Van Trees, Alexander Hardy, J. M. Barr and E. F. Meredith. Some of these are dead; others are located and in business elsewhere.

PRESENT MEMBERS OF THE BAR.

The personnel of the present bar of the Daviess circuit court will not suffer in comparison with the distinguished members who engaged in the practice here in other years. On the whole, the present bar is one of exceptional ability. Most of the attorneys in the practice are on the sunny side of middle age and the larger opportunities and possible accomplishments of life are before them. The oldest member of the present bar is Judge William R. Gardiner. He is not only the oldest in years, but holds the record for having been the longest in continual practice of any present or past members of the Daviess county bar. Judge Gardiner is still in active practice, being associated with C. K. Tharp and Charles G. Gardiner, under the legal firm name of Gardiner, Tharp & Gardiner. Other members and law firms in practice here are the following:

M. G. and Hugh O'Neal, under the firm name of O'Neal & O'Neal; M. S. Hastings, J. G. Allen and E. E. Hastings, under the firm name of Hastings, Allen & Hastings; Padgett & Burris; F. A. Seal and J. M. Walsh, under the firm name of Seal & Walsh; William Heffernan; Ezra Mattingly and S. E. Myers, under the firm name of Mattingly & Myers; George A. Faith and E. C. Faith, under the firm name of Faith & Faith; John H. Spencer; Thomas D. Slimp; Charles M. Mears; Aikman & Rogers; Arthur H. Greenwood; J. Earl Thompson and William P. Dennigen, under the firm name of Thompson & Dennigen; Arthur Allen; Robert W. Tharp; T. M. Sears, Elnora; Edgar T. Laughlin, Odon.

CHAPTER XV.

PHYSICIANS AND SURGEONS.

In 1881 the Legislature passed a law requiring the registration of all the physicians in the state and each county was provided with a special record for the purpose of listing all the physicians within its limits. Since that time, all physicians have been required to register in a county before they could practice. The following list of physicians was registered in Daviess county in 1881, many of them having practiced in the county for a quarter of a century or more before this time.

This record, entitled "Register of Physicians and Accoucheurs Residents of Daviess County," gives the names and the places where they were practicing at the time of registration. Many of them moved to Washington later and, of course, many others practiced in the county only a short time. The list of those registering in 1881 follows: Jackson L. Moore, Washington; William L. Evans, Loogootee; William B. Walls, Alfordsville; William H. H. Strouse, Washington; Charles Scudder, Washington; Ira M. Clark, Epsom; John Fitzgibbon, Washington; James M. Achor, Cornettsville; Henry Gers, Washington; John S. Mitchell, Alfordsville; C. G. Barton, Washington; Sarah Perkins, Cornettsville; Jacob W. Clark, Glendale; John N. Killion, Cornettsville; William P. Hobbs, Ragelsville; Charles P. Scudder, Washington; George W. Willeford, Glendale; James F. Parks, Washington; Ozias Nellis, Washington; John B. Byrn, Montgomery; Edward D. Millis, Plainville; Harvey Taylor, Ragelsville; Elisha A. Riggins, Montgomery; David R. Carter, Epsom; Oliver H. McKittrick, Plainville; Wylie B. Killion, Washington; Francis A. Anderson, Washington; Thomas L. Eads, Washington; Allen K. Lane, Odon; Stephen O. Culmer, Odon; John Dearmin, Raglesville; Daniel J. Smith, Odon; Lewis A. Standley, Epsom; Francis M. Harned, Washington; Barton Sears, Owl Prairie; Samuel W. Peck, Washington; John A. Scudder, Washington; Michael Scanlon, Washington; G. M. Robinson, Cannelburg; Quinton Clayton, Montgomery; W. C. Willeford, Montgomery; Mrs. Emma Underwood, Washington; G. W. Walker, Cannelburg.

Since 1881 the physicians have registered as they came into the county and it is to be noted that there have been registrations every year with the exception of 1895, 1896 and 1909. The list from 1882 to 1914, inclusive, follows:

1882—Mark H. Ragsdale, Glendale; William F. Hargrave, Cornettsville; Elias L. Dagley, Odon; Cyrus D. Taylor, Washington; Harriet Chowning, Washington; Sabina Ann Washington, Washington; Magdalena Strauss, Cannelburg; Thomas G. Ray, Epsom; Maria Hildebrand, Washington (signed in German); Sina Ward, Cumback; Thomas K. Plummer, Washington; Katie Plummer, Washington; Charles W. King, Ft. Wayne; Lovey Hosler, Washington; John T. Hedrick, Alfordsville; Nancy Calloway, Washington; Elizabeth Isham, Glendale; F. M. Sears, Owl Prairie; Margaret Chiles, Scotland; Levi Burris, Alfordsville; W. H. Jones, Cornettsville; W. Underwood, Washington; August W. Bingham, Alfordsville; Mary Crosby, Washington.

1883—E. L. Dagley, Washington; A. L. Sabin, Washington (Indian doctor); W. S. Jones, Cumback; J. C. Trueblood, Raglesville; J. P. Steffy, Washington.

1884—Milton P. Tolliver, Owl Prairie; J. S. Taylor, Raglesville; Abraham H. Faith, Plainville; M. C. Kent, Odon.

1885—(There are no addresses given after 1884) Hamilton Wolf, Andrew Kempf, Thomas M. Sears, Horace H. Burrill, George L. Spaulding, Miranda C. Kemp, William B. Anderson, Thomas Spaulding, B. F. Keith, E. A. Oppeer, John C. L. Campbell, William C. Willeford, John M. Jones, A. W. Porter, Stephen A. Brittain, Joseph F. Reeve, George F. Culmer, Caroden L. Swartz, Llewellyn B. Staley, George A. F. J. White.

1886—Walter M. Hunter, William R. Avery, Franklin J. Whittemore, W. J. Thomas, John W. Marlow, J. Thomas Scott, Henry Pagan.

1887—Loron Burdick, William A. Horrall, Alfred N. Bonham, Purnell C. Willis, John W. Culbertson, Charles Franklin Winton, Solomon L. McPherson, Charles R. Van Trees, Frederick T. Hiner, O. A. Bingham, Samuel F. Harris, N. V. Turner, Joshua Curtis Ashcraft, John T. Laughridge, Simon B. Carlton, C. C. McCowan.

1888—Edward W. Ingram, Michael M. Dooley, T. J. Stewart, John F. S. Taylor, Noah Jefferson Goshorn, David Frost.

1889—R. S. Mitchell, B. B. Brannock, Charles W. Benham, William L. Young, W. O. Coffey, John McKeown, M. D. Rea, Thomas W. Flowers, Evan Griffiths.

1890—Dawson E. Barnes, Alexander F. Joseph, E. Peter Joseph, F. Della Claire, Charles W. Divens.

1891—Charles C. Moore, Nicholas N. Jensen, Charles C. Young, George L. Parr, J. B. Wells, James Henry Walker, E. E. Geugelback, John R. Smith, William B. Deffenball, T. B. Van Nuys.

1892—J. Barton Catb, Overton Ethan Gootee, A. B. Knapp, Melvin H. Young, George Knapp, William J. Tolliver, J. W. Anderson, John W. Way, E. W. Hilburn.

1893—Elijah P. T. Hollcroft.

1894—John H. Seneff, Richard Wood McCracken, George A. Thomas, Henry Herr, Charles H. Yenne, W. Winston Waggoner.

1897—C. E. Trainor, D. Brooks Smoot, H. I. Sherwood, R. D. Pope, Mc. G. Porter, Rebecca Gipson, M. H. Young, J. M. Pickel, Thomas B. Rankin, Jerome D. Motte.

1898—Vance May, Hilbert P. Klein, Martin L. Arthur, Hamilton M. Arthur, H. Wechsler, Stephen B. Elrod, Gilbert W. Edmondson, Clarence Dale Fulkerson.

1899—William Henry Meyer, Joseph F. Michels, Mark Schrum, Charles T. Wall.

1900—Henry C. Hargan, William H. Holder, A. J. McGauhy.

1901—Addison Hayes Hattery, Lewis C. Shutt, Ernest Hollingsworth, Calvin L. Rowland, Rufus J. Danner.

1902—T. F. Spink, Orris E. Lett, Lewis J. Downey, John W. Bell, W. H. McGhee, Marion N. Thayer.

1903—Hiram M. Johnson, Homer Frank Carr.

1904—George Riley Tubbs, John W. Shelton, Ringgold S. Mitchell, Albert H. Spears.

1905—John L. Evans, D. J. Hege, Ralph M. Willeford.

1906—Andrew Robinson, James Augustus Pickell.

1907—Daniel W. Bell, Hester T. Phillippe, Nora Maude Arthur, Willis H. Cole.

1908—Otto Florea Fleemer, Frederick J. Freshley.

1910—John P. Sellman, Bert D. Burress, Ira E. Bowman, Morton M. McCord.

1911—Andrew Jackson Lane, Jacob L. Odell, Ambrose C. Clifford, William T. Selfridge.

1912—Douglass Hart, Sarah Snider, Arthur A. Rang, Heilman Curtis Wadsworth.

1913—George Washington Bonner, William B. Clark.

1914—John W. Pahmeier, Evelyn Pearl Hyatt.

OPTOMETRISTS.

Since 1907 the law has required the registration of optometrists in the counties where they practice. The Daviess county record shows that only four have registered in the county, as follow: Thomas David Cloud, Andrew M. Keck, Charles W. Stone and Carl R. West.

DENTISTS.

The registration of dentists has been required since 1899 and in the sixteen years which have elapsed since that time the following have registered in Daviess county:

1899—Roland M. Smiley, W. H. H. Welch, S. L. Wilson, J. H. Shields, Loree E. Van Osdol, Otis T. Robinson, Julian L. Seals, W. F. Shepherd, Frederich J. Homann, Jr., Edward W. Meyer, Frank M. Welch.

1900—Henry C. Hargan, Edward F. Kendall.

1901—Walter L. Anderson, Charles A. Porter, John C. Mitchell, William S. Seal.

1903—Ralph C. Shepherd, John Henry Groscuth.

1904—J. J. Schneider.

1905—George W. Russell, Sarah Willey.

1906—C. O. Clemmer.

1907—Henry C. McKittrick, Jacob Burris.

1908—Roy D. Smiley.

1909—Henry C. Tolliver.

1912—Frank E. Robinson.

1913—Walter J. Wilson, George W. Amerman.

1914—Paul E. Vize.

CHAPTER XVI.

SECRET SOCIETIES.

FREE AND ACCEPTED MASONS.

Charity Lodge No. 30, Free and Accepted Masons, of Washington, has a history covering almost the entire period from the beginning of the town, if the claims of its members can be relied on. It is conceded that much of this claim to antiquity of origin is founded on tradition, but there are some reasonable grounds for credibility of the claim. At the meeting of members and friends of the order, December 27, 1895, Charles G. Sefrit gave a historical sketch, entitled, "The Story of Charity Lodge," in which some interesting matters pertaining to the origin and history of the lodge were presented. The following quotations from Mr. Sefrit's sketch are given as the most reliable history of the lodge obtainable:

"The story of the early years of Charity Lodge is but little more than tradition. Upon two occasions fire found the records unprotected, and each time some of them became part of the ashes of the building wherein the lodge had its home. The first of these fires occurred in 1860. The lodge room was then in a building that stood where the Washington National Bank now is. This time most of the lodge papers were saved. But six years later the disastrous Commercial row fire came, and the entire belongings of the lodge, together with the records, dissolved in smoke. The most serious loss to the lodge as a result of the second fire was the loss of the records which contained the proceedings of the early meetings. The pecuniary loss was trifling, as compared with the disappearance of these records.

"When it is known that the organization of Charity Lodge antedated by a score of years the time when the oldest member of this order now living first obtained the right to sit in the lodge of master Masons, the difficulty of obtaining any definite information will be readily understood. There is no scratch of a pen, except the meager statements which appear in the reports of the grand lodge, and a small blank book, used in early times to keep an account of the amounts due from members, that gives any light on the affairs of the lodge for the first thirty-five years of its life. The grand lodge reports state that an application was made on the 3d of October, 1826, for a charter for Charity Lodge, located at Washington, Indiana, and then working under a dispensation. The application was granted, the issue of a charter was authorized, and the number assigned to the lodge was thirty. The order also provided that the three principal officers of the new lodge should be, Joseph Warner, worshipful master; Nathan Bascom, senior warden; Cornelius Berkshire, junior warden.

"In 1833 an officer of the grand lodge visited Charity Lodge and found that, owing to the removal from this place of some of the original members, the organization had been suffered to go down, and no meetings had been held for many months. This officer seized the charter and lodge effects and returned them to the grand lodge, which body sustained his action. Matters remained in this condition for nearly ten years. In 1842, Joseph Warren, who was the first worshipful master, appeared before the grand lodge and asked for the second dispensation, which was granted. The following year the charter of the Washington lodge was restored, the old number and name given it, and Charity Lodge No. 30 again had an existence.

"The new organization began with the same worshipful master, Joseph Warren, who presided over the first lodge. The senior warden was James Calhoun, and the junior warden was Stephen Belding. The little blank book, all that is left of the early records, shows that the lodge first began working under a dispensation some time in the fall of 1825. The first name on that book is that of Joseph Warner. Other names in the book appear in the following order: Nathan Bascom, Cornelius Berkshire, James G. Read, William McCormick, John Whallon, James Calhoun, Rawley Scott, all under date of 1825. In 1826 the following names were entered: George A. Waller, Armory Kinney, James Whitehead, William H. Routt and Philip Barton; in 1827, Stephen Belding, William Quigley, William Forster, William Veale, Rev. Hezekiah Holland, John Van Trees and Michael Ruport; in 1828, Rev. Hiram Hunter, Henry Dubois and Thomas Leming; in 1829, William Kelty.

"From the time of the reorganization the lodge continued to grow in numbers, slowly and steadily. Each year saw it more closely interwoven with the social fabric of Washington. In 1864, Joseph Cruse, a wealthy member of the lodge, died, and in his will bequeathed to the lodge nearly all his estate, consisting of valuable town lots and a sum of money. The aggregate gift was nearly eighteen thousand dollars. The money was used for the erection of the present building, which was completed in 1868. It was at first two stories; a third story was added in 1888."

The present membership of Charity Lodge is three hundred and thirteen. The present officers are: Frank McGehee, worshipful master; Wallace Walker, senior warden; Charles F. Cochran, junior warden; Elisha L. Hatfield, treasurer; Henry Aikman, secretary; Charles A. Raney, senior deacon; Harry L. Alberty, junior deacon; John T. Dougherty, senior steward; James W. Mattingly, junior steward; William S. Waller, tyler; trustees, Milton S. Hastings, Clyde B. Kellar and Charles H. Yenne.

ALLIED ORGANIZATIONS.

Washington Chapter No. 92, Royal Arch Masons, was organized on April 21, 1875. It has a present membership of one hundred and ninety-one.

Washington Council No. 67, Royal and Select Masters, was organized on April 27, 1895. Present membership, seventy-one.

Washington Commandery No. 33, Knights Templar, was organized on April 19, 1890. Present membership, one hundred.

Washington Chapter No. 210, Order of the Eastern Star, was organized on April 28, 1898. Present membership, two hundred and fifty.

INDEPENDENT ORDER OF ODD FELLOWS.

Liverpool Lodge No. 110, Independent Order of Odd Fellows, at Washington, was organized on July 8, 1852, with the following charter members: Thomas A. Baker, E. Hitchcock, John Becket, Charles Childs and H. Robb. The first officers of the lodge were: Charles Childs, noble grand; Thomas Baker, vice-grand; William Helphenstine, recording secretary; John Beckett, treasurer. Others who were identified with the early organization of the lodge were: Oliver Taylor, W. K. Edwards, John Dixon, P. B. McChesney, P. H. Hackleman, S. Meredith, George L. Gibbs, Gamaliel Taylor, Charles Fravel, John Kelley, George Brown, Taylor W. Webster, Samuel W. Smith, I. H. Stanley, Marshall Sexton, Edwin M. Finch, J. Z. McLaughlin, R. N. Graham, A. H. Mathews, Daniel Moss, John M. Turner, J. R. Moverod, J. P. Chapmen, W. B. Moffitt and George B. Jocelyn.

There are three members of the lodge now living who have been members of the order for over fifty years, namely: Stansel Cosby, A. E. Johnson and W. P. Ellis. The present membership of Liverpool Lodge is two hundred and seventy-five. The present officers are: G. Klingingsmith, noble grand; Clay McCormick, vice-grand; Arthur Greenwood, recording secretary; E. E. Horral, financial secretary; W. P. Ellis, treasurer.

A few years ago the lodge purchased a piece of residence property on East Main street, which was remodeled and made into a beautiful home for the order, at a cost of about fifteen thousand dollars. This home is provided with all modern conveniences, with a commodious hall for lodge metings, reading rooms, dining rooms and appointments for social gatherings. Oak Grove cemetery, west of the city, is the property of Liverpool Lodge. The ground for the cemetery was purchased in 1870 and contained twenty acres. Thirteen additional acres were purchased by the lodge in 1915, which will be improved and platted for cemetery purposes. The affairs of the cemetery are under the present management of George E. Reeves, president; Dr. G. W. Russell, secretary; J. W. Dillard, board of trustees.

The Independent Order of Odd Fellows is represented by lodges at Elnora, Plainfield, Montgomery, Odon and other places in the county.

KNIGHTS OF PYTHIAS.

Pythagorean Lodge No. 118, Knights of Pythias, was organized on May 20, 1884, by a delegation from Dioscuri Lodge, of Vincennes. The charter members were: L. P. Beitman, H. H. Hyatt, Charles P. Scudder, C. S. Slayback, A. C. Barber, C. H. Jones, Harry Bray, J. W. Clark, George Geeting, O. E. Bon Durant, John T. Neal, Nathan Beitman, W. F. Hoffman, Gus Levy, Isadore Beitman, W. W. Marmaduke, Frank Colyer, Louis Hess, Clifford Markle, E. J. Yeager and J. P. Mathew.

Following are the names of the first officers: L. P. Beitman, past chancellor; H. H. Hyatt, chancellor commander; Charles P. Scudder, vice-chancellor; C. S. Slayback, prelate; A. C. Barber, keeper of records and seal; C. H. Jones, master of exchequer; Harry Bray, master of finance; J. W. Clark, master at arms.

The lodge started out with a large and active roll of members and has maintained a steady growth during all the years since. The present membership is two hundred and thirty-four, all active and working for the good of the order. The lodge does not own any building, but has a commodious and well-appointed hall in which meetings are held. The regular meetings are characterized by marked interest and efficiency; the method and manner of work conferred has received favorable comment by competent critics.

Pythagorean Lodge was never in a more prosperous condition than at present. Following are the names of the present officers: Walter Wallace, chancellor commander; C. J. Burris, vice-chancellor; H. W. Palmer, prelate; Willis Hoddinott, keeper of records and seal; John E. Ketchum, master of exchequer; W. W. McCarty, master of finance; Charles Connaughton, master at arms; Earl McCafferty, inner guard; W. E. Brennan, outer guard; James A. Colbert, A. C. Wise and O. M. Vance, trustees.

ANCIENT ORDER OF HIBERNIANS.

Division No. 1, Ancient Order of Hibernians, was organized on St. Patrick's day, in the year 1870, by the county delegates of Clay county. The first meetings were held in the old city hall building, on East Second street, opposite Cabel & Company's coal office. This division was the second Ancient Order of Hibernians lodge instituted in the state of Indiana, the first division in the state being instituted at Brazil, in Clay county. The object of the society is to teach patriotism and devotion to the Stars and Stripes, and to foster a love for the "Little Green Island, far o'er the Sea." The society also extends to its members praiseworthy benevolent features, by paying generous sick and funeral benefits.

The first officers were: James E. Maher, county delegate; P. T. Garaghan, president; Patrick Grimes, vice-president; Martin Cahill, general secretary; Eugene O'Brien, assistant secretary; Stephen Maloney, treasurer.

Division No. 1 now has seventy members in good standing, has a strong bank account and is in a prosperous condition in every way. The meetings are held on the fourth Sunday afternoon of each month in the Knights of Columbus hall.

KNIGHTS OF COLUMBUS.

Washington Council No. 630, Knights of Columbus, was instituted on Sunday, February 9, 1902, under the direction of William J. Mooney, territorial deputy supreme knight, of Indianapolis, a former Washington citizen. The first members of the Knights of Columbus order in Washington, prior to the institution of the local lodge, were: Rev. John W. Doyle, Julius P. McGrayel, John M. Costello, John A. Sinnott and Charles A. Kidwell, who received their degree in Evansville, Sunday, April 19, 1901, at the institution of Council No. 565; also A. J. Padgett and Anthony Kocher, Jr., who were initiated with the second class of candidates into Council No. 541, in the city of Terre Haute.

The installation ceremonies of February 9, 1902, were held in the spacious lodge room of the Independent Order of Odd Fellows, corner of Main and East Third streets. The first business meetings of Council No. 630 were held in the Masonic temple. In the year of 1907 the beautiful three-story building of brick and stone, at the southwest corner of Fourth and East Main streets, was completed. Ground was first broken for the erection of this structure, July 5, 1906. The purchase price of this building site was eight thousand dollars; the contract price for the erection of the building was two thousand six hundred dollars, to which five thousand dollars has been since added for changes and improvements. The building is well heated, lighted and ventilated, particular attention having been given to comfort and sanitary details. The dimensions of the building are sixty feet frontage on Main street and one hundred feet south on Fourth street. The building covers the entire lot owned by the order. There are three large store rooms on the first floor of the building. The second floor comprises thirteen well-appointed suites of office rooms, the third floor being used as the council home. Many educational entertainments of various kinds have been given here, to which the general public is always invited.

The first officers of Washington Council were: Arnold J. Padgett, grand knight; Thomas P. Walsh, deputy grand knight; Matthew F. Burke, chancellor; Albert M. Kocher, warden; Julius P. McGrayel, financial secretary; Charles A. Kidwell, recorder; Cyril J. Ward, treasurer; John W. McCarty, lecturer; Rev. John W. Doyle, chaplain; Joseph J. Keller, organist; John P. Cavanaugh, Thomas R. Walker and John Dosch, trustees.

The present membership of the local council is sixty insurance members and one hundred and forty associate members. The regular meetings are held every Tuesday night at eight o'clock.

CHAPTER XVII.

PATRIOTIC ORDERS OF DAVIESS COUNTY.

At the close of the Civil War the armies that had fought in that war to its successful conclusion, were disbanded and the soldiers returned to their several homes and resumed the vocations of civil life. But the fraternal tie that had been welded in the fire of battle was not severed by the disbanding of companies and regiments. There was a spirit of comradeship infused in the hearts and lives of those who had touched elbows in the fire and smoke of battle, and who shared the privations and hardships of the camp and the weary march—a spirit that was not dispelled by the disbanding of companies and the laying aside of military equipments. There was a desire to maintain this fraternity and comradeship, and this desire soon found expression in a movement for an organization of veterans to accomplish this purpose. Many organizations of companies and regiments were formed and reunions held in various localities, and the enjoyment found by comrades in these associations suggested a larger and more permanent organization of state and national character. From this suggestion the Grand Army of the Republic had its origin.

ORGANIZATION OF THE GRAND ARMY.

The founding of the Grand Army of the Republic was primarily due to Dr. B. F. Stephenson and Chaplain W. J. Rutledge, of the Fourteenth Illinois Infantry, who, in February, 1864, conceived the idea of its formation. Doctor Stephenson lived in Springfield, Illinois, and enlisted on May 7, 1862, serving as surgeon of his regiment until June 24, 1864, when he was mustered out. Doctor Stephenson conceived the plan of such an organization while he was still in the service. His idea was to unite the soldiers who fought in the battles of the Union into a grand brotherhood, which would be as effective in preserving the peace of the nation as the Union army had been in the prosecution of the war; to maintain and strengthen the fraternal feelings of the soldiers who united to suppress the rebellion; to perpetuate the memory of those who had died in the cause, and to lend assistance to the needy and to the widows and orphans of soldiers.

Doctor Stephenson foresaw the magnitude of the organization he had in mind and spent about two years in working out plans and drafting the ritual. In this work he had the counsel and assistance of a number of his comrades and others who were in sympathy with the movement. Among the latter, Governor Morton, of Indiana, was actively interested and prominently identified with the preliminary work. It is related by some who were on the "inside," that Governor Morton had much to do with the preparation of the manuscript for the rules and regulations, and that it was through his instrumentality that these were printed and put into shape for effective use. It is also a matter of history that the ritual and rules and regulations were first used in Indiana for the muster and organization of posts, and that the first department organized was the department of Indiana. This was in 1866, and from that year dates the beginning of the Grand Army of the Republic.

ORGANIZATION OF POSTS IN INDIANA.

It was sometime in the early part of 1867 before there was an attempt to organize a post of the Grand Army of the Republic in Washington, although there had been a sort of informal organization of the Grand Army prior to that time. This informal organization was before the adoption of the ritual and the rules and regulations, and there was very little ceremony connected with the initiation of members. There was simply the giving of the established "grip" and countersign, the several members subscribing to an obligation. Under the prescribed forms of initiation of the first ritual there was nothing lacking in the way of ceremony. The paraphernalia and necessary appointments for the initiation ceremony were of a character to make one's hair stand on end, if he should unexpectedly meet the outfit on a dark night, all alone. Part of the outfit was an old-fashioned gable-roofed coffin, with a grinning skeleton lying therein, and grave-digger's tools conveniently near. The candidate was led to this outfit, blindfolded, and, kneeling down, was required to take a solemn obligation of loyalty. The consequence of the violation of this pledge was revealed when the blind was removed and he caught a glimpse of the suggestive scene before him. The provisions for the muster of recruits under the old ritual were intended to be profoundly solemn and impressively "scary."

The first muster of recruits and the organization of posts under the old ritual was conducted under the administration of Gen. Nathan Kimball, then department commander of Indiana. There was quite an interest in the organization of Grand Army posts in Indiana, and in other states about this time, and the membership of the order increased rapidly during the years

1867 and 1868. But there was a decline in the years following and the organization was on the wane. This was due, largely, to politics, which was a predominant feature of the organization at that time, and it was intended to be such by those who were chiefly instrumental in forming the constitution and ritual. The organization, in fact, was largely in control of some who were prominently identified with one of the leading political parties of that time, and it easily degenerated into a political machine, operated and controlled by designing politicians for selfish purposes. Of course, such an organization would find no favor among soldiers who were inclined to affiliate with any other political party; and, in fact, it was not in the favor of many whose sympathies and affiliations were with the party largely controlling the organization. A secret political organization, however worthy its purpose, or however worthy its individual membership, can never be a permanent success; or, at least, should not be a success, nor have approval of true, loyal American citizens.

A few of the posts in this and in other states maintained their organization during these years of decline, and these formed the nucleus for the greater Grand Army of the Republic that the world knows today. In the meantime, wiser heads gathered in council and a new constitution and ritual, and new regulations, were prepared, by which politics was absolutely prohibited in the order. Fraternity, charity and loyalty were made the cardinal principles, the "broad foundation stone, on which the order rests." These new rules and regulations, with the revised and more sensible ritual, were adopted in the early seventies. These met with the approval of the intelligent soldier citizens, and from that time the Grand Army of the Republic took on new life. It increased in membership rapidly from that time until it became the greatest semi-military organization the world has ever known, commanding the respect of citizens throughout this and other lands, regardless of party, creed or nationality.

ORGANIZATION OF THE POST IN WASHINGTON.

The organization of a Grand Army post in Washington under the old ritual was affected by the unwise policy that controlled the order, and did not long endure. It was several years after the adoption of the new ritual, and the new rules and regulations, before definite steps were taken to revive the interest in the organization there. There was one duty, however, that the veterans of the Civil War had assumed that was not permitted to fall into decline. That was the custom of decorating with flowers the graves of deceased comrades on the 30th of May, each year. This custom was established the year after the close of the war and it has been sacredly observed by the veterans and their friends in Washington. Without some organization to take charge of arrangements for this observance, the Memorial Day exercises were not always as appropriate as the occasion required, and this, no doubt, had something to do with turning the thoughts of the veterans to the necessity of reorganizing the Grand Army post. It was immediately following Memorial Day, 1882, that this thought took definite form. Application was made to Gen. James R. Carnahan, then department commander of Indiana, for a charter for the organization of a Grand Army post at Washington. This application was approved and an order given for the muster of the post, a mustering officer being detailed for that purpose. Accordingly, on June 1, 1882, the organization was effected with twenty-three charter members, under the official title of "Gerber Post No. 72, Department of Indiana, Grand Army of the Republic." Following are the names of charter members: W. P. Ellis, J. L. Moore, P. B. Kelenberger, J. G. Miller, Joseph Bogner, John A. Scudder, D. V. Creager, J. W. Ramsey, S. R. McCormick, Rev. R. E. Hawley, Joseph T. Kendall, H. H. Hyatt, S. F. Horrall, Thomas C. Meredith, C. P. Van Trees, Edward Kennedy, Joseph Pierce, William Cox, J. H. Achors, John W. Creager, J. F. Herndon, Dennis Bun and J. M. Achor.

The first officers of the post were: W. P. Ellis, post commander; J. L. Moore, senior vice-commander; P. B. Kelenberger, junior vice-commander; J. G. Miller, quartermaster; Joseph Bogner, officer of the day; John A. Scudder, surgeon; D. V. Creager, officer of the guard; J. W. Ramsey, adjutant; S. R. McCormick, sergeant-major; Rev. R. E. Hawley, chaplain, and Joseph T. Kendall, quartermaster-sergeant.

The following have served as post commanders since the organization, eight or nine of those named having served for two or more terms, each: W. P. Ellis, Joseph Bogner, J. W. Ramsey, George W. Moran, James W. Barr, Edward Kenney, J. F. Herndon, Zack Jones, W. N. Guy, William H. Springer, Philip Hart, Aikman Carnahan, J. W. Kellems, John D. Berry, Joseph S. Streeter, Frank Wise, George W. Snider, John Sullivan, O. H. Brann, William H. Waller, Henry Bell, Charles E. Peek and John H. Davis.

The officers of the post for 1915 are: John H. Davis, commander; William H. Faris, senior vice-commander; William Wirts, junior vice-commander; Thomas Harris, officer of the day; Francis Holtzman, surgeon; Charles E. Peek, chaplain; W. P. Ellis, quartermaster; Joseph Church, officer of the guard; Frank A. Evans, adjutant; A. E. Johnson, sergeant-major, and Benjamin Tolson, quartermaster-sergeant.

Under the rules of the Grand Army of the Republic, posts may select names only from persons deceased, if individual names are chosen for the official title of posts. Names of distinguished soldiers of the Civil War are favorite selections for names of posts, but only one post in each department is permitted to use the same name, and that must be by the approval of the department commander. Names of posts can be changed only by the same approval. On the death of General Grant, in 1885, there was a great rivalry of posts in each department to have their name changed to that of this distinguished soldier. By the prompt action of J. W. Ramsey, who was post commander at that time, the Washington post secured this honor. On receiving news of General Grant's death, Post Commander Ramsey immediately wired Department Commander Foster, at Fort Wayne, requesting that Gerber Post be changed to U. S. Grant Post, which request was granted. Ramsey's telegram was the first of scores of others making like request.

OTHER POSTS IN DAVIESS COUNTY.

A number of other posts have been organized in the county. In almost every town and village, where there was a sufficient number of veterans of the Civil War, a Grand Army post was organized and the organization flourished for a time. But death and the infirmities of age have marked the passing years of the veterans, and so depleted their ranks that most of these smaller posts have given up their charters and disbanded. Some still retain their organization and charter, but do not hold meetings regularly. Among the posts organized in the county are the following: J. W. Thornburg Post No. 474, at Odon, organized August 16, 1886, with the following charter members: H. C. Correll, W. H. Kinnaman, G. W. Critchlow, J. D. Laughlin, H. N. Correll, B. R. Sears, Michael Wallick, Harrison Browning, Eli Helm, G. D. Abraham, Samuel Dunlap, William McBarron, A. K. Lane, Z. V. Garten, John Hubbard, James P. Taylor, William H. Briner, John Stout, John O'Dell, S. L. Ketcham, William Hubbard, Harvey Manning, William Gadberry, D. L. McCarter, Jacob Flinn, G. D. Elsivie, Elias Clark, John B. Phipps, John B. Williams, James Payne, Thomas Wadsworth, Clement Dunlap, William J. Slimp, B. F. McFarland, John Hitchcock, James S. Kinnaman, William Cox. Among those who have served as commanders of the J. W. Thornburg Post are the following: G. M. Critchlow, T. M. Brown, Aaron Hattery, J. P. Taylor.

Plainview Post No. 532, Grand Army of the Republic, was organized at Plainville, May 3, 1892. The present membership is fourteen. Meetings are held irregularly. David H. Dyer, Allen Daugherty and D. V. Ellis are among those who have served as commanders of this post.

M. B. Cutler Post No. 537, at Elnora, was organized in 1892, with a good list of charter members. The following have served as commanders of this post: John Edmondson, Milton Farris, William Slimp and W. New. The post's regular time of meeting is the first Saturday evening of each month.

McCarty Post No. 251, at Alfordsville, was organized in 1886. This post has a good membership and was in a flourishing condition for several years. The name does not appear in the Grand Army roster for 1914, and it is presumed that the charter had been surrendered and the post disbanded prior to that time. Among those who have served as commanders of McCarty post are the following: Alfred Webber, Joseph Arvin, G. W. Cochran, William Patrick, John G. Leming, Philip Scales and James W. Gilley.

LADIES OF THE GRAND ARMY OF THE REPUBLIC.

U. S. Grant Circle No. 19, Ladies of the Grand Army of the Republic, was organized on July 24, 1897, by Mattie C. Smith, of Lafayette, Indiana. This organization is allied with the U. S. Grant Post, Grand Army of the Republic, and its object is to work in harmony with the Grand Army in the relief of needy and distressed soldiers of the Civil War, and the families of those deceased, and to teach patriotism in the public schools and inculcate a spirit of patriotism and devotion to the flag among the people of the community. Eligibility to membership in this order is based on relationship to a soldier or sailor who had honorable service in the Civil War—a wife, or daughter, or lineal female descendant of a veteran. Following are the names of the charter members of U. S. Grant Circle: Mrs. Sudie P. Dowden, Mrs. Rebecca E. Hollis, Mrs. Hattie Schurz, Mrs. Mary C. Fitts, Mrs. Fay E. Wagoner, Mrs. Tillie Jacobs, Mrs. Clara Carnahan, Mrs. Margaret Gilley, Mrs. Lavinia Lemmon, Mrs. Eliza Ramsey, Mrs. Mary E. Gold, Mrs. Gertie Tilston, Mrs. S. S. Boaz, Mrs. Harriet Summers, Mrs. Edward Kennedy, Miss Maud Clark, Miss Mattie Roberson, Miss Edith Waller, Mrs. Maggie Berry, Mrs. Hugh Sullivan, Mrs. Mary E. Fullerton, Mrs. Emma Nixon, Miss Etta Blackwell.

The first officers were: Mrs. Mary C. Fitts, president; Mrs. Rebecca E. Hollis, secretary; Mrs. Lavina Lemmon, treasurer.

The present officers are: Mrs. Mary Ellis, president; Mrs. Sarepta Summers, senior vice-president; Mrs. Belle Farris, junior vice-president; Mrs. Sarah Jackman, chaplain; Mrs. Agnes Dove, conductress; Mrs. Harriet Burris, assistant conductress; Mrs. Fannie Bruner, guard; Hattie Eslinger, assistant guard; Mrs. Vina Truelove, patriotic instructor; Mrs. Etta Dearmin, treasurer; Mrs. Margaret Padgett, secretary.

The membership of the order on May 20, 1915, was one hundred and sixty-seven. This includes forty-one veterans and eleven sons of veterans, who are entitled to honorary membership in the order.

SOCIETY OF THE DAUGHTERS OF THE AMERICAN REVOLUTION.

The Society of the Daughters of the American Revolution was organized in Washington, D. C., October 11, 1890. It has for its object the perpetuation of the memory of those who achieved American independence, the collection of relics of earlier American days, the protection of historical spots, the encouragement of historical research in relation to the Revolution, and the preservation of the records of individual services of Revolutionary soldiers and patriots. The National Society of the Daughters of the American Revolution has members in every state, and in nearly every territory of the United States. The society as a whole has a charter granted by the Congress of the United States; a national constitution, a national treasury, and the governing body, the continental congress. Formal organization of the society occurred on October 11, 1890, and the dark blue and white of Washington's staff was chosen for the society's colors. The design of a golden spinning-wheel was chosen for a badge. The first chapter was formed in Chicago, Illinois.

ORGANIZATION OF THE WASHINGTON CHAPTER.

While the matter of organizing a chapter of the Daughters of the American Revolution in Washington was under consideration by those who would be eligible to membership for some time prior to 1906, it was not until the latter part of that year that definite action towards an organization was taken. In response to a call, several of those who were members of the order in other chapters held a meeting and decided to proceed to the organization of a local chapter. In accordance with this decision an organization was effected on October 2, 1906, under the name of White River Chapter No. 429, Daughters of the American Revolution. Following are the names of the charter members: Mrs. Matilda Scudder, Mrs. Elva Bon Durant Cabel, Miss L. Josephine Chapman, Mrs. Alice Evans Corning, Mrs. Elizabeth Scudder Hall, Miss Pansy Horrall, Mrs. Ella C. Peek McKernan, Mrs. Pearle Horrall Redford, Miss Margaret Ellen Scudder, Miss Lucretia Wood, Mrs. Mary C. Shirley, Mrs. Matilda Boyd.

The organization was perfected by the election of the following to serve as the first officers of the society: Mrs. Elva Bon Durant Cabel, regent; Mrs. Alice Corning, vice-regent; Mrs. Mary C. Shirley, recording secretary; Miss L. J. Chapman, corresponding secretary; Mrs. Matilda Boyd, registrar; Mrs. Elizabeth S. Hall, treasurer; Miss Pansy Horrall, historian.

Following are the names of those who have served as regents since the organization: Mrs. Elva Bon Durant Cabel, Mrs. Mary C. Shirley, Mrs. Mary F. Borders, Mrs. Stella McCafferty, Mrs. Elizabeth Bogner.

In the line of special work done by the chapter, the purchase of the old Lashly cemetery and the placing of markers at the graves of Revolutionary soldiers buried therein, are notable examples. One of these graves is that of George Lashly, a soldier in the Revolutionary War, after whom the cemetery took its name. The chapter has made contributions of money to the poor fund of the city and to the county hospital fund. It also has done a commendable, patriotic work in the presentation of silk flags to all the primary departments of the city public schools. The regular meetings of the chapter are on the first Friday of each month. It has a membership of thirty-seven, all actively interested in the work of the chapter and in the increase of its membership and usefulness. The regular work of the chapter is along historical lines, a program of topics for historical research for each meeting being outlined in their year-book.

The requirements for establishing eligibility to membership in the Daughters of the American Revolution, as prescribed by the rules of the national organization, are very strict. All applications for membership must be submitted to the national authority, and evidence of the eligibility of the applicant must be established by authentic documentary proof that the applicant is a lineal descendant of a Revolutionary soldier, or one who rendered patriotic service in that war. Traditional or hearsay evidence is not accepted as proof of eligibility. Because of the exact requirements to establish proof of their lineage, those whose applications have passed approval, and eligibility to membership verified, may be justified in feeling a considerable degree of pride in the inherited honor.

LINEAGE OF MEMBERS OF WHITE RIVER CHAPTER.

Following is a list of members of White River chapter, and the Revolutionary ancestor of each, by whom eligibility to membership is established: Mrs. Lillian Armstrong, descendant of Lieut.-Col. James Johnson, of Pennsylvania; Mrs. Elizabeth Bogner, descendant of Lieut. Henry Chase, of Massachusetts; Mrs. Matilda Boyd, descendant of Col. Nathaniel Scudder, of New Jersey; Mrs. Mary Borders, descendant of Sergt. John Scott, of South Carolina; Mrs. Elva B. Cabel, descendant of Lieut. Josiah Tanner and Corporal Darby McGannon, of South Carolina; Miss Josephine Chapman, descendant of Private John Wallace, of Virginia; Mrs. Mary K. Chapman, descendant of Lieut.-Col. George Wilson, of Pennsylvania; Mrs. Alice Corning, descendant of Private Joseph Neely, of Pennsylvania; Mrs. Elizabeth Hall, descendant of Col. Nathaniel Scudder, of New Jersey; Miss Pansy Horrall, descendant of Private John Wallace, of Virginia; Mrs. Nancy Horrall, descendant of Lieut.-Col. James Johnson, of Pennsylvania; Mrs. Anna Lycan, descendant of Captain Andrew Mann and Captain James Martin, of Pennsylvania; Mrs. Stella McCafferty, descendant of Sergeant John Waller, of Virginia; Mrs. Mary McKernan, descendant of Private John Wallace, of Virginia; Mrs. Ella Peek, descendant of Private John Wallace, of Virginia; Mrs. Pearl Redford, descendant of Private John Wallace, of Virginia; Mrs. Harriet Radspinner, descendant of Private Asa Shattuck, of Massachusetts; Mrs. Grace Rodarmel, descendant of Lieut.-Col. George Wilson, of Pennsylvania; Mrs. Cleo Reed, descendant of Lieut.-Col. James Johnson, of Pennsylvania; Mrs. Mary Shirley, descendant of Samuel Dakin, minute-man and sergeant, Private Daniel Brooks, Capt. Daniel Chute, Capt. Joseph Poore, James Chute, minute-man, all of Massachusetts; Miss Margaret E. Scudder, descendant of Col. Nathaniel Scudder, of New Jersey; Mrs. Sarepta Summers, descendant of Lieut.-Col. James Johnson, of Pennsylvania; Mrs. Lucretia Bonham, descendant of Surgeon John Anderson Scudder, of New Jersey; Mrs. Elizabeth William, descendant of Private John Wallace, of Virginia; Mrs. Charles Seifrit, Mrs. Harry Hyatt, Mrs. Joseph Graham, Miss Mary Waller, all descendants of Sergeant John Waller, of Virginia; Mrs. Edith Boultman, descendant of Lieut.-Col. James Johnson, of Pennsylvania; Mrs. Jennie Lemmon, Miss Anna Lemmon and Miss Edith Lemmon, all descendants of Sergeant Elijah Hammond, private secretary to Gen. George Washington; Miss Laura Davis, descendant of Spencer Lacey, drummer, of Delaware; and Mrs. Lucia Crawford, descendant of Lieut. Henry Chase, of Massachusetts.

CHAPTER XVIII.

TOWNSHIPS OF DAVIESS COUNTY.

VEALE TOWNSHIP.

Veale township was named after James Veale, who was one of the most prominent of the first settlers. He came to the territory now within the boundaries of this township about 1807-08. Other settlers who came about the same time were Parmenius Palmer, Christopher Coleman, a Mr. Lett and three sons, William and Elijah Chapman, Moses Morgan, Thomas Wallace and a Mr. Goodwin.

Veale township was organized on May 12, 1817. Its location is in the southwestern part of Daviess county, bounded on the west by Knox county and on the south by Pike county, the west fork of White river being the boundary line on the west, and the east fork of White river the boundary on the south. The junction of these two streams is at the extreme southwest point of Veale township. The first saw-mill established in Daviess county was built and operated by Eli Chapman, on Veale creek, in this township. Veale township was also the location of several other pioneer industries in Daviess county. In its primitive state the land in Veale township was heavily timbered with the finest quality of oak, poplar and walnut. It required no small amount of labor to clear the land and bring it into a state of cultivation, the timber being considered an incumbrance then. It would be considered of great value now. There are some sections of the township in which the land is hilly and broken, but part of it is fertile and productive. A good deal of the river bottom land is highly productive. In 1910 Veale township had a population of one thousand fifty-nine. Stanton Barber is the present township trustee.

FIRST DISTILLERY IN DAVIESS COUNTY.

The first distillery in Daviess county was erected by "Obe" Flint in 1810. Like most of the other early industries hereabout, this institution was established in Veale township, two miles south of Maysville. Prior to this there were various kinds of stills brought into use. These were generally known as "teapot" stills and were of simple construction and limited capacity. The capacity, however, was sufficient to supply home consumption. Liquor in the early days was a staple article, as much a family necessity as bread and meat. It was a favorite remedy for the various ills that were prevalent, chief of which were malaria and snake bite. For the latter the whisky was taken straight; for the former it was usually administered in the form of bitters.

The Flint distillery, with larger capacity, was necessary to meet the greater demands on account of the increase of the early settlers. Even with this increase of capacity for the manufacture of whisky, the Flint distillery found a local market for all of its product for several years. The home consumption of the early settlers kept pace with the increase of production. It was not before 1836 or 1838, that more whisky was made than the early settlers needed for home consumption.

WASHINGTON TOWNSHIP.

Washington township was established on May 12, 1817. It was organized by the county commissioners among the first business transacted after the organization of the county. The township comprised a large part of the territory of the county, as first established. The exact boundary lines are not very definite, as the description appears on the commissioners' record. The description reads: "Beginning at range 7 and 8, township 2, sections 7 and 8, running thence north with section line, including all the inhabitance [inhabitants] north of beginning line." However, this description was sufficiently definite to serve the purpose intended, and it is not probable that the "inhabitance" had any uncertainty as to whether or not they were included in Washington township.

Prior to the organization of Washington township a small village had been established within its boundary. This village was called Liverpool and the design, in the organization of the county, was to make this the county seat. Further details as to how Liverpool lost its identity, by being merged into the town of Washington, are set out in another chapter. The population of Washington township in 1910, including the city of Washington, was eleven thousand four hundred and four. The present trustee is James E. Gilley.

(18)

REEVE TOWNSHIP.

Reeve township was another division of the county established at the first meeting of the county commissioners. The boundary lines of this township, as described on the records, follow: "Beginning at Aikman's creek and running up said creek to the head, thence on a direct line to the mouth of Lick creek, thence down White river to the place of beginning."

This township took its name from the first settler in that territory, Joshua Reeve. He came from South Carolina to this part of Daviess county in 1808. He is said to have been an active and enterprising pioneer. He built a cabin in the forest, his neighbors being wild cats, bears, panthers, and other denizens of the wild woods around. Vincennes was the nearest point from which Mr. Reeve could obtain needed supplies, and where he could get in touch with people of his own race. Having frequent occasions to visit that place, the journey being made through the unbroken forest, Mr. Reeve blazed a track through the woods from his home to Vincennes. This track was afterward established as a main thoroughfare between these two points, and is now much traveled by the automobile.

James and William Alford came into this territory a year or two after Mr. Reeve. Their advent was about 1809 or 1810. About a year later James and Robert Gilley, and Peter Helphenstine joined this pioneer colony. "Old Bill" Allen, as he was called, came about 1812, and a Mr. Kelso came along soon afterward. The first land entry in the territory comprising the township was made by Joshua Reeve, April 13, 1812, and consisted of the north fraction of section 23, township 1, range 5. The next entry was made by Trice Stafford in 1814; two others in 1815, by Jacob Reeder and William Ballow, respectively. The following year entries were made by Joseph Hays, Isaac Hollingsworth, Edward Adams, Caleb Brock and Henry Foster. From this time on, the settlement increased rapidly and land entries were more frequent. The township has since kept pace with the rest of the county in the general march of progress.

Reeve township had a population of one thousand five hundred and seventy-six in 1910. David S. Jackman, at Alfordsville, is the present township trustee.

BARR TOWNSHIP.

Barr township was organized on August 4, 1819, the territory being taken from the east part of Washington township. Among the early settlers of this township were Hugh Barr, after whom the township was named.

BARR TOWNSHIP SCHOOL

Other early settlers were James Montgomery, William Dant, Nicholas Kidwell, Joseph Miller, John Shepard, John Allison, John R. Kendall and William Williams. These, and most of the first settlers, came from Kentucky. Williams prairie was named after William Williams, the first settler in that section, about two miles west of Montgomery. Barr township is the largest in the county, containing seventy-two sections, and the largest number of early land entries were made in this township. The splendid farming lands of Barr township have been developed by the industry and energy of the early settlers and those who have succeeded them. The township is not only endowed with a wealth of agricultural resources, but is underlaid with an inexhaustible bed of the finest coal. Some of the best coal in the state comes from mines located in Barr township.

Including Cannelburg and Montgomery, Barr township had a population of three thousand three hundred and thirty-five in 1910. The trustee is Daniel E. Carlin, at Montgomery.

AMUSEMENTS OF THE PIONEERS.

A story related by old inhabitants with a memory dating back to early times, illustrates some of the ways the pioneers had of amusing themselves, in the intervals of clearing the woods and mauling rails. This story relates to a barbecue held at the house of "Billy" Williams, one of the early settlers of Barr township, in 1820. The story has appeared in print before, but it is worthy of reproduction and preservation in the history of Barr township.

It is related that "Billy" Williams was the owner of a pet bear, and it was his boast that this bear could make a successful fight against all the dogs in the neighborhood. So confirmed was he in that belief that he made an open challenge to the owners of dogs in all the country around to come with their dogs on a certain day and he would show what the bear could do with the bunch. The challenge was accepted and about twenty or thirty dogs were gathered for the contest. The dogs were of all breeds, some of them champions in every fight in which they had engaged. The owners thought it would be rare sport to see how quickly either one of these champions could "chaw up" "Billy" Williams's pet bear. It was fierce and exciting while it lasted. But it didn't last long. Some of the champion dogs, of which their owners boasted, did not stay to see the finish. With an apparently instinctive realization that discretion is the better part of valor, they stuck their tails between their legs and went howling through the woods. One sight of that belligerent bear was enough. Other dogs, with more courage and less discretion, entered into the fight. One after another was laid out and the bear was victorious.

Of course "Billy" Williams was proud of his bear, but his pride did not overcome his sympathy for the humiliated owners of the mutilated and discredited dogs. To make things even, he proposed to have a barbecue and make a sacrificial offering of his champion pet bear. This generous offer was gladly accepted. The bear was killed, roasted and eaten by the forty or fifty people who had come to see the contest.

BOGARD TOWNSHIP.

A section comprising "all that part of Daviess county lying north of Prairie creek," was, by order of the board of county commissioners, May 9, 1820, organized in a township and given the name of Bogard. Among the first settlers in this township was Elias Myers, who came from North Carolina in 1816. The record shows that he made an entry of land in 1817, his entry being one-half of section 30, township 4, range 6. Others who came about the same time were Joseph Summers, John Benefield, John Anderson, John Burch, Smallwood Canwood and David Killion. The record shows that these all made land entries during the year 1817. Among other early settlers were Abraham Snyder, who settled immediately east of Epsom; John Ruminer, who settled west, and Joseph Myers, who settled immediately south of Epsom. The present school house in Epsom is on what was formerly John Ruminer's land. The township was named for W. Bogard, who was killed by the Indians.

By the United States census of 1910, Bogard township had a population of one thousand five hundred and seventy-four. Richard M. Williams, Plainville, is the present trustee of the township.

ELMORE TOWNSHIP.

In response to a petition presented to the board of commissioners another township was established, August 13, 1821, by taking a section of territory off the north part of Bogard township. The name given to this new township was Elmore, after the Elmore family, in the vicinity of whose homes the first voting precinct was located. It is claimed that the Elmores were not the first settlers within the boundaries of this township. Among those who are probably entitled to this distinction are Edward Johnson, William Paddock, Solomon Dixon and Joseph Taylor. Each of these made land entries as early as 1816. The first land entry made by an Elmore, as shown by the record, was that of Isaac Elmore, in October, 1818. For the next few years following, there was quite an immigration to this part of the county and land entries were of frequent occurrence. Among those who settled here during these years were James Robinson, Terry Tate, Alexander Rogers, Thomas Rogers, John K. Long, Christopher, Jonathan and Isaiah Johnson, and Pascal Rucker, the latter coming from Kentucky in 1825. The Rogerses did not remain many years. With a view of finding a better location, they built a flatboat and floated down White river, destiny not known. A Tennessee colony came in 1825, among them members of which were William Moore, Jackson Haynes and Stephen, Eleazar and Thomas Reason.

The people who settled in Elmore township in early times were an intelligent and industrious class. By their frugal habits and exemplary lives they established a community characterized by its good citizenship. This character has been maintained by the succeeding generations. As a class the citizens of Elmore township rank with the best.

This township, including the town of Elnora, had a population of two thousand two hundred and sixty-eight in 1910. Clifford Farris, Elnora, is the present township trustee.

MADISON TOWNSHIP.

This township was originally called Wallace, which was organized in 1823. On petition of citizens interested, the name of the township was changed to Madison in 1835. The territory included in this township lies in the northwest corner of the county. Baldwin Howard was among the first settlers of the territory included in this township. He lived about a mile south of the present town of Odon. The first land entry was made by Zebulon Jenkins. Soon following him entries were made by Robert Evans, Sr., Samuel Hughen and William Gilmore. These entries were made in 1821 and 1822. In the few years following other land entries were made by Benjamin Coombs, Joseph B. Van Matre, Joshua Manning, Joseph, John and Harvey Hastings, Reuben and George Rainey and William Webster, the latter about 1830. Jacob and Eli Kinnaman came to the township in 1838, coming directly from Stark county, Ohio; their father and the rest of the family traveling the entire distance in a four-horse wagon. It is related that Jacob was not highly pleased with the change of location. He declared that he would return to Ohio as soon as he had money enough to pay for the journey. It is also related that he was quite successful in making money here and soon had a sufficient amount to pay for his return, but he continued to live in the Daviess county settlement.

Madison township had a population of two thousand three hundred and seventy-one, including the town of Odon, in 1910. The present trustee is Rufus D. McCarter, of Odon.

Among the early settlers was a colored man by the name of Ben Perkins. According to a story, handed down from early times, Perkins was a general favorite, notwithstanding his color. It is related of him that he tried to pass himself off for a Portuguese, on account of his color, not being a full black. In this he was not very successful; but he was successful in voting regularly and without a challenge, before colored men had the right of franchise in Indiana. Ben's affiliations were with the Whig party, and he always voted that ticket. In the spring of 1856 the Know-Nothing party had candidates for the various offices in Madison township, the Whig party not being represented. This left Ben "up in the air" as to how he ought to cast his ballot. At that time the township elected three school trustees and a clerk. The Democrats, in order to run a bluff on the Know-Nothing party, made Ben their candidate for township clerk. To the surprise of the Democrats, and everybody else, Ben was elected. And it is said he made one of the best clerks the township ever had. At the Presidential election in the following fall the Democrats confidently expected that Ben would return the favor and fall in line for Buchanan. But in this they were disappointed. Ben cast his ballot for John C. Fremont, the first Republican candidate for President. It was several years after before Ben was entitled to vote legally.

STEELE TOWNSHIP.

Steele township was organized in 1835 by taking another slice off of Washington township. Steele lies north of Washington township and borders on White river. The fact that a considerable portion of the land in this township lies along the river, and is low and flat, accounts for the fact that the rush of early settlers to this part of the county was not as great as in other parts. Most of the early settlers of Daviess county came from Kentucky, Tennessee and the Carolinas. They had been reared among the hills and had been accustomed to the cultivation of land more or less elevated. In coming to this new country the hills and high ground appeared to them the most favorable place for settlement. The lower lands, especially the river bottoms, the early settler avoided; not only because of the greater difficulty in getting this kind of land in condition for cultivation, but because of the fear of malaria that was supposed to be more prevalent there. The newcomer to Indiana in those days, and for many days and years after, had a holy horror of the "ager" and the "milk sickness." The terror of wolves and wild cats was not a circumstance compared to the dread of these diseases. Whatever ground there may have been for the belief that malaria was more prevalent in the river bottoms than elsewhere, certain it is that when the low lands were cleared up and put in a condition for cultivation, the malaria disappeared. And the venturesome people who had the energy, enterprise and foresight to purchase these lands, and put them in a state of cultivation, were abundantly rewarded in the most valuable and productive land in the county.

Very few, if any, land entries were made in the territory of Steele township prior to 1820. Entries were made by Andrew Couchman, Abraham Case and Alexander R. Hinds in 1821, and by Elias Beddle and Josiah Culbertson in the latter part of the same year. Since the first settlement, Steele township has kept pace with the rest of the county in the way of improved farming. For several years the farmers were at a disadvantage because of the lack of transportation facilities. The construction of the Wabash & Erie canal through the township gave hopes of improvement, but the hopes were blasted when the canal went dry. Several years later the railroad came and relieved the situation. Plainville, a pretty little village in the township, is an important station on the railroad and a convenient shipping point for the abundant produce of the farms in the vicinity.

Steele township had a population of one thousand eight hundred and fifty-two in 1910. The present township trustee is Charles A. Banta, Plainville.

HARRISON TOWNSHIP.

Harrison township was created out of parts of Veale and Reeve townships, by order of the commissioners, in June, 1841. This was one of the early settled portions of Daviess county. The first to arrive, it is believed, were William and Lewis Jones, who came from South Carolina in 1812. A little later they were joined by Christopher and Jeremiah Gregory, from the same state. These were followed about a year later by others from South Carolina, among whom were Samuel Comer, John Edwards, Green, John and Thomas McCafferty, and Joseph and William Jones. Altogether there was quite a colony of people among the first settlers in this township from South Carolina. The first land entries in Harrison township were made in 1814, by Joseph Case, Robert Hays and Elias Stone.

The population of Harrison township in 1910 was one thousand one hundred and nine. The present township trustee is Bernard Gillooly, Montgomery.

VAN BUREN TOWNSHIP.

The last township organized in Daviess county was Van Buren. It was created out of parts of Barr and Madison townships, by order of the commissioners, in September, 1841, in accordance with a petition of citizens interested. Very few land entries were made within the limits of this township prior to 1820, and very few early settlers. That section of the country was frequently visited by hunters and trappers in early times, before there were any permanent settlers. Among these, two brothers, named Peterson, are mentioned. Jabez Osmon and William Baker are mentioned among the first to locate permanently in the township. Francis Williams was an early settler and also an early justice of the peace. Squire Bruce and Joseph Bruce came later, also Asbury Sims and Cyrus Crook, who came in 1827 and lived where Raglesville is now situated.

One of the early industries of Van Buren township was a small distillery. It was located in the south part of the township and was built and operated by a man named Lentz. What the capacity of this distillery was is not a matter of record, but the product was probably sufficient to supply the home demand. It is stated that there was quite a little settlement around the distillery.

Van Buren had a population of one thousand one hundred and ninety-nine in 1910. Albert M. Clark, of Raglesville, is the present trustee of the township.

CHAPTER XIX.

DAVIESS COUNTY TOWNS AND VILLAGES.

It will be something of a surprise to many people to know that nearly forty towns have been located on the Daviess county map since the organization of the county. Many of these were simply "locations," with an ambitious name, promoted by individuals in the community who entertained roseate visions of the future. Some of these visions were stimulated by the construction of the old Wabash & Erie canal, and the promise of the great commercial traffic that would be established by that watercourse. All along the canal route, little towns sprang up like mushrooms in a night. While the digging of the canal was in progress most of these mushroom towns did a flourishing business in supplying the canal diggers with the necessaries of life—the fruit of the still being one of the "necessaries." The building of the railroads through the county was the occasion for other little towns finding a location on the map. Several of these early municipal ventures proved a success and have become thriving towns, peopled with intelligent and enterprising citizens. Some of the best schools and the best churches in the county are found in these towns.

A brief history of the towns in Daviess county, including those that never made progress farther than to get a name, will be an interesting subject for this chapter. Taking them in alphabetical order, the first of the list is:

ALFORDSVILLE.

Alfordsville, in Reeve township, is the principal village in the southeastern portion of the county. It was laid off, June 3, 1845, by Isaac Harris. The original plat of the place shows sixty-four lots. To these, additions have been made, the first being an addition of eight lots by Joseph A. McCord, in 1867. The first settler in that vicinity was James Alford, after whom the town was named. Among the other early settlers were James P. Gilley and James Allen. These families came from North Carolina about the year 1828. In the early thirties James Alford built the first house on the ground now occupied by the town. This house stood for many years as one of the old landmarks. The establishment of a school was one of the first concerns of the early settlers of Alfordsville, and it is noted that Tol Bartle and Barton Alford were engaged in that occupation in the early days, these being the first resident school teachers in the town. At present a two-room school house accommodates the lower grades and another room is rented for the high school. Efficient teachers are employed. The Methodist, Baptist and Christian denominations each has a comfortable and well-appointed church in the town, and the Knights of Pythias order has a lodge with an active membership.

ALBRIGHT.

This is a station on the Chicago & Eastern Illinois railroad. One store supplies the trade of the community, and a grain elevator handles the produce of the surrounding farms. A considerable amount of business is furnished the railroad in the shipment of grain and melons from this point during the season. The shipment of logs is one of the active industries at this place, a considerable amount of good timber being found in the vicinity.

BLACK OAK.

This is a switch on the Baltimore & Ohio railroad, located in Barr township.

CANNELBURG.

Cannelburg is an incorporated town with a population of three hundred, by the census of 1910. It sprang into existence on account of the extensive operations of the Buckeye Cannel-Coal Company in the early seventies. The town was laid out by A. J. Shotwell, L. C. Harris and Anthony Moots, who composed the coal company. In 1872 ten blocks were platted and divided into one hundred and two lots. In 1884 an addition of forty-four lots was made. The principal industry of the community is coal mining, which furnishes employment for a large number of men, and furnishes support for most of the families in town. The cannel coal mined here is regarded as being superior to any in the state, and immense quantities of it are mined and shipped to various parts of the country. Both cannel and bituminous coal are worked from the same vein, the cannel-coal overlying the other in a vein from two and one-half to five feet thick. The Buckeye Cannel-Coal Company's mine was opened in 1870, by A. J. Shotwell and

Clapp & Bailey. It was purchased by Washington and Cincinnati capitalists in 1881. The late Austin F. Cabel, one of Washington's leading citizens, was connected with the company as secretary under this organization. Most of the property in Cannelburg is owned by the company and the only store is kept by them. In the winter of 1881-82, an epidemic of smallpox affected the town, causing a large number of deaths among the inhabitants. In late years there has been a decrease in the amount of coal taken from these mines and the number of men employed is much less than formerly. This has had a marked effect upon the prosperity of the town.

Cannelburg is well provided with educational facilities. In 1914 a new consolidated high-school building was erected, with all the modern improvements and educational equipment. This is a certified high school, recognized by the state educational authorities. The community is largely of the Catholic faith. They have a frame building, All Saints' church, as their place of worship.

CHELSEA.

This town had an air of aristocracy about its name, and inherited something of distinction from its founder and promoter. But it was not able to measure up to the one, nor to justify the ambition of the other. Chelsea was an effort to build up a great city at the junction of the Ohio & Mississippi railroad and the proposed "Straight-line" railroad, of which the well-known Willard Carpenter, of Evansville, was the promoter. A town of fifteen streets and sixty-four blocks, divided into lots, was laid out by Mr. Carpenter in 1857. A number of these lots were sold, a few houses were built and at least one store was opened in the town, of which John Meads was the proprietor. In the beginning of its career Chelsea was not without prospects, but these prospects were dependent upon the prospects of Carpenter's "Straight-line." But the "Straight-line" failed and the name of Chelsea was changed to "Ichabod."

CORNETTSVILLE.

This town, located in Bogard township, was laid out by John F. Myers and Samuel Cornett, in 1875. It is nine miles northeast from Washington and is very pleasantly located in an excellent farming community. It has a population of about two hundred, one store, a blacksmith shop, a two-room brick school building, two frame churches, one of the Methodist and the other of the Baptist denomination. One on the hunt for a nice, quiet and respectable place in which to live would overlook a chance if he should pass by Cornettsville.

CORBYTOWN.

Looking at the matter from a distant and disinterested standpoint, one can conceive of no reason why a town of this name should long exist. And it didn't long exist. It was located in Veale township, about six miles south of Washington, on the proposed route of the old "Straight-line." If it ever had any prospects they went glimmering with the failure of Willard Carpenter's railroad enterprise.

COSBY.

Cosby was another Veale township town that staked a chance on Carpenter's railroad project, and lost. It had a saw-mill and several houses, and enough open space around to build several more houses. But this space was found to be more profitable for raising corn. No more houses were built and Cosby is only a memory of the oldest inhabitant.

CORNING.

Corning is an unpretentious little village in the northwestern part of Reeve township, with a small population, mostly of the Catholic faith. St. Patrick's church, a brick building, and a brick parochial residence, are prominent buildings of the town. A new public school house is being built. One store supplies the trade of the people near by.

CUMBACK.

In the southeastern part of Veale township is another modest little village, designated on the map as Cumback. Whether the founders and promoters of this village ever came back to see how the project prospered is not a matter of record. As a town it never got very far on the road to prosperity, but has been able to hold its own and attract the notice of the map-makers of Daviess county. There are two stores and a few houses in the village, also a Methodist church. A public school is near by.

ELDON.

This is another town predicated on the proposition that the Wabash & Erie canal was going to do wonderful things in the way of development of the country and in the building up of prosperous towns and cities along the route. David H. Kennedy, William S. Turner and Seth H. Cruse were so impressed with that idea that, in 1857, they laid out, in a very elaborate manner, a plat for a town at the intersection of the canal and the Ohio & Mississippi railroad, and called the place Eldon. The plat showed eighteen streets and fifty-six blocks, divided into lots. It was a very beautiful plat, as it appears on paper, with lines carefully drawn and the names of streets and numbers of lots distinctly marked. With this plat in hand the possible purchaser would have had no trouble at all in locating his lot. But the collapse of the canal marked the failure of the scheme to make a metropolis of Eldon. If there were any purchasers of lots shown on this artistic plat the purchaser had little concern about the location of his purchase.

ELNORA.

Elnora is a live, enterprising town in Elmore township. It sprang into existence with the completion of the Evansville & Indianapolis railroad, in 1885, though a postoffice and two or three stores had been established on the site of the new town for several decades previous to that time. The name of the postoffice was Owl Prairie, but the hamlet was called Owltown. September 25, 1885, William C. Griffith and A. R. Stalcup laid out a town on the site of this little hamlet, the town plat comprising nine blocks and fifty-three lots. With wise foresight the founders realized that the new town could not outlive the gibes and ridicule suggested by the name of Owltown, and so they gave the new town the more sensible and appropriate name of Elnora. On the 1st of January, 1886, the name of the postoffice was changed from Owl Prairie to Elnora.

Elnora was incorporated in 1892, the election for corporation officers being held on January 6 of that year. The following were the first officials: Thomas J. Payne, Newton Shake and Milton P. Toliver, trustees; E. E. Earle, treasurer; Isaac Todd, marshal; Byron Green, clerk. At the meeting of the board for organization, July 9, 1892, Thomas Payne was elected president. Jasper Whitman, T. M. Sears and Lee Wadsworth were elected school trustees. Howard Williams was appointed by the board as corporation attorney.

The Elnora Citizens Bank was established, January 1, 1903, by James B. Abell, Aaron Hitchcock, Henry H. Beever and Harry Hitchcock. This was a private enterprise, with James B. Abell as president; Aaron Hitchcock, vice-president; Harry Hitchcock, cashier; H. H. Beever, assistant cashier. The bank began doing business in a frame building, located on the site of the present building, a one-story brick building, erected in 1908. The bank was reorganized in 1905, under the new banking law of the state, the list of stockholders being increased to seven at that time. The present officers are: Samuel Shufflebarger, president; Ransom Pope, vice-president; Harry Hitchcock, cashier; Myrtle Winklepleck, assistant cashier.

William Smeltzer built a small electric light plant in 1905, which served the town for lighting purposes until it was destroyed by fire in 1910. The plant was rebuilt, and two or three years later was sold to a company, composed, in part, of some citizens of Elnora. This company erected a new modern plant in the fall of 1914. This plant was built at a cost of about thirty-five hundred dollars and is now operated by the Elnora Electrical Company, of which Sam Shamffelberger is president, and Charles Ross is secretary and treasurer.

The two elevators in Elnora do a good business in handling the grain, of which the surrounding country is very productive. The excellent shipping facilities afforded by the two railroads enable the elevators to pay the farmers the highest prices for their produce. The merchants of Elnora are generally prosperous, many of the business houses being brick buildings and of modern structure. The Methodist denomination has a new brick church, erected in 1911, at a cost of twelve thousand dollars. Prior to that time the Methodists worshipped in a frame church, erected in the fall of 1887, at a cost of one thousand one hundred dollars. Reverend Hawes was the first pastor, followed by Miles Wood, L. B. Johnson, A. D. Hartsock, H. H. Allen, H. N. King, S. O. Dorsey, Reverend Louther and others. Rev. S. J. Shake is the present pastor; the membership is three hundred, with a Sunday school enrollment of two hundred.

The Christian church is probably the oldest religious organization established in the vicinity of Elnora. Nearly fifty years ago this denomination built a small one-story frame church northeast of the town. Several years later there was a division in the society and another church was built by the faction that withdrew from the original society. One of these churches was known as the "old" and the other as the "new" church. A frame building, erected several years ago, serves as a place of worship for the Christian denomination in Elnora.

A two-story brick school building, with modern equipment and an efficient corps of teachers, leaves nothing to be desired in the way of educational advantages. Elnora had a population of nine hundred and sixty-one, according to the census of 1910.

EPSOM.

This town got its name on account of the water from a well that was dug by a Mr. Pace, having the taste of the famous Epsom salts. The town is located about two miles from Cornettsville, in Bogard township. In its early days the town was nicknamed "Tophet," and it is still recognized by that town. The first settlement was made by Peter Yount, about 1815 or 1816. Epsom never made pretention of being other than a small hamlet, with a few scattered dwelling houses. But it has maintained its existence all these years and has made some progress. In the way of business enterprises it has three stores, a flour mill, and a coal mine near by. It also has a good two-story brick school house, with a commissioned high school, and two churches, one Methodist and one Christian, both frame buildings.

FARLEN.

Farlen is, or rather was, located in the eastern part of Madison township. It had a postoffice at one time, also one store, but these have long since passed away and Farlen is in the "has-been" class.

GLEN DALE.

This town, of romantic name, is located in the central part of Harrison township, eight miles southeast of Washington. It has something less than a dozen dwelling houses, two stores and a blacksmith shop. It has a two-room public school building with graded schools, and a three-year high-school course. The one church is a frame building maintained by the Methodist denomination. A Masonic lodge and an Odd Fellows lodge have been maintained there for many years. The Odd Fellows lodge was organized in 1862 and the Masons in 1878. Each of these orders has a building in which their respective meetings are held.

GRAHAM.

This is a flag station on the Chicago & Eastern Illinois railroad. It is a good shipping point for the products of farms near by.

HYATT.

Hyatt, a station on the Chicago & Eastern Illinois railroad in Steele township, has one store and an elevator. A considerable amount of grain is shipped from this place, and it is a convenient point for the shipment of melons, which are extensively cultivated in this vicinity.

HUDSONVILLE.

Hudsonville is located in the southern part of Harrison township. It was laid out by Nelson and Daniel Jackson. It has one store, a concrete-block school house of one room, and a frame Methodist church building. About a half dozen houses are sufficient to shelter all the inhabitants of Hudsonville.

JACOB.

Jacob is on the Chicago & Eastern Illinois railroad.

JORDAN.

Another station on the Chicago & Eastern Illinois railroad, located in Washington township. During the fifties and sixties a large flour-mill was located there. This mill was built by James Spink, who afterward sold it to M. L. Brett. A slaughter-house was one of the big industries of the place in the early days. Flour and meat were shipped from there on the canal, as long that famous ditch would hold water.

LASCA.

This was formerly a postoffice in the northwestern part of Van Buren township. It was named by Oliver H. Fulkerson, a Van Buren township teacher. He took the name from one of Longfellow's Indian poems. At one time there was a little cross-roads store at this place, but it is a thing of the past. A two-room brick school house affords facilities for the training of the youth of the community.

LETTSVILLE.

Another name for this town, and the one by which it is generally known, is "Hole-in-the-Wall." How the place came by this hyphenated cognomen is related by a historian familiar with facts: "Years ago, at Lettsville, a low-down saloon was kept in the basement, or a cellar, of a dwelling. There was no outside door to the cellar, and the proprietor, to remedy the defect, knocked out enough bricks from the wall to make a passage large enough to admit a man. On account of this circumstance, the place took the name of 'Hole-in-the-Wall,' which clings to it to this day." There is nothing of Lettsville now, not even that hole in the wall.

LIVERPOOL.

Liverpool was laid out before Washington and the plat is now a part of Washington, as is more fully described in the chapter regarding the county seat.

MARSH.

Situated on the township line between Bogard and Elmore townships is Marsh. A former postoffice at this place has been discontinued; only a little crossroad store there now.

MAYSVILLE.

This town was laid out in 1834 by John McDonald, on the land of Charner Hawkins. It was situated on the Wabash & Erie canal, and, in the days when the canal prospects were bright, Maysville was the most important business place in the county. But its business and bright prospects vanished when canal navigation closed. A few tumble-down houses remain as relics of a once thriving town's greatness as a business center. There is a brick school house there, and a strong congregation of Methodists, with a frame church building. The pumping station of the Washington waterworks is also located there.

(19)

MONTGOMERY.

The town of Montgomery is located in Barr township, on the line of the Baltimore & Ohio Railroad, seven miles east of the county seat of Daviess county. It was laid out by Valentine B. Montgomery, on land owned by him in 1865, and from him the town took its name. The town dates its origin, however, from 1854, at the time when the Ohio & Mississippi railroad was being surveyed through the county. The first house was built in that year by James C. Montgomery, a brother of Valentine, who used the house for a dwelling and also for a small store in which were kept supplies for the contractors and men working on the railroad. When the railroad was completed through the town, in 1857, there was a population of about twenty, occupying the four houses that were then in the town. According to the United States census, the population of Montgomery in 1890 was four hundred and fifteen; in 1900, six hundred and sixteen; in 1910, five hundred and eleven. The decrease in population in 1910 is due to the transitory character of many of the residents who are employed in the coal mines near by.

When first settled, the town was literally "in the woods," a heavy growth of timber surrounding it on all sides. Timber, at that time, was an incumbrance to landowners. After the railroad was completed a considerable impetus was given to the place, houses springing up on every side; the mechanic, the merchant, the dealer in country produce found Montgomery a desirable place in which to carry on their various vocations. Valentine Montgomery did an extensive business in the buying of grain at that station, shipping it to Louisville and Cincinnati.

Among the first marriages to take place in Montgomery was that of Patrick McCarty and Elizabeth Morgan, daughter of Col. James Morgan, one of the most prominent citizens of the county. Mr. McCarty, the party of the first part in this matrimonial contract, afterward represented the county in the Legislature. James McCarty, son of the union referred to, was the first child born in Montgomery, the date of his birth being 1857. The McCarty family removed to the West sometime in the sixties, where they or their descendants are still living.

In 1869, while Lloyd Clark was trustee of the township, the first public schools of Montgomery were founded, and these schools have always been a credit to the county. They have kept well in line with the advance of educational methods in the county, and now the town can boast of a fine two-story brick consolidated and high school building, and certified high school. A fine two-story parochial school building, the property of St. Peter's Catholic church, in which a school was conducted for several years, is not now used for school purposes. The school was discontinued on account of the removal of many families from the town and vicinity. St. Peter's Catholic church is a large brick building, accommodating a large congregation. The United Brethren is an old organization here. This organization has a frame church, erected about 1882, and a membership of sixty-five. The congregation never had a resident minister, being supplied by ministers from Washington.

One of the prominent industries of Montgomery is the Harris & Bell flour mill. This mill was built by Josiah C. Harris in 1876, operations having been begun in November of that year. It is a five-story brick building, with a basement. As first constructed it had four runs of burrs, and cost eighteen thousand dollars. About twenty-five years ago the equipment was remodeled, at a cost of about thirty thousand dollars, by putting in the roller process and complete modern machinery, which made it a mill of one-hundred-barrel capacity. Another remodeling in 1915 increased the capacity to one hundred and twenty-five barrels. Josiah C. Harris, the founder, died in 1911. E. C. Harris, a son of the founder, and two daughters of W. E. Bell now own the property and conduct the business under the firm name of the Harris & Bell Milling Company.

The First National Bank of Montgomery was established in 1901, with a capital stock of twenty-five thousand dollars, with Dr. J. M. Crawford, president; S. L. McPherson, vice-president; C. C. Martin, cashier. This bank went into voluntary liquidation in 1911 and the building and assets of the concern were purchased by the Farmers and Merchants Bank, a private bank established in December of that year. The officials of the Farmers and Merchants Bank, at the time of its organization, were: Oliver Walker, president; S. L. McPherson, vice-president; B. L. Spaulding, cashier, later succeeded by John W. Rudolph. Capital stock, ten thousand dollars.

The business of Montgomery is largely dependent upon the mining industry, that being one of the most important coal mining towns on the line of the Baltimore & Ohio Railroad. Montgomery is also fortunate in being situated in the center of an excellent farming section of the county. The agricultural resources of the surrounding country are hardly surpassed by any part of Daviess county and the shipment of the products of the farm, stock and dairy products, from that point is hardly excelled by any other shipping point in the county. Montgomery was incorporated in 1870. It is located in the geographical center of Daviess county, and is exactly midway between Cincinnati and St. Louis, the terminus of the main line of the Baltimore & Ohio Railroad.

ODON.

The town of Odon, in Madison township, is the next important in size to the city of Washington. It was laid out in 1846, by John Hastings, on land formerly owned by Dr. J. Townsend. The town was first called Clarksburg and the postoffice established there was called Clark's Prairie. In 1880 the name of the town and the postoffice was changed to Odon. Doctor Townsend was the first settler in the town, which at that time contained thirty-six lots, according to the original plat as surveyed by P. S. Agan. Additions were made by Henry B. Kohr of nineteen lots, in 1866; sixteen lots by Howard Crook, in 1867; eleven lots by Olly Crooke, in 1868; eight lots by Z. V. Garten, in 1877, and forty-two lots by Hugh McCoy, in 1875. Several additions have been made in later years, indicative of the town's steady growth. The first merchants of Odon were Howard Crooke and Z. V. Garten, who were engaged in business there in 1855. John V. Smith established a weekly newspaper in Odon, in 1855, called the *Prairie Scorcher*, but there is no evidence that it ever did anything of the kind. The *Odon Journal*, a well-named and well-conducted weekly newspaper, has furnished the town with local news for several years.

The town of Odon was incorporated on June 20, 1885. The first board of trustees were: Dr. John Dearmin, John Smiley and Samuel Dunlap. W. L. Stoy was elected clerk; C. L. Pierson, treasurer; Wiley Edmonson, marshal. At a meeting of the board, December 2, 1885, W. R. Neenimer, Caleb Odell and Joseph Kinnaman were elected school trustees. The First National Bank was first established as a private concern by Howard Crooke. It continued until the death of Mr. Crooke, about 1895, and then passed into the hands of other parties. The present organization was effected about a year later, with a capital stock of twenty-five thousand dollars. The first officials of this organization were: Lowry Cooper, president; Harry H. Cook, vice-president; Walter C. Garten, cashier; Alex. O'Dell, assistant cashier. On June 1, 1909, the capital stock was increased to fifty thousand dollars. The present officers are: Alonzo A. Lane, president; J. M. Winkelpleck, vice-president; B. D. Smiley, cashier; Miss Flossie Winkelpleck (who, on January 13, 1913, succeeded Alex O'Dell), assistant cashier. The Farmers Bank is another financial institution of the town. This is a private concern with a capital stock of ten thousand dollars, under the management of the following officials: Lowry Cooper, president; Reason Bennett, vice-president; J. A. McCoy, cashier. This bank was established, January 12, 1914.

Roy F. Myers built an electric light plant in 1912, at a cost of twelve thousand dollars. It is well equipped for service and furnishes light for the town and for private consumers. Among the other industries of Odon are a planing-mill, a saw-mill, a brick- and tile-factory and a monumental works. The town also is well provided with churches. The denominations most largely represented are the United Brethren, Methodist and Christian. Each of these has a strong congregation and a comfortable house in which to hold services. A more detailed history of the churches of Odon, and other towns, will be found in another chapter in this work. The secret and benevolent orders, so largely represented in Odon and other towns, are given proper mention under another chapter heading.

Odon is situated in the center of a splendid agricultural country and has a large trade from the surrounding farming community. The completion of the Southern Indiana railroad, now the Chicago, Terre Haute & Southeastern railroad, gave an outlet for the products of the surrounding farms and made Odon a splendid shipping point, the one thing that the town had long needed. From this point is shipped grain, stock, poultry and other produce, bringing trade to the town and a considerable revenue to the railroad. The population of Odon has had a steady increase in the last three decades, as shown by the United States census. In 1890 it had seven hundred and sixty-four; in 1900, nine hundred and twenty-three; in 1910, one thousand sixty-four.

PLAINVILLE.

Plainville is on the line of the old Wabash & Erie canal, and was quite an important business point more than fifty years ago, with a number of stores and a good flour-mill. It went into decline, however, like many other towns, with the ill-fated canal, that cost so many millions of dollars and hundreds of lives to build, only to be abandoned shortly after its completion. Notwithstanding the adverse conditions, resulting from the collapse of the canal, Plainville continued to be a trading point, with one or two stores and a postoffice. The completion of the Evansville & Indianapolis railroad (now the Chicago & Eastern Illinois railroad) through Daviess county gave Plainville quite a business boom, and a number of new buildings were erected in the fall of 1885. The railroad made the town of considerable importance; the price of lots increased and the town doubled in population in a few years. Among the important business industries of the place is the Plainville Milling Company's plant, a three-story brick building, erected in 1910; a canning factory, an elevator, lumber yard, automobile repair shop, besides several lesser industries. There are several business houses representing lines of trade adapted to the community. Excellent educational advantages are afforded in the fine brick school building, an efficient corps of teachers being found in the different grades, and in the commissioned high school. The religious denominations represented are the Methodist, Christian and Brethren, each owning a good frame building and supported by a substantial membership. The secret orders are also well represented. The Farmers Bank was established, April 13, 1908, with a capital stock of ten thousand dollars, represented by about forty stockholders. The first officers of the bank were Nathan E. Killion, president; Charles A. Banta, vice-president; Ernest E. Killion, cashier, and R. Elmer Killion, assistant cashier. The present officers are the same, except that Mr. Banta has been succeeded by John S. Goshorn, as vice-president.

RAGLESVILLE.

Raglesville is a pretty little village, of something less than two hundred inhabitants, situated in the northern part of Van Buren township. It has a three-room brick school house; a Methodist church and a United Brethren church, each a frame building; two or three stores and a blacksmith shop. There is a fine coal mine near the town, and it is claimed there is not a better quality of coal produced in the county than that which comes from this mine. An old history of Raglesville coupled a brass band with a flour-mill that was formerly located there, as one of the important industries.

Raglesville was laid out under the name of Sanford, June 21, 1837, by Ozias Crooke, who was the first school teacher, and also the first merchant in the place. Crooke kept a general store there in 1840. The first settler in the vicinity was Asbury Sims, in 1832.

SANDY HOOK.

Sandy Hook is a station on the Chicago & Eastern Illinois railroad, in Veale township, a few miles south of Washington. Travelers on the railroad observe that all the trains stop at Sandy Hook long enough to allow them to read the sign board giving the name of the station.

SMILEY.

Smiley was formerly a postoffice in Van Buren township, but when the rural route system was introduced Smiley lost its postoffice and the Smiley postmaster lost his job.

SOUTH WASHINGTON.

South Washington is situated on the Petersburg road, one mile south of Washington, and has a population of about one hundred. Thirty-two lots were laid off as a town by Levi D. Colbert, in 1874. There is a two-room brick school building located there, where school is conducted regularly for the education of the children of the community. There is no postoffice or church building in the place, the people of the village obtaining their mail by the rural route, and their religious teaching from ministers from Washton who hold occasional preaching service in the village.

THOMAS.

Thomas is a station indicated by a conspicuous sign board, located on the Chicago & Eastern Illinois railroad, in Washington township.

TRAINOR.

Trainor was formerly a postoffice and a cross-road store, situated in the southeastern part of Bogard township, but there is nothing of the kind there now. A brick school building and St. Michael's Catholic church are located there.

TOM'S HILL.

This was a collection of houses, a saw-mill and stave factory located near the Baltimore & Ohio railroad, on the west branch of White river. The place and all the surrounding belonged to the estate of Elisha Hyatt, and the inhabitants were all tenants of his and employed by him in the operation of the mill and factory. Tom's Hill was formerly a busy place.

WACO.

A former postoffice at Waco has been discontinued. Waco still holds its place on the map, however. It is located in the southwestern part of Harrison township, and contains a little store, a brick school building and a frame church, belonging to the Christian denomination.

POSTOFFICES IN DAVIESS COUNTY, OUTSIDE OF WASHINGTON.

Following are the names of those who have served as postmasters at the several postoffices in Daviess county, outside of Washington, and the dates of their appointments:

ALFORDSVILLE.

Office established, April 1, 1856. James P. Gilley appointed postmaster on that date, but was not commissioned. Isaac W. Jackman was commissioned, April 14, 1856; J. A. McCord, June 28, 1861; Florian Bartl, Jr., October 23, 1866; A. W. Bingham, July 8, 1867; William B. Walls, November 22, 1869; J. A. McCord, December 5, 1870; William B. Walls, April 17, 1871; Mason McCord, May 13, 1873; J. A. McCord, April 23, 1877; J. T. Hedrick, August 31, 1885; W. T. Brown, October 31, 1887; John W. Robinson, April 4, 1889; Spencer Jackman, March 30, 1893; Matthew McCracken, April 15, 1897; Wayne Gilley, February 13, 1899; J. W. Allen, March 3, 1906; Orian Hembree, July 16, 1914.

BLACK OAK RIDGE.

Established May 4, 1858, Alva Clark, postmaster; Thomas J. Lafferty, November 26; 1872. Name changed, April 10, 1873, to Cannelburg.

CANNELBURG.

John Sullivan, September 18, 1873; William F. O'Brien, July 16, 1875; Emma Clark, December 21, 1887; H. L. Tucker, November 1, 1889; Lizzie Harris, February 1, 1890; Emma Clark, April 14, 1893; L. P. Cahill, April 22, 1901; Anna A. Harris, July 21, 1905; Alodia F. Haag, June 17, 1908.

CORNETTSVILLE.

Established, April 9, 1878; William Critchlow, first postmaster; William R. Baker, October 23, 1878; Thomas Queen, Jr., June 14, 1893; Florence M. Achor, July 16, 1897; office discontinued, November 29, 1902.

OWL PRAIRIE.

Office established, Harvey Hagans, postmaster, December 20, 1831; Richard Fulton, March 25, 1835; Isaiah Johnston, June 4, 1839; Thomas

Elmore, November 9, 1840; William Watts, February 9, 1848; Thomas Elmore, May 11, 1849; Harvey Taylor, January 31, 1851; S. W. Elmore, June 30, 1851; A. M. Helphenstine, June 16, 1854; William D. Clary, November 7, 1857; office discontinued, December 24, 1862. Re-established, March 30, 1865, W. T. Franklin, postmaster; William H. Moore, March 6, 1866; O. H. McKittrick, November 9, 1868; William D. Clerry, May 9, 1870; J. P. Grayble, December 12, 1870; F. L. Killion, April 13, 1871; David Taylor, March 27, 1874; J. R. Wadsworth, December 10, 1874; A. R. Stalcup, March 7, 1876; D. H. Taylor, September 8, 1885; name changed, December 11, 1885, to Elnora.

ELNORA.

Asa Haig, April 18, 1889; J. F. Danner, March 31, 1893; John W. Robinson, April 16, 1897; J. E. Pershing, September 16, 1902; Francis A. McMullen, February 11, 1914.

HUDSONVILLE.

Office established, January 5, 1901, P. J. Bradfield, postmaster; William F. Colbert, November 5, 1901; office discontinued, December 31, 1904.

HYATT.

Office established, February 20, 1904; Hiram Simpson, postmaster; O. M. Albright, November 15, 1894; William A. Frets, April 12, 1898; A. L. Vickery, July 6, 1899; O. M. Albright, December 4, 1903; office discontinued, July 15, 1910.

MONTGOMERY STATION.

Office established, February 16, 1859; James C. Montgomery; William Wizard, August 11, 1871; William Ward, March 6, 1872; William Done, May 22, 1872; Howard Love, March 27, 1874; James C. Montgomery, October 22, 1874; name of office changed, February 12, 1880, to Montgomery; William C. Willeford, March 6, 1882; James Farrell, October 16, 1885; O. B. Nixon, April 4, 1889; Lawrence Weimer, May 28, 1892; L. B. Spalding, April 17, 1893; D. L. Weimer, April 15, 1897; James W. Kennedy, July 1, 1914.

PERKINS STORE

William A. Perkins served as postmaster from the time the office was established, July 25, 1856, to May 13, 1858, during which time the name of the postoffice was changed twice; first to Walnut Hill, July 29, 1857; then to Clark's Prairie, May 13, 1858. On this date W. B. Lutes became postmaster; Howard Crooke, June 5, 1862; Clement Correll, June 10, 1865; J. V. Smith, February 13, 1871; Alex. Odell, June 25, 1877; J. M. Crooke, February 16, 1881. Name changed, April 4, 1881, to Odon.

ODON.

Alex. Odell, November 24, 1884; C. L. Pierson, September 3, 1885; T. J. Hubard, May 28, 1889; C. E. Odell, September 15, 1892; William J. Danner, January 6, 1894; William T. O'Donald, October 19, 1894; George D. Abraham, May 10, 1897; H. H. Crooke, April 22, 1908; Daniel Gantz, May 20, 1913.

PLAINVILLE.

Office established, May 31, 1856; Clement Lee; James Webster, August 11, 1860; C. M. Reiley, December 9, 1864; L. H. Lester, August 15, 1866; T. L. Broyles, June 27, 1873; A. E. Dibble, April 24, 1876; L. H. Dilley, April 10, 1877; David Rankin, October 29, 1877; W. B. McRae, April 12, 1880; William Hildreth, February 21, 1882; William F. Killion, December 11, 1885; J. C. Wright, April 4, 1889; William H. Allen, March 30, 1893; William J. Hildreth, April 16, 1897; John A. Evans, June 22, 1901; W. H. Bunch, 1905; Charles McWilliams, 1914.

CHAPTER XX.

THE CITY OF WASHINGTON.

The county seat of Daviess county was formerly called Liverpool, this being the name of the town in Indiana territory, as laid out in the forks of White river, in Knox county, by Isaac Galland, George Curtis and David Flora. The original plat contained one hundred and eighty-six lots, each being sixty feet in width and one hundred and twenty feet in length; each street, sixty feet wide, to "remain open for the benefit of the public forever." The deed was recorded on November 11, 1815, and on May 9, 1816, the record says:

"Isaac Galland sold to David Flora one-half of this same tract of land for one thousand four hundred and seventy-four dollars, the same price for which David Flora had sold the entire tract seven months previous, and the deed to the land is described as being the land sold to said Galland and George Curtis by said Flora by deed October 16, 1815, and being the tract of land on which the town of Liverpool is now located." The deed to Galland and Curtis by David Flora on October 16, 1815, was witnessed by Emanuel Van Trees, William Wallace and John Wallace, as David Flora could not sign his name. The plat of the town was made by Galland, Curtis and Flora, on land purchased by them in 1813, lying within sections 27 and 24, township 3, range 7.

The plat of the town of Washington was made and recorded on March 31, 1817. It comprises portions of sections 26, 27, 28, 33, 34 and 35, township 3 north, range 7 west, consisting of one hundred and thirty-six lots, each lot being eighty by one hundred and thirty-two feet in size. Lots 5, 35, 40 and 65 belonged to Emanuel Van Trees. Lots 10, 15, 20, 25, 30, 45, 50, 55, 80, 85 and 90 belonged to Wilkins. The public square, lying between Walnut and Main and Second and Third streets, was not to be sold, and the rest of the plat was to be sold for the benefit of the county. Main street, in this plat, is now Hefron street, and the town boundaries were substantially Van Trees, Flora, Meridian and East Sixth streets. Four squares and four lots, however, lay west of Meridian street. This plat included the town of Liverpool, which was merged in the larger town of

Washington when that was designated as the name of the county seat, on the organization of Daviess county.

The first additions to the original plat of Washington were made by Emanuel Van Trees and Peter Wilkins, August 18, 1817. One hundred and sixty-five lots, each sixty-five by one hundred and twenty feet in size, were laid out in these additions. These enterprising pioneers found ready sale for their lots, at prices ranging from thirty-five to one hundred dollars. The record shows that Samuel J. Kelso was the first purchaser of a lot in the new town of Washington, his purchase being lot 49, located on the north side of Walnut street, midway between Fourth and Fifth streets. This sale was made by Emanuel Van Trees, November 13, 1816. Among the purchasers of lots in 1817 were: Michael Wiley, William Chapman, James G. Reed, Richard Palmer and John Allen.

On the 9th and 10th of June, 1817, a great public sale of lots was held. One hundred and eight lots were disposed of at this sale, ranging in price from ten to two hundred and thirty-five dollars. Lot 107 was purchased by James Street for ten dollars; lot 79 by John McClure and Blackford, for two hundred and thirty-five dollars. The total amount received for this sale of lots was about six thousand dollars.

There were several inhabitants of the town prior to this great sale of lots, but their names and the location of their residences have not been preserved. The first house that was built was probably located near the site of the present high school building. It was a log building, as were all other residences at that early time. This building, however, was of hewed logs and a little above the average in appearance, as compared to the log cabins of the time. The first store in the town was kept by James Read. His store building was a log structure, located on the southwest corner of Main and Second streets. This store was opened in 1817. After continuing in the business for about a year Mr. Read sold his store to Joseph Warner and Seth Rodick, who continued the business under the firm name of Warner & Rodick, until 1825. A second store was opened in 1818 by a Mr. Van Camp, from Kentucky; this store was located about one hundred feet from the southeast corner of Main and First streets. According to the memory of the oldest inhabitant, the first blacksmith to locate in the new town was Friend Spears. Oher blacksmiths who came about the same time were William Bratton and Thomas Brown.

EARLY BUSINESS INTERESTS

In 1823 the town had a population of about one hundred and was showing a steady and substantial growth. By this time there were four stores in the town. Isaac Hedden and Stephen Belding, shoemakers, had come in and established shops for their trade; William Ballow, James Calhoun and Robert Stephens were engaged in making hats. Stephens came from Pennsylvania, arriving in Washington on May 15, 1822. A few years prior to this Alexander Hinton and Alexander Bruce had opened "taverns" in the town. The Hinton tavern was located near the southwest corner of Main and East Second streets; the Bruce hostelry was at the corner of Main and East First street. Among those living along Main street about 1822 and 1823 were: Samuel Miller, a wheelwright; Colonel Berry, who kept a boarding house; Richard Weaver; Thomas Tuning, a saddler and harnessmaker; George Bruner, who kept a market and whiskey shop in the old blockhouse; a family named Blankenship, two of whom assisted "Uncle Dick" Palmer to kidnap Sam, the colored man; George Bradford, who kept a small store; A. C. Kinney, the lawyer, who procured the freedom of the two colored boys, an account of which will be found in another chapter in this volume. Emanuel Van Trees, whose name is most prominently connected with the early history of Washington, was also located on Main street; also John and Michael Murphy, general merchants. A Mr. Carr had a treadwheel grist-mill on Walnut street, near Friend Spears' blacksmith shop. A yoke of oxen on the treadwheel was the motive power that operated the grist-mill.

The professions were well represented in those early days. Reverend Pipher was an Episcopalian minister; Doctor Holland was a local preacher in the Methodist church, and also a practicing physician. The Washington circuit, in 1823, was in charge of Reverend Ray, from Kentucky; Reverend Martin was the resident minister of the Presbyterian church, and Rev. Hiram Hunter (father of D. Eckley Hunter, a prominent teacher known in later times) was pastor of the Cumberland Presbyterian church. The legal profession was represented by Judge Call, Judge Dewey, Judge Blake, John Ewing and A. C. Kinney, all men of marked ability.

SLOW GROWTH.

For a few years after the first sale of lots and the impetus given the town by the rush of early settlers, the interest in the new town began to decline. There was but small increase in the population of Washington from 1825 to 1857. There was little in the advantages afforded by the town to attract men of capital and business enterprise. There were no railroads and the products of the farm were sent in flat boats on White river to a southern market. Merchandise was brought in on wagons from Evansville, Louisville and other points. The stage coach was the only public utility afforded for travel to distant places. This was the condition until 1857, when the construction of the Ohio & Mississippi railroad through the town instantly awakened Washington and the surrounding country to real life. New men and fresh capital came in and the first real boom that Washington had long hoped for began to be a realization.

INCORPORATION OF THE TOWN.

Washington experimented with a form of government under a board of trustees for several years with indifferent success. There was complaint among the citizens that the board neglected its duties, which is not an unusual complaint against municipal authorities and it is not an unusual case for such complaints to be well-founded, as they probably were in this instance. Anyhow, the criticism of the official negligence of the Washington town board, by press and people, became so strong that a petition was made to the court for a dissolution of the board, and the petition was granted on March 15, 1867. Then a movement was immediately started to reincorporate, or to adopt a city charter, if, upon taking a census, a sufficient number of inhabitants were found to entitle them to such a charter. The citizens were not united on either of these propositions. Some favored one, some the other, and a great many were indifferent. The following extract from one of the papers published in the town at that time will serve to show the feelings of the citizens with reference to this question:

"Our citizens have tried the beauties of a corporation for some time past, and have found, to their sorrow, that it was impossible to find men for the various offices that would see the law strictly enforced. A seeming dread that they would get into difficulty, or that the corporation was not sound, would take possession of their minds, and violations of the law were disregarded by the officers, and the law set at defiance by rowdies. We hope that a census of the population of Washington and its additions will be taken, and if we have a sufficient population to entitle us to a city charter let us have it; and if not, revive the corporation and 'grin and bear it' until we are entitled to a city charter. By all means let us have law and order in our town."

Whether a census was taken or not, or whether there was at that time a sufficient number of inhabitants in Washington to entitle it to a city charter, is not a matter of record. It is probable that there were those who at that time were sufficiently informed to make a safe guess that Washington did not measure up to the requirements for a city charter, and that this guess of well-informed citizens was accepted in lieu of a census as proposed. At any rate steps were immediately taken for a reorganization of the corporation. A meeting of citizens was held on April 18, 1867, at the court house, at which it was agreed to circulate a petition to be presented to the board of county commissioners, asking for an election on the question of corporation or no corporation. Things then moved along pretty swiftly. The petition was presented to the board on May 13, showing a large number of signatures in favor of calling an election. An election was ordered by the board to be held on May 29, at which there were two hundred and nine votes in favor of the re-incorporation of the town, and only forty in opposition. An election was held, June 18, for trustees and other officers under the new organization, resulting in the election of the following:

Trustees: J. H. O'Neal, J. C. Spink, S. D. Wright, J. E. Thompson, Elisha Hyatt, Wilson Keith, A. B. Bruner. William E. Thompson was elected clerk; W. W. Feagans, assessor; George Kauffman, treasurer; John McCarty, marshal. The trustees organized, June 25, by the election of Elisha Hyatt as president of that body. There were several resignations and changes soon after the organiaztion was effected.

ORGANIZED UNDER A CITY CHARTER.

With an established form of government, organized as a town corporation, Washington enjoyed peace and prosperity for a few years. There was a continued growth of population during these years. In the spring of 1871 the population had become sufficient to entitle Washington to a city charter, with a mayor and six councilmen. Accordingly, the necessary steps were taken to organize under a city charter. The city was divided into three wards, two councilmen to be chosen to represent each ward. At an election held after the necessary preliminaries, David J. Hefron was elected mayor; J. C. Spink, William Tranter, Sr., Albert Logan, Henry Walter, John Hyatt and Elijah Eskridge were elected as councilmen. Mr. Hefron served as mayor until 1875, when he was succeeded by William D. Bynum, who served four years. From that time the following have served the city as mayor:

James W. Ogdon, 1879 to 1881; Arthur Beddoe, 1882 to 1883; William P. Ellis, 1884 to 1886; James W. Ogdon, 1887 to 1891; C. K. Tharp, 1891 to 1893; John H. Spencer, 1894 to 1898; Joseph Wilson (died during term), 1898 to 1900; John Downey, 1900 to 1902; Hale Clark, 1902 to 1906; Robert Russell, 1906 to 1910; John W. McCarty, 1910, the present mayor.

THE BANKS OF WASHINGTON.

The first banking enterprise in Washington was a private concern, organized in 1868 by William Sanford, Frank Overton and C. W. Levings, under the name of Sanford, Levings & Company. The capital stock of the firm was ten thousand dollars. Mr. Sanford was president, and C. W. Abell, cashier of this institution at the organization. Several changes in the proprietorship of this bank were made within a year or two after its organization. In 1870 Elisha Hyatt purchased a controlling interest and at that time the name of the concern was changed to the Washington Exchange Bank. Dr. A. M. Whitten and Elliott McCullough were taken in as partners about one year later, and, with their investment, the capital stock was increased to twenty thousand dollars. Two years later Mr. McCullough died and his interest was withdrawn; about a year later Doctor Whitten withdrew his interest. This reduced the capital stock to the original amount, ten thousand dollars. In 1874 Hiram Hyatt invested one thousand dollars, raising the capital stock to eleven thousand dollars, and the name of the firm was Hyatt, Levings & Company. This firm continued to conduct the business until November, 1884, when the bank closed its doors on account of failure to make collections on loans made. Concerning this unfortunate ending of Washington's first banking enterprise, an old historian makes this comment:

"The failure of the bank involved Elisha Hyatt's personal estate and, in order to make settlement, he submitted to his and the bank's creditors the proposition to pay his own creditors in full, and seventy cents on the dollar to those of the bank, an extremely liberal and altogether unusual proposition."

The failure of this bank, however, did not leave Washington without an institution of this kind. About twelve years prior to this time another banking enterprise had been established and was at this time in successful operation, and has continued as one of the permanent and successful financial institutions of Washington for more than forty years.

B. & O. SHOPS AND ROUNDHOUSE, WASHINGTON.

THIRD AND MAIN STREETS, LOOKING WEST, WASHINGTON.

THE WASHINGTON NATIONAL BANK.

The Washington National Bank was organized on August 28, 1872. The original stockholders were: F. W. Viehe, James Campbell, M. L. Brett, W. M. Tyler, W. J. Williams, C. Lee, and S. H. Taylor. F. W. Viehe, W. M. Tyler, S. H. Taylor and M. L. Brett were the first board of directors; F. W. Viehe, the first president, and M. L. Brett, the first cashier. This bank was organized with a capital stock of fifty thousand dollars, but on March 11, 1907, the capital stock was increased to one hundred thousand dollars. At the expiration of the original charter, August 28, 1912, the charter was renewed and extended for twenty years. The present directors are: J. N. Jones, F. M. Harned and W. R. Meredith; N. G. Read, president; F. M. Harned, vice-president; Louis I. Read, cashier; A. C. Wise, assistant cashier. The report of the condition of the bank at the close of business, May 1, 1915, shows the following:

Loans and discounts (notes held in bank), $365,118.50; other items included in resources, $521,813.18; capital stock paid in, $100,000.00; surplus fund, $130,000.00; undivided profits, $19,152.77; individual and time deposits, $538,778.91.

THE PEOPLE'S NATIONAL BANK.

The People's National Bank of Washington was organized on February 2, 1888, with a capital stock of fifty thousand dollars. The first board of directors were: Hugh Barr, James W. Ogdon, John Downey, George Kauffman, Richard C. Graham, Magness J. Carnahan and Alfred B. Davis. The first officers were: Hugh Barr, president; James W. Ogdon, vice-president; R. C. Davis, cashier. On February 12, 1907, the capital stock was increased to one hundred thousand dollars. The present officers are: M. F. Burke, president; E. L. Hatfield, first vice-president; C. F. Cochran, second vice-president; P. A. Hastings, cashier; T. R. McPherson, assistant cashier. From the report of this bank at the close of business, May 1, 1915, the following items are taken: Loans and discounts (notes held in bank), $369,754.67; other items included in resources, $211,229.31; capital stock paid in, $100,000.00; surplus fund, $60,000.00; individual and time deposits, $312,120.27.

(20)

THE CITIZENS LOAN AND TRUST COMPANY.

The Citizens Loan and Trust Company was organized on November 2, 1902, and was incorporated under the laws of the state, November 26, 1902, being authorized by law to conduct a general financial, savings, deposit, loan and trust business. The officers for the first year were: James W. Ogdon, president; Henry Aikman, vice-president; William Kennedy, secretary; William M. Aikman, assistant secretary. The first board of directors were: James W. Ogdon, John C. Hagerty, Ed F. Meridith, Henry Aikman, Harry H. Crooke, G. J. Nichols, John Murphy, Miles G. O'Neal and William Heffernan.

This company was organized with a capital stock of forty thousand dollars. In 1904 it was consolidated with the Washington Trust Company and the capital stock was increased to sixty-five thousand dollars. In 1907 the capital stock was increased to one hundred thousand dollars. The present board of directors are: James W. Ogdon, M. G. O'Neal, William Heffernan, J. A. Colbert, W. B. Deffendall, Jacob Beitman, J. N. Jones, L. E. Hamersly and William R. Meridith. The present officials are: James W. Ogdon, president; Miles G. O'Neal, vice-president; William Kennedy, secretary; W. M. Young, assistant secretary. From a statement of the condition of this company at the close of business May 1, 1915, the following items are taken: Loans and discounts, $229,912.87; other items included in resources, $36,687.41; capital stock paid in, $100,000.00; surplus and undivided profits, $37,352.05; demand and time deposits, $125,440.34.

STATE BANK OF WASHINGTON.

The State Bank of Washington was organized on January 16, 1910, with a capital stock of one hundred thousand dollars. The persons identified with the organization of this enterprise were: W. J. McCord, P. J. Cavanaugh, Basil B. Pritchett, Lewis W. Keith, William R. Gardiner, W. L. Jackson, Lewis H. Keith, Frank B. Fornwald, Marie H. Kelley, and others, comprising a list of sixty-five stockholders. The first officers were: George Godwin, president; H. F. Vollmer, vice-president; J. M. Twitty, cashier. Judge W. R. Gardiner succeeded Godwin as president, January 7. 1912; George J. Keith succeeded Vollmer as vice-president, July, 1914; William P. Walter was appointed assistant cashier, April 1, 1912. These, with John M. Twitty, cashier, compose the present bank officers. The present directors of the bank are: William R. Gardiner, C. K. Tharp, John Ormsby, A. O. Fulkerson, George J. Keith, R. J. Barr, Ezra Mattingly, M. D. Kelley and Martin Cahill. From the report of the condition of this bank at the close of business, May 1, 1915, the following items are taken: Loans and discounts, $159,093.58; other items included in resources, $37,864.99; capital stock paid in, $100,000.00; surplus fund, $5,500.00; demand deposits and certificates, $89,479.39.

FINANCIAL EXHIBIT, CITY OF WASHINGTON.

The following exhibit, showing the municipal indebtedness, receipts and expenditures, for the years 1913 and 1914, will furnish to the uninterested taxpayers of Washington information as to the management of the municipal affairs. Referring to the item of expenditures for the electric light plant, for 1913 and 1914, it should be stated that the increased expense for 1914 was caused by the payment of a claim of three thousand and six hundred dollars against the city for a damage suit, and also a considerable expense for an addition and improvement in the equipment of the plant:

	1913.	1914.
Indebtedness—		
City bonds	$41,500.00	$34,500.00
Cash on hand	14,427.39	13,436.63
Net indebtedness	27,072.61	21,033.37
Receipts—		
Cash on hand, Jan. 1, 1913	$19,838.14	$14,427.39
Taxes received	42,561.00	42,035.91
Electric light department	28,050.16	28,386.44
Retail liquor license	7,200.00	7,000.00
Interest on deposits	233.70	202.28
All other sources	7,346.69	6,071.51
Total receipts	$105,229.69	$98,123.53
Expenditures—		
Salary, city officials	4,580.00	4,651.31
Health department	338.29	292.92
Fire department	7,313.92	7,182.35
Police department	4,594.74	4,413.41

Electric light plant	26,593.13	32,697.97
Water rent	6,741.00	6,900.15
Paid on city bonds	8,500.00	7,000.00
All other expenditures	32,141.22	21,458.87
Total expenditures	$90,802.30	$84,686.98

PUBLIC UTILITIES.

The Washington street railway was built in 1894 by a stock company, composed of Louis C. Fritch, William McMahon and others. The franchise is now owned and operated by Ziba F. Graham. The line extends from the eastern terminus of Main street, running along that street to the Baltimore & Ohio railroad shops. Electric motive power is used and furnished by the city electric plant.

Washington has been furnished electric light and electric power for several years by a plant under municipal ownership and the experience has proven satisfactory to the patrons and profitable to the city. A small tax levy provides funds for expense of operation and for street lighting, without any increase in the usual rates of service charged private consumers.

An abundant supply of good clear water is furnished by the Washington Water and Light Company, from a pumping station located south of the city, near Maysville.

Telephone service is furnished by the Central Union Telephone Company and the Pike County Telephone Company.

THE RAILROAD SHOPS.

The greatest boom that Washington experienced in all its history was a result of the location of the Ohio & Mississippi railroad shops at this place. From the time of building this road the company had their machine and repair shops at Vincennes. As the business of the road increased it became necessary to build larger shops with increased capacity for handling their business. As the location of the extensive shops contemplated would be of great advantage to the town selected for the plant, the railroad company proposed that the favored town should put up a bonus that would in some measure compensate the company for the advantages offered. Vincennes had the old shops and the citizens of that town considered that was the logical situation for the enlarged plant. The railroad company asked for seventy-five thousand dollars to be added to whatever advantage there might be in the "logical situation." The same proposition was made to Washington. Vincennes let the golden opportunity slip; Washington city and township took a vote on the proposition and it was accepted by a substantial majority of the voters. The shops were erected in 1889. Shortly after this the Ohio & Mississippi road went into the hands of a receiver, and finally became the property of the Baltimore & Ohio Company, being now operated by that company.

The buildings of the Baltimore & Ohio shops, as the plant is now known, consists of a round-house, containing thirty-four stalls; a machine shop, erecting shop, tin, cooper and pipe shop, boiler shop, planing mill, passenger-car shop, paint shop, steel-car shop and freight-car shop.

In the several shops and departments there are at present something over six hundred men employed. The average monthly payroll of all the departments is forty-nine thousand dollars. The shops are equipped with facilities and machinery of modern design, with skilled workmen employed in all the manufacturing departments. They build locomotives, passenger cars, freight cars, dining cars—in fact, do any kind of work that is done at any of the large locomotive and car-building plants.

THE WASHINGTON POSTOFFICE.

The postoffice was established in Washington, October 9, 1817, James J. Read being appointed postmaster on that date. Following are the names of those who have served as postmaster in Washington, and the date of their appointment, since the first:

Seth Reddick, June 11, 1821; E. H. McJunkin, September, 1828; John Murphy, July 29, 1829; William C. Berry, April 4, 1838; Michael Murphy, May 22, 1840; S. A. Rodarmel, March 30, 1861; J. S. Berkshire, April 20, 1864; William A. Horrall, March 26, 1869; Albion Horrall, May 19, 1877; Stephen Belding, March 1, 1886; William P. Ellis, October 19, 1889; J. W. McCarty, February 5, 1894; Frank I. Sefrit, January 14, 1898; E. C. Faith, January 26, 1904; Benjamin J. Burris, January 30, 1912; Ernest E. Forsythe, July 30, 1913, the present postmaster.

Congress has made an appropriation of sixty thousand dollars for a postoffice building in Washington; five thousand of this has been used in the purchase of a site, and some money has been expended in the preliminary and foundation work. As soon as the other part of the appropriation is available the contract for the construction of the building will be awarded and in due time Washington will have a suitable place for the handling of the large amount of mail matter passing through the office, an accommodation that the city is very much in need of at the present time.

THE PUBLIC LIBRARY IN WASHINGTON.

The movement for the establishment of a public library in Washington had its origin in act of the Legislature, providing that a certain per cent. of the proceeds derived from the sale of town lots should be used for that purpose. This provision was incorporated in the act creating Daviess county, and it was provided that the library should be established and maintained as a county library. In accordance with the provisions of this act, a small fund was secured and a library was established in the early twenties. The making of many books was not as prevalent then as now, and the selection of books for this first library was confined to a very limited list.

If there was anything in the nature of light reading, in the catalogue of books, from which selections might have been made at that time, the persons who made the selections for the first library certainly overlooked the chance. Among the selections made were the following: "History of the Martyrs, " Buck's "Theological Dictionary," Wesley's "Sermons," "Pilgrim's Progress," Young's "Night Thoughts," Thompson's "Seasons," Harvey's "Meditations," "Charles the Fifth," Rollin's "Ancient History," Plutarch's "Lives," Grimshaw's "History of the United States," Addison's "Spectator," Locke's Essays, Jefferson's "Notes," Woodbridge's Geography, "Children of the Abbey," Byron's Works, Pope's Essays, Shakespeare's Plays, Josephus's Works, and the like.

The librarian, in charge of a library stocked with heavy literature of this character, would not be overworked in handling the rush of school children for books, if the children of that time were like the children of the present time.

An act of the Legislature of 1852, provided for the establishment of township libraries. The townships were required to pay a small sum toward the expense and make suitable provision for the care of the books and the maintenance of the library. The books were to be furnished at the expense of the state. In 1854 and 1855, under the provisions of this act, the state distributed about eight sets, of three hundred volumes each, to the several townships of Daviess county. In these sets were all the leading works of that period, including many volumes of high merit. The township trustee was the custodian of these libraries, and for awhile they were very popular and largely patronized. Remnants of these township libraries may still be found in the office of township trustees; but most of the books of value will be found in the private libraries of citizens of the several townships, the books apparently having been taken out and never returned. Through the negligence of the custodian, no record was kept, and the borrower in time became the undisputed owner of the books. The township library books were all in substantial binding, and, unless wilfully destroyed, are, no doubt, in good condition.

About the time of the distribution of the township library books, William McClure, a citizen of New Harmony, of great wealth, died, leaving a large fortune as a bequest for the founding of public libraries throughout the state for the benefit of the working classes. These were known as the McClure, or working men's libraries, and were very popular wherever established. Several of these libraries were obtained for localities in Daviess county and were maintained for several years, to the great advantage of the community in which they were located. Like the township libraries, in time the books of the McClure libraries got into the hands of persons who were careless or indifferent about returning them. The custodian of the library was alike careless and indifferent about keeping a record of the books, and they are now scattered about in private libraries. A remnant may possibly be found in public libraries of later establishment in the schools and towns of the county.

THE CARNEGIE PUBLIC LIBRARY.

The Carnegie public library of Washington originated in a suggestion made by the ladies of the Monday Afternoon Club. Acting upon the suggestion, a meeting of about twelve citizens was held, February 21, 1901, in the office of Gardiner & Slimp. At that meeting a committee was appointed, consisting of Rev. I. I. Gorby, Ezra Mattingly and John W. McCarty, to correspond with Andrew Carnegie, for the purpose of ascertaining the conditions, and the amount he would be willing to donate, for the establishment of a public library in the city of Washington. Mr. Carnegie promptly responded to the inquiry of the committee, making an offer of fifteen thousand dollars for the establishment of the proposed library, which amount was afterward increased to twenty thousand dollars. The usual conditions were imposed as a condition to this donation: that an amount equal to ten per cent. of this donation should be guaranteed annually by the city as a fund for the permanent maintenance of the library. The city council accepted the donation on the conditions named, and guaranteed an annual appropriation of two thousand dollars as a maintenance fund.

On June 14, 1901, Joseph Cabel generously donated a large tract of ground, located on West Main street, for a library site and a public park. In accordance with a provision of an act of the General Assembly of 1901, a library board of seven members was appointed, three of whom were appointed by the judge of the circuit court, two by the city council and two by the city school board. Judge William R. Gardiner and Mayor John W. McCarty were appointed by Judge Houghton, of the circuit court; William F. Hoffmann and Mrs. J. M. Wakefield, by the city council; Ezra Mattingly and Mrs. T. A. Ackley, by the city school board. Mr. Hoffmann died on October 24, 1901, and Hamlet Allen was appointed in his place. Mrs. Wakefield and Mrs. Ackley resigned and their places were filled by Mrs. Austin F. Cabel and Mrs. J. W. Corning.

Patton & Miller, of Chicago, were selected as architects, plans and specifications were adopted, and a contract was let to Bulley & Andrews for the construction of the building. The contract price was sixteen thousand four hundred and ninety-one dollars, for all the work except heating, lighting, plumbing, sewerage, gas and water fittings. Furniture and book cases, and the work of finishing the two basement rooms, were also in addition to the contract price. The first brick was laid by Hamlet Allen in May, 1902. The building was completed and ready for occupancy by the latter part of December, 1902. The structure is of stone and brick, and is well and carefully built, of durable material and of the most approved style of workmanship. The architectural design is for a building of a durable and substantial character rather than one in which the ornamental and artistic features are most prominent.

John H. O'Neal, acting for himself, and in compliance with the wishes of his father-in-law, the late Dr. G. G. Barton, delivered to the library board over one thousand volumes. Some of these were books belonging to Mr. O'Neal, and some that were left in his custody, years ago, by Doctor Barton, for library purposes. There are now about ten thousand volumes in the library, of which fifty are the property of U. S. Grant Post No. 72, Grand Army of the Republic, which have been placed in the library for use and for safekeeping.

The first librarian was Mrs. Annie H. Gibson, who was appointed in 1902, and began her work on January 7, 1903. Those who have served as librarians since the establishment of the Carnegie library are the following: Mrs. Annie Gibson, 1903 to 1910; Miss Lucia Bogner, 1910 to 1911;

CARNEGIE LIBRARY, WASHINGTON.

ODD FELLOWS HOME, WASHINGTON.

Miss Helen Allen, 1911 to 1913. Miss Mary E. Waller is the present librarian, having begun her work in 1913, succeeding Miss Allen. Miss Adelia Casto is the assistant librarian.

Members of the present board of trustees are Prof. Hamlet Allen, president; Mayor John W. McCarty, vice-president; Ezra Mattingly, secretary and treasurer; W. F. Axtell, Mrs. A. F. Cabel, Mrs. M. S. Hastings and Mrs. Mary C. Shirley.

LIBRARIAN'S REPORT.

The following report of the librarian for the month of March, 1915, shows the number of books in the library on that date. The comparison of circulation with the corresponding month of the previous year shows a marked increase in patronage, the increase, it will be noted, being about equally distributed between adult and juvenile publications:

Total number of books on hand, March 1, 1915	9,645
Books added by purchase	236
Books added by gift	5
Number of books in library March 31, 1915	9,886

Circulation of books in March, 1915—
Adult		2,455
Juvenile		2,035
Total		4,490

Circulation, March, 1914—
Adult	1,864	
Juvenile	1,419	3,283
Increase circulation, March, 1915		1,207

Number of borrowers at beginning of month	1,783
New borrowers registered during month	79
Total number borrowers	1,862
Average daily circulation for March, 1915	144.83
Average daily circulation for March, 1914	131.32

BIOGRAPHICAL

MAGNESS J. CARNAHAN.

The success of men in business or any vocation depends upon character, as well as upon knowledge. Business demands confidence, and where that is lacking business ends. In every community some men are known for their upright lives, strong common sense and moral worth rather than for their wealth or political standing. Their neighbors and acquaintances respect them, the younger generations heed their examples, and when they "Wrap the drapery of their couches about them and lie down to pleasant dreams," posterity listens with reverence to the story of their quiet and useful lives. Among such men of a past generation, in Indiana, was Magness J. Carnahan, of Washington, Indiana, a progressive man of affairs, successful in material pursuits, but a man of modest and unassuming demeanor, well educated and a fine type of the reliable, self-made American, a friend to the poor, charitable to the faults of his neighbors, ready to unite with them in every good work and laudable public enterprise. He was proud of the county in which he lived, zealous for its progress and prosperity. He performed valiant service in behalf of the Union cause during the Civil War and, at the time of his death, was survived by a widow and a daughter who revere his memory.

Magness J. Carnahan was born on February 10, 1844, in Washington, Indiana. He was a son of Robert and Eliza (Graham) Carnahan, both of whom are natives of Kentucky, and who came to Daviess county, Indiana, in pioneer days. Magness J. Carnahan had a varied career. At the breaking out of the Civil War, he enlisted in Company C, Fifty-fifth Regiment, Indiana Volunteer Infantry, and at the expiration of his term of enlistment, re-enlisted in Company K, One Hundred and Seventeenth Regiment, Indiana Volunteer Infantry, serving nine months. He returned from the war and engaged in the clothing business at Loogootee, Indiana, in partnership with a Mr. Sefrit. He continued this business but a short time, when he formed another partnership with Thomas Adams and founded the hardware business that is now known as the Reynolds-Brooks Hardware Company.

He purchased the interest of Mr. Adams in 1873 and worked alone till 1884, when Lewis C. Brooks and Hervey Trueblood became members of the firm under the name of Carnahan & Company. The O'Donnell-Barrows Hardware Company, of Washington, is the successor to M. J. Carnahan Company. He thus built up two of the largest implement stores in southern Indiana. At one time he was also engaged in the grain and lumber business at Loogootee, and established a line of saw-mills. Later, he established a planing-mill at Loogootee, and still later he established the Carnahan Manufacturing Company there. He resided in Loogootee until 1900, when he moved to Washington.

Magness J. Carnahan was twice married, the first time at Louisville, Kentucky, in 1872, to Hattie Dunn, who died in 1885. His second marriage was to Margaret Trippet, in 1889, and to this second marriage two children were born, Helen, a graduate of Wellesley College, and Ramona, who died in infancy.

For some years prior to Mr. Carnahan's death, he lived at Washington. He had a splendid and imposing residence on East Main street. Magness J. Carnahan was a member of the Presbyterian church, in which he was a trustee and elder. He was a charter member of the Grand Army of the Republic at Loogootee, and throughout his life was prominent in the affairs of this patriotic organization. While in Washington, Mr. Carnahan served as a member of the county council.

HON. EZRA MATTINGLY.

The life history of the Hon. Ezra Mattingly has been for many years closely identified with the history of Daviess county, Indiana. Throughout the years his life has been one of untiring activity and it has been crowned with a gratifying degree of professional success. By a straightforward, honorable course, Mr. Mattingly has built up a good legal business. His life affords a further example of what an American youth, unaided by wealth, but plentifully endowed with energy and determination, can accomplish when accompanied by sound moral principles.

Ezra Mattingly was born on August 27, 1864, in Washington township, Daviess county, Indiana, and was reared on his father's farm. He attended the district schools and the old Southern Indiana Normal School at Mitchell. After leaving school, Mr. Mattingly engaged in teaching for seven years.

He then studied law in Washington and was admitted to the bar at the age of twenty-six. He has practiced law in Washington since his admission to the bar. His first partner was William Heffernan, and this firm continued in business for sixteen and one-half years. Mr. Mattingly's present partnership with Stephen E. Myers began on December 1, 1908.

On September 8, 1892, Mr. Mattingly was married to Tillie Millis, a daughter of Dr. Edward D. and Eliza Ann (Burton) Millis, and to this union three children have been born, Caroline, Edward J., and George E. Caroline is a graduate of the Washington high school and also of Franklin College, graduating from the latter institution in 1914 with high honors, and is now principal of the high school at Greens Fork, Indiana. Edward J. died in infancy. George E. is a freshman in Washington high school.

Mr. Mattingly is the youngest of a family of nine children: Albert G., who died on April 16, 1896; Mary E., the wife of John L. Johnson, of Bicknell, Indiana; James W., of Washington; Laura C., the wife of William H. Cole, of Okmulgee, Oklahoma; Elisha, of Washington; Samuel, who died on January 5, 1905; and two who died in infancy. His father was James Mattingly, a native of Mason county, Kentucky, who, because he hated human slavery, came to Daviess county, Indiana, and located upon a farm.

James Mattingly was first married to Catherine Barr, who died, leaving him two children, John and Martha, both of whom died many years ago. On March 4, 1849, he was married to Mary Ann Berry. They lived in Washington, Indiana, where he engaged in carpenter work until four or five years before his death, when failing health compelled him to return to farming. He died on the home farm in Washington township on January 31, 1865, at the age of fifty-five years. His widow died on March 26, 1914, at the age of eighty-five years. She never remarried and was for many years an active member of the Baptist church.

The paternal grandparents of Ezra Mattingly were natives of Kentucky and pioneers of Mason county. They were the parents of four children, John, Augustine, Sylvester and James, all of whom came to Daviess county, Indiana. The maternal grandfather was Beverly Berry, who was born in Kentucky in 1800 and who died in Daviess county, Indiana, in 1858. He likewise fled from the land of slavery to the free soil of Indiana. His wife was Ann Eliza (Evans) Berry, also a native of Mason county, Kentucky, born in 1802, who died in Daviess county, in 1872. They had a large family of children: Arthur, Evaline, Henry, James M., Mary Ann,

Sarah, Walter, Susan, Louisa, Amelia and John D., all of whom are now deceased except Amelia and John D.

Mrs. Ezra Mattingly was born in Orange county, Indiana, January 20, 1868, and is the eldest of four children, Tillie, Burton J., Caroline and William E. Her father, Dr. Edward D. Millis, is a native of Orange county, and her mother of Lawrence county, Indiana. Her mother died on September 12, 1898, at the age of fifty-two; her father still resides at Plainville. Her paternal grandfather was Capt. John Millis, who married Nancy Cloud, and her maternal grandfather was Zachariah Burton, who, for his second wife, married Matilda Teegarden. Zachariah Burton was a native of North Carolina, born in 1801, who became a pioneer of Lawrence county, Indiana, where he died in 1888. His children were Ransom, Caswell R., Mary S., Hugh F., Virginia C., John C., Margaret, Zachariah, Juliette, Eliza A., Sarah J., William H., George W., Caroline and Shubil.

Mr. Mattingly is actively interested in the civic and commercial affairs of his home city; is a director in the State Bank of Washington, attorney for the Union Savings and Loan Association and a member of the board of the Carnegie public library. He and his family are members of the Missionary Baptist church and he is a member of the board of trustees of his church and is a deacon of the local congregation. For several years he has served as a member of the board of trustees of Franklin College.

Throughout his life, Mr. Mattingly has been identified with the fortunes of the Republican party. He served as county attorney for two years and was county chairman in 1892 and 1894. From 1906 until 1910 he was a member of the Indiana state Senate, representing the district of Daviess and Pike counties, where he made an honorable record as a legislator, for which he is well known throughout the state of Indiana.

PROF. EUGENE D. MERRIMAN.

Perseverance and sterling worth are almost always sure to win conspicuous recognition in any locality, especially in educational work. Prof. Eugene D. Merriman, superintendent of the Washington city schools, for years has been recognized as one of the leading educators of this state. After an extensive course of training for educational work and wide experience as a teacher in the schools of Indiana and Illinois, Professor Merriman was called to Washington, as superintendent of city schools, in the fall of 1913, and has made a splendid record as the head of the schools since arriving in that city. He is a fine example of the successful, self-made man and not only deserves the confidence reposed in him by his fellow citizens, but also possesses a degree of talent and forcefulness of character which have made him successful as an instructor and educator. Professor Merriman is a man of strong fiber and vigorous mentality and has achieved a signal success as a director of educational work.

Prof. Eugene D. Merriman was born on August 8, 1871, in Huntington county, Indiana, the son of Hixon and Angeline (Broughman) Merriman, natives of Indiana, who were the parents of five children, Prof. Eugene D., of Washington; Cyril, of Camden, New Jersey; May, the wife of Fred Stacey, of Camden, New Jersey; Leona, the wife of L. C. Bowman, of Chicago; Hortense, who is unmarried and lives in Chicago, and Forrest, who died in early childhood.

Hixon Merriman was reared in Huntington county, Indiana. He owned a farm of forty acres, which he improved and where he reared his family. He sold this farm and moved to Marion, Indiana, where he now resides. His wife died in 1904 at the age of sixty years. Both were members of the Methodist Episcopal church.

The paternal grandparents of Prof. Eugene D. Merriman were Micajah Merriman and wife, natives of Ohio, who came to Indiana as pioneers. They took up land in Huntington county and owned a large farm where they died, well advanced in years. Their children were Hixon, Newton, Wayland, Jacob, Douglas, George and Basil. The maternal grandparents of Professor Merriman also came from Ohio in an early day and settled in Huntington county, in the village of Plum Tree. Mr. Broughman was a blacksmith and died in Plum Tree at an advanced age. They were the parents of five children, Sylvester, Angeline, Fremont, Colonel and Charles.

Prof. Eugene D. Merriman was reared on his father's farm in Huntington county, Indiana, and attended the district schools. After graduating from the district schools, he was a student at the Indiana State Normal School at Terre Haute and finally at DePauw University and the Indiana State University at Bloomington. After leaving Indiana University, he began teaching in the district schools of his home county and taught there for several years. His first principalship was at East Chicago, Indiana, after which he became superintendent of the North township schools, including East Chicago and Whiting. He remained there for seven years and then became a student at Cornell University at Ithaca, New York, being graduated from this university in 1905, with the degree of Bachelor of Arts.

From Cornell, he went to Belvidere, Illinois, as superintendent of the city schools and was there for eight years. During this period he attended Chicago University, from which institution he secured the degree of Master of Philosophy in 1911. Professor Merriman was called to Washington, Indiana, in 1913, as superintendent of the city schools there. There are three hundred students in the high school and about fifteen hundred pupils in the public schools of the county seat, over whom Professor Merriman has direct supervision. Superintendent Merriman is at present in attendance at Chicago University, during the summers, working for his Doctor's degree.

Prof. Eugene D. Merriman was married on August 15, 1896, to Elizabeth Stout, daughter of Job C. and Mary (Brady) Stout. One son, Merrill V., has been born to this union.

Mrs. Merriman was born in Huntington county, Indiana. Her parents were natives of Ohio, and early settlers in Huntington county. Her father died in 1910, at the age of seventy years, and her mother is still living. They were the parents of six children, Ella, Jennie, Mattie, William, Elizabeth and Nettie.

Professor Merriman and wife are members of the Methodist Episcopal church and take an active part in the affairs of this church, to which they are liberal contributors. Fraternally, Professor Merriman belongs to Washington Lodge No. 30, Free and Accepted Masons, Washington Chapter No. 92, Royal Arch Masons; the Knights of Pythias; the Royal Arcanum and the Modern Woodmen of America. Professor and Mrs. Merriman are members of the Order of the Eastern Star. Professor Merriman is a member of the National Education Association and has been prominently connected with the proceedings of that associattion. Mr. and Mrs. Merriman are popular in the social life of Washington and leaders in the social and civic affairs of that city.

CHARLES P. SCUDDER, M. D.

The man who devotes his talents and energies to the noble work of ministering to the ills and alleviating the sufferings of humanity pursues a calling which in dignity and importance is second to none other. If true to his profession and earnest in his efforts to enlarge his sphere of usefulness, he is indeed a great benefactor to all of his kind, for to him more than to any other man are entrusted the safety, the comfort, and in many instances the lives of those who place themselves under his care. Among this class of professional men is Dr. Charles P. Scudder, who has stood for many years, with few peers and no superiors, among the physicians of Daviess county, Indiana. During this time he not only has gained wide distinction in his chosen vocation, but also has established a substantial reputation for uprightness and character in all the relations of life. Doctor Scudder early realized that to those who attained well-defined success in the medical profession there must be given not only technical ability, but also broad human sympathy—a sympathy which passes mere sentiment and which becomes an actuating motive for helpfulness, and ever has sought to live up to this ideal, thus adding dignity and honor to his profession by noble purposes.

Charles P. Scudder, M. D., physician and surgeon, of Washington, Indiana, was born in that city on November 8, 1859, a son of Dr. John A. and Helen (Van Trees) Scudder, natives of Daviess county, who were the parents of seven children, namely: Dr. Charles P., with whom this narrative deals; Tillie F., the wife of S. B. Boyd, of the *Washington Democrat;* Laura G., the wife of John L. Winston, of Washington; Anna V., the wife of R. C. Davis, of Indianapolis; Dr. David A., deceased, and two who died young.

The late Dr. John A. Scudder, was reared in Daviess county, Indiana, and was a physician practicing in Washington for thirty-five or forty years. He served throughout the Civil War as an army surgeon and died in 1896, at the age of sixty-three years. His widow still survives him. Both were members of the Cumberland Presbyterian church. He was pension examiner in Washington for more than thirty-five years.

The paternal grandfather of Dr. Charles P. Scudder was Jacob S. Scudder, whose wife was Matilda Arrell. The former was a native of Daviess county, Indiana, and the latter a native of Pennsylvania. They were pioneer farmers of Veale township, this county, their home being six miles southwest of Washington. Jacob S. Scudder died in middle life, while his widow lived to reach the age of seventy-five. They were the parents of Dr. John A., Mrs. Elizabeth F. Hall, James, Emma and Dr. Charles, of whom Mrs. Hall is the only survivor.

John Scudder, the great-grandfather of Dr. Charles P. Scudder, was born in Freehold, New Jersey, and moved to Daviess county, Indiana, in 1819. He was a surgeon in the Revolutionary army, serving in the regiment of his father, Col. Nathaniel Scudder, also a physician, who was born on Long Island. His parents moved to Princeton, New Jersey, when he was sixteen years of age, and he was graduated from Princeton University, in 1751.

The maternal grandparents of Dr. Charles P. Scudder were John and Laura (Prentiss) Van Trees, the former a native of Cincinnati, Ohio, and the latter a native of Indiana, pioneers in Daviess county. For many years John Van Trees was a merchant in Washington, and was county clerk for more than thirty years. Both died in Washington. The biographical sketch of Warren Van Trees, presented elsewhere in this volume, gives additional interesting details regarding the Van Trees family history.

Charles P. Scudder, M. D., therefore comes from two of the oldest and most highly respected families of Daviess county, and is descended from a long line of physicians and surgeons. He was born and reared in Washington, Indiana, where he attended the public schools, being graduated at the head of his class at the Washington high school, after which he took up the study of medicine. In 1881 he was graduated from the Miami Medical College at Cincinnati and has practiced continuously in Washington for thirty-four years.

On August 20, 1895, Doctor Scudder was married to Louise J. Stamper, a daughter of William W. and Bertie (Davis) Stamper, and to this union four children have been born, Charles P., John A., William W. and David Fenwick, the latter of whom died at the age of two and one-half years. Mrs. Scudder was born in Owen county, Kentucky. Her parents, who likewise were natives of that county, are now living in Louisville, Kentucky. They are the parents of four children, Louise J., who married Doctor Scudder; Mrs. Ruth Swope; Mrs. A. W. Ellen, and John, the latter of whom died when a child.

Mrs. Scudder's father is a native of Kentucky, and is one of two children born to his parents, William W. and Elwood Stamper, the latter of whom is connected with the Second National Bank, of Louisville. Mrs. Scudder's maternal grandfather was Alfred P. Davis, who was a native of Kentucky, in which state he spent his entire life. He was the father of four children, Richard C., John O., George and Bertie, by his first marriage; and by his second marriage he had two children, Harry and Mrs. Allie Jones.

The founder of the Scudder family in America was Thomas Scudder, who came from London, England, and who lived at Salem, Massachusetts, as early as 1635. There he resided until his death in 1658. His wife was Elizabeth Scudder.

Charles P. Scudder, M. D., is a member of the Daviess County Medical Society, the Indiana State Medical Association and the American Medical

Associatiton. He is surgeon for the Chicago & Eastern Illinois Railway Company, and fraternally, is a member of the Benevolent and Protective Order of Elks. Politically, Doctor Scudder is a Republican. Mrs. Scudder is a member of the Presbyterian church, of which the family are faithful attendants and to the support of which they are liberal supporters.

ERNEST E. FORSYTHE.

Among the enterprising, progressive and public-spirited men, whose activities in business and political circles, as well as in public affairs, have made Daviess county one of the thriving counties of Indiana, and the city of Washington an important center of commerce and industry, is Ernest Forsythe, who is at present holding the responsible position of postmaster at Washington, and who is regarded as one of the influential men of Washington and Daviess county.

Ernest E. Forythe was born on April 2, 1873, at Nineveh, in Johnson county, Indiana, the son of David P. and Mary L. (Logan) Forsythe, the former of whom was a native of Johnson county, Indiana, and the latter of Kentucky. Mrs. Mary L. Forsythe rode on the horn of a saddle with her mother, when a baby, in coming from Oldham county, Kentucky, to Johnson county, Indiana, where she grew to womanhood and was married, and where the rest of her life was spent, her death occurring in 1903. David P. Forsythe died on March 28, 1915, at the home of his son, the subject of this sketch. His wife was originally a member of the Baptist church (old school), but later identified herself with the Methodist church. They were farmers in Johnson county, Mr. Forsythe owning a farm of eighty acres, which he sold before moving into Nineveh. They were the parents of ten children, Thomas T., deceased; Martha L., deceased, who was the wife of A. C. Deer; Sarah J., deceased; who was the wife of W. D. Terhune; Flora, the wife of Frank Chambers, of Clermont, Indiana; Oscar D., of Washington, this county; Josephine, the wife of N. F. Houston, of Topeka, Kansas; John E., of San Diego, California; Margaret L., the wife of Marshall Deer, of Johnson county, Indiana; Ernest E., of Washington, and Gussie E., the wife of Dr. J. J. Deer, of Zionsville, Indiana.

The paternal grandparents of Ernest E. Forsythe were David and Margaret (Pritchard) Forsythe, natives of Kentucky and pioneer farmers of Johnson county, Indiana, where they died and were buried upon the farm upon which they settled upon coming to this state. They brought their slaves with them from the South, but upon arriving on free soil freed their bondmen. The latter remained with them, however, and were buried in the same graveyard with their former master and mistress. The children born to David Forsythe and wife were David P., Sarah and Betsey. David Forsythe was married, secondly, to a Miss Lawins and two children were born to this latter union, Andrew J. and Elkanah.

The great-grandfather of Ernest E. Forsythe was also David Forsythe. He was the original David of the American line of this family and his wife was a girl that he had cared for on the voyage across the ocean to America. The original David Forsythe was born in Ireland and was a member of the Protestant church. He moved from Ireland to Scotland and thence to America, to obtain religious freedom. He located in Virginia, married Margaret Gibbins and reared a family, the numerous progeny of which is now represented in many states in the Union.

Ernest E. Forsythe's maternal grandparents were John and Paulina (Sturgeon) Logan, the former of whom was a native of Ireland. They were married in Kentucky and were pioneers in Johnson county, Indiana, where he was a plasterer by trade and later a farmer. They died on the old home place in Johnson county. They were the parents of Harry, Mary L., John, Margaret, Elliot and Nancy Eaton.

Ernest E. Forsythe, the subject of this sketch, was reared in Nineveh, Indiana, but was brought up as a farmer lad. He attended the Nineveh public schools and the high school and then went to the Danville Normal school, where he took the teachers' course. Afterwards he taught in the public schools of Johnson county for one year and then accepted a position with the Rock Island Railroad, at Herrington, Kansas. He worked in the baggage and freight department of that road for a time and later in the general offices of the Santa Fe Railroad at Topeka, Kansas, which latter position he resigned to accept a proposition from a Chicago portrait company as state agent for Indiana, with headquarters at Indianapolis. While occupying this position he was married, on June 1, 1896, to Mabel C. Fisher, the daughter of William H. and Mary J. (Good) Fisher, of Franklin, Indiana, to which union two children have been born, Harold, now aged seventeen, and Paul, aged eight.

Mrs. Forsythe was born in Johnson county, Indiana, her parents also being natives of the same county. The latter now reside in Franklin, where they celebrated their fiftieth wedding anniversary in October, 1914. They have five children, Lester, Herbert M., Earl C., Nellie and Mabel C. Mrs.

Forsythe's paternal grandfather was Capt. William Fisher, who served with distinction in the Union army during the Civil War.

Mr. Forsythe is an efficient postmaster. He was appointed to that responsible office in August, 1913, and is now holding the position, his service proving very satisfactory to the patrons of the Washington post office. Mr. Forsythe is a Democrat and for years has been active in the councils of his party. Mr. and Mrs. Forsythe are members of the Christian church as also is their son, Harold. Mr. Forsythe belongs to Moore Lodge No. 304, Free and Accepted Masons, of Odon, Indiana; Washington Chapter No. 92, Royal Arch Masons; the Washington lodge of the Independent Order of Odd Fellows; the Odon lodge of Knights of Pythias, and the Washington lodge of the Modern Woodmen of America. Ernest E. Forsythe is not only an efficient postmaster, but he is a good citizen and is held in high esteem by a host of friends and acquaintances who know him best.

SYLVESTER A. WHISMAN.

In and around the town of Elnora, in Elmore township, Daviess county, and throughout that whole part of the county, there is perhaps no one who does not know the gentleman whose name is noted above. Mr. Whisman is not only the heaviest property owner in the town of Elnora, but is one of the most extensive farmers and stock raisers in the county, his business operations covering a wide range. As farmer, stock raiser, merchant and banker, he has been a successful manager in all he has undertaken and in consequence wields a large measure of influence in the community in which his activities for years have been expended. Not only is he widely known, but he is personally popular among all with whom he comes in contact and there are few men in the county who have a larger personal following than he. A large man, of exceptional physical endowment, he also is a man of large heart and his friends are limited only by the number of his acquaintances. It is a pleasure therefore for the biographer here to call the reader's attention to a brief review of the achievements of this notable personality, whose influence in behalf of better things in Daviess county has been for so many years so wisely and widely exerted.

Sylvester A. Whisman was born in Monroe county, Indiana, near the village of Elletsville, on January 23, 1852, the son of George and Lettie (Hightower) Whisman, the former of whom was a native of Virginia and the latter a native of Tennessee. George Whisman, who was a teamster in Virginia, emigrated to Indiana in his middle age and bought a farm near Elletsville, in Monroe county, where he spent the rest of his life. To him and his wife there were born four children, William G., Harondon L., Sylvester A., the immediate subject of this sketch, and Nicey.

Sylvester A. Whisman was reared in Monroe county, attending the township schools of the neighborhood in which his parents lived. The first school that he attended was equipped as to seats, or benches for the pupils to sit upon, with split logs upheld by pegs driven into the rounded side, the children perching themselves upon the split surface, which Mr. Whisman recalls was not always entirely free from splinters, to the no small discomfort of the wriggling urchins who were compelled to occupy these precarious benches. Upon reaching manhood's estate, Mr. Whisman started farming in Monroe county and remained there until 1862, in which year he moved to Morgan county, Indiana, taking a farm near Martinsville, on which he remained until the year 1893, in which year he came to Daviess county, taking a farm in Elmore township, about one mile west of Elnora, on which he ever since has made his home.

Mr. Whisman believes in doing things on a large scale and for years managed no less than one thousand acres of land in the vicinity of Elnora. As his other business interests grew, however, he gradually reduced his farm holdings until now he operates but four hundred and thirty-seven acres; his sons and farm employees doing the active work of the farm, to which general farming is added stock raising on an extensive scale, particular attention being paid to white-faced cattle and the big type of Poland-China hogs, Mr. Whisman giving his close personal attention to the direction of the various phases of the cultivation of his broad fields.

In addition to his large farming interests, Mr. Whisman is the heaviest individual property owner in Elnora, and is a stockholder in the Elnora bank and in the bank at Marco. For the past sixteen years he has been a full partner in the general store at Elnora, with W. H. Black, this business also having prospered, as have all the other enterprises with which Mr. Whisman has been connected. He finds time, in connection with his large business affairs, to give a proper degree of attention to public affairs and his voice ever is heard in behalf of all movements having for their object the advancement of the common welfare. He is a Democrat and takes a no inconsiderable part in the campaigns of that party in his part of the county. For some years Mr. Whisman has given his services to the public in his vicinity as a member of the township advisory board, his excellent executive ability and sound business judgment proving invaluable in that connection.

Mr. Whisman has been thrice married. By his first wife, who was Carrie B. Constable, he had one child, a daughter, Ella, who married Earl Melsheimer. He married, secondly, Nellie Dutton, to which union four children were born, Joseph, Richard, Harry and William, the latter of whom is deceased. By his third wife, Oma Williams, there were two children, daughters, Lucy and Mary. To all these children Mr. Whisman has been a most devoted father and his sons, under his careful training, are taking an earnest and active part in the affairs of the locality in which they were reared. There are few men in Daviess county who are doing a larger work than is Mr. Whisman and he is regarded with the utmost respect and esteem by all who know him.

JOHN L. CLARK.

Specific mention is made of the many worthy citizens of Daviess county, Indiana, within the pages of this book, citizens who have figured in the growth and development of this favored locality and whose interests are identified with its every phase of progress, each contributing in his sphere of action to the well-being of the community in which each resides and to the advancement of its moral and legitimate growth. Among this number is John L. Clark, the present county treasurer of Daviess county. Although Mr. Clark is not a native of Daviess county, he is a native of the grand old commonwealth of Indiana, and has contributed his best energies to the moral and civic advancement of this great state.

Mr. Clark was born on February 13, 1863, at Weisburg, in Dearborn county, Indiana, a son of John and Carolina (Coman) Clark, natives of Dearborn county, who were the parents of ten children, namely: Mary, the wife of W. H. Patterson, of Bogard township; Clara, the widow of Francis Ferguson; Emma, the widow of James T. Williams; Ollie, the wife of Frank P. Eaton, of this county; John L., of Washington; Howard, of East Chicago, and four who died while young.

John Clark, the father of John L., was reared in Indiana, and was a farmer in Decatur county. Later he became a merchant at Weisburg, and for some years before coming to Daviess county, operated a saw-mill. In his latter years he was a farmer in Steele township, where he owned a farm of eighty acres. He died there in 1898, at the age of seventy-four years.

His wife died in 1869. Both were members of the Methodist church. John Clark was a man of rather wide political influence in Daviess county, having served two terms as county commissioner, an office which he filled with exceptional ability.

John L. Clark's paternal grandparents were natives of North Carolina and early settlers of the eastern part of Indiana. Their children were William, John, Samuel and a daughter.

John L. Clark was reared mostly in Daviess county, Indiana, and has lived here from the time he was nine years old. He was reared as a farmer boy and attended the district schools, living at home until he reached his maturity. He then married and rented land for several years. Finally he purchased forty acres of land in Steele township, which he improved and then added thirty-eight acres, which he still owns. He lived there until the spring of 1913, at which time he was appointed to fill out an unexpired term as county treasurer, he having previously, in 1912, been elected to the same office, and he is still holding this office. Mr. Clark also served four years as trustee of Bogard township.

On February 26, 1885, John L. Clark was married to Mary E. Morgan, a daughter of James and Laura (Burris) Morgan, natives of Indiana, and to this happy union seven children were born, Len L., Raymond E., John V., Vivian, Edwin, Lyle and Emma. Len L. is a carpenter at Bickell, Indiana. He married Effie Dalton, and they have one child, Fred. Vivian died at the age of nine months and Emma at the age of four months. The other children are all at home.

Mrs. Mary E. (Morgan) Clark, the mother of these children, died on January 12, 1912, at the age of thirty-eight. She was born in Barr township and was a member of the Methodist Episcopal church. Her father died in 1909 at the age of seventy-six, and her mother is still living. James and Laura (Burris) Morgan were the parents of thirteen children, Della, Mary, William, Thomas, James, Lucretia, Hattie, John and Frank, twins; Lucinda, Martha, Sarah and Ethel.

On October 6, 1909, Mr. Clark married, secondly, Sarah E. Small, a daughter of William H. and Ann (Sanford) Small, and to this union two children have been born, Robert and Walter, the former of whom died at the age of eighteen months. Mrs. Sarah E. (Small) Clark was born in Barr township. Her parents are now deceased. They were early settlers in Barr township, and were the parents of eleven children, Joseph, Reuben, John, Benjamin, Virginia, Tabitha, Mary, Lucretia, Helen, Sarah E. and Thomas.

Mr. Clark is a member of the Christian church, while Mrs. Clark belongs to the Baptist church. Politically, Mr. Clark is a Democrat and for years has been a potent factor in the political affairs of Daviess county. He is a modest, unassuming man, although he has won more than ordinary success in life; first, having made a success in his life's vocation; secondly, having served the people of Daviess county in a satisfactory manner, in at least two important offices. His integrity is beyond question, and he is not only highly respected by the people of Daviess county, but he is much admired for what he has been able to accomplish in life.

REV. CHARLES H. BUCHANAN.

There is no station in life higher than that of the ministry of the Gospel; no life can do more dignified and uplifting than that which is devoted to the amelioration of the condition of the human race; a life of sacrifice for the betterment of the brotherhood of man, one that is willing to cast aside all earthly crowns and laurels of fame in order to follow in the footsteps of the lowly Nazarene. One of those self-sacrificing, ardent, loyal and true spirits is the Rev. Charles H. Buchanan, whose life forcefully illustrates what energy, integrity and a fixed purpose can accomplish, when animated by noble aims and correct ideals. He has ever held the confidence and esteem of the people among whom he labors, and his career may be profitably studied by the ambitious youth, standing at the parting of the ways.

Charles H. Buchanan is a native of St. John, province of New Brunswick, Canada, where he was born on November 5, 1875, the son of James and Mary J. (Gay) Buchanan, both of whom were of English descent. The father was born on November 27, 1842, in London, England, his father, James W. Buchanan, having been a native of Glasgow, Scotland, where he was engaged in the bookbinding business. James Buchanan was educated in the public schools of his native city and country and remained there until seventeen years of age, when he decided to leave England for Canada. At the age of twenty-three he entered the English army, was duly assigned and later became a sergeant, then was promoted to the ranks of major and drill-master of St. John's Infantry. He remained in the army service for a period of twenty-eight years and then established himself in the bookbinding business in St. John, New Brunswick, Canada, which he continued for twenty-three years and at the present time is working at that trade. He was the founder and organizer of what is known as the Scots company of the boy's brigade, of St. John. His wife, Mary J. Gay, was born on June 12, 1848, in Somerside, Prince Edward Island. To their union were born eight children named, in the order of their birth, as follow: George A., born on September 3, 1868, who married a Miss Crofoot and now lives in Syracuse, New York, where he is president of a chemical company; William J., August 28, 1870, who married Maud Hanna, now living in the city of Brooklyn, New York, where he is pastor of a Congregational church; Anna Maud, June 10, 1873, who married Alfred Buckle, and died in September, 1904; Charles H., the subject of this review; Minnie I., December 25, 1877, who is now Mrs. Edward Smith, of Springfield, Massachusetts; Elizabeth Gay, May 7, 1880, who married Percy W. Campbell and died in July, 1907; Agnes L., April 13, 1882, who is the wife of Elbridge Benn, and Victoria R., August 24, 1887, who married Walter Sproul. The parents of these children are living in Canada and are active and devout members of the Presbyterian church in their home city, where they enjoy the high regard and confidence of all who know them. Their lives have been ideal and and have been marked by the utmost devotion to their children.

Charles H. Buchanan received his early education in the public schools of St. John, New Brunswick, and lived with his parents until about the age of nineteen. During this time he was occupied for the term of five years as an apprentice in the tinsmithing and plumbing trades, but, having decided that his vocation lay in another line, he left St. John when twenty-one years of age and came to the United States, going to Lexington, Kentucky, where he became enrolled in a Bible college, where he remained during the years 1897, 1898 and 1899 preparing himself for the ministry. After his graduation, in 1899, he went to Elnoro, Daviess county, Indiana, having been assigned to the pastorate of the First Christian church of that place, and on January 27 of that year was married to Bradie Lane. During the years 1899 and 1900 he served as pastor for the church named, in Elnoro, and also took up work in connection with the First Christian church in the town of Odon, this county, and for four years preached for both congregations. In the year 1903 he organized a congregation in Plainville, this county, and kept this under his charge until 1912. At the present time Reverend Buchanan divides his time between his congregation in Elnoro, this county, and the congregation of the Christian church in Houston, Jackson county, Indiana.

Mrs. Buchanan was born on September 13, 1882, in Odon, this county, a daughter of Dr. Allen K. Lane, by his third wife. Doctor Lane was born on January 25, 1843, in Washington county, Indiana, a son of Richard and Jane (Martin) Lane, who were natives of Tennessee and Kentucky, born in 1811 and 1817, respectively. They were married about the year 1837, shortly after which they took up their residence in the town of Martinsburg, Washington county, Indiana, where the father lived until 1845 and the mother until 1873. Mrs. Buchanan's father, Dr. Allen K. Lane, remained with his parents in early youth and received his preparatory education in the public schools. At the age of seventeen he began the study of medicine under Dr. James McPheeters in Fredericksburg, Washington county, Indiana, and remained with this preceptor until the year 1865, when he began the practice of medicine for himself in Pitts Point, Kentucky, continuing to practice there until the year 1869, when he removed to this county. He first located in the village of Raglesville, where he stayed until 1876, in which year he moved to Odon, this county. Through the able teaching of his friend, Doctor McPheeters, and by constant study and research, Doctor Lane, acquired a thorough practical knowledge of medicine; and, on account of his sympathetic ministrations, gentle consideration and fine fellow-feeling for the sufferings of humanity, he inspired confidence and is held in the highest esteem by everyone who knows him. Doctor Lane retired from the active practice of medicine in 1911 and now devotes considerable time to his farm of two hundred acres, situated near Odon.

Doctor Lane has been married three times. His first wife was Angie Glenn, born in 1844; married in 1863 and died in 1875. To that union were born three children, Chester A., deceased at the age of five years; Maude, who married John T. Sears, to which union four children have been born, Dale, Verna, Hobart and Bessie, and Blanche, who married Ripple Sears, to which union three children have been born, Paul, Lettie and Margaret. The second wife was Mary J. Kelsey, born in 1853; married in 1876 and died in 1878. To that union was born one child, who died in infancy. The third wife, Sarah Kelsey, a sister of the second wife, is the mother of but one child, Bradie, the wife of the subject of this review. Doctor Lane is a member of the Christian church of Odon, and is a member of the Independent Order of Odd Fellows and the Free and Accepted Masons. Personally, he is held up by everyone in the community as example of right living, his honorable methods in all dealings with his fellow men having won for him the admiration of all, and he is eminently deserving of the high position he holds in this community.

Rev. Charles H. Buchanan and wife, who make their home with Doctor Lane, are the parents of two children, Allen K., born on March 9, 1908, and died on September 24, 1913. The Rev. Charles H. Buchanan is held in the highest regard throughout the wide field covered by his ministerial labors, and his devotion, as a worker in the cause of his Master, merits for him a place in any history touching upon the lives and deeds of those who have given the best of their powers and talents for the aid and betterment of mankind in this section of the state. To those who are familiar with his life there comes a feeling of reverence in the contemplation of his services and their beneficent results. His long labors in this community have endeared him to the hearts of everyone with whom he has come in contact and he is, in the most significant sense, regarded as a true friend of humanity.

ELMER E. HASTINGS.

The life of Elmer E. Hastings has been for many years closely identified with the history of Daviess county, Indiana. His life has been crowned with a degree of professional success attained by comparatively few of those who aspire to eminence in the legal profession. Although a comparatively young man, years of conscientious work as a lawyer have brought with them not only an increase of practice, but a higher and more eminent standing in the estimation of his clients and fellow citizens. Mr. Hastings' life is an excellent example of what may be accomplished by a young man endowed with common sense, energy and determination. He has achieved a splendid reputation before the bar, at an age when many are merely starting out on their life's work. He has always been methodical and unswervingly persistent in search of essentials.

Elmer E. Hastings, of the law firm of Hastings, Allen & Hastings, Washington, Indiana, was born in Bogard township, Daviess county, on March 4, 1870, a son of John A. and Laura (Allen) Hastings, whose family history is contained in the biographical sketch of M. S. Hastings, a brother of Elmer E., presented elsewhere in this volume.

Elmer E. Hastings was reared on his father's farm in Bogard township, and attended the public schools of this county and the Southern Indiana Normal School at Mitchell, as well as the Central Normal School at Danville, Indiana, being graduated from the latter school in 1891. While a student at the Danville school, Mr. Hastings took the scientific and literary courses. After graduation, he taught school; in fact, he had taught several terms before leaving Danville. Two years later, he began the study of law in the office of Hastings & Allen. Mr. Hastings was admitted to the bar in 1892, and on January 1, 1894, he became a member of the firm of Hastings, Allen & Hastings, which firm has continued in business in Washington since that time, a period of nearly a quarter of a century. It is one of the oldest and well-established law firms of Washington and enjoys a large and lucrative practice in the courts throughout this section of Indiana.

Shortly after his admission to the bar, Elmer E. Hastings was married, November 30, 1893, to Bertha J. Garten, who was born in Madison township, this county, the daughter of Capt. James H. and Mary E. (Booth) Garten, to which happy union three children have been born, Ralph G., John S. and Eleanor E.

Capt. James H. Garten was a native of Indiana, having been born in Lawrence county, but he grew to manhood in Davies county. His wife was born in Ohio and came to Daviess county when a child. Captain Garten died on April 15, 1914, at the age of seventy-seven. His wife had preceded him to the grave in 1892. Capt. James H. Garten was a soldier in the Union army during the Civil War. He enlisted as a private and was mustered out of the service as a captain. He and his wife were the parents of two children, James E. and Bertha J.

Elmer E. Hastings is a Republican and served as city attorney of Washington for two years; deputy prosecuting attorney for four years and prosecuting attorney for one term of two years. Mr. Hastings was city chairman of the Republican committee through four campaigns. He was president of the Lincoln League of Indiana in 1910 and 1911. Mr. and Mrs. Hastings are members of the Methodist Episcopal church. He is one of the trustees of the church and is president of the Brotherhood class. Fraternally, Mr. Hastings is a member of Charity Lodge No. 30, Free and Accepted Masons; Washington Chapter No. 92, Royal Arch Masons; Washington Commandery No. 33, Knights Templar; Liverpool Lodge No. 110, Independent Order of Odd Fellows, and Washington Lodge No. 933, Benevolent and Protective Order of Elks. He was grand master of the Indiana grand lodge of Independent Order of Odd Fellows in 1907. Mr. and Mrs. Hastings reside at 609 East Walnut street, Washington, Indiana.

Elmer E. Hastings is one of the influential figures in the councils of his party in the second Congressional district and has been so for many years. By reason of his connection with the Lincoln League of Indiana, he has the reputation which extends beyond the limits of the second district. He is genial in disposition and, by training and temperament, is well equipped for the duties of a public career.

HON. JAMES PORTER.

Indiana has been especially honored in the character and career of her men of industry and public service. In every section have been found men born to leadership in the various vocations; men who have dominated because of their superior intelligence, natural endowment and force of character. It is always profitable to study the lives of such men, to weigh their motives and to hold up their achievements as incentives to greater activity and higher excellence on the part of others. These reflections are suggested by the career of one who has forged his way to the front ranks and who, by a strong inherent force and marked business ability, directed and controlled by intelligence and judgment of a high order, has been recognized, for over a quarter of a century, as one of the leading men of the state. No citizen in southern Indiana has achieved more honorable mention or occupied a more conspicuous place in the public eye than Senator James Porter, of Washington. Success is the result of methodical and consecutive endeavor. Senator Porter's success was attained by normal methods and means—the determined application of mental and physical resources along correctly defined lines. To offer, in a work of this character, an adequate resume of the career of this man, would be impossible; but, with others of those who have promoted the civic, agricultural and commercial progress of Daviess county and this section of Indiana, we may well note the more salient points that have marked his life and labors. He is a prominent and influential factor in the public affairs of his county, as well as in the enterprises with which he has been connected; having gained success through legitimate and worthy means, he stands as an admirable type of the self-made man.

James Porter, state senator from this district, was born in Reeve township, Daviess county, Indiana, on May 3, 1845, son of James and Ann (McCoy) Porter, the former a native of Ohio, and the latter of Virginia, who came to Daviess county in 1832 and bought a farm of one hundred and sixty acres in Reeve township, which they cleared and improved and where they reared their family. James Porter was a man of enterprise and push and prospered from the start, adding to this farm until he owned about five hundred acres. He died on the home farm in 1890, at the age of eighty-nine years. His wife had preceded him to the grave, her death occurring in 1875, at the age of sixty-two. Both were members of the Presbyterian church. James Porter served as justice of the peace for Reeve township for a number of years. He and his wife were the parents of ten children, Robert, Calvin, John and William, all deceased; James, the subject of this sketch; Steward, deceased; Marion, of Oklahoma; Elizabeth, the wife of Joseph H. Watts, of Grand View, Alabama; George, of Fort Worth, Texas, and Joseph, of Enid, Oklahoma.

The paternal grandfather of Senator Porter was James Porter, Sr., a native of Ohio. He and his wife lived in Jefferson county, Ohio, and died there well advanced in years. They were farmers and had five children, James, Joseph, Calvin, Elizabeth and Margaret.

James Porter, the subject of this sketch, was reared on his father's farm. He attended the old-fashioned subscription schools, in a log cabin with puncheon floor and a fire-place with clay-and-stick chimney, the teacher "boarding around." There were slabs for seats and the writing desk consisted of a board placed along the wall and supported with wooden pins. Mr. Porter lived at home until grown. He made his first money by hard labor and considered himself fortunate if he received fifty cents for a day's work. He then took a lease on a piece of timber land and cleared it up, making the rails with which to build the fences, and continued to farm as he cleared the land. His first purchase was three hundred acres of land on the east fork of White river in Harrison township, in partnership with two of his brothers. They cleared two hundred and forty acres of this land and a few years later James Porter owned the whole place. He lived there some years and added to this farm until at one time he owned about seven hundred and forty acres. His children were all born in that neighborhood. In March, 1889, he bought a home in the corporate limits of the city of Washington, with six acres of land, which has been his home ever since. In the meantime, Senator Porter has sold all his other lands.

In 1863 James Porter enlisted in Company K, One Hundred and Seventeenth Regiment, Indiana Volunteer Infantry, and served about seven months as a corporal. There were five brothers in the Porter family who went into the service and all lived to return home. Two, however, were wounded.

On October 1, 1874, James Porter was married to Judith Lemmon, the daughter of Elijah and Isabel (Summerville) Lemmon. Five children were born to this union, one of whom died in infancy, the others being Eva, who died young; Artie and Bessie, both at home, and Clara, who married Robert Porter, of Enid, Oklahoma, and has one daughter, Thelma.

Mrs. Porter was born in DuBois county, Indiana, and her parents, both of whom are now deceased, also were natives of this state. They were the parents of six children, namely: James, deceased; Clay Houston, deceased; Scott, Judith and Elizabeth, the latter of whom is deceased. The paternal grandparents of Mrs. Porter were Jacob and Catherine Lemmon, both natives of Pennsylvania, the former being of German descent. They had four children, Elijah, Jacob, James and Judith. Jacob Lemmon, Sr., had been formerly married and had four children by that union, John, David, Abraham and Susan.

Mrs. Porter is a member of the Presbyterian church. Mr. Porter belongs to Charity Lodge No. 30, Free and Accepted Masons; Washington Chapter No. 92, Royal Arch Masons, and Washington Commandery No. 33, Knights Templar. Politically, he is a Republican. He has served the people of Daviess county as county commissioner and county councilman, and in 1914 was elected to the state Senate of Indiana, which office he did not seek. During the session of 1915 of the Indiana General Assembly, Senator Porter was one of the leaders of the Republican minority in the Senate.

PROFESSOR HAMLET ALLEN.

Perseverance and sterling worth are almost always sure to win conspicuous recognition in any locality. Prof. Hamlet Allen has a remarkable record as an educator. He has been teaching almost continuously for forty years and for more than twenty years has been principal of the Washington, Indiana, high school. His career affords a splendid example of the successful self-made man, who is not only eminently deserving of the confidence reposed in him by the people of Washington and Daviess county, but who also possesses the talents and forcefulness that have made him successful as an instructor and educator. He is a man of strong mental fiber and has achieved a signal success in the educational world. Professor Allen has earned a signal success in the educational world. Professor Allen has earned high words of commendation from those competent to form a proper estimate of his worth, and his long tenure as principal of the Washington high school is a distinct evidence of the esteem in which he is held by the people of this city.

Prof. Hamlet Allen was born six miles northeast of Washington, Indiana, in Washington township, Daviess county, on August 12, 1849, son of Johnson and Mary J. (Sanford) Allen, the former a native of Washington township and the latter of Mason county, Kentucky, who were the parents of four children, Hamlet; William, deceased; Anna J., who married M. J. Hayes, a merchant of Washington, and is now deceased, and Virginia C., the widow of Benjamin F. Strasser, now living in Denver, Colorado.

Johnson Allen was reared in Daviess county, Indiana, and became a substantial farmer, at one time owning a farm of two hundred and eighty acres, which he improved. He first cleared a farm of eighty acres in Harrison township and the three younger children were born in Harrison township. During the last twenty years of his life he lived in Washington, his death occurring there in 1897, at the age of seventy-three. His widow lives with her son and is now eighty-four years old. Johnson Allen was brought up as an old-school Presbyterian, but soon after his marriage he and his wife united with the Baptist church. He was township assessor at one time and a man of considerable political influence in the county. He was a Democrat and took an active part in the councils of his party.

Professor Allen's paternal grandparents were William and Elizabeth (Eads) Allen, the former a native of New Jersey and the latter of Ohio. They were pioneers in Daviess county, coming here in December, 1816. William Allen was a shoemaker and farmer and lived in Washington township. He and his wife died on the old homestead, she at the age of about sixty and he about seventy. Mrs. William Allen was the aunt of Capt. James B. Eads, who built the St. Louis and Brooklyn bridges. William and Elizabeth (Eads) Allen were the parents of twelve children, James C., John, William, Robert, Johnson, Firman, George, Mary Jane, Elijah R., Hannah A., Moses and Melville W.

William Allen was the son of Col. John and Rachel (Wykoff) Allen, natives of New Jersey, who came to eastern Indiana prior to 1810 and settled in Dearborn county. Colonel Allen assisted in laying out the town of Harrison, and came to Daviess county in 1816, bringing with him his family of fifteen children. The first Presbyterian church organized in the Whitewater valley was organized at his home in 1810.

(22)

The maternal grandparents of Professor Allen were Hamlet and Ann (Clark) Sanford, natives of Orange county, Virginia, who moved to Kentucky, settling in Mason county, where all of their children were born. They came to Indiana in November, 1832, and located two miles northeast of Washington, where they engaged in farming and where they reared their children. Hamlet Sanford was a carpenter, farmer and builder. He lived two miles northeast of Washington until July, 1849, when he died at a ripe old age. He had formerly been married to a woman in Virginia, who died leaving two children, Lucinda and Eliza, who, with all of the children by the second marriage, came from Kentucky to Daviess county, Indiana. The second group of children were Lucretia, Pierce, Reuben, William, Virginia, John C., Tabitha Ann, Mary Jane and Elizabeth.

The great-grandfather on Professor Allen's maternal side was Pierce Sanford. Ann Clark, who was Professor Allen's maternal grandmother, was the daughter of William Clark, whose wife's maiden name also was Clark. This brings the family back to Clarks mountain in Virginia, where the original Clarks held a valuable estate, which was finally settled only a few years ago.

Prof. Hamlet Allen was reared on his father's farm in Washington township, Daviess county. He first attended the district schools and later the graded schools of Washington. Upon completing the course in the local schools, he entered Franklin College and from there went to the Indiana State University at Bloomington. He began teaching in the country schools of Daviess county in 1866 and received his college training subsequently. In 1874 he organized the Washington high school and was the principal of this school for five years. He then removed to the farm and for a time taught in the country schools, later taking up grade work in the city schools. In 1886 and 1887, Professor Allen was deputy postmaster in the Washington postoffice, and four years later served a term as deputy clerk of the circuit court. In 1894 he again was elected principal of the Washington high school, and has served continuously in that capacity since that date.

On December 26, 1878, Professor Allen was married to Rebecca Hyatt, daughter of William and Rebecca (Read) Hyatt, to which union two children have been born, Bessie Read and Helen Hyatt. Bessie married Stephen E. Myers, a lawyer in Washington, a biographical sketch of whom is presented elsewhere in this volume. Helen married Dr. C. J. Burris and they live with Professor Allen. They have one child, Eleanor Rebecca.

Mrs. Allen died on May 28, 1893, at the age of thirty-four. She was born on a farm adjoining the north edge of Washington. Her father was born in Mason county, Kentucky, and her mother in Washington township, Daviess county. They were the parents of five children, Mary, George, Margaret, Helen and Rebecca. William Hyatt had been married twice, his first wife having been Margaret McClure, of Knox county, near Vincennes, to which union there was born one son, Thomas. William Hyatt was the son of Thomas Hyatt, who married Margaret McFerren. They were natives of Maryland and came from Kentucky to Daviess county in 1819, settling on what is still known as the old Oyatt farm, at the edge of Washington. They were the parents of seven children, Lucinda, Eliza, John, Elisha, Mary Ann, William and Margaret. Mrs. Allen's maternal grandparents were Nathan and Mary (Weaver) Read), the former of whom was a native of Vermont and the latter of Daviess county. Their children were Martha, George C., Sarah, Miriam, Richard N., Nathan G. and Rebecca. Mrs. Allen was a member of the Baptist church, of which Professor Allen is also a member, serving the congregation as a deacon and clerk of the church.

Professor Allen is a Democrat but, with the exception of four years, during which time he was a member of the Washington city council, he has never been especially active in politics, having devoted his life and energies to the cause of education.

SAMUEL BROWN BOYD.

Samuel Brown Boyd, editor of the *Daily and Weekly Democrat*, at Washington, this county, was born in Yorkville, Dearborn county, Indiana, March 14, 1858, being a son of John and Elizabeth (Miller) Boyd, who were natives of Ireland and Ohio, respectively. The family numbered nine children, three of whom are living, Mrs. John S. Goshorn, Mrs. Millie B. Johnson and Mr. Boyd, all of Daviess county, Indiana. The parents are dead.

Mr. Boyd moved from Dearborn county to Daviess county with his parents in 1871. Both parents died shortly after the removal, the father in 1871 and the mother in 1875. At the age of seventeen Mr. Boyd found himself entirely upon his own resources. He worked on a farm in the summer and went to the country schools in the winter until he succeeded in securing a license to teach. He continued at school work for ten years, teaching in country schools for four years; principal of the Odon school for one year, in the grammar school, Washington, one year and county superintendent of schools four years—1883-87. In the meantime he attended school two summers at Danville, Indiana.

In 1885 he bought a third interest in the *Democrat;* in 1887 this was increased to one-half interest, and in connection with Stephen Belding and B. F. Strasser, respectively, he published the *Daily and Weekly Democrat* until 1891, when he purchased the entire plant. In 1906 he sold a half interest in the plant to Henry Backes and the publication has been issued since then under the firm name of Boyd & Backes.

Mr. Boyd was married on December 29, 1887, to Miss Tillie Scudder, eldest daughter of the late Dr. John A. Scudder, of Washington. To this union five children were born, two of whom are dead and three are living— Samuel, Jr., John Scudder and Polly Ruth, aged, respectively, twenty-two, nineteen and seventeen.

Mr. Boyd is a prominent member of the Democratic Editorial Association of Indiana, in which he served as president in 1895 and was secretary for several years. He has been an Odd Fellow since 1882 and is an ardent member of the Episcopal church. He served as a trustee of the Southern Indiana hospital for the insane during Governor Matthews' administration—1893-97; also on the city school board of Washington.

GEORGE W. DYKE.

Specific mention is made of many of the worthy citizens of Daviess county within the pages of this book, citizens who have figured in the growth and development of this favored locality, and whose interests are identified with its every phase of progress; each contributing, in his sphere of action, to the well-being of the community in which he resides and to the advancement of its moral and legitimate growth. Among this number is the gentleman whose name appears above, peculiar interest attaching to the fact that he has spent but a few years of his life within the borders of this county.

George W. Dyke was born on November 11, 1876, in Centerton, Morgan county, Indiana, the son of James and Sarah (Dyer) Dyke, the former born in 1840, in Mill Springs, Kentucky; the latter born in 1842, in Morgan county, Indiana. James Dyke was the son of William Dyke, a native of England, who emigrated to this country and first settled in the state of Maryland, where he and his family remained for some time, then went to the state of Kentucky, from which state they came to Indiana, locating in Hendricks county, later moving to Morgan county, whence they went to the state of Illinois where William Dyke died, after which his widow returned to Morgan county, where she spent the rest of her life. The maternal grandparents were George and Maria (Russell) Dyer. George Dyer's father emigrated, in an early day, to Morgan county, Indiana, where he took up a grant of land from the government, spending the rest of his life there. George Dyer died some years ago and his widow is living to the present day.

James Dyke was a blacksmith by trade and came from Kentucky to Indiana, locating at Brooklyn, Morgan county, where he continued to work at his trade and reared a large family. He was somewhat active in politics and while disposed to cast his vote in an independent manner, yet his leaning was towards the principles of the Republican party and to it gave his support. He and his family were members of the Methodist church. To his union with Sarah Dyer were born the following children, named in the order of their birth: George W., Angie, deceased; Josephine, Carl, Ebenezer, deceased; an infant, deceased; Mary, deceased; Norman and another infant, deceased.

George W. Dyke lived with his parents and received his early education in the public schools of Morgan county, later acquiring a good working knowledge of the blacksmithing trade, which he followed for a number of years, after which he took up the study of mechanical and electrical engineering. Having acquired a splendid knowledge of these latter lines, he was appointed to the position of manager of the plant of the Central Union Telephone Company in the town of Brooklyn, and continued as manager there until the company transferred him to Washington, this county, where he has been located since 1913. During the year 1914 he was appointed manager of the office of the Western Union Telegraph Company at Washington, but on account of a statute opposing dual employment in public service corporations, he was prevented from holding the management of the two branch companies, and had to give up the telegraph project.

On October 22, 1896, George W. Dyke was married to Effie Dalton, a native of Orange county, Indiana, daughter of S. W. Dalton, of Brooklyn, Morgan county, and to their union have been born five children, named, in the order of their births, as follow: Agnes, deceased; Gladys, Dons, Geneva, deceased, and George.

Since being transferred to the town of Washington, Mr. Dyke has taken an active part in the promotion of all meritorious enterprises that tend to the welfare of the public. Politically, he has always identified himself with the Republican party and although not an aspirant for public office, takes an aggressive and active part in political matters. Fraternally, he is a member of the Knights of Pythias, the Order of Red Men, and is a thirty-second-degree member of the Masonic order, going up through the York and the Scottish rite. Personally, Mr. Dyke is a man who, in all the relations of life, has been an advocate of wholesome living and cleanliness in politics as well; and has ever been outspoken in his antipathy to wrong doing, whether by the humble citizen or by the incumbents of influential offices. In every respect he has merited the esteem in which he is universally held, for he is a man of public-spirit, intellectual attainments and exemplary character.

ANDREW J. BIDDINGER.

It is the progressive wide-awake man of affairs that makes the real history of a community. His influence as a potential factor in the body politic is difficult to estimate. The examples such men furnish of patient purpose and steadfast integrity strongly illustrate what is in the power of each to accomplish. And there is always a full measure of satisfaction in advertising, even in a casual way, to their achievements in advancing the interests of their fellow men, and in giving strength and solidity to the institutions which make so much for the prosperity of the community. Such a man is Andrew J. Biddinger, a prominent real-estate dealer and insurance agent at Washington, Indiana. Mr. Biddinger's business has naturally brought him in touch with the public and today he enjoys an enviable reputation for honesty and square dealing. Perhaps no class of people contribute more to the material progress of a community than those persons who buy and sell real estate. No class of business men contribute more to the improvement of the community than real estate dealers, of which Mr. Biddinger is a leader in Daviess county. In every respect he is a representative citizen of Washington and of Daviess county.

Andrew J. Biddinger was born on November 10, 1855, in Butler county, Ohio, the son of George W. and Caroline (Hancock) Biddinger, the former a native of Pennsylvania, born near Carmichaeltown, and the latter a native of Drewersburg, Franklin county, Indiana. They were the parents of six children, John W., of Washington; Deborah A., deceased, who was the wife of William F. Trauter; Solomon A., a farmer in Washington township; Melinda, who died at the age of sixteen years; Andrew J., of Washington, and Almira, the wife of R. D. Cleaver, of Washington.

George W. Biddinger was reared in Butler county, Ohio, where he owned and improved a large farm. He sold out there in 1861, and came to this county, purchasing a farm in Washington township, where he died in 1872, at the age of fifty-eight years. His widow died in 1875, at the age of fifty-one. He was a member of the Lutheran church and his wife was a member of the United Brethren church. The parents of George W. Biddinger were Frederick and Catherine (Hoover) Biddinger, natives of Pennsylvania, and of German descent. They were early settlers in Ohio, and their eldest son was a soldier in the War of 1812, and also a soldier in the Mexican War. Frederick Biddinger, the son of Frederick Biddinger, was a soldier in the Patriot army during the Revolutionary War, and also served during the War of 1812, later emigrating to Ohio, where he became a farmer in Butler county, and died there, his wife dying in Hamilton county, Ohio. The former died at the age of seventy-six and the latter at the age of eighty-four. They had a family of eleven children, being: Jacob, Solomon, Michael, Jonathan, James, George, Andrew, Frederick, Mrs. Catherine Cann, Mrs. Mary Wall and Mrs. Elizabeth Cann. Frederick Biddinger's parents were born in Germany. Following his services in the Revolutionary War, Frederick Biddinger cut a hickory cane from a tree in the war zone to serve as a staff on his long walk home. Andrew J. Biddinger is now the possessor of this stout staff, a relic of the Revolution, which he prizes quite highly.

The maternal grandparents of Andrew J. Biddinger were John W. and Deborah (Stansberry) Hancock, natives of Maryland, the former of English and the latter of German descent. They lived to rear a large family in Franklin county, Indiana. John W. Hancock was a merchant and also owned a farm of five or six hundred acres. He shipped a great quantity of produce by wagon and operated a large number of huckster wagons. He died at the age of fifty and his wife at the age of eighty-seven. Their children were Phinx, Lloyd, Green, Charles, Seneca, Caroline and Julia Ann.

Andrew J. Biddinger was reared on his father's farm in Washington township. He attended the district schools and later Fort Scott College at Fort Scott, Kansas. He then returned to Daviess county and began farming, continuing in this vocation until 1889, when, for a time, he sold sewing machines. Since November, 1889, he has been engaged in the insurance business, and for twenty years he also has been engaged in the real estate business.

On April 5, 1894, Andrew J. Biddinger was married, to Dora Henry, a teacher in the Washington schools; daughter of Isaiah and Nancy (Taylor) Henry. She died in 1904, and on October 28, 1906, Mr. Biddinger married, secondly, Ruth Waller, who was born on a farm in Barr township, this county, daughter of George and Lucretia (McDonald) Waller, natives of this county, and both of whom are now deceased, she being their only child. Mrs. Biddinger's paternal grandfather was John Waller, who married Mary A. Goodwin. Their children were George, William S., Edward F., John M., Richard, James, Anna E., Mary and Margaret. Mrs. Biddinger's great-grandparents were Aaron and Margaret (McCullough) Goodwin.

Mr. and Mrs. Biddinger are members of the Christian church, in which Mr. Biddinger is serving as a deacon. Fraternally, he belongs to Liverpool Lodge No. 110, Independent Order of Odd Fellows. Politically, he is identified with the fortunes of the Prohibition party. Andrew J. Biddinger is highly respected in Daviess county and has been foremost in all worthy public enterprises.

WILLIAM H. KIEFER.

Washington, the metropolis of Daviess county, has a unique character in the person of William H. Kiefer, the clerk of the Daviess county circuit court and a man known throughout the country as a successful composer of band and orchestra music. According to the *Musical Messenger*, Mr. Kiefer is "a band organizer, instructor, director and cornetist." "Either designation or title is distinction enough for any one man to wear, if he bears it as well as Mr. Kiefer," says the *Musical Messenger*. "We don't know which he prefers, but we suspect that the public will call him composer, for he has certainly made himself popular with his compositions, and thousands are influenced through his writings, where hundreds are possibly benefited by his directing or cornet playing."

William H. Kiefer was born into a musical family and inherited the musical spirit, absorbing musical notation and rules with his alphabet and arithmetic. Living in a musical atmosphere, he began as a child to play on everything he could get hold of that would produce a musical sound. At ten years of age he played in a boys' band that had been organized and instructed by an uncle, Joseph P. Kiefer. This uncle took a special interest in him and instructed him privately in the rudiments of music, teaching him violin and cornet. William was an apt pupil and fully appreciated his uncle's interest. Mr. Kiefer attributes most of the credit for his musical attainments to this good uncle who encouraged and directed him during the formative period of his career. The ambition to write a band or orchestra piece took hold of him at the age of fifteen years and at that early age he began work on a composition. It was a march and when finished was called, "Salute to Washington," which was played by his home band and was well received. Later Mr. Kiefer began to publish band and orchestra selections. Most of his selections have been published by C. L. Barnhouse, of Oskaloosa, Iowa, whom Mr. Kiefer met during a three-years' sojourn at Oskaloosa.

William H. Kiefer, one of the many stars in the firmament of Hoosier authorship, was born in this county on July 22, 1872, a son of Gustave and Mary (Beck) Kiefer, the former a native of Baden, Germany, and the latter a native of Knox county, Indiana, who were the parents of eleven children, namely: William H., the immediate subject of this biographical sketch; Rose, the wife of George Pensenneau, of East St. Louis, Illinois; Leonard, of Indianapolis; Carrie, the wife of Charles Gill, of Washington, Indiana; Gustave, of Indianapolis; Catherine, the wife of Charles Dant, of Indianapolis; Benjamin, of Washington, Indiana; Mary, the wife of Alfred Helbig, of Vincennes; Albert, of Washington, and two children, Emma and Clarence, who died in infancy.

Gustave Kiefer came to America when eight years old with his parents, who located on a farm in Dubois county, Indiana, where he grew to manhood. He engaged in the lumber and saw-mill business near French Lick for a few years and then moved to Washington, where, for some years, he engaged in the manufacture of bricks. Subsequently he engaged in the butcher business and afterward conducted the German Hotel, on West Main street, which burned some years ago. He died in 1903, at the age of sixty. His widow died in 1910, at the age of fifty-nine. They were members of the German Catholic church.

The paternal grandparents of our subject were Anton Kiefer and his wife Caroline. Anton Kiefer was a brick-maker and died at Washington at an old age. He and his wife were the parents of five children, Gustave, Mary, Joseph, Lawrence and Stephen. The maternal grandfather of William H. Kiefer was William Beck, a native of France. He was a general merchant in Parkville, Indiana, and died there. William Beck was twice married, Mary and Christ being the only children born to the first union, and Rose and Nellie to the second union.

William H. Kiefer was born and reared in Washington, and attended the parochial and public schools. Later he took a course in the Jasper Business College. He served as a deputy in the county recorder's office for two years and was city clerk for four years, from 1902 to 1906. Upon retiring from this office he entered the real estate business, in which he was engaged from 1907 to 1912, in which latter year he was elected clerk of the Daviess circuit court on the Democratic ticket. Mr. Kiefer is the leader of the Citizens band and has served very acceptably in this capacity during the past twenty years.

On December 24, 1906, William H. Kiefer was married to Maud Helphinstine, daughter of John and Mary (Hyatt) Helphenstine, to which union two sons, William R. and John C. have been born.

Mrs. Kiefer was born in Washington, Indiana. Her parents, both of whom were born in this county, are now living at 100 John street, Washington. Of their children, Mrs. Kiefer is the only one now living. The paternal grandparents of Mrs. Kiefer were William and Maria (Aikman) Helphenstine, pioneers of Daviess county. The maternal grandparents of Mrs. Kiefer were William and Rebecca Ann (Read) Hyatt, who were the parents of the following children: Mary, George, Margaret, Helen, Rebecca and Thomas.

Mr. Kiefer is a member of the Knights of Columbus, the Benevolent Protective Order of Elks, the Fraternal Order of Eagles, the Woodmen of the World and the Modern Woodmen of America. He and his sons are members of the Catholic Church and Mrs. Kiefer is a member of the Presbyterian church.

As the *Musical Messenger* says: "The man who writes pleasing music, music that becomes popular, endears himself to a great host of his fellows whom he may never have the pleasure of meeting personally. Yet there is a sense of comradeship felt by him with those who play his music. The knowledge that comes to him of his music played in various sections of the country establishes a bond of fellowship between himself and these unknown friends, for a real friendship has been established. When we play music that we like we want to know to whom we are indebted for it. We seek the name of the author and finding it we remember it and begin to form in imagination a picture of him; that is, if no picture of him is furnished us with his music." Thus is the name of William H. Kiefer known throughout the country. Mr. Kiefer makes himself useful musically wherever he may be. For years he has been identified with, if not the chief leader in, the musical performances by local talent in and about Washington, his home city, such as light operas, minstrel performances and the like, and is personally very popular. His latest march, "The Specialist," was published in the *Musical Messenger* for September, 1914, and had a very large sale.

MILTON SIMPSON HASTINGS.

The welfare of our country depends in a great measure upon those men who in an unassuming manner work steadily away in their chosen field of endeavor, and who are yet broad-minded men; not blind to the needs of their community, nor to those things that stand for real progress. Daviess county has reason to be proud of the many true men she has produced who now are engaged in various lines of activities, among whom is Milton Simpson Hastings, a well-known and successful lawyer of Washington.

Mr. Hastings was born in Bogard township, Daviess county, Indiana, on April 25, 1862, the son of John Arthur and Lauretta (Allen) Hastings, natives of Indiana, who had seven children, four of whom are living: Mary E., wife of Andrew T. Myers, of Plainville, Indiana; Milton S., of Washington, Indiana; Paris A., of Washington; Elmer E., of the firm of Hastings, Allen & Hastings, and three children who died young.

John Arthur Hastings was reared in Lawrence and Daviess counties, Indiana, and was a teacher for many years. He lived most of the time in Bogard township, this county, where he also ran a farm. During the latter part of his life he was for several years, a merchant at Cornettsville, but teaching was his principal work. He lived a few years in Washington. He was admitted to the bar in 1857, but never practiced law. John A. Hastings died in 1891, at the age of fifty-nine. His widow died in 1905, aged sixty-five. They were originally members of the Christian church, but later of the United Brethren church. Mr. Hastings' father was a Quaker.

The paternal grandparents of Milton S. Hastings were Howell and Edith (Edwards) Hastings, natives of North Carolina, and pioneer farmers of Lawrence and Daviess counties. Howell Hastings also was a mechanic, being very handy with tools. He lived in what was then Clarksburg, now Odon, in Daviess county, where he died in middle age. His widow survived him many years and moved to Leavenworth, Kansas, where she died at an old age. They were the parents of six children, William Henry, Joshua Thomas, Zachariah Simpson, Rufus, Elizabeth and Charlotte.

The maternal grandparents of Mr. Hastings were Hiram and Keziah (Cook) Allen, early settlers of Daviess county, Indiana. Hiram Allen was a farmer and did some teaming from New Albany and Louisville to Washington. He died a young man. His widow remarried and lived to an old age. Hiram Allen and wife were the parents of three children, Lauretta, Milton L., and Mary E.

M. S. Hastings was reared on his father's farm, attending the district school of his home neighborhood, the public schools of Washington, and the Southern Indiana Normal at Mitchell. While going through the normal school he taught three terms of school. After being graduated from the normal school he taught one year, as principal of the public schools of Clay City, Illinois. He then returned home and began the study of law in the office of Gardiner & Taylor, at Washington, and was admitted to the bar of the Daviess circuit court in 1886. He and Josiah G. Allen formed a partnership on September 20, 1897, and have practiced together ever since, a period of twenty-seven years. The firm is now composed of M. S. Hastings, J. G. Allen, E. E. Hastings and A. W. Allen, a son of J. G. Allen.

On September 16, 1886, M. S. Hastings was married to Edith Laville Jackman, who was born in De Kalb county, Indiana, the daughter of Wesley and Sarah M. (Baxter) Jackman. Wesley Jackman was a native of Ohio and his wife a native of Pennsylvania. Mrs. Hastings is a graduate of the Lebanon (Ohio) Normal School and taught in both Indiana and Ohio, being instructor in literature, Latin and Greek in Lebanon, Ohio, in Mitchell, Indiana, and in other normal schools. She is a woman of culture and refinement and well educated. Her father died in 1907, aged eighty years, in DeKalb county. Her mother is still living at Auburn, Indiana, at the age of eighty-five. Mrs. Hastings is one of a family of eight children, Edith Laville, Mary E., Florence V. and a twin sister, Florida, who died when a young woman, Charles S. and Harry E. (twins), Minnie and Addie.

To Milton S. and Edith L. C. (Jackman) Hastings one child has been born, a daughter, Lois, who was graduated from the Washington high school, attended Butler College, at Indianapolis, and Indiana State University, at Bloomington, from which last institution she also was graduated. She taught English in the Washington high school for two years. Lois Hastings married Oliver F. Slimp, of Cleveland, Ohio, and to this union has been born one child, a daughter, Edith Elizabeth.

Mr. and Mrs. Hastings are members of the Christian church, the congregation of which Mr. Hastings serves as deacon. He also is a teacher in the men's Bible class, in which there are over one hundred men enrolled. He belongs to Charity Lodge No. 30, Free and Accepted Masons; to Washington Chapter No. 92, Royal Arch Masons; Washington Council, Royal and Select Masters, and to Washington Commandery No. 33, Knights Templar, of which latter society he was eminent commander during the years 1912 and 1913.

Mr. Hastings is a Republican and was deputy county prosecutor for two years. He was chief clerk of the Indiana House of Representatives in

1907. The firm of Hastings, Allen & Hastings acts as attorneys for the Peoples National Bank of Washington and the Washington National Bank, and practices in all the courts, having been called before the state supreme court in a large number of cases. M. S. Hastings, although a prominent and able lawyer, is quite modest and unostentatious in his general demeanor. Frequently he has been called upon to preside as judge of the circuit courts of Daviess and adjoining counties, in special cases, and is generally known as Judge Hastings, but his retiring and modest disposition makes him prefer to leave off the title, "judge", and to be known simply as Mr. Hastings. He is genial and kindly in his attitude toward all and no one is too humble to receive his attention and respectful consideration.

While Mr. Hastings' ambition as a lawyer is to continue to grow and be eminently successful, there is perhaps nothing that gives him more satisfaction and enjoyment than teaching his splendid Bible class and looking after the interests of his family; his exemplary home life being a source of infinite gratification to them. M. S. Hastings is held in highest esteem by the citizens of Washington for his integrity, his genuine Christian character and his real moral worth.

LEONIDAS SEXTON HORRALL.

The subject of this review is a representative farmer and stock grower of Washington township, Daviess county, Indiana, who is known as one of the alert, progressive and successful agriculturists of this favored section of the Hoosier state. In his labors he has not permitted himself to follow in the rut in a blind, apathetic way, but has studied and experimented and thus secured the maximum returns from his enterprising efforts; which he has so ordered his course at all times as to command the confidence and regard of the people of the community in which he lives, being a man of honorable business methods and advocating whatever tends to promote the public welfare in any way.

Leonidas Sexton Horrall was born in this county on March 18, 1871, the son of Edwin Ray and Johanna (Alexander) Horrall, both natives of this county. The paternal grandfather of Mr. Horrall was Cleaver Horrall, who arrived in Washington in an early day, and conducted a tannery on the site where the Baltimore & Ohio railroad station now is situated. In the early days he would haul leather to Evansville, Indiana, for the markets. He and his wife died in Washington. The maternal grandparents of Mr.

Horrall also were early settlers of this county, being farmers in Veale township.

Edwin Ray Horrall, the father of Leonidas S., was educated in the schools of Washington, where he grew to maturity, and began life for himself on a farm in Veale township, operating one hundred and twenty acres of land which he owned in 'Possum Hollow. Later he purchased another farm on one hundred and forty acres in the same township and moved to it. In addition to his farming interests, Mr. Horrall, in partnership with Hiram Hogshead, owned and operated the first steam threshing machine south of Washington, in this county. Mr. Horrall also operated a saw-mill in Veale township. He moved to Oklahoma, but later returned to Daviess county, locating on the farm where his son is now living. He served in the Union army during the Civil War as a member of the Forty-second Regiment Indiana Volunteer Infantry. Edwin Ray and Johanna (Alexander) Horrall were the parents of eight children, Cynthia Ann, Daniel Cleaver, Alfred, Elizabeth, Carrie Belle, Leonidas S., Lawrie Isaac and Videtta, all of whom are still living with the exception of Carrie Belle.

Leonidas S. Horrall grew to manhood on his father's farm in Veale township, receiving his education in the district schools of his home township. He assisted his father in the operation of the home farm and also with his thresher-machine and saw-mill, and before his marriage had bought and paid for forty-seven acres of land. In 1895 he engaged in farming on his own account. His wife owned one hundred acres of land, and to this Mr. Horrall added until they owned three hundred and ten acres of land in Harrison township. Later they sold this farm and purchased one hundred and forty-eight acres, where they now live, on the Portersville road, about one and one-fourth miles out of Washington. The family moved to this place in 1904, and Mr. Horrall now does a road contracting business in connection with his farming.

In 1895 Mr. Horrall married Anna Wilson, who was born and reared in Harrison township, a daughter of William Wilson, a pioneer of Harrison township. William Wilson came from Ohio in an early day, making the trip on foot, with all his belongings in a small carpetbag, which he carried. He settled in Harrison township, where he gradually accumulated a competency, and at the time of his death was the owner of eight hundred acres of land. He was an influential citizen in his day and generation, being a man of sterling integrity and of much strength of character.

To Leonidas S. and Anna (Wilson) Horrall have been born six children, Steward Sexton, Ermel Ethel, Lily Jewel, Glenn Irene, Roy and Nellie Lissie. The family are all loyal and earnest members of the Methodist Episcopal church, in whose welfare they are actively interested, and to whose support they are liberal contributors.

Mr. Horrall is a Republican, and for years has taken an active part in the political affairs of his county. On January 1, 1915, he assumed the duties of the office of county commissioner, to which office he had been elected in the previous election. He is a member of the Independent Order of Odd Fellows and also of the encampment, and takes an active interest in the welfare of those fraternal organizations. As a citizen Mr. Horrall stands high in the esteem of his fellow men, being public-spirited and progressive, and at all times willing to lead his aid and influence in behalf of enterprises for the material advancement of his county, and for the intellectual, social and moral good of the people.

PARIS A. HASTINGS.

Paris A. Hastings is a man, who, by close attention to business, has achieved marked success and has risen to an honorable position among the leading men of the county with which his interests are identified. It is a plain record rendered remarkable by no strange or mysterious adventures; no wonderful and lucky accidents and no tragic situations. Mr. Hastings is one of those estimable citizens whose integrity and personality must force them into an admirable distinction, which their modesty never seeks. He is one of that type of men who command the respect of contemporaries and posterity alike and leave the impression of their individuality upon the age in which they have lived.

Paris A. Hastings, the cashier of the Peoples National Bank, of Washington, Indiana, was born in Bogard township, this county, on August 13, 1865, the son of John A. and Lauretta (Allen) Hastings, the former a native of Lawrence county and the latter of Daviess county, who were the parents of eight children, four of whom grew to maturity, Mary, the wife of Andrew T. Myers, of Plainville, Indiana; Milton S., a judge, of Washington; Paris A., the subject of this sketch, and Elmer E., of Washington.

John A. Hastings was reared in Lawrence county, Indiana, and was a school teacher for about twenty-five years. He later operated a general store at Cornettsville, Daviess county, for a few years, and died there in

1891, at the age of fifty-nine. His wife survived him and died in Washington in December, 1905, at the age of sixty-five years. In their early days they belonged to the Christian church but later united with the United Brethren church.

The paternal grandparents of Paris A. Hastings were Howell and Edith (Edwards) Hastings, natives of North Carolina, who were among the first settlers of Madison township, this county, where they owned considerable land in the Odon neighborhood. Howell Hastings died in middle life, after which his widow moved to Kansas with her children and lived at Wellington for a time. She died in Kansas, at an advanced age. They were the parents of six children, Henry H., who died on his eighty-fifth birthday; Thomas, who died in the service of the Union army, during the Civil War; John A., Zachariah S., a Christian minister; Elizabeth and Charlotte. The maternal grandparents of Mr. Hastings were Hiram and Keziah (Cook) Allen, natives of North Carolina and early settlers in Van Buren township, this county. Hiram Allen died in 1849, while still a young man. His widow married, secondly, William Wilson. By the first marriage there were three children, Lauretta, Milton L. and Mary. By the second marriage there were four children, George, Keziah, John and Cordella.

Paris A. Hastings was reared on his father's farm in Bogard township and attended the district schools and the Southern Indiana Normal School at Mitchell. Later he attended the Northern Indiana Normal School at Valparaiso and was graduated from the Central Normal College at Danville. He taught school for two years, the last year at Cornettsville. He then served as deputy county auditor for two years and finally went into the newspaper business, for a number of years acting as business manager of the *Washington Gazette*, subsequently becoming the owner of that paper, continuing as sole owner until 1905, in which year the *Gazette* was consolidated with the *Herald*. Mr. Hastings was connected with this latter newspaper until July, 1912, when he sold his interest to C. G. Sefrit, and in January, 1913, became cashier of the Peoples National Bank, of Washington, a position he still occupies.

In the campaign of 1902, Mr. Hastings was chairman of the Republican county central committee, of Daviess county. He was elected to the Indiana Legislature at a special election that year, serving in the session of 1903. He was a city treasurer of Washington for four years and was interested, while in the newspaper business, in road building. He built more than one hundred miles of gravel and rock road in Daviess county, in partnership with M. H. Wilson.

On August 28, 1891, Paris A. Hastings was married to Cora A. Hendricks, of Hendricks county, the daughter of Milton and Mary E. (Sparks) Hendricks, to which union six children have been born, Frank H., Mary, Laura, Charles, Edith and Paul. Frank H. is a graduate of the Central Normal College and is now principal of the high school at Arcadia, Indiana. Mary and Laura were graduated from the scientific course at Central Normal College in 1913 and are in school there now, taking the classical course. Mary taught one term of school in Barr township. Charles is a junior and Paul a freshman in the Washington high school. Edith died in infancy. During Laura's twelve years in school, she never missed a day; never missed a session of her Sunday school, nor was she tardy at either place in the entire twelve years. This is a remarkable record.

Mrs. Hastings was born in Hendricks county, Indiana, December 5, 1861. Her parents were natives of Indiana. Her father died in 1908 at the age of seventy-eight and her mother is still living. They were the parents of six children, Cora A., Myra Jane, Orestes H., Vada, Lora and Grace.

Mr. and Mrs. Hastings and all of their children are members of the Christian church, the local congregation of which Mr. Hastings is serving as an elder. He was superintendent of the Bible school for six years. He is a member of Charity Lodge No. 30, Free and Accepted Masons; Washington Chapter No. 92, Royal Arch Masons, and the Washington council, Royal and Select Masters. He and his wife are charter members of Washington Chapter No. 210, Order of the Eastern Star.

Because of his long experience in public and semi-official life, Paris A. Hastings is well known in Daviess county, and it is only fair to say that he enjoys the unqualified esteem of the people of this county. He has made success of many ventures and, although still in middle life, has earned a competence which is his reward for his toil and planning.

ELMER BUZAN.

The men of most influence in promoting the advancement of society and in giving character to the times in which they live are of two classes, students and men of action. Whether we are more indebted for the improvement of the age to one class or the other is a question of honest difference in opinion. Neither class can be spared and both should be encouraged to occupy their respective spheres of labor and influence, zealously and without mutual distrust. In the following paragraphs are briefly outlined the leading facts and characteristics in the career of a gentleman who combines in his make-up, the elements of the student and the energy of the public-spirited man of affairs. Elmer Buzan, although formerly a teacher in the public schools of Daviess county, has enjoyed a successful career in business and at present is the treasurer-elect of Daviess county. He is not unknown to the wider educational circles of the state and, in political affairs, occupies a prominent place in Daviess county.

Elmer Buzan was born on May 13, 1879, in Washington township, Daviess county, Indiana, the son of Albert and Sarah Adaline (Jones) Buzan, both natives of this county, the former of whom was born in Barr township, and the latter in Washington township. The parental grandfather of Elmer Buzan was John Buzan, an early settler of Daviess county, who died in this county, his wife dying in Kansas. John Buzan and wife had six children, Maria, Albert, William (deceased), Lafayette (deceased), John and Mattie A. John Buzan served as a soldier in the Union army during the Civil War for about three years. The maternal grandparents of Elmer Buzan were Thomas and Lorraine (Freeland) Jones, pioneers of this county, who were the parents of five children, Mary C., Hosea, Elijah, Theodore and Ella. Theodore Jones, now deceased, was a one-time treasurer of Daviess county.

Albert Buzan, the father of Elmer Buzan, was formerly a farmer and a coal prospector. Though self-learned, his early educational opportunities having been limited, he is a well-informed man. He and his wife, the latter of whom is now deceased, were the parents of four children, Theodocia (deceased), Elmer, Bertha S. and Maria S. (deceased). Albert Buzan is a member of the Christian church, as was his wife, and their children were reared in the faith of that church.

Elmer Buzan was reared on a farm and was educated in the public schools of Daviess county, as well as in the Indiana State Normal School at Terre Haute, where he spent more than three years. Mr. Buzan began teaching when twenty-one years of age and was engaged in teaching until 1911, when he was made deputy county treasurer, by appointment, a position he held for two years, at the end of which time he was employed by the Prudential Insurance Company. In 1914 Mr. Buzan was elected county treasurer of Daviess county and will take office on January 1, 1916. He is a man who is well known throughout Daviess county and who has made a host of friends. The people of Daviess county have absolute confidence in Mr. Buzan, and he will be the last man to abuse that confidence.

On October 17, 1909, Elmer Buzan was married to Edna Pearl Ficke who was born in Topeka, Kansas, September 22, 1883, the daughter of William H. and Glendora (Hogshead) Ficke, now residents of Washington township, this county. To this union two children have been born, Ruby Alberta, born on February 1, 1911, and Norwood Howard, August 7, 1913.

Upon attaining his majority, Mr. Buzan identified himself with the Republican party and for years has been active in local councils of that party. He and his wife are members of the Christian church.

NATHAN E. KILLION.

The true measure of individual success is determined by the character of work in which one has been engaged. The measure of success is what one has accomplished. An enumeration of the living residents of Daviess county, who have succeeded in various spheres of endeavor, and who at the same time are impressing their personalities on the citizenship of this county—men who have been conferring honor on the localities where they reside, would be incomplete were there failure to make specific mention of Nathan E. Killion, president of the Farmers Bank of Plainville, and one of the most influential citizens in that section of Daviess county. The splendid success which has come to him has been the direct result of great physical and mental energy. Mr. Killion has a mind capable of laying judicious plans, and a will strong enough to carry them into execution. His, energy, foresight and perseverance carry him forward to a position in the front rank of the successful men of this county. Nathan Killion has carried forward to successful completion whatever he has undertaken. His business methods have ever been in strict conformity with the standard ethics of commercial life. He has taken an intelligent interest in the civic life of the community and has earned the high regard in which he is held by all who know him.

Nathan E. Killion was born on March 12, 1862, in Steele township, Daviess county, Indiana, the son of Alexander and Jemimah (Caywood) Killion, the former of whom was born on November 9, 1822, in Steele township, Daviess county, Indiana, and died on April 21, 1903. Jemimah (Caywood) Killion was born on June 29, 1829, and died on January 6, 1892. She was the second wife of Alexander Killion, who was married three times.

The grandfather of Nathan E. Killion and the father of Alexander

Killion was William Killion, a native of North Carolina, who married Dicey Ballard, and who, after their marriage, moved to Tennessee for a year. While the Killions were in Tennessee, one of William Killion's sons traveled to Indiana. He wrote back to his father that he had found a splendid place in which to live. William Killion, wife and family then moved to Indiana. His children were Alexander, Alfred, David, James, Sallie, Eva, William, Betsie, Frank and Wiley. The first wife of Alexander Killion was America Burch, who bore him three children, Dicey, John and Rachel. After her death Mr. Killion married Jemimah Caywood, and she bore him six children, Martha J., William, Nathan, Albert, Eva and Cora. Upon the death of his second wife, Alexander Killion married Mary Myers, but no children were born to this last marriage. Alexander Killion was a farmer of great wealth and owned four thousand acres of land in Daviess county, the most of which was in Steele township.

Many interesting things are to be recorded in the life history of Alexander Killion. He started in life with a small farm, which his father had given him. It was covered with timber and the only way he was able to secure the money with which to pay living expenses was by "working out" at twenty-five cents a day. Alexander Killion went back to his father and asked the latter to take part of the farm back and give him the money, but the father refused to do this. Alexander and his wife lived in a hollow sycamore tree for a time, and finally erected a log hut. After many years Alexander Killion became very wealthy and his life was continually in danger of thieves and robbers, who sought to get hold of his money. A letter was once thrown into his yard demanding five thousand dollars at once, this money to be placed under a certain culvert, death being the threatened penalty for failure to comply with the terms of the letter. Nothing ever came of the incident, however. On another occasion Alexander Killion was held up on his return from Washington, Indiana, but it happened that Webb Ogden and his son, Nathan, were nearby, one of them throwing a rock which fractured the skull of the robber and relieved Alexander from danger. It is said that this highwayman was a man from Martin county, Indiana.

Nathan E. Killion was educated at the Central Normal College at Danville, Indiana, and was married on March 5, 1885, to Cordeli Singleton, daughter of George and Lyda (Ragsdale) Singleton, who were Indiana farmers. George Singleton was a soldier in the Union army during the Civil War. To Nathan E. and Cordelia (Singleton) Killion three children have been born, Ernest E., Clarence E. and Ralph A. He is cashier of the bank there and a biographical sketch of him is presented elsewhere in this volume. Clarence is deceased. Ralph A. married Eula Barnes, and they live in Steele township, this county. They have three children, Ralph, Jr., Clarence and Mildred. Nathan E. Killion lived for twenty-one years on White river, on a bottom farm in Steele township, owning seven hundred acres of the richest soil in Steele township and two hundred acres in Knox and Pike counties, Indiana. Mr. Killion is president of the Farmers Bank of Plainville, a position he has occupied since the establishment of that sound financial institution in 1907! He also is a large stockholder in the Plainville Flouring Company, which is one of the most up-to-date mills in the state of Indiana.

Mrs. Killion is a member of the Methodist Episcopal church. Mr. Killion is a member of the Independent Order of Odd Fellows and both he and Mrs. Killion are members of the order of the Daughters of Rebekah.

Nathan E. Killion is known throughout the length and breadth of Daviess county, and in fact throughout this section of the state; not only as a successful farmer, but as a successful banker, a man who is well-informed on all current, political and civic questions and one whose advice and council is sought upon all sorts of questions. Naturally, he is a man who enjoys the confidence and esteem of a large number of people.

JAMES HARVEY GARTEN.

The character of a community is determined in a large measure by the lives of a comparatively few of its members. If its moral and intellectual status be good, in a social way it is a pleasant place in which to reside; if its reputation as to the integrity of its citizens has extended into other localities, it will be found that the standard set by the leading men has been high and their influence such as to mold the characters and shape the lives of those with whom they mingle. In placing the late James Harvey Garten in the front ranks of such men justice is rendered to Mr. Garten. Although a quiet and unassuming man with no ambition for public position or leadership, he contributed much to the material, civic and moral advancement of his community, while his admirable qualities of head and heart and the straightforward, upright course of his daily life, won for him the esteem and confidence of the circle in which he moved. Although he is now sleeping the sleep of the just, his influence still lives and his memory is revered by many.

The late James Harvey Garten was born in Lawrence county, Indiana, near Springville, on September 13, 1837, the son of James and Lydia (Gray) Garten, the former a native of Lawrence county, who came to this county many years ago and located permanently in Madison township, owning a large farm, most of which is now included within the limits of the village of Odon.

James Harvey Garten was first married to Lucinda Sears. They located on a farm about one mile from Odon, and to their union was born one child, Delight. Mr. Garten was married, secondly, on May 27, 1894, to Mrs. Mary Eleanor (Dunlap) Kohr, of Ohio, widow of Henry Booth Kohr, and to this union two children were born, Bertha Jane and James Edward.

James Harvey Garten was a farmer and stock raiser and was very successful. He was a soldier in the Civil War, and at one time was township trustee. He owned two hundred and forty acres of the land in the home place and another farm in the river bottoms. Mr. Garten died on April 15, 1914, and was widely mourned, for he was one of the best known men in that part of the county, for years having taken a prominent part in community affairs. He was a Republican and had served his township as trustee. He was a member of the Grand Army post at Odon.

Henry Booth Kohr, the first husband of Mrs. Garten, was born in Tuscarawas county, Ohio, in 1839, the son of James and Rachel (Booth) Kohr, the former a native of Ohio and the latter of Virginia. The Kohrs were of German descent. Jonas Kohr and wife died in Ohio, where they were farmers.

Henry B. Kohr was educated in the common schools of his home neighborhood and in a normal school. Before his marriage he came to Indiana and located at Odon, where he lived for some years before the Civil War. He was a teacher in Daviess county and followed this vocation all his life, clerking in stores during vacations. About three years before his death he moved to Tennessee in order to teach in a normal school there, but about two weeks after his arrival sickness seized him and after a period of invalidism of about three years he died on March 4, 1879.

Henry B. Kohr was married in 1865 to Mary Eleanor Dunlap, who was born on January 13, 1843, in Ohio, the daughter of Ray and Ruth (White) Dunlap, the former a native of Ohio and the latter of Virginia.

Ray Dunlap was the son of James Dunlap, a native of Ohio, who lived in the village of Leesburg, where he was closely connected with the public schools. Ruth White was the daughter of Thomas White, native of Virginia, who moved to Ohio, where he was a farmer. Ray Dunlap and Ruth White were married in Ohio, and in 1856 settled at Raglesville, this county, where Mr. Dunlap followed the trade of blacksmith. He later lived at various places about the country, including Loogootee. He finally returned to Odon and operated a blacksmith shop there for many years. He was a soldier in the Civil War and served as a drum major, but was discharged on account of ill health. He and his family were all members of the Methodist Episcopal church. The children of Ray and Ruth Dunlap were Drusilla, Mary Ellen and Samuel. Samuel served as a substitute during the closing days of the Civil War.

To Henry B. and Mary Eleanor (Dunlap) Kohr were born four children, namely: Walter Preston, who married Lela Harshey and lives at Cleveland, Ohio, where he is employed as a bookkeeper; Edgar Ray, deceased, and Della, who married Walter Breden, of Odon, this county. Mrs. Garten is a member of the Methodist Episcopal church at Odon and takes an active interest in all the good works of the community. She is a woman of much force of character and is highly esteemed by all who know her.

JEROME DEMOTTE, M. D.

There is no class to whom greater gratitude is due from the world at large than to the self-sacrificing, sympathetic, noble-minded men whose life work is the alleviation of human suffering and the administering of comfort to the afflicted. There is no standard by which their beneficent influence can be measured. Their helpfulness is limited only by the extent of their knowledge and skill, while their power goes hand in hand with the wonderful laws of nature and springs from the very source of life itself. Some one has aptly said, "He serves God best who serves humanity most." Among the physicians and surgeons of Daviess county who have risen to eminence in their chosen field of endeavor is Dr. James DeMotte, of Odon. Doctor DeMotte's career has been marked by broad-minded and conscientious service in a sphere to which his life's energies have been devoted. His profound knowledge of his profession has won for him a leading place among the distinguished medical men of his day and generation in Daviess county.

Jerome DeMotte was born in Pike county, Indiana, in 1869, the son of Albert and Elizabeth (Anderson) DeMotte, the former a native of Pike county and the latter of Dubois county, Indiana. Albert DeMotte's parents were Lawrence and Phoebe (Banta) DeMotte, who came from Mercer county, Kentucky, and settled on the farm where, two generations later, Dr. Jerome DeMotte was born, entering their land at the Vincennes land office on January 15, 1818. Lawrence DeMotte entered about two hundred acres of land, cleared it and established a home in the wilderness, and there he spent the rest of his life, his death occurring in 1872. The father of Lawrence DeMotte was John DeMotte, of Mercer county, Kentucky, who lived and died in that county, where he was a farmer. The family originally came from France and settled in New Jersey and from that state certain members of the family moved to Kentucky.

The maternal grandparents of Doctor DeMotte were William and Elizabeth (Harris) Anderson, who came from Kentucky to Dubois county, Indiana, in 1816, and entered a tract of three hundred acres of land. The home which they established in the wilderness is still in possession of the family. Both William Anderson and his wife died upon this farm. Upon coming from Kentucky to Indiana, William Anderson drove seventy hogs through from Kentucky and these were the first tame hogs in this section of the country. The following winter was very severe and bears killed all except five of the number.

Albert DeMotte received only a very limited education in the early schools of his day, it being necessary for him to go through the woods three and four miles to school. He was a farmer all of his life on the old DeMotte farm, which is still owned by the family. The children of Albert and Elizabeth (Anderson) DeMotte were Ella, Clara, Elvis, Jerome and Sebastian.

Jerome DeMotte received a common school education and in 1889 attended the Southern Indiana Normal School, now extinct, at Mitchell, Indiana. He also was a student at the Princeton Normal College in 1890 and 1891 and was graduated from this institution in the latter year. Subsequently he taught school for three years and then, in 1892, entered the University of Michigan, remaining there until 1895. He then spent one year at the Ohio Medical College and was graduated with the degree of Doctor of Medicine. He took up the practice of medicine in 1896 at Odon and has been engaged continuously in the practice of his profession there since that date, a period of about twenty years.

In 1899 Dr. Jerome DeMotte was married to Olive Vest, of Barr township, the daughter of A. J. Vest, a farmer of that township. To this happy union three children have been born, Russell, Pauline and Calvin, all of whom are living at home.

Doctor DeMotte is a member of the Daviess County Society and the Indiana State Medical Association, and he and his family are members of the Christian church. Doctor DeMotte has acquired an enviable standing among the professional men of Daviess county. He possesses, in the highest degree, the confidence and respect of his patients, and enjoys a large and flourishing practice in that section of Daviess county.

EDGAR T. LAUGHLIN.

Indiana has always been distinguished for the high rank of her bench and bar. Perhaps none of the newer states can justly boast of abler jurists or attorneys, many of whom have been men of national fame. Among those whose lives have been passed on a quieter plane, there is scarcely a town or city in the state that cannot boast of one or more lawyers capable of crossing swords in forensic combat with many of the distinguished legal lights of the country. While the growth and development of the state in the last half century has been most marvelous, viewed from any standpoint; yet of no one class of her citizenship has she greater reason for just pride than her judges and attorneys. In Edgar T. Laughlin, a well-known attorney of Odon, Indiana, are found many of the rare qualities which go to make the successful lawyer and jurist. He possesses perhaps few of those brilliant, dazzling, meteoric qualities which sometimes flash along the legal horizon, riveting the gaze and blinding the vision for the moment, then disappearing, leaving little or no trace behind; but rather has those solid and more substantial qualities which shine with constant luster, shedding light in the dark places with steadiness and continuity.

Edgar T. Laughlin was born at Odon, Indiana, on December 8, 1875, the son of Joseph D. and Lakie J. (Ledgerwood) Laughlin, and was educated in the Odon public schools, spending a short time, in the years 1886-87, in the Washington public schools. His father was county prosecuting attorney a part of this time. Young Laughlin took the honors of the county in the eighth-grade examination in the year 1893, and was graduated from the Odon high school in 1895. He studied law in his father's office and was admitted to the Daviess county bar at the age of twenty-one years. He practiced under his father for three years, or until the elder Laughlin retired in June, 1910, since which time Edgar T. Laughlin has conducted an individual law practice with his office and residence at Odon. In 1904 he was elected prosecuting attorney for this county, and was re-elected in 1906, serving from January, 1905, to January, 1909. He has taken an active part in community affairs and is a stockholder in the First National Bank of Odon and in the Farmers' Bank of Odon, as well as in the Farmers' Bank of St. Bernice.

On September 30, 1902, Edgar T. Laughlin was married to Elva Pearl O'Dell, daughter of John W. O'Dell, and to this union two children, Cleta D. and Nora Blanche, have been born.

Mr. Laughlin has been for some time city attorney of Odon. He also is the attorney for the trustees of Van Buren and Madison townships. Mr. Laughlin and family are members of the Methodist Episcopal church. He is a member of the Independent Order of Odd Fellows and the Improved Order of Red Men.

Edgar T. Laughlin's father, Joseph Dunn Laughlin, was born in Martin county, Indiana, February 1, 1845, the son of John O. M. and Elizabeth (Giege) Laughlin, the former a native of Kentucky and the latter a native of Tennessee. John O. M. Laughlin was the son of John Richard and Sarah (Gilis) Laughlin, the former a native of Virginia and the latter of Kentucky. John Richard Laughlin, a soldier in the War of 1812, emigrated from Virginia to Kentucky, and there was married. In 1818 he moved to Lawrence county, Indiana, purchasing land near Bedford. Incidentally he was engaged in the manufacture of salt, boiling down the water from one of the numerous salt springs thereabouts. After a time he began farming and he and his neighbors were accustomed to float live stock and merchandise on rafts to New Orleans. In 1832 he made a trip to New Orleans and walked back to Memphis, where he and his partner died of cholera.

Mrs. Elizabeth (Geiger) Laughlin, the wife of John O. M. Laughlin, was the daughter of a soldier of the War of 1812, who married a Henderson and emigrated from Tennessee to Lawrence county, Indiana, where he entered land near Bedford. Three sons of this family, Isaiah, George and Wiley, were soldiers in the Civil War. Though John O. M. Laughlin had very little education, he having attended school altogether about three months, he nevertheless became well informed. He was a preacher in the Church of God and also a farmer. He entered land in Martin county and accumulated altogether a hundred and sixty acres. He and his wife died in Martin county in 1895. They had lived in Morgan county for some time, probably for five or six years. They were the parents of ten children, namely: George, who died in infancy; Sarah F.; Matilda E.; John D., who served in Company B, Twenty-seventh Regiment, Indiana Volunteer Infantry, lived until 1909; Joseph D., who also served the same company; Merinda C., Ulysses G., Rufus J., Minerva E. and Ausman A.

An uncle of Joseph D. Laughlin, Joseph G. Laughlin, had three sons in Company B, Twenty-seventh Regiment, Indiana Volunteer Infantry. They were James B., John R. and Joseph H. James B. was wounded at Buckton Station and at Antietam, but survived the war. John R. was wounded at Antietam and some years after the war died of his wounds.

Joseph D. Laughlin was educated in the common schools of Martin county and at the Dover Hill Academy and Zion Seminary at Zion, Illinois. He taught school altogether eight years, the last year at Odon, Indiana. After quitting the teaching profession he began practicing law at Odon, and, with the exception of the time he was prosecuting attorney of Daviess county, has lived at Odon. He was prosecutor from November, 1886, to November, 1888. He practiced twenty-six years, retiring in 1900.

On October 26, 1873, Joseph D. Laughlin was married to Lakie Jane Ledgerwood, who was born in Greene county, this state, the daughter of Charles and Amanda (Chambers) Ledgerwood, both natives of Tennessee. Charles Ledgerwood was the son of Joseph and Margaret (Hayes) Ledgerwood, natives of Tennessee, who settled near Scotland, Greene county, this state, during pioneer times, being among the first settlers there. Joseph Ledgerwood was killed by a falling tree, and his widow died at the home of her son, Charles Ledgerwood, in the eastern part of Madison township, this county, at the age of ninety-three years. Mrs. Laughlin's maternal grandparents were Thomas and Lakie Janes Chambers, both natives of Tennessee, who died near Jelico, that state, the former at the age of one hundred and four years. Thomas Chambers owned five or six hundred acres of land and ninety slaves. He was a Union man and freed his slaves at the beginning of the war. Charles Ledgerwood married in Tennessee and came to Indiana about 1831, locating in Greene county, where he owned considerable land. About 1855 he removed to Madison township, this county, where his wife died about 1864 and he died two years later. They were the parents of eleven children, as follow: Eliza Jane, Margaret, Thomas, Barbara, Elizabeth, James, William, Amanda, Charles, Lakie Jane and Milton. James Ledgerwood, who lived until 1910, served in Company C, Ninety-first Indiana Volunteer Infantry, during the Civil War.

Eleven children were born to Joseph D. and Lakie J. (Ledgerwood) Laughlin, as follow: Laura, Edgar T., Lily, Maude, Bertha, Oliver O., Elizabeth, Jane, Nellie, Cora and Daisy Fay. Joseph D. Laughlin and family are members of the Methodist Episcopal church, and he is a member of J. W. Thornburg Post No. 474, Grand Army of the Republic, at Odon, Indiana. Mr. Laughlin is the man who obtained the construction of the railroad into Odon. It was through his efforts that the name of Clarksburg was changed to Odon.

HIRAM HYATT.

Among the men of sterling worth and strength of character who created a profound impression on the communal life of this locality, no one achieved a larger meed of popular respect than the late Hiram Hyatt. His life-long residence in one locality gave the people an opportunity to know him in every phase of his character. That he was true to life in its every phase is manifest by the esteem and regard in which he was held during his life and the respect that is paid to his memory. He won success by his own honest endeavor and indomitable energy. He placed himself in the front rank of the enterprising citizens of Daviess county by exercising these excellent qualities. He outstripped the less active plodders on the highway of life and achieved a marked success. His is a name that all men who remember him delight to honor because of his upright life and wholesome habits.

Hiram Hyatt was born on June 6, 1847, and died on February 16, 1896. He was a son of Elisha Hyatt, Sr., a large landowner of Daviess county. Hiram Hyatt was educated in the common schools of Daviess county, and when a young man entered a bank in Washington. Later he became a grain merchant, and looked after his father's estate. He was city treasurer of Washington for a number of years and prominent in the councils of the Republican party in Daviess county. He was a prominent member of the Masonic fraternity and was a Knight Templar, being past eminent commander at the time of his death. At the age of eighteen he became a deacon in the Presbyterian church and served throughout his life in that capacity. He was also a great Sunday school worker and every Sunday was to be found in his accustomed place in the Sunday school.

The late Hiram Hyatt was married on February 11, 1873, to Emma B. Van Trees, the daughter of Colonel Van Trees, and to this happy union two children were born: William A., a well-known real estate dealer of Washington, Indiana, and Harry V., a manufacturer of Chicago, Illinois.

Col. John Van Trees, the father of Mrs. Hyatt, was born on September 4, 1804, on the Little Miami river, near Cincinnati, Ohio, a son of Emanuel and Julia (Storms) Van Trees. Emanuel Van Trees was a native of Pennsylvania, and his father was a native of Heidelburg, Germany. Emanuel Van Trees came to Daviess county in 1819 and helped lay out the town of Washington. He had come west, however, about nine years previously. He died in a log house that stood on what is now the corner of East Sixth and Main streets, in the county seat. He was the first clerk of the court in Daviess county, and was succeeded in that office by his son, Col. John Van Trees, at the time of his death.

Col. John Van Trees was educated in the pioneer schools of Daviess county, but was almost wholly self-educated. He stood high in the educational affairs of Daviess county in his day and generation. He was a thorough master of the German language, as this language was spoken in his home. After retiring from the office of county clerk he became a merchant, and for many years was engaged in the mercantile business. He died on January 18, 1895, at the advanced age of ninety years. Col. John Van Trees erected a fine house in the colonial style in the place of the log house which his father had built, and lived there the rest of his life, this house still being owned by the family. Early in life Colonel Van Trees was a Whig, but later became a Republican, and was once a candidate for state treasurer. Colonel Van Trees had two sons, Charles R. and Henry E., who participated in the Civil War. His family consisted of five sons and five daughters, all of whom lived to reach middle age. Three sons and three daughters are still living, namely: John, of St. Louis, Missouri; Henry E., a resident of California; William L., of Washington; Mrs. Helen S. Scudder, of Washington; Lida, living on the old home place, and Mrs. Emma B. Hyatt, the widow of Hiram Hyatt.

Col. John Van Trees was married in May, 1830, to Laura G. Prentiss, who was born in Lexington, Kentucky, a daughter of Thomas Green and Laura G. (Porter) Prentiss, natives of Rutland, Vermont, who settled in Lexington, Kentucky, and built the woolen mills in that town. Subsequently they came to the banks of the White river, in this county, and there, with certain other New England settlers, established a town, which has now vanished. Mrs. Emma B. Hyatt is a descendant of Capt. John Prentice, a Revolutionary soldier who changed the spelling of the name from Prentice to Prentiss.

GEORGE GODWIN.

The career of George Godwin, head of the firm of George Godwin & Son, contains no exciting chapter of tragic events, but is replete with well-defined purposes which, carried to successful issue, have won for him an influential place in the business circles of Washington and Daviess county, as well as high personal standing among his fellow citizens. His life work has been on of unceasing industry and perseverance. The systematic and honorable methods which he has ever followed have resulted not only in winning the confidence of those with whom he has had dealings, but also in building up a large and profitable business in the sale of dry goods and groceries.

George Godwin was born in Reeve township, Daviess county, Indiana, on May 5, 1862, a son of Edward and Esther (Allen) Godwin, the former a native of Maryland, and the latter of Indiana, who were the parents of five children: Alfred M., deceased; Emma Jane, deceased, who was the wife of Reuben A. Perkins; George, of Washington, this county; Jesse, of Mitchell, Indiana, and Martha, the wife of James E. Gilley, of Washington.

Edward Godwin came to Indiana with his parents in 1831. They settled in Barr township, this county, and soon afterward moved to Knox county, near Edwardsport; but before the breaking out of the Civil War they returned to Daviess county, and here Edward Godwin grew to manhood and became a substantial farmer. He first purchased a claim of forty acres and added to it until at one time he owned about two hundred and forty acres of land in Reeve township. There he reared his family, and there he died at the age of seventy-three years. His widow still survives and now lives with her daughter, Mrs. Martha Gilley. Both were members of the Christian church, in which Mr. Godwin was an elder for more than forty years.

The paternal grandfather of George Godwin was Jesse Godwin, who married in Greenwood and came from Liverpool, England, to the United States, settling first in Maryland. Subsequently they came to Daviess county, arriving here in 1831. Jesse Godwin's wife died at Edwardsport, Knox county, Indiana. He afterwards returned to Daviess county, where his death occurred at the age of seventy-six. Jesse Godwin and wife reared a large family of children, among whom were Edward, George, John, Jesse and Thomas.

The maternal grandparents of George Godwin was Joseph and Susan (White) Allen, natives of Kentucky and Tennessee, respectively, and pioneers of Daviess county, they having been early settlers in Reeve township, where both died, the former at the age of seventy-nine and the latter at the age of eighty-four. Joseph Allen was a merchant, and when he came to this county started a horse-power grist-mill, which he presently changed to a water-power mill, finally erecting a steam-power mill. He was a very successful miller and after awhile erected a second mill. During the time that he was thus engaged as a merchant and miller he also continued as a farmer and stock raiser. He and his wife were the parents of thirteen children, namely: Esther, John, Malinda, Tolbert, Eliza, Jane, Mary, Stancil, James, Charles, Emma and two who died young.

George Godwin was reared on his father's farm in Reeve township, attending the district schools, and lived at home until he was twenty-four years of age. He began his career as a merchant in the town of Alfordsville, where he conducted a general store for two years before his marriage. On the 5th of January, 1885, this store was destroyed by fire and Mr. Godwin lost all his goods. On April 19, 1885, he opened the business again on the same spot, where he continued in business until 1907, in which year he moved to Washington. In 1906 Mr. Godwin was elected county treasurer, serving four years, comprising two terms. He became connected with the State Bank of Washington in the meantime, having assisted in its organization, and acted as its president for two years. Subsequently he resigned this office and purchased his present dry-goods and grocery store in 1912. Mr. Godwin has associated with him in this business his three sons, Neil, Keith and Ralph.

On April 11, 1885, George Godwin was married to Mary Lannum, a daughter of Robert and Matilda (Chandler) Lannum, and to this union five children have been born, Maud, Helen, Neil, Keith and Ralph. Maud married Bernard L. Spalding, of Montgomery, to which union two children have been born, Helen and Carl. Helen Godwin died at the age of eighteen years. The mother of these children died on April 26, 1911, at the age of forty-nine. She was a member of the Methodist Episcopal church, being a devoted and active worker in the church. She was born in Maysville, Kentucky; her parents wer natives of the same state and died there after the war. They were the parents of five children, Lizzie, Mary, John, Perry and Jennie, all of whom are dead save John.

On January 15, 1912, Mr. Godwin married, secondly, Mrs. Carrie B. Danley, widow of Joseph Danley, and a daughter of Eli and Sarah Gill. She was born in Ohio, of which state her parents also were natives, the latter moving to Illinois about the time of the Civil War, settling at Flora. Her father died there at the age of seventy-one, while her mother is still living. Mrs. Carrie B. Godwin is a member of the Westminster Presbyterian church in Washington. Mr. Godwin is a member of Loogootee Lodge No. 626, Free and Accepted Masons, and of Liverpool Lodge No. 110, Independent Order of Odd Fellows. He also belongs to the Improved Order of Red Men, the Ben Hur Society, the Modern Woodmen of the World, and the Modern Woodmen of America.

Few men living in the city of Washington are better known than George Godwin and few men more thoroughly deserve the confidence and esteem of their fellow citizens than he. He has been successful in business affairs, and has managed to acquire a substantial competence for his old age, when that time comes. His success in life is founded upon a reputation for honesty and square-dealing. Mr. Godwin's three sons, who are now associated with him in business, are equally devoted to the methods which have been established by their worthy father, and are regarded as among the rising young business men of the county seat.

ALVA OTIS FULKERSON.

Perseverance and sterling worth are almost always certain to win conspicuous recognition in any locality. Alva Otis Fulkerson, the present county superintendent of schools of Daviess county, Indiana, and formerly a well-known teacher in the Washington high school, is a splendid example of the successful self-made man. He not only eminently deserves the confidence reposed in him by the trustees of the various townships of Daviess county and the people of Daviess county as well; but he also possesses the talents and forcefulness which have made him one of the leading county superintendents in the state of Indiana. He is now president of the State County Superintendents' Association. He was a successful instructor and in his present position has done much to raise the standard of the public schools of Daviess county. He is a man of strong fiber and vigorous mentality.

ALVA O. FULKERSON.

He has achieved a signal success in the educational field and has earned splendid words of commendation from those who are competent to form a proper estimate of the man and his accomplishments.

Alva Otis Fulkerson, county superintendent of schools, of Washington, Indiana, was born in Van Buren township, Daviess county, Indiana, on March 18, 1868, the son of Isaac and Margaret L. (Allen) Fulkerson, natives of Indiana. He is one of nine children, born to his parents, namely: Eldon, of Hoquiam, Washington; Alice C., the wife of D. H. Courtney, of Elnora, Indiana; Alva Otis, the subject of this sketch; Arthur L., of Lawrence, Massachusetts; Clarence D., of Salem, Oregon; Oliver H.; Effie L., of Washington, Indiana; Allen B., of Indianapolis; Z. Roy, of Montreal, Canada; and Edgar L., who died from the effect of being scalded when about four years old. Edgar L. and Clarence D. were twins.

Isaac Fulkerson, the father of Alva Otis Fulkerson, was born and reared in Daviess county, Indiana, and was always a farmer. At the time of his death he owned a farm of seventy acres in Van Buren township. This farm he had improved and there he reared his family. He died in July, 1911, at the age of over seventy-three years. His wife survives him and resides in Washington. She is a member of the Methodist Episcopal church. Isaac Fulkerson was a soldier in the Civil War, serving as a private in the Fourteenth Regiment Indiana Volunteer Infantry at first, and later as a member of the Forty-fourth Regiment Indiana Volunteer Infantry; serving in all about three years. He received a fall on Cheat Mountain and for disability suffered by reason of this injury received a pension. His service during the war was mostly performed in Virginia and Tennessee. He always took a prominent part in politics, and was identified with the Democratic party, but never held office, except that of constable.

Alva Otis Fulkerson's paternal grandfather was James Fulkerson, who married Pantha Ann Evans. James Fulkerson and his wife were early settlers in Daviess county and were farmers. The former died in middle age and the latter after reaching the age of seventy-eight. They had a large family of children, among whom were Isaac, Marion, Michael, Ziba, Jacob, Henry, William and Irene E. A. O. Fulkerson's maternal grandfather was Cyrus Allen, who married Lodusky H. Compton. Cyrus Allen came to Indiana from North Carolina when about seven years old. His wife was a native of Indiana. They resided in Daviess county the greater part of their lives and were farmers. Cyrus Allen was past fifty when he died, but his wife lived to be eighty-three. They had a large family of children, as follow:

(24)

Oriena, Margaret L., Katherine, Clementine, Kezia, Theresa, Logan, Oliver P., Banner B., Willard Robert and Ellsworth.

Alva Otis Fulkerson was reared on his father's farm and attended the district schools and the Odon high school. He spent one term at the Southern Indiana Normal College at Mitchell; one year at DePauw University, and was graduated from the Indiana State Normal School at Terre Haute, in 1893, further pursuing his studies he was graduated from Indiana University in 1897 and in 1910 did some post-graduate work at Chicago University.

Alva Otis Fulkerson began teaching in 1889, and in 1899 went to Washington, this county, as principal of the Southside school, after he had taught in the district schools and served as principal of the schools at Raglesville, Staunton, and Elnora, Indiana. For five years he served as principal of the Southside school, and after that served for five and one-half years as teacher of history in the Washington high school. In January, 1911, he was elected by the county board of education, as county superintendent of schools to fill out a vacancy. He was re-elected in June, 1911, by the unanimous vote of the trustees, for a full term of four years. During this incumbency the Legislature extended the term of county superintendents two years, so that Superintendent Fulkerson's present term will not expire until 1917.

On September 5, 1900, Mr. Fulkerson was united in marriage to Minnie Ellen Casey, who was born in this county, a daughter of Thomas Walker and Delilah (Keiser) Casey. Thomas W. Casey came to Indiana, from Tennessee, when he was about eight years old. He became a successful merchant and was a veteran of the Civil War. He took part in some of the most important battles of the war, among which were Antietam and Gettysburg, being wounded during the second day of the latter bloody battle. He was mustered out as a first lieutenant. Mrs. Fulkerson's mother was a native of Ohio, but she came to Indiana when young. Mr. Casey was married twice. Clara, Albert R., Minnie E., Homer F., and Louella were the children by the first marriage and Effie, Fred E., Millie and Herschel D. were the children by the second marriage.

Mr. and Mrs. Fulkerson are members of the First Methodist Episcopal church of Washington. Mr. Fulkerson is a member of the official board of this church; superintendent of the Sunday school and president of the Epworth League. He was president of the district Epworth League for two terms and has twice represented his church as lay delegate at the annual conference. Mr. Fulkerson belongs to Charity Lodge No. 30, Free and Accepted Masons, and is also a member of the Royal Arcanum. In politics he is identified with the Democratic party, and during one campaign served as county chairman of his party. Mr. Fulkerson is a director in the State Bank of Washington, and a director in the Union Savings and Loan Association of the same city. He is prominent, not only in the educational life of Daviess county, but in the social, financial and commercial life as well.

DANIEL W. HAYES.

Among the men of sterling worth and strength of character in Daviess county who have made an impression upon the life of the locality in which they live, none has achieved a larger meed of popular respect and regard than Daniel W. Hayes, the president of the Odon Realty Company. His life-long residence in Daviess county has given the people an opportunity to know him thoroughly, and that he has been true to life in its every phase is manifested by the confidence and regard in which he is held by those who know him. In a business way, Mr. Hayes is a man of unusual attainment and has achieved a splendid success in life.

Daniel W. Hayes was born in Van Buren township, Daviess county, Indiana, April 25, 1866, the son of John and Rosanna D. (Snyder) Hayes, the former of whom was born in Wurttemberg, Germany, and the latter at Strausburg, in Tuscarawas county, Ohio. The paternal grandparents of Daniel W. Hayes never came to America. His maternal grandparents were Frederick and Sevilla Snyder, natives of Wurttemberg, Germany, who came to America before their marriage and who, after their marriage, resided in Ohio, where they were farmers.

John Hayes was educated in Germany and there learned the bleacher's trade. He came to America at the age of eighteen years and located in Ohio. He lived in that state until 1865, in which year he came to this county, and purchased land in Van Buren township. He farmed there until 1893, when he moved to the village of Odon, where his death occurred about one year later. He was a member of the United Brethren church, to which faith his family adhere, though while living in Ohio he was identified with the Lutheran church. To John and Rosanna D. (Snyder) Hayes were born the following children: Mrs. Sarah Evans, who lives near Raglesville, this county; Fred G., who lives at Nevada, Iowa; Mrs. Julia Dyal, of Raglesville; Mrs. Mary Rasler, deceased, who lived at Raglesville; Gideon, who lives at Cody, Wyoming; Mrs. Dolly Ward, of St. Louis, Michigan;

Charles, of St. Louis, Missouri; Mrs. Viola Ward, of Odon; and Daniel W., the subject of this sketch.

Daniel W. Hayes was educated in the public schools of Daviess county and in the Southern Indiana Normal School, now extinct, at Mitchell, Indiana. He also attended the normal school at Odon and later a business college at New Albany, Indiana. Mr. Hayes taught school in Daviess county for four years, after which he entered the mercantile business at Odon, having served one year's business apprenticeship at Washington, with Cable & Coffman, previous to going to Odon. Mr. Hayes operated a general store at Odon for seventeen years, and in 1907 he went into the realty business, having been elected to the office of president of the Odon Realty Company, which office he still holds.

In 1891 Daniel W. Hayes was married to Cora B. Ward, daughter of Philip S. and Margaret Ward. To this union seven children have been born, Beatrice, Dow, Dwight, Harold, John, Robert and Margaret. Mr. and Mrs. Hayes are members of the United Brethren church, active in both the work of the church and the Sunday school, and their children have been reared in that faith. Fraternally, Mr. Hayes is a member of the Knights of Pythias and of the Tribe of Ben Hur. In his capacity as president of the Odon Realty Company, he has done much toward promoting the material growth and prosperity of this community. He is honored and respected by his fellow townsmen and is entitled to rank as a representative citizen and business man of Daviess county.

GEORGE W. CORRELL.

It is interesting to note from the beginning the growth and development of a community; to note the lines along which progress has been made and to take cognizance of those whose industry and leadership in the work of advancement have rendered possible the present prosperity of the locality under consideration. George W. Correll, of this review, is one of the strong, sturdy individuals who has contributed largely to the material welfare of Daviess county, and particularly to the welfare of the vicinity of Odon, where he resides. He is an up-to-date business man, public-spirited as a citizen, and progressive in all that the term implies.

George W. Correll was born at Mt. Helsia, Ohio, on September 24, 1848, the son of Clement and Nancy (Shroy) Correll, the former a native of Ohio and the latter a native of Maryland, born in 1816. Clement Correll was a son of Jacob and Eleanor (Poter) Correll, both natives of New York state, who moved to Ohio after their marriage, and located at Cherryville. Jacob Correll was a tailor by trade. Mrs. Nancy Correll was a daughter of John and Rachel (Glass) Shroy, both natives of Germany, who settled in Indiana, near Sharpsburg. Late in life, about the year 1817, they removed to Ohio, settling near Strausburg with the first colony that landed west of the Tuscarawas river. They entered land in that vicinity and died there. John Shroy served in the War of 1812.

Clement Correll learned the tailor's trade from his father, and was engaged in working at this trade and in the mercantile business all his life. He made many uniforms during the Civil War. In 1859 he removed to Odon and from that time until his death he was in business in that village, being engaged in tailoring until about 1863, after which he engaged in the general mercantile business. He also was an auctioneer and a justice of the peace. Clement Correll was drafted by the authorities for service in the Union army during the Civil War, but was rejected on account of his weight. He and his family were members of the United Brethren church. Clement and Nancy (Shroy) Correll were the parents of four children, Harvey, Charles, George W. and John. Harvey Correll served three years in the Union army during the Civil War. Charles Correll, also a soldier, died in a hospital following the battle of Chattanooga.

George W. Correll was educated at Odon, and began learning the stone-cutter's trade in 1865. He started working at Odon, but subsequently moved to Bedford, and worked there and at other places. In 1872 he established a business for himself at Odon and in 1880 moved the business to Loogootee. In 1891 he returned to Odon and established his present business, in partnership with J. A. Burrell, under the firm name of Correll & Burrell. This firm deals in Bedford rock in a wholesale way, and has business dealings all over the country. It also is engaged in an extensive retail trade in monuments. This firm erected the memorial bridge at Atlanta, Georgia, in honor of Archibald Butt, President Taft's aide-de-camp, who went down with the ill-fated Titanic.

In 1872 George W. Correll was married to Rachel Wallick, of Odon, daughter of Michael Wallick, and to this union six children have been born: Ira, Richard, Beldwin, Walter, Roberta and Mary, of whom Walter and Mary are deceased.

Mr. Correll was assessor of Van Buren township while living upon the farm. Formerly he was a member of the Knights of Pythias. He and his family are connected with the Methodist Episcopal church. In a business way George W. Correll is well known, and in a personal way he is much liked and highly respected by his neighbors, and by all the people with whom he has had either social or business dealings.

ALFRED E. JOHNSON.

A respect which should always be accorded the brave sons of the North who left their homes and the peaceful pursuits of civil life to give their services and their lives, if need be, to preserve the integrity of the American Union, is certainly due Alfred E. Johnson, a well-known retired farmer and a member of a very old family at Washington, this county. Mr. Johnson proved his love and loyalty to the government on the long and tiresome marches, on the lonely picket lines, on the tented fields and amid the flames and smoke of battle, and then, returning to civil life, manfully took up the struggle of agricultural life, in which he was rewarded with a degree of success commensurate with his efforts. The great secret of his success has been his devotion to duty, whether that duty pertained to his own private affairs or matters affecting the public welfare. In war and in peace, his record has been signalized by honesty of purpose and integrity of thought and action; so that he has fully deserved the exalted position which has been accorded him by the people with whom he has lived so long.

Alfred E. Johnson was born on a farm four miles south of the city of Washington, in Daviess county, on March 27, 1840, the son of Elijah and Mildred (Horrall) Johnson, the former a native of Indiana, born in Vincennes in 1796, and the latter a native of South Carolina, born in 1808, who were the parents of nine children, namely: Anson B., who died at the age of ninety-two; Hulda, who died in July, 1914, at the age of nearly ninety-two, was the wife of William Singleton; Malina, who died at the age of eighty-six years, was the wife of William R. Thomas; Ezra, who died in 1853, at the age of twenty-four; Matilda, who died at the age of sixty-two, was the wife of J. B. Houts; Nelson, who died at the age of seventy-four; Norvan, who died at the age of seventy-four; Alfred E., the subject of this sketch, and Lenson, who died in California in 1913, at the age of sixty-nine years and six months.

Elijah Johnson was a farmer and a great hunter, his prowess as a deer-slayer having been widely recognized throughout this section. He came to Daviess county in 1816, and was married in 1820. He died in 1848, being crushed to death by a falling tree. His wife died in 1855. Both were devout Methodists, and all their children were members of the same church. All were old line Whigs and later Republicans, the husbands of the girls being members of the same party. The eldest son, Anson B., who lacked a few days of being ninety-two years old, voted for every Republican President from Harrison to Taft, except that, up to 1860, the presidential candidates were Whigs. Elijah belonged to the old territorial militia.

Alfred E. Johnson's paternal grandparents were James and Polly (Lindsey) Johnson, natives of Pennsylvania who came to Indiana in 1785 and settled in the then small village of Vincennes. James Johnson was a lieutenant-colonel in the Revolutionary army, attached to a Maryland brigade. Both he and his wife were buried at St. Francisville, Illinois; he at the age of eighty-three and she at a somewhat younger age. They were the parents of fourteen children: John L., William, Friend, Joshua, James, Elijah, Reuben, Abner, George, Rebecca, Maria, Polly, Sally, and one whose name is lost to the present generation.

Mr. Johnson's maternal grandparents were John M. and Polly (Horrall) Horrall, first cousins and natives of North Carolina, the former of whom was born in 1780. He and his wife came to Daviess county in 1812, four years before Indiana became a state, and settled on the farm now owned by the Shanks heirs, three miles south of Washington, where he died. His widow went to Illinois with a son-in-law, and died in that state. They were the parents of six children: Jason, Mildred, William, Nancy, Elvira, and one who died in infancy.

Alfred E. Johnson was born and reared on his father's farm in Washington township. He attended the old-fashioned subscription school, which had a big writing desk, made from a board, extending entirely across the side of the room. Later he attended the county public schools.

At the age of twenty-one Mr. Johnson enlisted as a Union soldier in the Civil War, and served three and one-half years. He enlisted as a member of Company E, Fifty-eighth Regiment, Indiana Volunteer Infantry, and later was attached to Companies D and C, Twenty-fourth Regiment, Indiana Volunteer Infantry. He participated in many battles, and was wounded slightly at the battle of Champion's Hill, Mississippi.

After the war Mr. Johnson farmed until 1897, when he retired and moved to Washington. He bought a nice home at 621 West Main street, where he still resides.

On October 13, 1870, Alfred E. Johnson was married to Frances E. Batchelor, daughter of John T. and Indiana (Purcell) Batchelor, both of whom belonged to pioneer families of this county, and to this union five children were born, Hugh Clinton, Lena, Elva Myrtle, Edith Llewellyn and Grant C. Hugh Clinton carried the mail for eighteen years and is now a piano tuner. He married Maud L. Winterbottom and they have two children, Malcolm and Norma. Lena died at the age of two and one-half years. Elva Myrtle married E. R. Wright, a conductor in the service of the Baltimore & Ohio Railroad Company, living at East St. Louis, Illinois. Edith L. is bookkeeper for the Vose Piano Company in Chicago, Illinois, and receives a splendid salary. Grant has a fine position with the Burroughs Adding Machine Company and travels out of Chicago.

Mrs. Johnson was born in Daviess county, Indiana, on August 10, 1854. Her father was born in Ohio and her mother in Indiana. They died in Daviess county, he at the age of sixty-nine, and she at the age of seventy-five. They were the parents of eight children, Sarah J., Minerva, Martha, Enoch, John, Mary, Laura and Frances. Mrs. Johnson's paternal grandparents were William and Catherine (Buher) Batchelor, natives of Ohio, who were among the pioneer settlers of this county. Subsequently they moved to Iowa, where they died. They were the parents of eight children, John, George, Catherine, Rachel, William, Abel, Julia and Sarah. Mrs. Johnson's maternal grandfather was Jesse Purcell, a native of North Carolina and a pioneer in Daviess county, who lived to be ninety-two years of age. He and his wife were the parents of eight children, Indiana, Rachel, Benjamin, William, Charlotte, Prudence, James and Hiram.

Mr. and Mrs. Johnson are members of the Methodist Episcopal church, and for more than forty consecutive years Mr. Johnson was an officer in the church. He has been a member of the Independent Order of Odd Fellows for fifty years. He is a Republican, and was a school director for ten consecutive years; also serving one term of three years as a member of the board of education in Washington. He was elected to one term of four years in the city council of Washington. No man in Daviess county is more highly respected or merits more honor than Alfred E. Johnson, a man who has lived a consistent life and who has taken a worthy interest in important public matters.

RINGGOLD SCOTT MITCHELL, M. D.

No other profession has accomplished, during the last half century, the progress and development that has been made by the medical profession. The man of original thought and action, whose text-book forms but the basis of future work, has ever moved forward, taking advantage of and utilizing new discoveries in the science of medicine and looking always for better methods and surer means to the desired end. Such a man is Dr. Ringgold Scott Mitchell, a physician and surgeon of Washington, Indiana. In considering the career and character of this eminent member of the medical fraternity, the impartial observer will not only be disposed to rank him among the leading members of his profession in Daviess county, but also as one of those men of broad culture and mental ken who have honored mankind in general. Through a long and busy life, replete with honor and success, he has been actuated by the highest motives and in the practice of his profession, he has brought rare skill and resource, his quick perception and almost intuitive judgment enabling him to make a correct diagnosis in practically every case. He has always been a close student of medical science, keeping in close touch with the latest progress and has been uniformly successful in practice. Because of his high attainments and exalted personal character, he is eminently entitled to representation in a work of this character.

Ringgold Scott Mitchell was born at Corydon, Indiana, on August 8, 1851, son of John S. and Martha A. (Elliott) Mitchell, natives of New York and Indiana, respectively, who were the parents of eight children, Charles S., of Flora, Illinois; Dr. Ringgold S., of Washington, Indiana; Emma A., who died at the age of ten years; Laura, the wife of S. C. Allen, of Jasonville, Indiana; Leonidas S., deceased; Edwin S., deceased; Indiana, wife of J. C. Chandler, of Washington; and Belle, who died at the age of seventeen.

John S. Mitchell was reared in New York state and when a young man, came to Indiana, settling in Floyd county, where he studied medicine. He began practicing in Harrison county and moved to Haysville, Dubois county, in 1853. Two years later he came to this county, locating at Hudsonville, where he practiced for twelve years, at the end of which time he moved two miles north and laid out the town of Glendale. A few years later he sold out to Doctor Clark and located at Mitchell, Indiana. In 1888 he returned to Daviess county and settled at Alfordsville, where he died in

1890, at the age of sixty-two years, his widow dying three months later, at the age of fifty-eight. Both were active members of the Methodist church. Dr. John S. Mitchell had given his services to the Union army as assistant surgeon of the Sixty-fifth Regiment, Indiana Volunteer Infantry, during the Civil War. He was one of the leaders in the Independent Order of Odd Fellows in this state, having served as district deputy. Doctor Mitchell was a son of Solomon and Mehitable Mitchell, the former a native of Ireland and the latter of Scotland, who were the parents of three children, Ambrose, John S. and Emily. Solomon Mitchell died in middle life and his widow married, secondly, George I. Wolf, to which latter union no children were born. Both George I. Wolf and his wife died at the age of seventy-five years and from the same cause, a fracture of the hip, their deaths occurring six weeks apart. Dr. R. S. Mitchell's maternal grandfather, Elliott, died when a comparatively young man, leaving a wife and two children, Martin A. and John. His widow married, secondly, a Mr. Moulden, but to this latter union no children were born.

Ringgold Scott Mitchell was reared in the village of Glendale, Daviess county, and attended the common schools. When a young man, he began studying medicine under his father, and in 1888 was graduated from the Kentucky School of Medicine, at Louisville. He had practiced, however, twelve years before his graduation. He was practicing in Garden City, Kansas, when the hot winds of 1888 burned up the crops in three days' time and he moved to New Albany, Indiana, where he practiced for a short time, when he was called home, to Alfordsville, on account of the sickness of his father. He remained there until after the death of his father and mother and then located at Flora, Illinois. He practiced there for six years, or until 1904, at the end of which time he returned to this county, locating at Washington, where he has practiced since that time.

On May 22, 1872, Doctor Mitchell was married to Lucy Cross, the daughter of Albert Cross, whose wife was an Akester, and to this union three children were born, Clare, Claude and Charles. Clara married S. H. Burton, of Washington township, this county. Claude is a farmer in Minnesota, living near Pine River postoffice. He is married and has four children. Charles is unmarried and is farming with his brother in Minnesota. He is city clerk of Pine River. The mother of these children was born in Iowa, and her parents, both now deceased, were natives of Indiana and Iowa, respectively. They were the parents of seven children, Laura, Lucy, Alfred, Judson, Glendora, Carrie and Lizzie.

Upon the death of his first wife, Doctor Mitchell married, secondly,

Elizabeth Wilson Gill, who was born at Carthage, Ohio, daughter of Eli and Sarah Gill, both natives of Ohio. Eli Gill was a well-known merchant and dealer in live stock, who has been dead for some years, his widow making her home with Doctor and Mrs. Mitchell. Eli Gill and his wife were the parents of the following children: Frank, Jacob (deceased), Albert, Fred, Carrie, Elizabeth, Maggie and Lucy.

Although Doctor Mitchell was reared a Methodist, he and his wife are members of the Presbyterian church. He is vice-president of the board of trustees of the church and is a teacher of the ladies' class in the Sunday school. Doctor Mitchell has a fine tenor voice, and has sung in choirs since he was twenty years old. Fraternally, he belongs to Charity Lodge No. 30, Free and Accepted Masons, and to Liverpool Lodge No. 110, Independent Order of Odd Fellows, at Washington. He also is a member of the county and state medical societies. Formerly a Republican, Doctor Mitchell became a member of the Progressive party at its formation, and has been active in the councils of that party since 1912.

Not only does Dr. Ringgold S. Mitchell stand high in the esteem of the people of Washington and vicinity, professionally, but in the civic and religious work of his home city, he has performed a worthy part. He is honored and respected by the hundreds of people who know him for this unselfish work.

JAMES A. BURRELL.

In examining the life records of self-made men it will invariably be found that indefatigable industry has constituted the basis of their success. True, there are other elements which enter into and conserve the advancement of personal interests, as perseverance, discrimination and the mastering of expedients, but the foundation of all achievement is earnest and persistent labor. At the outset of his career, Mr. Burrell recognized this fact, and he has never sought any royal road to the goal of prosperity and independence. He began work earnestly and diligently in order to advance himself, and the result is that he is now numbered among the progressive and influential business men of Daviess county.

James A. Burrell was born at Coshocton, Ohio, on May 29, 1854, the son of John W. and Sarah (McCoy) Burrell, both of whom were born in Ohio, John W. Burrell being the son of Richard Burrell. J. A. Burrell came to this county in his youth, locating at Odon, and was educated in the public schools. He entered the marble business, learning the technical points of the same under G. W. Correll, his present partner. In 1881 he started business in Odon for himself, first taking as a partner W. H. Wagy. The firm was known as Burrell & Wagy, and the partnership continued until 1892, in which year the present firm of Correll & Burrell was formed. This firm does an extensive wholesale business in Kentucky and Bedford stone, and a large retail business in monuments.

In 1880 J. A. Burrell was married to Sarah Crooke, daughter of Howard Crooke, to which union four children have been born, Carl H., a dentist of Jasonville, Indiana; Nellie, who married C. R. O'Dell, of Indianapolis; Carrie, who married Edward Love, of Odon, and Harry, who died at the age of two years. Mr. Burrell and family are members of the Methodist Episcopal church, and he is a member of the Knights of Pythias and of the Tribe of Ben Hur.

Reverting to Mr. Burrell's parentage, his father, John W. Burrell, was born in Tuscarawas county, Ohio, January 3, 1829, the son of Richard and Sarah (Keniristrick) Burrell, both natives of Maryland, who moved to Tuscarawas county, Ohio, where they both died on their farm in that county, when John W. was a small boy. John W. Burrell was educated in the public schools of Tuscarawas county, Ohio, and on July 7, 1853, was married, at Dover, Ohio, to Sarah McCoy. In 1859 they moved to this county, locating on a farm two miles east of Odon, and in 1861 moved to Odon, where they have since made their home. John W. Burrell was an undertaker and cabinetmaker, having learned the business in Dover, Ohio. As long as he was able to work this was his trade, but he has been disabled since the year 1910. Sarah (McCoy) Burrell was born in Carroll county, Ohio, the daughter of John and Ruth (White) McCoy, the former a native of Ireland and the latter a native of Wheeling, West Virginia. John McCoy was a son of Hugh and Elizabeth McCoy, natives of Ireland, who located in Belmont, Ohio, after coming to America. He was a preacher in the Methodist Episcopal church. Both he and his wife died in Belmont county, Ohio. Mrs. John W. Burrell's maternal grandparents were Thomas and Sarah White, both natives of Virginia, the former of whom was a slave-holder in that state and a captain in the patriot army during the Revolutionary War. He emigrated to Ohio about 1816 and located in Belmont county, from there moving to Tuscarawas county, Ohio, where he and his wife both died.

To John W. and Sarah (McCoy) Burrell six children were born, Albert, Richard, Anna, Harley, Samuel and Hilbert, all of whom are still living, and are members of the Methodist Episcopal church. John W. Burrell was a charter member of the Independent Order of Odd Fellows at Odon and is the only charter member now living.

James McCoy, a brother of Mrs. John W. Burrell, was a soldier in the Union army during the Civil War, having enlisted in the Fourteenth Regiment, Indiana Volunteer Infantry, under General Kemble. He was made a prisoner by the enemy and confined in Libby prison. This was the last ever heard of him. All the members of the Burrell family are well known and highly respected citizens of Daviess county.

ELISHA HYATT.

One of the beauties of our government is that it acknowledges no hereditary rank or title; no patent of nobility except that of nature, leaving every man to fix his own rank by becoming the artificer of his own fortune. Places of honor and trust, rank and preferment, thus happily placed before every individual, high or low, rich or poor, to be striven for by all, but earned only by perseverance and sterling worth, are most always sure to be filled with deserving men. Business responsibility in a community is won only by prodigious energy, by those possessing the ability, perseverance and industry of the very highest order. Elisha Hyatt, the proprietor of many splendid farms in Daviess and Knox counties, is a man who has had a large part in the business life of Washington and vicinity and affords a conspicuous example of the successful, self-made American. He not only deserves the confidence reposed in him by his fellow citizens, but this confidence in a large measure has been the basis of his splendid success. He is a man of vigorous mentality, and this quality has been a large factor in his career. Mr. Hyatt not only enjoys the distinction of belonging to one of the oldest families in this county, but he is one of the wealthiest citizens of the county and has been liberal with his money.

Elisha Hyatt, a farmer, now living at 406 East Grove street, Washington, Indiana, was born in that city on September 8, 1856, the son of Elisha and Martha (Beasley) Hyatt, the former a native of Kentucky and the latter a native of this county. They were the parents of the following children: Elizabeth, deceased, who was the wife of I. M. Parsons; Thomas, deceased; Theodore F., deceased; Hiram, deceased; Lydia, the wife of

Hugh Rogers, of Washington, Indiana; Richard, deceased; Adelaide, who died young; and Elisha, Jr., the immediate subject of this sketch.

Elisha Hyatt, Sr., was nine years old when he came with his parents to Daviess county. They settled just north of Washington on what is called the old Hyatt homestead, where he grew to manhood. He was a merchant during his earlier years and accumulated considerable property. He owned, at one time, eight thousand acres of land and was one of the organizers of the private bank of Hyatt, Levings & Company, which, on account of its failure in later years, lost Mr. Hyatt considerable money. He operated a stave factory and saw-mills and bought grain, in addition to running flatboats to New Orleans, being regarded as one of the leading men in Daviess county in his day and generation. He died at Washington on December 31, 1885, at the age of seventy-six years and two months, and his wife died on her birthday, August 20, 1901, at the age of eighty-four years. She was a member of the Presbyterian church and her husband, while not a member of the church, was also partial to that faith. He was a Republican and was at one time a member of the city council, but did not like to hold public offices.

The paternal grandparents of Elisha Hyatt, Jr., were Thomas Hyatt and wife, natives of Kentucky and pioneers of Daviess county. They bought land just north of Worthington, as above mentioned, and there they lived the remainder of their days, Thomas Hyatt's death occurring as a result of injuries received from the kick of a colt. They were the parents of seven children, Elisha, John, William, Eliza, Mary, Ann and Margaret. The maternal grandparents of Elisha Hyatt, Jr., were Edwin and Elizabeth Beasley, natives of Pennsylvania, who emigrated from that state to Kentucky, coming thence to Daviess county, at a time when the Indians were still here. They located in Maple Valley, south of Washington, and engaged in farming and tanning. They were the parents of but two children, Martha and a son, who died young.

Elisha Hyatt, Jr., was reared in Washington and attended the public schools of that city. He remained at home until he reached his majority, at which time his father gave him a start, and he later fell heir to a share of his father's estate, which he helped to settle. He has always followed farming, stock raising and buying of grain, but has kept his residence in Washington. He now owns about six hundred acres in Knox and Daviess counties.

In 1886 Mr. Hyatt was married to Etta Nixon, daughter of M. A. and

Elizabeth (Williamson) Nixon, born in Knox county, Indiana, in 1863. Her mother died in 1891 at the age of forty-eight and her father died on December 25, 1914. Mr. and Mrs. Nixon were the parents of seven children, Etta, Clara, Eliza, Myrtle, Ruth, Elizabeth and Elisha.

To Mr. and Mrs. Hyatt five children have been born, Clarence, Martha E., Evelyn Pearl, Elisha and Robert. Clarence, who married Alta Smith, conducts a grocery store at Indianapolis. Martha E. is at home. Evelyn P. is a physician in Syracuse, New York, and is now an interne in the women's and children's home there. Elisha, Jr., is in the automobile business, and Robert is a student in the Washington high school.

Mr. Hyatt is a member of the Republican party and was a city councilman for two or three terms. Mrs. Hyatt is a member of the Presbyterian church and is interested in all church work. Mr. and Mrs. Hyatt are well and favorably known in Washington and Daviess county, and are highly respected and esteemed by all who know them.

ROBERT J. BARR.

The gentleman whose name appears at the head of this biographical review needs no introduction to the people of Daviess county, since his entire life has been spent in this community, a life devoted not only to the fostering of his own interests, but also to the welfare of all. An honorable representative of one of the esteemed families of his section and a gentleman of high character and worthy ambitions, he has filled no small place in the public view, as the important official positions he has held bear witness. He is a splendid type of the intelligent, up-to-date, self-made American, and is regarded as one of the very best business men the county can boast of, being progressive and abreast of the times in all that concerns the commonwealth and, very properly, possesses the unqualified respect and confidence of all.

Robert J. Barr, the son of John and Julia (Burris) Barr, was born in Daviess county, Indiana, November 14, 1846, and has lived here all of his life. John Barr was a native of Kentucky, while Julia Burris was a native of Indiana, her birth having occurred in what is now Martin county.

The paternal grandfather of Robert J. Barr was James Barr, who came from Kentucky to Indiana about 1816 and located in what is now Barr township, Daviess county. He cleared the land and made a home for himself and family in the wilderness. He was a farmer all his life and was a prominent and influential citizen in the early days in the township which bears his name. The maternal grandparents of Mr. Barr were Robert and Mahala Burris, natives of Kentucky who came to Indiana in an early day and located in what is now Martin county, near the Daviess county line. They were pioneers in that section, and spent the rest of their lives there.

John Barr was reared on his father's farm in Barr township. He had very little opportunity for securing an education in that early day, attending school only three weeks all his life. He learned to read and write, however, and being a man of close observation, managed to become very well informed. As a young man he took up farming in Reeve township, and continued to reside there the rest of his life, he and his wife dying on the homestead in that township. John and Julia (Burris) Barr were the parents of seven children, namely: Eliza, deceased, was the wife of W. H. Godwin, and lived in Edwardsport, Knox county, Indiana; Jane, deceased, was the wife of Frank Prater, and lived in Reeve township, this county; William W., of Montgomery, Indiana; Susan, deceased, was the wife of Samuel Potts, of Reeve township; James, deceased, was a farmer of Reeve township; Juda, the wife of A. J. Burris, a farmer of Reeve township, and Robert J., with whom this narrative deals. William and James both served in the Union army during the Civil War, both surviving the struggle and becoming substantial citizens of Daviess county.

Robert J. Barr received his education in the common schools of Reeve township, and after he grew to maturity took up farming in Reeve township. In 1891 he sold his farm and moved to Washington. For the past fifteen years he has been engaged in fruit growing, and has a fine apple orchard of thirty acres two miles out of Washington. Mr. Barr is also a director in the State Bank of Washington.

In 1870 Mr. Barr was married to Emily H. Cole, of Reeve township, the daughter of Rev. Jacob Cole, of Floyd county, Indiana, and to this union have been born six children, Florence E., O. W., Estella A., Annie L., Glenn E. and Robert C., all of whom are living, with the exception of Florence E., who died at the age of thirty-seven. The family are all members of the United Brethren church.

Mr. Barr is an adherent of the Republican party, and for years has been actively interested in public affairs. He served his fellow citizens two terms as trustee of Reeve township, and in 1890 was elected to the office of county treasurer, serving one term. He also served two terms as county commissioner. Mr. Barr is a man of high moral character, persistent industry and excellent judgment, and throughout the locality where he has lived for so many years he occupies an enviable position among his fellow men.

WILLIAM S. WALLER.

The Union soldier during the great war between the states builded wiser than he knew. Through four years of suffering and wasting hardship, through the horrors of prison pens and amid the shadows of death, he laid the superstructure of the greatest temple ever erected and dedicated to human freedom. The world looked on and called these soldiers sublime, for it was theirs to reach out the mighty arm of power and strike the chains off from the slave, and preserve the country from dissolution and to keep unfurled to the breeze the only flag that ever made a tyrant tremble. For all their unmeasured deeds the living present will never repay them. Attention and political power may be thrown at their feet; art and sculpture may preserve upon canvas and in granite and bronze their unselfish deeds; history may commit to books, and cold type may give to the future the tale of their suffering and triumph, but to the children of the generations unborn will it remain to record the full measure of appreciation and undying remembrance of the immortal character carved out by the American soldiers in the dark days of the sixties, numbered among whom was William S. Waller, the tyler of the Masonic lodge at Washington, Indiana.

William S. Waller was born at the corner of First East and Van Trees streets, Washington, Indiana, the town at that time being known as Liverpool, on February 4, 1837, the son of John W. and Mary Ann (Goodwin) Waller, the former of whom was a native of Kentucky and the latter of Pennsylvania, who came to this county from Kentucky in 1817, locating at Liverpool, now Washington. John W. Waller was a merchant and held several public offices in the early days, among which were those of city treasurer and county assessor. He assessed the taxables of the county at a time when he received only ninety dollars for the entire work. He also served as justice of the peace for a number of years, and was a man of large influence in the early affairs of Daviess county. Later he purchased a farm east of Washington, consisting of a hundred and twenty acres, which he improved, and where he died in 1874, at the age of seventy-six.

(25)

His widow died in 1882, at the age of eighty-two. She was a Methodist and for many years was an influential factor in the good works of the community.

The paternal grandparents of William S. Waller were John W. and Mary G. (Mathis) Waller, natives of England, and pioneer settlers in Kentucky, to which state they emigrated at the close of the Revolutionary War, they first having settled at Plymouth, Virginia. John W. Waller, Sr., served as a captain in the Revolutionary War and died in Kentucky at an old age, in the year 1810. His widow came to this county, locating in Liverpool (now Washington), where she died at a very advanced age. They were the parents of the following children: John, George, Edward, Nellie, Nancy Mary, Jane, Patsey, Hannah and Elizabeth.

The maternal grandparents of Mr. Waller were Aaron and Margaret (McCullough) Goodwin, the former of whom was a native of Ireland and the latter of Scotland. Aaron Goodwin was a tanner by trade, who moved from Pennsylvania to Marietta, Ohio, and thence to Liverpool, now Washington, Indiana, where he operated a tannery, the first in the town. This tannery was on the corner of what is now First West and West Main streets. Both he and his wife lived to very advanced ages, and were prominent in the early affairs of Washington. They were the parents of the following children: William, Aikman, Aaron, Jane, Mary Ann, Ruth, Laura and Matilda.

William S. Waller was born and reared in Washington and that city has always been his home. He attended the old-fashioned subscription schools and lived at home until he was grown, after which he started for himself by farming on his father's farm. Later he worked at the carpenter trade for several years and still later engaged in the meat business for a number of years. After, for a little more than four years, he was street commissioner of Washington. For the past twenty-two years Mr. Waller has been the tyler for all the bodies of the Masonic lodge at Washington. He was made a Mason in 1874, his father having also been a prominent member of that body. He is a member of Charity Lodge No. 30, Free and Accepted Masons; Washington Chapter No. 92, Royal Arch Masons; Washington Council No. 67, Royal and Select Masters; Washington Commandery No. 33, Knights Templar, and Washington Chapter No. 210, Order of Eastern Star.

Mr. Waller enlisted in the Union army on April 19, 1861, for a period of six months' service during the Civil War. He first served in Company G, Sixth Regiment Indiana Volunteer Infantry, and at the expiration of his term he re-enlisted in Company I, Twenty-fourth Regiment Indiana Volunteer Infantry, serving until November, 1865. Mr. Waller was in many hard-fought battles during the Civil War, in which he received a few slight flesh wounds, but had no bones broken. After the war he returned to Washington and took up his life work as heretofore mentioned.

On March 4, 1858, William S. Waller was married to Mary Kendall, daughter of John and Nancy (Dyer) Kendall, to which union only one child was born, Adda, who married John W. Coleman, a resident of Washington, to which union has been born one daughter, Helen. Mrs. Mary Kendall Waller, who died in September, 1859, was born on a farm in this county, east of Washington. Her parents were natives of Kentucky, who came to this country in pioneer days and spent the rest of their lives here. They were the parents of seven children, Enoch, William, George, Joseph, Sarah, Mary and Martha.

While home on a furlough, during the war, Mr. Waller married, secondly, February 5, 1864, Isabell Campbell, daughter of William and Mary (Coventry) Campbell, to which union five children were born, John W., Mary, James, Ella and Edith. John W. is a coal miner in Pike county, this state, near Oakland City. He married Melissa Thompson, and they have four children, Charles, Odell, Mary and Ione. Mary died unmarried. James is a carpenter in Washington and is unmarried. Ella married J. W. Walker, a machinist. They have two sons, William and Charles. Edith married Charles W. Quick. They live at Orange Grove, Mississippi, and have no children.

Mrs. Isabell Waller was born in Mexico, twenty miles from Mexico City, in 1842. Her parents emigrated from Aberdeen, Scotland, and settled in Mexico. They were the parents of three children who lived to maturity, William, Robert and Isabell.

Mr. and Mrs. Waller are members of the Baptist church. Though Mr. Waller is a Republican, he was made street commissioner by a Democratic administration, and served in that capacity for four years. Mr. Waller comes of a long line of Masons, and has in his possession his grandfather Waller's Masonic apron. He also is a member of U. S. Grant Post No. 72, Grand Army of the Republic, and was commander of the post for three years. Washington has been Mr. Waller's home for seventy-eight years. He is a prominent and exemplary citizen. He and his good wife are among the oldest citizens in point of residence now living in Washington, and are honored and respected by the people of that community.

JOHN P. CAVANAUGH.

In the history of Washington the name of John P. Cavanaugh occupies a conspicuous place in the business circles, for during a number of years he has been one of the representative citizens in the city's commercial life, progressive, enterprising and persevering. Such qualities always win success sooner or later and to Mr. Cavanaugh they have brought a satisfactory reward for his well-directed efforts. While he has benefited himself and the community, in a material way, he has also been an influential factor in the moral, educational and social progress of the community. Left an orphan when he was seven weeks old, John P. Cavanaugh has achieved a worthy success, overcoming handicaps and surmounting obstacles.

John P. Cavanaugh, a well-known general merchant of Washington, was born on April 20, 1857, in Saline county, Missouri. He is a son of Patrick and Margaret (Cavanaugh) Cavanaugh, natives of Wexford county, Ireland, and Cincinnati, Ohio, respectively. John P. Cavanaugh was the only child of his parents, both dying when he was but seven weeks old. His father was reared in Ireland and came to America when a young man. He settled first in Kentucky, and was married in Cincinnati. In company with some other men he went to Pettis county, Missouri, where he was among the first settlers. They intended to take slaves there, but Mr. Cavanaugh died soon after his arrival in Missouri, in 1857, at the age of forty years. His wife afterward came to Indiana to live with her people, who had moved to this state and settled in Daviess county, and her death occurred two weeks later in 1857, at the age of twenty-seven. Both were devout members of the Catholic church.

The paternal grandfather of John P. Cavanaugh was John Cavanaugh, who died in Ireland. He had four children, Patrick, Daniel, Richard and Bridget, the latter of whom married a Mr. Keenan, of Cincinnati. She died in the latter city, leaving a son, J. J. Keenan, who was for some time employed in the Peoples store, of Cincinnati. The brothers of Patrick Cavanaugh disappeared, and their history is lost. Patrick spelled his surname with a K, while his wife spelled hers with a C, and they were not related.

The maternal grandfather of John P. Cavanaugh was James Cavanaugh, who married Elizabeth Maloy in Ireland and came to America with two children. They started on the voyage, however, with three children, but one died in mid-ocean. They settled in Cincinnati in 1833, where he was employed as a bookkeeper, and here he spent the remainder of his life. After his death, his wife came to Daviess county, Indiana, where her death occurred in 1894, in her ninetieth year. They were the parents of five children, William, Dennis, Mary, Margaret and Sarah.

John P. Cavanaugh was reared by his grandmother on her farm, attending the district schools of his home neighborhood. Later, he was a student in the parochial schools. Subsequently, he came to Washington and drove a mule in the coal mines for the firm of Cabel & Kauggman for some time. He next drove a delivery wagon for this same firm for three years, after which he was employed as a clerk in this company's store for a period of eighteen years. At the end of that time he conducted a general store in partnership with Leonard Farmwald and J. E. Crane, on the corner of Fourth and Main streets, Washington. Two years later Mr. Cavanaugh sold his interests in this store and moved to the corner of Fifth and Hefron streets, where he had formerly purchased a lot. At this time he opened a general store which he is still operating. The people who reared Mr. Cavanaugh, owned this property, and he purchased it later at a court house sale. He has been a resident of Washington for about forty-five years.

Mr. Cavanaugh's maternal grandmother married a second time, her second husband being Peter Fee, and to this union two children were born. John P. Cavanaugh was married, on the 10th of November, 1880, to Mary Riley, a daughter of Terrence and Bridget (Lenahan) Riley, and to this union eight children were born, William, Margaret, John, Clara, Joseph, George, John and Charles. The first four of these children died in infancy; Joseph is connected with the Boston store in Chicago, and is unmarried; George is employed in the store with his father; John is a student in the high school and Charles is a student in the parochial school.

Mrs. Cavanaugh was a native of County Mayo, Ireland, and her parents were also born there. They came to America during the Civil War and settled in Daviess county, where they lived the remainder of their lives. They were the parents of six children, Michael, Mary, Bridget, John, Anthony and William.

In addition to his mercantile business, Mr. Cavanaugh owns a farm of one hundred and sixty acres in Washington township, in this county, to which he devotes considerable attention. He is also interested in the dairy business, and has made a notable success in this line.

Mr. and Mrs. Cavanaugh and family are devout members of the Catholic church, and contribute liberally to the support of this denomination. Mr. Cavanaugh belongs to the Knights of Columbus and the Ancient Order of Hibernians. He is identified with the Democratic party, but has never taken an active part in politics, and has never held nor aspired to office. He is devoted, primarily, to the welfare of his family and the interests of his business. In every respect, John P. Cavanaugh must be regarded as one of the best living citizens of Daviess county.

GEORGE J. KEITH.

The name Keith has long been connected with the progress and development of Daviess county, and the name has been borne by men who have reflected great credit upon the state and upon their respective communities. It is a well-attested maxim that the greatness of a community lies not in the machinery of government, nor even in its institutions; but rather in the sterling quality of the individual citizen in his capacity for high and unselfish effort and his devotion to the public welfare. Among the citizens of Daviess county, who have not only won success and honor for themselves in their specific fields of endeavor, but who have also conferred honor on their respective communities, is George J. Keith, one of the prominent members of the Keith family, a substantial and successful farmer and a well-known banker. Although Mr. Keith resides in Washington, he owns nearly twelve hundred acres of land, and devotes a considerable amount of attention to the details of directing operations on this land.

Mr. Keith is a son of Jarit and Rhoda Jane (Lester) Keith, and was born on March 14, 1849, in Knox county, Indiana. His father and mother, natives of Daviess county, moved to Knox county, where they lived for about fifteen years, at the end of which time they returned to Daviess county, and in 1860 purchased from the heirs of Jarit Keith's father the farm in Washington township, still known as the Keith farm. Mrs. Keith died in 1902, and from that time until his death in 1913 Mr. Keith lived with his different children. At the time of his death he was nearly ninety-three years of age. He owned about two thousand acres of land.

The paternal grandfather of George J. Keith was George H. Keith, and his wife was Abbie (Perkins) Keith. They were natives of Kentucky and pioneers in Daviess county. They improved the old Keith farm in Washington township and there reared their family. George H. Keith died in Washington in 1858, at the age of seventy years. His wife survived him some twenty years, and died at the age of eighty-seven. George H.

Keith was a very stout and hearty man, and died from a congestive chill two hours after he was attacked. He and his wife were the parents of a large family of children, as follow: Lucinda, Emily, Martha, Jarit, George, Ann, Wilson, Charles and two or three who died in infancy.

The maternal grandfather of George J. Keith was William, Lester, whose wife was Julia (Wayman) Lester. They were both natives of Kentucky and were also pioneers in Daviess county. In fact, there were only three houses in the town of Washington when they arrived in Daviess county, and these three houses were built of logs. They settled in what was known as the Dutch settlement, seven miles northeast of Washington, and later moved farther north into Steele township, where he died well advanced in years. His wife survived him and lived to be eighty-five years old. They reared three children, Rhoda Jane, Louisa Ann and William Harrison.

George J. Keith was reared on his father's farm and attended the district school of Daviess county and also of Knox county, where he lived until he was twenty-four years old.

Mr. Keith rented a farm of his father in Knox county after his marriage and lived there two years, when Mrs. Keith died, and he then moved to Sugar Land, in Daviess county, on one of his father's farms. Eventually he purchased part of this farm and later inherited the remainder.

Mr. Keith's first marriage was to Mary Frances Carroll, the daughter of Benjamin Rufus and Harriet Carroll. She died in March, 1873, and left no children.

Again, on December 2, 1874, Mr. Keith was married to Martha A. Banta, daughter of Abram T. and Eliza Ann (Juvenall) Banta. Six sons were born to this union, Charles W., Ephraim J., Elmer F., James A., Oscar H. and Ray A. Charles W. is a farmer on the home place. He married Lucretia Parsons and they have two sons, Arthur and Benjamin; Ephraim J. is a farmer and real estate dealer in Sikeston, Missouri; he married Dicey Tommy and they have two children, Bonnie and William; Elmer is a farmer in Steele township and also a dairyman; he married Lilly McDonald; they have three children, Harley, Russell and Ruby; James is likewise a farmer in Steele township; he was formerly a locomotive engineer, and married Mildred Perine and they have one son, James Prime Keith; Oscar was in the navy for a time, but is now farming near Sikeston, Missouri, and is unmarried; Ray is farming in Sugar Land on his father's farm, and married Dicy Wilson.

Mrs. Martha A. (Banta) Keith was born in Sugar Land, Daviess county, but was reared in Barr township. She died on August 2, 1899, at the age of forty-six years and ten months. Her parents were born in Daviess county and died here. They had ten children, William, Dell, Martha, Etta, Dora, Henry, Eliza, Charles, Thomas, and another who died in infancy.

The husband of Betsey (Juvenall) Banta was a Mr. Banta, grandfather of Mrs. Martha (Banta) Keith. They were natives of Kentucky and pioneers in Daviess county, and had a family consisting of the following children: Abram, John, Jackson and Margaret.

Mrs. Margaret Keith's maternal grandfather was a Mr. Juvenall, whose wife was Betsey (McCracken) Juvenall. They were natives of Kentucky and pioneers in Daviess county. He was a stage driver in the early days. They had only one child, Eliza A. Mr. Juvenall died some time after his marriage and his widow afterward married a man by the name of Peachy.

Mr. Keith was married the third time to Mrs. Jane Chad, whose maiden name was Potts. She died on October 31, 1909.

On January 10, 1912, Mr. Keith was married the fourth time to Mrs. Lola M. Underwood, the widow of Marshall Underwood and a daughter of Griffin and Mary Anna (Williams) MacKinney. She had three children by a former marriage, Corinne, Marshall K. and Lucile Underwood. Corinne married Fred S. Clapp, and died leaving one child, Alice Mary; Marshall K. died at the age of twenty years and ten months, and Lucille lives at home.

The paternal grandfather of Mrs. Lola M. Keith was Archibald McKinney, whose wife was Margaret (Edwards) McKinney. He was a Scotchman and his wife was of Welsh stock. They had five children, Archibald, Robert, Griffin, Margaret and Catherine. Mrs. Lola M. Keith's maternal grandfather was Vincent Williams, and his wife was Elizabeth (Hart) Williams.

After moving back to Sugar Land, Mr. Keith continued to farm there until 1909, when he rented out his farm and moved to Washington, where he purchased a comfortable home and where he now lives, at 507 North Meridian street. He owns four hundred and seventy-six acres of the home farm in Sugar Land, and also seven hundred acres in Steele township. Mr. Keith is vice-president and a director of the State Bank of Washington.

Mr. and Mrs. Keith are members of the Christian church of Washington. He is one of the trustees of this church, and is identified with the Republican party. He is a member-at-large of the county council.

George J. Keith is one of the very prominent farmers and stock men of Daviess and Knox counties, in both of which he is well known. He is a man of engaging personality, and one who enjoys the esteem and confidence of all the people of Daviess and Knox counties, where he has lived, and with whom he has come into contact.

WARREN VAN TREES.

It is frequently maintained by those accustomed to superficial thinking that the history of so-called great men only is worthy of preservation, and that little merit exists among the masses to call forth the praises of the historian or the cheers and the appreciation of mankind. A greater mistake was never made. No man is great in all things, but many by a lucky stroke achieve lasting fame who, before that, had no reputation beyond the limits of the immediate neighborhood. It is not a history of a lucky stroke which benefits humanity most, but the long study and effort that has made the lucky stroke possible. It is the preliminary work, the method, which serves as a guide for others. Among those of Daviess county who have achieved success by consistent, steady effort, is Warren Van Trees, a well-known druggist and pharmacist as well as a farmer of Washington.

Mr. Van Trees was born on February 11, 1868, at Washington, and is the son of Thomas P. and Sarah Deane (Albertson) Van Trees, natives of Washington, and Salem, Indiana, respectively. They have three children, Harry, deceased; Warren and Thomas, Jr., deceased.

Thomas P. Van Trees, the father of Warren, was reared in Washington, where his father was a pork packer. Thomas P. was employed by his father to take pork and poultry down the White river and the Ohio and Mississippi rivers to New Orleans. During the war he was a prospector in the mountains of Colorado and Mexico. He also ran a hotel in Denver when it was a small village. He finally returned to Washington and engaged in the milling business for a number of years after which time he moved to his father's farm in Washington township, just north of town, and died there in 1911, at the age of eighty-one years. His wife survived him and now is eighty-one years old. Mrs. Thomas P. Van Trees is a devoted member of the Presbyterian church as was also her deceased husband.

The paternal grandfather of Warren Van Trees was John Van Trees. His wife was Laura (Prentiss) Van Trees. The former was a native of

Pennsylvania and the latter of Indiana, both of whom were pioneers in Daviess county, and where he purchased one hundred acres of land for one hundred dollars. This land had been sold for taxes amounting to nine dollars and eighty cents. Two hundred dollars an acre has lately been refused for this same land. John Van Trees owned several farms, but made his home in Washington, where he had a beautiful house and other property. He started a pork-packing business in Washington which he conducted for many years. He was also an extensive dealer in general merchandise and operated a store. John Van Trees was county clerk for twenty years. His penmanship was exceptional and almost like copper-plate. He lived to be ninety-one years old and his wife died at the age of sixty-eight. They had a large family of children as follow: Thomas P., John M., Charles R., Henry, Helen, Lydia G., Ann Eliza, Laura, Emma B., William, and one who died in infancy, the first born.

The maternal grandfather of Mr. Van Trees was Nathaniel Albertson, whose wife was Miss (Forsythe) Albertson. They were early settlers in southern Indiana, the wife having come from England to America in 1800. Nathaniel Albertson was a congressman from Floyd and Harrison counties, Indiana, and lived on a farm on the old turnpike near New Albany. His home was a stopping place for travelers hauling goods for which he charged them a picayune, worth about five cents. He died in the Rocky mountains at Central City, Colorado, while prospecting there, at the age of sixty-eight years. His wife lived to be ninety-one years of age. They had one son and five daughters, Eliza, Sarah Deane, Carrie, Laura, Alice and George.

Warren Van Trees, the subject of this sketch, lived in Washington until seven years old and then grew to manhood on his father's farm where he lived until twenty-seven. He attended the district school and the Washington public and high schools, and after leaving the farm he came to Washington and clerked for his uncle, John A. Scudder, in the drug store of Scudder & Company, for several years. He then purchased the store himself. He sold this store, finally, and was out of the business for seven years. Subsequently, he bought it back again and has continued in the drug business since that time.

Mr. Van Trees was married on December 14, 1910, to Mrs. Martha Glenn Morris, a widow of Robert Morris, and the daughter of John A. and Indiana (Mitchell) Chandler. Two children have been born to this union, Sarah Deane and Warren, Jr.

Mrs. Van Trees was born near Alfordsville, Indiana. Her parents were natives of this state and now live in Washington. They were the parents of the following children, Martha Glenn, Raleigh, Fred, Lillian, Mabel, Loran, Earl and Marie.

Mr. Van Trees is an ardent Democrat, but he has never taken an especially active part in politics. Mr. and Mrs. Van Trees are members of the different churches. Mr. Van Trees is a Presbyterian, and his wife is a member of the Methodist Episcopal church.

A large and flourishing drug business has been built by Mr. Van Trees in Washington. He enjoys, to the utmost, the confidence of his patrons and has always been kind and courteous to all his customers. He belongs to one of the old families in Daviess county, a family which has always stood for the very best things in the life of the community.

ERNEST G. RITTERSKAMP.

It is by no means an easy task to describe within the limits of this review a man who has led an active and eminently useful life, and who, by his own exertion, has reached a position of honor and trust in business with which his interests are allied. But biography finds justification, nevertheless, in tracing and recording such a life history, since the public claims a certain interest in the career of every individual. The time invariably arises, therefore, when it becomes advisable to present the careers of men who are leaders in business enterprises. It is with a certain degree of satisfaction that the chronicler essays the task of touching briefly upon the career of Ernest G. Ritterskamp, who, for many years, has been a prominent and influential citizen of Daviess county.

Ernest G. Ritterskamp, a well-known furniture dealer of Washington, was born on August 3, 1865, at Vincennes. He is the son of Fred and Louisa (Kercher) Ritterskamp, the former a native of Alberfeld and the latter a native of Mettmann, Germany. They had ten children, five of whom lived to maturity. Fred lives in Kansas City, Missouri; Otto is a furniture dealer in Vincennes; Emil is president of the Vincennes Furniture Company; Ernest G. is the subject of this sketch; Louisa, who died in her twenty-sixth year, was the wife of Frank Berry.

Fred Ritterskamp, the father of these children, was reared and married in Germany. He came to America with his wife and located in Vincennes. Here he was a contractor and builder. He was a carpenter by trade. He died in Vincennes at the age of fifty-five years. His wife survived him and died on August 26, 1904, at the age of seventy-four. They belonged to the German Evangelical church. The paternal grandparents of Ernest G. Ritterskamp were born and lived and died in Germany. The maternal grandfather, who was Gottfried Kercher, also lived and died in Germany. He was a baker. He ran a bake shop at Mettmann. His wife was Louisa Kersher.

Ernest G. Ritterskamp was reared in Vincennes and attended the public schools of that city. Early in life, he learned the carpenter trade, which he followed until after his marriage. For some time he was also engaged in railroad work, and during this period was a fireman for the Iron Mountain railroad and lived at De Soto, Missouri.

Mr. Ritterskamp married Altha Jackson, a daughter of John Jackson. One daughter was born to this union and died in infancy. Mrs. Ritterskamp died fifteen months after her marriage.

In January, 1891, Mr. Ritterskamp was married again to Amelia H. Schulte, the daughter of Fred and Mollie (Ritterskamp) Schulte. Ten children were born to this union, Viola, Ella, Otto, Walter, David, Oscar, Carl, and three who died young. All these children are now living at home.

Mrs. Amelia H. Ritterskamp was born at Evansville, this state. Her parents were natives of Germany, who came to America and settled there early in life. Here they were married after which they moved to Freelandsville, Indiana. The father died in Freelandsville, in 1909, but his wife is still living. They had a number of children, among whom were: Amelia H., William, Fred, Emma, Clara, Lydia and Louisa. Mrs. Amelia Ritterskamp's paternal grandfather was Christ Schulte. Her maternal grandfather was William Ritterskamp, whose wife was Amelia H. Ritterskamp. Their children were Fred, Harriet and Mollie.

Mr. and Mrs. Ritterskamp are members of the United Brethren church. Fraternally, Mr. Ritterskamp is a member of Pythagoras Lodge No. 118, Knights of Pythias; also the Woodmen of the World, the Ben-Hur Society, and the Modern Woodmen of America. Both Mr. and Mrs. Ritterskamp are members of the Knights and Ladies of Security. Ernest G. Ritterskamp carries a large stock of furniture, stoves, etc., and does a large business in Washington, and in Daviess county. He is well respected as a business man and in every respect is a good citizen of Daviess county. Mr. Ritterskamp has never been active in political affairs, but has devoted his attention rather to his own private business and to the welfare and comfort of his family, to which he is very much devoted.

LUTHER JOHNSON.

Among the well-known young business men of Daviess county whose enterprise and industry have won him distinctive prestige in the business circles of this county is Luther Johnson, a well-known clerk for the' I. W. Lutz & Son Furniture Company. None stands higher in the life of Washington and vicinity or higher in the esteem and confidence of this community than Mr. Johnson.

Luther Johnson was born on May 8, 1872, in Washington township, Daviess county, the son of Milford D. and Osee (Wise) Johnson, both natives of Indiana. They had six children, Ola, the wife of Otto Oberst, of near Evansville; Mollie, who died in early childhood; Stella, the wife of William Solomon, of Herrington, Kansas; Luther, of Washington; Edward H., who died at the age of fourteen years, and Pearl, who is the wife of W. B. Allen, of Washington township.

Milford D. Johnson, the father of these children, was reared in Daviess county, and was a carpenter by trade. He lived on a farm in Washington township until a few years before his death. He died in 1900, and his wife is still living at the age of seventy-three. Mrs. Johnson and her deceased husband were members of the Baptist church, as are all the family. Milford D. Johnson was in the service of the Union army during the Civil War as a bridge carpenter.

The paternal grandparents of Luther Johnson were Edward H. and Nancy (Murphy) Johnson, natives of Kentucky and early settlers in Daviess county, where they were farmers. They both died in this county well advanced in years, and were the parents of five children, Milford D., Anthony, Robert, Susan and Flora. The maternal grandparents of Mr. Johnson were John and Della Wise, who were also early settlers in Daviess county and were farmers. They had seven children, Henry, William, Alfred, John, Mary Ann, Lucinda and Osa.

Luther Johnson was reared on the farm and attended the district schools. He lived at home until grown and then came to Washington and worked for a transfer company for three or four years. Finally he began clerking in the furniture store of F. B. Fornwald, who recently sold out to C. W. Keach, and where he worked for several months when he left this employment and entered the store of I. W. Lutz & Sons. Mr. Johnson has been in this store for fourteen years, and is well known for his courteous dealings with the public and his upright, honorable conduct in all of his business relations.

Luther Johnson was married on June 25, 1905, to Nettie Whayne, the daughter of Nathan and Alice (Haynes) Whayne. One daughter, Thelma, has been born to this union. Mrs. Johnson was born in Kentucky. Her parents were natives of that state and came to Daviess county about 1888. They are now living in Washington. They have three children, Nettie, Eunice and Lucile. Mrs. Johnson's paternal grandparents were natives of Kentucky, where they died.

Mr. and Mrs. Johnson are members of the Baptist church. Fraternally, Mr. Johnson is a member of the Royal Arcanum and is an ardent Republican.

JOHN W. DILLARD.

Specific mention is made of many of the worthy citizens of Daviess county within the pages of this book, citizens who have figured in the growth and development of this favored locality and whose interests are identified with its every phase of progress, each contributing in his sphere of action to the well-being of the community in which he resides and to the advancement of its normal and legitimate growth. Among this number is John W. Dillard, peculiar interest attaching to his career from the fact that for quite a number of years he has been prominently identified with the real estate and insurance business in Washington, during which time he has also taken a prominent part in the civic and moral advancement of his community.

John W. Dillard was born in Bowling Green, Kentucky, November 20, 1856, the son of Henry and Mary (Combs) Dillard, natives of Kentucky. They were the parents of five children, Fannie, deceased; John W., of Washington; Ida, deceased, who was the wife of William Gleason; William, of Terre Haute, and Addie, deceased.

Henry Dillard, a tanner by trade, was the father of John W., and was reared in Kentucky. He came to Indiana about 1868 and located in Jackson county and engaged in farming. He served as a teamster in the Civil War. He died in 1869 and his wife died on February 18, 1913, at the age of seventy-six years. She was a member of the Christian church.

John W. Dillard, the subject of this sketch, spent his boyhood days in Jackson county, Indiana, and came to Daviess county in 1871. He resided in Washington, where he attended the public schools and grew to manhood. After reaching maturity, he engaged in various business pursuits. He first clerked for one year for John C. McCafferty and then took the position of superintendent of Oak Grove cemetery, which he held for ten years. He then owned and operated a monumental business in Washington for fourteen years in partnership with F. W. Kelle. He then entered the real estate, insurance and loan business, which he has followed since that time.

On June 15, 1876, he was married to Miranda E. Weddell, the daughter of Gabriel L. and Rebecca A. (Hall) Weddell. Two children have been born to this union, Dyanthia, who died in infancy, and Vassall Edgar, born on March 14, 1878. He is a teacher of vocal and instrumental music and is director of music in the Washington high school. He married Estella Talbott and they have two children, Amadeus Byron and John Warren.

Mrs. Dillard was born in Jackson county, Indiana. Her parents were natives of Virginia and Tennessee, respectively, and were early settlers in Jackson county. Her father, who was born in 1812, studied to be a lawyer, but on account of throat trouble gave up that profession and started farming. He was the owner of two large farms in Jackson county. He and his wife moved to Texas and settled in Belle county, where they lived the remainder of their lives. Gabriel L. Weddell was twice married and, by his first marriage, had three children, Jasper, Columbus and Lavina. By his second marriage there were twelve children, Hamilton, who was killed in the Civil War; Mary; Willis; Ella; Maria; Dora; Mirand E.; Warren; Sherman; Sheridan; Benjamin and Newton. He and his wife were members of the Christian church. She died at the age of sixty-one and he died a few years later at the age of eighty.

The paternal grandparents of Mrs. Dillard were David Weddell and wife, natives of Virginia and pioneers in Jackson county, Indiana, where they were farmers. He was in the War of 1812 and died at an old age. They were the parents of seven children, Gabriel; Claybourn; John A., who was a Christian minister; Nancy, Sarah, Martha and Stephen. The maternal grandparents of Mrs. Dillard were natives of Tennessee and pioneers in Jackson county, Indiana. They were the parents of five children, Rebecca A., Captain Willis, who was a soldier in the Civil War; Dyanthia, Dovie and William, who died in the Civil War.

Mr. and Mrs. Dillard are members of the Christian church. Mr. Dillard served as an elder for a number of years, as a deacon and as superintendent of the Sunday school. Fraternally, he is a member of Liverpool Lodge No. 110, Independent Order of Odd Fellows; of the encampment;

of the Pythagorean Lodge No. 118, Knights of Pythias; of the Modern Woodmen of America, and of the Tribe of Ben-Hur. He is a Democrat and is now serving as councilman-at-large. Mr. Dillard is well known and highly respected by a large number of friends and acquaintances in Washington and throughout Daviess county.

MARTIN LUTHER BONHAM.

The character of a community is determined in a large measure by the lives of a comparatively few of its members. If its moral and intellectual status be good, if, in a social way, it is a pleasant place to reside, if its reputation as to the integrity of its citizens has extended into other localities, it will be found that the standard set by the leading men has been high and their influence such as to mold the characters and shape the lives of those with whom they mingle. In placing the late Martin Luther Bonham among the foremost men of his day and generation, only simple justice is done to the memory of this worthy man. Although quiet and unassuming in manner and with no ambition for public position or leadership, he contributed much to the civic, material and moral advancement of his community. For many years he was a successful undertaker and funeral director in the city of Washington and Daviess county. His admirable qualities of head and heart and his straightforward, upright course won for him the esteem and confidence of the circle in which he moved and, although he is now sleeping the sleep of the just, his influence still lives and his memory is greatly revered.

The late Martin Luther Bonham was born on March 4, 1827, at Logan, in Dearborn county, Indiana. He was the son of Zedekiah and Amelia (Cullom) Bonham, the former a native of Tennessee and the latter of Ohio. Both were pioneers in Decatur county, Indiana, where he was a farmer, a justice of the peace and a man of considerable influence. His wife died here well advanced in years. He died later at a very advanced age. They had three sons and three daughters, Mrs. Rhoda Thompson, Mrs. Maria Keen, Martin Luther, Washington, Allen and Mrs. White.

The late Martin Luther Bonham was reared in Dearborn county, Indiana, where he lived until eighteen years of age, when the family moved to Harrison, Ohio, where he learned the cabinetmaker trade. Afterward he engaged in the undertaking and furniture business at Harrison for eighteen years. In 1863, Mr. Bonham removed to Washington, Daviess county, Indiana, where he entered the employ of John Mattingly for a time. He soon formed a partnership with Mr. Mattingly and, just prior to his death, became his successor. Mr. Bonham conducted the business alone for a time and then associated with him Mr. Joseph Gill, which partnership continued as Bonham & Gill for a number of years. In 1891, Mr. Bonham's sons, Z. A. and C. O., purchased Mr. Gill's interest, when the firm became M. L. Bonham's Sons, and this firm continues at the present time.

Martin Luther Bonham was married to Selana Lincoln in Harrison, Hamilton county, Ohio. They had four children, George H., now a resident of Wyoming and a man who has traveled extensively over the world; Mary L., deceased, who was the wife of John Krets; Zedekiah A. and Clifford O. Mr. Bonham died in Washington, this state, December 20, 1898, at the age of seventy-one years and nine months. His wife died some years previously, in Harrison, Ohio. After her death, he was married again to Mrs. Sarah Sours, but no children were born to this last union. Martin L. Bonham was a strong Republican. His first wife, Selana Lincoln, was born in Harrison, Ohio, and was a third cousin to Abraham Lincoln. Her parents were Henry and Mary Lincoln, natives of Maryland, and pioneers in Hamilton county, Ohio. They were the parents of four children, Mrs. Siren Bowlbey, Mrs. Mary Cruikshank, Mrs. Jane Johnson and Mrs. Selana Bonham. Zedekiah and Clifford Bonham were the successors of their father in the undertaking business which is still operated under the old firm name of M. L. Bonham's Sons.

Zedekiah Bonham married Marguerite McDaniel, who died leaving one child, Martin Luther. After her death, Mr. Bonham married again to Lucretia Wood.

Clifford O. Bonham married Martha J. Carnahan and they have had five children. The first two were twin boys, who died in infancy; the next two were twin girls, Fanny May and Frankie Maud, and the fifth child was Alma Inez, who was born eleven years after the birth of the last twins. Fanny May married Earl Hair and lives in Cincinnati. They have three children, Dorris, John Clifford and Marguerite, twins. Frankie Maud married Edward Clore and lives in Washington, Indiana; Alma Inez is a school teacher.

Zedekiah Bonham and his family are members of the Presbyterian church and Clifford O. Bonham and his family are members of the Methodist church. Clifford O. and Zedekiah were both born in Ohio and reared in

(26)

Washington, Indiana, where they attended the public schools and received their education.

The paternal grandfather of Mrs. Clifford O. Bonham was Robert Carnahan and her maternal grandparents were George and Anna (Morgan) Macklin.

Clifford O. Bonham is a Republican in politics and served three terms in succession as coroner of Daviess county. The Bonham family has been connected with the history of Daviess county for many years and they have been equal to every duty, public and private. The family is highly respected in Daviess county, where two enterprising sons are carrying on successfully the work of a worthy and highly respected father.

JOHN WICHMAN.

One of the most enterprising of our younger generation of farmers in Daviess county, who has believed, from the outset of his career, that the wisdom of yesterday is sometimes the folly of today and that, while the methods of our grandfathers in tilling the soil, were all right in their day, yet in the twentieth century, we are compelled to adopt new methods and farm along different lines, in view of the fact that conditions of climate, soil, grains, etc., have changed since the days of the pioneer. John Wichman has been a close observer of modern methods and is a student, at all times, of whatever pertains to his chosen life-work. He has, therefore, met with encouraging success all along the line and, judging from his past record, he will undoubtedly achieve much in the future years and take his place among the leading farmers of Daviess county, noted for its fine farms and progressive farmers.

John Wichman was born on June 28, 1871, in Decatur county, Indiana. He is the son of Anton and Elizabeth (Kuhlman) Wichman. His father who was born in Germany, about 1836, and came to America after receiving his early education in his native country; his mother is also a native of Germany. Anton Wichman and wife lived in Decatur county, Indiana, where they were farmers for a time. Subsequently, they moved to Daviess county, Indiana, and located in Steele township, where he owned eighty acres of land. They lived here until his death. He was a member of the Catholic church. Anton and Elizabeth Wichman were the parents of nine children, Anton, Jr., Mary, Catherine, John, Joseph, Rosie, Angela, Elizabeth and Henry. Of these children, Anton, Jr., who owns about three hundred acres of land in this township, married Catherine Arlinghouse; Mary married Otto Luken and lives in Cincinnati; Catherine, Rosie and Angela are unmarried; Joseph, deceased, married Elizabeth Englehart; Elizabeth married Aloysius Sum and lives in this county; Henry married Mary Young and owns one hundred and sixty acres of land in Steele township.

John Wichman is unmarried. He received only a common-school education, but has improved his opportunities by home study and has become a well-informed man. He is a man highly respected in the township where he lives for his enterprising habits and good common sense. Mr. Wichman lives with his mother and unmarried sisters on the home farm in Steele township. He owns two hundred acres of land in Steele township which he rents. The Wichman family are all members of the Catholic church.

John Wichman is a man who is not hasty in making up his mind regarding a proposition, but when his mind is once made up, he is fairly inflexible. His conservatism and the care which he takes to decide a proposition have been responsible largely for his splendid success as a farmer. Mr. Wichman is not only well known in Steele township, but he is a man honored and admired for his frugal habits and his good business management. In every respect, he deserves to rank as a representative citizen of this section of Daviess county and is, therefore, entitled to representation in a volume of this character.

JAMES WITSMAN.

The twentieth century farmer knows very little of the disadvantages which surrounded the pioneer farmer of this state. No longer is the farmer compelled to rise early in the morning and continue his labors into the evening. The farmer of today can do as much work in a half day as his father could, fifty years ago, in a whole day. The free mail delivery leaves the daily paper on his doorstep each morning. His telephone puts him into communication with his neighbors, while the interurban cars and automobiles enable him to participate in all of the features of city life. The present generation of farmers has no forests to clear, few swamps to drain, while hundreds of inventions, designed to lighten the labors of the farmer, have been put into their hands. The flail of our fathers has given way to the threshing machine of today and even the old-fashioned corn-cutter is laid on the shelf and the corn is now cut by machinery. The old-fashioned shucking-peg has given way to the modern corn-husker and, surrounded by such conditions, the farmer of today can have all the advantages of the citizens in the cities with few of their disadvantages. One of the modern farmers of Daviess county, is James Witsman, of Steele township.

James Witsman, who lives near Plainville, Indiana, on a splendid farm, was born on February 24, 1852, in Lawrence county, Indiana. He is the son of Oliver and Walter Ann (Evans) Witsman, the former a native of Lawrence county, Indiana, and the latter the daughter of a sergeant in the Revolutionary army. Oliver Witsman died while young or when he was about thirty-four years of age. He belonged to the Christian church and was active in its affairs. He was a splendid singer, a good talker and an efficient school teacher. He also followed farming in Lawrence county, Indiana, four miles west of Bedford, where he owned one hundred and sixty acres of land. He moved to Fayetteville, Indiana, and entered the mercantile business in 1857, after which he soon died. He was a member of the Masonic fraternity. Oliver and Walter Ann Witsman had five children, Sarah Jane, Clara, James M., Owen Homer and Morris Trimble. Of these children, Sarah, who married Z. T. Williams, lives in Lawrence county; Clara died in infancy; Owen Homer, who married Anna Pierce, died in 1889, and Morris Trimble, who married a daughter of William Henshaw, lives in Williams, Indiana, where he is a rural mail carrier.

James Witsman was educated in the common-schools and has been a farmer all of his life. Mr. Witsman was married to Rachel McCormick, who was born on October 1, 1856, and died on November 10, 1910. She was the daughter of Andrew and Elizabeth (Hastings) McCormick, the former of whom, at one time, owned a farm of three hundred and sixty acres, near Plainville. He was a man of strong religious convictions and an influential figure in the life of the community where he lived.

After the marriage of Mr. and Mrs. Witsman, they began housekeeping on the farm where Mr. Witsman now lives. They had six children, Goldie, born on October 13, 1885; Walter Lyle, November 30, 1887; William H., July 5, 1890; James Oliver, April 15, 1893; Sadie Pearl, April 26, 1896, and Lewis Norvell, May 30, 1898. The last is now a student in the high school. All of these children are living and all are still unmarried.

Mr. Witsman owns one hundred and eighty-five acres of land at the edge of Plainville, where he is engaged in farming and stock raising. He handles a high grade of live stock and has been very successful in the stock business.

All of the members of the Witsman family are identified with the Christian church and active in both the church and the Sunday school. They are all living upon Mr. Witsman's farm near Plainville. No family in Plainville is more highly respected than that of James Witsman.

CHARLES A. LITTELL.

It is the farmer who makes it possible for men in other occupations to live. Farming was the original occupation of man, and it is the only business which could exist independently of the others. Indeed every other occupation is dependent upon the farmer. The products of the farm have made our railroads what they are today, and the great bulk of manufacturing is made necessary because of the farmer's needs. The people of the city could not live a week without the farmer's products. He holds not only the purse strings of the nation, but even the very life itself of the people. For this reason, the farmer has, in reality, the most important business of all. Daviess county has fine farms and as good farmers as can be found anywhere in the state. And among the good farmers of this section, is Charles A. Littell, of Steele township.

Mr. Littell was born on July 7, 1870, in Clark county, Indiana. He is the son of John G. and Hannah (Burns) Littell. His father was born on October 9, 1830, in that county, and his mother was born on May 3, 1836, and died on January 12, 1907. She was the daughter of Michael and Francis (Robinson) Burns. Michael Burns was a farmer of Clark county, Indiana, and an influential member of the Christian church. John G. Littell, the father of Charles A., was the son of Josiah T. Littell, who was born in Pennsylvania on May 21, 1794, and who died in 1863. Josiah T. Littell was the son of Absalom Littell, born on September 12, 1751, in Pennsylvania, and who served seven years in the Continental army under Col. John Washington. After the war he was paid off in the Continental currency, and with it paid five hundred dollars for a cow and two hundred and fifty for a snuff box. It is a tradition that Absalom's father ran off from France because he did not believe in St. Bartholomew Day. Absalom Littell, the great-grandfather of Charles A. Littell, married Mary Norris, and they had seven children as follow: Amos, born on November 12, 1784; Abraham, July 25, 1786; Absalom, Jr., July 23, 1788; John T., June 16, 1790; Ann, July 12, 1792; Josiah T., May 21, 1794, and Margaret, January 23, 1797.

Absalom Littell moved from Pennsylvania to Clark county, Indiana, in 1797, and there remained until his death. He entered one hundred and ninety acres of land in Clark county.

Josiah T. Littell, the grandfather of Charles A., married Elizabeth Gilmore, who was born on January 27, 1801. They had ten children, Absalom, born on December 25, 1823; Mary J., March 7, 1825; Lucinda K., September 16, 1826; John Gilmore, October 9, 1830; Matilda; Anna M., April 10, 1832; William F., March 4, 1834; Josiah T., February 27, 1838; Margaret R., April 2, 1840, and Indiana, March 23, 1844. Josiah T. Littell was a farmer in Clark county, Indiana. He was a soldier in the War of 1812, and also a member of the state militia. He was a member of the Christian church, and identified with the Whig party. He owned one hundred and ninety acres of land in Clark county.

John Gilmore Littell, the father of Charles A., came to Daviess county in 1870, and owned two hundred acres of land at one time, but later in life, sold it and lived retired in Plainville, Indiana. He served in Company B, Twenty-seventh Indiana Volunteer Infantry, during the Civil War, and was a sergeant. He was a member of the Christian church. John G. and Hannah (Burns) Littell has five children, as follow: W. O., born January 18, 1855; Thomas E., born January 2, 1858; Ella A., born December 9, 1859; George C., born November 24, 1867, and Charles A., born July 7, 1870.

Charles A. Littell was educated in the common schools and at the age of thirteen learned the harness maker's trade. At one time he had a hardware store in Plainville, Indiana, but quit that business in 1906. After quitting the hardware business, he located on his present farm, in February, 1906. The farm consists of eighty acres and is located in Steele township. Mr. Littell is engaged in general farming.

Charles A. Littell was married on October 2, 1895, to Lillian Tomey, born on March 12, 1877, in Daviess county, Indiana, and the daughter of William P. and Mary E. (Hastings) Tomey, the former of whom was born on May 4, 1851, in Daviess county, and who died in August, 1905, and the latter of whom was born in Daviess county on May 22, 1857, and who is now living in Plainville. William P. Tomey was the son of John J. Tomey, who was born on November 29, 1824, and who died on December 27, 1877. He married Edith Roach. John J. Tomey was a shoemaker by trade and a farmer. He owned sixty acres of land. The children of John J. and Edith (Roach) Tomey were as follow: William P., born on May 4, 1851; Dollie L., March 12, 1854; Martha, April 25, 1857; Ida K., May 25,

1860; Joseph A., May 20, 1863; Mary E., December 13, 1866, and Margaret M., March 6, 1870. John J. Tomey was the son of Armistead Tomey and Dollie (Myers) Tomey, who had nine children, John J., Caroline, Elias P., William A., Elizabeth, Mary J., Martin, Martha and Frederick B. William P. Tomey, the father of Mrs. Littell, was a farmer and school teacher. He was educated at the Central Normal College at Danville, and lived in Daviess county during his entire life. He owned one hundred and fifty acres of land in Bogard township. He and his wife had five children, Oscar, born on April 5, 1875; Lillian, March 12, 1877; Ortho, October 21, 1879; Della, August 19, 1881, and Alma, June 27, 1884.

To Charles A. and Lillian A. (Tomey) Littell four children have been born, Verna Irene, on October 4, 1901; Mary Almira, January 13, 1911; Edith, March 29, 1898, died on August 17, 1900, and a son who died in infancy.

Mr and Mrs. Littell are members of the Christian church. Mr. Littell is a member of the Prohibition party, and a strong and ardent believer in temperance. The family are highly respected residents of Steele township, and are well known in this section of Daviess county.

JOSEPH EDWARDS.

A review of the life of the honored and lamented Joseph Edwards must of necessity be brief and general in its character; for to enter fully into the interesting details of his career, touching the struggles of his early manhood and successes of later days, would far transcend the limits of this article. He held a large place in the ranks of the enterprising and public-spirited men of his day and generation, and the luster of his deeds and the memories which attach to his name and character form no inconsiderable chapter in the history of the community where he did his work and achieved his success. Sufficient it is, we believe, to prove him entitled to the honorable position he long occupied among the brave and energetic self-made men of Indiana, who, by enterprise and unswerving integrity, forged to the front, despite all opposition, and won for the grand old Hoosier commonwealth a place second to none other in the bright constellation comprising the union of American states. That he did his part nobly and well cannot be gainsaid, and though dead, he yet speaks in the works which he accomplished and in the many kindly deeds and wholesome influences which, not only his friends, but the community as well, prize as a grateful heritage.

The late Joseph Edwards was born on November 25, 1840, in Daviess county, Indiana, where he also died on March 29, 1883, in Daviess county. He was the son of Thomas and Elizabeth (Dunkin) Edwards, the former a native of Kentucky, and the latter of Pike county, Indiana. Thomas Edwards lived in Daviess county, where he was a farmer, and an influential member of the Baptist church.

Joseph Edwards was educated in the common schools and was a farmer throughout his life. He owned one hundred and twenty acres of land. On February 7, 1867, he was married to Ava Byrer, who was born, March 4, 1846, and who is the daughter of Gottlieb and Matilda (Killgore) Byrer, the former of whom was a native of Pennsylvania, and who died in September, 1897, at the age of ninety-two, and the latter a native of Lawrence county, Indiana, died on April 28, 1882, at the age of sixty-four. Gottlieb Byrer was a farmer and also a merchant at Raglesville, Indiana, where he purchased the store of John Ragle, which was the first in that town. Gottlieb and Matilda (Killgore) Byrer had twelve children, William and Emily are deceased; Ava is the widow of the late Joseph Edwards; Demma, Phoebe and Henry are living; Noah and Hiram are deceased; Uretta is living, and John, Eliza and an infant, are deceased. Gottlieb Byrer was a member of the Universalist church. He was a son of Casper Byrer, a native of Germany, a member of the Unitarian church, who came to America and settled in the state of Pennsylvania. He had three sons, Frederick, John and Gottlieb. Matilda Killgore, Gottlieb Byrer's wife, was a daughter of Hiram Killgore, who was born in South Carolina, and who later moved to Indiana, settling on a farm in Lawrence county. Subsequently, he moved to Daviess county, Indiana, and settled in Van Buren township. He was a pioneer farmer. He married Nancy Grant, who was born in South Carolina, a daughter of William Grant, a southern plantation owner, and a soldier in the Revolutionary War. Hiram and Nancy (Grant) Killgore had ten children, Ina, Keturah, Pollie, Matilda, Reuben, Rollen, Perry, Eva, Sallie and Malinda. Hiram Killgore was a son of Charles Killgore, who also fought in the Revolutionary army.

After his marriage, the late Joseph Edwards settled near Plainville, where he purchased forty acres of land. He sold this farm and in 1871 removed to the farm where the widow and children now live. He owned one hundred and twenty acres of land at the time of his death.

Joseph and Ava (Byrer) Edwards had eight children, four of whom are deceased, Sarah Ellen, Emma, Dasie and Florence. Henry, Thomas, Anna and Josie are living. Of these children, Henry lives in Daviess county. He married Zella Clinton, and they have nine children, Gladys, Helen, Pearl, Augustus, Delphia, Lucile, Ava, Ruth and Edna; Anna lives in Plainville, Indiana. She married Lewis Disbrough, and they have no children. Lewis Disbrough was a soldier in the Civil War, having enlisted in August, 1861, serving for three years. After the war, he served five years in the regular army. The other children, who still live with Mrs. Edwards on the home farm, are Thomas and Josie, who assist in the farming.

The late Joseph Edwards was a soldier in the Civil War, having served with the One Hundred and Twenty-seventh Regiment, Indiana Volunteer Infantry, for three years. Mr. Edwards died on March 29, 1883, since which time the widow and children have been farming the place.

The late Joseph Edwards is remembered as a man of kind and generous impulses, one who was kind to his wife and to his family, who were his first consideration and his first care. He was a man who took a deep interest in public questions and has been missed in the community where he was so well known.

THOMAS O'BRYAN.

Among the influential citizens of Daviess county, the records of whose lives have become an essential part of the history of this section, Thomas O'Bryan occupies a prominent place. For years he has exerted a beneficial influence in the locality where he resides. His chief characteristics are keenness of perception, honesty of purpose and motive and every-day common sense, which have enabled him, not only to advance his own interests, but also, largely, to promote the moral and material advancement of Steele township, where he lives. Mr. O'Bryan is now living retired in Plainville, Indiana. He is well known by the people of Steele township.

Thomas O'Bryan was born on January 3, 1849, in Martin county, Indiana. He is the son of Sylvester and Sarah (Queen) O'Bryan, the former of whom was born in Kentucky, in 1804, and who died in 1876, and the latter, the daughter of Mason Queen, a native of Martin county, where he was a farmer and also a devoted member of the Catholic church.

After the death of Sylvester O'Bryan's father and mother in Kentucky, he was taken to be reared by an uncle in Indiana. When he grew up, he returned to his native state and lived there for a few years, but, subsequently, returned to Martin county, Indiana, where he farmed the remainder of his life. He owned six hundred and forty acres in Martin county and during the latter part of his life, he was a member of the Catholic church. He was married twice, his first wife being Julia Clemons. To this union two children were born, Joseph and William. After the death of his first wife, he married Sarah Queen, and to this union were born two children, Thomas, the subject of this sketch, and James, who is now residing in Arkansas.

Thomas O'Bryan was educated in the common schools of Martin county and grew up on his father's farm. He performed the usual tasks which fall to the lot of the average country boy, working on the farm during the summertime and attending school in the winter.

On April 18, 1872, Mr. O'Bryan was married to Ann Burch, the daughter of Lemuel and Emily (Jones) Burch, both natives of Daviess county, and now deceased. Lemuel Burch was born on April 20, 1832, and died at the age of forty-nine years. He was a farmer and a devout member of the Christian church, and he and his wife were the parents of seven children, Ann, George, Eugene, deceased; Darius, Christopher, Wiley and Milletus. Lemuel Burch was the son of Christopher Burch, who was born in a fort, who was a farmer by occupation and a member of the Christian church. He married Mary O'Callahan, a native of Ireland. Christopher Burch was a soldier in the War of 1812. He was the son of Charles Burch, a native of Ireland.

Mrs. Emily Burch, the mother of Mrs. O'Bryan, was the daughter of Wiley R. and Ann (Fording) Jones, the former a native of North Carolina and a slave-holder in the South, and the latter a native of Kentucky. Wiley R. Jones was the son of Ebenezer Jones, a native of Wales and a Methodist minister who came to America and settled in South Carolina. Later he moved to Daviess county, Indiana, with his family, where he was probably the first settler in that county.

After his marriage, Thomas O'Bryan began farming in Daviess county and, with the exception of seven months, which he spent in Arkansas, he has lived in Daviess county during the entire time since. He is now living a retire life in Plainville, where he owns several lots. He also owns seventy acres of land south of Plainville in Steele township.

To Thomas and Ann (Burch) O'Bryan, six children have been born, James, Sarah, Nellie, John Wesley, Eugene, who graduated from the State

Normal School at Terre Haute in 1915, and Pearl. Of these children, James married Helen Hurst and they have three children, William, Mable and Geraldine; Sarah married Jacob Ragle and lives in Arkansas. They have five children, Bertha, Hazel, Alma, Alva and Thomas; Nellie, who lives in Plainville, was a teacher and married Roscoe McCormick and has three children, Cecil, Clyde and Gordon; John W., who lives in Bogard township, also taught school, and married Mary Boyd and has two children, Merle and Elva.

Thomas O'Bryan has lived a long and useful life and has been an influential figure in his community. He enjoys the entire confidence and respect of his neighbors and is admired by them for having reared a large family to useful and honorable lives.

ERNEST E. KILLION.

For many years Ernest E. Killion has been identified closely with the business affairs of Plainville and Steele township in Daviess county, Indiana. Atlhough a comparatively young man, his life has been one of untiring activity, and has been crowned with a degree of business success attained by comparatively few of those who aspire to eminence in business. Several years' conscientious work as a banker have brought with them not only increased business for his bank, but also a growth in banking knowledge and that wide and accurate judgment, the possession of which constitutes maturity in the business relations of life. By a straightforward, honorable course, Mr. Killion has built up a large and lucrative banking business, which is a splendid tribute to his progressive ideas and native executive ability. His life-work is a splendid example of what an American youth, plentifully endowed with good common sense, energy and determination, can accomplish.

Ernest E. Killion, the subject of this sketch, was born on January 9, 1887, in Steele township, Daviess county, Indiana. He is the son of Nathan E. Killion, a native of Daviess county, the life history of whom is presented elsewhere in this volume.

Ernest E. Killion, after receiving a good common-school education, attended the Northern Illinois Normal School for twelve weeks, and after that, returned to Plainville, Indiana, where he farmed for one year. In addition to the business and teachers' course at the normal, he also went to Vories Business College, at Indianapolis, for one year.

Mr. Killion now owns twenty acres of land adjoining the town of Plainville. He is the cashier and is a heavy stockholder in the Bank of Plainville. It was founded on April 13, 1908. He is also in partnership with Ollie Gilliatt, a well-known business man of Steele township, whose life history is recounted elsewhere. These two men own a general store in Plainville, which was purchased in 1911. They are also partners in the Plainville Canning Company, which was established by them in 1909.

Ernest E. Killion was married on June 3, 1904, to Alice Reeve, the daughter of S. T. Reeve, of Edwardsport, Indiana. Two children, Alice and Ernest E., Jr., have been born to this happy union.

Mr. Killion is identified with the Democratic party. He is a member of the Independent Order of Odd Fellows, the Masons and the Modern Woodmen of America. He is well known in Steele township, and is highly respected by all classes of people with whom he is very popular. The success of the Plainville bank, of which he is cashier, is largely due to the persistency with which he has sought business and to his keen discrimination in selecting only that business which would prove the best for his bank. Mr. Killion has the entire confidence, not only of the directors of his bank, but of the community at large.

GEORGE W. DOOLIN.

With the death of every pioneer, this age is losing touch with that period which saw the Middle West emerge from the wilderness. Because we have the things which much older communities enjoy and esteem as the marks of civilization, the younger generation may feel that the Mississippi valley is no longer virgin territory. Perhaps it is not, but its beginning and latest development can be spanned by the lives of a few men still known among us. One of these passed away a few years ago. George W. Doolin saw the first pike, the first railroad and the first canal built in this part of the country. He was one of the early settlers in Daviess county and in serene, but not inactive, old age, passed away in Steele township, Daviess county, Indiana. George W. Doolin belonged to the stock of which the conquerors of the West were made. Men of his kind were conquerors not merely of the physical aspects of the new country, but of the moral, religious and civic as well.

George W. Doolin was born on April 16, 1848, in Greene county, Indiana, and died on June 10, 1907. He was a farmer north of Plainville, Indiana, one and one-half miles and there owned one hundred and ninety-two acres of land. He was the son of William Doolin and Comfort Baker, who were farmers in Greene county.

George W. Doolin was educated in the common schools and grew up on his father's farm. He was married on July 4, 1870, to Martha Graham, who was born on March 5, 1853, and who is the daughter of John A. and Emerine (Cox) Graham. To this marriage, eight children were born, Nora E., Robert E., Rozella, John S., Myrtle, Diaz, Pearl and May. Of these children, Nora E. married Thomas E. English and has two children, Noble Alexander and Ernest; Robert E., who lives in 'Steele township, married Laura Cox and has three children, Bertha May, Irene and Hazel A., twins; Rozella, who lives in Elnora, married Elbert Dyer and has six children, Pearl, Claude, Susan, Irmel, Walter and Mary A.; Myrtle, who lives in Washington, Indiana, married Charles Itskin and has two children, Virgil and Claude; Pearl, who lives in Steele township, married Leonard Powell, by whom she had one child, Emerald. Mr. Powell had been married before and had one child by his first wife, Leon; Mary Frances, who lives in Epsom, married Clay Dougherty and has one child, Leonard; Diaz, who married Ina Cooper, the daughter of Joseph and Nancy (Burks) Cooper, of Odon, who had one son, Robert. The wife and son live with Mrs. George W. Doolin.

Mrs. Doolin was the daughter of John A. Graham, who was born in Tennessee. He married twice. The second time to Emerine Cox, the daughter of Gabriel Cox, of Kentucky. John A. Graham located in Knox county, Indiana, where he owned eight hundred acres of land. By his second marriage, John A. Graham had four children, Sarah Angeline, Mary Lavina, Melissa and Martha. Of these children, Martha is the only one living. The first wife of John A. Graham was Elizabeth Sloven. By this union there were five children, Nathan, Stephen, Franklin, Rebecca and Elizabeth, the last of whom is the only living child.

Mrs. Martha A. Doolin, the widow of George W. Doolin, lived on the old homestead farm and looks after the operations upon it. She is a woman of keen business judgment and is highly respected in Steele township. George W. Doolin and wife were members of the Christian church. He was a Democrat.

WILLIAM CHARLES FOUST.

There is no occupation which gives a man the same independence of life, which brings him closer to nature, than does farming. In pioneer times farming was very much of a drudgery, but with all the modern improvements the farmer is relieved of much of the hard work which was the portion of his forefathers. Then, too, farming has risen in dignity, until now it is often referred to as a profession rather than as an occupation. For fifty years the science of agriculture was in its mere infancy, and the idea that a man had to take a course in college in order to be a successful farmer, would have been laughed at, but today our colleges are teaching agriculture as a science and are turning out thousands of young men who are well trained in the scientific methods of farming. Another advantage which the present-day farmer commands, which was totally unknown to his pioneer forefathers, is the matter of quick transportation. Good roads are running through every portion of our state, and the interurban and automobile keep the farmer in close touch, not only with his neighbors, but with the life in the city as well. Daviess is one of the oldest counties in the state, and, consequently, has many fine farms and good farmers within its borders. Among the enterprising and progressive farmers of Daviess county, there is none who stands in higher esteem than does William Charles Foust, of Steele township.

William Charles Foust was born on March 19, 1877, near Anderson, Madison county, Indiana. He is the son of John N. and Susan E. (Damewood) Foust, the former of whom was born near Knoxville, Tennessee, and who died, April 1, 1904, and the latter of whom was also born near Knoxville, Tennessee, and who died, April 1, 1910. She was the daughter of Boston and May (Cacaryn) Damewood. John N. Foust was the son of Daniel Foust, a native of North Carolina, and a soldier in the War of 1812. He moved to Tennessee, where he lived the remainder of his life, and it was in Tennessee that he reared his family.

John N. Foust received a common-school education and, at the outbreak of the Civil War, enlisted in the Union army. By birth and by location he was by rights identified with the interests of the Confederacy, but he did not believe in slavery, so he escaped by night to the North and to the Union army and served during the entire war. He enlisted in the Third Regiment, Tennessee Infantry, as a private soldier. He was hit by a spent ball, and the wound on his foot caused him a great deal of trouble during the remainder of his life. After the close of the war, he moved to

Indiana, and settled in Madison county, where he purchased eighty acres of land and where he lived, until 1883, when he sold his farm and came to Daviess county, Indiana, locating near Plainville. Here he bought one hundred and twenty-five acres. He was a member of the Methodist Episcopal church, in which he was very active. He was also active in local affairs and especially in those of Daviess county. At one time he was a guard at the hanging of an innocent man in Madison county, which afterward changed his whole attitude toward capital punishment. He was a member of the Odd Fellows, both subordinate lodge and the encampment. John N. and Susan E. (Damewood) Foust had four children, B. L., William Charles, Theodore Claude, and Mary Edna. The last two are deceased. B. L. Foust has been married twice, the first time to Anna Heinbough, who bore him one child, Ralph, deceased, and the second time to Nora Standley, by whom four children, Cleo, Standley, Lyman and Juanita have been born. B. L. Foust lives in Plainville, and is in the dry goods business.

William Charles Foust was educated in the Plainville schools and in the high school, where he was able to obtain a good education. Mr. Foust was married on April 19, 1904, to Florence Hastings, the daughter of John and Ellie (Littell) Hastings, who are farmers of Bogard township, Daviess county. Mrs. Foust is the only child of her parents who grew to maturity Mrs. Ellie (Littell) Hastings is the daughter of John G. Littell, and a sister of Charles A. Littell, whose life history is told elsewhere in this volume.

After his marriage, Mr. Foust moved to the farm upon which he now lives, which is located about one-half mile north of Plainville, and consists of one hundred and twenty-five acres. William Charles and Florence (Hastings) Foust had five children, Mildred Alzora, Florence Margarite, named after her mother; Charles Hastings, and twin brother and sister, Dorothy Ellen and John Donald. The mother of these children is a faithful and devoted member of the Christian church, while Mr. Foust belongs to the Methodist Episcopal church. Mr. Foust is a member of the Masonic lodge and of the Knights of Pythias.

Besides Mr. Foust's farm, he also owns a store building and lot No. 99 in Plainville. William Charles Foust is commonly known as Charles. His buildings are perhaps the most up-to-date of any in the community in which he lives and are equipped with electric light, while the new home in which Mr. and Mrs. Foust and children live, has all modern conveniences.

Mr. Foust is an enterprising farmer and a public-spirited citizen. He is a man who is honored by the people of Daviess county, among whom he is well known and respected for his many good qualities of heart and head.

NATHAN G. READ.

Nathan G. Read is one of those strong, self-reliant and determined characters who are occasionally met with and who are of such a distinct type as to become leaders of their fellowmen. Not that Mr. Read courts this distinction, for he is entirely unassuming, but his great force of character, his zeal and energy in whatever he undertakes, naturally place him in the front rank of those men who have been potent factors in the development of Daviess county. Mr. Read has long maintained his home in this county, and here he is well known to all classes by reason of his honorable and industrious life, both in his public and private capacity.

Nathan G. Read, the president of the Washington National Bank, of Washington, Indiana, was born in Washington township, Daviess county, Indiana, on March 30, 1842, the son of Nathan and Mary A. (Weaver) Read, the former a native of Massachusetts and the latter of Pennsylvania. Nathan Read and his wife were early settlers in Daviess county and were the parents of the following children: Richard N.; George C.; Nathan G.; Martha, who was the wife of Thomas H. Bradford; Mary, who was the wife of William Hyatt; Miriam, who married William Sanford; Sarah D., who was the wife of Elijah Arthur; Lydia, who died when a child. Of these, Nathan G. Read is the only one now living.

The elder Nathan Read was reared in Massachusetts and came to Daviess county when a young man. Here he purchased two hundred acres of land, two miles northeast of Washington. He improved this farm and there he reared his family.

Nathan G. Read was reared on his father's farm in Washington township. He attended the district schools and the Washington public schools. After leaving the farm, he became deputy county auditor under his brother, Richard N. Read, and served in this capacity for four or five years. He was then elected county auditor, November 1, 1867, and served two terms in this office, or until November 1, 1875. In August, 1877, Mr. Read was elected sheriff and held that office for two years. After his term as sheriff expired, he engaged in the general mercantile business, and, for a few years, was in partnership with William W. Feagans. Mr. Read entered the Washington National Bank on January 10, 1888, as assistant cashier. In January, 1897, he was elected president and has held this office since the date of his first election. He served on the Washington board of education from 1885 to 1907, and during that period was instrumental in forwarding

NATHAN G. READ.

improvements by which the standard of the Washington schools was raised to a very much higher plane.

Nathan G. Read was married on January 21, 1878, to Mrs. Fannie T. McCulloch, the widow of Elliott McCulloch and the daughter of John and Mary Teney. Two children have been born to this union, Robert Roy and Louis I. Robert Roy died when about eight years old. Louis I is now cashier of the Washington National Bank. He was graduated from the Washington high school and attended Purdue University for some time. He married Cleo Horrall and they have two children, Richard H. and Mildred.

Mrs. Nathan G. Read died on November 3, 1913. She was born near Aurora, Indiana, and was a woman of strong Christian character and much loved by all who knew her. Mrs. Read was a member of the Presbyterian church practically all of her life. Mr. Read also is a member of this church and is an elder in the congregation with which he is associated. Nathan G. Read is a Democrat and is a man of quiet and modest demeanor, but of sterling worth. He has lived all of his life in Daviess county and is one of the best-known men within its borders. "Still waters run deep," says an old proverb, and this particularly applies to Mr. Read. By the things he has accomplished in a material way; by his wholesome everyday life, his strict integrity and genuine, manly, Christian character, he has drawn around him a host of friends who hold him in the highest esteem. He has been a good citizen in every sense of the word, public-spirited and benevolent, and throughout his life has always taken an interest in the upbuilding and welfare of his city and county.

JOHN THOMAS.

The following is a brief sketch of the life of one, who, by close attention to business, has achieved a satisfactory degree of success in the agricultural life of Daviess county, Indiana, and who has arisen to an honorable position among the enterprising young farmers of Daviess county, with which his interests are identified. His record is a plain one, rendered remarkable by no strange or mysterious adventures, no wonderful and lucky accidents, no tragic situations. John Thomas is one of those estimable characters whose integrity and personality must obtain for them an admirable public notice which their modesty never seeks. Mr. Thomas commands

(27)

the respect of his neighbors and fellow citizens and has left the impression of his individuality upon the community where he lives.

John Thomas was born on September 13, 1876, in Morgan county, Indiana. He is the son of Harrison and Martha A. (Bothwell) Thomas, the former of whom was also born in Morgan county on April 25, 1852, and the latter of whom was born in the same county on June 4, 1854. Martha A. Bothwell was the daughter of John and Martha (Hinds) Bothwell. John Bothwell was born in Ireland on March 17, 1803. He and his first wife, Nancy Loraign, came to America and settled in Pennsylvania in Montgomery county, where his wife died. He was married, a second time, to Martha A. Bothwell, the widow of Richard Weathers. John Bothwell had twelve children by his second wife, Samuel, Anna, Mary, David, John, Hugh, Sarah, James, Isabelle, Ann, Martha and Margaret.

John Bothwell moved to Washington township, Morgan county, in 1838.

The father of Harrison Thomas, and the grandfather of John Thomas, the subject of this sketch, was John Thomas, Sr., a native of Tennessee, born on January 2, 1817. He was married the first time to Nancy Maxwell, the daughter of Thomas and Elizabeth Maxwell. By this union three children were born, Sarah, Harrison and an infant daughter. He was a farmer by occupation and was married a second time to Lucy Harper, the widow of Joshua King. The great-grandfather of John Thomas, the subject of this sketch, was Peter Thomas, who was born in North Carolina. He and his wife came to Ohio in 1823.

Harrison Thomas was educated in the common schools of Morgan county, Indiana, where he was a farmer. He owned eight hundred acres of land, about five hundred in Morgan county and two hundred and seventy in Steele township, Daviess county. He was a member of the Presbyterian church. Harrison and Martha A. Thomas have had four children, John, the subject of this sketch; Harry, who died in 1904, married Daisy Hanna and had one child, Harry, Jr.; William, who married Mary Cramer, and Jessie, who is single and lives at home.

John Thomas was educated in the common schools and is a farmer by occupation. He was married on October 23, 1907, to Mary Ada Hart, who was born on July 6, 1883, and who is the daughter of A. S. and Emeline (Shireman) Hart, the former of whom was born on December 12, 1845, and who died on June 12, 1911, and the latter born in Morgan county on June 10, 1848, and who died December 19, 1904.

Emeline Shireman was the daughter of Maxwell Shireman, who was born in North Carolina on November 2, 1821, and who married Sarah Cramer, who was born in New Jersey. Maxwell Shireman and wife were farmers in Morgan county, Indiana, and were members of the Methodist Episcopal church. Abraham Hart, Mrs. Thomas' paternal grandfather, was born in North Carolina and married Sarah Chipps. He and his wife were farmers in Morgan county, Indiana, and members of the Methodist Episcopal church. Mrs. Thomas' father, A. S. Hart, was a farmer and owned one hundred and thirty-five acres in Morgan county. He was a Democrat in politics and was active throughout his life. He served at one time as county chairman and represented Morgan county in the state Legislature. He and his family were members of the Methodist Episcopal church. A. S. Hart and wife had six children, Ora, Margaret, Laura, Mary Ada, Victor and Everett. Of these children, Ora married Nettie Avery and lives in Indianapolis, Indiana; Margaret married Bert Leonard and lives in Martinsville; Laura married Miner Leonard and lives in Martinsville; Victor married Ida Pringle and lives in Martinsville, and Everett married Cecile Unversaw and lives in Martinsville.

Mr. and Mrs. John Thomas lived in Morgan county until three years after their marriage, when they came to Steele township, Daviess county, Indiana. They moved to Daviess county, about 1911, and purchased one hundred and one acres, a part of the old Killion farm. They have no children. Mr. Thomas is engaged in general farming in Steele township and is a young and progressive citizen. He has very good land and is known as a successful farmer in this community.

JAMES A. GILL.

Among the representative citizens of Washington, Indiana, whose residence has contributed in no small degree to the moral and civic advancement of the city, is James A. Gill, a well-known funeral director of Washington. While laboring for his individual advancement, Mr. Gill has not forgotten his obligation to the public and his support of such measures and movements as have been made for the general good of the community, has always been depended upon. Although his life has been a busy one, he has never allowed it to interfere with his obligation as a citizen and neighbor. Through his long years of residence in this locality, he has ever been true to the trust imposed in him whether of a public or private nature and his reputation has been unassailable. Possessing in a marked degree those sterling traits which have commanded the uniform confidence, regard and sympathy, necessary to his vocation, he is today honored by all who know him and is numbered among the representative men of Daviess county.

James A. Gill was born on November 29, 1873, in Washington, Indiana, the son of Joseph H. and Mary E. (Carnahan) Gill, the former a native of Illinois and the latter of Indiana, who were the parents of six children, Jennie, the wife of D. H. Bennett, of Logansport; James A., of Washington; Charles, of Washington; Laura, the wife of Russell L. Schwindler, of Logansport; Helen, who is unmarried and lives at Tipton, and Joseph, of Washington.

Joseph H. Gill was partially reared in Illinois. His parents died when he was ten years old when he came to Washington, before the war, learning the cabinetmaker's trade here. When the war broke out, he enlisted for three years and re-enlisted for three additional years, serving altogether four years and three months. He was a sergeant and served in many of the hard-fought battles of the war. After the war, he returned to Washington and resumed his trade until 1872, when he went into partnership with M. L. Bonham in the furniture and undertaking business, which firm continued in business until 1892 under the name of Bonham & Gill. He later purchased the old establishment of William Foster and soon afterward associated with him his son, James A., under the firm name of Joseph Gill & Son. This firm continued until Mr. Gill's death, August 16, 1899, at the age of fifty-nine years. His wife died on March 9, 1911, at the age of sixty. Both were devoted members of the Methodist Episcopal church.

The maternal grandparents of James A. Gill were James and Elizabeth (Warner) Carnahan. The former died in Washington, where his widow is still living at the age of eighty-four. They were the parents of the following children: Mary E., Mrs. May Lutz, Mrs. Jennie Barber, Nellie and Florence, who died when a young woman.

James A. Gill was born and reared in Washington and has lifed here all of his life. He attended the public schools, but subsequently worked at the machinist's trade for about three years. He then went into the undertaking business which he has followed ever since, a period of twenty-one years. Mr. Gill does a large business and is an active member of the State Funeral Directors Association.

On June 25, 1902, James A. Gill was married to Mayme G. Hayes, the daughter of William M. and Winifred (Lee) Hayes. Five children have been born to this union, William H., James C., Ruth, Robert and Edward, twins.

Mrs. Gill was born in Washington, and her father and mother were natives of this state. Her mother died in 1891 at the age of thirty-eight years, and her father is still living. They had three children, Mrs. Helen McGaughey, Mrs. Mayme G. Gill and Mrs. Estella Keller. Mrs. Gill's mother was one of five children born to her parents, Mrs. Addie Buckner, Mrs. Alice V. Foster, Mrs. Stella Hoffman, Mrs. Winifred Hayes and James.

James A. Gill belongs to Charity Lodge No. 30, Free and Accepted Masons; Washington Chapter No. 92, Royal Arch Masons; Washington Council, Royal and Select Masters; Washington Commandery No. 33, Knights Templar; the Murat Temple, Nobles of the Mystic Shrine; Pythagorean Lodge, Knights of Pythias; Liverpool Lodge, Independent Order of Odd Fellows; the Daughters of Rebekah; the Order of the Eastern Star; Ogeechee Tribe No. 58, Improved Order of Red Men; Benevolent and Protective Order of Elks, and the Fraternal Order of Eagles. Mr. Gill is a member of the Presbyterian church and his wife is a member of St. Simon's Catholic church. Mr. Gill is a Republican. As a funeral director, James A. Gill is not excelled in this section of the state of Indiana. He enjoys the confidence of the people of his county and this confidence explains, to a large extent, his success as a funeral director in this section of Indiana.

WILLIAM E. LOUGHMILLER.

William E. Loughmiller is recognized as one of the energetic well-known business men of Daviess county, who, by enterprise and progressive methods, has contributed in a material way to the commercial advancement of Daviess county and the city of Washington, where he lives. In the course of an honorable career, he has been successful in business and enjoys a unique prestige among the representative business men of his community. It is eminently proper that attention be called to his achievements and due credit be accorded him as a representative citizen of Daviess county. Mr. Loughmiller is connected with the firm of W. J. Bacon & Company, dealers in hardware and implements.

William E. Loughmiller was born on December 31, 1870, at Fredericksburg, Washington county, Indiana. He is the son of Joseph C. and Lida E. (Morgan) Loughmiller, the former a native of Tennessee and the latter of Fredericksburg, Indiana. They had eight children, William E., the subject of this sketch; Clara B., the wife of John Shull, of Barr township, Daviess county; Sarah Elizabeth, the wife of Thomas Ratcliff, of Barr township; Mary, the wife of George McCracken, of Barr township; Nettie May, the wife of Ephraim Williams, of Barr township; Edith, the wife of Claude Ragle, of Barr township; Harry and John, both of Barr township.

Joseph C. Loughmiller, the father of these children, was four years old when he came with his parents from Tennessee to Washington county, Indiana, where he grew to manhood. He has been a farmer most of his life, came to Daviess county in the fall of 1871 and located first in Washington. He worked a while at coal mining and also followed farming. About 1884 he moved to Barr township and, subsequently, bought a farm of eighty acres south of Montgomery and still resides in this neighborhood, where he reared his family. Mr. Loughmiller has sold all but twenty acres of his farm. His wife died on December 24, 1907, at the age of fifty-five. Both were members of the Methodist church.

The paternal grandparents of William E. Loughmiller were John and Sarah (Stillwater) Loughmiller, natives of Tennessee and pioneers of Washington county, where they died well advanced in years. They had six children, Mary, Joseph C., Maggie, Willie Ann, Lafayette and Rachel. The maternal grandparents of Mr. Loughmiller were John and Margaret A. (Bright) Morgan, natives of Louisville, Kentucky, and pioneers in Washington county, where he died, his wife afterward coming to Daviess county with her children. She died in this county at the age of ninety years. They had eight children, Richard, Lizzie, John, William, Sarah, David K., Valentine E. and Lida. These children had one half-sister, Nettie. The grandmother married a second time, her last husband being a Mr. Brown.

William E. Loughmiller was reared in Daviess county, in Washington and Barr townships, on his father's farm. He attended the district schools and remained at home until grown. After reaching maturity, he rented a farm, married and operated this farm for seven years. In the meantime, he purchased a farm of eighty acres in Barr township and farmed there, until 1910, when he rented out the farm and moved to Washington, where he engaged in the hardware and implement business. Mr. Loughmiller still owns a half interest in the farm.

William E. Loughmiller was married on December 5, 1894, to Clara

Quilliam, the daughter of John J. and Anna Elizabeth (Myers) Quilliam. One son, William Russell, has been born to this union. He graduated from the Washington high school at the age of seventeen years and is now a student of music.

Mrs. Loughmiller was born in Washington, Indiana, August 10, 1871. Her father was born on the Isle of Man and her mother in Ohio. Her father died in December, 1913, and her mother is still living. They had seven children, Clara, Frank, William, James, Roy, Bernard and a daughter who died young.

The paternal grandparents of Mrs. Loughmiller were John and Lillian (Quirk) Quilliam, natives of the Isle of Man and early settlers in Daviess county. They had four children, Richard, John, Ellen and Jane. The maternal grandparents of Mrs. Loughmiller were Absalom and Nancy (Gorsage) Myers, natives of Ohio and early settlers in Daviess county, where they both died at advanced ages. They had three children, Anna Elizabeth, Frank A. and Grant.

Mrs. Loughmiller is a devoted member of the United Brethren church. Mr. Loughmiller is a member of the Modern Woodmen of America. In politics, he inclines to the independent. William E. Loughmiller is a modest man and a good citizen. The firm of W. J. Bacon & Company does a large business, carrying a well-selected stock of hardware and implements. Mr. Loughmiller has been an important factor in the growth and development of this business. He enjoys the confidence and esteem of the people of Daviess county, where he is well known and is entitled to rank as a representative citizen of this community.

CHARLES HENRY YENNE, M. D.

Devoted to the noble work which his profession implies, Dr. Charles Henry Yenne, physician and surgeon of Washington, Indiana, has been faithful and indefatigable in his endeavors. He has not only earned the due rewards of his efforts in a temporal way, but has also proved himself eminently worthy to exercise the important functions of his calling by reason of his ability, his abiding sympathy and his earnest zeal in behalf of his fellow men. His understanding of the science of medicine is regarded by those who know him as being broad and comprehensive. The profession and the public accord him a distinguished place among the men of this class in Daviess county. His has been a life of earnest and persistent endeavor, such as always brings a true appreciation of the real value of human existence, a condition that must be prolific of good results in all the relations of life.

Charles Henry Yenne was born on November 30, 1858, in Martin county, Indiana. He is the son of George and Sarah (Albaugh) Yenne, the former a native of Westmoreland county, Pennsylvania, and the latter of Carroll county, Ohio. They had nine children, Sabina, deceased, who was the wife of Leander C. Fish; John W., of Long Beach, California; Mary C., the wife of James Williams, of near Shoals, Indiana; Samuel P., of Shoals; Joseph A., of Ft. Morgan, Colorado; Eli P., deceased; Charles H., of Washington; Sarah J., the widow of William T. Acre, of near Shoals, and one who died in infancy.

George Yenne, the father of Dr. Charles Yenne, when a small child, went to Ohio with his parents, who settled in Carroll county. Here he grew to manhood and was married in the town of Kilgore. He worked at the wagonmaker trade in Ohio, and came to Indiana, in 1854, settling near Shoals on a farm.

Upon the breaking out of the Civil War, George Yenne enlisted in Company A, Seventeenth Regiment, Indiana Volunteer Infantry, under Captain Henley in Colonel Wilder's brigade. Colonel Wilder afterward became General Wilder, and this brigade became famous in the annals of the Civil War. Mr. Yenne died in Murfreesboro, Tennessee, of typhoid fever. He left a wife and eight children at home. At the time of his death he was a corporal in the Union army. He had blazed the way and built the buildings on the farm which his sons afterward developed and there grew up.

The paternal grandfather of Doctor Yenne was John George Yenne, who came from Germany when a young man and settled in Pennsylvania. He was married in Westmoreland county to a Miss Johnson, who was of German descent. Subsequently, he moved to Indiana and died in this state at the age of eighty-two. His wife lived to be about sixty-five years old. They had a large family of children namely: Henry, Joseph, George, Catherine and Elizabeth, twins, Susan and Anna.

Doctor Yenne's maternal grandfather was William Albaugh, whose wife was a Miss Simmons. They were natives of Ohio and farmers. Both died in Carroll county, Ohio, the grandfather at the age of seventy-nine, and the grandmother at the age of eighty-four. They had eight children, Melinda, Elizabeth, Lavina, Sarah, Samuel, Basil, Peter and Eli.

Charles Henry Yenne was reared on his father's farm and attended the district schools near Shoals. He also did some high school work at the Shoals high school, after he taught school for five years in the district schools of Martin county. He graduated from the Medical College of Ohio at Cincinnati, and began practicing at Shoals. After two years he moved to Owensburg in Greene county, and practiced there for nine years. In 1894, Doctor Yenne came to Washington, and has practiced here continuously for more than twenty years.

Dr. Charles Henry Yenne was married on April 25, 1883, to Dora Shirey, daughter of Michael and Araminta (Davidson) Shirey. Five children have been born to this happy union, Ralph V., Edna, Claudia M., Harlan S. and Sheldon who died at the age of five years. Ralph is a teacher in the technical schools in Indianapolis. He graduated from Purdue University. After his graduation he married Myrtle Bennett, of Washington. They have two children, John Oliver and Robert. Edna manages the household for her grandfather Shirey. She graduated from the Washington high school. Claudia M. married Guy W. Courtright of Grant, Nebraska, and they have three children, Edna Alice, Mary Louise and Charles Henry. Harlan S. is a teacher of English in the high school at Goshen, Indiana.

Mrs. Dora Yenne died on June 18, 1896, at the age of thirty-eight. She was a member of the Methodist church, and was born at Dover Hill, Indiana, on September 20, 1858. Her parents were natives of Ohio, and moved to Indiana in their early married life and settled in Martin county. Mrs. Yenne's mother died about 1904, at the age of sixty-nine. Her father is still living at the age of eighty-three. He was a soldier in the Civil War and served his country in the Sixty-fifth Regiment, Indiana Volunteer Infantry. He was with Sherman on his famous march to the sea. Michael Shirey and wife were the parents of seven children, Frank M., Addie, Dora, Siegel, Claudia, Merlin D., and Charles V.

Doctor Yenne was married the second time, May 2, 1897, to Mary E. Yenne, the widow of his brother Eli P. Yenne, and the daughter of Manley Marley and Elizabeth (West) Marley. Two children have been born to this union, Leah and Sarah Elizabeth Yenne. Mrs. Yenne had two children by her former marriage, May, who died in early childhood, and Madge Janet Yenne, now a teacher of English and Latin in the Washington high school. She graduated from the Indiana State University in 1912, with the degree of Bachelor of Arts.

Mrs. Mary E. Yenne (*nee* Marley) was born on April 19, 1868, at

Old Harrisonville, Martin county, Indiana, now Trinity Springs. Her father was a native of North Carolina, her mother of Indiana. Both are now deceased. They had six children as follow: Susan, Melissa, Benjamin B., Walter T., William and Mary.

Dr. Charles Henry Yenne is a member of the Daviess County and the Indiana State medical associations and also of the American Medical Association. He is a Republican. The only office which he has ever held was that of city councilman. Doctor Yenne is a member of the Methodist church while Mrs. Yenne is a member of the Christian church. Doctor Yenne belongs to Charity Lodge No. 30, Free and Accepted Masons; Washington Chapter No. 92, Royal Arch Masons; Washington Council No. 67, Royal and Select Masters; and Washington Commandery No. 33, Knights Templar. He is a member of Liverpool Lodge No. 210, Independent Order of Odd Fellows, of Washington, Indiana, and is a man who is not only well known, professionally, in Washington, and in Daviess county, but he is a man who enjoys the confidence and respect of all the people of the county wherein he lives.

FRANKLIN S. GREGORY.

It is a well-authenticated fact that success comes as a result of legitimate and well-applied energy, unflagging determination and perseverance in a course of action when once decided upon. Success is never known to smile upon the idler or the dreamer and never courts the loafer. Only the men who have diligently sought her favors are found with her blessings. In tracing the history of Franklin S. Gregory of the firm of F. S. Gregory & Son, it is plainly seen that the success which he enjoys has been won by commendable qualities of heart and head. His personal worth has gained for him the high esteem of the people of Daviess county.

Franklin S. Gregory, senior member of the firm of F. S. Gregory & Son, grain dealers of Washington, was born on January 4, 1863, in Daviess county, Indiana, is the son of Robert and Zylpha (Hill) Gregory, the former a native of South Carolina and the latter a native of Tennessee. They had fifteen children, William, deceased; George W., of Washington; Julia Ann, the widow of Jacob White, of Washington; Laura, the widow of Spillman Jones, and later of Henry Arms, of Washington; Bennett lives at Jonesboro, Arkansas; Melinda is the wife of James R. Steen of Washington; Alford is deceased; Mary is the wife of Perry Risley, of Oakland City, Indiana;

Sanford also lives at Oakland City; Franklin S. is the subject of this sketch; John died during the Civil War in the service of his country, and four children died in infancy. The father of these children, Robert Gregory, was a small boy when he came from South Carolina to Daviess county, Indiana. At the time of his arrival the Indians and deer were numerous in this section of the state. Robert Gregory was reared in Daviess county and was a farmer. He owned nine hundred and sixty acres of land at the time of his death. His home was in Harrison township, where he reared his family. He died on September 8, 1881, at the age of sixty-six. His wife died on April 14, 1900, at the age of eighty-one. Both were members of the Baptist church.

The paternal grandfather's history is lost as is also that of the paternal grandmother. It may be said, however, that they came from South Carolina and were pioneers in Daviess county, Indiana. They died on the place where they first settled, a farm in Harrison township. The paternal grandfather drove two-year-old steers from Daviess county to Louisville and sold them for ten dollars per head. He purchased land at two dollars an acre. There were two children by the first marriage, Robert S. and Lettie. The grandmother married again, her second husband being George Huston. Two more children were born, George and Catherine.

The maternal grandfather of Franklin S. Gregory was Bennett Hill. He lived in Tennessee. He and his wife had three children, Henry Hill, who was once a very prominent man in Washington; Bennett, Henderson and Zylpha.

Franklin S. Gregory was reared on his father's farm in Harrison township. He attended the district schools and lived at home until he was grown. Two months after he was married, his father died and Franklin inherited a part of the homestead and farmed it for sixteen years. He then traded the farm for a grain elevator in Washington and has been in this business since that time. In March, 1914, he associated himself in business with his son, Oral W.

Franklin S. Gregory was married on June 5, 1881, to Florence M. Horrall, a daughter of Joseph and Melvina (Eubanks) Horrall. Eight children were born to this union, Clarence E. died at the age of eighteen; Morton S. died at the age of twenty-nine; the other children are Elsie, Oral W., Minnie E., Dora B., Charles and Lawrence M. Morton married a Mrs. Goldie Ferrell and died about two months later; Elsie married Millard Webber. They live in Washington and have two children, Helen and Reba L.; Oral W. married Lucy M. Ennis. They have two children,

Thelma Mary and Dorothy May; Minnie married Ray Wey, of Terre Haute. The other children are at home.

Mrs. Florence Gregory was born in Veale township. Her parents, who are deceased, were natives of Daviess county. They had six children, William, Florence, Anna, George, Ella and Sarah.

Mr. Gregory's second marriage was to Mrs. Melissa E. Grubb, the widow of Eli Grubb. She had three children by her former marriage, Mrs. Bessie Ray, Virgil and Della. Mrs. Melissa E. Gregory was born in Daviess county. Her parents were natives of Ohio, and both are now deceased. They had five children, John, Frances Ann, William, Sarah and Melissa.

Mr. and Mrs. Gregory are members of the Christian church. Mr. Gregory is a member of Liverpool Lodge No. 110, Independent Order of Odd Fellows, and also of the Woodmen of the World. Franklin S. Gregory was reared as a Republican, but he has never been especially active in political affairs. To a large degree he enjoys the confidence of the people of Daviess county.

THOMAS C. MYERS.

Thomas C. Myers is a plain, honest man of affairs, who, by correct methods and a strict regard for the interests of his patrons, has made his influences felt in Washington and has won for himself distinctive prestige in the business circles of this city. Mr. Myers would be the last man to permit extravagant eulogies. Nevertheless, his life presents much that is interesting and valuable and which may be studied with profit by young men, whose careers are yet to be made. He is one of those men whose integrity and strength of character must force them into admirable notice which their modesty never seeks. Mr. Myers commands the respect of his fellow townsmen and will leave the impression of his individuality deeply stamped upon the life of the community where he lives.

Thomas C. Myers, a well-known grocer and the proprietor of a saw-mill, was born on April 2, 1866, in Bogard township, Daviess county, Indiana. He is the son of Joseph M. and Nancy L. (Adkins) Myers, natives of Daviess county. They had thirteen children, Thomas C.; Charles H., of Indianapolis; Oliver E., of Washington; Alfred C., of Bogard township; Arnold W., of Washington; Flora J., the wife of J. G. Loudermilk, of Clinton, Indiana; Emma and Della, twins, the former the wife of John Rogers, of Bogard township, and the latter the wife of Benjamin Bennington, of Jasonville, Indiana; Cecil, the wife of Arnold Killian, of Indianapolis; and Effie G., who died single. Besides these there were three who died in infancy.

Joseph M. Myers, the father of Thomas C., was born and reared in Bogard township, Daviess county, where he was a druggist in Epsom. He owned a good farm of one hundred acres. Mr. Myers died in 1900 at the age of fifty-eight and his wife is still living. Both were members of the Methodist church. The paternal grandparents of Mr. Myers were Joseph and Mary (Sifrit) Myers, natives of North Carolina. Born in 1802, he came to Indiana when quite young, when he engaged in farming in this state. He built the first house in Bogard township outside of the Dutch settlement. He and his wife both died at advanced ages, he at the age of eighty and she at the age of eighty-four. They had a large family, among whom were the following children: Joseph M., Elias, William, George W., Christina and Elizabeth. The maternal grandparents of Thomas C. Myers were Christopher and Nellie (Lee) Adkins, he a native of Kentucky and she of Virginia, and both were early settlers in Daviess county. He died at the age of fifty-eight and she at the age of seventy-four. They had two children, John, who died while comparatively young; and Nancy L., the mother of Mr. Myers.

Thomas C. Myers was reared on his father's farm in Bogard township and attended the district schools. He lived at home until twenty-one years of age and then worked in a store at Elnora for one year. Subsequently, Mr. Myers went into the saw-mill business in partnership with his brother, Charles H. They were together some twenty-six years, during which time they were also engaged in the mercantile business. Together they built the first flour-mill at Epsom and conducted it for four years. This mill was traded for a store in Mecca, Indiana. Soon afterward they dissolved partnership. Thomas C. Myers then went to Terre Haute and worked for the Kauffman Grocery Company for a short time and finally returned to Washington and started a restaurant. He then moved to Michigan and lived there for a few months when he came back to Washington and traded for his present grocery. He and his brother, Alfred C., are in the saw-mill business at the present time.

Thomas C. Myers was married on July 24, 1887, to Flora J. Wilson, the daughter of Andrew J. and Eleanor (Perkins) Wilson. One daughter, Lola A., has been born to this union. She married Charles Everett Miller, who died in April, 1913, leaving a son, Ivan. A daughter, Doris, was born after his death.

Mrs. Myers was born in Daviess county, Indiana. Her father was born in Missouri and her mother in this county. Her father died when he was a young man and her mother is still living, in Martinsville. Mrs. Myers is the only child born to this union. Her paternal grandparents were James Wilson and wife, natives of Indiana, who moved to Missouri in an early day, where they died. They had the following children: Andrew J., and Mary. Mrs. Myers' maternal grandparents were Asbury Perkins and wife, who were the parents of two children, Eleanor and John A.

Mr. and Mrs. Thomas C. Myers are members of the Christian church. Mr. Myers is a Republican. He is a good business man, a good citizen and belongs to two of the early pioneer families of this county. He is a representative citizen of this county and is therefore entitled to representation in a volume such as this.

ROLAND M. SMILEY, D. D. S.

Roland M. Smiley, D. D. S., a well-known dentist of Washington and a member of R. M. Smiley & Son, has practiced his profession in Daviess county for a period of nearly thirty years. By his professional ability and high personal character, he has made a distinctive mark in the community where he has lived so long and where he is so well known. In the realm of dentistry he has achieved a splendid reputation. Trained in the first instance as a public school teacher, Doctor Smiley later qualified himself admirably for his present profession. Among his professional colleagues in Daviess county, he is held in the highest regard. Associated with him in the practice of dentistry is Roy D. Smiley, his son, who also well trained for his profession. Dr. R. M. Smiley and son enjoy a large and lucative practice in Washington and Daviess counties.

Roland M. Smiley was born on February 12, 1859, in Tuscarawas county, Ohio. He is the son of Abner G. and Esther B. (Bair) Smiley, natives of Pennsylvania. They had five sons and two daughters, Payson A., of Raglesville, Indiana; Wilson S., of the same place; Roland M., Reisin P., of Raglesville; Wallace, of Odon, Indiana; and two daughters who died in infancy.

Abner G. Smiley, the father of these children, was a farmer and was reared in Tuscarawas county, Ohio. He came to Daviess county in 1863, locating in Van Buren township, where he purchased a farm of one hundred and sixty acres, which he improved. He had added forty-six acres to this tract and now has one of the best farms in the county. It was on this property that the Smiley family was reared. Abner Smiley died in Odon, in 1908, at the age of seventy-eight and his wife is still living at the age of eighty-one. Both were members of the United Brethren church.

The paternal grandparents of Dr. Roland M. Smiley were William and Elizabeth (Swyhart) Smiley, natives of Pennsylvania and pioneers of Tuscarawas county, Ohio. They died in that county, he at the age of forty-five and she at the age of eighty-three. They had a family of seven children, Lafayette, Abner G., Nancy, Jane, Martha, Harvey and Andrew J. The maternal grandparents of Doctor Smiley were Jacob Bair and wife, natives of Pennsylvania and early settlers in Tuscarawas county, Ohio, where they were farmers. They had sixteen children, Jacob, Benjamin, Kizzie, Mary, Catharine, Leah, Esther, Jonas, John A. and others who died young.

Roland M. Smiley was four years old when he was brought to Daviess county, by his parents, and this county has been his home since that time. He grew up on the farm and remained there until seventeen years old, attending the district schools. Subsequently, he was a student at the Northern Indiana Normal School at Valparaiso and later the Normal School at Lebanon, Ohio. Still later he took a one-year course in Dana's Musical Institute at Warren, Ohio. Doctor Smiley then taught in the public schools for two years and taught music for one year. Finally he took up dentistry and graduated from the Indiana Dental College in 1886, when he began practicing in Washington and has practiced in that city since that date.

Doctor Smiley was married on December 30, 1886, to Clara Danks, the daughter of Rev. Thomas C. and Emma (Young) Danks. Six children have been born to this union, Roy D., Karl, Clara, Charles, Paul and Esther. Roy D. is a graduate of the Indiana Dental College and is a member of the firm of R. M. Smiley & Son. He married Marguerite Scoble; Karl died at the age of twenty years; Clara died at the age of sixteen months; Charles is a student at Indiana University; Paul and Esther are students in the Washington high school.

Mrs. R. M. Smiley was born in Pittsburgh, Pennsylvania. Her father was a native of Wales. Both her father and mother are now deceased, her father dying in 1908 at the age of seventy-two and her mother in 1907 at the age of sixty-nine. They were the parents of six children, Joseph, Mayme, Clara, Belle, Charles and Lydia.

Mr. and Mrs. R. M. Smiley are members of the First Methodist Episcopal church and Doctor Smiley is a trustee of the church. He has also been choir director for twenty-six years, and is now teacher of the young men's

Bible class in which there are about sixty enrolled. Fraternally, he belongs to Charity Lodge No. 30, Free and Accepted Masons; Washington Chapter No. 92, Royal Arch Masons; Washington Commandery No. 33, Knights Templar. His son, Dr. Roy Smiley, is also a Knights Templar and belongs to Washington Council No. 67, Royal and Select Masters. Both men and their wives belong to the Order of the Eastern Star No. 210. Dr. R. M. Smiley is also a member of Pythagorean Lodge No. 118, Knights of Pythias.

ALBERT KILLION.

Prominent in the affairs of Daviess county and distinguished as a citizen whose influence extends beyond the limits of the community honored by his residence, the name of Albert Killion stands out conspicuously among the successful farmers and stock breeders. All of his undertakings have been actuated by noble motives and high resolves and are characterized by breadth of wisdom and strong individuality. His success and achievements but represent the results of utilizing his natural talents and directing his efforts along those lines where mature judgment and rare discrimination lead the way.

Albert Killion was born on May 19, 1865, in Steele township, the son of Alexander Killion and the brother of Nathan Killion, the latter of whom is referred to elsewhere in this volume.

Educated in the common schools of Daviess county, Albert Killion was reared on the farm and attended school in the winter, working on the farm during the summer. At the age of twenty-two, Mr. Killion was married to Mary Kettery, November 24, 1887. Mrs. Killion was born on February 27, 1869, in Madison county, and is the daughter of Jacob and Dialtha M. (Foust) Kettery, the former of whom was a farmer of Madison county and a native of Tennessee. He died on February 23, 1911. To Albert and Mary (Kettery) Killion three children have been born, Ethel, on April 4, 1900, died on December 5, 1908; Virgil, November 9, 1896, and Vernon, February 21, 1903.

After their marriage, Mr. and Mrs. Killion lived in Steele township and moved from there to Bogard township, Daviess county, in what is known as the Ten-mile house. While living upon this farm, Mr. Killion had charge of five hundred and forty-nine acres of land. They removed to Plainville in 1910. Mr. Killion owns in all eleven hundred acres of land, the most of which is in Steele and Bogard townships, Daviess county. Ninety acres of this land, however, is situated in Knox county. Besides farming, Mr. Killion is also a prominent stockholder in the Plainville Flouring Company, which was established in 1910. At the present time, however, he spends most of his time in buying and selling stock for the Tarr-Downs Company, in which he is financially interested.

Jacob Kettery, Mrs. Killion's father, married Dialtha M. Foust, and to them three children were born, Mary, the wife of Albert Killion; Joseph E., who lives in Bogard township, and who married Laura Hardy, and Charles, who married Hattie Chestnut and who lives in Odon, Indiana. Jacob Kettery and wife were members of the Methodist church. Mrs. Killion's paternal grandfather was Joseph Kettery, a native of Germany, who married Catherine Burk, also a native of Germany. Joseph Kettery was a farmer in Wayne county, Indiana, and a member of the Lutheran church. Of his children, only one, Lizzie D., is still living. The other children were John, Mary H., Lydia H., Joseph, Jacob and Jane.

Albert Killion has a comfortable home just at the edge of Plainville. He is a modest, unassuming man, but well liked and cordial in his manner. He is one of the enterprising and progressive citizens of Steele township and his work, as a farmer and business man, well deserves to be recorded in a volume of historical annals dealing with the lives of the people of Daviess county. Mr. Killion is the very soul of integrity and honor and is respected by his neighbors and fellow townsmen.

EDWARD B. SMITH.

Among the citizens of Daviess county who have lived long and useful lives in this community, is Edward B. Smith, now living retired at Washington, Indiana. Whether the elements of a success in this life are fundamental to the individual, or whether they are quickened by a process of accidental development, it is impossible to determine, yet the study of a successful career, whatever the field of endeavor, is none the less interesting and profitable by reason of this uncertainty. Edward B. Smith started in life unaided, and in his youth learned the correct principles of living. He has always been devoted to principles of right living and industrious habits. He has believed in education and morality, and in loyalty to the national government. Some of the best months of his life he gave to the defense of his country as a Union soldier. He is honored and respected in the city of Washington, where he lives, and is clearly entitled to specific mention in the annals of his county.

Edward B. Smith was born on July 6, 1846, in Clarington, Monroe county, Ohio. He is a son of Ira and Mary Ann (Bates) Smith, the former a native of Pennsylvania, and the latter a native of the Isle of Man. They had several children: Lydia, the wife of Clem Allen, of West Virginia; Mortimer, who died at Cheat Mountain, was a soldier in the Civil War; Edward B., of this review; Elisha, a resident of Murphytown, West Virginia, and Mary Ann, deceased.

Ira Smith, the father of Edward B., was reared near Clarington, and was a river man, following steamboating on the Ohio river, and was an officer on a boat. His death occurred at the age of forty-five years.

Little is known of the paternal ancestors of Mr. Smith, but his maternal grandfather's name was Edward Bates. Both he and his wife were born in the Isle of Man, and were early settlers in Monroe county, Ohio. They came to this country in a sailing vessel, the trip requiring six months. Both died in Monroe county at an advanced age, he being about sixty-five, while his wife lived to be nearly a hundred years old. They were the parents of the following children: Benjamin, Mary Ann, Caroline and William. Edward Bates served in the War of 1812.

Edward B. Smith was reared at Clarington, Ohio, receiving his education in the public schools of that place until he was seventeen years of age, when he began working in a hotel. In 1861 he enlisted for service in the Union army by joining Company A, Seventy-seventh Regiment, Ohio Volunteer Infantry, in which he served one year, lacking five days.

After the close of the war, Mr. Smith returned to Clarington, where he married and he and his young wife moved to Walker Station, West Virginia, where he engaged in farming for one year. He then engaged in drilling oil wells, following this occupation until 1868, when he moved to Xenia, Illinois, where he purchased a farm of eighty acres. However, he sold this farm soon afterward, and moved to Xenia, where he became engaged in buying ties for the Baltimore & Ohio Railway Company. In the fall of 1874, he moved to Washington, Indiana, and has since made this city his home, a period of more than forty years. When Mr. Smith first came to Washington he began clerking in the store of Hyatt & Cosby, later taking up the same work with Cable & Kauffman, remaining with the last named firm from 1875 until 1903, at which time he began working for the

Baltimore & Ohio Railway Company at his trade of carpentering in their shops in the city of Washington, continuing at this occupation until September 15, 1914.

On the 20th of August, 1863, Mr. Smith was married to Lovina T. Smith, daughter of Mahala Smith and husband, and to this union nine children were born, Alma Lenora, Charles, Fred, Herbert, George, Denva, Frank, Gussie and John. Alma Lenora married Harvey Lochridge, of Washington, and they have four children, Leo, Irene, Maxine and Robert; Charles is a machinist by trade, but is now operating a farm near Malta, Montana; he married Maud Lyons, and they have one son, Leavitt; Fred is also a machinist living at Springfield, Missouri; He married Anna Crager, and to them were born Edda, Lavern, Walter and one unmarried. Herbert died at the age of thirty-one years. George is a machinist living at Washington. He married Jennie Purcell, and they have three children; Deenva became the wife of Edward T. Gillick, of Cincinnati, and they are the parents of the following children: Melvin, Genieve and Mary; Frank is a machinist by trade, but is now engaged in farming in Montana, near Malta, where he and his brother, Charles, each owns three hundred and twenty acres. Frank first married Clara Allen, who died, leaving one child. His second wife was a Miss Keiser; Gussie died at the age of ten years, and John died in infancy.

Mrs. Smith was born in Monroe county. Her parents were natives of Ohio, and had four children, Jane, Elizabeth, Thomas and Lovina T. Mr. and Mrs. Smith are active members of the Christian church, in which Mr. Smith has been ordained elder for many years. Mr. Smith's mother, Mary Ann Bates, was one of the early members of the Christian church in the beginning of the Restoration movement, even before the days of Alexander Campbell, and died in that faith. She was twice married, her second husband being Sylvester Spears, to whom two children were born, John and Rosetta.

Mr. Smith has always been an adherent of the Democratic party, but has never taken an active interest in public affairs, preferring to devote his time and attention to his own interests, but nevertheless, has been an ardent supporter of all worthy movements having for their object the betterment of his community. Fraternally, he belongs to Charity Lodge No. 30, Free and Accepted Masons, and was made a member of the Independent Order of Odd Fellows in 1868. He is also a member of the Knights of Pythias, in the workings of which orders he takes an active interest.

WILLIAM J. BACON.

It is the progressive wide-awake man of affairs that makes the real history of a community. His influence as a potential factor in the body politic is difficult to estimate. The example such men furnish of patient purpose and steadfast integrity strongly illustrates what is in the power of each to accomplish. There is always a full measure of satisfaction in adverting even in a casual way to their achievements in advancing the interests of their fellow men and in giving strength and solidity to the institutions which make so much for the prosperity of a county. Such a man is William J. Bacon, of W. J. Bacon Company, dealers in hardware and implements at Washington, Indiana. It is proper that a review of his career be accorded a place among the representative citizens of Washington and Daviess county, where he is so well known.

William J. Bacon, of W. J. Bacon Company, was born on October 24, 1874, near Evansville, in Vanderburg county, Indiana, and is a son of Joseph D. and Sarah C. (Holcomb) Bacon, the former a native of Kentucky and the latter a native of Indiana. They had seven children, Howard J., who lives near Washington; Lulu, the wife of F. A. Williams, of near Henderson, Kentucky; Mary J., wife of W. P. Coan, of Harrison township; William J., of Washington; Charles D., of Pontiac, Illinois; Edward S., of Chenoa, Illinois, and Elizabeth A., the wife of Elmer Russell, of Chenoa. The father of these children, Joseph D. Bacon, for a part of his life was reared in Kentucky. He came to Indiana in an early day, locating first at Evansville. Subsequently, he came to Washington, arriving in 1884, where he was employed to run an engine on the Chicago & Eastern Illinois railroad for several years. Later, he was a farmer in Veale township, where he purchased a farm of fifty acres. He died a few years afterward, in 1904, at the age of sixty-two years. His wife still survives him and lives with her son William J. Bacon. Mrs. Joseph D. Bacon is a member of the Regular Baptist church, as was her deceased husband.

The paternal grandfather of William J. Bacon was James Bacon. His wife was Mary Ann (Dobson) Bacon, and both were natives of Salem, New Jersey. They moved to Kentucky and afterward to Indiana, dying at an advanced age soon after their arrival in this state. They had a large family of children among whom are the following: Theophilus, Charles, Mary Jane, Joseph D. and Thomas J. The maternal grandfather of Mr.

Bacon was Jerry Holcomb, a native of Indiana who died in Warrick county well advanced in years. He had several children, among whom were: Sarah C., William, John, Timothy and Anna.

William J. Bacon was reared on his father's farm. He attended the district schools and lived at home until grown. He then began running a country store in Pike county, five miles east of Petersburg, and here lived for four years. Subsequently, he sold his interests, and, in 1901, Mr. Bacon came to Washington, working for C. L. Littell & Son in the hardware business. In 1906, he purchased a half interest in the business together with L. C. Aikman, and the firm then became Bacon & Aikman. In 1908, Mr. Bacon purchased Mr. Aikman's interest and operated the business alone until 1913, when it was incorporated as W. J. Bacon Company. The company was organized with a capital stock of ten thousand dollars. The firm handles hardware and farm implements of all kinds. William E. Loughmiller is associated with Mr. Bacon in this business.

William J. Bacon was married on November 1, 1905, to Mary Ethel Hyatt, a daughter of George and Florence R. (Carter) Hyatt. Four children have been born to this union, Alice Marie, William Hyatt, Ralph Vance and Doris Margaret.

Mrs. Bacon was born on her father's farm just north of the city of Washington. Her father was born in Washington, and her mother in Bogard township, Daviess county. Her father died in 1911, at the age of sixty-two. His wife is now living on the old homestead. They had six children, William C., Mary Ethel, Alice Rosetta, George Read, Eliza and Charles Winton.

The paternal grandfather of Mrs. Bacon was William Hyatt and his wife was a Miss Graham. They were pioneers in Daviess county and had five children, Mary, Margaret, Helen, George and Rebecca. The maternal grandfather of Mrs. Bacon was a Mr. Carter. His children were David, Sarah, Florence, Mattie and Alice.

Mr. and Mrs. Bacon are devoted members of the Christian church and are active in the work of both the church and the Sunday school. Fraternally, Mr. Bacon is a member of the Independent Order of Odd Fellows and the Knights of Pythias. He is a Democrat. Mr. Bacon's prominence in the business life of Washington and Daviess county has attracted to him a host of friends. Although hardly in the prime of life, he has accomplished what most men do not achieve until they have arrived at the age of fifty or sixty. Mr. Bacon is in every respect worthy of the confidence of the people of Daviess county.

MARY CAMPBELL SHIRLEY.

Devoted to the noble and humane work of teaching, Mary Campbell Shirley has made her influence felt in the public schools of Daviess county, Indiana, and is not unknown to the wider educational circles of the state, occupying as she does a prominent place in her profession and standing high in the esteem of educators in other than her own particular field of endeavor. For many years she has pursued her calling with all the interest and enthusiasm, thoroughly in harmony with the spirit of the work, and has a proper conception of the dignity of the profession to which her life and energies have been unselfishly devoted. She always keeps in touch with the trend of modern thought along its various lines and, being a woman of scholarly and refined tastes, is acquainted with the literature of the world in general, while her familiarity with the more practical affairs of the day makes her feel at ease with all classes and conditions of people with whom she meets.

Mary Campbell Shirley was born on December 23, 1863, near Loogootee, Martin county, Indiana, and is a daughter of Dr. John C. L. Campbell and Emily (Brooks) Campbell. Her father was a native of Iredell county, North Carolina, born on October 27, 1828, and her mother was a native of Orange county, Indiana, born near the town of French Lick on May 6, 1832. Her paternal grandfather, Milton Campbell, was a son of Archibald Campbell, a Scotchman by birth and belonging to the great Argyle family. His uncle was the Duke of Argyle. In the year 1757 Archibald Campbell came to the United States. He landed in Delaware, where he grew up and married Jane Evans in that state. Later they moved to Stokes county, North Carolina, during the same year that "Continental" money was discontinued in this country. His name is entered in the census of North Carolina of the year 1790. Here he raised a large family. His last years were spent with his son Milton on his estate in Iredell county. Milton Campbell was his son—subject's grandfather—who married Margaret Smith. He had accumulated considerable of this world's goods, and it was his pleasure to care for his father in his declining years. Milton had won the title of colonel and died in 1860. He was colonel of the state militia, county surveyor and one of the five "magistrates" of the county. Mr. Campbell was familiarly called "Colonel" Campbell and was known everywhere in that section.

Mary Campbell Shirley's father, Dr. John C. L. Campbell, spent his early days on the North Carolina estate and when quite a young man began reading up on the subject of medicine. At a later date he enrolled as a student in the Louisville University, in Louisville, Kentucky, where he studied medicine and where he graduated in 1853. He then began the practice of medicine in the town of Mt. Pleasant, Indiana, and was married in 1855 to Emily Brooks. He enlisted in Company B, Eightieth Regiment, Indiana Volunteer Infantry, in 1862, where he served as corporal. In 1863 he was transferred to the Twenty-first Regiment, Heavy Artillery, as assistant surgeon. After being mustered out of service he returned home and finally began the practice of medicine in the town of Loogootee, Indiana, where he remained until the time of his death, February 15, 1893. His wife was the daughter of Jefferson Brooks, who came from Lincoln, Massachusetts, to Hindoostan, Indiana, where he engaged in business as a "flatboat" merchant and, later, moved to Mt. Pleasant, Indiana, where he died in the year 1882, having previously lost his wife by death in the year 1874. To Jefferson Brooks and wife were born the following children: Emily; Lewis, who was captain of Company C, Fourteenth Regiment, Indiana Volunteer Infantry (succeeding Captain Nathan Kimball, afterward General Kimball) and afterward became colonel of the Eightieth Regiment, Indiana Volunteer Infantry; Susan, who married Sanford Niblack; Thomas Jefferson, who was captain of Company B, Eightieth Regiment, Indiana Volunteer Infantry, who died as the result of a wound received in the battle of Perryville, Kentucky; Hannah Eustace, who married Eunice Trueblood, a sister of H. C. Trueblood; Seymour Waldo; Grace, who married P. R. Gibson, of Topeka, Kansas, now of Vincennes, Indiana, and whose wife is deceased.

Thomas Jefferson Brooks, Mary C. Shirley's maternal grandfather, was a descendant of Patriarch Puritan Thomas Brooks, who landed at Marblehead, Massachusetts, in the year 1634, and was one of a committee of seven who selected the site and laid out the town of Concord, Massachusetts. It was he that chose the land on the hill between Lincoln and Concord, which is now called Brooks Hill, and Brooks Inn is the place where Paul Revere stopped during his famous ride. The inn was kept by John Brooks, who married Lucy Hoar, a great aunt of George Frisby, which makes Thomas Jefferson Brooks a second cousin to Senator Hoar. He was prominent in the early history of Martin county, Indiana, active in all public affairs and a stanch supporter of the policies of Abraham Lincoln. He was married to Susan Poor, a native of Massachusetts, who came to Indiana in the year 1816 with her parents, John and Hannah (Chute) Poor. The father died in 1817 from heart lesion, due to an accident received in rolling logs, and his wife died some time later.

To Dr. John C. L. Campbell and wife were born the following named children, in order of their birth: Harlan Anderson; Ida; Eugenia, who married S. W. Chappell, now living in Pike county, Indiana; Mary, the subject; Susan Brooks, who married Samuel A. Chenoweth, deceased, and she lives in Shoals, Indiana; Ethel, the wife of Dr. Harvey J. Clemens and living in Salem, Oregon; John Milton, of Coalinga, California.

Mary Campbell Shirley received her early education in the public schools and Mt. Pleasant Academy, attended the county normal schools, the Indiana State Normal, the Indiana State University, Winona College and the Normal College, Valparaiso, Indiana. She began her teaching career at the age of sixteen years, and for three years was a teacher in the schools of Martin county, Indiana. She was married on June 13, 1887, to James L. Shirley, a son of John and Mary (Hatchett) Shirley, both natives of the state of Kentucky. His father was John Shirley, of Scottish descent, who came from North Carolina, where he was a large slave owner, and settled in Kentucky; his mother was a daughter of Archibald and Jane (Love) Hatchett, natives of Virginia, who came to Kentucky, where they received a grant of land and where they both died. Archibald Hatchett was actively engaged in the War of 1812, and his mother came with her parents to Virginia when a little child. John Shirley and wife came to Indiana in the year 1859, and to them were born the following named children: Jasper, who was a soldier with the Union army during the Civil War; Johanna, who married George Brown and now lives in Clay county; Susan, who married Marion Harbert and to whom were born Albert, deceased; Imogene, who married Harvey Trueblood, of Washington; James L., subject's deceased husband; Robert P., who married Emily Christ, of Clay county, now living in Tulsa, Oklahoma; Laura E., who married W. G. Wharton, and now lives in Portland, Oregon.

James L. Shirley was educated in the public schools of Clay county, after which he engaged in the mercantile business in the town of Columbus, Indiana, where he spent the last two years of his life and died on July 1, 1890. To James L. and Mary C. Shirley were born the following children: Herman Vincent, on May 22, 1888, a graduate of the Washington (Indiana) high school, attended Purdue University for two years, and is now engaged in the service of a large oil company in Fresno county, California; Mary Lois, born on February 25, 1891, a graduate of the Washington high school and the Indiana State Normal in 1914, now specializing in public school music. She will finish the supervisor's course in school music at Cornell University in August of 1915.

That singers are born and not made, cannot be more fitly demonstrated than in the instance of the long line of successive teachers of that art as set out in this biography. Professor Chute, an English vocal teacher, became the tutor of James I of England about 1603. Professor Chute was lineally descended to the old Puritan Dominie, one of the first settlers of our country and the ancestor of Daniel Chute, father of Conrad Baker's wife, who organized the schools of Evansville. Mary Campbell Shirley is a descendant of a sister of Daniel Chute, Hannah Chute. History portrays the unusual fact that for seven generations in America and the generations from that time back to the time to which reference is made above there has been an unbroken line of teachers. Mrs. Shirley takes great pride in the fact that her daughter has refused to break this beautiful line of teachers and has declined to consider any other vocation in life except that for which she is qualified, the art of teaching those about her to become proficient in the art of singing.

Since the death of her husband, Mrs. Shirley has devoted the past twenty-three years to teaching in the Washington (Daviess county, Indiana) schools, where her services have given eminent satisfaction and where she is held in the very highest esteem by all who know her. She is particularly well fitted to the duties of teaching and her early educational training has served her to the greatest advantage and to the great benefit of the schools of this town. Personally she is quite popular, possessing to a marked degree those characteristics that win and retain warm friendships. By her kindness and courtesy she has won an abiding place in the esteem of her fellow citizens and by her intelligence, energy and enterprising spirit, has made her influence felt during her residence in Daviess county, occupying no small place in the public favor.

WILLIAM ALEXANDER KILLION.

Splendid achievements always excite admiration. Men of deeds are men whom the world delights to honor. Ours is an age representing the most advanced progress in all lines of material activities, and the man of initiative is the one who forges to the front in the industrial world. Among the distinctive captains of industry in Daviess county, Indiana, a place of priority must be given to William Alexander Killion, of Steele townshp. He is in the fullest sense of the term a progressive, self-made American.

thoroughly in harmony with the spirit of the advanced age in which he lives and conducting all of his business matters carefully and systematically. In all of his acts he displays an aptitude for successful management. Mr. Killion has not permitted the accumulation of fortune to affect, in any way, his actions toward those less fortunate than he. He is most sympathetic and a broad-minded man in every respect. William A. Killion has a host of warm and admiring friends in Daviess county. Although he had the misfortune, some time ago, to lose an arm, it has not affected his remarkable ability to get from place to place, and he is able to drive a motor car with rare skill, by this means directing the operations upon his vast farm properties.

William Alexander Killion was born on November 9, 1857, in Daviess county, Indiana, the son of Alexander Killion and the brother of Nathan Killion, referred to elsewhere in this volume.

Educated in the common schools, Mr. Killion lived on the farm during the early part of his life.

William A. Killion was married on January 18, 1880, to Mary Dyer, the daughter of William and Mary Jane (Baker) Dyer. To this union five children have been born, Ivy May, Claude E., Elmer, Ora and Jessie. Iva May is unmarried and lives at home; Claude E., who lives in Plainville, married Elsie Artermann and has two children, Earl and Alvin; Ora, who lives in Harrison township, married Effie Brooker and has one child, Harley; Jesse, who lives at home, married Catherine Hummer and has one child, Louisa.

William A. Killion owns one thousand acres of land in this section of the state, of which acreage nine hundred acres are in Daviess county, sixty in Pike county and fifty acres in Greene county. Besides his extensive farm property, Mr. Killion owns a third interest in two sections of land at Panhandle, Texas. He also owns several shares in the Plainville Farmers Bank, and for some time was in the flour business in Washington, but sold out in December, 1897, and returned to the farm.

It was while he was in the milling business in Washington that he lost his right arm, February 20, 1896. The accident occurred in his mill when his hand was caught in a cog-wheel. It was necessary to amputate his arm below the elbow.

Mr. Killion is authority for the statement that there are nine William Killions in Daviess county, Indiana, and three William A. Killions. Physically, William A. Killion is a large man and possesses a genial, good-natured disposition at all times. He is very popular in Steele township, but is well known outside the boundaries of the township where he lives. Mr. Killion owns a splendid home one mile northeast of Plainville, where he and his family have lived since they removed from Washington, in 1897. Mr. Killion's quickness of perception and the dispatch with which he goes about his business are traits of character which he has inherited from his father before him, who was also a well-known business man in this section of the country. The Killion family is popular socially in Steele township.

Mr. Killion is identified with the Democratic party. He has never held office, however, and has never been interested in politics to this extent. His heavy financial and agricultural interests have kept him too busily engaged for participation in politics. He does, however, take a commendable interest in the civic and moral development of his community.

JOHN A. LAWYER.

Poets often tell the truth and the old song which contains the refrain, "The farmer feeds them all," states a very fundamental and economic truth. Without the farmer the rest of the country would starve within a week, despite the large amount of food in cold storage. Every occupation might be done away with but farming and people could live, but a total cessation of farming, for a very short time, would actually depopulate the whole world. A man can live without banks all of his life, but deprive him of his bread and his career is soon ended. Farming is becoming an honored profession, our district schools are teaching it as a science and our colleges are granting degrees for agricultural courses. The farmers of any community sustain the people dependent upon every other profession. Without the farmer, the banker would close his doors, the manufacturer would shut down his factory and the railroads would suspend operations. Among the honored farmers of Daviess county who help to keep the banker, the manufacturer and the railroad, is John A. Lawyer, of Steele township.

John A. Lawyer was born on August 15, 1848, near Louisville, Kentucky. He is the son of Joseph and Louise (Mathers) Lawyer, the former of whom was a native of Pennsylvania and a soldier in the Civil War, who died in 1863. Joseph Lawyer was confined, for a time, in the prison at Andersonville. He was a member of a company in the Indiana Volunteer Infantry, serving for more than a year. He farmed mostly in Washington county, and was an influential member in the Methodist church. His wife, who before her marriage was Louise Mathers, was the daughter of Nathan Mathers, of Washington county, who was a farmer, school teacher and a justice of the peace. Joseph and Louise Lawyer had five children, Rebecca; John A., the subject of this sketch; Bernetta, deceased; Abner, deceased; and Bishop. Of these children Rebecca, who married Howard Taylor, now deceased, lives at Linton, Indiana; Bernetta, who married James Cropp, lives in Washington; Abner, who married Anna Decker, lives in this county; Bishop, who was twice married, lives in Jasonville, Indiana.

Educated largely by home study and in the school of experience and hard knocks, John A. Lawyer has been a farmer all his life, and in this vocation has been more than ordinarily successful.

Mr. Lawyer has been married three times, the first time on October 5, 1865, to Martha Osman, who died on May 5, 1875, and who was the daughter of Charles and Margaret (Seiferd) Osman, farmers in Van Buren township, Daviess county. Charles Osman died while in the service of the Union army in the Civil War. By his first wife, Mr. Lawyer was the father of six children, Bernetta, Richard, Louise, Frederick and two who died in infancy. Mr. Lawyer was married a second time to Laura Wheeler, who died in 1878. One child, Ida, was born to this marriage, but she is now deceased. After the death of his second wife, Mr. Lawyer was married a third time to a half sister of his second wife, Huldah Wheeler, who was born on July 18, 1858, at Princeton, Indiana. By this third marriage, thirteen children have been born, John, Mattie, Maggie, Joe, Flora (deceased), Raleigh, Austin, Leonard, Pearl, Anna, McKinley, Charles and Ralph.

Mr. Lawyer enlisted in the Union army on October 8, 1864, first enlisting in Company D, Thirty-seventh Regiment, Indiana Volunteer Infantry, and later was transferred to the Eighty-second Regiment, Indiana Volunteer Infantry, and served about nine months. He also served in Company B, Twenty-second Regiment, Indiana Volunteer Infantry, and was discharged in August, 1865. At the time of his discharge he was with Sherman's army. He made the march with Sherman from Atlanta to the sea while in service. Mr. Lawyer belonged to the Eighty-second Indiana Volunteer Infantry.

Reverting to the parentage of Mr. Lawyer's third wife, Mrs. Lawyer was the daughter of Lemuel and Nancy (Balsh) Wheeler. Lemuel Wheeler was a farmer near Princeton, and served four years in the Civil War. His children were Marion, Laura, who died in 1878, and Huldah. Mrs. Lawyer's grandfather was Samuel Wheeler.

John A. Lawyer moved to his farm of three hundred and thirty-seven acres in 1894, where he now lives and is engaged in general farming. He formerly lived on the Ziab Graham farm. He has always been extremely prosperous. John A. Lawyer is a member of the township advisory board, and in politics is a Republican. Both he and his wife, as well as the members of his family, are affiliated with the Christian church. Mr. Lawyer is not a man who takes hold of new things quickly. He has always been conservative in his business dealings, but is in every respect reliable and dependable. He is much admired and highly respected in the community where he lives.

Mr. Lawyer built a fine residence in 1898 and also built a good barn, besides making many valuable improvements on the farm. He is a member of the post of the Grand Army of the Republic at Plainville, Indiana, where he enjoys getting around the campfires with the "old boys."

WILLIAM C. AUTERBURN.

Of high intellectual and professional attainments and ranking among foremost teachers of Steele township, Daviess county, Indiana, William C. Auterburn has achieved marked success in the work to which his talent and energy have long been devoted. As a teacher and principal of public schools, he has made his presence felt. His influence in Steele township has always tended to the advancement of the community and the welfare of the people of this township. Mr. Auterburn has a wholesome and stimulating influence on the pupils who have come in contact with him. His name with eminent fitness occupies a conspicuous place in the profession to which he is devoted, and in the historical annals of Daviess county.

William C. Auterburn was born on April 4, 1892, at Plainville, Indiana. He is the son of Samuel P. and Laura A. (Faith) Auterburn, the former of whom was born at Epsom on March 27, 1855, and the latter of whom is the daughter of Abraham and Frances C. (Myres) Faith, who are well-known farmers living near Epsom.

William C. Auterburn was educated in the public schools of Daviess county and in the high school at Plainville. For some time he has been a student in the Indiana State Normal School at Terre Haute, and will be graduated in one more year. For the last four years he has been teaching in the common schools of Daviess county, and during the present year is principal of the Plainville (Indiana) school. Mr. Auterburn was married on April 3, 1915, to Nell McBride, daughter of Wiley and Ida May McBride, of Spokane, Washington. He is a member of the Modern Woodmen of America, the Free and Accepted Masons, and religiously is a member of the Christian church.

Reverting to Mr. Auterburn's ancestors, his grandfather was Isaac Henderson Auterburn, who was born on July 16, 1817, at Louisville, Kentucky, and who died on May 22, 1872. Isaac Henderson Auterburn married Mary Jane Reynolds, who was born on August 25, 1825, and who died on March 13, 1875.

William C. Auterburn's great-grandfather was William Thomas Auterburn, who was born in Virginia, and who married Mary Jane Bledsoe, also a native of Virginia. William T. Auterburn and wife were members of the Christian church. They were farmers and lived near Louisville, Kentucky, most of their lives. Isaac Henderson Auterburn was a cabinetmaker in Louisville until the age of thirty-seven years, when he came to Epsom, in Bogard township, Daviess county, where he became a farmer. He owned two hundred acres of land at the time of his death, and throughout his life was active in the affairs of the Methodist Episcopal church. William C. Auterburn had five children, Samuel P., George W., Sarah S., Martin A. and Mary Jane. Of these children, Samuel P. is the father of William C.; George W. is living in Sikeston, Missouri. He married Dicie Bugher; Sarah E. lives in Bogard township. She married E. L. Grove; Martin A. married Mary Jane Killion, and is living in Sikeston, Missouri; Mary Jane is living near Epsom. She married Joseph T. Browning.

Samuel P. Atterburn, the father of William C. Atterburn, was educated in the common schools in Odon, Indiana, and also in the normal schools. When a young man he obtained a teacher's license, but never taught. He has been a farmer during his entire life, and an active and devoted member of the Methodist church. He is now living retired in Plainville.

To Samuel P. and Laura A. (Faith) Auterburn eight children have been born, Clay H., Alson, Maud J., C. Harvey, Hallie (who died at the age of six years), Roy A., Chauncey and William C. Of these children, Clay H. married Anna Hoover and lives at Bicknell. They have five children, Norman A., Lowell, Thelma, Constant H. and Charles. Clay H. is principal of the schools at Bicknell. Alson married Ola Orender, and they have one child, Opal. Maude J. died on August 10, 1914. She married James S. Watson, who died on April 1, 1914. They had five children,

Alson, Pearl, Laura, Lyle and Rex. C. Harvey married Mattie Orender. They had one child, Ora. Roy A. lives in Chicago. He married Hattie Dawson, and they have two children, Ralph and Harry. Chauncey also lives in Chicago. She married J. C. Rink. They have two children, Joe Merel and Charles J.

Samuel Auterburn is a member of the Independent Order of Odd Fellows and the Knights of Pythias.

STEARER Y. CALLAHAN.

The following is a sketch of a plain, honest man of affairs who, by correct methods and a strict regard for the interests of his neighbors and fellow citizens, has made his influence felt in Madison township and has won for himself distinctive prestige in the agricultural circles of this township. S. Y. Callahan would be the last man to sit for romance or become the subject of fancy eulogy. Nevertheless, his life presents much that is interesting and valuable and which may be studied with profit by young men whose careers are yet to be formed. He is one of those men whose integrity and strength of character must attract to him admirable notice— a notice which modesty never seeks. He commands the respect of his neighbors and, although suffering keenly from a severe affliction, he has maintained his optimism unimpaired. Mr. Callahan has been a hard worker throughout his life and is now in a position to enjoy the fruit of his early labors.

Stearer Y. Callahan was born on April 27, 1852, in Lawrence county, Indiana, and is the son of S. E. and Margaret (Sears) Callahan, the former of whom was born in Lawrence county in 1832, and the latter also a native of Lawrence county, the daughter of Andrew Sears, who was a well-known farmer of that county and a prominent member of the Christian church.

The paternal grandfather of S. Y. Callahan was Isaac Callahan, a native of Kentucky who married Jane Boyd, in that state, and came to Lawrence county, Indiana, where they were farmers. He owned one hundred acres of land and was influential in the Christian church of his county. They had ten children, John T., Elisha B., Southey E., Fannie, Martin, Henry, Sarah, Nancy Jane, Eveline and Polly.

The father of S. Y. Callahan was educated in the common schools of

Lawrence county, where he lived for one year after his marriage. He then moved to Daviess county and settled in Madison township near Odon, where he purchased eighty acres of land. After a few years, he sold this farm and moved to another farm of eighty acres south of Odon, where he lived the remainder of his life. S. E. Callahan was a quiet man who had little to say, but he was an optimist in all things and well satisfied with life, having made a commendable success. He was an ardent Republican. He died about 1899 at the age of sixty-four years. During the Civil War, he served nine months in the service of the Union army. He and his wife had thirteen children: S. Y., William, Annias, deceased; Peter, James, Grant, Joseph, Rebecca Jane, Tabitha, Mary, Stella, Lucinda and Maggie.

Goolie and Mary Ann (Adams) Cunningham are the parents of twelve children: William Thomas, Robert Wesley, Alonzo, Archa, John, Lewis, Mary, Julia, Martha, Lizzie, Alvira, Nancy. Mr. Cunningham was a farmer all his life, an elder in the Christian church and was a stanch Republican. He was born in 1816 and died in 1867, his wife was born in 1821 and died in 1892.

Stearer Y. Callahan, during his youth, was prevented from getting a very extensive education. He lived with his father on the farm and from the time he was a mere lad, was known to be very industrious and painstaking in all that he did.

Mr. Callahan married Martha Cunningham on January 18, 1872, who was born in Daviess county, Indiana, on November 13, 1849, is the daughter of Goolie and Mary Ann (Adams) Cunningham, early settlers in Madison township, Daviess county. To this union four children have been born, Anna, Arla, Daisy and Alva. Anna married Andrew Williams and has one child, Ira. They live in Madison township; Arla, who also lives in Madison township, married Homer Pershing and has two children, Calvin and Raymond; Daisy married Charles Kirk, of Madison township, and has three children, Cletus Verne and Ruth, Olva, who lives in Madison township, married Lula Riggins and has one child, Harold. They live in Madison township.

Mr. and Mrs. Callahan are members of the Christian church. In political affairs, Mr. Callahan is a strong Republican. He owns one hundred acres of land, one mile west of Odon, in Madison township, where Mr. Callahan and his family live. They are among the best-known citizens of Madison township, in which locality Mr. Callahan is respected for his industry, his good management and his kind-hearted, genial disposition.

OLLIE GILLIATT.

If a resume were to be written of the successful and influential business men of Steele township, Daviess county, Indiana, the name of Ollie Gilliatt would occupy a high position. Mr. Gilliatt has added to his natural business ability a wealth of common sense. He is a young man who understands thoroughly all of the interesting details of business principles, and is thoroughly capable of executing any plans which he has previously laid out. Mr. Gilliatt has won for himself a reputation of rare integrity. His courteous, affable nature, favored with a fund of keen analysis, have won for him countless friends and growing patronage among the good people of his community.

Ollie Gilliatt, a prosperous and enterprising young business man of Plainville, Indiana, was born near English, Crawford county. He is the son of J. H. and Sarah (Crems) Gilliatt, the former a native of Orange county, Indiana, and the latter a daughter of David Crems, who was an old-time blacksmith and a farmer in Crawford county. Ollie Gilliatt's grandfather was Harvey Gilliatt, a native of Virginia, born near Lynchburg, who married Amanda Leach, of Kentucky, when they came to Indiana and were among the early settlers of Orange county. Both belonged to the Methodist Episcopal church. Their children were: Leach, Samuel, and James.

J. H. Gilliatt and his wife are both living near Hyatt Station, Indiana. He is a farmer and owns ninety-seven acres of land. They are members of the United Brethren church. Of the eight children born to J. H. and Sarah Gilliatt, Ollie, the subject of this sketch, was the second. The others were Darinda, Leona, Ottis, Myrtle, Maudie, Harvey and Hazel. Mandy and Hazel are deceased.

Ollie Gilliatt was educated in the common schools of Daviess county and at the Indiana State Normal School at Terre Haute. He did not graduate, however, from the latter institution. He taught school in Daviess county for four years, and since that time has been engaged in many different business enterprises. Since 1911, Mr. Gilliatt has been associated with Ernest Kilhon, a well-known banker of this county, in the operation of a general store at Plainville. Since 1909 Mr. Gilliatt and Mr. Kilhon have also been associated together in operating a canning factory. Mr. Gilliatt, however, is a heavy shareholder in the Plainville Flouring Company.

Ollie Gilliatt was married to Catherine Henderson, the daughter of Seth Henderson, a native of Ireland, who came to this country early in life and who was married after his arrival in this country. To Ollie and Catherine (Henderson) Gilliatt three children have been born, Opal, Olene and Lenore, who are all living at home.

Mr. Gilliatt owns a comfortable home in Plainville, where he and his wife and family live. His experience as a teacher in Daviess county naturally accentuated his interest in educational affairs, and in 1909 Mr. Gilliatt was elected trustee of Steele township, serving for six years, or until 1914. He made a splendid record in this office and is given credit for greatly improving the standard of the Steele township schools. He is popular with all classes of people and is especially popular with the teachers of this township who worked for six years under his direction.

Mr. and Mrs. Gilliatt and family are members of the United Brethren church. Mr. Gilliatt is a member of the Free and Accepted Masons, the Independent Order of Odd Fellows and the Modern Woodmen of America. He is also a member of the Knights of Pythias.

JOHN D. MONTGOMERY.

It is a well-authenticated fact that success comes as a result of legitimate and well-applied energy, unflagging determination and perseverance in a course of action when once decided. Success is never known to smile upon the idler or dreamer and never courts the loafer. Only men who have diligently sought her favor are crowned with her blessings. In tracing the history of John D. Montgomery, it is plainly seen that the success which he enjoys has been won by those commendable qualities which will win success anywhere or in any vocation. His personal worth has gained for him the high esteem of many people. Mr. Montgomery, however, is a modest man and lays no great claim to accomplishment or personal achievement, though by virtue of his own perseverance and intelligence he has succeeded in many things.

John D. Montgomery was born in Barr township, Daviess county, Indiana, on October 2, 1858. He is a son of Valentine B. Montgomery and Harriett (Wathen) Montgomery, the former of whom was a native of Washington county, Kentucky. Valentine B. Montgomery's wife died in 1903. She was the daughter of Ceda and Rose Spalding of Kentucky, the former of whom was related to Archbishop Spalding, also to Catherine Spalding, one of the founders of Loretta Academy in Kentucky.

John D. Montgomery's grandfather was James Montgomery, who is thought to have been born in Maryland, where the Montgomery family originated. James Montgomery was a farmer who came to Barr township, Daviess county, in 1816, and located on what is now known as the Doctor McPherson farm. James Montgomery entered this land from the government and lived there the remainder of his life. In 1856 he fell dead while chopping down a tree. James Montgomery was a member of the Catholic church. He married Ann Howard. and to this union were born eight children, Mrs. O'Brian, Valentine B., Rose Ann, Josephine L., Mary E., James, William and John.

Valentine B. Montgomery, the father of John D., reecived very little education during his early life. For a time he was engaged in farming, and owned three hundred and twenty acres of land in Barr township. Later he engaged in the mercantile business with Patrick Larkin at Mt. Pleasant. While in this business he was captain of the boat that carried their merchandise up and down the river. After a time he left the merchandise business and engaged in pork packing for twenty years. He was the father of six children, Henry and Frank W. are deceased; John D. is the subject of this sketch. The other children are Mary E. and Sadie F.; James W. Montgomery lives in California, and is in the insurance and real estate business. He married a Miss Rose, who was the daughter of Senator Rose of California. Senator Rose had the reputation of owning some of the finest racehorses in the world. Mary and Sadie are unmarried and live on the Montgomery homestead farm.

After John D. Montgomery passed through the common schools of Daviess county he attended Notre Dame University for three years, soon after which time he was married to Rose Disser, the daughter of Michael Disser, of Barr township, the latter of whom was a farmer and an ardent member of the Catholic church. He was born near the Rhine river in Germany.

To John D. and Rose (Disser) Montgomery five children have been born. The eldest, Ambrose and Mary, are deceased. The other three children are: Frank, Cletus and Corinne. Of these children, Cletus is living at Hammond, Indiana. He married Thresa Kuntz, and they have one child, John, who is named after his grandfather, John D. Montgomery. The other two children are unmarried and live at home.

Mr. Montgomery has recently gone into the drug business at Montgomery, Indiana. In the earlier part of his life he taught school in Daviess county for seven years, during two years of which time he was principal of the schools at Cannelburg, in Barr township.

Mr. Montgomery is a Democrat, served as surveyor of his county at one time, and was very successful in this office. He and his wife and family are members of the Catholic church.

CHARLES A. BANTA.

An enumeration of the representative citizens of Daviess county would be incomplete without specific mention of the influential and popular farmer, Charles A. Banta, of Steele township. Mr. Banta is a well-known farmer who has been active in politics and who has been a tower of influence in the community where he lives. He is a member of one of the old and highly esteemed families of this township, and for many years has been a public-spirited man of affairs. He has impressed his individuality upon the community and added luster to the honorable name which he bears. Mr. Banta has always been actuated by a spirit of fairness in his dealings with the world in general, and has left no stone unturned whereby he might benefit his own condition as well as that of his friends in this favored section of the great Hoosier commonwealth. Straightforward and unassuming, genial and obliging, Charles A. Banta enjoys the good will and respect of a wide circle of friends throughout this part of the state of Indiana.

Charles A. Banta, a farmer of Steele township, was born on February 29, 1868, in Daviess county, Indiana. He received a good common school education, and when a young man performed the usual tasks which fall to the lot of the farmer boy.

Charles A. Banta is the son of Abraham T. and Eliza Ann (Stephens) Banta, the former of whom was born on December 31, 1823, in Daviess county, and who died on July 24, 1904, and the latter of whom was born on May 10, 1830, and who died on May 25, 1887. They were married on October 2, 1845. Abraham Banta was an active member of the Christian church at Bethany, and was an elder in the church at that place. He was also a soldier in the Civil War. To Abraham and Eliza Ann (Stephens) Banta the following children were born: Elizabeth Jane, on December 20, 1847, died on August 16, 1849; William W., October 8, 1849; Susan Dell, September 27, 1851; Martha Ann, December 18, 1853, died in 1899; Glen

Dora, May 19, 1859; Henry B., October 21, 1862; Sarah Etta, May 22, 1865, died on November 2, 1895; Charles A., February 29, 1868, and Thomas S., March 25, 1871.

The grandfather of Charles A. Banta and the father of Abraham Banta was Henry D. Banta, an early settler in Barr township, Daviess county. He was born in 1790, and died on September 20, 1875. Henry Banta's wife was born on April 30, 1812, and died on January 20, 1877.

At the age of twenty-one Mr. Banta was married to Ida M. Shanks, a daughter of Edward J. Shanks, a farmer of Washington township, Daviess county. The marriage took place on March 31, 1889. Mrs. Banta was born on May 8, 1870. After their marriage, Mr. and Mrs. Banta began housekeeping on the old E. J. Shanks farm in Washington township. In 1893, they moved to Steele township, near Plainville, on a farm of one hundred and sixty acres, southwest of that place, which farm Mr. Banta purchased from James Rink. Later Mr. Banta purchased what is known as the old Booker farm, comprising forty-nine acres. Subsequently, he purchased ten acres from the Rumner farm, and still later, bought one hundred and ten acres of what is known as the Van McHenry farm. Mr. Banta now owns a total of three hundred and twenty-nine acres, and is engaged in general farming and stock raising. It is obvious that Mr. Banta has been very successful from the fact that he has been able to acquire so many farms in a comparatively brief period.

The marriage of Charles A. and Ida M. (Shank) Banta has been blessed with the birth of one son and two daughters, as follow: Noah F. was born on June 8, 1890. He was killed at the age of nineteen in a runaway accident; Garnetta B., June 13, 1897, and Mary B., October 8, 1901.

The father of Mrs. Charles A. Banta, as heretofore noted, was Edward J. Shanks, who was born in Fayette county, Pennsylvania, on November 14, 1830, and died on November 11, 1888. He was one of the early settlers of Daviess county, and also one of those men who went to the gold fields of California, in 1850. He worked four years in the gold mines where he made his start in life. After he returned home, he was married to Celina G. Arison, of Fayette county, Pennsylvania, December 17, 1857. She was born in 1838, and died on August 12, 1879. To them were born one son and six daughters, Sarah Catherine, on January 10, 1860, died on January 17, 1864; Emma Jane, October 17, 1861, died on January 10, 1864; John Franklin, March 15, 1863; Mary Elizabeth, April 3, 1866; Laura Belle, April 24, 1868; Ida May, May 8, 1870, and Anna Martha, January 24, 1873.

The father of Edward J. Shanks was H. N. Shanks, who was born in 1802, and who died on October 4, 1852. The mother of Edward J. Shanks was Sarah Jordan Shanks who was born in 1805, and who died on February 5, 1885.

Charles A. Banta, the immediate subject of this sketch, was elected trustee of Steele township in 1904, and served for four years, until 1908. In that year he was elected a representative in the Indiana State Legislature from Daviess county, and served for two years as a Republican. In 1914, Mr. Banta was again elected trustee, and is now serving in this capacity in Steele township.

The prominence of Charles A. Banta extends beyond the boundaries of Steele township. He is well known throughout Daviess county, not only for his activity in politics, but as one of the substantial farmers of the county. He is a man of strong political convictions, yet a man who is admired and respected by an appreciative people.

OLIVER WALKER.

A review of the life of Oliver Walker must of necessity be brief and general in its character, since to enter fully into the interesting details of Mr. Walker's career, touching the earnest and persistent efforts of his earlier years and successes of later days, would far transcend the limits of this article. He has filled a large place in the ranks of the enterprising and public-spirited business men of his day and has been an important factor in the growth and development of Barr township's agricultural and commercial interests. He is a representative of that sterling type of the world's workers who has furnished much of the bone and sinew of the county and added stability to our country and its institutions. Yet, in spite of his many activities, he has never allowed the pursuit of wealth to warp his kindly nature, but has preserved his faculties and the warmth of his heart for the broadening and helpful influence of human life.

Oliver Walker is a plain, honest business man of affairs, who was born in Daviess county on August 16, 1865, the son of Joseph D. and Margaret (Compton) Walker, the former of whom was born in Daviess county, and the latter in Mt. Pleasant, Indiana, the daughter of Joseph Compton.

Ignatius Walker, the paternal grandfather of Oliver Walker, was a native of Virginia. While a resident of that state, he operated a flat-boat, but after coming to Daviess county, he began farming and was one of the earliest settlers. He was a member of the Catholic church and was married to Mollie Ann Masters.

Joseph E. Walker, the father of Oliver Walker, was educated in the common schools of Daviess county. He was a young man at the outbreak of the Civil War and enlisted in Company D, Twenty-fourth Regiment, Indiana Volunteer Infantry, serving two years, during which time he was seriously injured and came home much impaired in health. Joseph E. Walker was a man of considerable influence in his community and served as justice of the peace of Barr township for many years; he was a member of the United Brethren church, and died on November 3, 1896, at the age of sixty-three. The children born to Joseph E. and Margaret Walker were Oliver, the subject of this sketch; Anna, who is now living at Montgomery, Indiana; Jennie, who lives at Vincennes; Lewis, who lives at Linton,, and Isabella, who is a nun.

After receiving a common school education, Oliver Walker has, throughout his life, been interested in farming. More recently he became interested in the banking business, in which he has been active for the past eight years. For the first five years of that time he was a heavy stockholder in the Montgomery bank, which institution went out of business three years ago, which bank was succeeded by the Farmers and Merchants Bank of Montgomery, Oliver Walker being chosen as its first president. This bank has a flourishing business among the farmers and business men of Barr township.

Oliver Walker was married to Catherine Lanham, the daughter of Levi Lanham, a farmer of Barr township. Two children have been born to this union, both of whom died in infancy.

Mr. Walker owns eighty acres of land in Barr township just on the edge of Montgomery and, while he is active in the bank, also finds time to direct the operations on his farm. From 1893 to 1903 Mr. Walker conducted a saw-mill and lumber business. Previously he was a contractor and builder for about ten years.

There is nothing about the manners or demeanor of Oliver Walker which is in the least pretentious. He is a plain business man of keen discrimination and far-sighted business judgment. For all of these reasons, he has proved a very efficient and popular president of the Farmers and Merchants Bank, and during which time that institution has enjoyed a season of unrivaled prosperity. Mr. Walker deserves to rank as a representative citizen of Daviess county.

JOSEPH E. KETTERY.

Success in this life comes to the deserving. It is an axiom demonstrated by all human experience that a man gets out of this life what he puts into it, with a reasonable interest on the investment. The individual who inherits a large estate and adds nothing to his fortune cannot be called a successful man; he that falls heir to a large fortune and increases its value is successful in proportion to the amount he adds to his possessions; but the man who starts in the world unaided and, by sheer force of will, controlled by correct principles, forges ahead and at length reaches a position of honor among his fellow citizens, achieves success such as representatives of the two former classes can neither understand nor appreciate. To a considerable extent the subject of this sketch is a creditable representative of the class last named—a class which has furnished much of the bone and sinew of the country and added to the stability of our government and institutions. Joseph E. Kettery had the good fortune to be born of worthy parents, and this was his first great start in life.

Mr. Kettery was born on February 7, 1873, in Madison county, Indiana. He is the son of Jacob and D. M. C. (Foust) Kettery, the former of whom was born on August 2, 1848, in Wayne county, Indiana, and the latter in 1851, in Tennessee, the daughter of Joseph Foust, a farmer of that state. Jacob Kettery was educated in the common schools, and throughout his life was a farmer. The first part of his life was spent in Madison county, this state, the last twenty years of which have been spent in Daviess county. He died on February 23, 1900, while his wife, the mother of Joseph E., is still living in Plainville. She is a member of the Methodist Episcopal church, and has been active in the work of this church throughout her life. Her deceased husband was also a member of this church. He was a Democrat, and owned eighty acres of land in Bogard township. This is the farm upon which Joseph E. Kettery now lives.

The grandfather of Joseph E. Kettery was Joseph Kettery, Sr., a native of Germany, who came to America, before his marriage, with one brother. After arriving in America they were separated and never again saw each other. Some of the present generation of Ketterys have learned that the missing brother settled in Madison county, Indiana, and the other brother in Orange county, Indiana. Joseph Kettery lived in Madison county and was among the first settlers of that county. He owned one hundred and sixty acres there. His children were John, Joseph, Jacob, Lydia, Jane, Mary and Elizabeth. Mary and Elizabeth are the only living children.

Joseph E. Kettery was educated in the public schools and, early in life, spent three years in railroad work. At the age of thirty-four, or in 1910, Mr. Kettery came to Daviess county to his present farm.

On December 15, 1897, Joseph E. Kettery was married to Laura F. Hardy, who was born on December 15, 1875. She was the daughter of Francis and Hannah (Sparks) Hardy, of Daviess county, where they are farmers. They are devoted and prominent members of the United Brethren church.

To Joseph E. and Laura F. (Hardy) Kettery four children have been born, Ruby May, Pearl Angeline, Ruth Sunshine and Earl Elsworth.

Mr. Kettery owns eighty acres of land in Daviess county and also farms the farm which his mother owns. He owns a large amount of personal property and a share in his mother's estate. Fraternally, Mr. Kettery is a member of the Ben-Hur tribe.

WILSON S. SMILEY.

Well-defined purpose and consecutive effort in the affairs of life will inevitably result in attaining a true measure of success. In following the career of one who has won success by his own efforts, there comes into view the strong individuality which made such accomplishments possible and there is thus granted an objective incentive and inspiration, while at the same time there is enkindled a feeling of respect and admiration. The qualities which have made Wilson S. Smiley one of the prominent and successful farmers of Van Buren township, Daviess county, Indiana, have also won for him the esteem of his fellow citizens. His career has been one of well-directed energies, strong determinations and honorable methods. He has filled a large place in the political, civic and moral life of his community, and has especially done very much in behalf of the educational standards of Van Buren township, which he served for six years as trustee.

Wilson S. Smiley was born on February 20, 1857, in Tuscarawas county, Ohio. He is the son of Abner G. and Esther B. (Bair) Smiley, the former of whom was born in Tuscarawas county and died in 1908, at the age of seventy-eight years, and the latter of whom was a native of Ohio, whose parents came from Pennsylvania.

George Smiley, the grandfather of W. S. Smiley, was a native of Ohio, where he has lived during his entire life. He was a farmer and a devout member of the Lutheran church.

Abner G. Smiley, the father of W. S., was educated in the common schools and, as a young man, worked in a store at Winfield, Ohio. Later he entered into partnership with the owner of the store, and after a few years lost all of the money he had saved in this venture. He then took his family to a farm in Tuscarawas county, where he succeeded so well that he was able to purchase eighty acres of land. He paid for this farm in small installments of five and ten dollars each, until the debt was all paid off. Subsequently this farm was sold and he undertook to purchase a much larger one. His neighbors who owned the farm, however, refused to sell it to him because it was thought that he could not pay for it and was entirely too big an undertaking. At this time Abner G. Smiley declared that there was land in other states, and brought his family to Daviess county, Indiana, where he purchased one hundred and sixty acres of land in Van Buren township. This farm is still held by the Smiley family. The last eight years of Mr. Smiley's life he lived retired in Odon. He was never physically strong, but was possessed with great energy and was a hard worker always. He was a member of the United Brethren church and was a liberal contributor to the support of this church. He was an ardent Democrat. He and his wife were the parents of five children, Payson, W. Seward, Royland, R. P. and Wallace. Of these children, Payson married Angeline Bigler, of Van Buren township; Royland married Clara Darks and lives in Washington; R. P. first married Sarah Trueblood and later Mary Oliver; he lives on the old homestead. Wallace is unmarried and lives in Odon with his mother.

Wilson S. Smiley was educated in the common schools and taught two terms in Van Buren township. He was married, at the age of twenty-two, to Emma Danner, who died on June 15, 1911, at the age of fifty years. She was the daughter of Joseph and Amelia (Vandever) Danner. Joseph Danner was a farmer in Van Buren township. By this marriage five children were born, Curtis, Irwin, Addie, Eva and Raleigh. Of these children, Curtis lives in Indianapolis, and married Emma Hall; Irwin married Myrtle Kelsey and lives in Van Buren township; Addie married E. W. Montgomery and lives at Bedford, Indiana; Eva and Raleigh are still single.

After the death of Mrs. Emma Smiley, Mr. Smiley was married a second time to Dove Satterfield, of Plainville. Her maiden name was Dove Trueblood, she being the daughter of Mark Trueblood. No children have been born to this second marriage. Mrs. Smiley is a graduate of the Terre Haute Normal School and taught school for fifteen years in Loogootee, Franklin and Elwood.

Mr. Smiley owns one hundred and twenty acres of land in Van Buren township and is a general farmer. He devotes considerable attention, however, to stock raising.

Mr. and Mrs. Smiley are members of the Methodist church. Mr. Smiley is a Democrat in politics and served one term of six years, from 1908 to 1914, as trustee of Van Buren township.

ADOLPHUS G. WILLIAMS.

To write the personal record of men who have raised themselves from humble circumstances to a position of trust and responsibility in a community is no ordinary pleasure. Self-made men who have achieved success by reason of their personal qualities, and who have left the impress of their individuality upon the business and agricultural development of their home, neighborhood and township, and who affect for good the institutions of their community, unwittingly perhaps, built monuments more enduring than marble obelisk or granite shaft. To such it is unquestionably proper to say that Adolphus G. Williams belongs.

Adolphus G. Williams was born on March 25, 1850, in Franklin county, Indiana. He is the son of Solomon Williams and his second wife, who was Hannah Vanmeter, the latter of whom is a daughter of a well-known farmer living in Michigan. By this second marriage of Solomon Williams seven children were born, Adolphus G., John (deceased), Clarence Lee, Charles, Eugene, Augusta Bradfoot and Ada Palmer. Of these children, John married twice, the first time to Callie Johnson, who died; the second time he married Callie Giddings; Clarence Lee lives in Terre Haute; he married Anna Courtney; Charles lives in Missouri; he married Anna Hollingsworth and after her death was married to Janie Alford; Eugene lives in Indianapolis; he married Pearlie Barmore.

Solomon Williams's first wife was a Miss Clemens. By this marriage six children were born, Isabella, Louisa, Henrietta, Missouri and Sarah Ann. Solomon Williams was educated in the common schools and was a man of wide political influence in Daviess county, having served in many important offices. He was county recorder of Daviess county for a period of four years, and assessor of Bogard township. He was identified with the Republican party during his entire life. He moved to Daviess county in 1861, and settled in Steele township, where he owned one hundred and sixty acres, but after a time moved to Washington township, where he owned one hundred and ten acres. Here he remained the rest of his life and died in 1888.

Adolphus G. Williams, the subject of this sketch, was educated in the public schools of Daviess county, and with the exception of three years, during which he was in the mercantile business at Epsom, he has been a farmer all his life. Mr. Williams owns one hundred and forty acres in Bogard township, and is engaged in farming at the present time. He has made a rather unusual success of his chosen vocation.

Mr. Williams has been twice married. He was first married, in 1876, to Mary Sheppard, but no children were born to this marriage. Subsequently he was married, in 1882, to Anza M. Cummings, born on July 24, 1861, and a daughter of Malachi and Elizabeth A. (Robinson) Cummings. By this second union eight children were born, Walter, Maud, Richard, Bert, Bertha, Joseph, Edna and Alma. Of these children, Walter married Lula Williams, who, however, was not a relative; they live in Linton, Indiana; Maud married Austin Osmon; they live in Bogard township; Richard married Josephine Clossman; Bert married Lucy Templin and they live in Indianapolis. The remainder of the children are single and live at home.

Mrs. Adolphus G. Williams, as heretofore stated, was a daughter of Malachi and Elizabeth A. (Robinson) Cummings, the former a native of Jackson county, and the latter a native of Brown county, having been born near Nashville. Malachi Cummings moved to a farm within one mile of Odon, consisting of two hundred acres. In addition to being a farmer, he was also a preacher in the Christian church, and was active in politics, having held many local offices. Malachi Cummings was twice married. Mrs. Williams is a daughter by his second wife. The other children by the second wife were Robert, John, Susan, William, Levi and Joseph. Mr. Cummings' first wife was Polly Brown, who bore him two children, Evaline, who lives at Odon, Indiana, married John Sears, and Jane, the latter of whom is deceased. Malachi Cummings was the son of David Cummings, who was born in 1756 and who died in 1840. He was a native of Virginia, and moved to Tennessee in 1808. He married Sarah Keithly, and their children were as follow: John K., Joseph, Malachi, Eliza, Tabitha, Mary, Rosanna, Catherine, Rebecca and Jemimah. David Cummings moved to Lawrence county in 1815, and was elected county commissioner in 1816. He was one of the first commissioners of this county. He died at the age of eighty-four years. The land which he owned near Bedford he entered from the government. David Cummings was the son of Joseph Cummings, a soldier in the Revolutionary army, who was present at the surrender of Cornwallis at Yorktown.

Adolphus G. Williams, although a man well advanced in years, is a man who has earned for himself, by honorable and exacting toil, a substantial competence in life. He enjoys the esteem of the people in his community, and is entirely worthy of the confidence which his neighbors have placed in him.

He votes the Republican ticket and is a member of the Christian church.

CECIL S. SMITH.

Perseverance and sterling worth are almost sure to win conspicuous recognition in any locality and in any vocation. Cecil S. Smith, one of the most successful teachers in Daviess county, Indiana, although a very young man, is already recognized as a promising leader in the educational affairs of this section of the state. Mr. Smith has worked hard for success and his present attainments are only the natural results of his well-applied efforts. He had the advantage, however, in the beginning, of having been endowed with an unusually alert mind, and this he has used to the very best advantage. He possesses the talent and character to carry him upward in educational work. A young man of strong fiber and vigorous mentality, it may be said truly that he has already achieved a signal success, whatever his future accomplishments.

Cecil S. Smith was born on September 23, 1894, in Sullivan county, Indiana. He is the son of John V. and Catherine (Sproatt) Smith, the latter of whom is the second wife of John V. Smith, a native of Sullivan county, Indiana, whose present wife is a native of New Russellville, Illinois, the daughter of Reason R. Sproatt, a well-known farmer of Knox county, and one of the leading members of the Christian church in that county.

James Smith was the grandfather of Cecil Smith. He was a native of Clark county, and settled in Sullivan county, where he became an influential farmer and a leader in the Baptist church of Greene county. He and his wife had nine children, William S., John V., Martha, Margaret, Eliza, James, Nancy B., Ida I. and Louis M.

John V. Smith, the second son of his parents, and the father of the subject of this sketch, attended Franklin College when a young man and also took a normal course at various places. He taught thirteen years in the public schools of Sullivan and Knox counties and made a splendid record in this vocation. He was first married to Laura E. Miller and by this union three children were born: Leon V., Laura Fay and Blanche, all of whom are now deceased. The children of John V. Smith by his second marriage are: Cecil S., Mary J., and Ralph E. Mr. Smith is a member of the Baptist church, and an active member of the Socialist party. John V. Smith's second wife was the widow of George Eastridge, of Knox county, and to this union one child was born, Redmond R. He is located in Chicago, Illinois, as a telegraph operator for New York Central lines, Lake Shore & Michigan Southern Railroad Company. He is a graduate of Oaktown high school and took a course in telegraphy at Valparaiso. Fraternally, he is a member of the Independent Order of Odd Fellows. In 1911, he moved from Knox to Daviess county, and purchased eighty acres of land in Van Buren township, where he is now engaged in farming. He is a man of more than average attainment and well informed regarding all political and economic issues. His son, Cecil S., has inherited many of the intellectual qualities of the father.

Cecil S. Smith was graduated from the Odon high school in 1912, and has been teaching school since that time. During the summers of 1913-14, he was a student of the Danville Normal School at Danville, Indiana, where he was further equipping himself for his vocation as a teacher. He is now teaching in Van Buren township, district No. 7, and is popular among the patrons and pupils of this district. It is the young men of the present generation upon whom depend the future progress and prosperity of our country and no young man in Daviess county has a more promising career or is more certain to bear his share of the responsibility than is Cecil S. Smith.

A. L. STANDIFORD.

There is no positive rule for achieving success and yet, in the life of a successful man, there are always lessons which might well be followed. The man who gains prosperity is he who can see and utilize the opportunities which come in his way. The essential conditions of human life are ever the same. The surroundings of individuals differ but slightly, and when one man passes another on the highway of life to reach the goal of prosperity before others who perhaps started out before him, it is because he has the power to use advantages which probably fall within the purview of the whole human race. Among the prominent citizens and successful business men of Steele township, is A. L. Standiford, a well-known merchant of Plainville. The qualities of keen discrimination, sound judgment and executive ability enter very largely into his makeup, and have been contributive elements to the material success which has come to him.

Mr. Standiford was born on September 30, 1871, in Clark county, Indiana. He is the son of Cornelius Standiford, a native of Floyd county, this state, who in turn was the son of Nathan Standiford, a native of Kentucky.

Nathan Standiford was a school teacher and farmer in Floyd county, and a local Methodist preacher. He and his wife had six children, James, Eliza, Aquilla, Martha, Tabitha and Cornelius.

Cornelius Standiford, the youngest child born to his parents and the father of the subject of this sketch, was educated in the common schools of Floyd county, where he was a successful farmer before moving to Daviess county, where, in 1871, he was married to Martha Swim, who died in 1879, at the age of thirty-five years, he had died, previously, in 1875, at the age of thirty-nine years. Cornelius Standiford belonged to the Methodist church, and was always active in the work of that church and the Sunday school. Of the eight children born to Cornelius and Martha (Swim) Standiford, only three are living, James, Martha and Aquilla L. The deceased children are Nathan, Elizabeth, Katurah, William C., Eliza. Cornelius Standiford was a soldier in the Civil War, where he served three years in the Fifty-third Regiment, Indiana Volunteer Infantry. During a severe engagement he received a painful wound in the right hand, a bullet having passed through four of his fingers. Aquilla L. Standiford was educated in the public schools of Indiana, and for several years was a successful farmer, but finally gave up this vocation for other things.

Mr. Standiford was married to Demia Mallet, the daughter of W. W. and Phoebe (Byrer) Mallet, the former a well-known farmer of Bogard township, where he lived after his marriage, and worked by the day until 1893, when he went into the mercantile business at Epsom. He was in business for about six years, and then returned to a farm near that place. The following year he moved to Houston, Texas, and remained there for about four months, after which he returned to Epsom, and finally to Plainville, in 1910, when he opened a general supply store. In addition to his general business, Mr. Standiford also owns eighty acres of land in Steele township, which is well improved.

To Aquilla L. and Demia (Mallet) Standiford six children have been born, Pearl, Ruth, Mamie, Omer, Bessie and Eugene. All of these children are unmarried and live at home.

Mr. Standiford is identified with the Democratic party, and has been honored by the people of Bogard township on two occasions, having been elected assessor in 1910, and trustee of the township in 1904. He was in office, therefore, during the period of eight consecutive years, from 1900 to 1908. Mr. Standiford is a member of the Christian church. Fraternally, he is a member of the Knights of Pythias.

CHARLES GREEN SEFRIT.

Charles Green Sefrit, of Washington, general manager of the Gazette and Herald Company and editor of the newspapers printed by the company, the *Washington Herald* (daily) and the *Washington Gazette* (weekly), was born in Barr township, Daviess county, Indiana, in a log house that stood on the bank of Prairie creek, February 18, 1860. His father was Moses L. B. Sefrit, who died in 1892, and his mother was Eleanor McDonald, whose death occurred two years later. Both the Sefrits and the McDonalds belong to the earlier of the pioneer families of Daviess county. George Sefrit, the first of the name in Daviess county and the great-grandfather of the subject of this sketch, came with his children from Pennsylvania and settled in Daviess county. George Sefrit's parents were natives of Holland. In the time of the American Revolution his father was assassinated by a Tory. George Sefrit lived to be one hundred years old, and even at this great age his death was an unnatural one, for it resulted from injuries received in a fall. George Sefrit's funeral sermon was preached by the Rev. John Poucher, then a young Methodist preacher riding his first circuit; now an aged man, but yet in the service of the church, at this time stationed at Salem, Washington county, Indiana.

George Sefrit's son Charles was the father of Moses L. B. Sefrit. Charles G. Sefrit was named for his grandfather Sefrit and his mother's brother, Capt. Green McDonald, a Union veteran, who served the full term of the Civil War. Mr. Sefrit's maternal grandfather was Francis McDonald, who married Asenath Allen. The Allens were among the first of the white citiens of Daviess county, as were the Everetts, from which family came Mr. Sefrit's grandmother on his father's side, Elizabeth Everett, who

CHARLES G. SEFRIT.

kept up the family record for longevity by living to her ninety-sixth year. Francis McDonald, Mr. Sefrit's grandfather on his mother's side, came with his father, whose name also was Francis, from Kentucky in 1815. Francis McDonald I, however, was born in Scotland. He started with his parents for the United States when he was twelve years old, but all the other members of his family perished on shipboard from a pestilence that broke out when the vessel was on the high seas and caused the death of nearly all the passengers and part of the crew.

Charles G. Sefrit was married in 1880, his wife being Sarah Mulholland, daughter of Capt. Samuel H. Mulholland, a Union veteran, captain of Company I, Sixty-fifth Regiment Indiana Volunteer Infantry, and Ellen Kidwell. Mr. and Mrs. Sefrit have four daughters: Mrs. Ethel Hyatt, wife of Harry V. Hyatt, of Chicago; Mrs. Nell Graham, wife of Joseph B. Graham, of Evansville; Mrs. Claire Scoble, wife of Roy Scoble, of Washington, and Miss Ruth Sefrit. They have four granddaughters, Elinor, Virginia and Sara Elizabeth Graham and Sara Emily Hyatt, and one grandson, Joe Graham, Jr.

Mr. Sefrit enjoys the unusual distinction of having had a personal acquaintance with six generations of his own family—his great-grandfather Sefrit, who died when Charles G. Sefrit was seven years old; his grandfather Sefrit; his father; his own brothers and sisters; his own children, and his grandchildren, the eldest of whom at this writing is seven years old. Mr. Sefrit has one brother living, Frank I. Sefrit, manager of the *American Reveille*, published at Bellingham, in the state of Washington. His parents are dead, but two of his father's sisters and three of his mother's sisters are living, all of them far along in years.

Charles G. Sefrit has been in the newspaper business nearly all his life. He began as a reporter on the old *Washington Gazette*, when he was eighteen years old, and, except for brief intervals, has been associated with that paper since that time. He has been closely connected with Indiana politics, and was writing political editorials before he reached his majority, but never has held a public office, save for a period when he was the financial agent of the Southern Indiana Hospital for the Insane at Evansville, which situation he relinquished in 1904 to return to Washington and become the manager of the *Herald*. A year later the *Herald* and the *Gazette* were consolidated, with Mr. Sefrit as the managing editor.

Mr. Sefrit has done some newspaper work outside of Washington. For a time in 1908 he was engaged as the special representative of the *Cincinnati*

Enquirer, supplying that paper with letters from the Southern states in the preliminaries of the presidential campaign of that year. He also has had much service with the Indiana Republican state committee; was a member of the Republican state executive committee in 1906 and chairman of that committee in 1910. He is one of the best known of the newspaper men of Indiana.

BENJAMIN H. RITTER.

The life of a professional man seldom exhibits any of those striking incidents that seize upon public opinion and attract attention to themselves. His character is generally made up of those qualities elicited by the exercise of the peculiar duties of his vocation or the particular profession to which he belongs. When a young man has so impressed his individuality upon his fellow men as to gain their confidence and, through that confidence, has been able to advance to the front ranks of his profession, he becomes at once a conspicuous figure in the locality where he works and where his labors are performed. Benjamin H. Ritter is a well-known young man of Bogard township, Daviess county, Indiana, who has made remarkable progress as a teacher and who expects shortly to turn his attention to law, in which he may be expected to experience a like success. His friends predict that he will forge to the front in this responsible and exacting vocation and earn for himself an honorable reputation as a leader in the legal fraternity of any community where he chooses to practice.

Benjamin H. Ritter was born on July 3, 1888, in Bogard township, Daviess county, Indiana. He is the son of W. H. and Jennie (Bugher) Ritter, the former of whom is a native of Bogard township and the latter the daughter of Asa and Elizabeth (Myres) Bugher, pioneer farmers in Bogard township and prominent members of the Methodist Episcopal church and of the Grange. Asa Bugher was a soldier in the Civil War and, during his service in the Union army, was shot through the arm. This wound disabled him for some time and finally resulted in total paralysis.

The grandfather of Benjamin H. Ritter was Jacob Ritter, a farmer, whose parents were early settlers in Indiana. He married Elizabeth Schneider and became the father of four children, Jennie, Mary, W. H. and James. Jacob Ritter was also a soldier in the Civil War and was killed in the service in a powder explosion in the state of Kentucky.

W. H. Ritter, the father of Benjamin H., has always been a farmer.

His opportunities for an education during his youth were limited, but he has improved his time by home study and is very actvie in the local affairs of Bogard township. He was instrumental in bringing about the consolidation of the Bogard township schools in Epsom and the erection of the large school building at that place. Mr. Ritter is an influential member of the Methodist Episcopal church, as are his wife and children, five of whom have been born to them: Benjamin H., Walter J., Minnie, Clay and Roscoe. All of these children are single, except Walter J., who married Versie Mallett and they have three children, Ola, Olive and an infant daughter.

Benjamin H. Ritter was educated in the common schools of Bogard township and later graduated from the Northern Indiana Normal University, at Valparaiso. He has taught school for eight years, the last four of which he has been a teacher in the high school, one year of which was spent at Center, Indiana. Prior to that time he taught in the common schools of Bogard township. The last three years he has been engaged as principal of the high school at Epsom, in Bogard township.

Benjamin H. Ritter is a brilliant young man and a successful teacher. He is popular in Bogard township among all the people, and especially among the students and patrons of the Epsom high school. He has never married. Fraternally, he is a member of the Free and Accepted Masons, is a member of the Methodist Episcopal church, and is a young man who thoroughly merits the confidence which has been reposed in him by the people of his community. He is industrious, genial in nature and democratic in his manner. In the future, Mr. Ritter expects to turn his attention to law and in this connection it is only fair to say that a large measure of success awaits him.

ALBERT BUZAN.

Albert Buzan is a prosperous farmer, widely known in Bogard township, and is one of the honored citizens of Daviess county, where he is living after a life of strenuous activities in farming. His well-directed efforts in the practical affairs of life, his capable management of business interests and his sound judgment, have brought to him more than an ordinary measure of prosperity. His life demonstrates what may be accomplished by a man of energy and ambition, a man who is not afraid to work and who has the perseverance to continue his labors in the face of disaster and discouragements. In all the relations of life Mr. Buzan has commanded the confidence and respect of those with whom he has been brought in contact. A biographical history of this locality would not be complete without a record of his career.

Albert Buzan was born on February 16, 1852, in Barr township, Daviess county, Indiana. He is the son of John W. and Sarah (Perkins) Buzan, the first wife of John W., who himself was a native of Barr township, Daviess county, born on August 6, 1831. Sarah Perkins was born on February 16, 1832, in Barr township, Daviess county. She was the daughter of Alfred and Rebecca (Ellis) Perkins, the former of whom was a native of Kentucky. John W. Buzan was the son of William and Elizabeth (Waller) Buzan, the former a native of Kentucky, who came to Indiana early in its history and entered one hundred and sixty acres of land in Van Buren township in Daviess county. He was a well-known hunter and Indian fighter, and one time during his life swore vengeance against the Indians. The children of William and Elizabeth Buzan were: George, Martha, William and John W.

John W. Buzan was educated in the common schools of Daviess county, was a well-known farmer and owned in excess of one hundred acres in Daviess county. He was a devoted member of the Christian church. He served three years in the Union army during the Civil War. While in the service he became speechless. He was a sharpshooter attached to Sherman's army in his march to the sea, belonging to Company I, Sixty-fifth Regiment, Indiana Volunteer Infantry, and serving directly under Captain Childs and under Capt. Samuel Munholland. John W. and Sarah Buzan had seven children, Albert, Maria, Lafayette, William, Nettie, John W. and Martha F. All of these children, except Albert and Martha F., are deceased. Martha F. lives near St. Louis Crossing, Bartholomew county, Indiana.

Albert Buzan was educated in the common schools and throughout his life has been a farmer. He lived in Washington township, Daviess county, until thirteen years ago. In 1902 he purchased a farm of one hundred acres in Bogard township and has lived upon this farm since that date. Mr. Buzan is a man who is willing to take his share of public and civic responsibility. He is well and favorably known in Bogard township.

Albert Buzan was married on October 6, 1875, to Sarah A. Jones, the daughter of Thomas and Ruth (Freeland) Jones, well-known farmers of Daviess county and influential members of the Christian church. To this union four children have been born, Elmer H., Bertha S., Theodosia and Maria. Theodosia and Maria are deceased; Elmer H., who lives in Washington, married Pearl Fickey and has two children, Ruby Elbert and Norwood. He is treasurer of Daviess county at the present time, and a man of wide political influence; Bertha S. is unmarried and is keeping house for her father. Mrs. Buzan died some years ago.

Albert Buzan is a well-known and prominent member of the Christian church, and is a Republican in political affairs.

WIRTSEL V. ROSENBURY.

One of the well-known young men of Van Buren township, Daviess county, Indiana, is Wirtsel V. Rosenbury, a man of unassuming manners and extremely modest in his claim to preferment. He was graduated from the Odon high school in 1914, and subsequently attended the Indiana State Normal School at Terre Haute. He is now a successful young school teacher in Van Buren township and has charge of the Patterson school.

Wirtsel V. Rosenbury was born on September 10, 1895, in Van Buren township, Daviess county. He is the son of George William and Clementine (Overton) Rosenbury, the former of whom was born on December 4, 1869, in Van Buren township, and the latter of whom was born on October 14, 1871, in Madison township. Wirtsel Rosenbury's mother is the daughter of Anderson Overton, a farmer of Madison township, who owns about one hundred and sixty acres of land. The Overtons were early settlers in Madison township.

Wirtsel V. Rosenbury's grandfather was Josiah Rosenbury, a native of Ohio, who lived in Tuscarawas county, and who was married to Sarah Penrod. They moved to Indiana after their marriage and were pioneers in Daviess county. In 1860 Josiah Rosenbury purchased land near Raglesville. He was a member of the United Brethren church, and an active worker in that church. He and his wife were the parents of eight children, Harry Belden, who is deceased; Emma, George William, Sallie, Bertha, Joseph E., Minnie and Mary.

George William Rosenbury was the third child born to his parents. He was educated in the common schools and throughout his life has lived in Daviess county. He owns one hundred and thirty acres of splendid farming land in Madison township and Van Buren township. While he has engaged in general farming he also operates a dairy and keeps a great number of Holstein cattle. Seven children have been born to George W. Rosenbury and wife, Wirtsel being the eldest. The other children are: Wallace, Arnold, Harry, Irene, Myrtle and Edith.

George William Rosenbury and his family are all active members of the United Brethren church and Sunday school. Fraternally, George William is a member of the Modern Woodmen of America. Wirtsel V. Rosenbury is unmarried. He is a young man who is very fond of the vocation he has chosen and who promises to become one of the successful teachers of Daviess county. He has inherited from his father and mother the good qualities of body and mind, and is a close student of all current historical events. He is not only popular with the pupils and patrons of the Patterson school, where he is now teaching, but he is likewise popular in the neighborhood where he was born and reared and where he is so well known.

HAMAN WOODLING.

It was once remarked by a celebrated moralist and biographer that there has scarcely passed a life of which a judicious and faithful narrative would not have been useful. Believing in the truth of this opinion, expressed by one of the greatest and best of men, the writer of this review takes pleasure in presenting a few facts in the career of a gentleman who, by industry, perseverance, temperance and integrity, has worked himself from an humble station to a successful place in life, and who has won an honorable position among the well-known and highly esteemed men of Van Buren township, Daviess county, Indiana.

Haman Woodling, the subject of this sketch, was born in Stark county, Ohio, on January 20, 1842. He is the son of Andrew and Catherine (Kern) Woodling, the former born in Pennsylvania in 1800, and the latter born in that state, three miles from the Delaware Water Gap, in 1807. Catherine Kern was the daughter of John Kern, a native of Prussia, where he was a farmer. He was a member of the Lutheran church and, after coming to America, settled in Pennsylvania, where he lived the rest of his life. The grandfather of Haman Woodling was Andrew Woodling, Sr., a soldier in the War of 1812, and a farmer by occupation, who lived and died in Pennsylvania.

Andrew Woodling, Jr., the father of Haman Woodling, was educated in the common schools. He removed from Pennsylvania to Stark county, Ohio, in 1833, where he owned two hundred and sixty acres of land. Later he removed to Stark county, where he lived the remainder of his life. He and his wife had seven children. The first three, Bernard, Amos and Julia Ann, are deceased. Rachel and Daniel are also deceased, Daniel dying when an infant. Haman and Simon P. are still living. Of these children, Amos was county surveyor of Tuscarawas county, Ohio, for nine years, and also a justice of the peace in Franklin township. The late President McKinley practiced law in the court of Amos Woodling when a young man; Bernard was a farmer in Ohio; Simon Peter is a farmer in Daviess county, Indiana. Andrew Woodling, Jr., the father of these children, was a member of the Lutheran church and active in its affairs. He was an ardent Democrat throughout his life. Andrew Woodling died in October, 1872. His wife died in February, 1880.

Haman Woodling was educated in the common schools and lived with his father until he reached maturity. He was married on June 23, 1864, to Mary Jane Allen, the daughter of Samuel Allen, a native of Scotland, who came to America where he was a farmer. By this first marriage seven children were born, Andrew A. is deceased; Mary B. is also deceased; the other children are: William Oscar, Edgar Evans, Rachel Minerva, Flora May and Frank Haman. Of these children, William Oscar lives in St. Louis, Missouri; he married Emma Henry, of that city, and they have one child, Mable; Edgar Evans lives in Daviess county on a farm; he married May Perkins, and they have four children, Norman, Viola, Ray and Frank; Rachel Minerva lives in Greensburg; she married Harry Kretsch, and they have one child, Russell; Flora May lives in Indianapolis; she married Cass Kretsch, a brother of Harry Kretsch, and they have one child, Madge; Frank lives in St. Louis; he is unmarried, and is employed in the office of the Missouri Pacific & Iron Mountain Railroad.

Haman Woodling was married the second time to Catherine (Wrape) Morgan, who was born on January 17, 1848, in Jennings county, and who is the daughter of Henry and Ann (Bible) Wrape. Henry Wrape was a native of Ireland and a devout member of the Catholic church. His wife was a native of Germany. They lived in Jennings county all their lives, where they owned eighty acres of land. Their children were John, Robert, Catherine and Henry. Henry Wrape, Sr., was the son of Robert Wrape, who was a native of Ireland and who never came to America.

In 1866 Mr. Woodling came to Daviess county and purchased one hundred and fifty-nine acres of land in Van Buren township, where he now lives. Mr. Woodling taught two terms of school in Stark county, Ohio, before coming to Indiana, and one term after his arrival here. He represented Daviess county in the Indiana Legislature in 1883, and was a Democrat and served one term as county councilman from 1910 to 1914. He and his wife are members of different churches. He is a member of the United Brethren church and his wife a member of St. Michael's Catholic church of Bogard township. By his second marriage Mr. Woodling was the father of one child, Calvin, who died at the age of one year.

Haman Woodling is now retired upon his farm. He is a keen student of government and is a well-informed man regarding political questions. He is a prominent citizen in Van Buren township. He has been active in Sunday school work and has been its superintendent many years.

HENRY POINDEXTER.

In the daily laborious struggle for an honorable competence and a substantial career on the part of the average farmer, there is little to attract the casual reader in search of a sensational chapter, but to a mind thoroughly awake to the reality and meaning of human existence, there are noble and imperishable lessons in the career of an individual who, without other means than a clear head, strong arm and true heart, directed and controlled by correct principles and unerring judgment, conquers adversity and, toiling on, finally wins not only pecuniary independence, but what is far greater and higher, the deserved respect and confidence of those with whom his active years have brought him in contact. Such a man is found in the person of Henry Poindexter, the proprietor of a fertile farm in Bogard township, Daviess county, Indiana.

Henry Poindexter was born on February 27, 1873, in Martin county. He is the son of Paton and Elizabeth (Keutch) Poindexter, the former of whom was born about 1848, in Martin county, and the latter of whom was the daughter of Finley Keutch, a farmer of Martin county. Paton Poindexter was the son of Christian Poindexter, a native of Ireland, who married Lucinda Keck, a native of Martin County, this state. He was a farmer, owning about five hundred acres of land, and an extensive dealer in live stock, a business in which he accumulated a substantial fortune. Mr. Poindexter was a member of the Methodist church and active in its work. He served as county commissioner of Martin county at one time. Fraternally, he was a member of the Masonic fraternity. Christian and Lucinda Poindexter had eleven children, Ida, deceased; Amelia, Lorinda, deceased; Whitton, Rufus, John, Christian, Tillman, William, Paton and Wiley. Christian Poindexter was the son of Samuel Poindexter, a native of Ireland, who came to America, after his marriage, with his family. He settled in Martin county, north of Loogootee on a farm, was a soldier in the Revolutionary army and an influential member of the Christian church.

Henry Poindexter, the subject of this sketch, was educated in the common schools and has been a farmer all of his life. He moved to the farm where he now lives eleven years ago and rented it for nine years, purchasing it two years ago, which farm comprises one hundred acres. Henry Poindexter is engaged in general farming and stock raising. He has made a specialty of Duroc-Jersey hogs.

Henry Poindexter was married on December 16, 1901, to Anna E Hatry, the daughter of Aaron Hatry, a carpenter and contractor of Raglesville. Mr. and Mrs. Poindexter have had two children, Flossie May and Irwin, an infant, who died in 1908.

Henry Poindexter and wife are members of the Christian church, while Mr. Poindexter is a member of the Independent Order of Odd Fellows and of the Knights of Pythias. Henry Poindexter is a man who is popular in the community where he lives, because of his genial good nature and his sympathy in the progress and prosperity of his neighbors. He occupies one of the richest farms in the community and is making rather a complete success in his chosen profession.

Reverting to Mr. Poindexter's father, Paton Poindexter, it may be said that he is still living in Epsom in Bogard township. He came to Daviess county twenty-seven years ago and, although he was at one time a man of considerable wealth, he had the misfortune to lose most of his property.

LOUDA BEEKER.

Among the prosperous farmers of Daviess county, Indiana, who have built up comfortable homes and surrounded themselves with the comforts of life, few have attained a higher degree of success than Louda Beeker, of Bogard township. With few opportunities, except what his own efforts and those of his wife were capable of mastering and with many difficulties to overcome, he has made a success of life, and in so doing has earned the universal respect and esteem of all with whom he has come in contact. He is a man of tireless energy and strong courage and one whose career shows that he is an able and conscientious worker. As a citizen, he is public spirited and enterprising to an unwonted degree. As a friend and neighbor, he combines those qualities of head and heart that have won confidence and commanded respect. His life affords a splendid example of what an American youth, plentifully endowed with good common sense, energy and determination, can accomplish when accompanied by good moral principles.

Louda Beeker was born on March 7, 1869, in Bartholomew county. He is the son of Frederick and Matilda (Shaffer) Beeker, both natives of Germany. The latter died in 1883. She was the daughter of John G. Shaffer, a native of Germany, who came to America and settled near Columbus, Indiana, on a farm. He owned two hundred and forty acres of land and was a member of the Lutheran church. Frederick Beeker was educated in the common schools of Germany. He was married twice, the first time to Matilda Shaffer, who bore him six children, Clara, Louda, the subject of this sketch, Pauline, Lewis, John and Mary. The mother of these children died and Frederick was married to Margaret Shank, the daughter of Peter Shank, a farmer living near Columbus, this state. One child, Anna, was born to this second marriage. Frederick Beeker owned two hundred and fifty acres of land in St. Louis Crossing, Indiana, near Columbus. He was a member of the Methodist church and of the Independent Order of Odd Fellows.

Louda Beeker was educated in the common schools of Bartholomew county, and when a young man, performed the customary duties of the average farmer boy and grew up amidst the surroundings of a country lad. When Mr. Beeker reached maturity, he was married to Tessie Fox, the daughter of Adam and Laura (Treon) Fox. Adam Fox was a butcher at Hope, Indiana. To Mr. and Mrs. Louda Beeker, five children have been born, Florence E., Anna Grace, deceased; Edna Laura, Eula May and Ora L.

Mr. Beeker owns two hundred and seven acres of land in Daviess county, Bogard township, where he does general farming and stock raising. For several years he was engaged extensively in the horse-racing business, but quit that business because he could not be successful without gambling, and his conscience would not permit him to engage in it. Nevertheless, Mr. Beeker has made more than an average success as a farmer and has acquired a substantial competence. Mr. Beeker moved to Daviess county from near Columbus in 1907.

Louda Beeker is a Democrat, and he is a member of the Independent Order of Odd Fellows. Mr. Beeker is a man who enjoys the confidence to the highest degree of his neighbors and the people of Bogard township. His genial manners and goodness of heart have won for him a host of friends.

AUSTIN B. OSMON.

Though nature affords excellent opportunities for carrying on certain lines of labor, in every locality there is demanded of any man great industry and diligence if he succeeds. Competition makes him put forth his best efforts and it requires great care to conduct any business enterprise along profitable lines. This is especially true of farming. From the time of earliest spring planting, until the crops are harvested, the farmer's life is a very busy one. Even through the winter months he prepares for the labors of the coming year, and thus lays the foundation of his success for the ensuing year. And yet, the farmer lives the most independent existence, and always has the satisfaction of getting a day off when he desires. Daviess county has as fine farms as may be found anywhere in the state of Indiana, and one of the very progressive farmers of Daviess county, whose property is kept in a very high state of repair at all times, is Austin B. Osmon.

Austin B. Osmon was born on August 21, 1879, in Bogard township, Daviess county. He is the son of George W. and Cordelia (Wilson) Osmon, the former a native of Bogard township, and the latter the daughter of William A. and Keziah Wilson, who were farmers of Barr township, Daviess county, and large landholders. They were members of the Christian church.

Austin B. Osmon's grandfather was Charles Osmon, a native of Daviess county, born in 1821, and who married Margaret Seifrit, also a native of Daviess county, Indiana, and a daughter of Charles and Elizabeth (Evert) Seifrit. Charles Seifrit and wife came to this county in an early day. They were of Dutch descent and were members of the Methodist Episcopal church. Austin Osmon's great-grandfather was Jabus Osmon, a native of Ohio, who married Mary Baker. Jabus Osmon was a farmer and one of the early settlers of Daviess county. Jabus Osmon and a man by the name of Eagle were engaged extensively in trade with the Indians, who eventually killed Mr. Eagle, at which time Jabus Osmon swore vengeance. He killed a large number of them, eleven, at one time. He afterward entered about three hundred and sixty acres of land in Van Buren township, and lived there the remainder of his life. He and his wife had nine children, Dyer, John, Wesley, Thomas, Isaac, David, Philip, Sarah and Elizabeth. Jabus

Osmon was a member of the Methodist church and one of its pioneer leaders. He was a great hunter, and when there was to be a log-rolling he was the man whose duty is was to kill the game for the dinner. He dressed and acted a great deal like an animal while he was in the woods. Indians were continually on his trail, but he was never caught unawares.

Charles Osmon, the grandfather of Austin B. was educated in the common schools, was a farmer in Bogard township, Daviess county, and owned one hundred and forty acres of land. He and his wife had eight children, Martha, Ellen and Elizabeth are deceased; Alice, Lorie, George and Charles are still living. Isaac is also deceased. Charles Osmon was a member of the Methodist Episcopal church, was active in local Republican politics, and died on January 2, 1863, while in the service of the Union army. His wife, Mrs. Charles Osmon, born on July 4, 1824, is still living in Epsom, Daviess county.

George W. Osmon, the father of Austin B., was educated in the common schools, and was a farmer. He owned about six hundred acres of land, while he and his wife and family were members of the Methodist church. He was a member of the Independent Order of Odd Fellows and the Knights of Pythias. George W. Osmon was a quiet and unassuming man and was married at the age of twenty-five to Cordelia Wilson, as heretofore related. Her father, William A. Wilson, was a farmer in Barr township, and a large landowner. He was a member of the Christian church. George W. Osmon and wife had eight children, Austin B., the subject of this sketch; Ada, Bessie, Nora, Homer, Everett, Bonnie and Charles. Bessie is deceased. Of the other children, Ada married John E. Cox and lives in Montana; Nora married R. J. Crist, and lives in Montana; Homer lives on the home place. He married Clotie Wadsworth. The remainder of the children of George W. Osmon are single.

Austin B. Osmon was educated in the common schools, and after leaving the common schools took a normal course at Vincennes University, which he attended for one term. He taught school for five terms in Daviess county.

On November 24, 1904, Mr. Osmon was married to Maud Williams, the daughter of Adolphus G. and Angeline (Cummings) Williams, of Cornettsville, Bogard township. Mr. and Mrs. Austin B. Osmon have five children, George, Robert, Benson, Roena and Pauline.

Mr. Osmon removed to his present farm of one hundred and seventy-five acres when he was married. In 1914, he built a comfortable and commodious home. He is an extensive breeder of Shorthorn and Polled-Durham cattle, and of Poland-China hogs and Shropshire sheep.

Mr. and Mrs. Osmon and family are members of the Methodist Episcopal church. Mr. Osmon is a member of the Masonic lodge. Mr. Osmon is now living upon the farm and owns the farm which his father formerly owned. He is an enterprising, progressive young farmer, well known and highly respected.

DANIEL I. MYERS.

Among the representative farmers of Daviess county, Indiana, is Daniel I. Myers, the owner of a splendid farm in Bogard township. Mr. Myers has carried on the various phases of farming with that discretion and energy which are certain to find a successful issue. Mr. Myers has been a hard worker and a good manager. He is a man of economical habits and is highly respected in the community where he lives, and where for many years he enjoyed an unusual influence for good. Mr. Myers has been fortunately situated in a thriving farming community, and has always made the very best of his opportunities. Early in life, his opportunities for a thorough education were limited, but he has supplemented the education of his younger days by home study and is a well-informed man today. He is the father of S. E. Myers, a well-known lawyer of Washington, whose lifework is recited elsewhere in this volume.

Daniel I. Myers was born on September 12, 1860, in Bogard township in Daviess county. He is the son of Elijah H. and his first wife, who was Asemeth (Eaton) Myers. Asemeth Eaton was the daughter of Joseph and a Miss (Boyd) Eaton. Joseph Eaton was the son of Joseph Eaton, Sr., a Daviess county farmer and an early settler in Daviess county. He in turn was the son of Isaac Eaton.

Elijah H. Myers, the father of Daniel I., was a son of Daniel Myers, a native of North Carolina, who entered land where Cornettsville in Bogard township is now situated. Daniel Myers and wife had nine children, Elijah, Tempa, Isabella, Mary, Frank, Daniel A., Josiah, Thomas and William.

Elijah H. Myers, the father of Daniel I., was educated in the common schools. By his first wife six children were born, Frank P., Mary S., Elijah N., James (deceased), Daniel I., the subject of this sketch, and Josiah. By his second wife, who was Clara Carp, the daughter of Wilson Carp, five children were born, Wilson C., Anna K., Stella, May and Olive. Elijah

H. Myers was a prominent and influential member of the United Brethren church. He was also influential in the political affairs of Bogard township, having served both as trustee and as constable. In addition to operatnig a mill, he was an extensive stock buyer in this community and owned about four hundred acres of land, and was a farmer of large affairs.

Daniel I. Myers was educated in the common schools. His opportunities for obtaining an education were meager and he was not able to pursue his studies as far as he wished. Mr. Myers was married on October 22, 1882, to Ada Jane Williams, who was born on August 14, 1862, in Daviess county, on a farm. She was the daughter of Joseph and Eliza (Peachee) Williams. Joseph Williams owned two hundred acres of land, the farm upon which Daniel I. Myers now lives and the farm which he owns. He was a local preacher in the Methodist church. Joseph Williams was married twice. By his first wife, who was Sarah Maston, he had four children, all of whom are now deceased. Stephen, the eldest son, was killed in the battle of Bull Run. Alfred, John and Martha were the other children. By his second wife, Ada Jane Williams, the mother of Mrs. Myers, four children were born, Lewis, Rosie, Rachel and Ada Jane.

Joseph Williams died in 1876, and was a son of Archibald Williams, a native of Kentucky and an early settler in this part of Indiana. He married Mary Ross, and they had eight children, John, William, James, Joseph, Presley, Debby, Matilda and Ada. Archibald Williams entered land in Washington township. He was a prominent member of the Methodist church and a strict doctrinarian, all of which he practiced.

After his marriage, Daniel I. Myers removed to the form where he now lives. Mrs. Myers inheriting thirty acres, Mr. Myers purchased the interest of the other heirs, or in all one hundred and thirty acres.

Daniel I. and Ada Jane (Williams) Myers have had six children, Stephen E., the eldest, who is a prominent lawyer in Washington; Pearl May; Verna Grace; Alva E., deceased; Nelson L. and Ernest L. Stephen married Bessie Allen; he was educated at the Indiana State Normal at Terre Haute and at the State University at Bloomington; Pearl May married William Lester and they live in Washington; Verna is the primary teacher at Cornettsville, having been educated in the Indiana State Normal at Terre Haute.

Daniel I. Myers served six years as trustee of Bogard township, from 1909 to 1915. During this period the schools of Bogard township made the most rapid progress during any similar period in their history. Mr.

Myers erected the new school building at Epsom, which has been made a commissioned high school, and is a credit to any community, which is fully equipped. Mr. Myers also built a graded school at Cornettsville, in Bogard township. At the end of his term of office as trustee, the teachers presented him with a large Bible, which Mr. Myers prizes very highly. He was popular as a trustee, and is much admired as a citizen. Mr. and Mrs. Myers and their family are all of strong religious inclinations. Mr. Myers is a member of the United Brethren church, and Mrs. Myers is a member of the Methodist church. Mr. Myers is a member of the Independent Order of Odd Fellows and the Woodmen of the World. In politics he is an ardent Republican.

WILLARD E. ISENOGLE.

Among the farmers of Daviess county who believes in following twentieth century methods, is William E. Isenogle, of Bogard township. Mr. Isenogle comes from a splendid family and one that has been foremost for right living and industrious habits, for education and morality, as well as for all they contribute to the welfare of the commonwealth. Such people are welcome in any community for they are empire builders and as such, push the frontier of civilization ever westward and onward, leaving the green, wide-reaching wilderness and the far-stretching plains populous with contented people and beautiful with green fields. They have constituted that sterling horde which caused the great Bishop Whipple to write the memorable lines "Westward the course of empire takes its way."

Willard Isenogle was born on January 19, 1870, at Coshocton, Ohio. He is the son of John and Martha (Schultz) Isenogle, the former of whom was born on October 17, 1840, in Jefferson county, Ohio, and the latter born on January 7, 1848, in Coshocton county, Ohio. Mrs. Martha Isenogle was the daughter of Jacob Schultz, whose wife was a Cook, and the former of whom was a farmer and owned two hundred acres of land in the state of Ohio, and the latter a daughter of one of the pioneer families, known for their thrift and industrial tendencies. He was a valiant soldier in the Civil War. Mrs. Isenogle died on January 22, 1904, and after her death, Mr. Isenogle married Sadie McCully. No children have been born to this second marriage By the first marriage of John Isenogle, four children were born, Alonzo C., deceased; Willard E., the subject of this sketch; Lawrence Bell, deceased, and Nora Eddie, who is at present living in the state of

California. John Isenogle is a member of the Methodist church and served three years and eight months in the Union army during the Civil War. He was with General Sherman on his memorable march to the sea and, during his service, was taken a prisoner and confined at Andersonville. After having been imprisoned for a time, he was exchanged on account of having contracted typhoid fever.

John Isenogle is the son of Jacob Isenogle, a native of Carroll county, Ohio. Jacob Isenogle married Rachel Engeling and was a farmer who came to Daviess county, during the Civil War, where he rented land for a time and was a well-known farmer. He was identified with the Democratic party. The children of Jacob and Rachel (Engeling) Isenogle were: Stephen, John, Abigail, Adeline, Gideon, Catherine, Rachel, Lavina, Cyrus, Adam and Jane.

Willard E. Isenogle was educated in the common schools of Daviess county, where he obtained a good common school education, and when old enough, took up farming, where he worked until the time of his marriage, March 19, 1893, to Etta McCall, who was born on August 28, 1871, in Bogard township, and who is the daughter of George W. McCall, a native of Pennsylvania who came to Indiana from that state after serving courageously as a Union soldier during the Civil War. He settled on a farm in Daviess county in Bogard township. He and his family were all members of the United Brethren church. He married Martha A. McCall, who was born in Veale township, Daviess county.

After his marriage, Mr. Isenogle rented his father-in-law's farm, on which he now lives and which he owns. This farm is well improved and consists of one hundred and four acres. Mr. Isenogle has been conservative in his business relations and frugal in his living, and is a modest, unassuming man who lays no great claim to worthy achievements.

To Willard E. and Ettie (McCall) Isenogle two children have been born, Arba, on December 9, 1898, died on January 19, 1910, and George E., on November 11, 1905.

Mr. and Mrs. Isenogle are devoted members of the United Brethren church and are active both in the church and Sunday school. They contribute liberally of their means to the support of this church. Mr. Isenogle is a member of the Modern Woodmen of America and active in the affairs of this organization. Willard Isenogle is well known in Bogard township as a substantial farmer in the community where he lives. From any standpoint he deserves to rank as a representative citizen in this section of Daviess county.

ANDREW McCALL.

It is a well-authenticated fact that success comes as a result of legitimate and well-applied energy, unflagging determination and perseverance in a course of action when once decided upon. Success was never known to smile upon the idler or dreamer and never courts the loafer. Only those who have diligently sought her favors are crowned with her blessing. In tracing the history of an influential citizen of Daviess county, Indiana, now deceased, it is plainly seen that the success which he enjoyed was won by all of those commendable qualities. It was also his personal worth, which gained for him the high esteem of his neighbors and, in fact, of all the people of Daviess county, among whom he was so well known.

The late Andrew McCall was born at New Huntington, Pennsylvania, on February 10, 1839, and died on March 18, 1913. He was the son of William A. and Margaret (Donaldson) McCall, both of whom were natives of Pennsylvania and farmers. William A. McCall and wife moved from Pennsylvania when Andrew McCall, the subject of this sketch, was nine years old, and settled first in Illinois and then moved to Daviess county, settling in Washington township. They finally moved to Bogard township, where they purchased land. William A. McCall owned two or three hundred acres of land. He and his wife had seven children, Sarah, Ellen, Elizabeth, Martha, Andrew, John and Alexander.

The late Andrew McCall was educated in the common schools and throughout his life was a successful farmer. He was married on October 2, 1871, to Mary C. Peachee, who was born on January 28, 1850, and the daughter of James and Martha Ann (Allison) Peachee, the former a native of Kentucky and the latter of Daviess county. James Peachee was the son of Benjamin Peachee, who married Rebecca Rigdon. He was a farmer, who first lived in Kentucky and who, later in life, moved to Daviess county. Benjamin Peachee and wife were members of the Methodist Episcopal church. They had eight children, Eliza, Sophia, Retha, Mirrah, James, John, Benjamin and Alfred. James Peachee, the father of Mrs. Andrew McCall, was educated in the common schools. He was a carpenter, blacksmith and cooper. He was an influential member of the United Brethren church and active as an exhorter in this church. He belonged to the Independent Order of Odd Fellows. His children were Sarah, deceased; Mary, C., the wife of Mr. McCall; Matilda J., deceased; Osiah; Martha A.; Isaiah; William and Hiram, deceased.

The late Andrew McCall, after his marriage, settled on the farm where his widow and son now live and where he lived until his death. Mr. and Mrs. McCall had six children, all of whom are deceased with the exception of the youngest, John Austin, who is unmarried and who lives at home with his mother. The deceased children were Rose, Edward, Everett, Eva and Lula.

Altogether, the late Andrew McCall owned five hundred acres of land in Daviess county, three hundred acres of which comprised the home farm. He was a member of the United Brethren church and a very active man in local affairs, political and otherwise. Since the death of Mr. McCall, Mrs. McCall and her son, John Austin, have lived on the farm, which the son is now operating. The late Andrew McCall was a very progressive and prosperous farmer. During his life he erected the very best house and barn in his community. The farm is located about one mile south of Epsom. It is highly productive and its present splendid improvements are due to the untiring energy and unselfish devotion of the lamented husband and father, who gave his life not only in behalf of the happiness of his wife and son, but who lived in behalf of the community where his labors were performed. He is remembered as a man of generous and kind impulses, and one who enjoyed to an unaccustomed degree the confidence of all of his neighbors.

MILTON L. ALLEN.

One of the distinctive functions of this volume is to take cognizance of those citizens of Daviess county who stand eminently representative in their chosen spheres of endeavor. In this connection there can be absolute propriety in according to Milton L. Allen the consideration which is due him as one of the representative farmers of Van Buren township. He is numbered among the leaders in the agricultural life of Daviess county, and is one of its most prosperous farmers. Mr. Allen's farm in Van Buren township is kept in a splendid state of repair, which applies especially to his buildings. His land is well drained and well fenced and equipped for the operations of the progressive, up-to-date farmer.

Mr. Allen was born on June 15, 1843, in Van Buren township, Daviess county, Indiana. He is the son of Hiram and Keziah (Cook) Allen, who was the second wife of Hiram Allen. The former was born in Virginia and the latter in North Carolina, the daughter of William Cook, who was one of the earliest settlers in Daviess county. William Cook entered eighty acres of land and at the time of his death owned one hundred and forty acres. He was a member of the Baptist church. Hiram Allen was the son of James and Tabitha (Lytton) Allen, the former born in North Carolina, and married in 1794. There were ten children born to this union, four sons and six daughters, all of whom grew to maturity. James Allen was a farmer and early settler in Daviess county. He entered one hundred and twenty acres of land from the government in Bogard township and here he lived until his death. Among his ten children were Elihu, Hiram, Cyrus, Alkinah, Mahalia, Polly and Elizabeth.

Hiram Allen was educated in the common schools and was a farmer throughout his life. He owned five hundred acres of land in Van Buren township, was identified with the Whig party and active in local politics. He and his wife were members of the Baptist church. His brother, Elkanah, was a Baptist minister and conducted church every two weeks in the barn owned by Hiram Allen. The first wife of Hiram Allen was Mahalia Newland and by this union there were three children, James, Eliza and Isabel, all of whom are deceased. By his second marriage, there were three children, Laura, deceased; Milton L. and Mary. Mary lives in Seattle, Washington. Hiram Allen died in October, 1844, and his wife, the mother of Milton L., died in 1895.

Milton L. Allen was educated in the common schools and reared on the farm. He was married in August, 1860, to Amanda Laytton, who was born in Daviess county, Indiana, and the daughter of Hosea Lytton, a farmer of Daviess county and a devout member of the Christian church. Seven children were born to this union, Lucetta, Gordon, Mason, Walter. Maryette, Florence and Susie. Only two of these children, Lucetta and Gordon, are living. Lucetta married George Coffin and lives in Indianapolis, and Gordon married a Miss Orr and lives in Toledo. They have three children.

After the death of Mrs. Amanda Allen, in 1878, Mr. Allen was married, a second time, to Susie Hinton. The marriage took place, May 28, 1895. Susie Hinton was the widow of Wallace Hinton, and had two children by her first marriage, Loueda and Forrest. Mrs. Susie Allen was Susie Gootie before her first marriage, and was a native of Martin county. By her second marriage, she has had three children, Orrin P., Roy D. and Ross, the last of whom is deceased. The other two children are at home.

Mr. Allen enlisted, August 9, 1861, in the Twenty-seventh Regiment, Indiana Volunteer Infantry, and was assigned to Company B., in which company he served three years and two months and was engaged in the battles of Chancellorsville, the Battle of the Wilderness and Antietam. He was severely wounded during the war at Antietam on September 17, 1862, by a gun-shot wound in the right breast, which was of such a nature as to cause him to be sent to the hospital at West Philadelphia for six months.

Mr. Allen owns two hundred and thirty acres of land in Van Buren township and is still engaged in farming it. Mr. Allen is a Republican. He has always been active in local politics and served as constable of his township at one time. Formerly, he was a member of the Independent Order of Odd Fellows. He is a member of the Christian church, while Mrs. Allen is a member of the Catholic church. The Allens are well known in Daviess county and Mr. Allen is highly respected as one of Daviess county's most enterprising farmers. He is a member of the Grand Army of the Republic post at Loogootee.

THOMAS G. WADSWORTH.

Farming, to which practically all of the life of Thomas G. Wadsworth, one of the well-known and highly respected citizens of Van Buren township, has been devoted, is the oldest pursuit for a livelihood known to mankind and one in which he will ever be most independent. Thomas G. Wadsworth is a native of Daviess county, having been born in Van Buren township and here has spent all of his life. His life has been largely devoted to his fellow men and Mr. Wadsworth has been untiring in his efforts to inspire a proper respect for law and order, and has been ready at all times to uplift humanity along civic and social lines.

Thomas G. Wadsworth, the subject of this sketch, was born on April 11, 1863, in Van Buren township in Daviess county. He is the son of Thomas, Jr., and Elizabeth Jane (Odell) Wadsworth, the former of whom was born on June 30, 1828, in Lawrence county. He was married first to Elizabeth Jane Odell, who was born in 1832, in Indiana. She was the daughter of Emsley and Sarah (Gray) Odell, early settlers in Madison county.

The grandfather of Thomas G. Wadsworth was also Thomas Wadsworth, who was born in Pennsylvania in 1782 and who was a farmer by occupation. After living for some time in Kentucky, he moved to Indiana, and finally located on one hundred acres of land in Van Buren township, Daviess county, where he lived until his death in 1841. He married Nancy

Skaggs and to this union were born five children, Thomas, Peter, Silas, Joseph and Margaret.

The father of Thomas G. Wadsworth, Thomas Wadsworth, was reared on a farm and received a common-school education. He remained at home with his parents until reaching maturity and was married on April 12, 1850, to Elizabeth Jane Odell, as heretofore mentioned. To this union were born nine children, John, Emsley, Peter, Martha, William, James, Thomas, Mary and Silas. John, Martha, Mary and Silas are all deceased. The mother of these children died on December 26, 1868. She was a devoted member of the Methodist church throughout her life. After her death, Mr. Wadsworth was again married, January 2, 1870, to Sarah J. Killion, who was born in 1841, in Indiana. To this union were born two children, Bloomer and Hubert, the latter of whom is deceased. Mr. Wadsworth owned two hundred acres of land, on which, in 1882, he erected a beautiful home. He was a Republican and cast his first vote, however, for Franklin Pierce. In the Civil War he was a strong Union man and served in Company C, Ninety-first Regiment, Indiana Volunteer Infantry. He fought in a number of very severe battles and was discharged in August, 1864. Thomas Wadsworth was a local Methodist preacher for more than forty years. He died on November 14, 1908.

Thomas G. Wadsworth, the subject of this sketch, was educated in the common schools. He taught in the country schools for one year and was married on December 14, 1889, to Catherine Keck, born on November 18, 1867, the daughter of William and Harriett (Poindexter) Keck. William Keck was a native of Tennessee and a farmer there. He came to Martin county and located in Brown township. He was an influential member of the Methodist Episcopal church during his life. William Keck was the son of Christian and Catherine (Yond) Keck.

To Thomas G. and Catherine (Keck) Wadsworth one son, Forest K., has been born. He was born on June 12, 1894, and is now a public school teacher.

Mrs. Wadsworth is a devoted member of the Methodist Episcopal church as have been so many of the ancestors of both Mr. and Mrs. Wadsworth before them. She is a member of the church at Raglesville. Mr. Wadsworth is a member of the Masonic lodge. He was appointed trustee at one term and served out the unexpired term. He is now engaged in the fire insurance business for the Fidelity Phoenix Fire Insurance Company, of New York, and has been for the past sixteen years. Mr. Wadsworth has built up a large and lucrative business in Van Buren township. In addition to his insurance business, he is also a notary public. He owns seven acres of land and a home in Raglesville.

Thomas G. Wadsworth is a pleasant man, modest and unassuming and a worthy citizen of the community wherein he lives.

HUGH MORGAN.

Daviess county, Indiana, enjoys a high reputation because of the splendid order of her citizenship and none of her citizens occupy a more enviable position in the esteem of his fellows than Hugh Morgan, the son of wellknown pioneers of Daviess county. A residence here of more than sixty years has given his fellows a full opportunity to observe him in the various walks of life in which he has been engaged and his present high standing is due solely to the honorable and upright course he has ever pursued. As a leading citizen of his community, he is eminently entitled to representation in a work of this character.

Hugh Morgan was born on February 25, 1862, in Barr township, Daviess county, in that portion of the township, however, which is now embraced by Bogard township. He is the son of Hugh, Sr., and Margaret (McAvoy) Morgan, the former of whom was born in County Down, Ireland, and who was a farmer in that country before coming to America. After landing at New Orleans, in this country, he came up the river to Cincinnati and then to Covington, Kentucky, where he helped construct the Covington & Lexington railroad. He also conducted a boarding-house for some of the employees engaged in the construction of this railroad. About 1850, he moved to Daviess county, and entered eighty acres of land in Barr township. On account of a revision of the township line, this land is now embraced in Bogard township. This farm is now owned by Hugh Morgan, Jr., and his two brothers, Patrick and James.

The children born to Hugh Morgan, Sr., and wife were as follow: Patrick, Hugh, Jr., James, Catherine, Anna, Mary and John. Of there children Catherine is the only one who married. She married James Healy and they live in Bogard township, Daviess county, and have one child, Hugh; James, Patrick and Hugh, Jr., live on the home farm; Anna, Mary and John are deceased. The father of these children died on August 6, 1882, at the age of seventy-five. His wife, the mother of these children, died on December 29, 1900, at the age of eighty years. They were members of St. Michael's Catholic church, of Bogard township.

At the time Hugh Morgan, Sr., entered this land, it was covered with forest and no roads were to be found anywhere. Mr. Morgan, Sr., improved his land and transformed a wilderness into a fertile and productive farm.

Hugh Morgan, Jr., was educated in the common schools and was graduated from the Southern Indiana Normal School at Mitchell. This institution is no longer in existence. Here Mr. Morgan took both a business and teacher's course. He has taught in the common schools of Daviess county for thirty-one years and in Bogard township for the past twenty-three years. He is unmarried and is living on the homestead farm entered by his father and owns it in partnership with his two brothers.

Mr. Morgan is a member of the Knights of Columbus. He is a devout and faithful member of the Catholic church, and identified with the Democratic party.

JOHN A. SIMS.

Not too often can be repeated the life-story of one who has lived honorably and usefully and who has attained notable distinction in the county of his residence. John A. Sims, a former assessor of Daviess county, has been a busy and useful man, not only in Van Buren township, where he lives, but in Daviess county as well. The office of biography is not to give voice to a man's modest estimate of himself and his accomplishments, but rather to leave upon the pages of history the opinion of his neighbors and friends. John A. Sims occupies a high place in the esteem of his fellow citizens. He has always been loyal to trust imposed upon him and upright in his dealings with his fellow men. He is a representative citizen of Daviess county, and from many standpoints is entitled to representation in this volume.

John A. Sims was born on November 1, 1872, in Van Buren township. He is the son of Zachariah and Sarah E. (Cox) Sims, the former of whom is a native of Van Buren township, and the latter of whom is a native of Bogard township, the daughter of John and Elizabeth (Fore) Cox. John Cox was a farmer in that township and a valiant soldier during the Civil War. He died in the hospital at Vicksburg.

The paternal grandfather of Mr. Sims was Asbury Sims, a native of Kentucky. Asbury Sims' father was Starlin Sims, a native of Georgia, who moved to Kentucky and later to Lawrence county, where he was a farmer and pioneer settler in that county. Asbury Sims was a member of the Christian church. He married Katurak Kilgore, and they had a number of children, among whom were the following: Starlin, Abbey, Sallie, Alfred, Edward, Polly, Zachariah, Nancy, Malinda, Noah and Hiram. Asbury Sims moved with his family to Daviess county, near Raglesville, and there entered two hundred acres of land. He lived in this place until his death.

The father of John A. Sims, Zachariah Sims, was educated in the common schools and lived near Raglesville in Van Buren township his entire life, where he owned one hundred acres of land. Zachariah and Sarah E. (Cox) Sims have five children, Hiram, Mary, Clara, Emma and John A. Of these children, Hiram married Susan Toon, and they live at Raglesville. He is the postmaster at Raglesville and has a general supply store; Mary married John Beasley. They live in Van Buren township and are farmers; Clara married Thomas Beasley, and they live in Bogard township; Emma married Harvey Riggins and they live in Van Buren township. Zachariah, the father of these children, died on September 15, 1891, at the age of forty-three years. He owned and lived on a part of the farm entered by his father, and the subject's grandfather. Mrs. Zachariah Sims is still living in Raglesville.

John A. Sims, the subject of this sketch, was educated in the public schools of Van Buren township in Daviess county. He spent one year in the schools of Ellmore township, and, subsequently, attended the normal school at Odon, as well as the Central Indiana Normal College at Danville.

Mr. Sims was married on September 16, 1893, to Enola Overton, the daughter of William Overton, a farmer of Van Buren township, and a prominent member of the United Brethren church.

To Mr. and Mrs. John A. Sims five children have been born: Russell, Clarence, Valda, Alden J. and Roscoe. Mr. Sims now owns eighty acres of land, adjoining Raglesville. It is a splendid farm and well kept in every respect, which shows him to be an enterprising farmer.

Mr. Sims is a Republican. From 1907 to 1911, he was county assessor of Daviess county. He is a man well known throughout Daviess county, of good appearance, affable and courteous to all and is especially popular in the community where he lives, and enjoys the confidence and esteem of all his neighbors and all of those who have come in contact with him, either socially or politically or even in a business way.

THOMAS F. BARLEY.

Thomas F. Barley, a well-known farmer of Bogard township, is a Hoosier by birth and may justly bear the title of a self-made man, having worked his way unaided from the humble ranks of the toiler to and through the vicissitudes and adversities of life, to an admirable and influential position among the enterprising farmers of Daviess county. The success attained by him in his business affairs has been due greatly to his steady persistence, stern integrity and excellent judgment, qualities which have also won for him the confidence and esteem of the public, to a marked degree.

Thomas F. Barley was born on June 29, 1873, in Bogard township, Daviess county, Indiana. He is the son of John and Malintha (Standley) Barley, the former of whom was born in 1835, in Tennessee, and who died in 1875, and the latter born on October 9, 1834, is still living. Malintha Standley is the daughter of George and Ann (Rector) Standley, who lived in Anderson, and were pioneers and farmers there. John Barley was the son of Thomas and Parlina (Franklin) Barley, the former of whom was a native of Tennessee and an early settler in Van Buren township, Daviess county. They had four children, John, Pauline, Plas and William.

Thomas F. Barley's mother was married three times. John Barley was her third husband. Her first husband was James McBride and to this union five children were born, Kaiser, Sarah, Mary, Martha and George. Her second husband was Patrick Tomy and to this union one daughter, Jane, was born. Her third husband was John Barley and to this union five children were born, Susan, William P., John H., Thomas F. and Edward. Susan is living in Bogard township and is unmarried; William P. married Jennie Allen and lives in Washington township; John H. married Rettie Mallet and lives in Bogard township; Thomas F. is the subject of this sketch and Edward married Sarah Rosenberry and lives in Bogard township.

John Barley, the father of Thomas F., was a soldier in the Civil War. He served ninety days in the Union army and, on his return home, was taken with pneumonia and died very suddenly. John Barley was an active man in local politics and was identified with the Democratic party. He served as township trustee, as constable of Bogard township and held other minor offices. He was a member of the Grange and owned one hundred and sixty acres of land in that township.

Thomas F. Barley was reared in Bogard township and there received his education. He was married on January 6, 1906, to Lovina L. Scott, who was born on November 2, 1871, also in Bogard township, and who is the daughter of William and Frances D. (Faith) Scott, farmers in that township and active members of the Methodist church. William Scott was educated in the common schools and was known as one of the finest scribes in Daviess county. He owned one hundred and twenty acres of land. He died, October 14, 1877, at the age of forty years, and his wife is living at Epsom, in Bogard township. William Scott was a thirty-second-degree Mason and a stanch Republican. Thomas F. and Lovina L. (Scott) Barley had seven children, Elias A., William T., Laura J., Francis P., George A., Lavina L. and Harrison D. After the death of William Scott, Mrs. Scott married, a second time, George W. Bell, who was a soldier in the Civil War in the Sixty-second Regiment, Indiana Volunteer Infantry. He was wounded at the battle of Gettysburg and carried a bullet in his hip until his death. He died on October 14, 1914, at the age of seventy-five years. No children were born to this second marriage.

William Scott was the son of James Scott, a native of Martin county, a farmer there, and while he owned three hundred and fifty acres of land there he was one of the very earliest settlers in this county and spent the latter part of his life in Bogard township. He was the sixth child born to James Scott and wife. The others were Reason, James, Lucinda, Joseph and Malintha. Frances D. Faith, the mother of these children, was the daughter of Abraham and Fannie (Myers) Faith, who were well-known farmers in Bogard township and active members of the Methodist church. Abraham Faith was a member of the Independent Order of Odd Fellows at Plainville. His children were Louisa, Thomas, Frances D., Laura, Lavina and Harrison.

Mrs. Thomas F. Barley, before her marriage to Mr. Barley, was married to Amos D. Thomson, who was born on October 12, 1873, at Greenville, Illinois, and who died on October 14, 1904, in Daviess county, Indiana. They first lived at Salem, but, subsequently, came to Bogard township. By this marriage there were two children, Jessie H., born on April 9, 1898, and Lawrence D., born on October 9, 1902.

After his marriage, Thomas F. Barley settled on a small tract of land south of Epsom, in Bogard township. After one year he moved three miles northeast of Epsom, on a farm of thirty-seven acres, where he remained for nine months and then moved to the Parry Creek bottoms on a thirty-acre farm owned by his wife. He was here thirty-five months when they sold out and moved to their present farm of forty acres. Since that time, they have added forty acres more in one tract, and forty-eight in another, as well as seven acres in a third tract. All of this land is located in Bogard township.

Mr. and Mrs. Barley are members of the Methodist Episcopal church at Epsom. Mr. Barley is a member of the Modern Woodmen of America They have one child, Bertha Ellen, who was born on October 6, 1909.

WILLIAM W. REED.

In the respect which is accorded to men who have fought their own way to success through unfavorable environment, we find an unconscious recognition of the intrinsic worth of character which cannot only endure so rough a test, but gain new strength through the discipline. William W. Reed was not greatly favored by inherited wealth or the assistance of influential friends, but by perseverance, industry and wise economy, he has acquired a comfortable station in life and made his influence felt for good in his community in Bogard township where he has long maintained his home. Because of his honorable career, he is eminently worthy of a place in this volume.

William W. Reed was born on April 13, 1865, in Fort Wayne, Indiana. He is the son of William A. and Eliza (Bear) Reed, the former of whom was a native of Pennsylvania, who, in his younger days, came to Ohio, where he was married. His wife was born in Ohio. William A. Reed's parents died early in life and left him an orphan. He received but little education and shortly after his marriage, he removed from Toledo, Ohio, to Fort Wayne, Indiana, where he remained for eight years. He then came to Daviess county, and located in Van Buren township, where he purchased one hundred and thirty acres of land, where he lived until his death. William A. Reed died in 1895, at the age of sixty-five years. His wife died two years later at the age of sixty-nine. They had six children, Francis; Sarah, deceased; William W.; Charles; Wallace and Elizabeth. Of these children, Francis is living at Fort Wayne; Charles is living in Greene county; Wallace lives in Owen county and Elizabeth lives in Greene county.

William W. Reed, a well-known and prosperous farmer of Bogard township, was educated in the common schools and was married, in 1886, to Sarah J. Perkins, the daughter of Albert and Louisa (Hovey) Perkins, of Daviess county. Albert Perkins was a farmer, and while she was a native of that county, both have since died. To them were born six sons and one daughter, four of whom are now living. The children are: Albert, Mary, Charles, John, Stella and Clara. Of these children, Albert Laverne, who lives in Van Buren township, married Ada May Browning and has one child, Carlton; Mary married Freely Poindexter, of Bogard township, and has two sons, Elmer and Clay. Charles, who lives in Barr township, married Nellie Potts, and they have two girls at home.

William W. Reed is one of the most extensive farmers of Bogard township and owns two hundred acres of land in this township, most of which he has acquired by his individual efforts. He has always been a good manager and is a close student of modern agricultural methods. His farm is kept in a wide state of repairs. In fact, Mr. Reed is well informed upon all questions, agricultural, political, or civic. Because of his large store of information, which he has gained from careful and well-ordered reading, he is one of the leading men of his township and one who is admired and respected by his neighbors. He is aggressive, broad-minded and liberal in all his views and enjoys the confidence of all the people of this section of Daviess county. He votes the Democratic ticket.

PETER RAGLE.

No other county in Indiana produced braver men to serve in the Civil War than did Daviess county. This state sent over two hundred thousand men to the front during that terrible conflict and Daviess county contributed its quota without any difficulty, meeting every call of Governor Morton with a promptness that spoke well for the patriotic zeal of her sons. They left their homes to serve and save their country and hundreds of them sacrificed their lives that the stars and stripes might continue to wave over a united nation. We cannot forget that they fought a brave fight for human liberty and that they deserve all the praise and honor that can be given them. They are fast answering the last roll call and within a few years, we can only honor their memory. It seems eminently fitting in this volume to set forth the lives of these gallant veterans who are still living. Among the brave boys in blue who enlisted from Daviess county, there is none who is more worthy of an honored place in this volume than the subject of this sketch.

Peter Ragle was born near Raglesville, Daviess county, Indiana, June 5, 1842. He is the son of Peter and Margaret (Wadsworth) Ragle, both natives of Tennessee. Peter Ragle, Sr., was a son of James Ragle, of Tennessee, who was a farmer, and who died in his native state. He served in the Indian wars and, on one occasion, was attacked by two Indians. He killed one of them, knocked the tomahawk from the hand of the other and killed him, and sat on him until he regained his strength. James Ragle married a Miss Parrot and after his death, she married a Mr. Watt. They came to Daviess county, Indiana, and located near Raglesville, where he was an early school teacher and here they both died.

Peter Ragle's maternal grandparents, the parents of Margaret Wadsworth, were Thomas and Nancy (Skags) Wadsworth, who came during pioneer days to Indiana and entered land near Raglesville. They owned one hundred acres of land and erected the first building upon the land.

Peter Ragle, Sr., the father of the subject of this sketch, was educated in Tennessee and reared on a farm. He was yet unmarried; he went to Orleans, Indiana, and was a farmer in that neighborhood for a time. After his marriage, about 1820, he located near Raglesville, Indiana. His brother, John, settled a little later in this community and was the first merchant at Raglesville; in fact, he established the town. He hauled his goods from New Albany, Indiana. Peter Ragle, Sr., entered forty acres of land and continued entering forty acres at a time, until he had two hundred acres in all. He erected the first buildings upon his land and continued to clear it until his death. Peter and Margaret Wadsworth had thirteen children, John, Thomas, Robert, Jacob, who was a captain in Company K, Eightieth Indiana Volunteer Infantry; Rhoda, Alonzo, who was a sergeant in the same company with his brother, Jacob; Nancy, David, Peter, Susan, Nathan S., who was a corporal in the same company with his brothers; Margaret and Mary. All of these children were born on the old farm and all were devout members of the Methodist Episcopal church.

Peter Ragle, Jr., enlisted on July 4, 1861, in the Twenty-seventh Indiana Volunteer Infantry, in Company B, as a private and was, subsequently, promoted to sergeant and finally to color-bearer. He was wounded, in the shoulder, in the battle of Resaca, Georgia, the bullet cutting an artery. Mr. Ragle bled so profusely that he was unable to stand for six weeks and was in the hospital for one year. He was discharged from the hospital at Madison, Indiana, May 25, 1865. He served in all of the battles of the Army of the Potomac up to the time his company was transferred to the Army of the Cumberland.

Peter Ragle was educated in Daviess county, Indiana, and after the war, he came back to his father's farm and began farming. He was soon married and purchased a farm adjoining his father's. Peter Ragle, Sr., gave his son, Peter, Jr., forty acres and to this Peter, Jr., added forty acres. Subsequently, he moved to Martin county, Indiana, where he purchased one hundred and forty-seven acres. He resided there for twenty years and was then elected county treasurer on the Republican ticket and re-elected at the expiration of his first term, serving in all for four years. After filling this office for four years, Mr. Ragle returned to the farm in Martin county and remained for six years. At the end of this time, he sold out and moved to Elnore, where he still lives. He returned to this county in 1897 and for five years sold machinery. He then traveled five years for the Deering Harvester Company and at the expiration of this period, engaged in the real estate and insurance business and is still so engaged.

Mr. Ragle was married in 1866 to Martha Trueblood, who lived near Raglesville. She is the daughter of Jesse A. Trueblood, a farmer of this county. To this happy union seven children were born: Jerome and Jesse, deceased; Addie, who is now Mrs. Boyle, of Greencastle, Indiana; Margaret, deceased; Mattie, deceased, who married a Mr. Corbin; Dovey, who is now Mrs. John Pate, of Loogootee, and Grace, who is now Mrs. Guthrie, of Odon.

Mr. Ragle was married a second time in 1880, Emma J. Groover, of Martin county, becoming his wife on this occasion. She died on November 29, 1914. To this second marriage, twelve children were born, Mrs. Maude Jones, of Kentucky, and Myrtle, a twin sister of Maude, who died at the age of six months; Sarah R., who died at the age of fifteen years; Flossie, who is now Mrs. Robinson, of Palestine, Illinois; Charles A., who is a partner with his father in the real estate business; Harley, who is a bridge carpenter on the Chicago & Eastern Illinois railroad; Hazel, who is now Mrs. Albert Persing, of Elnore; Peter, who died young; Hattie, who is now Mrs. Parsons, of Daviess county; Paul, who is a student in the Elnore high school, and an infant. Pearl died at the age of ten years. All of the members of the family are members of the Methodist Episcopal church.

Back in the pioneer days, Peter Ragle, Sr., was a member of the vigilance committee, which whipped several local thieves and undesirable citizens, and finally gave them a certain length of time to leave the country. Some time during the operations, one of those who was being chastised, called out, "Pete Ragle, you are the cause of this and for it you will drop dead behind your plow before the leaves are as big as a squirrel's ear." This remark was made in the early spring. The undesirable left the country and some years afterward Peter Ragle was going to Vincennes to enter a forty-acre tract of land. He was unarmed and some distance ahead, he recognized the man who had made the threat coming on foot with a gun on his shoulder. When the latter recognized the former, he greeted him heartily and passed on, but each looked anxiously over his shoulder until they were out of sight of one another.

Peter Ragle, Jr., has had a considerable part in the progress and prosperity of this section of Daviess county. He is an honored and respected citizen of this community and has been a member of the Masonic lodge for a period of more than forty years.

Mr. Ragle has been a life-long Republican; his first vote was cast for Abraham Lincoln, for his second term. He is a member of M. B. Cutler Post No. 537, Grand Army of the Republic.

EMERY LETT.

Among the farmers of Daviess county, Indiana, who have to their credit many long years spent industriously and intelligently tilling the soil, is Emery Lett, of Veale township. Mr. Lett comes from a good family, one that has always stood for right living and industrious habits, for morality and all that contributes to the welfare of the commonwealth. Such people are welcome in any community for they are empire builders and, as such, have pushed the frontier of civilization ever westward and onward, leaving the green, wide-reaching wilderness and the far-stretching plains populous with contented people and beautiful with green fields. They have constituted that sterling horde which moved the great Bishop Whipple to write the memorable lines, "Westward the course of empire takes its way."

Emery Lett was born on the farm where his mother still lives, in Veale township, in 1864. He is the son of Hamilton and Arilla (Coleman) Lett, the former of whom was born where Emery Lett now lives, and the latter near by. They were married in 1849. The paternal grandparents of Emery Lett were James and Nancy (Veale) Lett, the former a native of North Carolina and the latter one of the early members of the Veale family of Veale township. The maternal grandparents of Mr. Lett were John B. and Frances Coleman. Hamilton and Arilla Lett had eight children, Eli, Ellis, Artimecy, Ida, Gibson, Emery, Laura and Dora. Hamilton Lett died on

December 24, 1884. At the time of his death, he owned two hundred and fifty acres of land.

Emery Lett was educated in the public schools of Veale township at the Lett school and became a farmer early in life. He has always been engaged in this vocation and is a heavy raiser of grain and live stock.

Mr. Lett was married, in 1889, to Dora M. Gregory, the daughter of George and Etta (Robinson) Gregory. George Gregory was born in Harrison township, in 1850, and was the son of Robert and Mournen (Hill) Gregory. Robert and Mournen Gregory were married at the ages of fourteen and thirteen, respectively, and neither could read or write at the time of their marriage. They were practically penniless when they were married and at the time of their death, were the richest people in Harrison township and owned many hundred of acres of land and a great deal of live stock, including hogs and cattle. Their son, John, was killed in the Civil War, being a soldier in the Union army. George Gregory's wife, who before her marriage was Etta Robinson, was born near Washington, this state, and was the daughter of Elijah and Lucretia (Sanford) Robinson, both natives of Kentucky and early settlers in Harrison township, where they remained until their death. George Gregory was educated in Harrison township and was a farmer until he moved to Washington and lived retired. He then married Leva Releford and now operates a dairy at the edge of Washington. By his first marriage there were ten children, Anna; Dora; Elijah; Austine, who died in infancy; Hamlet, who died in infancy; Ona; Walter; Pearl; Hallie and Lydia, deceased. George Gregory and family were all members of the Baptist church and their ancestors on both sides were also members of that church.

To Emery and Dora M. (Gregory) Lett three children have been born. Everett, who is a graduate of Indiana University and a school teacher. He is having splendid success in the Indianapolis high schools, and in many instances has served as judge on debates; Ethel, who is deceased, and Hamlet, who is now a student at the University of Illinois.

Mr. Lett was a candidate for the state Legislature, in 1914, on the Democratic ticket, but was defeated with the remainder of his ticket. He was also, at one time, a candidate for county commissioner of Daviess county, on the Democratic ticket, but was defeated at that time. Emery Lett owns about two hundred acres of splendid farming land, in Veale township, and is a highly respected and enterprising farmer. He is a member of the Independent Order of Odd Fellows and of the Modern Woodmen of America.

FREDERICK J. FRESHLEY, M. D.

Among those who stand as distinguished types of the world's workers is Frederick J. Freshley, M. D., one of the able and honored young physicians and surgeons of Daviess county. He is a man of fine intellectual and professional attainments, of most gracious personality, of strong and noble character and one who has labored with zeal and devotion in the alleviation of human suffering. He is clearly entitled to representation among the progressive and enterprising citizens of his county. Doctor Freshley is devoted to his chosen profession and has added honor and dignity to the medical profession. At all times he has had due regard for the high standard of professional ethics common to the medical profession and has exhibited a marked skill in treating disease.

Frederick J. Freshley was born on July 1, 1884, at Grandview, Indiana. He is the son of Frederick J. and Mary A. (Miller) Freshley, the former of whom was a native of Germany and the latter a native of Spencer county, this state, the daughter of Michael Miller, a native-born German, a farmer by vocation, and an influential member of the United Brethren church. Michael Miller, after landing in New Jersey, came to Ohio, where he remained a few years and then removed to Spencer county, Indiana, where he died in 1903.

Dr. Frederick J. Freshley's grandfather was Frederick Freshley, a native of Germany, who, after his marriage, and after rearing a family, came with his family to America, finally settling in Spencer county, where he was a farmer and owned one hundred and twenty acres of land. His son, Frederick J. Freshley, the father of Dr. Frederick J., was educated in the common schools. He was an influential member of the United Brethren church and prominent in the local politics of that county. He died on October 25, 1884, and his wife is still living at Grandview, this state. They had seven children, Catherine, George, Flora, Carrie, Ida, Oscar and Dr. Frederick J. All of these children are now living. Oscar married Irma Helbig, the daughter of Valentine Helbig, of Sellersburg, Indiana. They live at Plainville, where he is in the drug business with Dr. Frederick J.

Frederick J. Freshley was educated at Grandview, and after completing the common and high school courses of study, graduated from the Central Normal College at Danville, and also from the University of Louisville, in 1908. Doctor Freshley received a diploma of pharmacy in 1909.

He has specialized in diseases of children and, in the practice of his profession, has made a pre-eminent success, enjoying a large and lucrative patronage throughout this section of the state.

On February 3, 1909, Dr. Frederick J. Freshley was married to Bessie P. May, who was born in Spencer county, and who is the daughter of John and Mamie (Pleiss) May, prominent citizens of Spencer county. To Doctor and Mrs. Freshley no children have been born.

Doctor Freshley is a member of the Knights and Ladies of Security, the Independent Order of Odd Fellows and the Modern Woodmen of America, and also the Woodmen of the World. Doctor Freshley has been a practicing physician at Plainville for about six years. He not only practices his profession, but, as heretofore related, is in the drug business, at Plainville, with his brother, Oscar. Doctor Freshley is a clean-cut, young physician of charming personality, enterprising in his ideas and keenly devoted to the welfare of his section of the state. From many standpoints, he deserves the confidence and esteem which have so graciously been bestowed upon him by the people of his community.

JAMES E. GILLEY.

Of high intellectual and professional attainments and ranking among the foremost teachers of Daviess county, James E. Gilley, the present trustee of Washington township, achieved marked distinction in his chosen calling before his election to his present office. As a teacher, he made his presence felt and as a citizen in the daily walks of life, his influence has always tended to the advancement of the community and the welfare of his fellow men. Not only has he wielded a wide and beneficient influence for many years as an instructor in Daviess county, but he has also had a wholesome and stimulating effect on the students who have come in contact with him. The name of James E. Gilley, with eminent fitness, occupies a conspicuous place in the ranks of the teachers of Daviess county, and this rank was extenuated when he was elected to the important office of township trustee.

James E. Gilley was born near Alfordsville, Indiana, on April 20, 1879. He is the son of Alvin P. and Mary J. (Shively) Gilley, the former a native of Daviess county, born near Alfordsville, and the latter a native of Barr township. James E. Gilley's paternal grandparents were Ebenezer Picket and Elizabeth (Parsons) Gilley, the former a native of Daviess county and the latter probably of Barr township. The paternal great-grandparents of James E. Gilley came from South Carolina. His paternal great-grandfather was James P. Gilley, who settled in Reeve township more than one hundred years ago. He came by wagon from South Carolina and entered land in this county, where he is clearing it preparatory to making a home. James P. Gilley fought in the battle of Cowpens, in the Revolutionary War. Ebenezer P. Gilley, the grandfather of James E., was educated in the pioneer schools of Reeve township. He entered land early in life and built flatboats which he operated. He butchered hogs that were raised in Indiana and shipped them to New Orleans. He resided in this locality practically all of his life, with the exception of the period of five years, from 1875 to 1880. He was also an extensive dealer in real estate and, at his death, owned one hundred and sixty acres of land.

The maternal grandparents of James E. Gilley were Sanford and Elizabeth (Allen) Shively, the latter of whom was born near Alfordsville. Mr. Gilley's maternal great-grandfather was Henry Shively, born in Kentucky. He subsequently came to Indiana, locating in Bogard or Van Buren township, where he was a farmer, and also preached in the pioneer Christian church, then called the Disciples church. Elizabeth Allen, the maternal grandmother of Mr. Gilley, was the daughter of James and Mary (Hyser) Allen, of Kentucky, who located near Alfordsville, Indiana. There they lived until their deaths. He was a farmer and the father of a large family. Elizabeth Allen's mother, Mary Hyser, was the daughter of Jacob and Elizabeth Hyser, natives of Tennessee, who came first to Kentucky and finally to Indiana, locating near Alfordsville.

Alvin P. Gilley, the father of James E., was educated in Reeve township and also in Martin county. He began farming early in life and is still engaged in this business. He has lived at his present home practically all of his life, with the exception of three years, from 1875 to 1878, spent in Kansas. He has fifty acres of land. Six children have been born to Alvin P. and Mary Gilley, Ulysses G.; Ira, who died at the age of two weeks; Levi; John M., who died at the age of four years; James E., and A. O.

James E. Gilley received his elementary education in Martin county, but later was a student in the public schools of Reeve township, Daviess county. After leaving the public schools, he taught school for eighteen years in Daviess county. During this period he attended the Southern Indiana Normal School at Mitchell; Carnegie College at Rodgers, Ohio, and Indiana State Normal School at Terre Haute, and has done some work at Indiana

University. He attended the summer sessions at these various places, teaching school during the winter. When he was twenty-eight years old, he was deputy county treasurer, but aside from the services in this capacity, he has been a teacher all of his life, and was actively engaged, until January 1, 1915, when he became trustee of Washington township, this county. Mr. Gilley is discharging the duties of this office in a most commendable manner and has won the approval and commendation of all the people of Washington township.

James E. Gilley was married on March 31, 1901, to Martha A. Godwin, who lived near Alfordsville, the daughter of Edward and Esther Godwin. To this happy union, one child, Crystal Juanita, was born, but she died at birth.

James E. Gilley is an ardent Republican and has been identified with this party all of his life. Fraternally, he is a member of the Independent Order of Odd Fellows and the Modern Woodmen of America. Mr. and Mrs. Gilley are devoted members of the Christian church and are active in both the work of the church and the Sunday school.

JOHN CARESS.

It is a well-attested maxim that the greatness of a community or a state lies not in the machinery of government nor even in its institutions, but rather in the sterling qualities of the individual citizen, in his capacity for high and unselfish effort and his devotion to the public welfare. In these particulars he whose name appears at the head of this review has conferred honor and dignity upon his locality, and as an elemental part of history it is consonant that there should be recorded a resume of his career, with the object in view of noting his connection with the advancement of one of the most progressive and flourishing sections of the commonwealth, as well as his official relations with the administration of the public affairs of the community honored by his citizenship.

John Caress, manager of the Lemon Elevator Company, of Elnora, Indiana, was born in Lawrence county, this state, about ten miles east of Bedford, on August 22, 1862. He is a son of Simon and Sarah (Williams) Caress, natives, respectively, of Kentucky and Lawrence county, Indiana.

The Caress family originally came from the South, and Simon Caress, the father of John, came from Kentucky to Lawrence county, in an early day, as a school teacher. He was considered one of the best educated and informed men in Lawrence county, in the pioneer days, and followed the occupation of a teacher all his life after coming to Lawrence county, where he also engaged in other clerical work, auditing books at the court house. He died in Lawrence county in 1874. He and his family were Baptists in their religious faith, and active workers in this denomination in the early days. Simon Caress was a Democrat until the organization of the Whig party, after which he was an adherent of that political faith, and took an active part in the public affairs of his community. He was married three times, and to his first marriage, to Martha Pague, the following children were born: Abraham, Tabitha, Johanna and Jerome; his second wife was a Miss Williams, and to this union one child was born, Frances Margaret; his third wife was Sarah Williams, whose parents were early settlers of Lawrence county, having come to this state from West Virginia. Simon and Sarah (Williams) Caress were the parents of three children, Elizabeth, Simon and John, with whom this narrative deals.

John Caress received his education in the schools of Lawrence and Martin counties, having left Lawrence county at the age of thirteen years. He first started in life for himself in Martin county, engaging in farming and saw-milling, in which latter occupation he continued until 1888, when he moved to Elnora, Daviess county, where he engaged in carpenter work for four years, after which he went into the grain and mill products business. In 1892, he became connected with the company in which he is now employed, and has been manager of this business since that time. The company was first known as the C. M. Lemon Company, who put up their first elevator in this place about twenty-two years ago. In 1904, the company erected a new elevator, larger and more commodious, to accommodate their growing business, and is now known as the Lemon Elevator Company.

In 1882 John Caress was married to Eliza Flummerfelt, who is also a native of Martin county, her birth having occurred near Dover Hill, Indiana. To this union have been born six children, James, William H., Sarah Isabel, Maud May, Eldina and Hadden, all of whom are residents of Daviess county.

Mr. Caress and family are earnest and loyal members of the Methodist Episcopal church, while fraternally, Mr. Caress is a member of the Knights of Pythias and the Modern Woodmen of the World. He was a Democrat until President McKinley's administration, since which time he has been a Republican. He has always taken an active interest in public affairs, and has served efficiently in several public positions. He was treasurer of the city schools for some years, and is now serving as city treasurer.

Judged by his labors, Mr. Caress is a busy man. None has done more to advance the material interests of his section of the county, and as a citizen none stands higher in the esteem and confidence of the people generally.

LEW HARRIS.

Agriculture has been an honorable vocation always and at the present time the agricultural output of the United States is more than equivalent to the output of all of the factories of the country. There is one thing in the life of a farmer which distinguishes it from that of any other occupation and that is the ability to exist independently of any other vocation. The merchant, the banker, the manufacturer all depend absolutely on the farmer's crops. A famine throughout the country would bankrupt the strongest merchant, wreck the largest bank and close the most extensive factory. Business men can see their business collapse within a week, but nothing short of an earthquake can ruin the farmer. Land is, as it always has been, the most favorable financial investment. Panic may sweep the manufacturer out of business over night, but the farmer can survive when every other industry fails. Therefore, the farmer is the backbone of the nation, and he who can make two blades of grass grow where but one formerly grew, is performing the most useful mission known to man. Daviess county farmers are equal to those found anywhere in the state. Their history is largely the history of the material advancement of any county. Among her excellent farmers, there is none more deserving of recognition in this day than the Honorable Lew Harris, a member of the Indiana General Assembly from Daviess county.

Lew Harris was born near Cannelburg, in Daviess county, on August 17, 1874. He is the son of Lewis C. and Mary (Murray) Harris, the former of whom was born in Daviess county and the latter in Louisville, Kentucky. The paternal grandparents of Lew Harris were Nathan and Elizabeth (Burri) Harris, the former a soldier in the War of 1812, and the latter a native of one of the eastern states. Nathan Harris located near Cannelburg in pioneer times. He purchased government land and owned altogether at one time, two hundred and forty acres. This land he cleared and improved and upon it he established his home in the wilderness. Mrs. Mary

(Murray) Harris, mother of Lew Harris, died in January, 1875, after which time Lew was reared by Martha Murray Moots, an aunt, sister of his mother, with whom he lived until her death, on July 20, 1907.

The maternal grandparents of Lew Harris were Samuel and Ellen (Allison) Murray, both natives of Kentucky. Samuel Murray was engaged in building flat-boats at Maysville, in pioneer times, at a period when that town was at its zenith of growth and prosperity. He was among the first settlers of that vicinity, although he first settled at Mt. Pleasant and, subsequently, removed to Maysville. During the latter years of his life, he retired, to a large extent, from the boat industry and gave his attention to building wagons in Maysville, where he died.

Lewis Harris, the father of Lew Harris, was educated near Cannelburg and became a farmer. He was a farmer practically all of his life in Barr township, where he owned sixty acres. He and his wife died in this township. Lewis and Mary Harris had seven children, William, Elizabeth, Edward, Joseph A. and Lew, and two died in infancy. After the death of his first wife, Lewis Harris married Sarah Beasley, and to this union three children were born, Morton, Robert C. and Fred C. All of the members of this family are identified with the Christian church and active in its affairs.

Lew Harris was educated in the public schools of Barr township and, during his youth, performed the usual tasks which fell to the lot of the average country boy. Early in life he began to farm and has been engaged in this vocation, continuously, since his youth. Mr. Harris owns one hundred and twenty-six acres, which is known as the old Anthony Moots place. It is a fertile and productive farm and Mr. Harris has made many substantial improvements upon it. He is one of the leaders of the agricultural life of this community.

On December 24, 1903, Mr. Harris was married to Cora B. Hunter, the daughter of Francis M. Hunter, and to this union two children have been born, Wilbur Murray and Otto Marion.

For the past twenty years, Lew Harris has been active in politics. In 1914 he was elected from Daviess county as a member of the Indiana Legislature on the Republican ticket and served during the session of 1915. During this session he served on many important committees and was known as one of the leaders in drafting and passing legislation at Indianapolis. Mr. Harris is a member of the Christian church as well as his wife and family, while fraternally, he is a member of the Independent Order of Odd Fellows at Montgomery and the Modern Woodmen of America at the same place.

SILVESTER SWANN.

Agriculture has been an honored vocation from the earliest ages and, as a usual thing, men of honorable and humane impulses, as well as those of energy and thrift, have been patrons of husbandry. The free out-of-door life of the farm has a decided tendency to foster and develop that independence of mind and self-reliance which characterises true manhood. No richer blessing can befall a boy than to be reared in close touch with nature in the healthful life of the field. It has been from the fruitful soil that the moral bone and sinew of the country has sprung. The majority of our nation's great warriors, renowned statesmen and distinguished men of letters were born on the farm and are indebted largely to its early influence for the distinction which they have attained.

Silvester Swann was born on May 20, 1866, in Veale township, Daviess county, Indiana. He is the son of Joseph and Jane (Traylor) Swann, the former of whom was born in Washington township on September 10, 1839. Joseph M. Swann, the father of Silvester, was the son of William and Jane (McIntyre) Swann, the former of whom was born in Mason county, Kentucky, and the latter on the line between Fayette and Bourbon counties, in that state.

Joseph M. Swann and his brothers, Thomas and Lewis, served in the Civil War and all survived, but Lewis left the army broken in health and died many years ago. He served in Company G, Forty-second Regiment, Indiana Volunteer Infantry, in which Joseph M. also served. Thomas served in the Twenty-seventh Regiment, Indiana Volunteer Infantry. Joseph M. enlisted in 1862 and was discharged in 1865. After the war, he came home and began farming in Veale township. He purchased a home and worked hard to acquire a competence, and as a result of his untiring efforts, he had more than two hundred and fifty acres of land at one time, and he made all of his own money. He was a general farmer, but made a specialty of hog and cattle raising and feeding. Joseph M. Swann moved to Washington in November, 1908, and purchased the property where he now lives. He was married, in 1859, to Mary Palmer, who lived only ten months after their marriage. He was married again, in 1861, to Mrs. Jane (Harrall) Traylor, the daughter of William Harrall, who was called "Uncle Buck" Harrall. He was a great hunter and pioneer of Veale township and came from North Carolina. His wife was Elizabeth Stone, of South Carolina. To the second marriage of Joseph M. Swann, five children were born,

Frank, Ellen, Silvester, Ettie and Samuel. He was married a third time, November 14, 1889, to Sallie Alexander, of Veale township, but no children were born to this marriage. Joseph M. Swann and his family were members of the Methodist Episcopal church. He was a member of the Grand Army of the Republic.

William Swann, the grandfather of Silvester Swann, was educated in Mason county, Kentucky, and was married in that state. Immediately after his marriage, he came to Washington township, Daviess county, where he arrived about 1830, and bought a farm of one hundred and sixty acres, which he cleared and improved. He died in Washington township and his wife also died there when Joseph M. was about fifteen years old. William Swann was the father of nine children.

Silvester Swann was educated in Veale township and took up farming on the land where his brother, Samuel, now lives. Subsequently, Silvester Swann and his brother bought a good farm, but later sold it. He then purchased the farm known as the old Graham place, where he now lives. He owns one hundred and forty acres and is engaged in general farming.

On September 15, 1891, Silvester Swann was married to Cora Dell Barber, the daughter of Nelson and Mary (Batchelor) Barber. The complete history of the Barber family is to be found in the life story of Lew W. Barber, a brother of Mrs. Swann, contained elsewhere in this volume.

To Silvester and Cora Dell (Barber) Swann, four children have been born, Mrs. Cleo Chattin, Nelson, Jesse and Clifford.

All of the members of the Swann family are affiliated with the Bethel Methodist Episcopal church and throughout their lives they have been active in its affairs. They are earnest, Christian people and highly respected citizens of Veale township.

ZADOCK D. VEALE.

Among those men who are eminently entitled to a place in a work of this character, is Zadock D. Veale, whose name initiates this paragraph. The name of Veale will continue to adorn the annals of Daviess county for all time, from the fact that the family was so intimately connected with the pioneer history of this locality and from the further fact that all the members of the family have performed well their part in the drama of civilization and have led lives that were exemplary in every respect. Zadock D. Veale, one of the younger generation of the Veale family, has set an excellent example in this community where he has been a leader for many years, and in a conservative manner has done what he could to promote the advancement which his worthy forbears so successfully began.

Zadock D. Veale was born on the farm where he still lives in Veale township, September 12, 1875. He is the son of William Thomas and Susan (Dickerson) Veale, the former of whom was born on a farm adjoining that on which his son now lives, and the latter, a native of Barr township, born five miles east of Washington. William Thomas Veale was the son of James C., Jr., and Ella (Aikman) Veale. James C. Veale, Jr., was born in the Carolinas and came to Indiana when a boy of eighteen years. His father, James C. Veale, Sr., however, had preceded him by one year, having arrived in Daviess county in 1807. James C. Veale, Sr., was a soldier in the Revolutionary army. He married a Miss Townsend, possibly in Virginia. James C. Veale, Jr., taught the first school in Veale township, in fact, in the whole county. The family settled on what later became Veale creek and also in Veale township, which took its name from James C. Veale, Sr. James C. Veale, Sr., and children all entered land, cleared the forest and established homes in the wilderness. James C. Veale, Jr., was a farmer in that township until his death.

The maternal grandparents of Zadock D. were Zadock and Elizabeth (Cole) Dickerson, the former a native of Maryland and the latter of Kentucky. Mrs. Veale's maternal great-grandparents were Serat and Elizabeth (Smith) Dickerson, natives of Maryland, who moved to Kentucky where Serat Dickerson died. His widow, with her son Zadock, came to Daviess county. Elizabeth Cole was the daughter of James Cole, of Kentucky, who came to Indiana and, after settling here, died in Daviess county.

William Thomas Veale was educated in the public schools of Daviess county and was a farmer throughout his life. He owned one hundred and sixty acres of land where Zadock D. Veale, the subject of this sketch, now lives. He made the most of the improvements upon this farm, including the erection of the buildings which are now standing. The children of William Thomas and Susan Veale were Ella, Elizabeth and Zadock. Ella lives at home with her mother on the old place; Elizabeth married S. G. Wilson, is living in Memphis, Tennessee, and they have one daughter, Susan V., and Zadock D., the subject of this sketch, who never married. Five children were born to William Thomas Veale by a former marriage to Amanda Murphy. They were Alonzo, Willis, Ada, Laura and James.

The Veales were originally Presbyterians, but the family of William Thomas Veale came to be members of the Christian church, which is an offshoot of the Presbyterian church, having been established by Alexander Campbell, who was a prominent member of the Presbyterian church at one time. William Thomas Veale had a brother who was a Presbyterian minister, whose name was James Aikman Veale.

Zadock D. Veale was educated in the local public schools of Veale township, Daviess county, and after completing the common school course, attended a commercial school at Washington. With the exception of two years, he has always lived on the home place. During this two years he was on what might be called a scouting expedition in the West. Mr. Veale has never married. Fraternally, he is a member of the Independent Order of Odd Fellows and the Daughters of Rebekah. He is well known in this community and enjoys the confidence and good will of all his neighbors.

ISAAC ALLISON.

The best title one can establish to a high and generous esteem of an intelligent community is a protracted residence therein. Isaac Allison, one of the best-known and highly esteemed young farmers, has resided in Veale township all his life. His career has been a most commendable one in every respect, well deserving of being perpetuated on the pages of a historical work of the nature of the one in hand. Like his sterling father before him, he has been a man of well-defined purpose and has never failed to carry to successful completion any work or enterprise to which he has addressed himself. He has applied himself very closely to his work and waited for the future to bring its rewards. Together with his brother, also a young man of sterling reputation, he owns the farm which at one time was possessed by his father and to this farm he and his brother have added some forty acres.

Isaac Allison was born in Veale township, Daviess county, Indiana, in 1871. He is the son of John A. and Mary (Carroll) Allison, the former a native of Washington township, and the latter a native of Veale township. John A. Allison was educated in Daviess county and was a teacher for about five years. Subsequently, he became a farmer and followed this vocation until his death. He accummulated one hundred and eighty acres of land, which Isaac Allison and his brother, Owen C., own. Since their father's death, however, they have added forty acres to the farm where the buildings are now located. John A. and Mary (Carroll) Allison became the parents of seven children, Smith M., the eldest; Robert, the fifth, and Dickson, the last child, are deceased. The others are Owen, Isaac, Laura G. and Lillie. The family of John A. and Mary (Carroll) Allison were all members of the Methodist church.

The grandfather of Isaac Allison was Joseph Allison, who was born in Pennsylvania and who came to Kentucky with his parents. He operated a flat-boat and made several trips to New Orleans, walking back. He came to Daviess county before his marriage, and located in Washington township, south of Washington. He owned eighty acres of land there. His wife was Mary Ragsdale, who lived west of Washington in the Maple valley. She was born in South Carolina, in 1800, and was the daughter of Hezekiah Ragsdale, a pioneer of Maple valley, who came here in 1806. He was a mill-wright and made looms, spinning, etc. In 1854, Joseph Allison purchased the old Chapman farm of eighty acres in Veale township, where William Allison's sons now live. Joseph Allison served in the War of 1812. He was the father of ten children. Nancy is ninety-four years old. The other children are Harriette, Martha, Elizabeth, William, Jane, Sarah, Mary, John and Joseph. Joseph was a soldier in the Civil War, having enlisted in Company G, Forty-second Regiment, Indiana Volunteer Infantry, in 1862. He served a little less than a year and went through the campaign in Kentucky and Tennessee. He was also at the battle of Stone's River, and was never wounded or taken prisoner. Joseph Allison was just recovering from sickness when the battle of Stone's River occurred. Although his comrades wanted him to stay back, he insisted on going into the battle. He rode an old horse the day before the battle to keep up with the regiment. At this battle he contracted a cold which caused him to have broken health throughout his life.

Mary (Carroll) Allison, who was the mother of Isaac Allison, was the daughter of Dickson and Leutitia (May) Carroll, both of whom were natives of North Carolina, and who were married there. They came to Indiana in 1837, with five children, and located near Washington township. A short time later they purchased a farm in Veale township, where Owen Allison now lives. They owned one hundred and sixty acres there, only a little of which was cleared when it was purchased from a man who had entered it from the government. Dickson Carroll's sons, Nathaniel, William, John, Robert and Dickson, all served in the Civil War and all survived this war. Another son, Rufus, paid a substitute to go in his place.

Isaac Allison was married, in December, 1904, to Martha G. Ennis.

Three children, Mary Elizabeth, John Albert and Beula Pearl, have been born to this union. All the family are members of the Methodist church. Martha G. was a daughter of Albert W. and Mary Jane (Samples) Ennis. They both lived in Washington township, this county. He was a farmer and died on April 15, 1915. His wife is still living. They were the parents of ten children, seven of whom are now living. He was a Democrat and was interested in the general welfare of his community.

Owen C. Allison, a brother of Isaac, who is associated with him in agricultural enterprises, was born on January 5, 1869, in Veale township. He was educated in the public schools of Veale township and became a farmer. Originally, Smith Allison, a third brother, was associated with Isaac and Owen in their farming enterprises. Smith is now deceased, and the remaining brother continues in partnership. They now operate seven hundred and forty acres, and make a specialty of Shorthorn cattle, as breeders and feeders.

On April 6, 1890, Owen C. Allison was married to Lillie Wilson. Two children, Luther M. and Charles Ray, have been born to this union. The family of Owen Allison are all members of the Methodist church. Mr. Allison formerly was a member of the Independent Order of Odd Fellows.

JOSEPH H. MEADS.

By hard and laborious effort and continuous and well-directed energy, the subject of this review has risen from an humble station in his early life to a position of independent retirement. His unswerving loyalty to right principles of living and fidelity to duty has won him the respect and confidence of the people with whom he has been associated for so many years, and he is fully entitled to recognition in a work of this character, on account of his enterprise and achievements, which have brought him into prominence and earned for himself a conspicuous place in the lives of the men who have been successful and are the leaders in this community.

Joseph H. Meads was born on October 14, 1846, in Washington township, Daviess county, Indiana, the son of William C. and his first wife, Deliah (Hays) Meads. His father was born in 1830, in Washington township, this county and state, and received his early education in the neighboring schools. He began farming as a very young man and owned a farm here which he sold out at a later date and decided to remove to the state of

Kansas, where he purchased two hundred acres of land near Topeka, where he continued to farm until the time of his death in the year 1900. His first wife lived until the year 1849, and during her life had given birth to the following named children: Alfred D., born in 1844, who was in the Civil War as a member of Company E., Sixth Regiment Indiana Volunteer Infantry, was wounded in the battle of Dallas, Texas, and served his country three years; Joseph, the subject of this review, and, John who died in infancy. His second marriage was to Sarah Grow, daughter of Christopher Grow, and to that union were born, Christopher, drowned at the age of seventeen; William, living in Oklahoma; Rousseau, a resident of Kansas; Sentna, now residing in Oklahoma, and Emanuel, postmaster at North Topeka, Kansas. He was a practical member of the Christian church, an advocate of the principles of the Republican party, and personally, a man who was held in the highest esteem by all who knew him.

Receiving his early education in the public schools of Washington township, this county, and when quite a young man, Joseph H. Meads left the parental home and went to the state of Illinois where he secured employment with the Illinois Central Railroad Company. In 1863 he went to New Albany, Indiana, where he clerked in a store for about a year. With the exception of a few months spent in the town of Harrisonville, Indiana, Joseph Meads had farmed all of his life and until the time of his retirement from active work in 1912. During this time, he acquired a farm consisting of one hundred acres in Washington township, this county, where he lived until he sold out in 1912 and removed to Washington, and where he resides with his daughter, Lillian. The subject's wife was born on November 27, 1845, and her maiden name was Theresa McClellan. She was a native of Barr township, Daviess county, and died on December 10, 1910. To their union were born the following named children: Anna, who died at the age of seven years; James M., whose life history is given elsewhere in this volume; Lillian; Charles, who married Claudia Porter and lives on a farm in Barr township; Afred, who married Belle Edwards and lives in Washington where he makes his headquarters as a railroad fireman; Harry, who died about the age of seven years; Elwood, who married Bettie Edwards and lives in Veale township, this county, and Gertrude, who is the wife of Elwood Williams.

Joseph H. Meads bears the reputation of having been a successful farmer, due to his untiring energy and good management, and was able to retire with a fair competence. He has always been identified with the Republican party, but never took any active interest in its affairs. He is a member of the Christian church and renders support to that denomination in accordance with his means. Personally, Mr. Meads is congenial and unassuming in his relations with his fellow men, leads a quiet life and is highly respected by all of his neighbors and acquaintances for the honorable and praiseworthy life he has led.

DANIEL CADDEN.

There are certain qualities which a man must possess who wishes to make a success of any profession. Among these are honesty and determination. The career of Daniel Cadden, a passenger engineer on the Baltimore & Ohio railroad, living at Washington, Indiana, has been strongly marked by these two characteristics. He has never known what it is to lay aside the cares of life and retire to ease, having been a hard-working man all of his life. Because of his honest endeavor to lay aside a comfortable competency for his declining years and because he has spent such a life as to win the commendation of his fellow men, he is eminently worthy of representation in this volume.

Daniel Cadden was born in West Marietta, Ohio, on January 24, 1865, the son of William and Bridget (Coleman) Cadden, both natives of County Mayo, Ireland, and who both came to America when young and were married in Wheeling, West Virginia. Martin Cadden, the paternal grandfather of Daniel Cadden, made a visit to America, but did not locate, returning to his native land, where he remained the rest of his life and where he was a farmer. The maternal grandfather of Mr. Cadden was Daniel Coleman, also a native of Ireland, who came to the United States in his younger days, but remained only a short time, returning to his native land, where he was engaged in the produce business.

William Cadden, the father of Daniel, was a railroad man nearly all his life. He came to America, in 1847, and lived for a time in New York, but later went to Wheeling, West Virginia, where he was engaged in railroad construction work, afterward working at this business in various parts of the United States. Later in life, he retired to a farm in Ohio, and still later moved to Chillicothe, Ohio, where his wife died, after which he came to Washington, Daviess county, Indiana, and lived with his son, Martin, until his death. Both he and his wife were devout members of the Catholic church.

Daniel Cadden was educated in the public schools of Marietta, Ohio, and assisted his father on the farm until he was twenty years of age, when, in 1886, he became a fireman on the old Ohio & Mississippi railroad, now the Baltimore & Ohio, and since that time his name has never been off the pay-roll of this company. He became an engineer in 1895, between Cincinnati and Washington, Indiana, and, in 1908, became a passenger engineer, and has since held this important and responsible position. In 1907, he built his present modern and attractive home in Washington and has made his home there ever since he entered the employ of the Baltimore & Ohio Railway Company, with the exception of a few years when he lived in Jeffersonville, Indiana.

In 1894, Mr. Cadden was married to Agnes Swords, the daughter of Joshua and Mary (Conlin) Swords. They were Ohio people and have always lived there, both of whom are now deceased. He was a blacksmith by trade. They have six children, William, George, Harry, Mary, Annie and Agnes.

Mr. Cadden is a Democrat, but has never taken a very active part in political affairs. He is a member of the Brotherhood of Locomotive Engineers, in which organization he takes an active interest. Both Mr. Cadden and his wife are devout and loyal members of the Catholic church, in whose welfare they are actively interested.

HENRY BACKES.

A review of the life and career of Henry Backes must of necessity be brief in character. To enter fully into the interesting details of his career, the early struggles and the successes of later years, would transcend the limits of this article. Mr. Backes has filled a large place in the ranks of public-spirited citizens and successful newspaper men of his day and generation in Daviess county. His career has been a long, busy and useful one. Although he is a comparatively young man, Mr. Backes has been keenly devoted to the progress and prosperity of his native city, and as a joint owner of the *Washington Democrat*, has been in a position to contribute materially to its growth and prosperity.

Henry Backes was born on February 19, 1873, in Washington, Indiana, a son of John P. and Laura (Maher) Backes, who were married in Washington, Indiana, on January 30, 1871. The paternal grandparents of Henry Backes, Henry and Katherine (Barens) Backes, were among the early set-

HENRY BACKES.

tlers of Washington, coming from Bitburgh, Germany, in July, 1854, after a seventy-two-day voyage on a sailing vessel. No railway passed through Washington then, and the trip from Little Orleans, Indiana, to Daviess county's capital was made by wagon.

Henry Backes received his education in the public schools of his native city, and served his apprenticeship as a printer in the offices of the *Gazette* and the *Advertiser*. On January 1, 1906, he purchased a half interest in the *Democrat* from S. B. Boyd, and since then he and Mr. Boyd have been associated together as equal partners in the enterprise. Mr. Backes has been identified with the *Democrat* in the capacity of printer, foreman, city editor and business manager since 1891. Although an ardent Democrat and active in the councils of his party, and especially in organization work, he has never sought political reward in the form of an elective or an appointive office. He has been content, rather, to work in the trenches for the party's welfare.

On May 29, 1893, Mr. Backes was married to Laversa J. Quick, the ceremony being performed by the Rev. Francis Torbeck, pastor of St. Mary's church. Mrs. Backes was born in this county on September 24, 1874, a daughter of John and Mary Ellen (Johnson) Quick, who were married at Pleasant Hill, Daviess county, on May 2, 1872. Mr. Quick served his country during the Civil War as a member of Capt. James K. Brown's Company L, Fifth Regiment Illinois Cavalry. He died at Fort Leavenworth, Kansas, on October 24, 1909. Mr. and Mrs. Backes are the parents of three children, Bertha Katherine, John Joseph and Richard Paul.

Mr. and Mrs. Backes are members of St. Simon's Catholic church, and Mr. Backes is a member of the Knights of Columbus. He is also a member of the Royal Arcanum.

ALFRED SIMS.

The attention of the reader is called, at this point, to the following brief biography of the gentleman whose name appears above, one of the most progressive farmers of that fine agricultural section comprised in Elmore township, Daviess county, a section dotted with fine farm houses, comfortable homes, spacious and well-filled barns, overflowing granaries; a section on whose rolling pastures sleek cattle graze and in whose happy homes a contented population find life very well worth living. Among the agriculturists of that section, who are carrying on their operations in a large way, few are better known than Alfred Sims, and few families thereabout are more popular and well-liked than his. Having realized, in his own life, something of the hardships attending the efforts of the struggling farmer, but having courageously and industriously faced and overcome the difficulties which confronted him in the earlier part of his career, Mr. Sims is happy in the thought that he is able to give to his family advantages that he did not possess in his day of small things, his children being given a chance to acquire a college training.

Alfred Sims was born on a farm situated on the line separating Daviess and Martin counties in Brown township, on July 10, 1864, the son of Starlin and Susan (Holt) Sims, the former of whom was a native of Lawrence county, a member of one of the most prominent pioneer families of the county, and the latter of whom was born in Tennessee, the daughter of Henry and Catherine (Gray) Holt.

Asbury Sims, father of Starlin Sims and grandfather of the immediate subject of this biographical sketch, was of English descent and born in Laurel county, Kentucky, near London, on March 29, 1808. He moved to Indiana with his father, Starlin Sims, Sr., and located on the site of Bedford, Indiana, about 1820, and died on December 31, 1897. He was one of the early settlers in Lawrence county, Indiana, but not finding conditions there just to his liking, after a brief residence, removed to Daviess county, settling in the Raglesville neighborhood, where he, eventually, purchased a farm and spent the remainder of his life. His wife, who was Katura Killgore, was of Scottish-Irish descent and was born in Sequacha valley, in Tennessee, on May 15, 1811, and died on January 6, 1897. She came to Indiana with her parents, Hiram and Nancy Killgore. One of the immediate ancestors of Mrs. Asbury Sims was Nancy Grant, who was born in South Carolina in 1790. Hiram Killgore was born in Tennessee in 1790. The mother of Asbury Sims was Sarah Howard, a native of Kentucky. This lady had large-jointed or crooked fingers, a peculiarity incident to a great many of the younger generation, among them the subject of this sketch. Starlin Sims, Jr., was a native of Georgia, who came to Kentucky on foot, when a young man. Asbury Sims had four brothers, John, Nicholas, William and Zachariah. John and William moved west in an early day; Nicholas and Zachariah remained in Indiana, spending their entire lives in Martin county. Zachariah was a soldier in the Mexican War and a captain in the War of the Rebellion. Asbury Sims also had four sisters, who lived in Martin county. Charlotte married a Crook; Cynthia Ann married a Rector; Patsy married a Payton, and Elizabeth married a Rainey. Asbury Sims is believed to have cleared the first ground where Raglesville is now located. The grandfather of Asbury Sims' wife was killed and scalped by the Indians in what is now the state of Tennessee.

Asbury and Katura (Killgore) Sims had twelve children, Starlin; Alfred; Edward, who died in his early youth; Zachariah; Noah; Hiram; Sarah, who married Aaron Williams; Abbie, who married Joseph Hastings; Malinda, who married James H. Holt; Nancy, who married Michael O'Connor; Elizabeth and Mary, who died young. Elizabeth married William Marshall.

Starlin Sims was reared on the paternal farm in Van Buren township and as a young man started farming and stock raising for himself, a vocation which he followed all his life, save for the period during which his services were given to the nation in the dark days of the sixties, he having served as a soldier in the Union army. At the close of his military service, Starlin Sims returned to Brown township, Martin county, Indiana, eventually becoming a large landowner in that part of the county, and in Daviess county, where he and his wife also were prominent in all good works, their memory being cherished by many in that region for the good they did during their lives.

Henry Holt, who married Catherine Gray, and who was the father of Mrs. Starlin Sims, was born about 1785, and died in 1880. He was of English descent and a native of the Sequacha valley, in Tennessee. Catherine Gray was of Irish descent also. They had thirteen children, eight sons and five daughters, as follow: Dawswell, Calvin, Henry, Jr., James, Chrispen, John, Emerson, Drury, Sarah, Margaret, Elizabeth, Anna and Susan. Of these children all are deceased except two: Mrs. Anna Woodruff, of near Epsom, who is eighty-seven years old; and Mrs. Sally Ledgerwood, of Scotland, who is ninety-two years old. Susan, the last named and the youngest of the family, was the mother of Alfred Sims.

The Holt family came to the wilds of Martin county and settled one and one-half miles northeast of Burns City about 1833. There was not a spot of cleared land to be found anywhere on the heavy wooded tract which was selected as a homestead. There was a small tract of three or four acres of the homestead very nearly surrounded by a high protective cliff with a fine spring. The family appropriated this enclosure for their few head of live stock, and the projecting rock gave the family their only shelter from spring until the following fall. The first essential was to clear some ground and raise some bread-stuff for the coming winter. Meat was plentiful for the killing. There was the howl of wolves and the scream of panthers on all sides. Susan, being the youngest, slept with her father and mother in the wagon under the cliff and felt somewhat more secure. Other members of the family had to be content with whatever arrangement of their beds could be made. The dogs stood guard. By late fall the family had constructed a substantial hewn log house into which they moved and where they felt more secure at least from the numerous rattlesnakes of the time.

Henry Holt was accustomed to have his young cattle killed by the wolves and at such times made it a point to take a portion of the carcass and bait one of his large bear traps to catch a wolf. He had much better success in catching them by setting his trap in a stream or pool of water. These traps were constructed so that there were two or three steps of stone for the wolf to start in on. A small footing was then made of leaves off the trees encircled by small stakes. The wolf would step on this footing, thinking it was secure, falling into the water would next land in the trap. On one occasion, Henry Holt and his sons took a wolf home alive, thinking they would permit the family to admire it at close range. They cut the tendons in his hind legs and put him down in the yard, thinking he would be helpless. No sooner had he reached the ground than, in some mysterious way, he sprang up and caught one of the children by the arm, pulling her from the door. At this turn of affairs the boys dispatched him at once. On another occasion, one of the sons was watching a deer lick far out in the woods at night. He had constructed a scaffold in a tree, at the side of the lick, upon which he hid himself with a gun in hand and lay in wait for the coming deer. Before climbing the scaffold he had made a trip around the brush to obtain dry material from which he might make a little light, should he hear a deer at the lick, in order to facilitate his aim. While waiting he heard something making the same rounds that he had made in search for material for a torch, and which finally trailed him to the very tree in which he had his scaffold. The animal leaped high up the tree and made a second leap. The son, who by the way was Henry, Jr., had discovered by this time that he was confronted by a panther which was ready to spring upon him at the next jump. Being very much frightened and not knowing what else to do, he screamed at the top of his voice, whereupon the panther dropped to the ground and slowly slunk away. Henry got no deer that night and did not venture down until morning.

To the union of Starlin and Susan (Holt) Sims there were born ten children, as follow: Sarah A., who died at the age of nineteen; William, who married Rosa Burns; Francis, who married Mary Cowan; John, who married Nancy Bowman; Alfred, the immediate subject of this sketch;

Elizabeth, who married Willet Shiveley; Harvey, who married Effie Williams; James, who died in his youth; Anna, deceased, and Margaret, who married William H. Bowman. Starlin Sims was a life-long Republican and gave close attention to the political affairs of the county, state and nation, ever being interested in all movements which promised the betterment of the conditions surrounding the lives of the common people. He reared his family in the faith of the Christian church and he and his wife were actively interested in all the beneficences of the congregation to which they were attached.

Alfred Sims grew to manhood on the paternal farm in Van Buren township, receiving his education in the excellent schools of that township, and, as a young man, started to farm for himself, his first venture being made on a tract of eighty acres. This he cultivated so diligently and so successfully that he has been able to add to his original holdings until now he owns a farm of three hundred and sixty and one-half acres, practically all of which is under a high state of cultivation. In addition to his work as a general farmer, he has engaged extensively in stock raising, his production of Percheron horses, Shorthorn cattle, Shropshire sheep, the large type of Poland China hogs and mammoth jacks and jennets having more than a local reputation for excellence. In 1895, Mr. Sims built his present fine residence in which his family is very pleasantly and happily situated and has built two large barns and two silos, the other outbuildings and general appointments of the farm being in keeping, so that he has today one of the most attractive places in that part of the county.

On March 15, 1888, Mr. Sims was united in marriage to Laura A. Ketcham, daughter of Seth L. and Almira (Benham) Ketcham, the former of whom was born in this county on November 8, 1839, the son of Daniel and Elizabeth (Goodwin) Ketcham. Daniel Ketcham, who was born in the year 1810, came to Daviess county from Shelby county, Kentucky, the place of his birth, in the year 1838, and spent the rest of his life here, becoming one of the largest land owners in the county, owning at the time of his death in October, 1865, six hundred acres of land. His wife, who was Elizabeth Goodwin, was a native of Jackson county, this state, born in 1817, a member of a prominent pioneer family of that part of the state.

Seth L. Ketcham received his early education in the schools of Daviess county, which he supplemented by a two-years' course in the Indiana State University at Bloomington, following which he entered the ranks of the school teachers in this county and for twenty years was one of the county's best-known instructors. When the Civil War broke out, Mr. Ketcham enlisted in Company B, Twenty-seventh Regiment Indiana Volunteer Infantry, but after a service of seven months was discharged on account of chronic rheumatism. On July 16, 1864, Seth L. Ketcham was united in marriage to Almira Benham, who was born in 1839, the daughter of Ira and Mary Benham, and who died in 1881. To this union there were born five children, Mary, Daniel W., Laura A., John M., and W. Evert, the second daughter becoming the wife of Mr. Sims.

To the union of Alfred and Laura A. (Ketcham) Sims there have been born nine children, as follow: Firman C., who married Eldena Caress, has two children, Samuel K. and Sara Cathleen; Susan Almira, who married R. Elmer Killion; Luava; Seth D.; Adolphus, who died at the age of twelve; Laura Bernice; a son who died in infancy; Janet and Madge.

Mr. Sims is a Republican in politics and is a member of the Christian church. He is one of the most prosperous farmers of Elmore township and is counted among the leaders in the social and civic life of his community, being interested and taking a prominent part in all movements which are designed to better the general condition. He is a good citizen who well deserves the high position he occupies in the regard of his neighbors.

OSCAR HANEY.

In the anxious and laborious struggle for an honorable competency and a substantial career on the part of the average professional man fighting the every-day battles of life, there is but little to attract the idle reader in search of a sensational chapter, but for a mind fully awake to the reality and meaning of human existence, there are noble and immortal lessons in the life of the man who, without other means than a clear mind, a strong mind and a true heart, conquers fortune and gains not only temporal reward for his toil, but also that which is greater and higher, the respect and confidence of those with whom his years of active life have placed him in contact. One of the well-known young citizens of Daviess county, Indiana, who has made a record for himself as a teacher in the schools of Daviess county is Oscar Haney.

Oscar Haney was born in Clay county, near Brazil, Indiana, November 15, 1890. He is the son of George and Mary (McCullough) Haney, the former of whom is a farmer in Clay county.

Educated in the common schools of Jackson township, Clay county,

Oscar Haney subsequently spent a year and a half in the non-commissioned high school of his home township and then four years at the Indiana State Normal School at Terre Haute, graduating in 1913.

After Mr. Haney had graduated from the Indiana State Normal School he came to Montgomery, Indiana, in the fall of 1914, as assistant principal of the schools of that place. Subsequently he was appointed as principal of the Cannelburg schools and is now filling that position with credit to himself and to the school he is serving. Mr. Haney is popular, not only with school officials and patrons of the Cannelburg schools, but likewise with the pupils of the school. He is devoted to his chosen profession, and although a comparatively young man, is destined to become one of the foremost leaders in the educational circles of this section of the state of Indiana. Oscar Haney is industrious, well trained for his professional work and possessed of unusual native ability to become a leading instructor.

WILLIAM J. SHANKS.

It is proper to judge the success of a man's life by the estimation in which he is held by his fellow citizens. They see him at work, in his family circle, in church, hear his views on public questions, observe his code of morals, witness how he conducts himself in all the relations of society and civilization and are, therefore, competent to judge of his merits and demerits. After a long period of years, during which daily observations are carried on, it would be out of the question for his neighbors not to know of his worth, for, as has been said, "Actions speak louder than words." In this connection it is not too much to say that William J. Shanks has passed a life of exceptional honor. He has been the recipient of meritorious recognition from the people of Daviess county, who elected him to the office of county surveyor. He possesses the confidence of every one who has had the pleasure of his friendship.

William J. Shanks, the present surveyor of Daviess county, Indiana, was born in Washington township, three miles south of Washington, on April 16, 1887. He is the son of John G. and Mary E. (Carnahan) Shanks, both natives of Daviess county,

John G. Shanks was the son of William and Katherine (Graham) Shanks. William Shanks, subject's grandfather, a native of Fayette county, Pennsylvania, was born June 29, 1827. He was a son of John and Sarah

(Jordan) Shanks, and of German-Irish extraction. Of four children born to John and Sarah Shanks, William was the third. John Shanks was born in the northern part of Pennsylvania in 1801 and his wife was born in 1802 in the same state. In 1837 he came to Daviess county, Indiana, and entered one hundred and sixty acres of land. Aside from being a farmer, he was also a tanner and followed this trade in this state. Subsequently he returned to Pennsylvania in 1838, and remained there until 1846, when he returned with his family and located in Washington township, Daviess county. Here he died in the fall of 1852, and his wife died in 1883.

William Shanks, the grandfather of William J., remained at home and worked for his father until he was twenty-three years of age, after which he taught school for three terms. In 1849, he was appointed deputy surveyor and served for two years. In 1852 he went to California and engaged in mining, but returned in 1856 and began farming. In 1858 he settled on a farm in Washington township, where he remained until his death. He owned three hundred and twenty-six acres of land, of which two hundred and twenty-six acres were in a fine state of cultivation. In 1868 he was elected county surveyor of Daviess county and re-elected in 1872. He was married in 1857 to Katherine Graham, a native of Pike county, Indiana, who was born on October 31, 1827, and who is the daughter of John and Ann M. Graham. John Graham was born in 1779 in Scotland, and his wife was born in Maryland in 1801. The children of William and Katherine Shanks were: Anna and Sarah E., twins, born in February, 1861, and John G., in 1862. William Shanks was an ardent Republican.

Mrs. John G. Shanks, who, before her marriage, was Mary E. Carnahan, was the daughter of John G. and Ellen (McLin) Carnahan, both of whom were natives of Daviess county. John G. Carnahan was the son of Robert and Rebecca Carnahan, natives of Ireland. Ellen McLin was the daughter of George and Anna (Morgan) McLin, the former a native of Kentucky and an early settler in Daviess county. He was a soldier in the American Revolution.

John G. Shanks, the father of William J., was educated in the Daviess county public schools and the Washington high school. He began farming early in life on the old home place of his father south of Washington. He owns two hundred and twenty-five acres and is engaged in general farming. He is a republican and was commissioner of Daviess county from 1906 to 1910. All of the members of the family are active in politics; in fact, William Shanks served sixteen years as surveyor of his home county.

Mrs. John G. Shanks is a devoted member of the Presbyterian church, but the children are mostly members of the Methodist church. John G. and Mary E. (Carnahan) Shanks have had six children, Ethel K., who married Oren Peek; William J., the subject of this sketch; Clifford J., who married Ethel Barber and is now farming the old home place; Bertha, who died at the age of two and one-half years; Frank C., who is a student in the high school, and Russell, who is at home.

William J. Shanks was educated in the common schools of Daviess county and in the high school at Washington. He was also a student for some time at the Washington Commercial College. He took private lessons in surveying under Grant, Ed and George Faith. Mr. Shanks was deputy county surveyor and city engineer for four years under George Faith. William J. Shanks has also been a prodigious student at home. Grant Faith was county bridge engineer when Mr. Shanks was a student under him, and Ed Faith was an attorney who had received a course in surveying in college.

Three years ago William J. Shanks quit surveying and worked as a farmer until January 1, 1915, when he took the office of county surveyor, to which he had been elected in the fall of 1914. William J. Shanks is a man well known throughout Daviess county, and few young men have accomplished more in the same length of time than he. He is a member of the Methodist Episcopal church of Washington.

JOHN FITZPATRICK.

Descended from honored ancestry and himself numbered among the leading agriculturists of Daviess county, Indiana, John Fitzpatrick is entitled to specific recognition in a work of this character. A residence in this county of many years has but strengthened his hold on the hearts of the people with whom he has been associated and today none here enjoys a larger circle of warm friends and acquaintances, who esteem him for his sterling qualities of character and the honorable methods he has always pursued in his dealings with his fellow men.

John Fitzpatrick was born on February 20, 1870, on his present farm in Washington township, Daviess county, and is the son of Ternes and Helen (Mahony) Fitzpatrick. His paternal grandparents were John and Mary (Fitzpatrick) Fitzpatrick, both natives of the state of Ohio, who came here about the year 1851, and settled on the farm at present owned by John Fitzpatrick. It is observed that the grandmother's maiden name was the same as her husband's family name, but they were of no relation. To their union were born the following named children: Elizabeth; Bettie; Ternes, deceased; Susanah; Patrick, deceased; William, deceased; John, deceased; Mary and Nicholas.

Ternes Fitzpatrick was born on the old place in Ohio, in the year 1838, and received his early education in the neighboring public schools. As a young man, he started as a farmer and pursued that calling his entire life, and after coming to Daviess county with his parents, he not only farmed, but having purchased a complete threshing outfit, made this his business, which afforded him an opportunity for increasing his income and, at the same time, gave him a large acquaintance. His original farm consisted of one hundred and thirty-five acres of fine land, and on this place he made a great many improvements. He was regarded as a successful agriculturist in his day and, after living a most useful life and one full of kind consideration and devotion to his family, he died in 1878, being then but forty years of age. His wife, Helen Mahony, was born on May 26, 1836, in County Tipperary, Ireland, and was a daughter of James Mahony and Julia (Sause) Mahony, natives of Tipperary county, Ireland, where the former was a herder. It was in the year 1851 that they immigrated to American soil and settled in Daviess county, this state. To them were born six children, Ellen, John, James, Catherine, Mary and Michael. To Ternes Fitzpatrick and wife were born, William, who died at the age of two and one-half years; John, the subject of this review; Frank J., who graduated in the Washington county high school, attended the Catholic College in Jasper, Indiana, and who is now living in the city of Indianapolis, where he is occupied as a boiler maker.

John Fitzpatrick received his early education in the public schools of Washington township, Daviess county, assisted his father around the farm and, at the age of sixteen, engaged in farming to his exclusive interest. He has always raised a general line of crops and, in addition to this, takes a keen interest in raising good stock. On February 20, 1900, he was married to Celia Wathan who was born on July 28, 1870, and was a daughter of Raphael and Mary (Cavanaugh) Wathan, the former a native of the state of Maryland and the latter a native of the city of Cork, County Cork, Ireland. To their union were born Sarah K., Anna, Thomas, Mary, Celia and Rose. To John and Celia (Wathan) Fitzpatrick have been born the following named children: Doyle, on March 23, 1901; Helen, August 17, 1903; James, October 7, 1905, and Alma, February 4, 1908.

Mr. Fitzpatrick and his family continue to reside on the home farm in Washington township this county, and in the past few years have made a number of decided improvements on the place, including the erection, in 1905, of a fine new modernly-constructed barn building. Everything about the place takes on the aspect of the occupant possessing a fair measure of this world's goods. Mr. Fitzpatrick has the reputation of being a hard-working, industrious and successful agriculturist, and, in the matter of production, he is able to get the maximum results from his lands. The entire family and all of the ancestors have been true to the teachings of the Catholic church and the living members in Washington township are regular attendants at St. Simon's Catholic church in Washington. He is faithful to the principles of the Democratic party, but does not take an active interest in politics. Personally, he is a gentleman in every sense of the word, a warm supporter of all movements tending toward the advancement and welfare of his fellow men and is eminently deserving of the respect and high esteem of everyone.

ARTHUR H. GREENWOOD.

The biographies of enterprising men, especially of good men, are instructive as guides and incentive to others. The examples they furnish of steadfast purpose and inflexible integrity, strongly illustrate what is in their power to accomplish. Some men belong to no exclusive class in life. Apparently insurmountable obstacles have awakened and developed their faculties and served as a stimulus to carry them to ultimate success. Arthur H. Greenwood has lived to good purpose and achieved a much greater degree of success than falls to the lot of the ordinary individual. By a straightforward and commendable course, he has made his way to a respectable position in the world and has won the esteem and admiration of his fellow citizens. His character and steadfast integrity, the public has not been slow to recognize and appreciate, for today, although a young man, he enjoys a large and lucrative law practice in Daviess county, Indiana.

Arthur H. Greenwood was born on January 31, 1880, in Steele township, Daviess county, the son of Richard H. and Eliza J. (Davis) Greenwood, the former a native of Daviess county, and the latter of Crawford county, Ohio. They had six children, who are living, Martha D., the wife of John A. Dilley, of Corydon, Iowa; Franklin K., of Washington; Charles B., of Bogard township; Harry P., of Washington; Theodore, of Bogard township; and Arthur H. Four children died in infancy.

Richard H. Greenwood, the father of Arthur H., was reared in Daviess county. He was a farmer, a blacksmith and operated a saw-mill. He served two terms as trustee of Steele township and was then elected county treasurer, serving two terms. He was a soldier in the Civil War and belonged to the Twenty-seventh Regiment, Indiana Volunteer Infantry. He served in two companies and was in the service altogether three and one-half years. He was wounded at the battle of Antietam, having been shot through the hip. Richard H. Greenwood now lives in Bogard township with his son, Theodore. He is seventy-eight years of age, having been born in 1836. His wife died in 1904, at the age of sixty-six years. Both joined the Methodist church when they were young.

Mr. Greenwood's paternal grandparents were William and Sarah (Wingfield) Greenwood, the former a native of Virginia and the latter of North Carolina. Both were of English stock. They came to Daviess county in 1830, and were farmers. They died at advanced ages, he at the age of eighty-six and she at the age of seventy-six. They had eleven children, Richard H., John W., Catherine, Martha, Theresia, Sina, Elizabeth, William, Mack, Lydia and Elisha H. The maternal grandparents of Mr. Greenwood were Christian and Charity (Felts) Davies, natives of Ohio, where they lived in Crawford county. She and her husband died in Ohio and had a family of seven children, Mary A., Levi, Charity, Eliza J., mother of subject of this sketch; Elias, Julia, and one, Christian, who died while young.

Arthur H. Greenwood lived in Washington township, Daviess county, until twelve or fourteen years of age, when his parents removed to Washington, where he grew to manhood. He attended the public schools and was graduated from the Washington high school with the class of 1898. He then entered Indiana State University, at Bloomington, and graduated from the law department in 1905 with the degree of Bachelor of Laws. Between the time Mr. Greenwood was graduated from the high school and the time he entered the university, he was a clerk for Cabel & Kauffman, in Washington, Indiana. He worked in this capacity from 1898 till 1902, or three and one-half years. In 1905, Mr. Greenwood was admitted to the bar in Daviess county, in the state and federal courts, and has practiced law in Washington since that time.

Arthur H. Greenwod was married on September 30, 1906, to Nettie B. Small, the daughter of Joseph W. and Annetta B. (Brown) Small. Three children have been born to this happy union, Ruth, Joseph R. and Arthur H., Jr.

Mrs. Greenwood was born in Washington. Her parents were natives of Daviess county and now live two miles west of Washington. They have six children, Naomi, William, Nettie, Joseph W., Ella and Thomas. Mrs. Greenwod's paternal grandparents were William and Ann (Sanford) Small, both natives of Daviess county. They had eleven children, Joseph W., Tabitha C., Mary, Lucretia, John, Thomas, Helen, Jennie, Reuben, Benjamin and Sarah. The maternal grandparents were Alonson and Margaret Brown, natives of Indiana and former residents of Fredericksburg. Mrs. Small is the only living child born to this union. Margaret Brown had been formerly married to a Mr. Morgan and had eight children by that marriage, Elizabeth, David K., Lydia, Richard, John, William, Sarah and Volney.

Mr. and Mrs. Arthur H. Greenwood are members of the Baptist church, of which Mr. Greenwood is a deacon. He is also assistant superintendent of the Sunday school. Mr. Greenwood belongs to Washington lodge of the Independent Order of Odd Fellows. His affiliations are with the Democratic party. At the present time he is county attorney of Daviess county and is also acting as treasurer of the Washington board of education.

During his college course, Mr. Greenwood distinguished himself as a leader among his fellow students. Since his graduation from college he has fulfilled the expectations of his friends during his college days. He has become a leader, not only in his profession, but in the political life of the county where he resides. He is a man of well-pronounced convictions and a man who does not deviate from these convictions.

JOHN W. BILLINGS.

Among the representative farmers and stock growers of Washington township, Daviess county, Indiana, is the man whose name appears as the caption for this review. He is known as one of the alert, progressive and successful agriculturists of this favored section of the Hoosier state. In his labors he has studied and experimented with intelligence and thus secured the maximum returns from his enterprising efforts. At all times his course has been so ordered as to command the confidence and regard of the people of this community, being a man of honorable business methods and advocating whatever tends to promote the public welfare in any way.

John W. Billings was born in the state of Illinois on November 26, 1850, and is the son of Jesse and Sarah (Miller) Billings. His father was born in Lawrence county, Indiana, on August 19, 1831, and was the son of

William and Mary (Davis) Billings, the former a native of the state of Tennessee and the latter of Wales, who were married in Tennessee in the year 1820. Two years after their marriage, they moved to Lawrence county, and made an investment in two hundred acres of land, situated near the town of Mitchell. It was in this neighborhood that John Billings' father was born and where his mother died when he was but eight years of age. Jesse Billings continued to reside with his father, received his early education in the public schools of Lawrence county, learned farming, and remained with the father until he attained the age of nineteen years, and was married, February 7, 1850, to Sarah Miller. She was born on November 22, 1833, and was a daughter of John and Susannah (Tyre) Miller. Soon after his marriage, Jesse Billings moved from Lawrence county to Illinois, where he bought land and remained for the following four years. It is said that he had erected the largest barn building in Illinois, also, that when he left Indiana he carried all of his belongings in a red bandana handkerchief and returned to Indiana with four thousand dollars in gold coin. Upon his return to this state, he settled in Daviess county, where he purchased one hundred and thirty-five acres of land and added to it from time to time until the total acreage he owned amounted to five hundred and sixty. To Jesse and Sarah (Miller) Billings were born the following named children: John W., the subject; Abram R., who married Bettie Thomas; Mary S., who married Dora Dant; George W., who married Eva Beckett; Annie A., who married James Meade; Annetta B., who married Jefferson Bates; Morton E., who married Turrie Hayes; Charles S., who married Lovina Osborn; Lillie M., who married John Kemper; Louis S., who married Belle Arnold; Jesse Frank, who married Rettie Rindinger. Jesse Billings was a member of the order of Free and Accepted Masons, a supporter of the Republican ticket, and a member of the Christian church.

John W. Billings received his early education in the public schools of Washington township, Daviess county, and afterward devoted a year to the teaching of school. Owing to his deep interest in farming, and not caring to continue teaching for a livelihood, his father purchased for him one hundred and fifteen acres of land in Washington township, and it is on that place John W. has devoted his entire life. Since beginning here, he has acquired considerably more land, and today, his holdings consist of four hundred acres of exceedingly high-grade farming land. A number of well-constructed buildings are on the place and everything is kept up to the very highest point of efficiency. The residence, which is one of the finest in the community, is modern in every particular, and a source of pride to the owner and his family. John W. Billings has been twice married, the first union was with Ellen Cosby, a daughter of Overton Cosby and wife, to whom were born, Oscar, who married Nora Allison, they have two children, Nellie and Mary; James, who married Mary T. Holder, who now live in Evansville. Their children are Lillian, Arthur and Lessie; Harry, who married Jennie Blackwell and is living in the West. Their children are Dorothy, Floyd and Stewart, and William. Subject's second marriage was to Elizabeth Rogers, born on March 21, 1860, who was the daughter of William and Mary Suddith, and occurred in the year 1895. The children by the second marriage are Dewill and Gladys.

Though an ardent supporter of the Republican ticket, John M. Billings does not take a very active part in politics. He and his family are members of the Baptist church. Mr. Billings is a man who keeps well abreast of the times, being a wide reader of current topics and has won the respect and esteem of all who know him for his friendly manner, his business ability and upright living, and he is regarded by all as one of the substantial and progressive citizens of this section of the county. He is a popular member of the circles in which he moves and ever alert to promote anything that tends to benefit the welfare of mankind.

JOHN WILLIS WILLIAMS.

It is a well-attested fact that the greatness of a community or state lies not in the machinery of government nor even in its institutions, but rather in the sterling qualities of individual citizens; in their capacity for high and unselfish efforts, and in their devotion to the public welfare. In these particulars John Willis Williams has conferred honor and dignity upon his locality and as an elemental part of history it is fitting that there should be recorded a resume of his career, with the object of noting his connections with the advancement of one of the most flourishing and progressive agricultural sections of the commonwealth.

John Willis Williams, a well-known and progressive farmer of Barr township, Daviess county, Indiana, was born in the township where he is living on November 13, 1855, the son of John Robert and Emmeline (Gates) Williams, the former a native of Louisville, Kentucky, and the latter a native of Beardstown, that state.

The paternal grandparents of Mr. Williams were William and Elizabeth (Hethington) Williams, both natives of Ireland, who were married there, and who, after their marriage came to America about 1832. He later returned to Ireland, but came to the United States a second time, settling near New Albany, Indiana. He was the owner of a farm near Palmyra.

The maternal grandparents of Mr. Williams were John and Nancy Ellen (Brown) Gates, of near Beardstown, Kentucky, who came to Indiana by covered wagon about 1834, locating in Barr township, in the woods just a little west of Loogootee. Here he acquired one hundred and twenty acres of land in the wilderness and cleared and improved it. He owned several farms at the time of his death, but before this time he had removed with his family to Perry township, Martin county, Indiana.

John Robert Williams, the father of John Williams, was reared in Washington township by his grandparents on his mother's side of the family. At the outbreak of the Civil War he enlisted in Company E, Eightieth Regiment, Indiana Volunteer Infantry, at which time he was living in Martin county. He returned to this state, after the war, and followed the carpenter trade until 1869, and then became a farmer, following this occupation, in Martin county, until 1875, when he located in Barr township, south of Cannelburg. John Robert Williams was a well-known farmer and highly esteemed in this community. He was a man of industrious and frugal habits and devoted primarily to his own personal interests. Nevertheless, he had a keen interest in the welfare of his neighbors and friends and was greatly beloved by them.

John Willis Williams was educated in the public schools of Martin county and began his own personal career in Barr township as a farmer. In the beginning, Mr. Williams was a renter. Subsequently, he purchased twelve acres of land, a part of the splendid farm upon which he now lives. This land was purchased in 1881, to which Mr. Williams has added until he now owns one hundred and sixty-five acres of fine farming land. The farm is well equipped with modern, up-to-date buildings for general farming, and Mr. Williams also makes a specialty of dairying. During late years he has begun to establish a herd of Holstein cattle, and has been very successful.

Mr. Williams was married on November 27, 1877, to Ann Brown, the daughter of William and Scholastica (Gough) Brown, the former of whom was born and reared in Washington. His brother, Joseph Brown, was at one time sheriff of Daviess county. William Brown's parents were early settlers in Washington, Indiana.

John W. and Anna (Brown) Williams are the parents of seven children, Lewis Vitus, Anna Mary, John Leo, Ernest, Frances Helen, Bridget Louisa and Cassie.

Mr. Williams has never been active in public affairs in the community where he lives and especially in politics, but served a term of two years as road supervisor. He, together with his family, are members of St. Peter's Catholic church, to which they are earnestly devoted and are liberal contributors to its support. John W. Williams is a man who is highly respected in Barr township.

CHARLES W. KEITH.

It is proper to judge of the success of a man's life by the estimation in which he is held by his fellow citizens. They see him at his work, in his family circle, in church, hear his views on public questions, observe the operation of his code of morals, witness how he conducts himself in all the relations of society and civilization, and are, therefore, competent to judge of his merits and demerits. After a long course of years of such daily observations, it would be out of the question for his neighbors not to know of his worth, for, "Actions speak louder than words." In this connection it is not too much to say that the subject of this sketch has passed a life of honor, that he has been industrious and at the same time liberal, and that he has the confidence of all who have the pleasure of his friendship.

Charles W. Keith was born on October 11, 1877, in Washington township, Daviess county, Indiana, and is the son of George J. Keith and wife, whose life record is given elsewhere in this work.

Having received his education in the township schools of Daviess county, Charles W. Keith began his career as a farmer when quite a young man. It was about four years ago that he moved to his present location, which farm contains two hundred and eighty-five acres of first-class land, the greater portion of which is kept under cultivation and used for grazing stock. A general line of crops is raised and he also gives his attention to live stock. Since moving to this place, a number of improvements have been made in the way of new buildings, and the home is well situated, strictly modern and a source of considerable pride to the owner and his family.

Charles W. Keith was married on January 27, 1901, to Lucretia R. Parsons, who was born in Barr township, Daviess county, and is a daughter of Benjamin and Vienna (Hannah) Parsons, who are the parents of eight

(34)

children, as follow: William A., who married Elizabeth Mattingly; Lucretia, subject's wife; Mary, who married James Quilliams; Ervin A., who married Ora Jones; Austin R., who married Hattie Ragles, and Dovie L. To Charles W. and Lucretia (Parsons) Keith have been born the following named children: Charles Arthur, on April 25, 1902; George Benjamin, April 12, 1906, and Prentis S., October 17, 1908, died on May 3, 1909.

Mr. Keith believes in the principles of the Republican party and has supported that ticket through the various campaigns since his first vote. He does not take an active part in political matters, but is always ready to lend his influence in the proper direction, and according to his view. He and the family are members of the Christian church and lend their support to that denomination. Personally, he is a broad-minded, liberal man, possessing a splendid, good-natured disposition and ever ready to lend a helping hand to his less fortunate fellow citizens. He is well and most favorably known throughout this entire section and has always been regarded as a man of sound business principles, upright in all his dealings and congenial in his relations with his acquaintances. He has a host of friends and, because of his high character, progressiveness and enterprise, is entitled to representation in the history of the county in which he lives.

GEORGE ALVIN FAITH.

There are individuals in nearly every community who, by reason of pronounced ability and force of character, rise above the heads of the masses and command the unbounded esteem of their fellow men. Characterized by perseverance and a directing spirit, virtues that never fail, such men always make their presence felt and the vigor of their strong personalities serves as a stimulus and an incentive to the young and rising generation. To this energetic and enterprising class, George Alvin Faith, a well-known lawyer of Washington, Indiana, very properly belongs. Mr. Faith has devoted himself to his adopted profession and to the public duties to which he has been called and because of his personal worth and accomplishments he is clearly entitled to representation among the enterprising and progressive business men of his locality. Mr. Faith received a good education. He was a successful school teacher and an efficient civil engineer and in late years has built up a flourishing practice as a lawyer.

George Alvin Faith was born on December 3, 1878, in Bogard township, Daviess county, Indiana. He is the son of Thomas W. and Matilda J. (Strange) Faith, the former a native of Daviess and the latter a native of Martin county, Indiana. They have seven children, Grant, of Pimento, Indiana; Edward C., a lawyer of Washington; Milton Z., of Veale township; Henry C., of West Point, Mississippi; George A., of Washington, and Hugh G., a farmer of Washington. One son, John, died in infancy.

Thomas W. Faith, the father of George Alvin, was reared in Daviess county and was a farmer and lumberman. He owned a farm of one hundred and twenty acres in Bogard township, near the village of Epsom, where he reared his family. Besides this old homestead farm, Thomas W. Faith owned other farm property. He now lives at the edge of the city of Washington, and is retired. He and his wife are members of the Methodist Episcopal church. Thomas W. Faith was a soldier in the Civil War, serving three years. He was a private and was with Grant at Vicksburg.

The paternal grandfather of George Alvin Faith was Abraham H. Faith, whose wife was Frances (Myers) Faith. The former was a native of Ohio, of English descent, and the latter of German parentage. They were married in Daviess county. He died about 1897, his wife died October 11, 1886. They had a large family, consisting of the following children: Louisa, Dianah, Melissa, Laura, Lavina, Thomas W. and Abraham H.

George Alvin Faith's great-grandfather was Thomas Faith, who was a pioneer of Daviess county, and who owned the old Brett farm. He was not only a farmer, but a successful cabinetmaker. He came to Daviess county from Pennsylvania. His wife was Catherine (Boos) Faith. Thomas Faith was a soldier in the War of 1812, and fought with Harrison at Tippecanoe. His father was a Revolutionary soldier. The maternal grandfather of George Alvin Faith was John Joseph Strange whose wife before her marriage was a Miss Scott, with natives of Kentucky. John Joseph Strange's wife, through her mother, was connected with the famous Price family and a relative of the Confederate General Price's family. They were pioneers in Martin county, Indiana, and there died. They had a large family, consisting of these children: John S., Thomas, Melinda E., Elizabeth, Sarah, Margaret, Martha, Lewis, Lucinda, Susan and Matilda.

George Alvin Faith was reared on his father's farm in Bogard township, and there attended the district schools. He graduated from the Washington high school with the class of 1897, and then taught school for six years. Subsequently, he was engaged in civil engineering for some time. He studied law and practiced his profession in Washington for twelve years.

During this time Mr. Faith has built up a large and lucrative practice and established himself as one of the leading lawyers in Daviess county. He is well versed in the law and does a general practice, not only in the city of Washington, but throughout Daviess and adjoining counties.

George Alvin Faith was married on December 21, 1907, to Virginia Hays Head, a daughter of Hillary and Sarah (Hays) Head. Three children have been born to this happy union, John Head, George Alvin, Jr., and Helen Virginia.

Mrs. Faith was born in Daviess county. Her parents were natives of Kentucky. Her father died in 1909, at the age of sixty-eight years. Her mother is still living in Parshall, Colorado. Mrs. Faith is one of four children, Hallie, Nellie, Virginia and one who died in infancy. Mrs. Faith is a member of the Baptist church.

Although George Alvin Faith is not an active farmer, nevertheless he owns a splendid farm of one hundred and seventy-five acres in Washington township and directs the operations on this farm. He is a Republican and has served as county surveyor for four years and was civil engineer of the city of Washington for four years. George Alvin Faith is well known in Washington and Daviess county. His activity in politics has brought him a well-deserved recognition and his ability as a lawyer has brought him a well-merited practice.

JOSEPH D. FRANKLIN.

The science of agriculture, for it is a science, finds an able exponent and an able and successful practitioner in the person of Joseph D. Franklin, who is widely known in Daviess county, Indiana. Mr. Franklin has a very fertile and productive farm, located in Veale township. He comes from one of the highly honored and respected families of Daviess county, the members of which have played well their part in the general development of this favored section of the great Hoosier commonwealth. Mr. Franklin has lived in this county for more than fifty years and is well known to all classes and conditions of men.

Joseph D. Franklin was born on September 25, 1862, in Veale township, Daviess county, Indiana, and is the son of John F. and Laura J. (Ragsdale) Franklin, the former a native of Germany, born in 1823, and the latter a native of Veale township. Joseph D. Franklin's paternal grandparents were born, lived and died in Germany. His paternal grandfather was killed in a flour-mill. His widow, with her son, John F., the father of Joseph D., and a half-sister came to America in 1827, when John F. was only four years old. Joseph D. Franklin's maternal grandparents came to this county in the early days and located near the old Bethel church, in Veale township. Mr. Franklin's maternal grandfather was a Methodist minister and a farmer.

John F. Franklin, the father of Joseph D., landed at Baltimore upon the arrival of himself and his mother in this country, but a few years later they came to Cincinnati. At the age of twelve years, he started in life for himself. At this time he had no shoes, only two shirts and a sealskin cap. He remained for a time in Cincinnati and then came to Veale township, where he entered forty acres of land, where his son, Joseph D., now lives. John F. Franklin added to his original forty acres until at one time he owned over six hundred acres. He was a hard and industrious worker and was accustomed to be up in the morning before daylight and to wait for the light to come so that he might cultivate his crops. His mother died when he was eight years old, and until he was twelve years old, he was cared for by an uncle. He helped to build the canal between Evansville and Indianapolis. He was an officer during the time Alton B. Parker was nominated and died sitting in his chair on the old home farm soon after making the remark that he thought the Democrats should nominate Bryan. John F. and Laura Franklin had six children, Joseph D., the subject of this sketch; Mrs. Charity Van Trees; Mrs. Mary E. Taylor; Susan A., Cora H., deceased, who graduated from the Academy of Music at Cincinnati, and Estella.

Joseph D. Franklin was educated in the common schools of Veale township. He took up farming early in life and, except for one or two years, has always lived on the old home place. For fourteen years he has operated coal mines on his land. He has sixty-one acres in his own farm and his mother, who lives in Washington, also owns land.

Joseph D. Franklin was married in 1897 to Martha M. McCain, of Pike county, Indiana. To this union three children have been born, Floyd Frederick, who is a student in the second year of high school at Washington, and who is sixteen years old; Jewell Dott, seven years old, who is attending the home school, and Alvin Marshall, who is five years old.

The Franklin family are members of the Methodist Episcopal church at Pleasant Hill. Mr. Franklin is a member of the Independent Order of Odd Fellows and belongs to Star lodge, at Glendale. He is also a member of the Improved Order of Red Men and the Woodmen of the World, both at Washington. Joseph D. Franklin is well known and highly respected throughout Daviess county. He is a Democrat and has served as a notary public for the past eight years. Mr. and Mrs. Franklin carry a joint endowment policy of sixteen thousand dollars.

JAMES M. MEADS.

Examples that impress force of character on all who study them, are worthy of record. By a few general observations may be conveyed some idea of the high standing and intellectual qualities of James M. Meads in the community where so many active years of his life have been spent. United in his composition are so many elements of a solid and practical nature which, during a series of years, have brought him into prominent notice, and earned for him a conspicuous place among the enterprising men of Daviess county, Indiana, that it is but just recognition of his worth to speak of his achievements.

James M. Meads was born on February 16, 1869, in Washington township, Daviess county, and is the son of Joseph H. and Theresa (McClellan) Meads, whose life history appears elsewhere in this volume under the caption of Joseph H. Meads.

When quite a young man, James M. Meads, educated in the public schools of Washington township, this county, started his agricultural career, by renting a farm in Barr township, which he cultivated for a period of five years. In the month of December, 1892, having been economical and thrifty, he purchased a forty-eight-acre tract of land in Washington township; in 1900, he purchased an adjoining thirty-seven acres, and, in December, 1905, made a further purchase of adjoining land of twenty-three and three-quarter acres, giving him a total of one hundred eight and three-quarters acres in this township. From time to time, needed improvements were made and it was in 1895 that he erected a splendid barn building and a residence. The barn was struck by lightning and as a consequence the building was burned and quite a severe loss was sustained. This structure was replaced by a new barn, which was again destroyed on June 30, 1913. A new barn was erected September, 1913. In addition to general farming, James Meads is interested, to some extent, in the raising of fine cattle. He has ample barn, shed and granary room and the buildings are all kept in the best of repair and paint. Everything about this place gives the observer the impression that the owner is a good manager and prosperous.

James H. Meads was married on February 2, 1890, to Anna Billings, a daughter of Jesse and Sarah (Miller) Billings, whose life history appears elsewhere in this work under the caption, John W. Billings.

Identified with the Democratic party since 1896, and during the years of 1912, 1913 and 1914, James H. Meads served on the board of county commissioners of Daviess county. He is an ardent supporter of the progressive principles set forth by his party and always lends an aggressive, helping hand to his party's interests. Personally, Mr. Meads is a man of great popularity in his community and can be depended upon, by his friends and acquaintances, to give, from memory, exact data pertaining to the dates of happenings of any consequence. His intelligence along these lines is particularly marvelous. From a social standpoint he is a man who makes friends easily, is genial and pleasant to meet, well informed on all current topics, and a man in whom the utmost confidence is reposed by all who know him.

STEPHEN HENRY BATCHELOR.

The best title one may establish to the high and generous esteem of a community is a protracted residence therein. Stephen Henry Batchelor has resided in Daviess county since he was fifteen years old. His career has been a commendable one, well deserving of perpetuation on the pages of a historical work of this nature. Knowing that the county was destined to take high rank in the productive and rich localities of the North, Mr. Batchelor has applied himself very closely to his work and waited for the future to bring to him its reward. Today he is one of the substantial farmers and dairymen of this county.

Stephen Henry Batchelor was born on August 27, 1871, in Orange county, Indiana. He is the son of George and Katherine (Scarlett) Batchelor, both of whom were natives of Orange county. Stephen Henry Batchelor's paternal grandparents were natives of Orange county, where they lived and died. His paternal grandfather was a farmer and a soldier in the War of 1812. His maternal grandfather was also a native of Orange county and a farmer. He was also a soldier in the War of 1812. Mr. Batchelor's paternal and maternal grandparents all lived and died in Orange county.

George Batchelor, the father of Stephen H., was educated in the public schools of Orange county. He died when Stephen H. was but eight years of age and his wife also died in Orange county. George Batchelor was a farmer and is the father of eight children, four children having been born to each of two marriages. The mother of Stephen H. Batchelor was George Batchelor's first wife.

Stephen H. Batchelor was educated in the public schools of Orange county and also in the schools of Daviess county, to which county he came when he was about fifteen years of age, in company with his step-mother.

From the time Stephen H. Batchelor was fifteen years of age, until his marriage, he worked at different places and for different people, but he has made his own way in the world practically since he was ten years old. Mr. Batchelor first purchased a farm of seventy acres in August, 1900, where he now lives. It is well located and Mr. Batchelor has comfortable and commodious buildings, where he also makes a specialty of raising small fruit and is engaged in the dairy business. His dairy cattle are almost all Jerseys.

On April 4, 1895, Stephen H. Batchelor was married, when he was twenty-four years old, to Etta May Rutherford, a native of Ohio. To this happy union one child, Ernest Henry, has been born. The Batchelor family are all members of the Methodist Episcopal church and active in the work of both the church and Sunday school, he being a liberal contributor to the support of this church. Mr. Batchelor is a Republican, but has never aspired to office. His own personal affairs have taken up his time and he has preferred to devote his spare moments to the welfare of his wife and child.

CHARLES L. STUCKEY.

The biographies of successful men are instructive as guides and incentives to those whose careers are yet to be achieved. The examples they furnish of patient purpose and consecutive endeavor strongly illustrate what is in the power of each to accomplish. Charles L. Stuckey, whose life story herewith is briefly set forth, is a conspicuous example of one who has lived to good purpose and achieved a definite degree of success in farming, to which vocation his accomplishments and energies have been directed.

Charles L. Stuckey was born in Washington, Indiana, on June 18, 1869. He is the son of William S. and Deborah A. (Johnson) Stuckey, the former a native of Pike county, in this state. William S. Stuckey was a son of George P. and Permelia (Traylor) Stuckey. George P. Stuckey was born on February 25, 1806, and his wife on August 1, 1808. Sarah A. (Johnson) Stuckey was the daughter of the Rev. Levi Johnson, who for many years was a Methodist preacher in southern Indiana. He preached at Bethel, on what was called the Washington circuit.

William S. Stuckey, father of Charles L., came as a boy to Daviess county, where he was educated in the public schools. He was a school teacher for some time and later a wagon maker in Washington. Finally he became a farmer in Veale township and followed this vocation until his death. He was a justice of the peace for many years and acquired a wide reputation on account of the number of people he married. He also served in the capacity of township assessor. William S. Stuckey and his wife were the parents of several children, among whom were George L., Lawson H., Charles L., Leonard N., Willison L., Elmer L., Mary B., Emma Grace, Myrtle, Edward, Elsworth and two others.

George P. and Permelia (Traylor) Stuckey, the paternal grandparents of Charles L. Stuckey, were the parents of eleven children, Elizabeth J., born on March 26, 1828; William S., July 29, 1830; Samuel Ray, July 3, 1832; Jacob A., October 8, 1834; Simon D., November 26, 1836; Lemmon, date unknown; Jessie, February 2, 1839; Polly H., February 14 1841; Frances C., in 1843; Noah P., November 6, 1845; Eliza Ellen, October 6, 1848. Eliza Ellen is the only one of this family who is still living. She lives at Spokane, Washington.

Rev. Eli Johnson, the maternal grandfather of Mr. Stuckey, was born on August 28, 1813, and married Primmellar Wright, who was born on February 22, 1819. They had fourteen children, as follow: J. Wesley, born on March 28, 1837; James, October 5, 1839; David E., September 10, 1841; Charles D., October 11, 1843; William H., February 19, 1845; Deborah, February 13, 1847; Mary H., June 12, 1849; Lucian B., January 1, 1851; Maria J., November 7, 1853; Susan C., February 28, 1855; Emma C., January 13, 1857; Sarah N., June 17, 1859; George McClellan, December 1, 1851; and Elmer K., August 2, 1863.

Charles S. Stuckey, the subject of this sketch, was educated in the public schools of Veale township and in the normal schools at Odon and Princeton. He taught school for thirteen years, beginning in 1892. In 1903 Mr. Stuckey was elected township trustee, and served one term, during which period he had much to do with raising the standard of the schools. He gave entire satisfaction as trustee of this township and was remembered by the people for the services he performed. During this time he was engaged in farming, and, in fact, has been a farmer since his retirement from this office. He owns seventy-two acres of land and has erected good buildings on the farm. Mr. Stuckey is entitled to the full credit for his success, because he has received no outside assistance from anyone.

Charles L. Stuckey was married in 1900 to Carrie B. Peek, the daughter of Charles E. Peek and Julia A. (Thomas) Peek. Charles E. Peek is the son of John and Winnie (Palmer) Peek, and his wife is the daughter of William Wright Thomas. To this union three children, Donald J., Russell D. and Elva P. have been born.

Mr. Stuckey is a member of the Independent Order of Odd Fellows. He and his wife and family are members of the Methodist Episcopal church. The Stuckeys are prominent farmers in Daviess county and are clearly entitled to representation in a volume which purports to preserve the history of the people of this county.

THOMAS G. HORRALL.

It is certainly interesting to note in the series of personal sketches in this volume, the varying conditions that have compassed those whose careers are here outlined. An effort has been made in each case to throw well-focused light on each individuality and to bring into proper perspective the scheme of each career. Each man who strives to fulfill his part in connection with human life and activities is deserving of recognition whatever may be his field of endeavor, and it is the function of works of this nature to perpetuate for future generations an authentic record concerning those represented in its pages. The value of such publications is certain to be cumulative for all time to come and will present the individual and specific accomplishments from which generic history is derived.

Thomas G. Horrall, the subject of this sketch, was born on the farm where he now lives in Veale township, in 1851. He is a son of Thomas and Elizabeth (Jones) Horrall, the former a native of South Carolina and the latter a native of Daviess county, Indiana. Thomas G. Horrall's paternal grandparents came from South Carolina and settled in Daviess county. They lived in Washington township, near what is now known as the Lillie farm, at which time there was a fort upon the farm. Mr. Horrall's maternal grandfather, William H. Jones, was a pioneer farmer in Daviess county.

Thomas Horrall, Sr., the father of Thomas G. Horrall, came to Daviess county when a boy and from here enlisted in the Federal army, during the War of 1812. He was a farmer throughout his life. He entered forty acres where Thomas G., the subject of this sketch, now lives, but owned several farms at different times. At his death, he owned one hundred and fifteen acres, where Thomas G. now lives. The brick that were used in constructing the house, on this farm, Thomas Horrall, Sr., burned on the place. He also built the house, but in the division of the farm, at the death of the father, Thomas G.'s sister took that portion of the farm.

Thomas G. Horrall was educated in the Veale township schools, has lived on the old farm all his life, and has never been away from home more than two weeks at a time. Thomas G. Horrall owns sixty-five acres of land and rents considerable tracts of land from different neighbors. He has erected the present buildings on the farm and is engaged extensively in dairying.

In 1884 Thomas G. Horrall was married to Emmor Kelso, of Reeve township, Daviess county. To this happy union, one child, Edith, has been born. She is now Mrs. Ezra Bingham. All of the Horrall family are identified with the Methodist Episcopal church and they are all prominent in both the work of the church and the Sunday school. Mr. Horrall is a liberal contributor. Politically, he is a Republican, but he has never been active in the councils of any party.

MATTHEW L. BRETT.

One of the best-remembered men of a past generation in Daviess county, Indiana, is the late Matthew L. Brett, who served many years as auditor of Daviess county, several terms in the Indiana Legislature and as treasurer of the state of Indiana. Of Mr. Brett, personally, it may be said that he was a man of strong and active sympathies. His sentiment was warm and ardent, his feelings deep and intense, and these and other attractive characteristics unconsciously drew him a large number of devoted friends upon whom, under all circumstances, he could rely, and who, now that he has passed from earthly scenes, revere his memory. He was a close student of human nature and comprehended with little effort the motives and purposes of men. He was a lover of truth and sincerity and the very soul of honor. In brief, he is remembered as a manly man of pleasing but dignified presence, a student of many subjects and an influential man in the circles in which he moved. Of sound character and unflagging energy, he stood as a conspicuous example of symmetrically developed manhood. His position as one of the state's representative citizens was conceded by all who knew him.

The late Matthew L. Brett was born on January 5, 1823, in South Carolina. He was the eldest of seven children born to Patrick M. and Mary Brett, who came to America from Ireland immediately after their marriage, in 1820. They lived in South Carolina for about ten years and then came to Daviess county. Patrick M. Brett was a lawyer and professor and a prominent man in South Carolina and also in Daviess county. He held many important offices, among which was that of county auditor. He died in 1844 and his wife in 1868.

Matthew L. Brett was reared on a farm in Daviess county, where he spent most of his life. He was educated under the direction of his father and, although he was unable to attend college himself, he was able to afford that privilege to his brother and five sisters. At the age of twenty-one, he succeeded his father as county auditor of Daviess county, in 1844, and held this office continuously for fifteen years. During the time he was auditor of Daviess county, he also carried on farming, milling and in the mercantile business. In 1860, Matthew L. Brett was elected to the Indiana Legislature and served during the regular and special sessions. He served two years on a committee appointed by the Legislature to audit the expenses incurred by the state on account of the war. In 1862, Mr. Brett was elected treasurer of the state of Indiana and held this position two years. In 1872, he was elected to the state Legislature again and served during two sessions. Shortly after his service in the Legislature, he became a cripple and from this time on, until his death, he gave his entire attention to farming. He owned two hundred and fifty acres, a part of which was located near Washington, in Daviess county, and a part located in Warren county.

On June 1, 1858, Matthew L. Brett was married to Alice Hayes, of Vincennes. She was the daughter of William and Ann (Beckes) Hayes. Benjamin Beckes, the father of Ann Beckes and grandfather of Mrs. Brett, was said to be the first white child born in Vincennes. Two children were born to Matthew L. Brett and wife, both of whom are now deceased, Anna, who was the wife of Austin F. Cable, and William, who died young. Mr. and Mrs. Cable had one son, Brett, who is the only descendant of Matthew L. Brett. Brett Cable has always resided with his grandmother and operates the old home farm.

Matthew L. Brett is said to be the only treasurer of the state who did not take any interest for the money deposited to the credit of the state. After serving his last term in the Indiana Legislature, Matthew L. Brett purchased a farm at the edge of Washington. He made many improvements upon this farm and here died, July 25, 1896, where his widow still lives.

Matthew L. Brett was a devout member of the Catholic church, and his wife is also a member of this denomination. Mr. Brett was a Democrat.

Matthew L. Brett's success was not achieved without unflagging industry and persistent, painstaking and judicious effort. No history of Daviess county would be complete that did not present the facts in the career of the late Matthew L. Brett.

LEW W. BARBER.

The best history of a community or state is that which deals most with the lives and activities of its people, especially those who, by their own endeavor and indomitable energy, have forged to the front and won recognition as progressive citizens. In this brief review will be found the record of one who has outstripped the less active plodders on the highway of life and achieved a career surpassed by few of his contemporaries, a career of marked success in agricultural affairs and a name, which all men who know him delight to honor. Because of his upright life and habits of thrift and industry, Lew W. Barber is one of the best-known farmers of Veale township.

Lew W. Barber was born on the old homestead farm on September 27, 1862, the son of Nelson and Mary (Batchelor) Barber, the former of whom was born on the old homestead on June 12, 1833, and the latter in Knox county, the daughter of George Batchelor and wife, who died in California. Nelson Barber was the son of Aden and Eliza Katherine (Houts) Barber, the former of whom was born in New York and the latter in Kentucky in 1813. Eliza K. Houts was the daughter of George and Jennie (Graham) Houts, who came from Kentucky and entered what is called the old Barber homestead just south of where Lew W. Barber now lives. They entered one hundred and sixty acres. Stanton Barber, a brother of Lew W., now lives on this farm. The Houts family were of Scottish descent. Aden Barber was unmarried when he came to Veale township, where he purchased a farm from a man who had entered the land, and added to his original tract of forty acres until he owned one hundred and twenty-five acres.

Nelson Barber, the father of Lew W., was reared on the old home farm and educated in the public schools. He taught in Daviess and Franklin counties for several years, but soon took up farming and stock raising. He resided where his son, Stanton, now lives. He owned two hundred and twenty-five acres. Nelson Barber was a man of wide political influence in Veale township, having served as township trustee at one time. He and his family were members of the Methodist Episcopal church. Nelson Barber and wife were married in May, 1857. They had twelve children, Aden C., Frank, Ellis, Edgar, Lew W., George L., John N., Stanton, Cora D., Bertha A., Ottis C. and Jennie Pearl.

Lew W. Barber, the subject of this sketch, was educated in the common schools and in the commercial college at North Indiana Normal School at Valparaiso. After completing his education, he taught school three years.

Subsequently, he located on the farm where he now lives. Mr. Barber has erected excellent buildings upon this place and is engaged in general farming.

On October 6, 1886, Lew W. Barber was married to Emma J. Thomas, of Washington, who is the daughter of William R. and Malina B. (Johnson) Thomas, the former of whom was the son of John and Vina Thomas, who lived in Washington township, on what was known as the Ricks farm. Malina B. Johnson was born on the old Johnson farm, which was located on the Petersburg road, in Washington township. She was the daughter of Elijah and Mildred (Horrall) Johnson, the former of whom was born in Knox county, in 1796, and the latter in South Carolina, in 1802. Elijah Johnson was the son of Peter Johnson, who was born in Pennsylvania in 1758, and came to Indiana in 1790. He was a soldier in the Revolutionary War. The Johnson family is of Scottish descent.

Lew W. and Emma J. (Thomas) Barber are the parents of eight children, Jennie; Jessie, who died in infancy; Ethel; Hazel; Robert N.; Mary; Lillian and Mildred.

Fraternally, Mr. Barber is a member of the Independent Order of Odd Fellows. Throughout his life he has been identified with the Republican party and has served efficiently as trustee of his township. He and his family are members of the Methodist Episcopal church and are active in its affairs.

WILLIAM C. SCUDDER.

There are individuals in nearly every community who, by reason of pronounced ability and force of character, rise above the heads of the masses and command the unbounded esteem of their fellow men. Characterized by perseverance and directing spirit, two virtues which never fail, such men always make their presence felt, and the vigor of their strong personalities serve as a stimulus and incentive to the young and rising generation. To this energetic and enterprising class of men William C. Scudder very properly belongs. Mr. Scudder has never been seized with the roaming desires that have led many of Daviess county's young men to other fields of endeavor. He has devoted all his life to the industries at home and has succeeded remarkably well, which is evidenced by a study of his life's career.

William C. Scudder was born on the farm where he still lives, in Veale township, in October, 1851. He is the son of John and Alice (Arrell) Scudder, the former a native of New Jersey, the latter of Pennsylvania.

Mr. Scudder's paternal grandfather, John A. Scudder, was a son of Kenneth Scudder, who was a general in the Revolutionary army, in which army John A. was a commissioned surgeon. Kenneth Scudder was killed by the British in this war. About one hundred years ago John A. Scudder came to Daviess county and settled in the central part of Veale township. It is probable that he entered land here. It is known that he practiced medicine and it is likely that he was the first physician in this vicinity. He also was engaged in farming. John A. Scudder had ten sons. He owned two hundred acres of land, only a small part of which was cleared, and there was only a little hut on it when he removed to the farm in the wilderness.

The maternal grandparents of William C. Scudder came from Pennsylvania about one hundred years ago and settled in the western part of Veale township. Mr. Scudder's maternal grandfather likely entered what is now the Rodgers farm, which he cleared and where he made his home and died.

John Scudder, the father of William C., was educated in the pioneer schools of his day and generation. He was engaged in packing pork, which he floated in flat-boats down the Ohio and Mississippi rivers to New Orleans, upon which he also took corn and lard. Later in life, however, he gave all his attention to farming. He served in the Indiana Legislature, during the fifties, as a representative of the Whig party. He was a candidate for re-election after having served the first term, but about this time the American or Know-Nothing party was organized, and because he would not join in this movement he withdrew from the race. For many years he lived on a farm of two hundred acres where William C. now lives, which land he owned, as well as one hundred and twenty acres on the river in Veale township. He erected practically all of the present buildings. John Scudder was township trustee for some time and during his entire life was prominent in the councils of his party.

John and Alice (Arrell) Scudder had six children, Jacob F., Ellen, William C., Alice, Lydia and Carrie. Jacob F. was a soldier in the Civil War. He is still living at an advanced age.

William C. Scudder, one of the six children and one of the two sons born to his parents, was educated in the public schools of Daviess county, and after finishing the public schools took a commercial course in a college at Evansville. After finishing his education, he became a farmer and stock raiser, having upon his farm a great many hogs and cattle. In fact, Mr. Scudder is still engaged in raising hogs and cattle and found it a very profitable phase of farming. Mr. Scudder owns two hundred acres in the old home place and a hundred and sixty acres on the creek, all of which is in

Veale township. He is a Democrat and has been township trustee of the township and in this office made a record of which he and the people of his township have good reason to be proud. From time immemorial, almost, the Scudders have been members of the Presbyterian church, and William C. is no exception to the rule.

LOUIS GRANT TAYLOR.

Agriculture has been the true source of man's dominion over earth ever since the primal existence of labor and has been the pivotal industry that has controlled for the most part all of the fields of action to which his intelligence and energy have been devoted. Among the sturdy elements of Daviess county whose labors have profited alike themselves and the community in which they live, is Louis Grant Taylor, a well-known farmer and coal operator. In view of the consistent life lived by Mr. Taylor, all of which has been passed within the borders of ths county, it is particularly fitting that the following short record of his career be incorporated in a book of this nature.

Louis Grant Taylor was born on October 7, 1864, in Washington, Indiana. He is the son of John M. and Henrietta (Painter) Taylor, the former a native of Germany, and the latter of Virginia. The paternal grandparents of Louis G. Taylor were Michael Taylor and wife, natives of Germany, where he was a stone mason. Mr. Taylor's maternal grandparents came from Leroy, Virginia, and located first in Missouri. His maternal grandfather was a farmer, who died in Missouri, where he moved in 1850, and where he entered land.

John M. Taylor was born on January 4, 1827, in Wurttemberg, Germany, was the father of Louis Grant, and was educated in Michelbach, Germany, and there learned the stonemason trade, which his father had followed. He was a son of Jacob Frederick and Elizabeth M. Greiner. He came to America before his marriage, about April 5, 1854, and came first to New York city and, subsequently, to Louisville, Kentucky. There he began to work on the Ohio & Mississippi railroad, now the Baltimore & Ohio Southwestern, and assisted in building all the stone bridges from Seymour to Vincennes. He came to Indiana in November, 1854, and for about twenty-five or thirty years he was in the bakery business in Washington. Subsequently, he retired to a farm of eighty acres in Veale township, and there died in 1907. His wife is still living in Washington. Six children were born to John M. and Henrietta Taylor, as follow: John, Henrietta, Louis Grant, Elizabeth, William and Richard.

Louis Grant Taylor was educated in the Washington public schools, where, for a short time, he clerked in a store and then went to the farm. Mr. Taylor has an interest in the estate of his father, and, during the past fifteen years, has been a partner in the coal mining industry with his brother-in-law. They made a rather remarkable success of this business.

On December 23, 1888, Louis Grant Taylor was married to Mary E. Franklin, the daughter of John F. and Laura J. (Ragsdale) Franklin, the former a native of Germany, born in 1823, and the latter a native of Veale township. The paternal grandparents of Mrs. Taylor spent all of their days in Germany. Her paternal grandfather was a miller and was killed while operating a flour-mill. The maternal grandparents of Mrs. Taylor came to this vicinity in an early day and located near the old Bethel church, in Veale township. Her maternal grandfarther was a Methodist minister and a farmer. Mrs. Taylor's father, upon coming to this country, landed at Baltimore, but soon removed to Cincinnati, and at the age of twelve years started in life for himself. He became a wealthy land owner in Daviess county, and at one time owned over six hundred acres. He assisted in building the canal from Evansville to Indianapolis. He died while sitting in a chair on the old home farm in Daviess county.

To Louis G. and Mary E. (Franklin) Taylor, six children have been born, Anna, Pearl, Blanche, Fred, Lucile and William.

Mrs. Taylor is a member of the Methodist Episcopal church. Fraternally, Mr. Taylor is a member of the Tribe of Ben Hur. He is a Democrat. The Taylors are well known in this section of Daviess county and are highly respected citizens.

JOSEPH WILLEY.

Those who faced every danger and death itself upon the battlefield of the Civil War and bore suffering and made sacrifices for their country's sake, are especially deserving of mention in these annals. The younger generation should never forget that to them is due a debt of gratitude which can never be repaid, as the prosperity, liberty and happiness which we now enjoy is the direct outcome of their labors and loyalty. Among the honored veterans awaiting the last roll call, Joseph Willey, of Washington, Indiana, is one who gave nearly four years of his life in the service of his country, and who returned home after the war and has lived a life of usefulness and honor since that time.

Joseph Willey was born in Hamilton county, Ohio, on December 18, 1834. He is the son of Charles and Talitha (Stephenson) Willey, the former born near Boston, on August 1, 1800, and the latter in Cape May county, New Jersey, on February 12, 1802. The paternal grandfather of Joseph Willey was Hosea Willey, of Massachusetts, who removed to Hamilton county, and some time later moved to Kentucky, and there died. He was a farmer. Some of the Stephensons served in the War of 1812, and also in the Revolutionary War. The maternal grandparents of Joseph Willey were Stephen and Sarah (Lake) Stephenson, the latter of English descent. They came from New Jersey in 1806, and located in Hamilton county, where they followed farming and where they died.

Charles Willey, the father of Joseph Willey, was educated in the public schools of Ohio. He remained in Hamilton county until 1838 or 1839, where he was a farmer and cooper, and then removed to Daviess county, where he resided until the fall of 1845, when he moved to Knox county. He died in Knox county, January 9, 1846. While a resident of Daviess county, he lived in Veale township. After his death the family moved back to Hamilton county in March, 1846, and there Joseph Willey received his education.

In October, 1855, Mr. Willey located on the farm in Daviess county where he now lives. He worked by the month in the cooper shop near by, which was operated by his uncle, Peter Stephenson, who had a station of "the under-ground railway," and who at that time was assisted by Joseph Willey. Later, Joseph Willey ran a cooper shop near where he now resides. Since 1874, Mr. Willey has given his entire attention to farming. He now owns the farm of sixty-three acres upon which his father settled in Knox county, and fifty-five acres where he lives in Veale township.

Joseph Willey enlisted in Company E, Fifty-second Regiment, Indiana Volunteer Infantry, on December 16, 1861, and served till January 31, 1865. He was slightly wounded twice during the war, but was never in a charge that was repulsed.

On February 21, 1856, Joseph Willey was married to Jane Cummings, who was born and reared in Pike county, and who is the daughter of Charles and Delilah (Rhodes) Cummings, of that county. Charles and

Delilah (Rhodes) Cummings were early settlers in this county, and both came from North Carolina. On both sides of the family they were farmers. To Joseph and Jane (Cummings) Willey eight children were born: Talitha, on February 16, 1857, is now deceased; John R., January 16, 1859, is deceased; Mary Alice, November 17, 1865; Joseph died in infancy; Carrie, January 31, 1871; Sarah, May 17, 1873; Bertha, April 28, 1876, is deceased, and likewise Cora, June 12, 1880. The mother of these children died on February 15, 1900. She was a member of the Cumberland Presbyterian church and was a woman of rare refinement and one highly respected in the community where she lived, devoted to her husband and her children.

Formerly Mr. Willey was a member of the Grand Army of the Republic, but is no longer active. He served two terms as trustee of the township where he lives, having been elected in April, 1888, and re-elected in 1890, and because the Legislature extended the term of trustee, Mr. Willey served until 1895. He has also held other minor offices. Joseph Willey is an ardent Republican. Sarah Willey has always lived at home. Mrs. Willey attended the Indiana Dental College, and graduated in 1905. But on account of the death of her mother and two sisters she returned home to take care of the old home.

AARON W. LOCKWOOD.

That life is the most useful and desirable which results in the greatest good to the greatest number. Though all do not reach the heights to which they aspire, yet in some measure each can win success and make life a blessing to his fellowmen. It is not necessary for one to occupy eminent public positions to do so, for, in the other walks of life, there remains much good to be accomplished and many opportunities for the exercise of talents and influence, which in some way will touch the lives of those with whom we come into contact, making them brighter and better. In the list of Daviess county's successful business men, Aaron W. Lockwood has long occupied a prominent place and in his career there is much that is commendable. His career forcibly illustrates what a life of energy can accomplish, when plans are wisely laid and actions are governed by right principles, noble aims and high ideals.

Aaron W. Lockwood was born on September 4, 1872, in Barr township, Daviess county, Indiana. He is the son of Seymour B. and Phoebe J. (Houghton) Lockwood, the former a native of New Rochester, New York, born on August 29, 1826, and the latter a native of Mt. Pleasant, Martin county, Indiana, born on February 29, 1836.

The paternal grandfather of Aaron W. Lockwood was Aaron Lockwood, and his children were Phoebe, Katie and Dottie, by his first marriage. By his second marriage, to Catherine Houghton, there were three children: Enni, Eula and Clay. He died in 1897, at the age of ninety-one years, and his second wife died on June 2, 1913, at the age of ninety years. The maternal grandfather of Aaron W. Lockwood was a native of Davis county, Kentucky, and a pioneer near Mt. Pleasant, Martin county, Indiana, where he was a merchant. He was engaged in the packing business in Martin county.

The maternal grandfather of Mr. Lockwood was at one time a state senator. He owned the Houghton ferry near old Mt. Pleasant. He was a very prominent man during his time and was very successful in business. He was an active and influential member of the Christian church and an ardent Republican.

Seymour B. Lockwood, the father of Aaron W., was educated in the public schools of New York state. He came to Mt. Pleasant, Indiana, when a young man and worked in the store of Mr. Houghton. Later, he engaged in business with another man, under the firm name of Lockwood & Gibson. Subsequently, he came to Daviess county, Indiana, where he owned a farm, and died here in 1880. His wife died on September 3, 1887. He was a Republican in politics. His wife was a devoted member of the Christian church. They had twelve children: Catherine, deceased; Inez E.; Horace H., deceased; Jesse S.; Anna Laura; Greeley; Glenn, deceased; Ora, deceased; Odell, deceased; Delano, deceased; Aaron W., and Lewis Brooks.

Aaron W. Lockwood was reared on the farm and educated in the public schools of Daviess county, Indiana. He was engaged in the livery business at Loogootee for some years and subsequently worked in a hardware store for John Hibner. Later, he purchased an interest in the store known as the John Hibner Hardware Company and has been a traveling salesman for the International Harvester Company for a considerable period.

Mr. Lockwood was married on March 4, 1893, to Minnie Baker, who was born in Daviess county, Indiana, February 4, 1873. She is the daughter of William D. and Melvina (Alford) Baker, the former a native of Virginia, born on October 1, 1848, and the latter born on February 16, 1853. The paternal grandparents of Mrs. Lockwood were Isaac and Elizabeth (Bagnal) Baker, both of whom lived and died in Virginia. Mrs. Lockwood's maternal grandparents were John W. and Margaret (Bennett)

Alford, both natives of Kentucky and early settlers in Reeve township. Both died at Alfordsville, Daviess county. Mrs. Lockwood's father, William D. Baker, was a blacksmith. He and his wife live at Loogootee, Indiana. They were the parents of nine children, Mamie A.; William Franklin; Rolla M.; Margaret I.; Clara B., deceased; Hugh G.; Byron; Lilbert, deceased, and Helen.

To Mr. and Mrs. Aaron W. Lockwood six children have been born: John B., born on January 15, 1895, who is a graduate of the Loogootee high school and now working for the International Harvester Company; Bessie, born on October 25, 1897, who is a student in the high school at Washington; Eva, born on September 23, 1899; Gordon, born on February 26, 1901; Muriel, born on September 13, 1903, and died in infancy, and Charles Aaron, born on December 29, 1908.

In politics, Aaron W. Lockwood has been a Republican all his life. Fraternally, he is a member of the Independent Order of Odd Fellows and the United Commercial Travelers. Religiously, Mr. Lockwood and family are members of the Methodist Episcopal church.

ALONZO A. LANE.

The strong, earnest men of a people are always public benefactors. Their usefulness in the immediate specific labors they perform can be defined by leaps and bounds, but the good they do through the force they put in motion and through the inspiration of their presence and example, is immeasureable by any finite gauge or standard value. The gentleman, whose name introduces this sketch, is a man of that type. Although well known and highly esteemed, he is averse to any notice savoring of adulation, and prefers to let his achievements, rather than the fulsome praise of the chronicler, speak for him. Every life, however, if properly known, contains more or less of interest, and the public claim a certain property interest and right in the career of every citizen, regardless of his achievements or the station he has attained. In placing before the reader the brief review that follows, due deference is accorded the feelings of the subject, in conformity with whose well-known wishes the writer will endeavor to adhere strictly to facts and omit, as far as possible, complimentary allusions, at the same time realizing that the latter have been honorably earned and should form no small part of a like sketch in which it is sought to render nothing but what justice and meritorious recognition demand.

Alonzo A. Lane was born on September 12, 1863, a few miles south of Salem, the county seat of Washington county, Indiana, and is the son of Richard and Ellen (Lowery) Lane. Subject's paternal grandfather was Richard Lane, who was born in the state of Tennessee in 1813, and his paternal grandmother was Jane (Martin) Lane, also a native of Tennessee and born in the year 1811. The former was at one time a merchant, but believing that his vocation was to preach the gospel of religion, he studied for the ministry and was later ordained a minister in the Christian church and assigned to the town of Martinsburg, Washington county, Indiana. To the union of Richard and Jane (Martin) Lane five children were born, as follow: Cynthian, who died at the age of five years; Martin; Ruphus, who married Angie Glenn; Richard, subject's father; Allen K., who married Sarah Kelsey and who was a practicing physician in Odon, Daviess county, for forty-five years, now retired, and John Albert, who married Emma Gardener.

Subject's father was born in Martinsburg, Washington county, Indiana, in the year 1840. He attended the neighboring schools and remained under the parental roof until about the time of his maturity, and then engaged in farming in the county of his birth. About the year 1880, he decided to move to Daviess county, Indiana, where again he took up farming and continued agricultural pursuits for the rest of his life. To Richard and Ellen (Lowrey) Lane were born four children, Alonza Albert; Arthur W., who lives in Odon, Daviess county; Luetta, the wife of James Carroll, who lives in Odon; and, Harvey, who is married and lives in Odon. Subject's father and family are members of the Church of Christ, to which they lend their earnest assistance. Politically, Mr. Lane has always been a true advocate of the principles of the Republican party.

Alonzo A. Lane spent his boyhood days on his father's farm and received his preparatory education in the township schools of Washington and Daviess counties, Indiana, and later attended normal school. At Bloomfield, Greene county, this state, he began teaching school, and continued in that profession for a period of ten years. He was assigned to one of the township schools in Madison township, in Daviess county, where he taught for six years; at a later date, he was assigned to the school in Odon, Daviess county; he taught in three summer normals in Odon between winter terms. He discontinued teaching after four years in Odon schools. Following this, Mr. Lane formed a partnership with Mr. Lowery Cooper, who was a manufacturer of hardwood lumber and wagon-dimension stock, consisting of spokes, rims, etc., in the town of Odon and remained in that business for three years. After that, he bought a one-third interest in a local flour-mill in Odon and bought further interests until he owned three-quarters of this property. He then sold a quarter of his interest back to the miller, and, at the present time, is interested to the extent of an equal partnership. Mr. Lane bought a farm consisting of two hundred and sixty-five acres of fine land situated in Elmore township, Daviess county, bordering on the west fork of the White river, and this land he rents for cultivation purposes. In addition to the interests mentioned, he is also the owner of the Lane Poultry Company, of Odon, which makes a business of dealing in poultry, butter and eggs, and they also deal in the buying of hides and pelts. Mr. Lane is a member of the Bloomfield (Indiana) Building and Loan Association, and acts as the agent in this locality for that association. He is interested in the Elnora Grain Elevator Company, of Elnora, this county, and also acts as president of the First National Bank in Odon.

Mr. A. A. Lane was married to Minnie Garten, December 22, 1899. She was born on February 4, 1870, and is the daughter of Capt. Z. V. and Sarah E. (Smith) Garten. Captain Garten was born on November 18, 1829, and is the son of James Garten and Lydia (Gray) Garten. James Garten was born in the year 1788, and in his early days was a farmer in this state. Later, he married Lydia (Gray) Garten, as his second wife, who was born in 1806. To the first marriage, which was with Betsie Sears, there were two children born, Cyrena and Nancy B., and to the second union there were five children, Jane, Eliza, Zimri, James H., and Mary Ann, deceased.

Captain Garten spent his boyhood days with his parents and was educated in the subscription schools of the neighborhood. He spent four terms in these schools. When he arrived at the age of twenty-three, the Civil War was being waged, and in answer to the call of President Lincoln, he enlisted on August 15, 1862, and was assigned to Company C, Ninety-first Indiana Volunteer Regiment, and commissioned as captain. In a fierce engagement with the rebel forces, near Atlanta, Georgia, he was severely wounded in the left leg on September 29, 1864, and was honorably discharged. Returning to Odon, this county, he engaged in farming on a tract of land in Madison township, Daviess county, and which he afterwards purchased. This tract originally contained two hundred eighty-eight acres. At various times, portions of this land have been sold until now there remains but one hundred sixty-eight acres, which he still owns, but does not cultivate, having retired from active work in 1905, and now resides in the town of Odon. Captain Garten's wife, Sarah, was a daughter of Daniel J. and Catherine (Woody) Smith, and gave birth to a son, Walter Clarence, who is now married to

Elizabeth Crooke. They have four children: Bessie, Frank, Mage and Robert; they were also the parents of a daughter, Minnie, the wife of the subject of this review, who was born on February 4, 1870.

Alonzo A. Lane and Minnie Garten were married on December 22, 1889, and to them were born three children, as follow: Charles, born on December 24, 1890, who is the present manager of the Lane Poultry Company, since he left Purdue University; Nellie, who was born on November 28, 1893, attended college in Oxford, Ohio, and now resides at home, and Edith, born on February 23, 1900, and who resides with her parents. The family, including Mr. Lane, are stanch members of the Christ church, of Odon, and to this denomination lend hearty support. Politically, Mr. Lane is identified with the Republican ranks, and, while not an active worker in politics, he has served his community as school trustee for the past nine years and occupied the office of town clerk for one term. Personally, Mr. Lane is a broadminded man of wide acquaintance and bears the reputation of being absolutely upright and honorable in all his dealings with his fellow men. Quiet and unassuming in disposition, his great influence is felt throughout the community, and he is known to be a man firm in his convictions and upholds only those things that make for the material and moral good of the public.

HARRY H. CROOKE.

The best history of a community or state is that which deals most with the lives and activities of its people, especially those who, by their own endeavor and indomitable energy, have forged to the front and placed themselves in a position where they deserve the title of progressive men. In this brief review will be found the record of one who has outstripped the less active plodders on the highway of life and who has achieved a career of marked success in the business circles of Daviess county, and in the agricultural affairs of this county. His name, which all men who know him like to honor, on account of his upright life, stands for thrift, industry and enterprise.

Harry H. Crooke was born at Odon, then called Clarksburg, in 1867, and is the son of Howard and Anna (Culner) Crooke, the former of whom was probably a native of Lawrence county, Indiana, and the latter a native of England. The paternal grandparents of Harry H. Crooke were Ollie and Nancy Crooke, of Virginia, who immigrated to Kentucky in an early day and later to Lawrence county, Indiana, where they entered land and established a home. They reared a large family and the last years of Ollie's life were spent at Odon. The maternal grandparents of Mr. Crooke were Steven Culmer and wife, natives of England, who came to America and first settled in Pittsburgh, Pennsylvania. Later, they moved to Lawrence county, Indiana, and were pioneer farmers.

Howard Crooke, the father of Harry H., was educated in Lawrence county, and settled on Clark's prairie, near Odon, immediately after his marriage, and remained here until his death. He was a farmer, although his home was in Odon. In December, 1890, he opened the first bank in Odon. It was a private bank and was operated until his death, in 1895. He owned several farms and was a justice of the peace for many years. Howard Crooke was an active and enthusiastic worker in the ranks of the Republican party, and at one time made the race, on that ticket, for state senator, but was defeated by a slight margin. He was a member of the Methodist Episcopal church. Howard and Anna Crooke had five children, Mrs. Sarah Burrell, Mrs. Fannie Culmer, Mrs. Margaret Smiley, Mrs. Lillie Edgin and Harry H., the subject of this sketch.

Harry H. Crooke was educated in the schools at Odon and at Indiana University. After leaving the state university at Bloomington, he returned to Odon and entered the banking and real estate business. He assisted in the organization of the First National Bank at Odon and is a director in this bank. He also organized the Odon Realty Company in 1905 and he is secretary and treasurer of this organization. Mr. Crooke is also interested in farming. He is engaged all the time in buying and selling land and looks after his own agricultural interests.

Harry H. Crooke was married in 1890 to Maggie Mason, of Odon. To this union twelve children have been born, Hazel, Lela, Mason, Oren, Frank, Edith, Martha, Howard, Harry, Jr., Ned, Elizabeth and Joseph. All of these children are still living.

Harry H. Crooke served six years as postmaster of Odon, from 1906 to 1912. In 1905 he was elected to the Legislature from Daviess county and served one term. Throughout his life, Mr. Crooke has been identified with the Republican party. Fraternally, he is a thirty-second degree Mason and a member of the Knights of Pythias. Few men in this section of Daviess county are better known than Harry H. Crooke, and few men are more deserving of the confidence, esteem and good will of their neighbors and friends than is Mr. Crooke. He is possessed of a practical interest in all public improvements in this part of Daviess county. Mr. Crooke is well known throughout the county and has a host of friends.

LESTER LEE.

The "back-to-the-soil" movement, which is becoming so popular in all parts of the country, has no more devoted champion than the progressive and energetic young farmer whose name heads this brief biographical sketch. Reared on a farm and then attracted by what, many are foolish enough to claim, is the larger and the freer life of the city, he soon became disillusioned and has found great comfort and happiness in the life he at present is living on a small farm, which he is operating with much success and every prospect of enlarged opportunities. It is such young men as this that constitute the chief hope of the country, and it is fitting that in a history of Daviess county there should be presented a biographical reference to his life and to his experience, in trying both the rural life and then the urban life, and his decision to return to the life of the farm. The biographer, therefore, with pleasure, invites the reader to this modest sketch of the career of the young man whose name is noted at the top of this article.

Lester Lee was born in Decatur county, Indiana, November 4, 1874, the son of David R. and Sarah H. (Pearce) Lee, both natives of Decatur county, the former of whom was born on September 7, 1850, and the latter born on September 7, 1851.

David R. Lee is the son of John and Anna (McCoy) Lee, both of whom were natives of Mason county, Kentucky, the former born in 1809, and the latter born in July, 1811. John Lee was the son of Gashum Lee, a native of the state of New Jersey, who migrated from that state into Virginia, thence to Kentucky and thence to Decatur county, Indiana, where his memory, as one of the pioneers of that county, still remains. John Lee came into Indiana from Kentucky with his parents in the year 1819, and thus became one of the pioneers of Decatur county. He grew to manhood there, married Anna McCoy, and reared his family in that county, farming practically all his life, though in his later years he clerked in a store in the village of St. Omar. He died in 1862, his wife surviving him many years, her death not occurring until the year 1895. They were prominent members of the Baptist church and were active in all good works in their neighborhood, where the memory of their goodly lives survives to this day. John Lee was an active participator in the public life of his community. He was an ardent Republican and took an earnest interest in the affairs of that party.

To John and Anna (McCoy) Lee there were born thirteen children: William; Lodema; Lewis, who died in his youth; Eda; Manuel; Nancy;

Jessie; John T.; Sarah; Lloyd; David; Charles W., and one who died in infancy. The numerous progeny of these children, today, make the Lee family one of the most widely represented and best known in this part of the state.

David R. Lee, son of John and Anna (McCoy) Lee was reared on the paternal farm in Decatur county, acquiring an excellent education in the then well-organized schools of that county, and as a young man started farming in the neighborhood in which he was reared. He was married in Decatur county to Sarah H. Pearce, the date of the nuptials being January 9, 1874, and there all but one of his children were born. Thinking to better his condition, David Lee moved from Decatur county to Daviess county in 1883, but after an experience here of eighteen months, moved back to Decatur county, where he continued farming until the year 1889, when he returned to Daviess county, settling in Washington township, where he has made his home, living since 1893 on his present farm of thirty-one acres in that township, he and his wife being among the best-known persons in their neighborhood, and held in the highest regard by all. Sarah H. Pearce, whom Mr. Lee married, is the daughter of William M. and Charollete A. (Avery) Pearce, pioneers of Decatur county, to whom were born five children, the others being: Mary F., Herman A., Amanda and William W.

To David R. and Sarah H. (Pearce) Lee were born six children, as follow: Lester L., the immediate subject of this sketch, who married Mary Cuskaden; Lawrence H., born on February 25, 1877, who married Mary Emerling; Carlton M., born on July 17, 1880, unmarried and lives at home with his parents; Lottie A., born on February 12, 1884, married Joseph R. Westhafer, now deceased, by whom she had one child; Allen L., who lives at home and is a teacher in the Longfellow consolidated school; Orla H., born on July 30, 1887, died on September 9, 1891; Charles M., born on October 20, 1890, married Glenn Potts, and has one child, a son, Edgar L. The Lees are members of the Methodist church and the father and sons are all Democrats, taking an active part in the political affairs of the county, being deeply interested in all matters relating to the welfare of the community.

Lester L. Lee was educated in the public schools of Washington township, and as a young man started working on the farm. In 1909, he left the farm and began working in the railway shops in the county seat. One winter of such form of service, however, proved sufficient for him and he returned to the more wholesome life of the farm, on March 13, 1902, moving onto his present small farm of twenty-five acres near the city of Washington, where he and his small family are living in comfort and happiness, being very well circumstanced and independent of the "slings and arrows of outrageous fortune."

To Lester L. and Mary (Cuskaden) Lee one child has been born, a daughter, Lelia L., a bright little girl, who is the delight of the lives of her parents and the light of their happy home.

Mr. Lee is a progressive young man, an excellent farmer and is well known and popular in his neighborhood. He is a member of the Odd Fellows, the Modern Woodmen and the Eagles, and takes a hearty interest in the affairs of these several fraternal societies. He has been actively interested in the political affairs of his home township and county, and from the year 1908 to 1914, served the county very acceptably as township assessor.

FRANK KRAMER.

One of the well-known saloon keepers of the city of Washington, Daviess county, Indiana, is Frank Kramer, who was born in this county, April 23, 1883. Mr. Kramer was reared in Washington and educated in the public and parochial schools of this city. For eight years he has been engaged in the saloon business in Washington, and is now located at 311 West Main street. In politics, Mr. Kramer is a Democrat. He and the members of his family are all associated with the Catholic church. Mr. Kramer was married in 1904 to Stella Kidwell, a native of Washington, who was born in 1883. She is the daughter of John and Barbara (Dant) Kidwell, both of whom are natives of Washington, Indiana. John Kidwell is now living retired. To Mr. and Mrs. Frank Kramer three children, Mary, Harold and Bernard, have been born.

Frank Kramer is the son of Louis and Mary (Hack) Kramer, the former a native of DuBois county, born on February 3, 1848, and the latter a native of Cincinnati, born on January 2, 1853. Louis Kramer was educated in the public schools of DuBois county. He was identified with the Democratic party and affiliated with the Catholic church. For many years he was a coal miner, later a mining engineer, and still later a prospector. His wife died on February 8, 1891, and he now lives retired in Washington, Indiana. He and his wife had nine children: Helen, deceased; George; William, deceased; Henry J.; Catherine; Frank; John; Albert, deceased, and Ernest.

The paternal grandfather of Frank Kramer was Peter Kramer, who married Kate Lechner. Peter Kramer was born in Germany in 1814, and his wife was born in that country in 1825. Peter Kramer came to DuBois county when only nine years old. He grew to manhood in this county and engaged in the mercantile business. He also owned and operated a small packing house and was very successful. His only child was Louis Kramer, the father of Frank Kramer. Peter Kramer died in 1849, after which his wife married Miles Schuler. Two children were born to this marriage, Mary and Kate. Peter Kramer and his wife were members of the Catholic church.

Frank Kramer's maternal grandfather was a native of Germany, who married Victoria Hack, and they came to Jasper, DuBois county, early in life and here he died. His wife died in 1899. The paternal grandmother of Frank Kramer, Kate Lechner, was the daughter of Frank Lechner, who came to DuBois county in 1832, and settled in Jasper, where he died at the age of eighty-eight years.

The Kramer family has, therefore, been identified with the history of Daviess and DuBois counties, Indiana, for many years. The members of this family have been hard working, industrious citizens, devoted to the interests of their families and to the welfare of the community. Frank Kramer, the subject of this sketch, is no exception to the history surrounding the lives of his father and grandparents.

WILLIAM C. CAMP.

The gentleman, whose name appears above this sketch, belongs to that class of men who win life's battle by sheer force of personality and determination, coupled with soundness of judgment and keenness of discrimination. In whatever he has undertaken he has always shown himself to be a man of ability and honor, ready to lend his aid in defending principles affecting the public good. He has ably and conscientiously served his county in the capacity of deputy auditor, while in other phases of civic life he has earned the unqualified endorsement and support of his fellow citizens. Recently, Mr. Camp has been engaged in the real estate, insurance and abstract business and is well known throughout Daviess county as one of the leading business men of the city of Washington.

William C. Camp was born on March 9, 1872, in Reeve township, Daviess county, Indiana. He is the son of John B. and Sarilda (Myers) Camp, the former born on June 21, 1841, near Steubenville, Jefferson county,

Ohio, and the latter born in 1846, in Fleming county, Kentucky. The paternal grandfather of William C. Camp was Chester Camp, who was born in 1819 near Steubenville, Jefferson county, Ohio, and who came to Indiana from Ohio in 1846, settling in Reeve township, Daviess county. Chester Camp was a Republican, though earlier in life he had been a member of the Whig party. He and his wife were members of the Methodist Episcopal church. Their children were John R., Isaac, Lewis, William J., Harriet and Electa Jane. Mr. Camp's maternal grandparents were Henry and Susan (Sullivan) Myers, the former of whom was born in Fleming county, Kentucky, in 1825, and came to Indiana sixty years ago, and the latter born in Fleming county, Kentucky, in 1826. They were married on October 6, 1844, and were early settlers in Daviess county. He was a farmer and in politics was identified with the Democratic party. He and his wife were members of the Methodist Episcopal church. Their children were Sarilda and John.

John R. Camp, the father of William C., came to Daviess county, Indiana, with his parents. He was a farmer by occupation, a Republican in politics, and he and his wife were members of the Methodist Episcopal church. They now reside in Reeve township, on the old Camp homestead, a part of which was entered by Chester Camp, the grandfather of the immediate subject of this sketch. Nine children were born to Mr. and Mrs. John R. Camp, as follow: Charles C., Clara A., William C., John H., Bertha E., Ella, Mason H., Jesse and Harrison, all of whom are now living.

William C. Camp was born on a farm and educated in the public schools of Daviess county, principally. For some time he was also a student at the normal school at Mitchell, Indiana, and, later, was a student at DePauw University. Mr. Camp was a school teacher for eleven years, teaching principally in the district schools of Daviess county. He is well remembered as one of the most successful teachers in this county.

In 1903, Mr. Camp moved to Washington, after his appointment as deputy county auditor. He served continuously in this position for seven years, or until August, 1910, after which he went into the insurance, abstract and real estate business, at 115 East Main street. Mr. Camp has built up a large connection, and is one of the best-known business men in Daviess county. He is a director in the Industrial Savings and Loan Association, and to this, during late years, he has devoted considerable time and attention. Until the campaign of 1912, Mr. Camp was identified with the Republicans, but at the formation of the Progressive party, at Chicago, in August of that year, he became identified with and has since been a Progressive. He is a great admirer of Colonel Roosevelt and of ex-Senator Beveridge.

Fraternally, Mr. Camp is a member of the Masonic fraternity, the Independent Order of Odd Fellows, the Knights of Pythias, the Improved Order of Red Men, the Modern Woodmen of America, the Daughters of Rebekah, the Pythian Sisters and the Daughters of Pocahontas. Religiously, he is a member of the Methodist Episcopal church. At the present time, Mr. Camp is serving as a member of the Washington city board of health.

Mr. Camp is a well-informed man on all current political and civic questions, and is regarded as a leader in the political affairs in the city where he lives. He is honored and respected by his contemporaries in business and is widely admired for his genial good nature.

JAMES F. MACKELL.

One of the conspicuous names on the list of Daviess county teachers is James F. Mackell, one of the brilliant young citizens of Montgomery, Indiana. He is a young man of high standing in the community where he lives and one to whom has not been denied a rather full measure of success. He has long been recognized as a factor of importance in connection with the educational profession of Daviess county, and has been identified with the recent growth and development of the educational system of this county. For one who has been engaged in the educational profession a comparatively short time, James F. Mackell has to his credit achievements beyond those which fall to the average man.

James F. Mackell was born in Montgomery, January 24, 1888. He is the son of John and Katherine (Clarke) Mackell, both natives of Daviess county. James F. Mackell's paternal grandparents were James and Anna Mackell, natives of Ireland, who came to America from their native country and located in Barr township, Daviess county, where James Mackell was a farmer. Here he purchased one hundred and sixty acres of land which he cleared and improved and here he lived until his death. The maternal grandparents of James F. Mackell were natives of County Cork, Ireland, who came to America from their native country and first located in Philadelphia. Later, they moved to Barr township, Daviess county, where he was a farmer and entered the land upon which he lived.

John Mackell, the father of James F., was educated in the common schools of his day and generation. His wife, who, before her marriage, was Catherine Clarke, was also educated in the common schools of Barr township. He became a farmer upon the same land his father had owned and remained there until his retirement, in 1913, when he moved to Montgomery. He and his family are all members of the St. Peter's Catholic church. John and Katherine Mackell had two children, James F., the subject of this sketch, and Henry, a machinist.

James F. Mackel was educated in St. Peter's parochial school, which he attended for eight years. He was then a student in the Montgomery high school for two years and, after finishing his high school work, attended the Indiana State Normal School at Terre Haute. Continuing this work, he took the normal degree in 1912 and the degree of Bachelor of Arts in 1915.

Mr. Mackell began teaching in 1906 in Barr township and taught three terms in the district schools of this township. He also taught two years at Cannelburg in the grades and has been principal of the Montgomery high school for four years. In this latter place, Mr. Mackell has made an enviable record for himself and is popular not only with the patrons of the school, but also with the pupils and has endeared himself to the hearts of a great many people. Fraternally, Mr. Mackell is a member of the Knights of Columbus at Washington, Indiana. As a teacher, he is well known throughout Daviess county, not only for his professional attainments, but for his genial manners and democratic habits. He is a young man who is expected to make a rapid rise in his chosen profession.

WILLIAM E. ULRICH.

It should be interesting to note in the series of personal sketches appearing in this work the varying conditions that have compassed those whose careers are outlined, and the effort has been made in each case to throw well-focused light on the individuality and to bring out into proper perspective the plan of each respective career. Each man who strives to fulfill his part in connection with human life and human activities is deserving of recognition, whatever may be his field of endeavor. It is the function of works of this nature to perpetuate for future generations an authentic record concerning those represented in its pages, and the value of such publications is certain to be cumulative for all time to come, showing forth the individual and specific accomplishments, of which generic history is ever engendered. In presenting the life record of the late citizen of this community whose

WILLIAM E. ULRICH.

name forms the caption of this article the chronicler takes due consideration of his former humble station in life and his steady advancement by honorable methods to a position of high esteem, making his worthy of mention in a work of this nature.

William E. Ulrich was born in Germany on November 4, 1848, and came to this country in the year 1865. He remained for a while in Daviess county, Indiana, but being a single man and seized with the desire to see the country, he traveled over the various states of the Union before his marriage, on May 14, 1875, in Washington, Indiana, to Anna Fromme, a daughter of Henry and Christina (Kuhlman) Fromme, natives of Germany, who were married in Evansville, Indiana, after coming separately to this country. Their marriage occurred in the year 1847, after which they removed to Daviess county, settling in Washington township in 1860, where they spent the rest of their lives, the father dying on December 16, 1874, and the mother on August 7, 1889. Both were devout members of the Lutheran church, and he was a supporter of the Democratic party during his life. To their union were born nine children, named in the order of their birth as follow: Henry, Christina, Frederick, Anna, William, Gustina, Louis, Albert and Charles.

Soon after William E. Ulrich was married he engaged his services in the capacity of a miner and worked at this for a while; then went into the retail liquor business for a few months, and later entered the butcher business, which he continued until he started in the ice business, which he conducted for a period of twelve years; then bought fifty-seven acres of land near the town of Washington, Indiana, where his widow now resides, and farmed until the time of his death, on February 28, 1900. To this union of William E. and Anna (Fromme) Ulrich, were born twelve children, all of whom are living, named in the order of their births as follow: Bertha, Ada, Cora, Henrietta, William, Louis, Carl, Augusta, Maud, Adolph, Fredricka and Erustine, the three latter of whom live at home with their mother.

William E. Ulrich was an ardent supporter of the Democratic party. He was a member of the Lutheran church and his family also are members of this church. Personally, Mr. Ulrich was a man well thought of by all who knew him. He had a most genial disposition, and was truly devoted to his family, affording them a first-class living. He forged to the front in spite of all obstacles and was always held in high esteem by all classes, because of his honesty of purpose and genuine courtesy to everyone.

WILLIAM H. WILLIAMS.

The history of a county or state, as well as that of a nation, is chiefly a chronicle of the lives and deeds of those who have conferred honor and dignity upon society. The world judges the character of a community by those of its representative citizens, and yields its tribute of admiration and respect to those, whose works and actions constitute the record of a community's prosperity and pride. Among the prominent young business men of Daviess county, who are well known because of their success in mercantile affairs and the part they have taken in the affairs of the locality, is William H. Williams, the well-known proprietor of a flourishing laundry in Washington.

William H. Williams was born on December 22, 1875, in Washington, Indiana, the son of John and Martha (Cook) Williams, the former a native of Daviess county, born on February 14, 1842, and the latter of Zanesville, Ohio, born on January 21, 1841. They were pioneers in Daviess county, Indiana, and both died in this county. John Williams was a blacksmith by trade and owned a shop about three miles south of Washington, Indiana. Mrs. Martha Williams was the daughter of William Cook, who came to Daviess county, Indiana, in an early day. He was a carpenter by trade and worked at this occupation until his death. John Williams, the father of William H., was educated in the public schools of Daviess county, and was a well-known farmer during his active life. He enlisted at the outbreak of the Civil War, in Company E, Twenty-second Indiana Volunteer Infantry, and served throughout the war, and was wounded several times. In politics, he was an ardent Republican. John and Martha Williams, who now live in the city of Washington, have been the parents of two sons, Charles C., who lives in Indianapolis, and William H., the subject of this sketch.

William H. Williams was educated in the public schools of Washington and in the Washington high school. Early in life he engaged in the laundry business, and, in 1902, started for himself at 421 and 423 East Main street. In 1912, he erected the building in which his present business is housed, at 16 Southeast Fourth street. This building has a room sixty-three by ninety feet and employment is found for about sixteen people. Mr. Williams has been very successful in this undertaking and has a large and lucrative patronage.

William H. Williams was married to Frances L. Baker, who was born on December 28, 1875, in Virginia, and who is the daughter of Isaac and Elizabeth (Uttley) Baker, both natives of Virginia. Isaac Baker is now deceased, but his widow is living in West Virginia. They were the parents of four children, Barton, Uttley, Frances and Earl, all of whom are living.

To Mr. and Mrs. William H. Williams, one son, Carl, was born on September 10, 1902.

In politics, Mr. Williams is a Republican, but has never been an aspirant to public office and has never held office. Fraternally, he is a member of the Independent Order of Odd Fellows. William H. Williams, although a comparatively young man, has made an unusual start in life, and has a business which very probably will grow to much larger proportions in the years to come. He is a man who enjoys the entire confidence of the community in which he lives, because of his honorable and upright methods of business dealings.

A. LAWRENCE CLARK.

The final causes which shape the fortunes of individual men and the destinies of states, are often the same. They are usually remote and obscure, their influence wholly unexpected, until determined by results. When they inspire men to the exercise of courage, self-denial and industry and call them to play the higher moral elements; lead men to risk all upon conviction, faith in such causes lead to the planting of great states, great people, and great movements. That country is the greatest which produces the ablest and most manly men, and the intrinsic safety depends not so much upon methods and measures, as upon that true manhood from whose deep sources, all that is precious and permanent in life, must proceed. Such a result may not be consciously contemplated by the individuals instrumental in its accomplishment; each pursuing his personal good by exalted means, they work out as a logical result; they have wrought on the lines of the greatest good. What A. Lawrence Clark, a well-known school teacher of Van Buren township, Daviess county, Indiana, is doing for the people of this township, may be told in a few words, yet its far-reaching influence cannot be measured by any definite standard of value. Mr. Clark is a brilliant young man and well equipped for the profession he has chosen for a life's vocation.

A. Lawrence Clark was born in Van Buren township, October 7, 1895, and is the son of A. M. and Rosettie (Hobbs) Clark, the former a native of Ohio, and the latter the daughter of W. P. Hobbs, a physician and Methodist minister, who married a Miss Elrod, of Orange county, Indiana.

Lawrence Clark was educated in the common schools of Daviess county and was graduated from the Odon high school with the class of 1913. He spent a short time at the Indiana State Normal and one term at Indiana University. He has now been teaching for two years and, at present, is the principal of the Raglesville non-certified high school. Mr. Clark is unmarried and is prominent in the affairs of the Methodist church.

Reverting to Mr. Clark's ancestry, his grandfather, W. P. Hobbs and wife, were the parents of several children, among whom were Cyrus, William, Jr., Melvin, Mildred and Rosettie. W. P. Hobbs was a soldier in the Civil War, in which he served as assistant surgeon in Company A, Eighty-fifth Regiment, Indiana Volunteers.

Mr. Clark's paternal grandfather, John Y. Clark, was born in Pennsylvania and was a very early settler in Indiana. He married Belinda Correll, of Ohio, and to them were born eleven children. John, William, James, Marshall Lovina, Belle, Mary and Ellenor are still living. John Y. Clark was a blacksmith by trade and owned a small farm. He was a prominent member of the United Brethren church.

Mr. Clark's father, A. M. Clark, was educated in the common schools and was a student in the normal school for two or three terms. He taught in the common schools of Daviess county for twelve years and after quitting this profession, took up blacksmithing and is a blacksmith at the present time. He is now the trustee of Van Buren township, Daviess county, having been elected in November, 1914, on the Republican ticket. Mr. Clark also held this same office twenty-one years ago. He is an influential member of the Methodist church and very active in this denomination. He is also active in the Sunday school and at present is serving as superintendent.

Lawrence Clark is one of four sons born to his parents, the others being Charles A., John A. and Oliver H. Of these children, Charles A. is living in Indianapolis. He married Lillie Garten and they have two children, Donald G. and Harry Hobbs. Charles A. is the auditor of the *Indianapolis News*. John A. is cashier of the *Indianapolis News*. He married Clara Ida Paterson, and they have two children, Ralph Waldo and Myron. Oliver H. is also living in Indianapolis and is president of the Arian Realty Company. He married Delphia Menefee. The parents of these children are now living in Raglesville. Mr. Clark is prominent in the affairs of his township. Fraternally, A. M. Clark is a member of the Ben-Hur tribe and the Knights of Pythias.

The family of A. M. Clark have all made good in the world, and have brought additional honor and respect to their worthy parents. Lawrence Clark is a young man of unusual promise, with a bright future before him.

EDWARD T. O'CONNOR.

It is not always easy to discover and define the hidden forces that move a life of ceaseless activities and large professional success. Little more can be done than to note their manifestation, in the career of the individual under consideration. In view of this fact, the life of a man in public affairs, a man who holds public positions, such as Edward T. O'Connor, the subject of this sketch, affords a striking example of well-defined purpose. Mr. O'Connor has shown himself to have the ability to make that purpose serve, not only his own ends, but the good of his fellow men, as well. At present, the efficient superintendent of roads in Daviess county, Indiana, Mr. O'Connor has made a success in several lines of endeavor. He is well known throughout Daviess county, and is admired and respected by a host of people for his interprise, his industry and his genial good nature.

Edward T. O'Connor was born April 22, 1875, in Van Buren township, Daviess county, Indiana. He is the son of Michael and Anna (Sims) O'Connor, the former a native of Ireland, born in 1835, and the latter of Daviess county, Indiana. The maternal grandparents of Edward T. O'Connor were Asbury and Kitura (Kilgore) Sims, both natives of Kentucky and among the pioneers of Van Buren township, Daviess county, Indiana. He was a farmer and entered land from the government in Van Buren township, and lived on this farm the remainder of his life, dying at about the age of ninety-two. His wife, also, died at the age of ninety-two. The paternal grandparents of Mr. O'Connor were John and Mary (Brown) O'Connor, both natives of Ireland and both came to Indiana after their marriage, settling in Park county. He worked on the railroad and later moved to Daviess county, where he became a farmer. He owned a farm at the time of his death. He died in Van Buren township at an advanced age and his wife also died in this township at an old age.

Michael O'Connor, the father of Edward F., throughout his life, was identified with the fortunes of the Democratic party. He was a member of the Catholic church as was also his wife. She died in February, 1884, and he is now living on the old homestead. They had a family of five children, Edward F.; Mary K., deceased; John; Elizabeth, deceased, and Nora.

Edward T. O'Connor was reared on the old homestead in Daviess county, and educated in the Daviess county public schools. Early in life he became a farmer, and, later, he became a general contractor. He was not only a successful farmer, but he made an unusual success of contracting, and had a large business in this and adjoining counties. In 1912, Mr. O'Connor came to Washington, and was engaged in the livery business until 1913, when he was appointed by the board of county commissioners as superintendent of roads. He is now filling this position and is much interested in good roads, also being thoroughly familiar with the science of building highways that will last.

Edward T. O'Connor was married on April 30, 1900, to Mary B. Fanning, who was born in Reeve township, and is the daughter of Frank and Bridget (Flannigan) Fanning, early settlers of Reeve township. Mr. Fanning is now deceased and his widow still lives in this township. To Mr. and Mrs. Edward T. O'Connor seven children have been born: Marguerite Marie, Nora, Mary Kitura, Francis Fanning, Edmond, Estella and Vincent Edward, all of whom are living.

All of the members of the O'Connor family are identified actively with the Catholic church, to which Mr. O'Connor is a liberal contributor.

JOHN H. SPENCER.

In placing the name of John H. Spencer as one standing in the front ranks of the enterprising men of affairs and a leader of the bar at Washington, Indiana, one whose influences tend to the upbuilding of the city and the advancement of the affairs of his native county, simple justice is done. Mr. Spencer, who is now district collector of income taxes for the seventh district of Indiana, is recognized throughout Daviess county by all familiar with his history, as a man of real influence in this section of Indiana. His career presents a notable example of those qualities of mind and character which overcome obstacles and win success in the battle of life.

John H. Spencer was born on December 28, 1861, at Greenville, Tennessee, the son of William M. and Elizabeth (Jones) Spencer, natives of South Carolina. They had six children, Sarah, deceased, who was the wife of J. W. Canady; Jennie, who is unmarried; Ella, who is the wife of Milton M. Mitchell, of Washington; Tillie, who died unmarried; Elizabeth, deceased, who was the wife of Thomas L. Dant, and John H., of Washington.

William M. Spencer was reared in South Carolina and came to Rushville, Indiana, in 1867, where he lived for two years. He then came to Washington, Indiana, in 1869, and engaged in the lumber business, which he followed during the greater part of his life. He operated a saw-mill for many years. William M. Spencer died in Washington, January 2, 1895, at the age of sixty-seven, and his wife died in 1906, at the age of eighty-one. Both were members of the Methodist church. William M. Spencer was a soldier in the Confederate army, first, a captain and, subsequently, a colonel in this army.

John H. Spencer's paternal grandfather was John G. Spencer, a native of South Carolina, but removed to Kansas and settled on a farm between Iola and Humbolt. He was a farmer and died there at an advanced age. Mr. Spencer's maternal grandfather was Thomas M. Jones, also a native of South Carolina. He moved to Missouri and settled in Carroll county. In early life he was a carpenter and coffin maker, but later a farmer. He died in Missouri, as did also his wife. Both were very old at the time of their deaths,—perhaps ninety-four or ninety-five years.

John H. Spencer was born in Greenville, Tennessee, and came to Indiana when a child with his parents. He was reared in Washington and attended the public schools here. He graduated from the high school in 1880 and then began studying law in the office of Judge J. W. Ogdon. In 1882 he was admitted to the bar and has practiced in Washington ever since. He is a member of the Methodist church.

Politically, Mr. Spencer is a Democrat. He was clerk of the judiciary committee of the House of Representatives in 1885 and two years later, when the Legislature convened, he was chief journal clerk in the Indiana State Senate. In 1887 and 1891 he had charge of the engrossing and enrolling room in the Senate. From 1894 to 1898, he was mayor of Washington and also served as deputy prosecutor for five and one-half years. In 1900, he was a delegate to the Democratic national convention at Kansas City. He was the nominee for state senator in 1908, but was defeated. Mr. Spencer was city attorney for four years, or until 1914, when he was re-elected, but in February he resigned to take the position of income tax collector for the seventh district.

Thus it appears that John H. Spencer has been honored by the people of Daviess county and by the people of Indiana with many important positions of trust and responsibility. It is only fair to say, that he has performed the duties of all of these positions conscientiously and faithfully. In the first place, Mr. Spencer is a man of superior ability and in the next place, he is a man who puts into any duty, public or private, the very best energy and thought of which he is capable. John H. Spencer has never married, but has devoted the time which most men devote to their families, to matters of public interest and, in this respect, he has performed a notably good work in behalf of the people of Daviess county.

COURTLAND E. HAYES.

It is a well-established maxim, that the greatness of a community or a state lies not in the machinery of government or even in its institution, but in the sterling qualities of its individual citizens, in their capacity for high and unselfish effort, and their devotion to the public welfare. In these particulars, Courtland E. Hayes has conferred honor and dignity upon his locality and as an elemental part of history, it is fitting that there should be recorded a resume of his career, with the object of noting his connection with the advancement of one of the most flourishing and progressive sections of the commonwealth of Indiana. Mr. Hayes is a well-known business man of Washington, Indiana, who, by his personal efforts, has built up a large patronage in the city of Washington and vicinity.

Courtland E. Hayes was born on May 17, 1886, in Denver, Colorado. He is the son of Edwin and Flora (Cuppy) Hayes, the former a native of St. John, New Brunswick, Canada, born in 1861, and the latter of Shelburn, Indiana, born in 1859.

The paternal grandfather of Courtland E. Hayes was Edwin A. Hayes, Sr., who now resides near St. John, New Brunswick. His wife is deceased. The maternal grandparents of Mr. Hayes were Carter and Nancy (Carter) Cuppy. They settled first in Indiana, but later moved to Illinois. He died at Kemp, Illinois, and his wife is still living in that place.

Edwin Hayes, Jr., the father of Courtland E., is a general merchant at Kemp, Illinois. He left St. John, New Brunswick, Canada, when a young man and located at Idaho Springs, Colorado, where he was a teacher for several years. After his marriage at Idaho Springs, he removed to Denver and there was secretary of a large wholesale plumbing house for some time. In 1898 Edwin Hayes, Jr., removed to Kemp, Illinois, where he engaged in the general mercantile business, in which he has been engaged since that time, a period of practically seventeen years. Edwin Hayes, Jr., was formerly an ardent Republican, but during the last two or three years has been identified with the new Progressive party. He and his wife are members of the church of Christ. They have been the parents of four children, Courtland E., Glenn, Carter and Amelia, all of whom are now living.

Courtland E. Hayes received his early education at Kemp, Illinois, and also in the high school at Arcola, Illinois, and in the normal school at Marion, Indiana. In 1911, Mr. Hayes moved to Washington, Indiana, and engaged in the general mercantile business at 1 West Main street. Although a comparatively young man, he has thoroughly established himself as one of the enterprising business men in the city of Washington, and is honored and respected by the citizens of this county.

Mr. Hayes was married on September 8, 1909, to Bertha Hawkins, a native of Arcola, Illinois, born in 1886. She is the daughter of William W. and Mary (White) Hawkins, both residents of Arcola, Illinois. To this happy union, two children have been born, Pauline Elizabeth and Jack Edwin.

Mr. Hayes and his family are members of the Christian church at Washington and take an active part in the affairs, both of the church and the Sunday school. They contribute liberally of their means to the support of this denomination. In politics, Mr. Hayes is now identified with the Progressive party, though formerly he was a Republican. Fraternally, Mr. Hayes is a member of the Free and Accepted Masons and has been for several years.

LAWRENCE CHARLES GROSS.

It is an axiom demonstrated by all human experience that industry is the key to prosperity. Success comes not to him who idly waits for fortune's favors, but to the faithful toiler who, with cheerful celerity and sleepless vigilance, takes advantage of every circumstance calculated to promote his interests. Such a man was Lawrence Charles Gross, a well-known and highly-esteemed citizen of Daviess county, Indiana, who in a comparatively brief period of time, advanced from an humble station in life to a proud position among the citizens of this county. Faithfulness to duty and a strict adherence to fixed purposes, which always do more to advance a man's interests than wealth or position, were the dominating factors in his life, which was replete with honor and success worthily attained. He was known as a man of strictly honest business principles; industrious, pleasant and agreeable.

The late Lawrence Charles Gross was born on May 1, 1866, in Germany, where his parents died. He came to America early in life and after landing in this country, went immediately to Green Bay, Wisconsin, when he was fifteen years old. Subsequently, he removed to Louisville, Kentucky, and in October, 1889, came to Washington, Indiana. He died on May 29, 1909. His earlier education was received in Germany. He was a baker and engaged in this business on March 17, 1892, at 13 Southeast Second street, and continued in business until his death. Since his death the business has been carried on by his widow. In politics, Lawrence Charles Gross was a

Democrat. He was a member of the Free and Accepted Masons, a Knights Templar and a member of the Knights of Pythias. He attended the Presbyterian church, of which Mrs. Gross is a member all her life. The late Lawrence Charles Gross was married, March 9, 1892, to Louise Schuck, a native of Weis-Baden, Germany, born on October 26, 1868, and a daughter of Philip and Catherine (Alberti) Schuck, both natives of Germany, the former born on January 14, 1839, and the latter born on October 20, 1842. They were married in Germany and in 1869 they came to New Albany, Indiana. After living there for two years, they removed to Washington, Indiana, in 1871. Philip Schuck was a coal miner. Later in life he was engaged in the restaurant business in Washington, Indiana. In politics, Philip Schuck was a Democrat. He was a member of the Presbyterian church and active in the Independent Order of Odd Fellows. He was also a member of the German Benevolent Society.

The children of Philip and Catherine (Alberti) Schuck were as follow: Lena, who died in infancy; Henry and Louise, who were born in Germany; Peter, who was born in New Albany, Indiana; Mary, born in Washington, Indiana, and who is deceased; Louis, who is deceased, was born in Washington, Indiana. The father of Mrs. Lawrence Charles Gross died on September 13, 1888, and his wife died on April 16, 1909.

Mrs. Gross's maternal grandfather was Christian Alberti, born in 1810, who married Elizabeth Bernhart. He died in Germany in 1867. After his death, his widow came to the United States and located in Washington, Indiana, and died there on September 24, 1886. She was born on December 15, 1815. They had four children, Jennie, Louis, Catherine and Louise, all of whom are now deceased.

Lawrence Charles Gross was one of five children. The others were Caspar, Martin and two sisters.

The late Lawrence Charles Gross occupied a prominent place in the business life of Washington and his death was keenly lamented by the people of Washington and vicinity. Few men paid stricter attention to business, or were more thoroughly centered in their own personal affairs, than the late Mr. Gross. While he gave all his time and energy to business, he, however, was interested in the public welfare and loyally supported all worthy public movements. Mrs. Gross is a most estimable lady and is now living in Washington, Indiana. She has a host of friends, which she has won because of her gentleness of character and keen intellectual refinement. Mrs. Gross presented the memorial window to the Presbyterian church, in memory of her beloved husband.

WILLIAM DEARMIN.

It cannot be other than interesting to note in the series of personal sketches appearing in this work, the varying conditions that have compassed those whose careers are outlined. An effort has been made in each case, to throw a well-focused light on the individuality and to bring into proper perspective, the trend of each career. The man who strives to do his part in connection with human life and its activities, deserves recognition, whatever may be his field of endeavor. It is a function of historical works of the character of the one in hand, to perpetuate for future generations an authentic record concerning those represented in its pages. The value of such publication is intended to be cumulative for all time to come, and the work represents the individual and specific accomplishments of each generation.

William Dearmin, a well-known grocer, of Washington, Indiana, was born in Monroe county, Indiana, January 19, 1853. He is the son of Joseph and Eliza (Rainey) Dearmin, the former a native of Virginia, born in 1812, and the latter a native of Indiana, who died in Monroe county in 1855. Joseph Dearmin was the son of John Dearmin, a native of Virginia, who came to Monroe county, Indiana, in 1824. Here he died about 1857. John Dearmin's wife was Rebecca Pearcy.

Joseph Dearmin was twelve years old when he was brought to Monroe county, Indiana, with his parents. He was a farmer in Monroe county and identified with the fortunes of the Democratic party early in life, but later became a Republican. He died in 1876, in Daviess county, Indiana. By his first wife he had five children: Dr. John, who first lived in Monroe county and later in Daviess county, died in Indianapolis; George; James L., deceased; William, and Percy, deceased. After the death of his first wife, Joseph Dearmin married Mary Reeder and had two sons by this marriage, Thomas and Henry, both of whom are deceased.

William Dearmin was eighteen years old when his parents moved from Monroe county, Indiana, to this county, in 1875. He was educated in the public schools of Indiana, and, after completing his education, lived in Illinois for a few years. In 1876, he removed to Daviess county, where he was married. He settled at Raglesville, in 1877.

William Bearmin was married to Mary Critchlow, of Daviess county. She was the mother of five children, Carl L.; Martha F., the wife of Alfred M. Tarr; Ada P., the wife of A. H. Witsett, of Pittsburg, Kansas; Joseph

E. and Miles R., both of Washington, Indiana. Mrs. Dearmin died in 1896, and Mr. Dearmin was married again to Margaret V. McFadden, of Daviess county. No children have been born to this last marriage.

While living at Raglesville, Mr. Dearmin was engaged in carpenter and contracting work. For a time he was located at Elnora, Indiana, and was in the real estate and insurance business. In 1912, he came to Washington, Indiana, and engaged in the grocery business, operating two stores, one at 725 East Main street, and one at 14 Southeast Third street. His sons, Carl L. and Joseph E., were in partnership with him, under the firm name of Dearmin's Cash Grocery. Later, Joseph E. sold his interest in the firm to his father and brother, and he is now a traveling salesman. William Dearmin and his son, Carl L., are now in business at 14 Southeast Third street, under the firm name of Dearmin's Cash Grocery, and do a very extensive business. They began in a small way and now have one of the largest groceries in Washington. Mr. Dearmin and his son also own a good farm in Barr township, consisting of ninety-six acres.

The Dearmins are highly-respected residents of Washington and have built up an enviable reputation for honesty and square dealing. These qualities account in a large measure for their phenomenal success, since coming to Daviess county and particularly to Washington.

Mr. Dearmin is a member of the Independent Order of Odd Fellows, at Odon, Indiana, the Modern Woodmen of America, at Washington, and are also his three sons; he also holds membership with the Methodist Episcopal church at Washington, Indiana.

JAMES M. CONLIN.

The record of the subject of this sketch is that of a man who, by his own unaided efforts, has worked his way from a humble station to a position of influence in his community. His life has been one of unceasing industry, perseverance and toil, and the systematic and honorable methods he has followed have won for him the unbounded confidence of his fellow citizens of Daviess county, whose interests he ever has had at heart.

James M. Conlin was born May 8, 1871, in Martin county, Indiana, and is the son of James and Mary Anne (Feagan) Conlin. His father was born in Cincinnati, Ohio, September 17, 1846; his mother was born in Daviess county, September 12, 1844. His paternal grandparents were natives of Ireland, who immigrated to this country and first settled in Cincinnati, Ohio, and later came to Reeve township, this county, where both lived and died. Subject's maternal grandparents, Henry and Ellen (Sutton) Feagan, were natives of Daviess county, coming here in an early day, and here they both died.

Subject's father received his early education in the public schools of Daviess county and began his career as a common laborer, working in various places in Daviess and Knox counties, Indiana, on the railroads and after some years was promoted to foreman of a section gang. At a later date he became a locomotive fireman and continued in that capacity for some time. At the present time he is occupied in Vincennes, Indiana, as a stationary engineer and lives there. He has always supported the Democratic ticket and the entire family are members of the Catholic church. To their union were born the following named children: James M., Henry, deceased, William, Agnes, Sarah, Anna, Margaret, Mattie and Michael.

James M. Conlin received his early education in the public schools of Knox county, Indiana, and when quite young began work as a laborer in a local stave factory. At a later date, he secured employment in the Ohio and Mississippi shops in Vincennes, Indiana, and worked there during the years 1887-88, and on March 24, 1889, left there to go to work as a machinist in the Baltimore & Ohio Southwestern railroad shops in Washington, Indiana. While employed there, he was promoted to the position of assistant foreman of the round house, later promoted to foreman, and finally placed in the position as general foreman of the round house and director of the machine and erecting shops. In 1893, Mr. Conlin was married to Catherine Brennan, a native of Washington, Indiana, and a daughter of Owen and Catherine (Roarty) Brennan, both residents of Washington. To Mr. and Mrs. Conlin have been born four children: Rose May, Charles, Marguerite and Dorothy, deceased.

Mr. Conlin owns an attractive home at No. 110 Pearl street, in Washington, where he and the family have resided since 1908, and where every evidence of the kindest hospitality exists. Politically, Mr. Conlin is a supporter of the Democratic ticket, but at no time has he aspired to hold political office. Fraternally, he is a member of the Knights of Columbus and the Royal Arcanum. Religiously, the whole family are attached to the Catholic faith and contribute liberally to the support of that denomination. Personally, Mr. Conlin, is genial and unassuming in his relations with his fellowmen, easily wins friends and among the wide acquaintance which he enjoys, he has many warm and loyal admirers. Mr. and Mrs. Conlin are leading quite lives and they are highly respected for the honorable and praiseworthy lives they have led, and for the hospitality they have ever shown to the poor and needy, having long been worthy examples and influential for good, wherever they have resided.

FRANK MANGIN.

Enterprise and industry, coupled with well-directed purpose, will always be productive of some measure of success. In the pursuit of agriculture, the qualities mentioned are quite essential. Numbered among the successful farmers in Daviess county, Indiana, is the man whose name appears at the head of this review. He has so developed his holdings and cultivated his land so intensively, that he has attained a definite degree of success, and at the same time has greatly benefited the people of this county. Having always pursued honorable and upright methods in his dealings with his fellowmen, and having led an exemplary life, he is entitled to recognition in a work of the character of this history.

Frank Mangin was born on September 24, 1845, in Lorraine, France, and is the son of Frank and Katrina (Lawson) Mangin, both natives of France, where they lived and died. The subject of this review received his education in his native country and came to his country in 1867, first settling in Floyd county, Indiana, where he remained until 1870, and then came to Washington, Indiana. In 1878, he returned to France and was married there to Catherine Vourms, born on September 12, 1853, and a native of Lorraine, France. Returning with his wife to America in 1879, he went to the town of New Albany, Indiana, for a short time, then coming to Daviess county, entered, and at a later date bought his present farm consisting of forty acres. A number of improvements have been effected on the place and a general farming business is conducted. Mr. Mangin has a commodious and comfortable residence, well situated, and everything about the place is kept up in good shape, indicating a considerable degree of interest in his holding. To him and his wife have been born the following children: Mary, who died at the age of fourteen years; Frank, who died at the age of five years; Barbara, wife of George Rankle, of Washington township, whose children are: Frances, born on February 15, 1902; Margaret, March 15, 1905; Catherine M., March 23, 1908; Rosemary, July 4, 1911, and Vincent, July 19, 1914; Anna, wife of William C. Howard, whose marriage occurred on October 6, 1914; he is a machinist on the Baltimore & Ohio railroad at Washington, Indiana; Rose, who is a trained nurse and lives in Kokomo, Indiana, and Nicholas, who lives with his parents.

Politically, Mr. Mangin is a supporter of the Democratic ticket, but does not take any active interest in the political questions. Religiously, he and his family are devout members of the Catholic church. Personally, he is regarded as an unselfish, charitable man, of pleasing disposition and a gentleman in every sense of the word. His life in this community has resulted in a large number of friends, who hold him in the highest esteem and who recognize in him worthy motives, business ability, and high character. He is a man who is liberal in his views, believes in progress and improvement and does what he can to further these ends, taking an interest in whatever makes for the material advancement of the county, and the social, intellectual and moral good of the people.

JOSEPH SMALL.

While success cannot be achieved without unceasing industry, the futility of effort is often noticeable in the business world, and results from the fact that it is not combined with sound judgment. Many a man who gives his entire life to earnest and unremitting toil, never acquires a competence; but when his labor is well directed, prosperity always follows. Joseph Small is one whose work has been supplemented by careful management and today he is numbered among the successful agriculturists of the locality in which he lives. Descended from honored ancestry of Revolutionary days, and himself having won the high esteem of his community by honorable methods and right living, is entitled to recognition in a work of this nature.

Joseph Small was born on November 4, 1849, in Washington township, Daviess county, and is the son of William and Tabitha (Sanford) Small, the former born February 13, 1822, in Washington township, and the latter born in Mason county, Kentucky, February 11, 1829. Subject's paternal grandparents were Benjamin and Mary Small, the former a native of Virginia, who went to Kentucky in an early day and was married there. He removed to Daviess county, Indiana, where both he and his wife died. Subject's maternal grandparents, Hamilton and Tabitha Ann (Clark) Sanford, were both natives of Kentucky and came to Daviess county, Indiana, in an early day. They are both dead. William and Tabitha (Sanford) Small were the parents of the following children: One who died in infancy; Joseph W. and a twin who died in infancy; Tabitha Ann; Mary Jane; John W.; Lucretia; Thomas R., who died on March 12, 1914; another who died in infancy; Helen; Virginia; Reuben; Benjamin and Sarah.

The great-grandparents on both sides of Mr. Small's family were active during the Revolutionary War, and his great-grandfather was killed in the last battle.

William H. Small, died in January, 1881, in Washington, Indiana. The father had been a good provider for his family and lived an honorable and upright life. His early education had been neglected, but being a man of keen observation and quick to learn, he acquired considerable knowledge and was recognized as a bright and well-informed man. He was a member of the old Whig party and later became a Democrat. At one time he was engaged to assist in the building of the old Baptist church in Washington, Indiana, and belonged to that denomination, while for the most of his life he was engaged in farming.

Mr. Small received his education in the township schools of Daviess county, and at the age of twenty went to work in the southern Indiana coal fields. After laboring in the mines for a while, he secured a position as foreman for the firm of Cabel & Kauffman, and remained with that firm for twenty-three years, then went to work as foreman for the firm of Freeman & Wolford, where he remained for the following five years; then, for the next two years, acted as foreman for the United Fourth Vein Coal Company, mined for several months, and finally began farming and continues to farm to this day. He is the owner of two hundred eleven acres of land in Daviess county, and one hundred fifty-six acres in Owen county, Indiana. He carries on general farming and has made a good many improvements on his home place.

Joseph Small was married in 1877, to Annette Brown, who was born in Fredericksburg, Washington county, Indiana, a daughter of Alonzo B. and Margaret Brown, she being the only child. Her father went to Texas many years ago and is supposed to have died there, and her mother moved to Daviess county, Indiana, forty-three years ago and still lives there. To Mr. Small and his wife have been born the following children: Naoma, who married James B. Aikman, and lives in Washington, Indiana; their children are: George, Margaret, Josephine and Paul; William H., who married Ida Long, and is now engaged in farming; Annette B., now Mrs. Arthur Greenwood, living in Washington, Indiana, where he practices law; Theresa, deceased infant; Joseph, who married Sarah Shinefelt, and is a civil engineer, graduate of Purdue University, and now connected with the American Bridge Company, of Ambridge, Pennsylvania; Ella, who married Marvin Busic, and lives in Dayton, Ohio; Thomas Jefferson, who married Minnie Dover, and is mining coal in Linton, Indiana.

Politically, Mr. Small supports the policies ot the Democratic party. Personally, he is a man of clean character and of genial impulses, so that, unconsciously, perhaps, and without effort, makes friends with all who come into contact with him. He enjoys the respect and esteem of his fellow citizens and is regarded by all as one of the substantial and worthy citizens of the community in which he lives.

JOHN KOLLER.

Agriculture has been an honored vocation from the earliest ages, and men of honorable and humane impulses, as well as of energy and thrift, have been patrons of husbandry. The free out-door life of the farm has a decided tendency to foster and develop that independence of mind and self-reliance which characterizes true manhood, and no greater blessing can befall a boy than to be reared in close touch with nature in the healthful, life-inspiring surroundings of the fields. It has always been the fruitful soil from which have sprung the moral bone and sinew of the country, and the majority of our nation's great warriors, renowned statesmen and distinguished men of letters were born on the farm and were indebted largely to its early influences for the distinction which they subsequently attained.

John Koller was born on August 6, 1878, on his present farm, in Washington township, Daviess county, Indiana, and is the son of John and Mary (Smith) Koller. His father was born on March 22, 1842, in Alsace-Lorraine, Germany, and came to this country when a very young man, settling in Daviess county, Indiana. His first marriage was to Alberdina Sum, and resulted in the birth of two children, Frank and Mary, deceased. His second wife, Mary Smith, was a daughter of Peter and Elizabeth (Dornauf) Smith, both natives of Germany, who came to this country in 1869, and settled in the state of Pennsylvania, afterward removed to Daviess county, Indiana, and where they died in a few months. To them were born: Jacob, Peter, Mary, John and Elizabeth. John Koller's mother was born near the river Rhine, Province of Nassau, Germany, on September 8, 1849, and died on June 28, 1910, in Daviess county. She came from Pennsylvania to Daviess county. Subject's father owned the place which he now occupies and up to the time of his death had cultivated the soil for the raising of garden products. The father had acquired a complete knowledge of the shoemaker's trade, but did not follow it in this country. He died on July 18, 1895, on his place in Washington township, this county. He had always supported the Democratic ticket and belonged to the Catholic church.

John Koller received his early education in the parochial Catholic schools and spent a while in attending the public schools, then followed in the footsteps of his father and continued the truck farming business. In this he has been very successful and gives considerable attention to dairy products, having as many as ten cows to look after at this time. Subject farms the original twenty-five acres owned by his father, and also farms about fifty acres near Washington, Indiana. On January 22, 1907, Mr. Koller was married to Theresa Harter, who was born on March 30, 1879, in Germany, and who is the daughter of Ignatius and Christena (Baerle) Harter, both born in Germany, the former on January 17, 1843, and the latter on February 3, 1853. They were engaged in farming in the old country, but upon coming to America, in 1881, they settled in the town of Washington, Indiana, and Mr. Harter worked in the coal mines until his retirement from active business life. Politically, he was an independent voter, not taking sides with either of the leading parties, but preferring to vote as he thought best. Religiously, he was a devout member of the Catholic church and the family were brought up in that faith. To Mr. and Mrs. Harter were born five children, as follow: Joseph, Theresa, Caroline, Charles and Lena, all living. To the subject of this review and wife was born one child, John, on December 15, 1907.

Personally, Mr. Koller is a man of wide and accurate information on the questions pertaining to gardening and makes a careful study of this line. He is a keen observer and his success in gardening is due to his intelligent management, thrift and industry. Politically, he supports the Democratic party and is a firm believer in its policies. Religiously, he and his wife are members of the Catholic church and to that denomination lend their hearty support. Socially, Mr. Koller has the reputation of being a kind and pleasant gentleman and enjoys the respect and esteem of all who know him. His life in this community has been one above reproach, because of his honorable methods and satisfactory dealings with his fellow men.

EDGAR L. COVALT.

Among the citizens of Daviess county who have attained to positions of distinction in the community, in which their interests lie, is Edgar L. Covalt, who has lived in this county for so many years and has led an eminently active and busy life. This well-known gentleman has long ranked among the progressive agriculturists of this county and has always strived to fill his part in connection with local life and local activities. Not only has he achieved considerable success, in his chosen field of labor, but he has also established an imperishable reputation for uprightness in all the relations of life.

Edgar L. Covalt was born on August 16, 1869, in Steele township, Daviess county, Indiana, and is the son of Cheniah and Louisanna (Williams) Covalt. His father was born on October 16, 1842, in Henry county, Indiana, and his mother was born on December 12, 1838, in Franklin county, Indiana. After their marriage, and in February, 1867, they settled in Daviess county, where the father and mother died, July 26, 1913, and June 25, 1891, respectively. Subject's paternal grandparents, Cheniah and Elizabeth (Echelbarger) Covalt, came from the state of Ohio, and were early settlers in Henry county, this state, where both died and are buried near the town of Mooreland, Henry county. Mr. Covalt's father was a soldier with the Union forces, enlisted for the war in 1861, and assigned to Company C, Thirty-sixth Indiana Volunteer Infantry, with which he remained until the close of the war. He took part in the fiercest engagements of the Civil War, principally in the battles of Shiloh, Chickamauga and Lookout Mountain. The father was twice married, the first time to Lemoa Anna Williams, who gave birth to Lillian and Edgar L., and by his second marriage, to Ola Lucas, became the father of four children, Ferdinand, Hoyt, Myrle and Mildred.

Edgar L. Covalt received his early education in the township schools and later attended school in the town of Washington, Indiana, after which he engaged in farming and has continued in that business ever since. At the present time, he is the owner of one hundred twenty-seven acres of fine land in Washington township, and cultivates the soil in a general way and raises cattle and horses.

On November 26, 1889, he was married to Fannie M. Keith, who was born on April 22, 1868, and is the daughter of George H. Keith, Sr., and Sarah Jane (Willeman) Keith. The former was born in Daviess county, in the year 1828, and the latter was born in the same county in 1838. Her father was a son of George and Abierilla (Perkins) Keith, whose life record is given elsewhere in this work. To the union of George H. Keith, Sr., and wife were born the following children: Mary; John; Grant; Fannie, who is subject's wife; Charles; Abbie; George, and Louis H. The father died on March 17, 1914, and the mother died on March 24, 1910. The maternal grandparents of Mrs. E. L. Covalt were Hiram and Margaret (Crawford) Willeman, who came to Daviess county in an early day and settled on a farm in Washington township, where they died. To subject and wife was born one child, Nellie, on May 5, 1901, and who died on August 5, 1904.

Politically, Mr. Covalt is a stanch supporter of the principles of the Republican party and an ardent advocate of the progressive ideas set forth by that party. Religiously, he and his wife are members of the Methodist church in Washington, Indiana, and to which they lend their unstinted support. Personally, Mr. Covalt is honest and upright at all times, and he is not only held in high esteem for his sound business ability, but for his wholesome private and social life, and his position is established as one of Daviess county's most respected citizens.

HENRY ALBERTY.

Numbered among the people of Daviess county, who began their lives in an humble station and by sustained perseverance, well-directed energy and industry, attained positions of honor and responsibility, is the man whose name forms the caption for this review and whose life record has been brought to a close by the inevitable fate that awaits all mankind. The career of this gentleman was a strenuous and varied one, entitling him to honorable mention among the representative citizens of his day and generation in the county with which his life was so closely identified.

Henry Alberty was born May 22, 1866, in Germany, and was the son of Louis and Phillipena Alberty, both natives of Germany, and where his mother died. The father was born in the year 1841, and the mother was born on February 18, 1841, and died in 1880. His father was married a second time in Germany some time prior to their arrival in the United States. By the first marriage were born five children: Henry, Phillip, Louise, Louise, deceased, and Carrie. By the second marriage were born: Henrietta, Minnie and Kate. Together with his second wife and all living children, subject's father arrived in this country and settled on a farm in

Washington township, this county, and continued to farm until about the time of his death, June 11, 1895, at the age of fifty-four years. He became an ardent advocate of the principles of the Democratic party, and was a member of the Presbyterian church.

Henry Alberty was but a lad of fourteen when his parents arrived in Washington township, and having received an early education in the home country, at once sought work and was employed in 1889 as a fireman on the Baltimore & Ohio Southwestern railroad, and remained in that capacity until the year 1897, when he received promotion to the position of locomotive engineer. This occurred on March 17, 1897, and he held the position until the time of his death, October 6, 1913. In June, 1888, he was married to Anna M. Jones, who was born in Wales, July 24, 1866, and a daughter of Henry B. and Jane (Edwards) Jones, the former born in Wales in 1841, and the latter born in England in 1843. Her parents were married in Wales, April 6, 1862, and remained there until the year 1870, when they came to this country, first settled in Pennsylvania, and in 1873, came to Washington, Indiana, where the father worked as a coal miner and died here, October 14, 1914. The mother of subject's wife also died in Washington, October 20, 1914. Henry B. Jones became affiliated with the Republican party, although never active in party affairs. He and his wife and family were members of the St. John's Episcopal church of Washington. To them were born the following children: Harry L., Jessie C., Harriet, and Eugene. To the subject of this review and his wife were born four children: Harry, a tinner in the Baltimore & Ohio Southwestern railroad shops; Jesse C., a machinist; Harriet, a bookkeeper in the Hammersly store, and Eugene, who attends school.

Henry Alberty's brother, Phillip C. Alberty, was born on May 9, 1869, in Germany, and after coming to this country in 1882, with his father, went to work in the shops of the Baltimore & Ohio Southwestern railroad in Washington, Indiana, for a while, and then went to work as a coal miner. In November, 1893, he was married to Martha E. McAtee, who was born in Daviess county, Indiana, October 16, 1875, and is a daughter of Marce and Mary (Spaulding) McAtee, both natives of this county and wherein they died. To their union were born the following named children: John, Lizzie, Vina, Lucy, Martha and Daniel. Phillip McAtee's paternal grandfather was Daniel McAtee, a pioneer settler of this county. To Mr. and Mrs. Phillip Alberty have been born the following children: Katie, the wife of Martin Hochgesang, of Washington, Indiana; Alma; Louis Carl, who attends high school; Harry, Theresa, Walter, and two others, Roy and Mary, deceased.

Henry Alberty during his life was looked on as a man of exemplary habits, steady and industrious, and his character was such as to reflect the highest credit upon himself. All in all he was a worthy representative of the steady and progressive class. Politically, he was a Democrat in his views, but gave his support to the side whose policy he considered the best. Religiously, he was brought up in the Lutheran faith and his wife is a Catholic. Personally, he was generous-hearted, conscientious, fair and square in his business dealings, and a good provider for his family.

WILLIAM H. NEAL.

The student, interested in the history of Daviess county, does not have to carry his investigations far into its annals, before learning that William H. Neal has long been one of the most active and leading citizens in the stock-raising interests of this community. While attending to his large business, particularly dealing in horses, he has also found ample opportunity to assist in the material and civic welfare of the county. His life has been such as to elicit just approbation from those who know him best, owing to the fact that he has an established character for upright and honorable dealings with his fellow men, and thus becomes entitled to notice in a review of this kind.

William H. Neal was born on January 29, 1855, in Lawrence county, Indiana, and is the son of Asa and Anna (Fulton) Neal, the former a native of Kentucky, born in 1818, and the latter born in the state of Indiana. His father, who died in Kentucky, came, with his mother, to this state in the year 1820, and lived under the parental roof, received his education in the public schools of Lawrence county, and later farmed. He was a member of the old Whig party, later a Democrat, but voted for Abraham Lincoln. His wife was a devout member of the Baptist church and died in the year 1887, surviving her husband just three years. To their union were born the following children: Sarah, Maria, Alexander (deceased), Margaret (deceased infant), William H., Robert (deceased infant), Mary, James, Charles and Jane.

The subject of review was reared on his father's farm in Lawrence county, received his early education in the public schools, and made a business of farming, but gave special attention to live stock, particularly horses. He continued to deal in stock until the year 1882, and at one time owned the fastest pacing mare in the world, known by the name of "Flora Bell." In 1880, he came to Washington, Daviess county, where he engaged in the hotel business in 1884, in what is known as the Meredith House, and was proprietor of this hotel for several years. After disposing of this business, he went to the town of Olney, Illinois, where he engaged in the livery business the following year, then sold out and returned to Washington, Indiana, and for the past eighteen years has devoted his time and attention to dealing in live stock and has been always a great lover of horses.

In 1884, Mr. Neal was married to Della Harris, who was born on August 7, 1858, in the state of Wisconsin, but who was reared and educated in the town of Washington, Indiana. She is a daughter of William and Laura (Coval) Harris. Her father was a native of England, born 1832, and her mother a native of Daviess county, Indiana, born in Washington, August 31, 1837. William Harris immigrated from England to the United States and first went to Wisconsin. He was married in 1856 and came to Washington, Indiana, in 1859. It was here that he enlisted for service with the Union forces in 1861, and was assigned to Company E, Twenty-seventh Regiment, Indiana Volunteer Infantry, and served until the close of the Civil War; then returned to Washington, Indiana, where he took the proprietorship of what was then known as the Union Hotel and now called the Meredith House. He remained with the Meredith House until the year 1876, and then managed the Hyatt House of this town, until the year 1881, and where he died on June 10, 1882.

Mr. Neal's wife, Laura Coval, was a daughter of John and Delilah (Ruggles) Coval, both natives of Kentucky. They went to the state of Wisconsin in an early day and it was there that he died. She returned to Washington, Indiana, where she remained until her death, which occurred on September 28, 1893. Delilah Ruggles was a daughter of Thomas Ruggles and Rachael (Freeland) Ruggles, both natives of Kentucky, and who came to Daviess county, Indiana, in the year 1812, and, owing to conditions of the times and the continuous troubles with the Indians, they were obliged to live in a local fort. These grandparents were engaged in farming during their lives; the father died in 1813, the mother surviving until 1843. Both were members of the New Light Church. To their union were born, Elizabeth, Jacob, Delilah, Mary, Nancy and Aaron.

William H. Neal's great-grandfathers, Alexander Neal and Isaac

Edwards, were soldiers in the Revolutionary War. They served through the war and returned to Virginia, where they lived the balance of their lives.

The subject of review and his wife have not been blessed with children, but have taken the responsibility of raising a grandnephew named Louis Waller, who is attending the public schools at the present time. Mrs. Neal is an active member of the Methodist Episcopal church of Washington, and to which denomination she lends her hearty support, in which her husband liberally joins her. Politically, Mr. Neal is a firm believer in the principles of Democracy and is ever active in his support of that party's cause. On two occasions he was nominated by the people of his community to occupy the office of county sheriff, but failed to be elected, though making a close run with his opponent. Fraternally, he is a member of the Benevolent and Protective Order of Elks. Personally, he is a man of liberal views, believes in progress and improvement and does what he can to further these ends, taking a deep interest in whatever makes for the material advancement of the county and the social, intellectual and moral good of the people.

JOHN M. PEEK.

In the respect which is accorded to men who have fought their own way to success through unfavorable environment, we find an unconscious recognition of the intrinsic worth of character which cannot only endure so rough a test, but gain new strength through the discipline. The gentleman to whom the reader's attention is now invited has not been favored especially by inherited wealth or the assistance of powerful friends. In spite of this, by his perseverance, industry and economy, he has attained a comfortable station in life and has made his influence felt for good in Daviess county. Because of his honorable career and because of the fact that he is numbered among those patriotic sons of the North who assisted in preserving the integrity of the Union in the dark days of the Civil War, he is eminently entitled to a place in this volume.

John M. Peek was born on the farm where he now lives in Veale township on April 14, 1845. He is a son of Levi and Sallie (Veale) Peek, the latter of whom was a daughter of James C. and Eleanor (Aikman) Veale. James C. Veale was a son of James C., Sr., and Melvina (Townsend) Veale. James C. Veale, Sr., emigrated from South Carolina to the territory of Indiana, in the spring of 1806, and settled on a creek which was afterward known as Veale's creek, and is so known to this day. When Daviess county was organized into townships, Veale township was named in honor of James C. Veale, Sr., who built a mill on the creek to grind wheat and corn, and a saw-mill to manufacture lumber. He was married to Melvina Townsend, and to this union eight children were born, as follow: William T., who married a Miss Stevenson, had two children, Watis and Emily; Watis emigrated to Texas and there died at the age of sixty-two, and Emily married a Mr. Helphenstein, and is now living in Chico, California, at the age of eighty-three. Daniel married a Miss Coleman, and reared a family in Veale township, this county. James C., Jr., hereafter referred to, is the maternal grandfather of John M. Peek. John T. married a Miss Hyatt, of Washington, Indiana, a sister of Elisha and John Hyatt, early merchants of that city. Nancy married a Mr. Lett, and reared a family of several children. Elsie married a Mr. Wallace and reared a family. Katy married a man by the name of Arrell, who died, and she afterward married a Mr. Kilgore.

James C. Veale, Jr., was born in 1786, in South Carolina, and died in the spring of 1858. He came with his parents early in life to Veale township. At Comer's Fort, which was located near old Maysville, he was married to Eleanor Aikman, who was born in 1791, in Shepherdstown, in the Shenandoah valley of Virginia, and lived there during her early girlhood. Her family came west to the territory of Indiana in 1807, where she met James C. Veale, Jr. They were married in 1813, at Comer's Fort. There were a large number of Indians around that part of the country at that time, who made a great deal of trouble for the settlers. Most of the pioneers of that time lived either in or near a fort. James C. Veale, Jr., taught the first school ever located in Daviess county, the records of which show this fact. He was employed by the county commissioners. He enlisted in the Indiana Volunteers and served under Gen. William H. Harrison in the War of 1812. He was wounded while on duty near Vincennes, fighting the Indians, and when he died, the bullet was still in his body. James C. Veale, Sr., had also fought in the Revolutionary War.

James C. Veale, Jr., and Eleanor (Aikman) Veale were the parents of the following children: William T. married and reared a family, and lived to the ripe old age of eighty-four years; John M. was lost at sea at the age of twenty-nine years, and was unmarried. He was on a vessel loaded with cotton, bound from New Orleans to Pensacola, Florida, where they encountered a severe storm in the Gulf of Mexico, when the vessel took fire and burned to the water's edge, and all on board were lost; James A. married a Miss Newton for his first wife, and after her death, he married a Miss

Irons, of Huntington, Indiana; Sarah married Levi Peek, the father of John M. Peek, the immediate subject of this sketch; Julia died in infancy; Mary M. married a Mr. Johnson and reared a family; Elizabeth married a Doctor Whitton, of Washington; Eleanor died at the age of eight years; Anderson married a Miss Allen, a daughter of Moses Allen, and reared a family, living to the ripe old age of eighty-three years; George W., who now lives at Topeka, Kansas, was born on May 20, 1833. He married Nannie Johnson, of Evansville, this state, on January 20, 1857, and after living a short time in Indiana, removed to the Territory of Kansas, where they have lived ever since. George W. and Nannie (Johnson) Veale are the parents of two sons, George W., Jr., and Walter Johnson. George W., Jr., lives in Topeka, Kansas, and Walter J. lives in California. George W. Veale, Sr., is the last surviving member of his father's family. At the time this was written, 1915, he is living at Topeka, Kansas, but his eyesight has failed and he can neither see to read or write.

Levi Peek, the father of John M., was for many years a justice of the peace in Daviess county, and was always active in local affairs. The period of his career covers the years from 1812 to 1852, and during this period, he did much to promote the material progress and prosperity of Daviess county, and to make it a comfortable and inviting place in which to live.

John M. Peek received his education in the common schools of Daviess county, and at the age of seventeen, enlisted in Company I, Sixty-fifth Regiment, Indiana Volunteer Infantry, serving for three years in the Union army. After the close of the Civil War, he returned to the farm, where he has lived ever since. Mr. Peek has one hundred and seventy-six acres of land in his present farm. He has erected a fine group of buildings, a former group of buildings, equally fine, having burned. Throughout his life, John M. Peek has been extensively engaged in raising live stock for the markets, and in this has been very successful. For his declining years, he has a substantial and comfortable competence and, if necessary, will be able to live in honorable and peaceful retirement. Mr. Peek was married on September 13, 1883, to Ella Chapman, who was born in Martin county, Indiana, the daughter of James and Matilda (Wallace) Chapman. The Wallaces were early settlers in Veale township. John M. and Ella (Chapman) Peek are the parents of four children, Mary, Joseph, Richard and Louise.

All the members of the Peek family are faithful and earnest adherents of the Methodist Episcopal church, having their membership in the Bethel church of that denomination, in whose welfare they are deeply interested, and to the support of which they are liberal contributors. Mr. Peek is an active member of the Grand Army of the Republic, in which he has been deeply interested for many years. Levi Peek was one of the leaders in the Bethel church which he helped build and was active in church work. He also held office in the church.

GEORGE EMMERLING.

Among the citizens of Daviess county, who have attained a place of prominence in the community in which he lives, is the man whose name is used for the heading of this sketch. Coming to this county when but a child, and having led a life of unceasing industry, uprightness and honor, and acquired a fair measure of this world's goods as a result of his honorable methods and good business ability, he is entitled to recognition in a volume of the character now in hand. During his career, he has demonstrated his worth to his fellow citizens, and on account of his ability, integrity and progressive ideas, holds the respect and high esteem of everyone who knows him.

George Emmerling was born, December 12, 1856, in Lawrence county, Michigan, and is the son of Anthony and Bridget (Madden) Emmerling. His father was born in Germany in 1832 and came to this country with his parents when but a lad of four years of age. His mother was born in Ireland in 1836. The paternal grandparents, Joseph Emmerling and wife, were both natives of Germany and came to this country in an early day, settling in the state of Pennsylvania, where they both died.

George Emmerling's father received his early education and grew to manhood in Pennsylvania, where he was married. After his marriage, he removed to Lawrence county, Michigan; then in 1867, left there for Daviess county, Indiana, where he and his brother, George, engaged in the flour and saw-mill business in Maysville, and continued as partners for several years. George sold his interest and removed to Jasper, Dubois county, Indiana, where he again engaged in the flour-mill business. Anthony Emmerling continued business in Maysville for a few years and died there. He was a supporter of the Democratic party and a member of the Catholic church. His wife died in 1876 in Daviess county. To their union were born five children, John (deceased), George, the subject; Frank (deceased), Charles and Mary.

Mr. Emmerling received his early education in the public schools of

Maysville, Indiana, and, in 1880, was married to Lena Neighbor, who was born in 1860, in Daviess county, Indiana, the youngest daughter of William and Lena Neighbor, both natives of Germany, and who came to this country, first settling in Evansville, Indiana, then removed to Daviess county, Indiana. Her father died in 1880, and her mother is still living at the age of eighty-nine years.

To the subject and his wife have been born six children, as follow: Austin, who was educated in the Washington, Indiana, high school, later in the Central Normal School, Danville, Indiana, finished in the Indiana State Normal School and now engaged as a teacher in the consolidated schools of Washington township, this county; Effie and Gertrude, who reside with the parents; Lester, who is manager of his brother Austin's cigar and tobacco store on Main street, Washington, Indiana; Noble and George, both living at home and attending school in the Washington public schools.

Soon after his marriage Mr. Emmerling engaged in farming and now owns one hundred and twenty acres of fine farming land in Washington township. He carries on general farming and stock raising with considerable success. Politically, he is an active supporter of the Democratic ticket, though he does not aspire to public office. Religiously, the family are members of the United Brethren church and to which denomination he gives his liberal support. Personally, the subject is a man of pleasant manner, genial disposition and is well liked by everyone who knows him. He takes a deep interest in matters pertaining to the improvement of farming methods, and is ever ready to give consideration to the support of meritorious enterprises which tend to promote the interests of his fellow citizens.

CHARLES E. PEEK.

Daviess county, Indiana, was not lacking in loyalty during the dark days of the Civil War when the Ship of State was almost stranded on the rocks of disunion. She contributed her quota of brave and valiant me nto assist in preserving the integrity of the government, among whom was Charles E. Peek, at present an enterprising farmer of Veale township. Loyal to his country in its hour of peril and extremity, as was demonstrated on many bloody battlefields, he has ever been a stanch supporter in the times of peace. There are few ex-soldiers in Daviess county, who are more widely known than Mr. Peek. The ranks of the noble organization to which he belonged in the days of his youth, are fast diminishing by the one invincible foe. It is fitting that in a publication of this nature, special tribute be paid to those who served in the greatest civil war known to history.

Charles E. Peek was born in 1845, in Veale township, near Mt. Olive church. He is the son of John and Winnie (Palmer) Peek, both of whom were natives of South Carolina, and was born in 1808, and she in 1813. John Peek was the son of Cager and Mildred (Harrall) Peek, of South Carolina, who settled in Martin county and there died. Cager Peek was at one time a member of the Indiana Legislature and in political tendency was a Democrat. Mrs. Winnie Peek was the daughter of Perminus Palmer, who settled on the Petersburg road in 1818.

John Peek, the father of Charles E., came to Daviess county with two brothers. He was a prominent man in the early affairs of Daviess county, having served as county assessor and as a school teacher for many years. He was a shoemaker and operated a store with a shoe shop on the Petersburg road and had a large business in the early days and employed several shoemakers to care for his trade in which he continued until his death. Upon coming to Daviess county, he entered eighty acres of land on White river, about 1836, part of which is still held by the Peek family. John Peek was identified with the Know-Nothing party, but after the disintegration of that party, he became a Whig and, still later, a Republican. He was the father of six sons and four daughters.

Charles E. Peek was educated in the common schools and upon reaching maturity, took up farming as his life's vocation. He has always lived in Veale township, although he has traveled extensively, having visited thirty-three states in the union.

Mr. Peek enlisted in Company F., Tenth Indiana Cavalry, in the fall of 1863 and was discharged in the fall of 1865. He was attached to the One Hundred and Twenty-sixth Regiment and was never wounded nor taken prisoner during the war. He was in a train wreck en route to the south, in which accident he was slightly injured. Mr. Peek owns one hundred and thirteen acres of land where he lives and thirty-three acres in the bottoms, in Veale township.

Charles E. Peek was married to Julia A. Thomas, the daughter of William Wright Thomas, of Washington township. William Wright Thomas was born in Daviess county on June 4, 1826, the son of John and Vina Thomas, the former of whom was likely born in South Carolina. John Thomas was the son of David Thomas, who was a native of South Carolina, and who came very early to Washington township, where he entered land and farmed until his death. He and his wife are both buried in Bethel cemetery. William W. Thomas died at the age of forty-one. He was the father of seven children and he, together with his family, were members of the Methodist church. John Thomas was prominent in the organization of the Bethel church and deeded to the congregation the land upon which the first church was built.

Charles E. and Julia A. (Thomas) Peek have been the parents of nine children, Mrs. Viola Glenn Barber; William E.; John E.; Mrs. Carrie Belle Stucky; Mrs. Bertha E. McKown; Callie Eveline, died at the age of six years; Mrs. Cora E. Ackman; Mrs. Melina Opha Wood and Thomas J., who died in infancy.

Mr. and Mrs. Peek are members of the Methodist Episcopal church. Mr. Peek is a Republican and has served as road supervisor and constable of Veale township. He is a member of the Grand Army of the Republic, has been class leader in the Methodist church and Sunday school for forty years, and for thirty-five years, acted as treasurer of the board of trustees of the Bethel Methodist church. Charles E. Peek is a man of exceptional prominence in Veale township, not only because of his long residence here, but because of his many good, worthy qualities for which he is honored and respected by his neighbors and fellow citizens.

STANTON BARBER.

The occupation of farming to which the major part of the business life of Stanton Barber has been devoted, is the oldest pursuit for a livelihood known to mankind and the one on which man will ever be the most dependent. The Barber family has long been connected with the general growth of Daviess county of which Stanton Barber is a native and where, in fact, he has spent all of his life. While primarily attending to his own various interests, his life has also been devoted somewhat to his fellow man and he has been untiring in his efforts to inspire a proper respect for law and order and has been ready at all times to uplift humanity along civic and social lines. Stanton Barber is the present efficient township trustee of Veale township and in this office is making a commendable record for himself.

Stanton Barber was born where he now lives in Veale township on October 5, 1869. He is the son of Nelson and Mary (Batchelor) Barber, the former of whom was born on the old homestead, on June 12, 1833, and the latter in Knox county, Indiana, the daughter of George Batchelor and wife, who died in California. Nelson Barber was the son of Aden and Eliza Katherine (Houts) Barber, the former of whom was born in New York, and the latter in Kentucky in 1813. Eliza K. Houts was the daughter of George and Jennie (Graham) Houts, who came from Kentucky and who entered what is called the old Barber homestead, just south of where Lew W. Barber now lives. They entered one hundred and sixty acres. Stanton Barber, the subject of this sketch, now lives on this farm. The Houts family was of Scottish descent. George Houts was unmarried when he came to Veale township. He purchased a farm from a man who had entered the land and added to his original tract of forty acres until he owned one hundred and twenty-five acres. He put up part of the house which is still standing.

Nelson Barber, the father of Stanton, was reared on the old home farm and educated in the public schools. He taught in Daviess and Franklin counties, for several years, but soon took up farming and stock raising. He resided where his son, Stanton, now lives. He owned two hundred and twenty-five acres. Nelson Barber was a man of wide political influence in Veale township, having served as township trustee at one time. He and his family were members of the Methodist Episcopal church. Nelson Barber and wife were married in May, 1857. They had twelve children, Adon C., Frank, Ellis, Edgar, Lew W., George L., John N., Stanton, Cora D., Bertha A., Ottis C. and Jennie Pearl.

Stanton Barber was educated in the common schools and has spent practically all of his life on the farm where he now lives. He has one hundred and forty-five acres where his great-grandfather Houts entered land. Mr. Barber has a saw-mill and threshing machine and is also engaged in general farming. He has made an unusual success of his life's vocation, a success which is recognized by all of his friends and neighbors.

Mr. Barber was married, in 1890, to Hattie Ricks, and to this union one child, Fern, has been born, who died in infancy. Mrs. Barber died in 1892 and, subsequently, in 1895, Mr. Barber was married a second time, to Viola G. Peek, the daughter of Charles E. Peek. To this union seven children have been born, Virgil, Venus, Norman, Charles, Lester, Ruth and Thomas Dale.

Mr. Barber is a Republican and has served on the township advisory board, and on January 1, 1915, took charge of the office of township trustee, to which he had been elected, in the fall of 1914. All the members of the Barber family are identified with the Bethel Methodist church and are active in both the work of the church and the Sunday school.

WILLIAM M. SUTHERLAND.

There are several hundred different occupations at the present time, but there is only one of all this number that is absolutely necessary to man's existence. The three things without which man cannot live are food, clothing and shelter, and it is the farmer who not only controls the food supply, but also holds the clothing products of the world in his hands. His is the only occupation which can exist independently of all others. An increasing number of our best farming men are taking agricultural courses in college, thereby fitting themselves the better for scientific farming. The profession has taken on increased dignity within the past few years and more and more of our young men are applying themselves to the modern idea in husbandry. The farmer of today has the immense advantage of working with machinery which renders his work free from many of its former disadvantages. Daviess county has hundreds of splendid farmers and among them was the late William M. Sutherland.

The late William M. Sutherland was born on August 17, 1873, in Washington county, Pennsylvania, and was the son of George and Margaret Sutherland, both of whom were natives and lifetime residents of Pennsylvania, in which state they died.

William M. Sutherland was educated in Washington county, Pennsylvania, and was there married to Mary Hettington. About 1860 he moved to Coshocton county, Ohio, and was there engaged in the occupation of a farmer. William M. and Mary (Hettington) Sutherland had six children, Lucy Jane, Sarah Elizabeth, Laura Levina, George, William and David Campbell. Mr. Sutherland was married again in 1876 to Harriette A. Rutherford, who was born in Coshocton county, in 1855, and who is the daughter of Anthony and Elizabeth (Teaz) Rutherford, both natives of Ireland, who were married there and came to America and located in Ohio. They had two children born in Ireland and they came to America about 1850. Anthony Rutherford was a soldier in the Civil War and a member of an Ohio regiment. He came to Daviess county in 1883, and located at Washington township where he died. To William M. and Harriette A. (Rutherford) Sutherland two children, Ernest T. and James P., were born. Ernest T. is deceased. The late William M. Sutherland served as township trustee in Coshocton county, and was an active Democrat and died, April 21, 1900. He came to Daviess county in about 1890 and located where his widow still lives in Veale township. He had eighty-four and a quarter acres and erected buildings which are still standing on the farm.

James P. Sutherland, the son of William M. and Harriette A. (Rutherford) Sutherland, was born on May 14, 1887, and was educated in the public schools of Daviess county. He has always lived on the home place with the exception of four months. James P. Sutherland was married in 1909, on June 20, to Della May Dayton, of Daviess county. Two children have been born to this union, William Berton and Dorothy Belle.

James P. Sutherland and wife and children are members of the Methodist Episcopal church. Fraternally, James P. Sutherland is a member of the Independent Order of Odd Fellows. He is a well-known farmer and dairyman of Veale township.

FRANK A. McMULLEN.

Among the worthy citizens of Elnora, Indiana, whose residence here has contributed in no small degree to the prestige of the vicinity, is Frank A. McMullen, for, while laboring for his individual advancement, he has never forgotten his obligations to the public, and his support of such measures and movements as have been made for the general good has always been depended upon. Although his life has been a busy one, he has never allowed his private interests to interfere with his obligations as a citizen and as a neighbor. Through the long years of his residence in this locality, he has ever been true to the trusts reposed in him, whether of a public or private nature, and his reputation in a business way has been unassailable. Possessing in a marked degree those traits which have commanded uniform confidence and regard, he is today honored by all who know him and is numbered among the representative citizens of his community.

Frank A. McMullen, the present genial postmaster of Elnora, Indiana, was born in Lawrence county, Illinois, on June 13, 1878, and is a son of Archie and Laura (Shirkliff) McMullen, natives respectively, of Ohio and Indiana.

The paternal grandparents of F. A. McMullen were John and Mary (McCleary) McMullen, the former of whom was born in Columbiana county, Ohio, and the latter a native of Ireland. The paternal great-grandfather of Mr. McMullen, was John McMullen, who came from Ireland in an early day and located in eastern Ohio, where he followed the occupation of a farmer. In the late fifties, he settled near Dover Hill, where he again engaged in farming, and here lived the rest of his life, as well as his son, John, the grandfather of F. A. McMullen. Archie and John McMullen drove a team in the army.

The maternal great-grandparents of Mr. McMullen were John and Mary (Gough) Shirkliff, the former of whom was a soldier in the War of 1812, serving under Andrew Jackson, and at New Orleans received a bullet wound, which bullet he carried until his death. He was a native of Tennessee, the family having originally come from France to the United States, settling first in Carolina, from whence they moved to Tennessee, and later, John Shirkliff moved to Kentucky. After remaining in that state for a time, he moved to Indiana, but later returned to Kentucky, where his death occurred. The maternal grandparents of Mr. McMullen were Alex and Rose (Gough) Shirkliff, both natives of Kentucky. The Gough family came to Indiana more than one hundred years ago, settling in what is now Barr township, Daviess county, Indiana. Alex Shirkliff came from Kentucky also in an early day, settling near Mr. Pleasant, where he was engaged in watch making, and also conducted a blacksmith shop. He was a soldier in the Union army during the Civil War, while his wife, Rose Gough, had cousins who served in both the Union and Confederate armies during that great struggle, and who participated in the same battles.

Archie McMullen, the father of Mr. McMullen, has been a farmer all his life and is now living on a farm in Washington township in this county, where he and his wife are the parents of the following children, Charles, Rose, Laura, Mrs. Mary Ketchem and F. A.

Frank A. McMullen was educated in the common schools of his home township, and was a student in the University of Valparaiso, for two years. After leaving school, he engaged in teaching, which vocation he followed in Elnora township for ten years, and was very successful in his educational work. In 1914, he was appointed postmaster of Elnora, and is now efficiently serving his fellow citizens in that capacity.

Mr. McMullen was married in 1908 to Lola Sears, a daughter of Luther Sears, of Elmore township, and to this union have been born four children, Lois, Lewis, Gerald and Donald. Mrs. McMullen is a native of this county, and is a lady of much culture and refinement. She is an active member of the Church of Christ.

Mr. McMullen is an adherent of the principles of the Democratic party, and has always taken an active interest in its affairs. He is a member of the Free and Accepted Masons and the Independent Order of Odd Fellows, in the welfare of which organization he takes an active interest.

JACOB C. STILLWELL.

The greatest results of life are often attained by simple means and the exercise of ordinary qualities of common sense and perseverance. Practical industry, wisely and vigorously applied, never fails of success, and it brings out the individual character of the man to the end that it acts as a powerful stimulus to the efforts of others. Among the men of Daviess county, Indiana, who have attained a good measure of this world's success and who started in an humble way is the man whose name appears above.

Jacob C. Stillwell was born in Pike county, Indiana, near the town of Petersburg, on November 3, 1874, and is the son of Richard and Sarah (McKlin) Stillwell, the former a native of this state and the latter also a native of Indiana, Daviess county, and the wife by a second marriage. Jacob C. Stillwell's paternal grandfather was born in Germany and came to this country when a very young man, settling in Indiana where he engaged in farming to some extent, but gave closer attention to the race-horse business and was a familiar figure at county fairs and other exhibitions where horses are an important part of the entertainment. To their union were born four children, as follow: Thomas, at one time elected state representative on the Populist ticket; Richard, subject's father; Anna and Julia.

Richard Stillwell, was educated in the public schools of this state and remained with his father until about the age of twenty years, when he enlisted in the army of the United States and was in the service during the war with Mexico. When that war was ended he went out into the west part of the country, where he remained for a few years, then returned to Indiana and was married. After farming here for a number of years, the Civil War broke out and he enlisted again in the service of the Union as a cavalryman for a period of three years. After the war, he again returned to Indiana, and continued to farm for a number of years, then removed to Stoddard county, Missouri, where he farmed and raised live stock for the remainder of his life, and died there. To Richard Stillwell and wife were born, by the first marriage, four children, Anna, Gardener, Charles, and a child that died in infancy. After the death of the first wife, Richard Stillwell was married to Sarah McKlin and by this second marriage were born, Jacob, the subject of this review, John, who married Julia Bremmett and they have one child, Mary. The last named is engaged in farming in Washington township, this county.

Jacob Stillwell received his early education in the public schools of Daviess county, and began his career working as a farm hand wherever he could secure employment, and continued in this way until the year 1900. By constant saving and careful management, he was able to buy a farm known as the Carpenter farm, consisting of one hundred and sixty acres, in Washington township, which purchase was made in 1903, and has resided on this place ever since. This farm is located about two miles east of Washington, and Jacob Stillwell has devoted his entire time to making improvements to the extent that the observer is not slow to conclude that the owner has been a success in his calling as an agriculturist, and, secured a good portion of this world's goods. Mr. Stillwell has a commodious and comfortable home, in which he and his family take a great pride. Jacob Stillwell was married on August 6, 1900, to Susannah T. Wilson, who was born on December 31, 1876, and is the daughter of James H. and Susannah (Litten) Wilson. To their union have been born the following named children: Perry, August 6, 1902; Theodore A., August 30, 1913.

Jacob Stillwell is a member of the Independent Order of Odd Fellows, and the Woodmen of the World. He has always been a worker in the Republican ranks and lends his support to the progressive principles of that party. The family are regular attendants of the Christian church, to which Mr. Stillwell renders liberal contribution in accordance with his means. Personally, the subject is a quiet, unassuming and very pleasant gentleman to meet. He is a man of kindly disposition, charitably disposed to all classes, honest and thoroughly trustworthy, and is much admired by all who know him for his uprightness and business integrity.

THOMAS C. SINGLETON.

Indefatigable industry, sound business judgment and wise management have been the elements which have contributed to the success achieved by Thomas C. Singleton, of Veale township, who for many years has been an enterprising and progressive farmer of this section of the state. Mr. Singleton lives on a well-improved farm in Veale township, a farm, in fact, which is numbered among the best in the township. Because of his splendid character and unquestioned integrity, he enjoys, to a marked degree, the highest respect of the community. Mr. Singleton has paid particular attention to live stock and has been very successful in raising hogs and cattle for the market.

Thomas C. Singleton was born on the farm, where he now lives, in

Veale township, Daviess county, Indiana, on June 24, 1873. He is the son of Hunley and Lucinda (Hyatt) Singleton, the former a native of Kentucky and the latter of Veale township. Hunley Singleton was the son of William and Nancy (Tolbert) Singleton, natives of Kentucky, whose lives were spent in that state. William Singleton was a tanner and was twice married, his first union having been with Lucinda Hyatt, who was Thomas Singleton's grandmother, and his second union was with Delilah Thomas, the daughter of Charles Thomas and sister of William Thomas. Lucinda (Hyatt) Singleton was a sister of William and John Hyatt and of Mary Ann and Margaret Graham. Mr. Singleton's maternal grandparents were either born in Veale township or came there, early in life from the Carolinas, with their parents. His maternal grandfather was a farmer in Veale township where he owned a large tract of land. He entered this farm from the government, cleared and drained it and there died. The maternal great-grandfather of Mr. Singleton was James C. Veale, Sr., the founder of Veale township and whose life was so intimately connected with this section of Daviess county. James C. Veale was a member of the home guards during the Civil War.

Hunley Singleton, the father of Thomas C., when but a child, came to Indiana from Kentucky and was reared by John and Francis Coleman. He located in Veale township early in life and was there married. He was a carpenter by trade, but was principally engaged in farming. Hunley Singleton had a small tract of land where his son, Thomas C., now lives, a farm consisting of seventy-five acres. Aside from this he had a large tract of land in the river bottoms. He erected all of the buildings which are now standing on the farm owned by Thomas C. Singleton. Hunley Singleton had no military career, but was in the celebrated Morgan raid. He and his wife died upon this farm. They were the parents of eleven children, three of whom died in infancy. The others were Laura, John V., Nellie, Perry, Dennie, James W., Maude Glenn and Thomas C. Hunley Singleton had one sister, Nancy, who married Victor Buchanan, of Illinois.

Thomas C. Singleton was educated in the public schools of Veale township and in the Washington public schools. After finishing his education in the schools of Daviess county, he attended the university at Vincennes, and then taught school for five years in Veale township. Subsequently, he took up farming on the old home place. With the exception of the house, he has erected all the buildings on this farm. Mr. Singleton owns, in all, one hundred and seventy acres, seventy-five acres of which is comprised in the farm where he lives and the remainder of which is part of the Graham farm. Mr. Singleton is a general farmer and stock raiser.

Thomas Singleton was married on September 9, 1900, to Bertha Barber, who was born in Veale township and who is the sister of Lew W. Barber, whose sketch is found elsewhere in this volume, which gives the family history of Mrs. Singleton.

Throughout his life, Thomas C. Singleton has been an ardent Republican. He was one of those men who remained faithful to that party during the split in 1912, when the Progressive party was formed. As a consequence of his faithfulness and a reward for his many services which he has rendered in behalf of his party, Mr. Singleton was nominated by his party in Daviess county and triumphantly elected to the office of county recorder in the fall of 1913. His election to this office is only a fitting tribute to his years of service, interest and activities in behalf of that party. Mr. Singleton is a member of the Cumberland Presbyterian church, but Mrs. Singleton is a member of the Methodist Episcopal church. Mr. Singleton is a member of the Independent Order of Odd Fellows.

PORTER BUSSARD.

The record of Porter Bussard is that of a man who, by his own unaided efforts, has worked his way up from an humble beginning to a position of influence. His life has been one of unceasing industry and perseverance, and the systematic and honorable methods he has followed have won for him the unbounded confidence of his fellow citizens.

Porter Bussard was born on June 5, 1854, in Fairfield county, Ohio, and is the son of Christopher and Hannah (Nioninger) Bussard, who lived the greater part of their lives in the state of Ohio. To their union were born the following named children: Porter, Nelson, Thomas, Clark, Hattie, Ida, Nora, Della and two infant boys who died about the time of their births. The father of these children was a hard working man who labored from early to late and it was with great difficulty that he earned sufficient means to properly raise a family of these proportions. However, by the work of his hands, he was able to give his family the necessaries of life and otherwise provide for them, at the same time teach them habits of thrift and economy which served each one of them well in later years.

Porter Bussard received his early education in the public schools of Fairfield county, and began his career as an ordinary farm hand, working out wherever he could dispose of his services, and, by the practice of strict economy, was enabled to save enough from his earnings to begin farming for himself. After farming successfully, in his native state, for about three years, he went to Illinois where he remained for eleven years, then removed to Vermilion county, Indiana, where he purchased a farm consisting of three hundred and sixty-nine acres, after having worked in this county for ten years. Remaining here for the following five years, during which time he traded the original three hundred and sixty-nine acres for a more desirable place containing two hundred and forty acres, he continued to farm and added eighty acres, by purchase, which gave him a total of three hundred and twenty acres. Having received tempting offers for his Vermilion county land, he decided to sell out and then removed to Greene county, where he bought two hundred and eleven acres, on which he resided for the following four years. After making sale of this property, he came to Daviess county, in 1905, where he located in Washington, and established himself in the bakery business, which he conducted for a period of eighteen months. In connection with this business, it is said that he installed the largest and most complete baking oven ever used in the town of Washington. Concluding to discontinue the baking business, Mr. Bussard bought a farm consisting of ninety acres, which is situated about one and one-half miles east of the town of Washington, Daviess county, and has been occupied in farming this place since the year 1908, which piece of land required considerable improvement to make it highly productive, and in order to obtain the maximum results he began installing a system of tile drainage and making other necessary changes, until today this farm is regarded as one of the most profitable in this section of the country. The place has been fully enclosed with good fencing and new buildings have been constructed so that the observer cannot help but conclude the owner to be a man of careful management and industrious, to all appearances possessing a good share of this world's goods. In addition to general farming, Porter Bussard devotes considerable time and attention to the feeding of cattle and hogs. The farm buildings and large and comfortable home are situated on an elevation so that a view of the country can be had for miles around.

In October, 1875, Porter Bussard was married to Ada Valentine, a daughter of Noah and Sarah (Avis) Valentine, and to their union have been born seven children, named as follow: Ervin, who married Mazie Simpson; Letha, who married Allen McMasters and whose children are Carl, Blanche, Bessie, Mary, Raymond (deceased), Leta and the baby; Noah, who is married to Edna Pagett and has one child, Porter; Herbert, who married Beulah Coats; Florence, the wife of Robert Cross and they have two children, Iona and Merle; Elsie and Flossie.

Mr. Bussard is a supporter of the principles of Democracy, but does not take an active interest in politics. The family belongs to the Methodist church, to which they lend their support, according to their means. Personally, Mr. Bussard is a man who has proved himself somewhat better than the average man in the way of industry and management, and today is regarded as one of the most successful agriculturists of this county, and is able to get a proportionately larger return from his farm than many others, which are of much more acreage. This is the result of unceasing energy and careful experiment. On account of his genial disposition, sound business judgment, honorable and upright methods, Mr. Bussard is justly entitled to the praise and admiration of his fellow men and his friends are in number as his acquaintances.

NICHOLAS F. BARKLEY.

The prosperity and substantial welfare of a community are, in a large measure, due to the enterprise and foresight of its business men. It is the progressive, wide-awake men of affairs that make the real history of a community, and their influence in shaping and directing its varied interests is difficult to estimate. The well-known man whose name appears above ranks among the leading business men in the northern portion of Daviess county, Indiana, and it is to such enterprising spirits as he that the immediate locality is indebted for the high position it occupies in the activity of its trading and progress.

Nicholas F. Barkley was born on January 26, 1873, near the town of Massillon, Stark county, Ohio, and is the son of Joseph and Anna (Feller) Barkley. Joseph Barkley was born in 1840, in Allegheny county, near the city of Pittsburgh, Pennsylvania, and received his early education in the county schools of that locality. As a young man he worked as a farm hand until the breaking out of the Civil War, at which time he was ready and willing to offer his services to the Union cause. He did not enlist in the service of the country until about the close of the war and then served for a term of six months as one of the home guards. Some time after his discharge from the government service, he removed to Stark county, Ohio, where he bought a thirty-acre farm and it was here that he was married. After selling out his interests in Stark county, Ohio, he removed to Daviess county, Indiana, in 1886, where he established himself a home, raised his family and continued to follow agricultural pursuits until the time of his death which occurred on Easter Sunday, in the year 1914, at which time he was in the seventy-fourth year of his age. He survived his wife a number of years, her death occurring in 1905. To their union were born three children, Emanuel, who married Lena Keagy and now lives in Jasonville, Greene county, where he is occupied as a miner; Nicholas F., the subject of this review; and Joseph, who died at the age of eighteen. The father of these children was a man who was well thought of in the community for his honorable methods and kindly disposition. He was a supporter of the Democratic party and the family belonged to the Methodist church, to which they contributed liberally, according to their means.

Nicholas F. Barkley received his early education in the public schools of Daviess county and at a later date attended the Vincennes University, from which he went to the National Normal University, of Lebanon, Ohio, where he remained a full term. After this, he taught school for about eight years in his home community and put in a year in the normal school. Having decided to discontinue teaching, and believing his vocation lay in another line, he went to work as a clerk in one of the general stores of Odon, where he remained a clerk for the next four years when he formed a partnership with Albert Diefendorf, who was conducting a general store business. Mr. Diefendorf sold out his interest to Mr. J. A. Overton and Nicholas F. Barkley continued as a partner with him for the following five years. After buying out Mr. Overton, in the year 1912, Nicholas F. began to add to the general lines heretofore handled and it is said that a more complete stock of general merchandise is not to be found in any store of like kind anywhere for supplying the demands of such a community. The business was started in the year 1904, with a stock which invoiced to the amount of one thousand four hundred dollars and consisted largely of groceries and dry goods in a very small way. The dry goods line was increased at a later date and a total of two thousand eight hundred dollars was invested. The business continued to grow and the buying of stocks proportionately increased until the present stock would easily invoice sixteen thousand dollars; the annual business amounts to a gross figure of forty-five thousand dollars. This steady growth of business is the result of careful management, close attention to details and, above all, kind consideration for the demands of the public and marked courtesy to everyone. Mr. Barkley carries the reputation for honorable methods in all of his business dealings and is held in the highest esteem by his fellow men.

In September, 1899, Nicholas F. Barkley was married to Millie Ferguson, a daughter of John and Nannie Ferguson, and to their union have been born three children, Leland, in August, 1900; Esther, August, 1905, and Douglas, August, 1912. Mr. Barkley is a progressive advocate of the Republican party's principles, but does not take an active interest in these matters; however, he is always ready and willing to serve his party when needed and is strong on furthering the interests of his community and lends his influence in a quiet, unassuming manner. He is a devout member of the Christian church of Odon where his wife and family are regular attendants. Besides his general store business interest, Mr. Barkley is a stockholder and director of the Farmers Bank of Odon, and is a member of the Independent Order of Odd Fellows. Personally, he is a gentleman, in every sense of the word, of an extremely good-natured and affable disposition and his personality is pleasing to everyone.

HUETTE POINDEXTER.

We like to know how men succeed. Just as the child mind loves to wonder how Jack made his beanstalk grow until he could climb up on it and have all of those astonishing things happen, so there is a real fascination in trying to discover the processes or events through which a successful man has traveled in order to "arrive." And even in this unromantic age, there is enough of the hero worshipper in all of us to cause our admiration for the so-called prosperous to increase in proportion to the obstacles which had to be met and overcome. A strange thing is human nature after all. Everywhere in human life, as in the animal and vegetable kingdoms, is to be found inter-action between the individual and his environment, and the rule is that the individual follows the line of least resistance. Thus we have many sons of physicians becoming physicians, many sons of preachers becoming preachers, and many sons of farmers becoming farmers. Variations from the rule are, however, always more interesting than expected conformity, at least from a psychological viewpoint, for they invite study and speculation, and because Huette Poindexter chose to be a business man instead of a farmer, when all signs pointed to the farmer's career, gives his life a peculiar interest to the biographer.

A leader among the merchants of Odon, is Huette Poindexter, and yet both father and grandfather were farmers. The surprising fact in this connection is that the younger Poindexter did not change his destined vocation in order to improve upon the success of his father and grandfather, for both men were prosperous, and the latter was one of the most widely known men in Martin and Daviess counties.

Christian Poindexter, grandfather of the man under present consideration, was born in Tennessee, and came to this state with his parents when he was a mere lad of twelve years. When grown, he took up a farm known as "the old pigeon roost," and farmed there practically all of his life. The farm which he cultivated consisted of three hundred and seventy acres of land obtained from the government at the munificent sum of twelve and one-half cents an acre. He gave particular attention to the raising of sheep, cattle and hogs, and to stock buying. So correct were his judgments relating to stock, that his opinion and advice were frequently sought by farmers for miles around. But his interests were not limited to farming and stock raising. He was an active politician, and for two terms served as county commissioner of Martin county. He was a Republican. His wife was, previous to her marriage, Miss Luranda Keck, her birthplace being near Doverhill, Martin county. Their children were, Patten, father of the man whose life forms the theme of this biography; Early W.; Wiley; Rufus M.; Emelia; William; John S.; Christian; Lurinda; Tillman H., and double twins. The membership of this early branch of the family was in the Methodist church. The great-grandfather of Christian Poindexter was George Poindexter who came to this country from Ireland.

Coming down another generation, we find that Patten Poindexter, father of Huette, was born on July 27, 1847, in the same county in which his father had lived since boyhood. His wife was, before her marriage, Miss Elizabeth Kutch, who was born on September 14, 1861, the daughter of Melkard and Eleanor (Butcher) Kutch, the former having been born in Monroe county in 1823, died in 1855, and the latter born in the same county in 1820, died in 1894. Patten, finding himself on a splendid, large farm of over three hundred acres, decided very naturally to follow the example of his father, and after receiving his education from the schools of the county in which he was born, continued his residence there on the farm for ten years. At the expiration of that time, he and his family removed to Daviess county, where the same capacity for hard work characterizing his ancestors, brought him success, and in this county they still reside. He, too, is a Methodist and a Republican.

The eight children who came to bless the home of Mr. and Mrs. Poindexter are still living. They are: Mrs. Anna Hattery, whose husband is a farmer living in the northern part of Bogard township; Nettie, who became Mrs. S. G. Felix, of Muskogee, Oklahoma; Huette, the subject of this biography; Leotie, the wife of Walter Shiveley, lives in Greene county; Ainley, who married Alvin Smith and made their home in Washington; Freely, who was united in marriage to Effie Read, a well-known farmer living in Bogard township; Veecher, who was never married and who lives at present in Iowa, and Dimple, a single daughter living at home.

Huette Poindexter was born in Burns City, Martin county, February 3, 1878. As a boy he attended school in Daviess county, and then gave his attention to agriculture in Bogard county until 1907. And now comes the change in taste or ambition which lost to the state a farmer, and gave to it a merchant. For we find him for the next five years engaging in commerce. He removed to Loogootee, and went into a furniture store and undertaking establishment combined. In 1912, he found an opportunity to broaden his field of commercial activity by buying the stock of George D. Abrams, of Odon, and here he has lived and worked ever since. To the furniture store formerly belonging to Mr. Abrams, he added a fine undertaking establishment.

The next step was a still larger store, for in 1912, he bought out the H. E. Marks furniture business, at the same time going into partnership with O. R. Laughlin. This partnership lasted for one year, and then Edward Wilson bought out the interests of Mr. Laughlin. The firm name is now Poindexter and Wilson. Thus from a stock worth one thousand two hundred dollars, Mr. Poindexter has increased its value to five thousand dollars, and has a business which any town of the size of Odon might envy.

Mrs. Poindexter, who was Miss Clara E. Seneff, was born in Bogard township, Daviess county, on July 24, 1876. She is the daughter of Joseph H. and Amanda (Humerickhouse) Seneff. The family of Mr. and Mrs. Poindexter consists of five children, namely: Zela Irene, Ives T., Roy W., Paris E. and Verlin L.

It is not surprising that we find Mr. Poindexter a member of a number of organizations. He believes in and is a supporter of the Republican party, and is a communicant of the Methodist church. As a corollary of his profession of undertaker, Mr. Poindexter was elected as county coroner. He is also a prominent lodge member, being affiliated with the Odd Fellows, the Knights of Pythias and the Modern Woodmen of America.

Modern business methods are so exacting that in order to be a successful merchant one must be both enterprising and progressive. Therefore, it is not necessary to add that Mr. Poindexter has both of these qualities. Moreover, his personality is such as to make him popular in the best sense of the word. His intelligent grasp of subjects and situations, his interesting personality, and his constant energy and enthusiasm are some of the qualities which have made him the successful man that he is, and if he should leave the community in which he has made his home, he would be greatly missed.

FRANKLIN D. DILLON.

Among the worthy citizens of Daviess county who have built up a comfortable, splendid home and surrounded themselves with considerable landed and personal property, none has attained a higher degree of success than Franklin D. Dillon. Making the most of his opportunities and by careful management in the face of many discouragements, he has made an exceptional success of his life as an agriculturist. His life has been one of unceasing industry and perseverance, and the systematic and honorable methods he has pursued have won for him the unbounded confidence of his fellow citizens, whose interests he has ever had at heart and which make him worthy of mention in a work of this character.

Franklin D. Dillon was born on April 22, 1879, in Elmore township, Daviess county, Indiana, and is the son of Wesley T. and Evangeline (Arford) Dillon. His paternal grandparents were Captain William and Eliza (Satterfield) Dillon, the former born in 1798 in the state of Ohio and a descendant of Irish ancestors, the mother being born in Kentucky in the year 1812. This grandfather was twice married, the father of fourteen children and came in the year 1821 to Daviess county, where he became a great landowner and died in the year 1876.

Wesley T. Dillon was born on May 26, 1847, on his father's farm in Daviess county, and received his early education in the public schools, after which he taught school for a few years and then engaged in farming in Elmore township, this county, where he bought two hundred and five acres of good land. His first purchase consisted of one hundred and twenty acres of land, and it was immediately after he bought this tract that he was married to Evangeline Arford on July 26, 1871. She was born on March 5, 1855, in Daviess county, and was the daughter of Jacob and Catherine Arford. To their union were born the following children: Ada, who married Albert Malone and lives in Elmore township; William J., who married Margaretta Kimball, lives in Chicago, Illinois, where he is an attorney-at-law; Walter S., who married Agnes Nelson, lives in Atlanta, Georgia, where he is an attorney-at-law; Albert H., who married

Margaret Thompson, and died on September 11, 1908; Franklin D., the subject of this review; Arthur B., who married Blanche Dobbs and lives in Elmore township, where he is engaged in the hardware business; Inez, who married Clifford Farris and lives in Elmore township. The entire family are members of the United Brethren church, and Wesley T. Dillon is a stanch Democrat and a worker for the party. In the year 1874 he was appointed county assessor and two years later was elected to the office of township trustee, which he held for two terms and filled to the entire satisfaction of the community. Personally he is a man of genial disposition, always good-natured and easy to approach. His friends are as many as his acquaintances, and he is held in the highest esteem by all who know him.

Franklin D. Dillon received his early education in the public schools of Elmore township, this county, where he also attended the high school in Odon. He began farming at an early date in Elmore township, and continued there until 1904, when he decided to go to Mexico, where he remained the following four years. In that country the greater portion of his time was spent on a ranch and at one time he spent several months in the capacity of brakeman on a railroad. Returning to Indiana in the year 1908, he again engaged in farming in Elmore township and moved to his present tract in 1909, where he has made a great many improvements, including the building of his residence in the year 1911, and a modern silo in 1913. Mr. Dillon carries on a general farming business and gives considerable attention to the raising and shipping of live, and in this connection also buys live stock for shipping purposes. He has been very successful in his line, and the farm which he owns is one of the finest in this part of the country. The buildings and fences are all kept in repair and paint, and everything gives the aspect of prosperity as a result of good management. Mr. Dillon was married on August 30, 1910, to Mrs. Margaret (Thompson) Dillon, who was the widow of Albert H. Dillon, brother of Franklin D., who died on September 11, 1908. She was a daughter of Arthur D. and Emma (Piper) Thompson. The children of Mrs. Dillon of her first marriage are as follow: Harold, born on May 16, 1899; Ruth, August 12, 1901, and Dorothy, October 26, 1906. By the second marriage to Franklin D. one child was born, Clara, on September 23, 1911.

Mr. Dillon gives his support to the Democratic party, the principles of which he firmly believes to be for the best interests of the American people. His interests are with the United Brethren church, to which he contributes liberally. Personally, whole-souled and strictly honorable in his methods and dealings with his fellow-men, he enjoys a large circle of warm friends and always evidences the spirit of generous hospitality, old and young alike being at all times welcome to his home.

ROBERT W. MASON.

The young man whose name appears at the head of this review is widely known as one of the honored and progressive citizens of Odon, Daviess county, Indiana. He has lived in this locality all of his life, is a member of one of the leading families, and for a number of years has been prominently identified with the mercantile interests of this community. His careful efforts in the practical affairs of life, his capable management of his business interests and his sound judgment have brought to him a fair measure of prosperity, and in all the relations of life he has commanded the respect and confidence of those with whom he has been brought in contact.

Robert W. Mason was born on January 25, 1875, in Washington, Daviess county, Indiana, and is the son of William and Martha (Sturgeon) Mason. His grandfather on the father's side was Rankin Mason, a native of the state of Kentucky and who farmed the greater part of his life. His wife was Margaret (Cochran) Mason, and, after their marriage they made their home in the town of Richmond, Kentucky, which was the seat of a great many of the activities of Civil War days. To them were born nine children, as follow: William, Sarah, Jennie, John, Nancy, Robert, Gilbert, Rankin and Walker.

William Mason was born in Richmond, Kentucky, in 1843, received his early education in the public schools of his native state and, after passing the high school grades, attended the University of Richmond where he studied law. After graduation, he began the practice of law in the town of Washington, which practice he continued there until about the time of his death, in 1878. On September 15, 1869, William Mason was joined in wedlock to Martha Sturgeon, a daughter of Alford and Louvinia (Slaughter) Sturgeon. Her father was born on June 12, 1803, and died in the year 1875. Her mother was born in the year 1809. To their union were born the following named children: Mary L., Sarah L., Robert L., Mary M., Abrigle M., Frances L., Martha E., and Alford W. To William and Martha (Sturgeon) Mason were born the following named children: Margaret L., on October 19, 1870, who married H. H. Crooke; Evelyn P.,

September 14, 1872, the wife of Walter Dearmin; Robert W., January 25, 1874, who married Plesy McCoy; Jennie M., July 17, 1876, who married M. A. Wilson.

Robert W. Mason received his early education in the public schools of Odon, Daviess county, and began his business career as a farm hand about the year 1895 as an employee of his father and continued to work for him until about the year 1900 when he established a mercantile business with W. S. Haig, in Odon. In 1905, he went into the manufacture of building brick, in Odon, and discontinued this business in 1912, when he established a feed and grain exchange in Odon and has followed this business until April, 1915, when he sold out. Robert W. Mason married Plesy W. McCoy, in January, 1895, daughter of Hugh and Elizabeth (Booth) McCoy, and to their union have been born the following named children; William, deceased; Ruth; Dott; Ethel; Mary Alma; Robert; Margaret and Arnold. All are living, except as noted, and belong to the Methodist church of Odon.

Mr. Mason is a Democrat and is willing at all times to lend his support to the principles of that party. He is a member of the Free and Accepted Masons. Personally, he is regarded as a good business man, an excellent manager, and a man who possesses sound judgment and foresight, who believes in ever pressing forward. He enjoys the respect and esteem of those who know him for his friendly manner, his interest in the promotion of the public welfare, and is regarded by all as one of the substantial and worthy citizens of the community honored by his residence.

PAUL GOLLIHER.

One of the conspicuous figures in the history of Steel township, Daviess county, Indiana, during the last half century is Paul Golliher, a prosperous farmer of that township. His career has been useful and honorable, and he has conferred credit upon the community where he has lived for so many years. Strong mental powers, invincible courage, and a determined purpose, hesitating at no opposition, so entered into his make-up as to render him a dominant factor in the social and agricultural life of his community. He is a man of sound judgment, keen discernment, and possesses a fund of information far greater than that possessed by the average man educated during the days of his youth. Mr. Golliher is a fine scribe, and early in life, while a soldier in the Union army, during the Civil War, endeared

MR. AND MRS. PAUL GOLLIHER.

himself in the hearts of his comrades by writing their love letters to the girls they had left behind.

Paul Golliher was born on March 31, 1845, in Cook county, Tennessee, the son of William and Sallie (Paul) Golliher, the former of whom was born in Richmond, Virginia, and the latter of whom was William Golliher's second wife. William Golliher and Sallie Paul were married in 1838. By this second marriage there were nine children: Lettie, born on March 28, 1839; Pauline Ann, May 22, 1840; Marvin, March 28, 1842; John S., February 15, 1844; Paul, March 31, 1845; Amanda, May 19, 1846; Memory, April 27, 1848, and two who died in infancy.

By William Golliher's first marriage, to Catherine Massey, June 26, 1814, there were twelve children born: Margaret, born on May 15, 1815; Henry, October 9, 1816; William Washington, August 30, 1818; Jackson, October 31, 1820; James, November 16, 1822; Elizabeth, July 5, 1824; Sarah, September 21, 1826; Richard, June 8, 1828; Charles B., October 19, 1830; James, August 26, 1832; Catherine, June 14, 1835, and Frederick, June 11, 1837.

On March 15, 1850, William Golliher came to Indiana, locating in Orange county, in the neighborhood of Orleans, where he owned one hundred and sixty acres of land. Subsequently he went to Iowa and stayed there for twelve months. William Golliher's father was a soldier in the patriot army during the Revolutionary War. He was a native of Ireland, and his son was postmaster at Richmond, Virginia. The grandfather of Paul Golliher, on his maternal side, was William Paul, who was a soldier both in the War of 1812 and in the Mexican War. William Paul was a son of Thomas Paul, a soldier in the Revolutionary army, who after the war returned to England, and was there married.

Paul Golliher, the subject of this sketch, was named in memory of his mother's family name. He was educated in the common schools, and during his youth lived upon the farm, performing such work as usually fell to the lot of country boys of that day. He enlisted in the Union army in April, 1864, and shortly after his enlistment was poisoned. The effect of this poisoning left his breathing very much impaired. Mr. Golliher has been a farmer all his life and owns two hundred acres in Steele township. He started his successful career by renting for the first twenty years of his married life and moved to Steele township in 1879.

Paul Golliher was married twice, first on March 31, 1872, to Anna Spear, the daughter of Hiram Spear, of Orange county, this state. No children were born to this union. Mr. Golliher was married, secondly, on August 4, 1876, to Sarah C. Standiford, who was born on March 15, 1853, the daughter of Meriton and Mary (Crane) Standiford, farmers in Orange county, Indiana. Meriton Standiford is the son of William Standiford, a farmer and soldier of the War of 1812.

To Paul and Sarah C. (Standiford) Golliher the following children have been born: Nora E., born on June 18, 1877; William E., November 28, 1878; Ada D., January 16, 1880; Edward, November 16, 1881; Mary E., July 16, 1884; Stella M., January 26, 1887; John A., October 14, 1889; Benjamin, June 15, 1891, and Meriton, May 6, 1894. Mary E. died in December, 1884; Meriton died on May 8, 1894. Nora married Henry Transper and lives at Plainville, Indiana. William married Delight Rinks and lives at Battle Creek, Michigan. Ida married Theodore Slavens and lives in Plainville. Edward married Lolie Carlett and lives in Steele township, this county. Stella married Benjamin Brown and lives at Plainville. The remainder of the children are unmarried.

Mr. and Mrs. Golliher are members of the Christian church. Mr. Golliher's father, William Golliher, was a member of the Baptist church. Mr. Golliher is identified with the Republican party and is a member of the Odd Fellow lodge at Plainville and of Plainville Post No. 315, Grand Army of the Republic. He is well known in Steele township, and honored and respected by all his neighbors.

IRA E. BOWMAN, M. D.

Among the rising young physicians of Daviess county, there is one who by sheer force of his engaging personality and inherent capability, to which natural traits he has added a thorough schooling in the science of medicine, rapidly is forging to the front in the ranks of the followers of the healing art in this section of the state. A native of the county in which his capable services in the cause of ailing humanity are being so well directed, Dr. Ira E. Bowman is naturally sympathetic with his field and with those who come under his gentle and skillful ministrations, and as a consequence, has built up a practice during the short time he has had his office in Odon, that speaks volumes for the success of the ministrations and the personal popularity of the young physician. Among the great natural benefactors of the race, there is none who holds a closer relation to the individual thus benefited than does the thoughtful, considerate, studious physician, and that Doctor Bowman is filling all the requirements of his exacting profession is clearly demonstrated by the success which he has made in the field which he selected for his life's labors in his trying profession. It is not a cause for wonder, therefore, that his friends are predicting a notable future for him in the professional life of this county. This being true, no history of the present time, in Daviess county, would be complete without brief and modest mention of this young physician, and it is a pleasure for the biographer here to present a brief outline of the salient points in the life of Doctor Bowman.

Ira E. Bowman was born in Bogard township, Daviess county, Indiana, on January 27, 1881, the son of William H. and Margaret (Sims) Bowman, the former of whom was born on March 1, 1855, both of whom were natives of Martin county, this state, the latter of whom was the daughter of Starling and Susannah (Holt) Sims, members of one of the pioneer families of that county.

William Bowman, paternal grandfather of Doctor Bowman, was a native of Tennessee, born in March, 1820, who came to Indiana in an early day and settled in Martin county, where he entered six hundred acres of land, in which county he married Julianna Andis, and reared his family, being a farmer all his life. He was, for many years, one of the leading men in the community in which he lived. Both he and his good wife were earnest members of the Christian church, being ever prominent in the good works of their community. William Bowman lived to the ripe old age of eighty-two, his death ocurring in 1902, and his memory will long be treasured in the neighborhood in which he lived a life so long and so useful.

To William and Julianna (Andis) Bowman there were born nine children: Mary Jane; Pleasant, who was killed while serving his country as a Union soldier during the Civil War; John; Sarah; Amanda; Isaac; Elizabeth; William H., father of Doctor Bowman, and Jacob.

William H. Bowman was reared on the paternal farm in Martin county, receiving the benefit of the excellent township schools of that period, and upon reaching manhood decided to follow the life of a farmer. In the year 1879 he was united in marriage to Margaret Sims, one of the belles of that neighborhood, and started farming for himself on a tract of one hundred and twenty acres. Later he moved over into Daviess county, and now has an excellent farm of two hundred and sixty acres, part of which lies in Elmore township and part of which lies in Bogard township, the Bowman home being in the latter township. Mr. Bowman not only has been successful in his farming operations, being rated as among the leading farmers of the county, but he has been active in all the good works of his neighborhood and very properly is accounted among the most influential men in his community, his voice always being exerted in behalf of any movement having as its object the advancement of its general welfare. The Bowmans are all members of the Christian church.

To William H. and Margaret (Sims) Bowman were born seven children, as follow: Ira E., the immediate subject of this family history; Alpha O., a Bogard township farmer, who married Hazel McGee; Nora, who married John B. Stotts and lives at Odon; Sidney E., a well-known veterinary surgeon at Odon, who married Arla Myers; Victor V., at present a student at Purdue University, where he is taking the agricultural course; Starling E. and Allegra, who are still at home.

Ira E. Bowman was reared on the paternal farm and received his elementary education in the schools of Bogard township, which he supplemented by a course at the Odon high school, from which he was graduated, after which he attended the Central Normal School at Danville, Indiana, and then took the literary course at Indiana University, following which, for three years, he taught school at Epsom, in Bogard township, being very successful in this form of service. Mr. Bowman then, for four years, was engaged as money order clerk in the postoffice at Washington, this county; meanwhile giving much attention in his leisure hours to the study of medical works, his decision to enter the medical profession having been formed about this time. In pursuance of this laudable ambition, he entered the Indiana University School of Medicine, at Indianapolis, from which excellent institution he was graduated with the class of 1910, for proficiency in his studies being given an internship in St. Anthony's hospital, at Terre Haute. After acquiring some very valuable practical experience in his hospital work, Doctor Bowman entered upon practice for himself, his first office being opened at Elnora, where he continued for one year with very encouraging success. He then moved to the neighboring village of Raglesville, where he remained in practice for another year, repeating the successes which marked his residence in Elnora, and at the end of that time, in order to enlarge the field of his growing practice, moved to Odon, where he since has made his home and maintained his office.

On June 20, 1912, one year before locating in Odon, Doctor Bowman was united in marriage with Miss Pearl Myers, daughter of Lewis and Martha J. (Killion) Myers, prominent residents of this county, and to this union one child has been born, a son, Orin Howard, who was born on March 5, 1914.

Doctor Bowman is a member of the Masonic fraternity, and, though the exactions of his profession do not permit his giving much attention to political affairs, he is a Democrat and takes a good citizen's interest in all public matters, being active in the promotion of all movements designed to promote public welfare. Doctor and Mrs. Bowman are among the leaders in the social circles of their home town and are deservedly popular among all classes of the progressive community in which they live.

WALTER T. DEARMIN.

Numbered among the leading business men of Daviess county and worthy of recognition for his perseverance and sterling qualities, Walter T. Dearmin holds a place in the hearts of the people of this community and is eminently deserving of the confidence reposed in him by his fellow citizens. Being a self-made man of strong fiber and vigorous mentality, he has achieved signal success in his business and has earned the highest words of commendation from those competent to form a proper estimate of him and his accomplishments.

Walter T. Dearmin was born in the town of Sidney, Illinois, on September 15, 1869, and is the son of Dr. John and Eliza A. (Smith) Dearmin. His paternal grandparents were Joseph and Mary E. (Reiney) Dearmin, both natives of the state of Virginia and born there in the years 1812 and 1826, respectively. To their union were born three children: John, subject's father, George and William. The paternal grandfather left Virginia with his parents, who settled in the town of Bloomington, Monroe county, Indiana, in the year 1820, but later removed to Daviess county, in the year 1875, and died in the town of Raglesville, in 1876. His wife died in the year 1855, in Monroe county. John Dearmin was born in Bloomington, Monroe county, on April 27, 1845, where he received his early education in the public schools. While in his school work the Civil War broke out and he anxiously awaited the time when he could join the army of the North. On March 10, 1862, he enlisted and was assigned to Company B, Twenty-seventh Regiment, Indiana Volunteer Infantry, and remained in the service for three years. He was actively engaged in some of the fiercest struggles of those days, including the battles of Buckton Station, Winchester, Chancellorsville, Antietam, Gettysburg, Resaca and Atlanta. In the year 1864 he was transferred to Company C, Seventeenth Regiment,

Indiana Volunteer Infantry, and was on the memorable march with Sherman to the sea. On April 5, 1865, he was honorably discharged from service, at the town of Goldensburg, North Carolina. Shortly after his return from North Carolina he went to Sydney, Illinois, where he began the study of medicine under the tutorship of Dr. Howard Smith, and it was here that he remained for a term of three years. On September 15, 1865, he was married to Eliza A. Smith, daughter of William Smith, of Monroe county, to which union were born: Minnie, deceased, who was the wife of Noah Pate; Walter, the subject of this review; Elbert T., who resides in Indianapolis. The mother of these children lived until March 1, 1874. Doctor Dearmin was married a second time, on November 24, 1875, to Susan Pershing, daughter of Solomon and Magdaline Pershing, and to their union were born: May, who married Paul Paulson; Dott and Day. It was in 1872 that Doctor Dearmin began the practice of medicine in the town of Hindoostan, Indiana, and after a term of two years he removed to Daviess county, where he continued the practice of his profession. In 1882 he came to the town of Odon, where he established a good practice and remained until 1897, when he removed to the city of Indianapolis, where he died in the year 1899. He was a member of the Methodist church, was a member of the Free and Accepted Masons, belonged to the Republican party and was a stanch advocate of the progressive principles of that party.

Walter T. Dearmin received his early education in the public schools of Odon, Daviess county, where, after finishing school, he was employed by a local druggist, who taught him the business, and where he remained for a period of three or four years. Concluding to go into business for himself, he opened up a drug store in this town and continued in that line for twenty years, when, about the year 1900, he retired from this business. At a later date, Mr. Dearmin thought he saw possibilities of legitimate profit in the poultry and egg business and started into this on a very small scale. This business has grown, steadily and profitably, to such big proportions that he is identified with the large eastern markets, to which he makes a specialty of shipping poultry and eggs in carload quantities. In this business he has been very successful and is known throughout this region as a wholesale dealer.

On January 6, 1891, Walter T. Dearmin was married to Eva P. Mason, who was born on September 14, 1872, and is the daughter of William and Martha (Sturgeon) Mason, whose life record will be found elsewhere in this work under the caption Robert W. Mason. Walter T. and Eva P. (Mason) Dearmin have had born to them the following children: Rena

L., on June 16, 1893, who is teaching in one of the Daviess county schools; Russell Paul, January 1, 1897; Robert Mason, May 4, 1899; Maysel C., June 24, 1901; Walter Fred, August 8, 1902. All are members of the Odon Methodist church, to which denomination they lend their support.

Mr. Dearmin is a strong supporter of the Republican party, and though not particularly active in politics, he takes a deep interest in good legislation and is ever ready to lend his influence toward matters pertaining to the public good. He is a member of the Scottish Rite and is a thirty-second degree member of the Free and Accepted Masons, and his wife is a member of the Eastern Star. Personally, Mr. Dearmin is well known throughout this section of Daviess county, both in the farming and business world. He takes a full measure of interest in farming and owns an eighty-acre tract in Madison township, this county, where he takes pride in raising different grades of live stock. He owns a beautiful home in the town of Odon, where the many friends of the family are delighted to gather, for they are always assured of a hearty welcome and an enjoyable hour. Mr. Deamin is truly a gentleman, honest and upright at all times, and is held in high esteem for his exceptional business ability, and his position is secure as one of Daviess county's most prominent and influential men.

JAMES W. GILLASPIE.

Indiana University is a magnet, attracting to itself the youthful, the ambitious and the intellectual of many states. A great many farms lie within the radius of its influence, but many farmers' sons have continued to follow the plow under the very shadow of this great institution. Here and there, however, a lad there is who feels within himself something which responds to the force going out from the university, and once the hunger for a broader life is recognized, no farm, however attractive, can hold him. It was this ideality which gripped the enthusiasm of the man whose career is appropriately portrayed in this sketch, and which took him from the farm and eventually made him the center of the educational life of a whole community. James W. Gillaspie worked and attended school alternately, however, for many years before he attained the enviable position he now holds.

James W. Gillaspie, who is the superintendent of the schools of Odon, was born near Jamestown, Boone county, Indiana, on February 14, 1862.

He is the son of Francis C. Gillaspie, born on March 7, 1818, and Sarah Srout, born on March 5, 1825, both parents being natives of Kentucky. His grandfather, John Gillaspie, was a Virginian, and the father of a large family.

Francis Gillaspie, the father of the Indianian in whom we are concerned, was educated in the public schools of Kentucky. As farming was the most popular occupation in those early days, he first gave his attention to agricultural pursuits, afterward engaging in the carpenter's trade. The migratory instinct, however, became too strong to permit him to be contented as long as there was an unexplored country to the north, so one fine morning he loaded his household goods in wagons and, with his family, started northward. Arriving at Boone county, this state, he decided to go no further, and thus Jackson township became the home of this enterprising and hard-working pioneer. Thrift and industry brought its results, for it was not long before Francis Gillaspie was the owner of a fine farm of six hundred and forty acres where he worked and lived until June 1, 1884, the date of his death. Mr. and Mrs. Francis Gillaspie's family circle grew until it numbered ten children. These were: Mary A., deceased, who married James McReynolds and later Martin Whiteley; William A., also deceased, who married Georgia Young; Sarah A., deceased, who married Charles Bennington; John W., who became the husband of Ellen Shepherd, now deceased; Georgia and Fannie, twins, the latter of whom passed away in infancy, the former marrying Sanford Shockley; Simon A., deceased, who married Mary A. Gregory; James W., the man whose career is the topic of this sketch; Nettie Frances, who married Robert T. Ashley, and Jesse Omar, whose first wife was Della Heckathorne, and who afterward married Grace May. Mrs. Gillaspie, the mother, died on May 3, 1903.

That Francis Gillaspie was highly respected, and that he bequeathed to his children a name that they could honor, is shown by the fact that he was made township trustee on three different occasions, and was for one term county commissioner.

James W. Gillaspie's ambition could not be satisfied with what the Boone county schools had to offer, although they were on a par with other similar schools of their time. After attending the school nearest the farm, where he helped his father and brothers in their agricultural interests, he began the career which was to make him a recognized leader by matriculating in the normal school at Ladoga, where he studied for two years. About this time he was the recipient of a certificate from the State Normal at Terre Haute, in 1898, followed by a spring and summer term at the

State University at Bloomington, a summer term at Butler College, Indianapolis, and a term at the Winona Normal College.

It must not be imagined, however, that this educational process was continuous, or that the vacations were spent in idle dreaming, waiting for the next term of school. In reality, they meant hard, strenuous work, sometimes in the harvest field, sometimes in the schoolroom. But always was the dream tucked away somewhere in his consciousness, always the desire to become a man of force and influence, and the purpose to persevere until this end should be reached. Long after he became a teacher he was himself a student, for he began teaching in 1881, while we find him still seeking knowledge and inspiration in normal schools as late as 1900. He taught every winter following 1881, except one, and that was a winter spent in study and research. Who can help but admire the perseverance and determination of such a man? In 1910 Mr. Gillaspie began the superintendency of the Odon schools, and his continuance in service there is evidence enough of his efficiency.

Those who remember Mr. Gillaspie as a college student recall that he believed in an all-round education, and therefore was a man of splendid physique and abounding energy.

In 1883 Mr. Gillaspie married Ella Jacks, daughter of James Harvey and Nancy (Covey) Jacks. Mrs. Gillaspie was born on October 10, 1866. Her father was born on April 2, 1828, and died on June 18, 1899. The mother, who is still living, was born on May 31, 1832. It is rather unusual that a man and wife should both belong to such large families as in this instance, for Mr. and Mrs. Gillaspie had an almost equal number of brothers and sisters. The family Bible in the home of the latter shows that there were nine children born to Mr. and Mrs. Jacks. These were as follow: Mary A., who is the widow of Thomas Trusty, and resides in Indianapolis; Ella, wife of James Gillaspie; Emma R., who, with her husband, Charles W. Robbins, lives on a farm in Boone county; Milton H., who married Lina Davis and lives in Indianapolis; Ethelind L., who, after her marriage to Charles A. Bell, moved to Gurdon, Arkansas, where they still reside; Cora B. and Flora, the former of whom lives at home with her mother and has never married, the latter of whom died in infancy; Beatrice, wife of William M. Smith, living in Leesburg, Ohio, and Justina F., who, with her husband, James A. Starr, makes her home in Jamestown, Indiana. Mr. and Mrs. Gillaspie have no children.

Returning to the theme of our sketch, it is interesting to know that with all of his other activities, Mr. Gillaspie has found time for active church work, having been for some time an elder in the Christian church. He is a member of both the National and State Teachers' Associations.

Considering the years of preparation for his profession, it is not surprising to learn that Mr. Gillaspie, superintendent of the Odon schools, is a capable educator, a man of culture and refinement, and a citizen whose opinion is sought and respected. The main fact in this life is, it seems, that he, as a young man, did not wait for fortuitous circumstances to bring him fortune and happiness, but that he carved his destiny out of his early surroundings.

DAVID S. JACKMAN.

The student interested in the history of Daviess county does not have to carry his investigation far into its annals before learning that David S. Jackman has long been one of its most active and leading citizens in agricultural and stock raising affairs. His labors have been a potent force in making this a rich agricultural region. During several decades he has carried on general farming, gradually improving his valuable place, and while he has prospered in this, he also has found time and ample opportunity to assist in the material and civic betterment of Daviess county. David S. Jackman, however, before he became a farmer was a skillful carpenter, and in connection with his father, with whom he was in partnership, he got his start in life as a contractor and builder.

Mr. Jackman was born on May 7, 1865, in Jefferson county, Ohio. He was the son of Isaac W. and Martha (Walker) Jackman, the former of whom was born in 1832, in Jefferson county, Ohio, and who died on August 13, 1910, and the latter of whom was born in Jefferson county, Ohio, in 1839, and is still living.

David S. Jackman's paternal grandparents were David and Ruth (Cole) Jackman. In 1856 they came by boat to Cincinnati, and then by rail to Reeve township, Daviess county. They were accompanied by David S. Jackman's father and by many relatives. The grandfather of David S. Jackman purchased one hundred and sixty acres, and died on this farm at the age of seventy-four years. All of his family belonged to the Methodist Episcopal church. David S. Jackman's maternal grandparents lived and died in Ohio.

On account of the meager advantages offered during his youth, Isaac Jackman was unable to get a very extensive education. Early in life, however, he learned the carpenter's trade. He served a three years' apprenticeship and after his marriage moved to Iowa and worked at his trade for five years, after which he returned to Ohio. In 1866 he and his family, with his father, mother and other relatives, came to Indiana. Isaac W. Jackman first purchased twenty acres of land in Reeve township, but worked at his trade as a carpenter. He then traded twenty acres for fourteen and one-half acres south of Alfordsville and lived upon this tract of land until his death. He built the majority of the barns and houses in that community. Isaac W. Jackman was a large man, weighing more than two hundred pounds. He belonged to the home guards during the Civil War, when he lived in Ohio, and performed brilliant service on behalf of the Union. Isaac W. Jackman worked at his trade by contract. He and his son, David S., the subject of this sketch, for a time held a farm in partnership. His family were all members of the Methodist church.

Isaac W. Jackman and wife were the parents of nine children besides the subject of this sketch: Ella married Frank McCord, a farmer of Martin county; Ruth Anna married M. H. McCord and lives in Cincinnati, her husband being a mail clerk on the Baltimore & Ohio railroad; Jennie married James S. Gould and they live on a farm in Martin county, Indiana; Spencer O. is a farmer and lives in Reeve township; Robert died in 1899; Clara married Joseph Porter and lives in Cincinnati; Florain B. lives in Los Angeles, California, where he is a carpenter; Gertrude married S. M. Porter and they live in Vincennes, Indiana, he being head car inspector for the Baltimore & Ohio railroad.

David S. Jackman attended the public schools of Alfordsville and early began to learn the carpenter's trade with his father. When twenty years old he went into partnership with his father, doing carpentering and contracting. As his father grew older, David S. gradually assumed all the burdens of this work. They purchased together a farm and David S. finally purchased his father's interest in this farm. He built his present house on this farm, just south of Alfardsville, in 1900.

Mr. Jackman was married on June 4, 1891, to Emma B. Allen, the daughter of Alfred and Harriet (Burress) Allen, both of whom are deceased. Mrs. Jackman was born in Reeve township. To this happy union nine children have been born: Clyde E. was born on December 7, 1892, and is a student in the Loogootee high school; Olive E. was born in 1894 and married Harry Myers; Marvel Mattie was born in 1899; Constance B. was born in 1901; Beatrice died in 1912 of diphtheria; Garnet B. was born on

July 6, 1905; Ruth was born on March 17, 1909; Clara was born in 1911, and Bernard in May, 1913.

Politically, Mr. Jackman is a Democrat. He was appointed to serve an unexpired term of seventeen months as trustee of Reeve township in 1913, and in the following year was elected to the same office for a term of four years. Mr. Jackman has served on the advisory board of the township and has been more or less prominent for many years in the political affairs of this section of Daviess county. Fraternally, he belongs to the Independent Order of Odd Fellows, to the Royal Order of Moose and the Woodmen. In his farming operations Mr. Jackman makes a specialty of Poland China hogs, with which he has been unusually successful.

JOHN W. WALLS.

There could be no more comprehensive history written of a city or county, or even of a state and its people, than that which deals with the life work of those who, by their own endeavor and indomitable energy, have placed themselves in the category of progressive men. In this sketch will be found the record of one who has outstripped the less active and less able plodders on the highway of life, one who has not only not been subdued by many obstacles and failures, but who has made them stepping stones to higher things. At the time he was winning his way in material things, he had an enviable reputation for uprightness and honor.

John W. Walls, an enterprising citizen of Alfordsville, Indiana, was born September 7, 1857, in Crawford county, Indiana. He is a son of Dr. William Barnett and Mary Ann (Newton) Walls, the former of whom was born in Ohio in 1834, and who died in 1895, and the latter of whom was born in Crawford county, Indiana, in 1838, and who died in 1910.

The maternal grandfather of John W. Walls was John Newton, a farmer of Crawford county, Indiana. The paternal grandfather was William Walls, who was a native of Ohio, coming to Crawford county, Indiana, about 1840. He was a farmer there and lived in that county the remainder of his life. He and his family were active members of the Methodist Episcopal church.

Dr. William Barnett Walls taught school when a young man, then studied medicine in the office of a physician, and began the active practice of his profession in Haysville, Dubois county, Indiana, remaining there for two years. In 1867 he came to Alfordsville in Daviess county, where he continued in the practice until his death. He was typical of the better class of country physicians, and was much beloved by all the people. He had the entire confidence of all the residents of Alfordsville and vicinity, and served these people several years as postmaster. He spent much of his time on horseback, going over the hills and through the mud of Reeves township to see his patients, and these exposures shortened his life. Politically, he was a Republican, and throughout his life took an active part in the councils of his party. He and his family were all devoted members of the Methodist Episcopal church.

Dr. William Barnett and Mary Ann (Newton) Walls were the parents of nine children: Sarah, who became the wife of Foster Emery, who conducts a feed stable in Loogootee, Indiana; John W., the immediate subject of this sketch; Alice, the wife of Alexander Swickmond, of Alfordsville; George B., a Methodist minister living in New Harmony, Indiana; Belle, the wife of L. Harrell, of Cannelsburg, Indiana; Cony, a teamster residing in Alfordsville; Lou, the wife of W. T. Brown, deputy county auditor, and resides in Washington, Indiana; F. M., a farmer living in Reeve township, and Lena, the wife of Charles Newton, and lives in Bismark, North Dakota.

John W. Walls was seven years of age when his parents moved to Alfordsville, and here he grew to manhood and attended the schools of this village. Early in life he engaged as a hand in the timber business. For twenty years he was engaged in sawing out staves and headings, mostly in Reeve township. He afterwards engaged in the hotel business in Alfordsville, Indiana, for four years. He now owns and operates a coal bank on his thirty-eight-acre farm in Reeve township. In 1912 Mr. Walls purchased a one-half interest in the Rose Milling Company, of Alfordsville, and became manager of the flouring-mill. He has since acquired all of the stock and still operates the mill. He also manages his farm in Reeve township.

Mr. Walls was married in 1885 to Elvira Alford, who was born in Reeve township, and who is a daughter of T. J. and Lucy Ann (Perkins) Alford, both of whom are deceased. The town of Alfordsville was named for James Alford, the grandfather of Mrs. Walls.

Politically, Mr. Walls is a loyal Republican, and has always been interested in the affairs of his party. Fraternally, he belongs to the Independent Order of Odd Fellows and the Improved Order of Red Men. Religiously, he is a loyal and earnest member of the Methodist Episcopal church, in whose welfare they are actively interested and to the support of which they are liberal contributors. Mrs. Walls is a member of the Christian church.

Mr. Walls has built up an extensive business at Alfordsville and enjoys the good will of all the residents of the village and surrounding community.

PETER BERENS.

The two most strongly-marked characteristics of the East and the West are combined in the residents of Indiana. The enthusiastic enterprise which overleaps all obstacles, and makes profitable almost any undertaking in the comparatively new and vigorous states, is here tempered by the stable and more careful policy, that we have borrowed from our eastern neighbors. The combination is one of unusual force and power. It has been the means of keeping this section of the country on a par with the older East, and at the same time producing a reliability and certainty in business and agricultural affairs, which is frequently lacking in the West. This happy combination of characteristics was possessed to a notable degree by the late Peter Berens. He was too well known to the residents of Daviess county to need any formal introduction. He was recognized as a man of strong and alert mentality, deeply interested in everything pertaining to the welfare of the community, and regarded as one of the most progressive and enterprising men of his county.

The late Peter Berens was born in 1823, in Germany, and was a son of Peter and Anna Marie Berens, both natives of Germany, the former of whom died in Germany and the latter of whom spent her last days in Washington, Daviess county, Indiana.

Peter Berens was reared and educated in Germany, and when a young man he came to Washington, Indiana, and engaged in the boot and shoe business in Washington. This was in an early day. Mr. Berens was in business for about thirty-five years, and during this period built up a large and flourishing patronage in Washington and Daviess county. He was a man who is remembered for his many good qualities of heart and head, a man who was kind to his neighbors and charitable to a fault. His business success was founded upon that sturdy integrity so characteristic of the German people.

Mr. Berens was married in Evansville, Indiana, to Anna O'Callahan, who was a native of Ireland and whose parents died in Ireland. She came to Evansville, Indiana, when a young woman and shortly afterward was married to Mr. Berens. They had eight children, Mary B., Charles, Rose, Peter, Jr., William, deceased; Catherine, Thomas and John, deceased.

Throughout his life Peter Berens was active in the affairs of the Catholic church, of which he was always a member. He helped to build the old St. Simeon church, and also the new church. Peter Berens throughout life was identified with the fortunes of the Democratic party. He died in 1887, his wife having died nine years previously, in 1878.

Mary Berens, the eldest child of her parents, was married in 1898, to John E. Rickard, who, in that year, engaged in the book and stationery business at 112 East Main street, Washington, Indiana. He continued in this business for two years or until his death in 1900. Mrs. Rickard since his death has carried on the business alone, and has made a splendid success of it. Mrs. Rickard is well known in Daviess county as one of those women who have demonstrated what her sex may accomplish in a business way. She has undoubtedly inherited much of her business sagacity from her deceased father.

MICHAEL J. BENNETT.

Michael J. Bennett is a representative farmer and stock raiser of Harrison township, Daviess county, Indiana. He is known as one of the alert, progressive and successful farmers of this favored section of the Hoosier state. In his labors, he has not permitted himself to follow in a rut, in a blind and apathetic way, but has studied and experimented and thus obtained the maximum returns from his efforts. At the same time he has so conducted himself in all his undertakings, as to command the confidence and regard of the people of the community in which he lives. He is a man of honorable business methods and is an advocate of whatever tends to promote the public welfare in any way.

Michael J. Bennett was born on August 15, 1845, in Collinsville, Illinois. He is the son of Patrick and Ann (McCuen) (Galoony) Bennett, the former of whom was born in 1815, in County Meath, Ireland, and died in July, 1887, and the latter of whom was born in County Leitrim, Ireland, in 1817 and died in 1885.

Patrick Bennett grew up in Ireland. His father was overseer of a big estate. After his father's death, Patrick started for the United States at the age of twenty years. The sailing vessel upon which he came to this country was carried out of its course, and it took seven months to reach New York city. Patrick Bennett gradually came west, until he finally went to work for a Mr. Beasley, in Daviess county, Indiana. He then married in Washington, Indiana, and moved to Collinsville, Illinois, where he lived for two years. He then moved to Kankakee, Illinois, where he lived one year. From Kankakee, the family moved to Terre Haute, where Patrick worked four years in building the Evansville & Terre Haute railroad. After this he rented a farm in Harrison township, Daviess county, Indiana, and then purchased eighty acres and lived upon this farm until his death. He was a Democrat in politics, and a devout member of the St. Patrick's Catholic church.

Michael J. Bennett was one of two children born to his parents. He was the elder, and Elizabeth, who was the youngest, married John Colvin, and lives in Reeve township. Patrick Bennett's wife, Michael J. Bennett's mother, was first married to John Galoony and had one son living by this marriage, Bernard Galoony. He lives on a farm in Harrison township; three died—John, Ellen and William.

Michael J. Bennett attended school in the old log church at St. Patricks and grew up on the farm. He left home after attaining his majority and worked out on different farms until he was twenty-seven years of age. After this he came home and took care of his parents. Michael J. Bennett inherited the farm which his father had owned but it was heavily mortgaged and since their death he has been able to pay off the mortgage and has added to it, until he now owns two hundred and forty-two acres in Harrison township. Mr. Bennett keeps thoroughbred Hereford cattle and the very finest horses. He started without anything in life and has made a remarkable success. His present residence, which is one of the best in Daviess county, was erected in 1895.

Michael J. Bennett was married on February 4, 1873, to Catherine M. Donnolly, who was born in Harrison township, and who is the daughter of William and Mary Donnolly, both of whom were natives of Ireland, and early settlers in Daviess county, Indiana. To this happy union, eight children have been born: Ann, January 1, 1874, who married Martin Doyle, a wealthy farmer of Harrison township; William, April 5, 1875, who lives in Barr township; Mary, December 21, 1876, who married John Disser, and lives in Harrison township on a farm; Patrick, April 4, 1878, who lives with his father on the home place; Jerome, May 29, 1883, who is an electrician in Salt Lake City, Utah; James, June 18, 1885, who lives in Harrison township; John, June 5, 1887, who is an electrician in Ogden, Utah, and Catherine, April 17, 1881, and died September 25, 1904, who was the wife of John Downey.

Although Mr. Bennett is affiliated with the Democratic party, he has never taken an active part in its councils and has never cared to hold office. He has always been keenly interested in his vocation and has given it his entire time and attention. Michael J. Bennett is a man highly respected in Daviess county, where he is well known, and is a devout member of the Catholic church.

ANDREW HAAG.

In the daily laborious struggle for an honorable competence in any career, on the part of a business or professional man, there is little to attract the casual reader in search of a sensational chapter. To a mind thoroughly awake to the reality and meaning of human existence there are noble and imperishable lessons in the career of an individual who, without other means that a clear head, strong arm and true heart, conquers adversity and finally wins not only pecuniary independence, but what is far greater and higher, the deserved respect and confidence of those with whom his active years have been spent.

Andrew Haag was born in Princeton, Illinois, on April 30, 1853, and is the son of Andrew and Philomena (Drum) Haag, both natives of Germany, born on November 24, 1812, and June 20, 1820, respectively. His father came to the United States in the year 1839, being then but nineteen years of age, and first settled in the town of Williamsport, Pennsylvania, and his mother came to this country in the year 1841, also went to Williamsport, where they were married on October 15, 1844. The following year, on the 4th of June, they moved to Princeton, Illinois, where he engaged in the teaming business. They were the parents of the following children: George C., October 22, 1849; Andrew, April 30, 1853; William, June 17, 1856, who died in St. Joseph, Missouri, November 22, 1898; Henry, October 6, 1858, who died in Jefferson, Iowa, August 19, 1910. The father and mother were devout members of the German Lutheran church, and he was an ardent advocate of the principles of the Republican party.

Andrew Haag was reared in the town of Princeton and attended school there until the seventeenth year of his age, and then went to Creston, Iowa. When a few years older he secured employment as locomotive fireman on the Burlington system, and remained at that work for a number of years. In 1877 he received promotion to the position of locomotive engineer, and three years later was transferred to another division of the road and made his headquarters in the city of St. Joseph, Missouri, where he remained until the year 1889, and was then engaged in the same capacity with the Baltimore & Ohio Southwestern railroad, making his headquarters in Washington, Indiana, where he has continued as engineer to the present day.

In 1877 Andrew Haag was married to Carrie Hartsonrader, who was born on December 16, 1860, in St. Joseph, Missouri, a daughter of Nicholas and Margaret Hartsonrader, both of whom lived and died in St. Joseph. To Mr. and Mrs. Haag was born one child, Charles Andrew, on August 17, 1878. He received his early education in the Washington public schools, graduated from Purdue University, Lafayette, Indiana, and is now acting in the capacity of superintendent of the mechanical and engineering department of Purdue University. He married Madge Cox, of Lafayette, Indiana, born in the year 1882, and they have one child, Hellen Phillis, born on July 4, 1913.

Mr. Haag is the owner of an attractive home at No. 706 West Main street, Washington, where he and his wife take great pleasure in entertaining their large circle of warm friends, and where the greatest hospitality exists. Politically, Mr. Haag is a member of the Republican party and in thorough sympathy with the policy advocated by that party, but does not take any active interest in affairs of this kind. He and his wife are devout members of the Westminster Presbyterian church, to which denomination they contribute liberally. Personally, the subject is a man of generous disposition, pleasant and affable, and is numbered among the popular and most progressive citizens of Washington, Indiana. He takes a deep interest in current affairs, and is always ready to support meritorious enterprises that tend to the promotion of the public good. He has been a member of the Brotherhood of Locomotive Engineers since 1877, becoming a member at St. Joseph, Missouri, and is now a member of No. 289, at Washington. He was a delegate to the St. Louis convention. Mrs. Haag is a member of the Ladies' Auxiliary No. 349.

ALFRED DAVIS MEADE.

Indiana was not lacking in loyalty during the dark days of the Rebellion, when the ship of state was almost stranded on the rocks of disunion, but contributed her full quota of brave, valiant men to assist in preserving the integrity of the government, prominent among whom was the late Alfred Davis Meade, of Daviess county, Indiana. He was loyal to his country in the hour of peril and extremity, and this was demonstrated on many bloody battlefields. He was its stanch supporter in times of peace, and at the time of his death there were few soldiers of Daviess county as widely and favorably known and none who could boast of a more honorable record. The ranks to the noble organization to which he belonged, in the days of his youth, are fast being decimated by the one invisible foe, and it is fitting that in every publication of this kind special tribute be paid to those who served during the greatest civil war known to history.

Alfred Davis Meade, who was born in Washington township, Daviess county, Indiana, May 12, 1844, and who died on December 3, 1910, enlisted in Company E, Sixth Regiment Indiana Volunteer Infantry, in September, 1861. He was appointed corporal and later sergeant, and fought at the battles of Murfreesboro, Resaca, Chattanooga, Kenesaw Mountain, Atlanta, Shiloh, Chickamauga and in many others. He started on the march with Sherman to the sea, but on May 27, 1864, near Altoona, Georgia, he was severely wounded by a bullet, which passed through his body just below the heart. By the time he had recovered from this wound the war was practically over.

Alfred Davis Meade was the son of William and Delilah (Hayes) Meade, both of whom were natives of Maryland and early settlers in Washington township, Daviess county, Indiana. They were ardent members of the Christian church. Delilah (Hayes) Meade died early in life, and after her death her husband remarried. Two children were born to the first marriage, Alfred D. and Joseph, the latter of whom now lives retired in Washington, Indiana. The half brothers of Alfred Davis Meade are: William, Ruso, Emanuel and Sentony.

The late Alfred Davis Meade had a very limited education, consisting of a few months spent in the township schools. He improved his opportunities by home study and was a well-informed man. After the Civil War he returned to his father's farm and helped to operate it for some time.

Mr. Meade was married on September 12, 1865, to Sarah Shaw, who was born on July 12, 1845, and who died on March 28, 1879. Sarah Shaw was a daughter of Piney Shaw, an early settler of Barr township.

After the death of his wife Mr. Meade married Mary E. White. She was born on August 17, 1843, in Dearborn county, Indiana, and is the daughter of Joseph and Elizabeth (Bonham) White. They both died when Mrs. Meade was a very small child, and she remembers nothing about them.

In 1877 Mr. Meade purchased a hundred and thirty acres of land in Harrison township, Daviess county, Indiana, and later added eighty acres more to this farm. He lived upon this farm happily throughout his life and farmed until his death. His widow, Mrs. Mary E. (White) Meade, and a son, William, still live on the place. Alfred Davis Meade belonged to the Grand Army of the Republic and to the Independent Order of Odd Fellows. The Meade family are all members of the Christian church.

By his first marriage six children were born to Alfred Davis Meade:

James B., who was born on July 10, 1866, is a farmer in Harrison township; Minnie, who was born on December 26, 1867, was burned to death at the age of twenty-eight; Giles W., who was born on June 19, 1871, died young, as did also Charles E., was was born on April 19, 1873; Edward E., who was born on January 9, 1875, is a farmer in Rieve township; Frank S., who was born on July 15, 1878, lives at Bicknell, Indiana.

By the second marriage four children were born: Sarah E. was born on July 27, 1880, and died in infancy; Annie R. was born on January 24, 1882, married Edward Johnson, and they live at Portland, Oregon, and have two children, Marie and Alfred; William A. was born on May 7, 1885, and lives on the farm with Mrs. Meade; Martin L. was born on March 18, 1888; he married Grace Cummings and they live in Martin county and have two children, Milton, born on March 4, 1911, and Lucile, born on January 11, 1913.

Alfred Davis Meade lived a life of rare usefulness in the community where he was an active farmer for so many years. He was a stanch Republican, was highly respected by the citizens of Daviess county, and well known throughout the county.

HENRY JOSEPH KRAMER.

The utilitarian age has been especially prolific in men of action, clear-brained men of hig hresolves and noble purposes, who give character and stability to the communities honored by their citizenship, and whose influence and leadership are easily discernible in the various enterprises that have added so greatly to the high reputation which this county enjoys among her sister counties in this great commonwealth. Conspicuous among this class of men, whose place of residence in Daviess county has added to the business prestige of the community, is Henry Joseph Kramer, a well-known merchant of Washington, now engaged in the meat business.

Henry Joseph Kramer was born on August 18, 1879, in Washington township, Daviess county, Indiana. He is the son of Louis and Mary (Hack) Kramer and the brother of Frank Kramer, whose sketch appears elsewhere in this volume.

Henry Joseph Kramer was educated in the Washington public and parochial schools. He learned the meat business in Washington and began working at this business when sixteen years of age, and, with the exception of one and one-half years spent in Terre Haute, he has lived in Washington all of his life. In 1904 Mr. Kramer engaged in the meat business for himself at 414 East Main street, and he has built up a flourishing trade and enjoys a large patronage from the people of Washington and vicinity. Mr. Kramer is an expert butcher and a keen, far-sighted, capable business man. His reputation for square dealing has won for him an enviable place in the business circles of the city of Washington.

Henry Joseph Kramer was married on June 2, 1903, to Victoria Daugherty, who was born in Washington, Indiana, and who is the daughter of Eugene and Ann Daugherty. Mrs. Ann Daugherty died in 1904 and her husband now lives with Mr. and Mrs. Kramer, to whose happy union one son, Ralph Joseph, was born on March 30, 1904.

Although Mr. Kramer is identified with the fortunes of the Democratic party, he has never been especially active in political matters and has never held office. Fraternally, he is a member of the Knights of Columbus, the Benevolent and Protective Order of Elks, and the Fraternal Order of Eagles, all in Washington. He and his wife and son are devout members of the Catholic church and contribute liberally of their means to the support of this church.

FLORIAN B. WHITE.

One of the enterprising and successful farmers of Daviess county, Indiana, who has succeeded in his chosen vocation, wholly as a consequence of his own courage, persistence and good management, is Florian B. White. He is a man who believes in lending what aid he can to his neighbors and the general public, while advancing his own personal interests. As a consequence, he is acknowledged as one of the best citizens of Daviess county. Mr. White has acquired a substantial competence in life and, when his declining years come, he can be happy in the assurance that he can live comfortably without further labor.

Florian B. White was born on July 25, 1857, in Reeve township, Daviess county, Indiana. He is the son of Gilbert and Nancy (Alford) White, the former of whom was born in Tennessee in 1824 and died in 1902, and the latter born in Reeve township, Daviess county, Indiana, in 1827 and died in 1867.

Gilbert White was the son of John White, who was born and married in the state of Tennessee. When Gilbert White was eight years old, the family drove through from Tennessee to Indiana in wagons, drawn by oxen. They settled in Reeve township, Daviess county, along Sugar creek. John White was a farmer, but he later moved to a farm in Martin county, where he died. Nancy Alford was the daughter of William and Betsy Alford. The ancestors of the Alford family came from France and were the founders of Alfordsville in Reeve township. William Alford was born in Alfordsville and was a farmer in Reeve township. The family belong to the Christian church.

Gilbert White grew up on a farm in Reeve township and after his first marriage, farmed in this township. After the death of Nancy (Alford) White, the mother of Florian B. White, his father married again to Mary Emaline Jones, who died in 1911. There were nine children born to Gilbert White and his first wife, six daughters and three sons, and four children born to the second marriage. During his life, Gilbert White moved to Veale township, where he farmed for several years. Subsequently, he returned to Reeve township. All of the members of the White family were attached to the Missionary Baptist church.

Florian B. White was a mere lad when the family moved to the farm in Veale township. He lived upon this farm until he was twenty-three years old, and then rented a farm in Harrison township. He soon purchased sixty acres in that township but sold that subsequently and, in February, 1905, purchased eighty acres of the old Zinkans farm. Here he still lives. He has erected all of the buildings on the place and has a comfortable home with every convenience that is necessary for modern farming.

Florian B. White was first married to Zilphea Gregory, May 30, 1880. She died in October, 1902, and Mr. White was married again on March 25, 1906, to Nellie McClure, who was born in Pike county, Indiana, the daughter of William and Lucinda McClure, the former of whom was born in Kentucky and the latter in Daviess county, Indiana. Mrs. Lucinda McClure is now deceased. Her husband is a farmer in Pike county, Indiana.

Florian B. White's second wife was first married to William Harbison, born in Martin county, Indiana, August 11, 1873. He died on March 7, 1901. He was a farmer. There were two children by this union, Paris, born on March 7, 1896, and Lucile, born on July 21, 1897, both of whom are at home.

By his first marriage, Florian B. White was the father of six children, Martha Jane, born on September 10, 1881, who married Frank Emmick, and lives on a farm in Daviess county; Essie, born on May 18, 1885, who married Louis Spencer; Lydia, born on June 19, 1887, who married James

McBride; Nora, born on June 30, 1889, who married William McCracken and lives in Tulsa, Oklahoma; Phoebe, born on September 23, 1891, and Myrtle, born on August 20, 1893. By his second marriage, three children were born, Gilbert, born on January 1, 1907; Ray, born on November 11, 1908, and Susan, born on February 11, 1911.

Florian White is a loyal Republican but has never been especially active in political affairs and the only office which he has filled is that of road supervisor. Nevertheless, he is highly esteemed by the people of his community and honored and respected for his many good qualities. He is an enterprising farmer, a good citizen and merits the esteem and confidence bestowed upon him by his neighbors.

RETT A. ROBERTS.

Whether the elements of success in life are the inner attributes of the individual or whether they are taken by a process of circumstantial development, it is impossible to determine, clearly. Yet the study of a successful life, whatever the field of endeavor, is none the less interesting and profitable, by reason of the existence of this uncertainty. So much in excess of those successes are the records of failures and semi-failures, that one is constrained to analyze either case to determine the approximate cause. In studying the life history of Rett A. Roberts, a well-known educator of Daviess county, Indiana, we find many qualities that always win success if the career is properly directed. Evidently Mr. Roberts's career has been well directed, since it has resulted in much good to others as well as in attaining a comfortable competence for himself.

Rett A. Roberts was born October 11, 1886, in Reeve township, Daviess county, Indiana. He is the son of John Franklin and Louisa (Marklin) Roberts, the former of whom was born on May 27, 1843, in Louisville, Kentucky, and who is still living, and the latter of whom was born on April 4, 1853, in Washington county, Indiana.

The paternal grandparents of Rett A. Roberts were William and Maria Jane (Grismore) Roberts. William Roberts died when his son, John F., was eighteen months old, and J. F. Roberts remembers nothing concerning him. The mother died when J. F. Roberts was only four years old. His grandfather, George Grismore, kept him for a time, when he was finally taken by his uncle, Albert Grismore. Albert Grismore lived in Douglas county, Illinois, and John F. lived there for four years. From the time he was twelve years old, John Franklin Roberts worked as a regular hand, driving the horse-power on a threshing machine. He obtained only three months of schooling during his entire life. At the age of fifteen he went back to live with his Grandfather Grismore at Bloomfield, Greene county, Indiana. John Franklin lived with his grandfather until the Civil War broke out. On December 1, 1861, he enlisted in Company E, Fifty-ninth Indiana Volunteer Infantry, and served three years, nine months and fifteen days. He was at the siege of Vicksburg and was engaged here for forty days and forty nights. He was also in the Carolina campaign, and participated in the Grand Review at Washington at the close of the war. After the war he drove mules on a street car in Louisville and was married there. Subsequently he became an overseer on his uncle's farm in Washington county, Indiana, but finally came to Reeve township in Daviess county, Indiana, and rented a farm. He then purchased a farm in Reeve township, and in September, 1913, he retired, moving to Alfordsville, where he now lives. He is a Republican in politics, and served as a school director for several years. Fraternally, he is a member of the Grand Army of the Republic. He is a member of the Methodist church.

John Franklin Roberts and his wife were the parents of five children: Maud, who married J. W. Collins, and she is now deceased; Huldah May married H. Moore and lives at West Baden, Indiana, where he is a farmer; Robert Austin lives in South Dakota, where he is a school superintendent; Flora Nevada is unmarried and lives at home; Rett A. is the youngest child and is the subject of this sketch.

Mr. Roberts's maternal grandparents were William and Margaret (Tyron) Marklin, both of whom died when Mr. Roberts's mother was an infant. She was reared by her grandfather and grandmother Tyron. She was the only child born to her parents who lived beyond infancy.

Rett A. Roberts attended the graded school of Alfordsville, as well as the high school. When he was seventeen years of age he began teaching school, and has taught school more or less since that time. He attended Valparaiso University, graduating with the class in pharmacy in 1907. He also took a course at this institution. Later he took part of the course in medicine and surgery in Kentucky University at Louisville, Kentucky. In 1906 Mr. Roberts was instrumental in starting a high school at Alfordsville, and was the first principal of this high school. He has held this position continuously since the high school was founded. In August, 1914, Mr. Roberts purchased the drug store of Jesse Godwin in Alfordsville and still conducts this store. He is a registered pharmacist.

Rett A. Roberts was married, May 18, 1911, to Clara E. Mills, who was born in Martin county, Indiana. She is the daughter of William W. and Celia (Truelove) Miles, both of whom are living at Alfordsville, Indiana. He is a retired farmer. Mr. and Mrs. Rett Roberts have no children.

Politically, Mr. Roberts is a Republican. Fraternally, he is a member of the Knights of Pythias, the Modern Woodmen of America and the Improved Order of Red Men. Rett A. Roberts is a young man of rare talents, courteous in manner and genial in disposition. He is a competent instructor and a capable and painstaking business man, honored and respected in the locality where most of his work has been performed.

LOUIS W. KEITH.

One of the best titles a man can establish to the high and generous esteem of an intelligent community, is a protracted and honorable residence therein. Louis W. Keith, one of the best known and highly esteemed men of Daviess county, has resided in this locality all his life, and his career has been a most commendable one in every respect, well deserving of being perpetuated in a historical work of this nature. Like his father before him, he has been a man of well defined purpose, and never failed to carry to successful completion any work or enterprise to which he addressed himself. Beginning life under many unfavorable circumstances, he let nothing deter him and before the lapse of many years he had a fine farm under cultivation. Knowing that the county was destined to take a very high rank in the productive and rich localities of the North, he applied himself very closely to his work and waited for the future to bring its reward, and today he is one of the substantial men of the county.

Louis W. Keith was born in May, 1862, in Washington township, Daviess county, Indiana, and is the son of Jarit and Elvida (Lester) Keith, whose life history is recorded elsewhere in this work.

Mr. Keith began life under the parental roof, received his early education in the township schools of this county and applied himself to farm work from the very start. He is now the owner of one of the finest farming tracts throughout this section. His place consists of seven hundred acres, nearly all of which is under cultivation, and besides general crop raising, a good deal of attention is given to stock raising. While Mr. Keith does not deal especially in blooded stock of any kind, yet his herds of cattle are of standard breed and, and he finds a ready market for the produce. During the past few years a number of new buildings have been erected on the land, and the owner bears the reputation of having a place for everything and everything in its place. The home is a substantial, commodious and comfortable building, occupying a conspicuous place among the other well built and substantial looking barns and outbuilding.

Louis E. Keith was in his twenty-second year of age when married, in December, 1884, to Lillian Covalt. She was born in Henry county, Indiana, on October 5, 1866, and is the daughter of Cheniah and Louisanna (Williams) Covalt. Her father was born on October 16, 1842, in Henry county, Indiana, and her mother was born on December 12, 1838, in Franklin county, Indiana. Some time after their marriage they settled in Daviess county, Indiana (February, 1867), where the father died on July 26, 1913, and the mother passed away from this life on June 25, 1891. Cheinah Covalt was a son of Cheniah and Elizabeth (Echelbarger) Covalt, who came from the state of Ohio and were early settlers in Henry county, Indiana, where both died and are buried near the town of Mooreland, that county. His wife's mother was a daughter of Solomon and Sarah (Clements) Williams. Solomon was born on November 16, 1809, and his wife was born on October 15, 1812. They came from the state of Maryland and settled first in Franklin county, Indiana, then later moved to Daviess county, this state. Her mother died in Franklin county on June 30, 1846, and the father died in this county on February 11, 1888. Her father had been a prominent farmer, stock raiser and trader in his day, and was a soldier in the Civil War. He enlisted in 1861 and was assigned to a company in the Thirty-sixth Indiana Volunteer Infantry, with which he remained until the close of the war. He was in the fierce engagements against the Confederate forces and took active part in the battles of Shiloh, Chickamauga and Lookout Mountain. He was twice married, and by his first wife was the father of Lillian and Edgar L. Covalt; by the second marriage, to Ola Lucas, he became the father of four children: Ferdinand, Hoyt, Myrle and Mildred.

To the union of Louis W. Keith and wife have been born the following children: Ethel, September 28, 1885, the wife of Charles A. Aikman, and they have one child, Helen; Elmer, June 15, 1889, died on January 19, 1892; Clara, July 15, 1893, wife of Austin A. Twomey, to whom was born Wilma; Shirley, January 19, 1896, who was graduated from the high school and now lives in Washington, Indiana.

Politically, Mr. Keith has always been an ardent supporter of the Republican ticket, and, although he has never aspired to office, does considerable work toward advocating the sound principles of his party. Religiously, he and his family are members of the Methodist church and contribute liberally to that denomination. Personally, Mr. Keith is very widely known throughout Daviess county and has a large circle of friends, who esteem him for his splendid record as a business man and for the honorable methods he has always pursued in his dealings with his fellow citizens. He is numbered among this community's most prominent and leading people.

OLIVER MASON VANCE.

It is the progressive, wide-awake man of affairs who makes the real history of a community, and his influence as a potential factor of the body politic, is difficult to estimate. The examples such men furnish of patient purpose and steadfast integrity, strongly illustrate what is in the power of each to accomplish, but there is always a full measure of satisfaction in adverting, even in a casual way, to their achievements in advancing the interests of their fellow men and in giving strength and solidity to the institutions which make so much for the prosperity of the community. Such a man is Oliver Mason Vance, a real estate and insurance man of Washington, Indiana, and it is eminently proper that a review of his career be accorded a place among the representative citizens of the city and county in which he resides.

Oliver Mason Vance was born on November 12, 1864, in Daviess county, Indiana, and is the son of George Campbell and Lydia (Palmer) Vance, both natives of Daviess county, born in 1838 and 1841, respectively. Subject's paternal grandparents were Campbell A. and Letta (Gregory) Vance, both natives of the state of South Carolina, of Scottish descent, and who came to Daviess county, Indiana, in an early day and remained the rest of their lives. He died in the year 1865 and survived his wife by several years. To them were born Isaac, George C., Sarah, Elizabeth, Martha, Harriet and John, all of whom are now dead. Mr. Vance's maternal grandparents were Mason and Rachel Palmer, who were early settlers in Daviess county, where they lived and died. Their children were, "Captain" Joshua, Mary, Lydia, John F., Mason R., and Permenus Allen. Their father was engaged in farming as a regular business, and at one time was a poineer teacher in this district. He was a member of the Methodist Episcopal church as was the other members of the family.

The Vance family were all Scotch Presbyterian in their belief and the great-grandfather, Campbell Vance, came to Daviess county from the state of South Carolina, in a very early day, and took up a large tract of land in the southern part of this county. After remaining here a number of years, he returned to his old home in Union county, South Carolina, where he spent the rest of his life up to his death. Subject's grandfather being one of the pioneers of this section was a leading man in his neighborhood and was very active in Republican politics. He held the office of justice of the peace for many years and served the community to good advantage in this office. Subject's father and his wife are living in Washington, this county, and are devout members of the Presbyterian church. To them were born the following children: John M., Mattie J. (deceased), Oliver Mason, Etta, Perry W., Cora (deceased), Hattie (deceased), Ezra J. (deceased), and Emma I. (deceased).

Oliver Mason Vance was reared on the homestead farm in Harrison township, this county, educated in the public schools and attended the high school in Louisville, Illinois, where his parents had lived for a few years. He graduated from Vincennes (Indiana) University and followed the teaching profession for several years, and then engaged in farming in Washington township, where he and his wife now own a farm, consisting of two hundred fifteen acres. With the exception of two years spent in the city of Mobile, Alabama, where he was engaged in business and made an investment in Alabama lands. Mr. Vance has lived in Washington since 1905 and conducts a general real estate and insurance business and in which he is eminently successful. In 1891 Mr. Vance was married to Mary J. Keith, who was born in 1865, a native of this county and daughter of Jarat Keith, whose life record appears elsewhere in this review under the caption of George Keith. Subject and wife have one child, Oliver McKinley, born on February 3, 1898, and who is a student in the Washington high school at the present time.

Politically, Mr. Vance has always taken an interest in public affairs and at one time served the community for three years as a Republican member of the board of county commissioners. Fraternally, he is a member of the Independent Order of Odd Fellows and Knights of Pythias. Religously, he and his wife are members of the Methodist Episcopal church and contribute to that denomination according to their means and take an interest in the social affairs connected with the church. Personally, Mr. Vance is a man whom it is a pleasure to know, being generous hearted, kind, helpful, honest in all his dealings with his fellow men, and eminently worthy of the trust and respect reposed in him. He is regarded as having sound judgment in the actual values of real estate and is one of the county's most representative and valued citizens.

GEORGE WILSON FYFFE.

The career of the above well-remembered gentleman, was strenuous and honorable and, although his life record has been brought to a close by the inevitable fate that awaits all mankind, his influence still pervades the lives of a wide circle of friends and acquaintances who revere his memory. He proved his loyalty to his fellow citizens and was a man ever ready to advance the material interests of the community in which he so long lived. He is a worthy subject for review in a work of this character, and it is proper that he be accorded a place among the memoirs of representative citizens of Daviess county, Indiana.

George Wilson Fyffe was born in Lawrence county, Illinois, on December 23, 1839, and was the son of Edward Perry and Sarah (James) Fyffe. His parents lived and died in Lawrence county, Illinois, and to them were born the following children: Rebecca (deceased), Anne, Adaline, Martha, James (deceased), Marion, Benjamin (deceased), Mills and George Wilson (deceased).

George Wilson Fyffe came to Daviess county, Indiana, when quite a young man and was married to Julia Cane, who died on July 9, 1872. Mr. Fyffe married a second time, on December 23, 1875, to Nellie L. Wilson, who was born on June 25, 1857, in Barr township, Daviess county, and who is a daughter of James H. and Susannah Q. (Litten) Wilson. Her father was a native of Scotland, born on October 7, 1830, who came to this country and settled in Greene county, Indiana. Her mother was born on April 14, 1836, in Lawrence county, Indiana. Their marriage ceremony was performed in Daviess county, where they made their future home, and to them were born the following children: Angeline, Joseph, Nellie L., Decie, Milton H., Andrew Jackson, Emily Jane, Jacob Michael, James William, Thomas Theodore, Susan Tabitha and Martha Samantha (twins), and Mary, who died in infancy. The father has always been a supporter of the Republican ticket. Religiously, the entire family lend their support to the Christian church, and all are respected and honored citizens.

The subject of review received his education in the township schools and began farming when a young man. He acquired ownership of one hundred acres of land in Washington township, this county, and the family continues to reside there since his death, on January 8, 1912. To Mr. and Mrs. Fyffe were born the following children: Rillie Angeline, Lulie Bell, Harry Halcomb, Susan Adie, Sarah Ethel, Charles Edward, Lora Agnes, James Austin, George Ransom William A., Thomas Scott, Raymond Earl, and Milton Frederick.

Politically, Mr. Fyffe was a persistent advocate of the principles of the Republican party, but never took an active part in its affairs. Religiously, he was a member of the Christian church and his family also belong to that denomination. Personally, he was a man well thought of by all his friends and acquaintances, who held him in the highest respect and esteem. He had a reputation for being thoroughly progressive, in matters pertaining to the public welfare, and was ever ready to assist in the promotion of meritorious enterprises toward that end. All in all, he was a worthy representative of the steady, intelligent and progressive class that gives stability and character to the community in which they live.

George W. Fyffe was a justice of the peace for four years. He was a soldier in the Civil War, and served nearly four years in Company A, Sixty-third Illinois Volunteer Infantry. He was enrolled on December 1, 1861, and discharged on December 31, 1863, at Huntsville, Alabama, and re-enlisted and served to close of the war.

By his first marriage there were born three children; two died in infancy, Lafie, Edgar, who lives in Terre Haute, Indiana. He is an engineer on the Southern Indiana railroad.

JOHN G. SHANKS.

Among the enterprising and progressive farmers of the county there is none who stands higher in the esteem of his neighbors and fellow citizens than does John G. Shanks, who is also well known in this county and who has had a large part in the civic development of this favored region.

John G. Shanks was born in Daviess county, on the farm which he now owns in Washington township, on September 22, 1862. He is the son of William and Catherine (Graham) Shanks. William Shanks was a native of Fayette county, Pennsylvania, who was born on June 29, 1827, and was the son of John and Sarah (Jordan) Shanks, and of German-Irish extraction. Of the four children born to John and Sarah (Jordan) Shanks,

William was the third. John Shanks was born in the northern part of Pennsylvania in 1801, and his wife was born in 1802 in the same state. John Shanks was a son of William Shanks, who died in Pennsylvania in 1842. In 1837 John Shanks came to Daviess county, Indiana, and entered one hundred and sixty acres of land. Aside from being a farmer, he was also a tanner and followed this trade in Indiana. Subsequently he returned to Pennsylvania in 1838. He remained in Pennsylvania until 1846, when he returned with his family and located in Washington township, Daviess county. Here he died in the fall of 1852, his wife surviving until 1883.

William Shanks, the father of John G. Shanks, remained at home and worked for his father until he was twenty-three years of age, after which he taught school for three terms. In 1849 he was appointed deputy surveyor of Daviess county and served two years. In 1852 he went to California and engaged in mining, but returned four years later and began farming. In 1858 he settled on a farm in Washington township and remained upon this farm until his death. He owned three hundred and twenty-six acres of land, of which two hundred and twenty-six acres were in a fine state of cultivation. In 1868 he was elected county surveyor of Daviess county and was re-elected in 1872. He was married in 1857 to Catherine Graham, a native of Pike county, Indiana, who was born on October 31, 1827, and who was the daughter of John and Anna M. Graham. John Graham was born in 1779 in Scotland, and his wife was born in 1801 in Maryland. The children of William and Catherine Shanks were: Anna and Sarah E., twins, born in February, 1861, and John G., the subject of this sketch, born on September 22, 1862. William Shanks was an ardent Republican throughout his life and was always influential in the councils of his party.

William Shanks died in Washington township on May 9, 1888. His wife, Catherine (Graham) Shanks, died on August 28, 1900, in Washington township.

John G. Shanks was reared on the old homestead farm and educated in the Daviess county public schools. During his entire life he has been a successful farmer. Mr. Shanks believes very keenly in the modern spirit of farming and in modern methods of soil cultivation. This no doubt accounts for much of his success in life. John G. Shanks has two hundred and six acres of land, and is engaged in general farming and stock raising. He makes a specialty of Poland China hogs and is considered an expert judge, not only of thoroughbred hogs, but of cattle and, in fact, of all other kinds of live stock.

John G. Shanks was married on October 14, 1883, to Mary E. Carnehan, the daughter of John Carnehan, who died in 1873. To Mr. and Mrs. Shanks six children have been born, Ethel, William J., whose sketch is found elsewhere in this volume; Clifford J., Bertha, deceased; John Frank, and Russell C.

William J. Shanks, the eldest son, is county surveyor of Daviess county. John G. Shanks was county commissioner of Daviess county for six years, and has to his credit a very successful administration. He is well remembered by the people of Daviess county as a competent and efficient public official. During his entire life, John G. Shanks has been an ardent Republican, and during the split in the Republican party in 1912 he remained faithful to the old wing, and today is keenly interested in the revival of the party to its former power and strength, not only in this state, but in the country at large.

John G. Shanks, in every respect, is an up-to-date farmer. He takes great pride in keeping his farm in a first-class state of repair. He is thrifty, enterprising and alert, one of those men who have contributed very much to the spirit which makes for public improvement and, in fact, the improvement of the world in general.

JOHN HASTINGS.

In placing John Hastings in the front rank of worthy citizens of Daviess county, it is done after due consideration has been given to his career in this locality. John Hastings has long been numbered among the progressive citizens of this community and his reputation for integrity, and other admirable qualities, is such as to warrant the historian including him in a work intended to set forth the life work of men who have set high standards and whose influence is such as to mold the character and shape the lives of those with whom they mingle. Although a quiet and unassuming man, with no ambition for public position or leadership, he has contributed much to the material advancement of the community.

John Hastings was born on August 7, 1861, in Elmore township, Daviess county, Indiana, and is the son of William and Susannah (Slimp) Hastings. The paternal grandparents were Joseph and Hannah Elizabeth Hastings, who came to Indiana, when son William was but four years of age, and settled near the town of Odon, Daviess county. To their union were born

Alice, who married William Noblet; Elizabeth, who married Andrew McCormick; James, who married Elizabeth Hammersley; Celia, who married Nathan Hanners; Malhaly, who first married William Faith and then John Long; Isar, who married Nancy McCormick, and Harvey, who married Jane Wesmillan.

John Hastings' father began farming as a very young man, in Elmore township, and continued to farm all of his life. During his time he acquired a full section of land which he divided among his surviving children. First, was an infant child; Levi, who married Rebecca Slinkard; Nancy, who married George Feltner, who was killed during an engagement in the Civil War; her second husband, Martin Cox, died and her third husband is Robert Bratton; Jefferson, who married Elizabeth Slimp and who died, then married Sarah Manley; Hannah Elizabeth who married Samuel Skomp, their children are George (deceased), Jane (deceased), John, Albert, Charles (deceased), and Mary, the wife of William Lynch; Jams (deceased), who married Margaret Slinkard; George (deceased), who married Nancy Dillon; John, the subject of this sketch; Anna, who married Thomas Killion, and William who died in infancy.

John Hastings received his early education in the Elmore township public schools, began farming at an early age and has continued this business ever since, besides giving some particular attention to the raising of live stock, but at the present time a son Charles gives personal attention to the greater part of the details of farming. Mr. Hastings owns two hundred and fifteen acres of fine land and erected all the buildings thereon. His first wife was Sarah Courtney, a daughter of James and Frances (Moore) Courtney; she gave birth to one child, Charles. His second wife, Sarah Dunlap, is a daughter of Clemens and Martha (Robison) Dunlap, and by this marriage he is the father of William, who married Rosa Sharpless; Ada, who married Harvey Sims, and they have four children, Bonnie, Doras, John and Lloyd; Nellie, who married Alva Sims and they have two children, Julia and Louisa; Hattie, who married Ellis Malone; and Paris. Mr. Hastings' wife's parents gave birth to four children, Scott, Sarah, Hattie, deceased, and Cora.

John Hastings has never taken an active interest in politics, but has always been an ardent supporter of the principles of the Republican party. He and his family are stanch members of the Christian church and to that denomination lend their financial support. Personally, Mr. Hastings may well feel a sense of pride in his achievements and the honorable position he

(41)

holds among the enterprising and successful citizens of the county in which he lives. Unassuming and genial in disposition, he has ever attended strictly to his own affairs and makes better all who come within the range of his influence.

JAMES W. RUST.

There are individuals in nearly every community who, by reason of pronounced ability and force of character, rise above the heads of the masses and command the unbounded esteem of their fellow men. To this energetic and enterprising class the subject of this sketch very properly belongs. He has devoted himself to his adopted vocation as a farmer, and because of his personal worth and his accomplishments, he is clearly entitled to representation among the enterprising and progressive men of Daviess county.

James W. Rust was born on March 31, 1874, in Jackson county, Indiana, and is the son of Henry and Clara (Robertson) Rust. The former was born in Germany and came to this country when quite a young man and settled in Jackson county, where he died. The latter was a daughter of James and Phoebe (Jacobs) Robertson, early settlers, and entered government land in Jackson county and at one time possessed twenty-five hundred acres of land. To the marriage union of Henry and Clara Rust were born: James W., Lottie, Lillie, Andrew, and Grace, who is a teacher in the Washington (Indiana) public schools, and the youngest, Charles.

James W. Rust received his early education in the public schools and was married on July 11, 1897, to Eunice Rhoads, a native of Jackson county, Indiana, and daughter of John and Susan (Frank) Rhoads. Subject and wife have three children, John Henry, James Rhoads and Mary Millicent.

Soon after his marriage, Mr. Rust removed to Daviess county from Jackson county and engaged in farming on his present farm, which he purchased in 1911. This tract of land consists of two hundred and fifty acres of fine land, and is well improved, favorably located and its production is better than the average yield. Mr. Rust carries on general farming and stock raising, and is regarded as very successful in whatever he attempts. A number of new buildings have been added to the place in past years and everything is being kept up in good repair. The general aspect is one of prosperity, due to careful management, keen observation and special attention to the little details which go to make up the things of greater importance.

Mr. Rust has always been identified with the Democratic party, but does not take an active interest in political matters. Fraternally, he is a member of the Independent Order of Odd Fellows, and, religiously, is a member of the Christian church, to which he liberally contributes. Personally, Mr. Rust possesses to a large degree those characteristics which gain friends, and his friends are only limited by the number of his acquaintances. He is deservedly popular in the community in which he lives, and those who know him are unstinted in their praise of his genial disposition and superior ability, and he has ever held the confidence and esteem of the people with whom he has been associated for so long a period.

CLIFFORD FARRIS.

Numbered among the enterprising and progressive citizens of Daviess county, none are held in higher esteem than the young man whose name forms the caption of this review. He has long been actively engaged in agricultural and stock raising pursuits in this county, and his honorable career in this community has but strengthened his hold on the hearts of the people, consequently he is fully entitled to recognition in a work of this character.

Clifford Farris was born on September 28, 1885, on his father's farm in Elmore township, Daviess county, Indiana, and is the son of Milton and Alwilda (Porter) Farris. Milton Farris was the son of Sanders and Sarah (McGill) Farris, the former a native of Kentucky, who came to Indiana when a very young man and began farming in Greene and Martin counties. He farmed in these locations all of his life and at one time owned sixty acres situated in Greene county. To their union were born five children, namely: Milton, subject's father; Lindsey, who married Nauma McGuire; Clementine, who married William Henry; Caroline, who died when quite young, and Theodore. The mother of these children died soon after the birth of Theodore, and he was given to a family by the name of Giles, who reared him. All were members of the Christian church.

Milton Farris was born on February 10, 1845, in Greene county, Indiana, and his wife, Alvilda Porter, was born on February 26, 1846, in Carroll county, Ohio, and was a daughter of Nathan and Susannah (Nofsker) Porter. Mr. and Mrs. Farris are the parents of five children, as follow: John Leonard, born November 25, 1868, married Ella Strickland, and their children are Paul, Leonard and Clara, the last named living in Dalhart,

Texas; William E., born on November 22, 1870, first married Lovina Roberts and by whom two children were born, Roland and Gray, and for his second wife took Grace Pauley, to whom no children were born; they live in Buffalo, New York; Oscar, born on January 16, 1881, who married Maud Price, and to which union were born Helen and Marie, their residence being in Eureka, Kansas; Porter, born on November 28, 1882, who married Susannah Pershing; they have one child, Mildred, and live in Brazil, Indiana; Clifford, the subject of this review. Part of the family are members of the Christian church and part are members of the Methodist Episcopal church.

Milton Farris received his early education in the public schools of Martin county, Indiana, and later enlisted in the service of the Union. This occurred on July 21, 1861, and he was assigned to Company F, Twenty-first Regiment, Indiana Volunteer Infantry, and was engaged in military operations against the Confederate states during the following four and one-half years, and participated in the battles of Baton Rouge, Brazen City, and was captured and retained as a prisoner of war in the battle of that city. During the engagement at Baton Rouge he suffered a slight bullet wound in the hip and was honorably discharged on January 11, 1866. After his return from the battlefields he went to Knox county, where he farmed for a period of twenty years. He moved to his present farm on March 31, 1885, which is located in Elmore township, Daviess county. This farm consists of one hundred and fifteen acres of fine land and, while still belonging to him, he gave up active farming on the place and now leads a life of retirement in the town of Elnora.

Clifford Farris received his early education in the public schools of Elmore township, and afterward began his present occupation as a farmer in that township. He makes his place of residence on his father's farm, where, besides raising a general line of crops, he takes a deep interest in raising live stock, and is successful at it. Mr. Farris recently bought twenty-five acres of land for himself in Elmore township and expects to increase his land holdings from time to time. On February 23, 1907, he was married to Inez E. Dillon, a daughter of Wesley T. Dillon, whose life history is recorded elsewhere in this work under the caption of Franklin D. Dillon.

Having always given his support to the Republican party, Clifford Farris takes an active part in the workings of party affairs. In 1914 he was elected to the office of township trustee and, being possessed of more than average intelligence, will have no difficulty in discharging the duties of that office to the entire satisfaction of the community at large. Personally, Mr. Farris is regarded as a good business man, of excellent judgment and foresight and, being strictly progressive, keeps well abreast of the times. He has won the respect and esteem of all who know him for his friendly manner, genial disposition and is looked upon by all as a substantial and progressive citizen of this section of the county.

JAMES P. TAYLOR.

A career marked by earnest and indefatigable application to his life work has been that of James P. Taylor, a substantial and honored citizen of Madison township, Daviess county, Indiana. Although Mr. Taylor was born in Lawrence county, Indiana, he has long maintained his residence in Daviess county, during all of which time his life has been an open book to be read by his fellow men. He was a valiant soldier in the Civil War, and his fidelity was of the type which has characterized his actions in all of his relations and gained for him the confidence and esteem of the public and unbounded respect of all with whom he has been brought in contact. James P. Taylor is widely known throughout Daviess county and is well liked by a host of people who know him so well.

James P. Taylor was born on July 12, 1845, in Lawrence county, Indiana. He is the son of Samuel and Elizabeth (Garten) Taylor, the former of whom was born on August 13, 1820, in Monroe county, Indiana, and the latter born in June, 1827. Samuel Taylor's father, Matthew S. Taylor, was born in Pennsylvania. The father of Matthew S. Taylor was Robert Taylor, a native of Ireland, who was married in his native country and who came to America in pioneer times, locating in Pennsylvania. Matthew S. Taylor, the grandfather of James P., married when a young man and removed from Pennsylvania to Monroe county, where he farmed during the remainder of his active life. He died upon the farm where he settled upon coming to Indiana. His children were Robert, Henry, John, Samuel, Jane and Ann. Samuel Taylor, the father of James P., was educated in the district schools of his community and was reared on a farm. He attended school, however, less than six months altogether. When James P. was two years old, Samuel Taylor, his father, removed to Madison township, Daviess county, where he lived the remainder of his life. He owned a farm of two hundred acres. This community was a wilderness when he removed to it, and he cleared much of the land. Samuel and Elizabeth (Garten) Taylor had ten children: James P., the subject of this sketch; Mary Ann, who married George M. Critzlow; John, who married Elizabeth Hastings; Zimri M., who married Lucinda Conard; Lydia, who died in infancy; Almeda, who married John P. York; Lucinda, who died at the age of sixteen years; William H., who married Orpha E. Orsborn; Vivia E., who married Joseph Lawyer, and Samuel, who died young. Samuel Taylor was an old-line Whig and, later, a member of the Republican party.

James P. Taylor, the subject of this sketch, was educated in the district schools of Madison township. When a young man he enlisted in the Union army and served valiantly during the dark days of the Civil War. He enlisted on August 1, 1862, at the age of seventeen, and served about three years, being discharged on July 17, 1865. He fought courageously in the battles of Franklin, Tennessee, Nashville, Fort Fisher, Fort Anderson, Bluntville, Tennessee, Morristown, Raytown, Walkersford, Fort Zollicoffer and in the siege of Atlanta, eighteen battles in all. In 1864 he joined Sherman's army at Buzzard Roost and was in all of the engagements from Resaca to Atlanta. He served first in Company I, Sixty-fifth Regiment, Indiana Volunteer Infantry (mounted), but was dismounted when he joined the service. At Fort Anderson Mr. Taylor was wounded in the side of the head. After coming home from the war he started farming in Madison township and has farmed here ever since. He owns eighty acres of land and has comfortable, well-kept buildings on the farm, which he built with his own hands.

On November 24, 1887, Mr. Taylor was married to Agnes J. Cavnes, the daughter of Sion and Agnes (Gough) Cavnes. To this union two children have been born, Viola B. and Leota E. Viola B., who was born on December 27, 1868, died on April 10, 1900. She married William H. McCarter and they had three children, Paul T., Dewey R. and Delphia C., the latter being deceased. Since the death of his mother, Paul T. McCarter has lived with his grandparents, Mr. and Mrs. Taylor. Leota E. Taylor, who was born on July 28, 1873, married Dawson B. Ogden and has eight children, Rebecca Josephine, Phoebe B., Helvia, Pauline, Helen, Margaret, Vella J. and Autumn.

James P. Taylor is a Republican and served as justice of the peace in Madison township for sixteen years. He is now serving his fourth term as a notary public. He is a member of the Grand Army of the Republic at

Odon, of which he is commander. James P. Taylor is a man well known and well liked.

Mr. and Mrs. Taylor took Emery W. Montgomery to rear when he was a baby. They reared him to manhood and educated him, and he is now principal of the Bedford high school. He married Ada Smiley.

MILTON B. LEDGERWOOD.

Among the citizens of Madison township, Daviess county, Indiana, who have established comfortable homes and surrounded themselves with valuable personal and real property, few have attained a higher degree of success than Milton B. Ledgerwood, who comes from a very old family in this section of the state of Indiana. With no great wealth of opportunity and with many discouragements to overcome, Mr. Ledgerwood has made an exceptional success in life, and now as he is passing the meridian of life he has the gratification of knowing that the community in which he resides has been benefited to a large degree by his presence and by his council. He is one of the most highly respected citizens in this section of Daviess county.

Milton B. Ledgerwood was born on March 27, 1857, in the township where he now lives. He is the son of Charles and Manda (Chamber) Ledgerwood, the former of whom was a native of Virginia, born on August 15, 1806, and the latter of whom was a native of Tennessee, born on September 18, 1809. When a young man, Charles Ledgerwood moved from Virginia to Tennessee, and from Tennessee he came to Indiana. During the first few years of his residence in Indiana he lived in Greene county. About 1845 he removed to Madison township, Daviess county, where he entered about three hundred acres of land from the government. He lived in Madison township the remainder of his life, clearing and draining the land and improving his farm. Among other improvements, he erected many log buildings upon his farm.

Charles and Manda (Chamber) Ledgerwood had fifteen children, as follow: Eliza, born on February 23, 1830; Margaret, June 3, 1831; Thomas, February 13, 1833; Nathaniel, January 11, 1835; Elizabeth, September 15, 1837; Barbara, February 20, 1838; Rebecca, August 8, 1840; James, May 18, 1842; William Riley, February 11, 1844; Sarah Jane, August 4, 1845; Manda, May 1, 1847; Charles Hays, June 14, 1849; Laca Jane, April 9, 1851; Mary Jane, March 31, 1853, and Milton B., March 27, 1857, the youngest child of his parents, both of whom were devout members of the Baptist church. Charles Ledgerwood was an ardent Democrat.

Milton B. Ledgerwood was educated in the public schools of Madison township, Daviess county. After completing his education he began farming in that township, where he has lived all his life. He owns two hundred and three and one-half acres in Madison township, and is engaged in general farming and stock raising. He makes a specialty of Polled Angus cattle, and has become an expert with this particular breed. Mr. Ledgerwood and family live on their farm in Madison township. The present place he purchased in 1897.

Milton B. Ledgerwood was married on March 11, 1890, to Elizabeth Baker, who was born on August 30, 1868, and who is the daughter of John and Rolina (Thair) Baker, who came to Indiana from Ohio. They had six children: Mary, John, Alice, George, Jonas and Elizabeth, the wife of Mr. Ledgerwood. They were members of the Methodist church.

To Milton B. and Elizabeth (Baker) Ledgerwood six children have been born, as follow: Charles, on April 28, 1892; John, May 17, 1894; Edna, August 11, 1896; Ruth, December 1, 1900; Raymond, May 21, 1902, and Ralph, April 10, 1905, died on May 17, 1905.

All the members of the family are now living at home, and it is a happy home circle. Mr. Ledgerwood is a Democrat, and he and his wife and all the members of the family are connected with the Baptist church. The Ledgerwood family not only are all well known in this section of Daviess county, but they are highly respected and valuable citizens.

OSCAR M. WALLICK.

Self-assertion is believed to be absolutely necessary to success in life, and there are good reasons for entertaining such a belief. The modest man very rarely gets what is due him. The selfish, aggressive man elbows his way to the front, takes all that is in sight, and it sometimes seems that modesty is a sin, with self-denial as the penalty. There are, however, exceptions to all rules, and it is a matter greatly to be regretted that the exceptions to the rule are not more numerous. One notable exception is Oscar M. Wallick, a hustling young farmer of Madison township, Daviess county, Indiana, whose life history is here presented. Mr. Wallick possesses just a sufficient amount of modesty to be a gentleman at all times, and with sufficient persistency to win in the business world. As a result of these well and happily blended qualities he has won a host of friends in Daviess county. He is well known to all classes as a man of influence, integrity and ability.

Oscar M. Wallick was born on May 9, 1872, in Madison township, near Odon, Daviess county, Indiana. He is a son of William H. and Sarah E. (Taylor) Wallick, the former of whom was born in 1845, in Tuscarawas county, Ohio, and who was a daughter of Henry and Nancy (Garton) Taylor. Henry Taylor was born in Monroe county. William H. Wallick was the son of Michael Wallick, a native of Pennsylvania, who married Nancy Jane Boothe. They came to Indiana about 1851 and settled on a farm in Madison township, Daviess county. They had five children, William H., Rachael, Sarah, Ella and Harvey. Michael Wallick was one of the pioneer farmers of this community.

William H. Wallick was educated in the public schools of Daviess county, and especially in Madison township. When a young man he enlisted in Company B, Thirty-eighth Regiment, Indiana Volunteer Infantry, and served about one year in the Civil War. After his enlistment expired he came back and engaged in farming. He also worked as a carpenter for some time. He owned about five hundred acres of land in this county.

William H. and Sarah E. (Taylor) Wallick had six children, Oscar M.; Ada G., who married R. D. McCarter; Ray, who married Josephine Hasler; Lola, who married Thomas Summerville; Henry, who married Susie Ledgerwood, and Jen. William H. Wallick is a Republican in politics, a member of the Methodist church and a member of the Grand Army of the Republic.

William H. Wallick died on January 2, 1909. His wife is now living at Odon, Iowa. Mr. Wallick owns in all two hundred acres of land, all located in Madison township. He made all of the improvements just as they stand.

Oscar M. Wallick, the subject of this sketch, was educated in the public schools of Madison township. Later he attended the State Normal School at Terre Haute for one year, and after leaving school began teaching in 1895. He taught fourteen terms, quitting the profession in 1913. All of Mr. Wallick's professional labors were performed in Madison township, Daviess county. While he was a teacher he was also engaged in farming. About 1900 he purchased a farm of eighty acres. He now owns a stock farm of a hundred and twenty acres in Madison township, and is engaged in general farming and stock raising.

On March 26, 1898, Oscar M. Wallick was married to Larinda Ketcham, the daughter of John M. Ketcham, who married Minerva Laughlin, the daughter of Osman Laughlin. To this happy union two children have been born, Gleason was born on October 31, 1903, and Neva, born on September 1, 1911.

John M. Ketcham was born on February 1, 1845, on a farm in Madison township, Daviess county, Indiana. He is a son of Daniel Ketcham and Eliza Goodwin, the former born in 1810 in Kentucky, and the latter born in 1817 in Monroe county, this state. Daniel Ketcham was a son of Joseph Ketcham and wife, who had nine children, George, Lewis, Blaine, Daniel, Jane, Betsie Ann, Mary, Rebecca and Hettie. In his later life, Joseph Ketcham brought his family to Indiana and located in Monroe county. Joseph Ketcham had a brother killed by an Indian in Monroe county, Indiana. The Indian kept the scalp of his victim.

Daniel Ketcham attended the subscription schools of Monroe county, and when a young man worked as a farm hand. He came to Daviess county, immediately after his marriage, and located in Madison township. He made his home in the wilderness, and owned over seven hundred acres of land at the time of his death. Daniel and Eliza Goodwin Ketcham had eight children. Jane, who first married Jefferson Eaton and after his death James Allen; Lewis, deceased, who was married three times, first to Elmira Bennem, second to Mary E. Bennem, and third to Mrs. Sarah Johnson; Betsie Ann, who married Lowery Storm; John M., the father of Mrs. Wallick; Rebecca, who married Isaac Storm; Malinda, who married Lilburn Woodruff; Mary, who married Melkard Kutch; and Amanda, the eight child, married U. G. Laughlin. Daniel Ketcham and his wife were members of the Methodist church. He was a Democrat, and served as trustee of his township for many years.

J. M. Ketcham was educated in the common schools of Madison township, and when a young man started farming on the tract of land where he now lives. He has farmed here all his life. Mr. Ketcham owns two hundred and forty acres in Madison township. He has been engaged in general farming and stock raising, retiring from the former in 1913. He has erected all the buildings on the place where he now lives, the house being built in 1883. John M. and Minerva (Laughlin) Ketcham have had nine children. Rosetta married John B. Williams, and they have three children, Floy, Fred and Palmer. Lauranda married Oscar Wallick. Lucine married Henry Taylor and they have two children, James Russell and John Alvin. May married Arthur Trueblood and they have four children, Roger

K., Ralph H., Mary J. and Grace. William W. married Maud Hoffman and they have two children, Glendora R. and John W. Dollie M. married Samuel Scott, who have one child, Nona. The other children are: Grace, John S. and Britta M. Mr. Ketcham is a Republican. Mrs. Ketcham's family are all members of the Baptist church.

Mr. and Mrs. Wallick are devout members of the Baptist church and regular attendants at both the church services and the Sunday school. Mr. Wallick is an ardent Republican. Fraternally he is a member of the Knights of Pythias and a member of Lodge No. 303, Free and Accepted Masons, at Odon, Indiana.

WILLIAM HAM.

The office of biography is not to give voice to a man's modest estimate of himself and his accomplishments, but rather to leave upon the records of time the verdict establishing his character, determined by the consensus of opinion of his neighbors and fellow citizens. In touching upon the life history of William Ham, the writer aims to avoid fulsome encomium and extravagant praise, but desires to hold up for consideration those facts which have shown the distinction of a true, useful and honorable life, a life characterized by perseverance, energy, broad charity and well-defined purpose. William Ham is a successful merchant at Alfordsville, Indiana, and the proprietor of a modern country store.

William Ham was born on April 8, 1843, in Reeves township, Daviess county, Indiana, the son of James and Anna (Williams) Ham, the former of whom was born in 1820, in Bourbon county, Kentucky, and who died in 1895, and the latter of whom was born in 1820, in Maryland, and who died in 1897.

The paternal grandparents of William Ham were Peter and a Miss (Bennington) Ham. Peter Ham was born in Virginia and settled in Kentucky about 1830. Subsequently, he moved to Daviess county with his family. Peter Ham served in the War of 1812. He and his family were all members of the Baptist church. He was a man rather large in stature, weighing more than two hundred pounds.

The maternal grandparents of William Ham were Thomas and Anna (Burns) Williams, who were natives of Maryland, and who came to Indiana about 1825, where they took up land in Reeves township. They also were members of the Baptist church.

James Ham was a lad of ten years when his parents settled in Daviess county, where he grew to maturity in Reeves township, and where he purchased a farm. Later, he moved to Alfordsville and lived a retired life for some time, but still later he moved to Washington, and here his death occurred. Throughout his life he was a Republican, and was an influential and substantial citizen of his community.

James and Anna (Williams) Ham were the parents of thirteen children, as follow: Thomas, a farmer living near Shoals; Mary Ann became the wife of John R. Montgomery and lives at Loogootee; William M., with whom this narrative deals; Albert, who died at Vincennes in 1907; Emily, who became the wife of Charles Cohorn and died at Vincennes; Margaret, deceased, was the wife of William Williamson, of Wheatland; Delilah, the wife of William Cohorn, of Vincennes; Hannah, deceased; Edith, deceased, was the wife of a Mr. Fox; Melissa, deceased, was the wife of John Mullen; Sarah, also deceased, was the wife of Andy Hodge; David, of Carlisle, Indiana, and Charles, living at Terre Haute, where he is employed as a railroad foreman.

William Ham grew up on his father's farm in Reeves township, and was unable to attend school more than a few months. When he was eighteen years of age, in August, 1861, he enlisted for service in the Union army, in Company G, Forty-second Regiment, Indiana Volunteer Infantry, and participated in the battles of Perryville, Murfreesboro, Chickamauga and many others. At Chickamauga he lost his left leg and was confined in different Union hospitals for nearly a year. Finally he was mustered out of service with his regiment at Indianapolis.

After the close of the war, William Ham went to Washington, and there served three years as an apprentice at the shoemaker trade. He then came to Alfordsville, and for six years conducted a shoe shop. He afterward moved to Sedan, Kansas, where he operated a shoe shop, and finally to Orich, Missouri, where he lived for six years. He then came back to Alfordsville, and conducted a shoe shop in connection with a harness shop for several years. In 1900 Mr. Ham started a grocery in Alfordsville. Later he discontinued the grocery, but, in 1906, he started a general store, and is still conducting this store. It is the largest in the town and occupies two buildings. Mr. Ham has a large stock of goods and handles all lines of merchandise usually to be found in a store of this character. He has built up a large and lucrative business and is a good business man, giving his undivided attention to the details of his store.

William Ham was married in November, 1866, to Sarah Summers, who is a daughter of Charles and Margaret (Greeman) Summers. Mrs. Ham was born in Reeves township. To this union nine children have been born: Marcellus, who died at the age of one year; Talbot, who died at Washington, June, 1911, was a painter by trade; Walter, living in Washington; Al. J., a jeweler by trade, is assisting his father in the store; Margaret, the fifth child born to her parents; Albert, who was the sixth in order of birth; Rose, the wife of Henry Potts, of Alfordsville; Nellie, the wife of Emery Watham, of Springfield, Missouri; Thomas, unmarried, works in his father's store.

Mr. Ham is a Republican in politics, but throughout his life he has been too busy to devote much time to politics. He has never held office nor has he ever aspired to it.

WILLIAM ANDREW LaVELLE.

Practical industry, wisely and vigorously applied, never fails of success, but carries a man onward and upward, brings out his individual character and acts as a powerful stimulus to the efforts of others. The best results in life are often obtained by simple means and the exercise of the ordinary qualities of common sense and perseverance. The every-day life, with its cares, necessities and duties, affords ample opportunity for acquiring experience of the best kind, and its most beaten paths provide a true worker with abundant scope for efforts and self-improvement. William Andrew LaVelle is one of the enterprising young farmers of Barr township, but he is also one of the best and most popular teachers of the township.

William Andrew LaVelle was born on January 10, 1879, in Barr township, Daviess county, Indiana. He is the son of Michael and Elizabeth (Lamb) LaVelle, the former of whom was born in Barr township in 1849, and the latter in Harrison township in 1854.

The paternal grandparents of William A. LaVelle were Michael and Jane (Gaul) LaVelle, the former of whom was a native of County Mayo, Ireland, and who came to the United States when a mere youth. Michael LaVelle went overland to California with the "eighteen forty-niners," and soon saved ten thousand dollars from gold mining. He contracted the fever, however, and lost some money. Subsequently, he returned to Daviess county with two thousand dollars saved, and with this he purchased about six hundred acres of land in Barr township, where he lived until his death. William A. LaVelle's maternal grandparents were Edward and Catherine (Bradley) Lamb, both of whom were of Irish nativity. They owned a farm in Harrison township, Daviess county, in an early day. Michael LaVelle, the father of William A., grew up on his father's farm in Barr township. Subsequently he carried on farming for himself for a time in that township, but being a natural mechanic, he moved to Washington and obtained a position in the Baltimore & Ohio railroad shops, where he still works. He is a loyal member of the Catholic church, as are his parents and his wife's parents.

William A. LaVelle is the eldest of four children born to his parents. The others are: Mary, who married John Bies and lives in Washington; Thomas J. is married and lives in Washington, where he is a boilermaker; and James J., a telegraph operator, lives at Vincennes.

Attending the public schools of Barr township at an early age, William A. LaVelle made rapid progress with his education. In 1900 he studied law and was admitted to the bar, but never practiced the profession. When he was grown he began teaching school and has taught for the last fifteen years in Barr and Harrison townships. In the meantime, however, during the summer, he has farmed and attended school. In all, he has attended the State Normal School for three years and has also spent twenty-four weeks at the Northern Indiana Normal School at Valparaiso. Lately Mr. LaVelle has been teaching in Glencoe school in Harrison township. He is said to be the best and most popular teacher in that township. In 1912 Mr. LaVelle purchased eighty acres out of the Dan Smith farm in Harrison township, and now lives on this farm, which he operates in addition to teaching school. He and his family are members of St. Peter's Catholic church at Montgomery.

Mr. LaVelle was married in 1909 to Mary Catherine Drew, who is a native of Barr township and the daughter of John and Maria Drew, the former of whom is deceased. John Drew was a farmer in Barr township, and he and his wife are of Irish nativity. To William A. and Catherine (Drew) LaVelle three children have been born, Lucile Josephine, September 29, 1912; William Paul, October 27, 1914, and Louis Joseph, July 28, 1911, who died January 31, 1913.

William A. LaVelle is one of the promising young men of Daviess county. He has already got a good start in life, and with his commendable habits and sterling personal qualities, he is expected to achieve in the future larger and better things.

OLIVER A. TAYLOR.

Oliver A. Taylor is recognized as one of the energetic, well-known business men of Daviess county, Indiana, who, by his enterprise and progressive methods has contributed in a material way to the commercial advancement of this county. In the course of an honorable career he has been successful in agriculture and enjoys distinct prestige among the representative men of Daviess county. It is eminently proper that attention be called to the achievements of this prosperous young farmer of Madison township, in the annals of his county's history.

Oliver A. Taylor was born on April 15, 1877, on the farm where he now lives in Madison township, Daviess county, Indiana. He is a son of J. G. and Rebecca (Conard) Taylor, the former of whom was born on May 1, 1846, on the farm where Oliver A. now lives, and the latter of whom was born on June 4, 1848, in Harrison county, this state.

The grandfather of Oliver A. Taylor was Henry Taylor, who was born in Monroe county, and who married Nancy B. Garten. The great-grandfather of Mr. Taylor was Samuel S. Taylor, who was a native of Pennsylvania, and who came to Monroe county when a young man, living all his life, on the farm where he located. Samuel S. Taylor had six children, four sons and two daughters, Robert, Henry, John, Samuel, Jane and Anna.

Henry Taylor, the grandfather of Oliver Taylor, had five children, William, who died in the service of his country during the Civil War; Samuel A.; James G.; Sarah E., and Jane.

James G. Taylor was educated in the subscription schools of Madison township, Daviess county. Though he was unable to attend school but a short time, he supplemented his public school education by home study, and was a well-informed man and a man of wide practical intelligence, so far as the every-day affairs of life are concerned. When a young man he began farming in Madison township. After his father's death he removed to the farm where his son, Oliver A., now lives. He erected all the buildings on this farm, and owned, altogether, two hundred and sixty-seven acres, where he made a specialty of raising stock.

The children of James G. and Rebecca (Conard) Taylor were four in number: Laura E., who became the wife of Samuel A. Scott, is deceased; John Henry, who married Vine Ketchem, lives in Illinois; Oliver A., the immediate subject of this narrative, and Nancy M., who became the wife of Paris M. Laughlin. James G. Taylor is a Republican and is a member of the Baptist church.

Educated in the public schools of Madison township, Oliver A. Taylor was also a student for two terms at the Normal College at Odon, and when only eighteen years of age, began farming on the place where he is now living. He has farmed here continuously since that time, is an extensive breeder of Guernsey cattle, Poland China hogs, and has been very successful in the breeding of these animals. His farm consists of one hundred and twenty-seven acres, on which he has good buildings and a comfortable country home in every respect.

Oliver A. Taylor married Elsie E. Erwin, the daughter of Caleb Erwin, to which union one child has been born, Erwin Bowman, who died in infancy.

Mr. Taylor is a Republican, and he and his wife are earnest and devoted members of the Baptist church, Mr. Taylor serving as deacon in this church. He belongs to the Masonic fraternity and the Knights of Pythias. No young farmer of Daviess county is more highly respected than Oliver A. Taylor, and very few have worked harder for success, and not many have made greater progress than he in his chosen vocation.

NATHANIEL HUNT JEPSON.

It is interesting to note from the beginning the growth and development of a community; to note the lines along which progress has been made and to take cognizance of those whose industry and leadership in the work of advancement have rendered possible the present prosperity of the locality under consideration. Nathaniel Hunt Jepson, the well-known watchmaker, jeweler and optician of Washington, Indiana, is one of the strong, sturdy individuals who have contributed largely to the material welfare of Washington. Although well advanced in years, Mr. Jepson is still up to date in his business methods, public-spirited as a citizen and progressive in all that the name implies. He is a grand, good man, who has made a remarkable success of his business in the city of Washington.

Nathaniel H. Jepson was born on January 28, 1835, in Belmont county, Ohio, a son of John and Hannah (Hunt) Jepson, natives of Lancashire, England, who were the parents of eleven children, five of whom grew to maturity, as follow: John, now deceased; Hannah Elizabeth, who died unmarried on November 11, 1914, at the age of eighty-one years; Nathan-

NATHANIEL H. JEPSON.

iel H., of Washington; George, of St. Clairsville, Ohio, and Dr. Samuel L., the present secretary of the state board of health of West Virginia, now living in Wheeling.

John Jepson worked in a woolen factory in Utica, New York, his first place of residence in this country after coming to the United States, with his wife and two children, when about thirty years of age. Later he removed to Ohio and settled near St. Clairsville, where he engaged in farming, and where he spent the remainder of his life, his death occurring at the advanced age of ninety-one years. He was badly crippled by an accident at the raising of a barn. His widow survived him some years, her death occurring at the age of eighty-four. Both were stanch members of the Presbyterian church, as were all of their children. Both Mr. Jepson's paternal and maternal grandparents lived and died in England.

Nathaniel H. Jepson was reared in St. Clairsville, Ohio, and received a common-school education in the schools of that place. He began clerking in his father's grocery at the age of fourteen, and for some years followed this vocation. He then began learning the watchmaker's and jeweler's trade in Cadiz, Ohio, and has followed this business for more than fifty years. He moved to Washington, this county, in 1870, and has lived there for a period of forty-five years. In the first place he bought out a small concern, which has been considerably enlarged. Mr. Jepson carries a large and fine assortment of watches, clocks, jewelry, silverware and optical goods, and has a flourishing business in Washington and vicinity.

Mr. Jepson was married in 1863 to Elizabeth Black, the daughter of Samuel and Barbara Black, and to this union three children were born, John Samuel, Lucy and Jessie. John Samuel is deceased. He represented a wholesale jewelry manufacturing house in Newark, New Jersey, and was the Pacific-coast representative of that firm. Lucy also is deceased. She was the wife of Felix L. Cadou and the mother of three sons, Eugene Jepson, Edward Leon and Felix L., Jr. Eugene Jepson is now attending the Indiana State University, at Bloomington, and stands at the head of his class. Jessie, the youngest child of Mr. and Mrs. Jepson, married Harry S. Smith, chief train dispatcher at Seymour, Indiana. Mr. and Mrs. Smith have one daughter, Elizabeth.

Mrs. Jepson was born in Stark county, Ohio, in 1840. Her parents were natives of Pennsylvania and Ohio, respectively, her father having been a major in an Ohio regiment during the Civil War. He was later a captain of one of the gunboats on the Ohio and Mississippi river during the war. He died in Ohio, leaving five daughters and four sons, Lycurgus, Samuel, Frank, George, Elizabeth, Bertha, Emma, Alice and Mary.

Nathaniel Hunt Jepson was a soldier in the Civil War, a member of Company B, One Hundred and Fifty-seventh Regiment Ohio Volunteer Infantry, and served between four and five months. After the close of the war he returned to Ohio and located in Steubenville for a time. Mr. Jepson is a Republican and served for ten years as a member of the Washington city council, and for three years as a member of the Washington city school board. Mr. and Mrs. Jepson are members of the Presbyterian church in Washington, in which Mr. Jepson is an elder.

Nathaniel Hunt Jepson is a representative citizen of Daviess county. He is a man who has worked to good purpose and who in his declining years is able to enjoy the fruits of his early labors, but he has worked unselfishly through all these years. He has been a good citizen, a kind neighbor, a loving husband and father, and will go down in the history of Daviess county as one of its most substantial citizens.

EDWARD C. FAITH.

It is not an easy task to adequately describe the character of a man who has led an eminently active and busy life in connection with the great legal profession and who has impressed his individuality on the people of Daviess county in one of the most exacting fields of human endeavor. Among the truly self-made and representative men of Daviess county, none ranks higher than Edward C. Faith, a conspicuous figure in the civic life of the community. A man of tireless energy and indomitable courage, he has won and held the unqualified esteem of his fellow citizens. With the law as his profession, he has won a splendid reputation. Mr. Faith has also succeeded admirably as a civil engineer and performed efficient public service in this profession.

Edward C. Faith was born in Bogart township, Daviess county, Indiana, on October 12, 1868. He is the son of Thomas W. and Matilda J. (Strange) Faith, a history of whom appears elsewhere in this volume. Edward C. was reared on his father's farm in Bogard township, Daviess county, and attended the district school and the Southern Indiana Normal College at Mitchell, graduating in the teachers' class in 1887. He then taught school five years, during which time he was principal of the Plainville schools, from 1892 to 1893. He was elected county surveyor in 1894 and served two terms in that office. He graduated from the Indiana Law School of the University of Indianapolis in the class of 1897, and was admitted to practice in all the courts. Mr. Faith took the two-year law course in one year and was graduated with honors. He began to practice in Washington and has continued there since 1897. Three brothers, Grant, Edward C. and George A., were first associated together, but Edward C. is now practicing alone.

After returning from the law school Mr. Faith was elected city civil engineer of Washington in 1898, and served for four years. In February, 1904, he was appointed postmaster and served until 1912, eight years. Since that time he has devoted himself entirely to the practice of law.

Edward C. Faith was married to Lena Bach, at Bloomfield, June 14, 1894. She was the daughter of Emanuel and Laura (Stropes) Bach. Mrs. Faith was born in Bloomfield, Indiana. Her father was a native of Switzerland, who came to America, locating in Kilbuck, Ohio, when twelve years old. He later came to Indiana and located at Bloomfield. He was a soldier in the Civil War, and died in 1894, at the age of sixty years. His wife survives him and still lives at Bloomfield. They had six children, Rolla E., Sadie E., Jesse J., Leroy. Lena B., and Zula, who died in infancy. The paternal grandfather of Mrs. Faith was Emanuel Bach, whose children were as follow: Elizabeth, Eda, Emanuel, Mary, William, Eliza, Louis, Edwin and Caroline. The maternal grandfather of Mrs. Faith was Jeremiah Stropes. His wife was Sarah (Franklin) Stropes. Their children were: Adam, Laura, Serinda, Jeremiah, William and Sarah, who died in infancy.

Edward C. and Lena (Bach) Faith are the parents of two children, Don C. and Harold B. Don C. graduated when sixteen years old from the Washington high school in the class of 1912. He had a license to teach before that time. He is now teaching his third term of school at Maysville, in Washington township, and Harold B. is now sixteen years old and is employed in the automobile department of the Hatfild & Palmer Company.

Mrs. Faith is an active member of the First Methodist Episcopal church. Mr. Faith belongs to the Odd Fellows and the Elks and is a Republican. He has a farm of fifty acres in Washington township on the Maysville road, which is his home.

Edward C. Faith is a man of broad experience, a good lawyer and a man who commands the respect of his fellow citizens.

AARON D. BECHTEL.

Success is achieved only by exercising fundamental qualities of nature. Those by whom great epochal changes have been made in the agricultural world began early in life to prepare themselves for the peculiar duties and responsibilities. It has been only by the most persevering and continuous endeavor that they have succeeded in rising superior to obstacles and reaching the goal of their ambition. Such lives are an inspiration to others who are less courageous and more prone to give up the fight before their ideal is reached. In the life history of Aaron D. Bechtel there is much evidence of those peculiar characteristics which make for achievements and for success, such qualities, for instance, as persistency, fortitude and indefatigable industry. Mr. Bechtel is one of the best known and most highly respected citizens of Madison township, Daviess county, Indiana.

Aaron D. Bechtel was born on September 4, 1850, in Coshocton county, Ohio. He is the son of Abraham and Rachael (DeKamp) Bechtel, both of whom were natives of Pennsylvania. Abraham Bechtel was the son of Martin Bechtel, who married Elizabeth Williams. Martin and Elizabeth Bechtel had five children, Abraham, John, Elijah, Martin and Elizabeth. When Abraham Bechtel was a young man he started in life as a farmer in the state of Pennsylvania. He came to Indiana in 1862 and located in Daviess county, farming here the remainder of his life. Abraham and Rachael Bechtel had ten children: Samuel; Aaron D.; Sarah Ann, who died at the age of seven; Martha M.; Mary; William; Hester; James, who died in his youth; Jane and Benjamin F. Abraham Bechtel and wife were members of the Baptist church, while Mr. Bechtel was a Republican.

Aaron D. Bechtel was educated in Madison township, Daviess county. When a young man he farmed during a part of the time and at other times worked at the brick mason's trade. Mr. Bechtel purchased a part of the farm upon which he now lives in 1874, and owns two hundred acres of splendid land, which is highly productive. He is engaged in general farming and stock raising and has accumulated an exceptionally large competence.

Mr. Bechtel was married on January 1, 1874, to Mary Jane Taylor, the daughter of Henry Taylor. To this union seven children were born: Albert, deceased; Nancy, who married Frank Pugh and has had four children, Lester, Herford (deceased), Glenn and Neva; Iva, deceased; James, who married Blanche Bogle and has one child, Harold; Jacob, who married Lizzie Richison and has two children, Palmer and Russell; Zula, who married Claude Sipes, and Fay. The mother of these children died in 1912, and Mr. Bechtel was married, March 13, 1913, to Hannah Howard, a daughter of Daniel and Minerva (Brummett) Howard. At the time of her marriage, Mrs. Bechtel was Mrs. Hannah Ledgerwood, the widow of Henry H. Ledgerwood. By her first marriage, Mrs. Bechtel had six children: Sarah, who married John Vaughn and has two children, Darrell and Gladys; Minerva, who married James Maham and has one daughter, Catherine; John W., Candice, Henry and Ava.

Aaron D. Bechtel is a member of the Baptist church, while fraternally he is a member of the Independent Order of Odd Fellows. Mr. Bechtel is a Republican. Aaron D. Bechtel is a man not easily disturbed by passing fancies or present-day fads. He is a man who takes the world as it comes, who believes in the honesty and integrity of his fellow citizens, but who, nevertheless, has been wise enough in his personal and private relations to rely strictly upon his own personal resources. He has made an exceptional success of farming, and now has in his possession more than a sufficient competence for his declining years. He has been too busy with his own personal and private affairs to take much part in matters of public moment.

WILLIAM H. McCARTER.

An enumeration of those men of the present generation who have won honor and public recognition for themselves and at the same time have honored the locality to which they belong would be incomplete were there failure to make specific mention of William H. McCarter. The qualities which have made him one of the prominent and successful men of Daviess county have also won for him the esteem of his fellow men. His career has been one of well-directed energy, strong determination and honorable methods.

William H. McCarter was born on April 4, 1847, in Madison township, Daviess county, Indiana. He is the son of Moses and Sarah (Ketcham) McCarter, the former of whom was born on September 4, 1813, in Tennessee, and who died, December 27, 1856, and the latter of whom was born in Kentucky, of German descent, on June 21, 1812, and who died in 1863. Sarah (Ketcham) McCarter was the daughter of Joseph Ketcham. The grandfather of William H. McCarter was Joseph McCarter, a farmer of Tennessee.

Moses McCarter ran away from home at the age of seventeen years. He came to Indiana about 1830 and located in Monroe county. He was one of the early settlers in this part of the country. He settled in the woods in Madison township, this county, and cleared much of the land. Later he located on a farm of about five hundred acres in that township. Moses and Sarah (Ketcham) McCarter had eight children: Joseph; Catherine; Jane; Daniel L.; Nancy; William H., the subject of this sketch; John and George died in youth. Moses McCarter and wife were members of the Methodist church, and he was identified with the Republican party.

William H. McCarter was educated in the subscription and public schools of Madison township, Daviess county. When a young man he started farming in Madison township, and has farmed here all his life. He owns two hundred and sixty acres, which he has accumulated by dint of hard labor and careful management, as well as frugal and economical living. He does general farming and makes a specialty of raising a great deal of live stock. All of the buildings on Mr. McCarter's farm he himself has erected. They are a credit to his fertile and well kept farm and a credit to the community where he lives.

Mr. McCarter was married on March 29, 1866, to Miranda C. Laughlin, who was born on August 1, 1846, in Martin county, this state, and who is the daughter of John O. M. and Elizabeth Laughlin. To this happy union nine children have been born: Minerva E. married Philip Miller; Rufus D. married Ada G. Wallick and they have three children, Densel, Clenton and Glen; Ida A. married Edward Hubbard; John K. married Della Jollif; Edna married Ora Richardson; Walter is living at home; William, Thadius and Elizabeth, the last three, died young.

Mr. McCarter is a Republican. He has been honored by the people of Daviess county in a political way, having served two terms as commissioner of the county and two terms as trustee of Madison township, and in both of these offices Mr. McCarter acquitted himself as becomes one who is moved by the spirit of public service and honest consecration to the duties which he accepted at the time of his election.

William H. McCarter is one of the most highly respected citizens of Daviess county. His two terms as county commissioner and his two terms as trustee of Madison township have given him a wider experience in public life than falls to the lot of most men. Mr. McCarter's son, Rufus D., is a very prominent farmer of Madison township, and at present is the efficient trustee of this township.

GEORGE W. POWNALL.

Not too often can be repeated the life history of one who has lived so honorable and useful a life and attained to such distinction as George W. Pownall. As a private citizen he has been a pronounced success in everything with which he has been connected. There are individuals in nearly every community, who, by reason of ability and force of character, rise above the heads of the masses and command the unbounded esteem of their fellow men. Such individuals are characterized by perseverance and a directing spirit, two virtues which never fail. They always make their presence felt and the vigor of their strong personalities serves as a stimulant to the young and rising generation. To this energetic and enterprising class George W. Pownall very properly belongs, as he is one of the substantial and extensive farmers of Madison township, Daviess county, Indiana, and is still active at the age of seventy-three, and was doing a man's work when he sat down to give the outline of the facts set forth in this brief biography.

George W. Pownall was born on September 10, 1841, in Portage county, Ohio, the son of Jesse and Nancy (Swift) Pownall, the former of whom was born on April 15, 1815, in Virginia, and who died in 1905, and the latter of whom was born in Vermont. Jesse Pownall was a son of John Pownall, a native of Virginia, who died in Portage county, Ohio.

Jesse Pownall moved from Virginia to Ohio in 1827, and lived in Portage county until after his marriage, when he moved to Wabash county, Indiana, where he lived for sixteen years on a farm. In 1860, he came to Madison township, Daviess county, and lived there on a farm the remainder of his life. He was the owner of two hundred and forty acres of land in Madison township, and was a general farmer and stock raiser. He did most of the clearing of his land himself.

The children of Jesse and Nancy (Swift) Pownall were six in number: Louisa, who became the wife of Hiram Hughner; George Washington, the immediate subject of this review; Amy, the wife of Blackburn Ferguson; Melissa, the wife of William Moore; Byron, who married Mrs. Ketchem, and Elnore, who became the wife of John Lyle. Jesse Pownall and his family were earnest and loyal members of the Christian church. Mr. Pownall was a Democrat.

George W. Pownall attended school in Wabash county for about three months each year for two years. A few years before Mr. Pownall moved his family to Wabash county, it was a dense wilderness, over-run by Indians. When a young man, Mr. Pownall began farming on the tract of land where he has since lived, in Madison township. He is the owner of four hundred acres of land in that township, and does general farming and stock raising, making a specialty of breeding Shorthorn cattle and Poland China hogs. He also raises a great many mules. During Mr. Pownall's farming experience, he has cleared between two and three hundred acres of wild land, with his son's assistance, within the last twenty years.

On November 18, 1867, George W. Pownall was married to Alwilda Ferguson, who was born on November 26, 1849, the daughter of John and Salina (Conkle) Ferguson, and to this union four children have been born, Florence, who is the wife of Jonas M. Winklepleck; Clarence, who married Minnie Woodruff; Teletha, the wife of Daniel Osborn, and Theodore Clemens, who married Randa E. Pate.

George W. Pownall is identified with the Democratic party, while he and his family are earnest and loyal members of the Christian church. That Mr. Pownall has lived an honorable and upright life is evidenced by the fact that he is beset by no qualms of conscience, and is able to do a man's work at the age of seventy-three. In clearing and draining the land, George W. Pownall has done more for the prosperity and progress of Daviess county than any other man who may be living in it today. His service has been of the practical kind, not only the kind which counts, but the kind which can easily be measured.

THEODORE C. POWNALL.

To attain worthy citizenship by correct habits of living, even from childhood, deserves more than mere mention. One may take his place in public life as a consequence of some vigorous and untoward stroke and even abide in the hearts of friends and neighbors, but to gradually rise in the same position, winning one's way through sterling worth and faithfulness to daily trust rather than by craving for exaltation and popularity, is worthy of the highest praise and commendation. As such, the career of Theodore C. Pownall is viewed by the people of Madison township, Daviess county, Indiana, where he lives.

Theodore C. Pownall was born in Madison township, Daviess county, Indiana, on December 24, 1873. He is the son of George W. and Alwilda (Ferguson) Pownall, the former of whom was born on September 10, 1841, in Portage county, Ohio. George W. Pownall is at present one of the well-known farmers of Madison township and is still active at the age of seventy-three.

George W. Pownall is the son of Jesse and Nancy (Swift) Pownall, the former of whom was born in Virginia on April 15, 1815, and died in 1905, and the latter a native of Vermont.

Theodore C. Pownall was educated in the public schools of Madison township. When a young man, he started farming, and throughout his life has been engaged in farming in partnership with his worthy father. He owns eighty-two acres of land and does general farming and stock raising. On the place where he now lives in Madison township, he has erected all of the buildings, some of which were erected in 1913.

On July 10, 1900, Mr. Pownall married Randa E. Pate, the daughter of William Pate, and they have had four children, Herschel D., Hallet C., Georgia A. and Geneva.

Mr. Pownall is a Democrat. Fraternally, Mr. Pownall is a member of the Independent Order of Odd Fellows. He belongs to a very wealthy family in Madison township and one which is highly respected in this section of Daviess county. Theodore C. Pownall, himself, is a worthy young farmer and an enterprising citizen of his locality.

THOMAS E. RESLER.

The present generation has been especially productive in men of action, clear-brained men of high ideals and noble purposes, who give character and stability to the communities honored by their citizenship, and whose influence and leadership are easily noticed in the various enterprises that have added so greatly to the high reputation which Daviess county enjoys among her sister counties of this great commonwealth. Conspicuous among this class of men whose place of residence is in this community, is the progressive citizen under whose name this review is written.

Thomas E. Resler was born on April 2, 1876, in Stark county, Ohio, and is the son of Isaac J. and Susannah (Shanower) Resler, both natives of Tuscarawas county, Ohio, born on March 26, 1844, and November 19, 1848, respectively. To the paternal grandparents, John and Barbara Resler, were born the following named children: David, who enlisted in the service of his country and died during the Civil War; Isaac J., subject's father; John Henry; Jacob; Harvey, Mary, who married Joseph Rosenburg, and Phoebe.

Isaac Resler received his early education in the public schools of his native county and in his early manhood had a desire to become a cook in the army and actually started to join a regiment of soldiers. His father came after him and caused his return home on account of his youth. After this experience he began farming and settled down to hard work in this line in Ohio. At a later date he decided to move to Indiana and came to the town of Loogootee, Martin county, near where he lived on a farm for the ensuing four years and acquired one hundred and sixty acres of land. In 1890, he made a trade which brought him into possession of eighty acres of land in Elmore township, Daviess county, where he lived and farmed until the time of his death, December 15, 1903. His wife still survives him. To their union were born the following named children: David, deceased at the age of twenty-three years; Jacob, who married Clara Bechtel and lives in Elmore township; Cora, who married A. L. Fielder; Frank, who married Martha Fielder; Ellen B., who married Frank Bechtel; Jennine, who died at the age of sixteen years; Thomas E., the subject of this review; Isaac, who married Arla Roberts; Suda, deceased; Jessie, who married Minnie Bynum; Ida, who married Victor Bray; Roy, who died in infancy. They are members of the United Brethren church, and the lamented father also belonged to that institution. He was a supporter of the Republican ticket, but did not take any active part in politics. Personally, he was well thought of and held in the very highest esteem by all who knew him.

Thomas E. Resler was educated in the public schools, partly in Ohio, and later in Loogootee, then again he attended the schools in Elmore township. In his early manhood, and after leaving school, he secured a position in the city of Indianapolis, with the wholesale commission house of John W. Neumann & Company, where he remained for a period of five years. Following the work around the commission house, he went out as a traveling salesman and continued to travel for two years. At a later date, he purchased a general store in West Indianapolis, and which he conducted for about a year, then returned to the home farm in Elmore township, where he farmed for the next two years. In the year 1904 he went to Knox county, where he rented two hundred acres of river bottom land, which place he cultivated for four years; he then returned to Elmore township, Daviess county, and bought out the home place and sold it within the same year. After this sale Mr. Resler rented what is known as the John Swartz farm, in Elmore township, continued to farm this for a year and gave it up for the purpose of managing his father-in-law's farm, which consists of one hundred and seventy-six acres and where he makes his home at the present time. During the year 1904 Thomas E. Resler was married to Ethel Martin, a daughter of Doctor Simon and Sarah E. (Brumfield) Martin, and to their union three children have been born, Fred S., on February 10, 1906; Dorothy Eunice, March 22, 1911, and Florence, November, 1913, died January 1, 1914.

Dr. Simeon Martin was a son of Joseph and Nancy (McCray) Martin, and was born on April 29, 1852, near Little Eagle Creek, Marion county. His paternal grandparents, by first marriage, were William and Jane (Hall) Martin, the former a native of Pennsylvania, who spent most of his life in Ohio as a farmer, but in his declining years, was a resident of Indianapolis. His first wife gave birth to the following named children: John H.; Joseph; Ambrose S.; Ezra J., a university graduate; William; Phoebe J.; Lucinda. The second wife was Elizabeth Goldsberry, who gave birth to Colvin and Ella. Doctor Martin's father, Joseph Martin, received his early education in the public schools of Newton, Ohio, and farmed his entire life, coming to Indiana in the year 1835 or 1836, locating in Marion county, where he farmed on the land known as Haughville and which is now a part of the city of Indianapolis. It is said that he broke the ground and did the first plowing immediately west of the present site of the state capitol building at Indianapolis. He was twice married, the first time to Nancy McCray, who was born in 1825, in Connersville, Fayette county, who gave birth to two children, Simeon, subject's father-in-law, and Sarah J., who married Frank P. Wier and lived in Morton county, Kansas. The second marriage was to Minerva Messersmith, a daughter of Peter Messersmith, who gave birth to a son Richard, who died in infancy, and Luetta B., who married D. A. Castleman and resides in Indianapolis.

Dr. Simeon Martin was educated in a public school that formerly occupied a portion of the ground where Crown Hill Cemetery is located in the city of Indianapolis; later he attended school in Mount Jackson, an Indianapolis suburban town, then attended Battle Ground College and Commercial Institute for two years. After these years of schooling, he decided to teach and was a professional school teacher for nine years. He was married in 1877, to Minnie Caterson, a daughter of James P. Caterson, who was a Mexican War veteran and captain in the Civil War of 1860-1865. To their union was born one child, William, who died at the age of one year; his mother died in the year 1881. Doctor Martin's second wife was Sarah E. Brumfield, a daughter of Nathan Brumfield, and to this union were born Eva, who died in infancy; Ethel, subject's wife; Lulu, who died at the age of fourteen years, and Nora. After Doctor Martin discontinued teaching, he attended the College of Physicians and Surgeons, at Indianapolis, where he began the study of medicine and graduated in the year 1883, then established himself as a practitioner, first in the town of White Lick, Boone county, where he remained a year, then went to Daleville, Delaware county, where he remained four years, and again removed to the town of North Salem, Hendricks county, and continued to practice for the following fifteen years. He bought a farm from Robert W. Mason, consisting of one hundred and sixteen acres in Elmore township, Daviess county, after which he purchased sixty acres more and now owns one hundred and seventy-six acres of what is known as the Old Mason farm, situated about half way between the towns of Odon and Elnora, and where he now lives. He is an active member of the Christian church, a member of the order of Free and Accepted Masons, and is now serving the county as a Republican member of the county council. He is highly esteemed by all who know him.

Thomas E. Resler is an ardent advocate of the progressive principles of the Republican party, but does not take any active interest in politics. He is a member of the Modern Woodmen of America, and favors the belief of the United Brethren church and lends his support to that denomination. Personally, he is one of the popular young men of the community and particularly noted for his genial disposition, aggressiveness in the promotion of all meritorious enterprises tending to the welfare of the community, and, socially, is most hospitable, wins friends easily and, among the wide acquaintance which he enjoys, he has many warm and loyal supporters.

LEVI W. WEAVER.

Levi W. Weaver needs no introduction to the people of Daviess county, since his entire life has been spent in this community, a life devoted not only to promoting his own interests, but also the welfare of his neighbors. He is a man representative of one of the esteemed families of this section and a gentleman of high character and worthy ambition. He has held no small place in the public view and is a splendid type of the intelligent, up-to-date, self-made American. He is regarded as one of the very best business farmers in Elmore township. As a citizen, he is progressive and well abreast of the times. Mr. Weaver enjoys the confidence of all of his neighbors, by whom he is highly respected.

Born on March 9, 1875, in Elmore township, Daviess county, Indiana, Levi W. Weaver is the brother of Jacob C. Weaver, whose life history is told elsewhere in this volume, and the son of Abraham and Fannie (Barkey) Weaver, the former of whom was born in Mason county, Kentucky, on January 21, 1840, and died on July 20, 1908, and the latter born in 1841 in Ontario, Canada, died on August 14, 1906. Levi Weaver's grandfather was Jacob Weaver, a blacksmith, born in Westmoreland county, Pennsylvania, who married Charlotte Kinneman, also a native of that place. They were married in Pennsylvania, but subsequently moved to Kentucky, where they only resided a short time, when they removed to Indiana, settling in Madison township, Daviess county, at which place Jacob Weaver followed his trade the remainder of his life. He owned a farm of eighty-five acres, and was a devout member of the German Lutheran church.

Abraham Weaver, the father of Levi Weaver, was educated in the subscription schools of Daviess county and obtained only three months' schooling before he had arrived at the age of twenty-one. This education, however, he supplemented by home study and became a well-informed man, teaching school for four years. He was a builder and contractor and did most of his work in Greene, Martin and Daviess counties. He owned a farm of two hundred and ninety-five acres in Elmore township, was a Democrat in politics and a member of the United Brethren church.

Levi W. Weaver was one of three children born to his parents: Jacob C., whose history is given elsewhere, and Christina, who was born in 1870 and died in 1875.

Educated in the public schools of Elmore township, Daviess county, Indiana, Levi W. Weaver, after leaving the public schools, took a business course and went to Illinois, remaining there for twelve and one-half months, during which time he completed the course of stenography and typewriting. After leaving the business college he began farming on the tract of land where he now lives in Elmore township. He has lived upon this farm continuously since that time, the farm consisting of one hundred and fifty acres at the present time. Mr. Weaver does general farming and stock raising and is an extensive breeder of the large type of Poland China hogs.

Levi W. Weaver was married in 1899 to Catherine S. White, the daughter of James M. and Mary J. (Wood) White. To this union one son, Robert Donovan, has been born. He was born on September 3, 1901.

James M. White was born in Virginia, but removed to Kentucky and from that state to Illinois, where he was a farmer in Clark county. For the last twenty years he has lived a retired life in Westfield, that state. The children of James M. and Mary J. White were: William T.; Flora V.; Catherine S.; Lillian, deceased; Garett W., deceased, and Emma L. James M. White was the son of Garett and Martha (Marr) White, who were natives of France and who immigrated to this country.

Levi W. Weaver has been a hard worker, an industrious farmer and a good manager. In the broader sense of the word, Mr. Weaver considers himself the steward of the wealth and property which have been placed in his hands. He is interested in all public enterprises, a progressive, up-to-date citizen, thoroughly in sympathy with the spirit of the generation in which he is living. From many standpoints he is to be considered a representative citizen of Daviess county.

WILLARD BOWMAN.

In the brief sketch of any living citizen it is difficult to do him exact and impartial justice. Not so much, however, for the lack of space or words to set forth the familiar and passing events of his personal history, as for want of the perfect and rounded conception of his whole life, which grows, develops and ripens like fruit to disclose its truest and best flavor only when it is mellowed by time. Daily contact with a man so familiarizes us with his virtues that we ordinarily overlook them and commonly underestimate their possessor. It is not often that true honor, public or private —that honor which is the tribute of cordial respect and esteem—comes to man without a basis of character and deeds. The world may be deceived by fortune and by ornamental or showy qualities without substantial merit and they render to the undeserving the short-lived admiration, but the honor which wise and good men value and which lives beyond the grave must have its foundation in real worth, for "Worth maketh the man." Not a few men live unheralded and almost unknown beyond the narrow limits of the city or community wherein their lots are cast, who yet have in them, if fortune had opened to them a wider sphere of life, the elements of character to make statesmen or public benefactors of world-wide fame. Compared with the blazon of fame which some regard as the true stamp of greatness, there is a lowlier and simpler and yet truer standard whereby to judge them and to fix their place in the regard of their fellowmen. During a life of more than fifty years in Daviess county, Indiana, the people have had an opportunity to know what manner of man Willard Bowman is. Testimony is ample that he is a good citizen in the full sense of the term and worthy of honor and public trust. He is at present an intelligent farmer and one who, by dint of his intelligence, has accumulated a personal fortune.

Willard Bowman was born on March 13, 1859, in Brown township, Martin county, Indiana. He is the son of Michael and Mahala (Sulsor) Bowman, the former of whom was a native of Martin county, Indiana, and the latter a native of the same county and the daughter of Michael Sulsor. Michael Bowman was a son of Pleasant Bowman, a native of Tennessee, who came from that state when a young man and settled in Martin county. He was a farmer there and very successful during his life. Pleasant Bowman and wife had nine children, John, Michael, William, Howard, Cynthia, Susannah, Margaret, Hannah and Sarah Ann. Pleasant Bowman's wife was, before her marriage, Sally Raser.

Michael Bowman, the father of Willard Bowman, was educated in the public and subscription schools of Martin county. He was a well-educated man for his day and generation. He started farming in Brown township, Martin county, and farmed there all of his life. He was principally engaged in farming and stock raising, and owned about two hundred acres of land. During the winter season he engaged in buying furs, and also dealt some in the buying and selling of live stock.

The children of Michael and Mahala Bowman were Martin, who married Malinda Atkins; Milton, who married Cynthia A. Osborne; Willard, the subject of this sketch; Nancy Jane, who married John Sims, deceased; Sarah Alice, who married Absalom Sharpless, deceased.

Michael Bowman and family were active and devout members of the Baptist church. He was a Democrat and was trustee of Brown township, Martin county, at the time of his death.

Willard Bowman was educated in the public schools and especially at the Welsh school in Brown township, Martin county. His education did not cease, however, when he finished attending this school, for he practically educated himself by studying at night after doing a hard day's work. He began farming when a very young man, first about 1881 in Cameron township, Martin county. About 1885 he came to Daviess county and located in Madison township, farming there until 1910. In that year he traded for the farm of one hundred and sixty acres which he now owns in Elmore township. He still has fifty acres, however, in Madison township. Mr. Bowman does general farming and stocking raising. During his entire life he has bought and shipped horses and mules to Atlanta, Georgia, and at one time was heavily interested in this business, although he has not been active in it for several years. He ships some stock, however, at the present time.

Willard Bowman was married first to Laura Osborn, the daughter of James and Jane Osborn, and to this union two children were born, Edith, who married George Dillon and has three children, Mable, Sheldon and Frederick, and Grover, a farmer of Knox county, who is unmarried. After the death of Mrs. Bowman, Mr. Bowman was married to Sally A. Hastings, the daughter of Joseph and Addie (Sims) Hastings. By this second marriage one child, Paul, was born, on March 27, 1895. He is living at home and graduated from Odon high school on April 29, 1915.

Willard Bowman is a Democrat. In 1896 he was elected sheriff of Daviess county and served for three years. During the last ten years he has made nine trips to Arkansas on hunting expeditions. Mr. Bowman is commonly called "Governor Bowman" and is well known throughout Daviess county. He is a great lover of sports, especially hunting, and has a small pack of registered dogs that he takes with him to Arkansas on his hunting trips. At home he hunts foxes and other game. There is an unusual coincidence in the family birthdays. Mr. and Mrs. Bowman's birthdays, the birthday of one daughter, two sons and a grandchild all fall on the same day of the year.

ALBERT MALONE.

When one pauses to consider the enormous influence for good that must have been exerted by the conscientious, talented and well-trained man in a service of more than a quarter of a century in the school room, the thought inevitably arises leading up to the conclusion that here perhaps has been exercised one of the most potent factors in the development of the neighborhood in which such service has been extended that can be imagined. What a wonderful thing it is to have had in charge the educational training of the countless youth who have been placed under the gentle care of the conscientious teacher whose service has extended over such a period as here set out. The far-reaching influence of such a service can never adequately be estimated. It easily is conceivable that in an indirect way this influence may reach all corners of the earth, for in a quarter of a century there no doubt passes before a district school teacher youth who, in their after experiences, literally do reach the uttermost parts of the earth. There is no gainsaying the local influence of such a service, however, and in the northern part of Daviess county there is to be found no one who will deny to the gentleman whose name introduces this interesting biographical sketch, the honor of having touched and influenced the lives of more of the youth of that section of the county than any other person in it. Since the year 1888 Albert Malone has been a teacher in the schools of Elmore township, and in that time has endeared himself to all, old and young alike. He has had the honor and the pleasure of receiving under his scholastic care the children of those who once were pupils under his charge, and, reasonably enough, may expect yet to receive into his charge even the grandchildren of some of his original pupils. This is indeed a form of public service that is worth while, and the biographer takes particular pleasure in inviting the attention of the reader of these pages to the following brief and modest review of the life of the well-known Daviess county teacher here referred to.

Albert Malone was born in Madison township, Daviess county, Indiana, on November 1, 1867, the son of Frederick and Martha C. Leon (O'Sullivan) Malone, the former of whom was born in Tuscarawas county, Ohio, on July 5, 1843, the son of Elias and Susannah (Freed) Malone, natives of Ohio, the latter of whom also was born in Ohio, the daughter of Robert and Mary O'Sullivan.

Elias Malone, who was born in Ohio, where he grew up as a farmer, came to Daviess county about the year 1850, and settled on the farm in Madison township on which his son Frederick now resides and on which he spent the rest of his life. He was a man of forceful character, upright and energetic, who quickly became one of the most prominent and influential men in that part of the county. He and his good wife were active in all movements having to do with the betterment of local conditions and were admired and respected by the citizenry throughout that region, the memory of their good deeds being cherished by many thereabout to this day.

To Elias and Susannah (Freed) Malone there were born nine children: Frederick, Samuel, John, Henry, Jacob, Mary, Catherine, William and Amy, the descendants of whom today form a quite numerous family, many men and women of large influence in their respective communities being included in the list.

Frederick Malone, the father of the immediate subject of this interesting biographical review, was but seven years of age when his parents moved from Ohio to this county, therefore practically his whole life has been spent here. He grew to manhood on the paternal farm in Madison township, receiving his education in the excellent district schools of that neighborhood and still lives on the home farm, which for many years has been in his name, which is a well kept property of ninety acres, practically every foot of which is in a state of excellent cultivation. Mr. Malone is not only an excellent farmer, but a citizen of worth, whose influence in the community in which he so long has lived is ever exerted for good, so that he is recognized as one of the leading citizens of that section. He and his wife are members of the Baptist church, in which faith they reared their children, and are warmly interested in the various beneficences of the congregation to which they are attached. Mr. Malone is a Democrat and, though never included in the office-seeking class, is deeply concerned in all matters relating to good government, and takes a good citizen's interest in the campaigns of his party.

To Frederick and Martha C. Leon (O'Sullivan) Malone seven children were born, as follow: Albert, the subject of this sketch; Elias, who married Eva Ketcham; Leonard, who married Dossie Graham, to which union two children have been born, George and Ruth; Mary, who married Sheridan Todd; Grover C., who married Mattie Graham; George, who died in infancy, and Day B.

Albert Malone was reared on the home farm, receiving his elementary education in the district schools of Madison township, later attending the high school at Odon, supplementing this course of instruction by a course in the normal school at Mitchell, Indiana, which was followed by a course in the college at Hartsville, this state. Thus admirably equipped for the profession of teaching, to which he had decided to devote his life, Mr. Malone, in the year 1888, began in the district schools of Elmore township, and has been teaching ever since. His winters thus occupied, Mr. Malone has, during all this time, devoted his summers to farming, and owns a fine tract of one hundred and thirty acres in Elmore township, where he makes his home and where he built an excellent and comfortable house in 1914.

In 1890 Mr. Malone was united in marriage to Ada E. Dillon, daughter of Wesley Dillon, a member of one of the old families of this county, further genealogical details of which may be found by turning to the biographical sketch of F. D. Dillon, presented elsewhere in this volume. To this union there have been born two children: Ellis, who was born on February 23, 1891, was graduated from the Elnora high school, attended the Indiana State Normal at Terre Haute, and is now following his father's example and is teaching school in Elmore township. He married Hattie Hastings and has a very pleasant home. Lyman, the other child, died in infancy.

Mr. Malone is not only one of the oldest teachers in Daviess county, but—and this is stated without fear of offending his confreres on the county educational board's staff of teachers—one of the best liked. Certainly in the neighborhood in which for so many years he has been teaching there is none to gainsay his popularity, and the people of that part of the county will be quite content to have him continue for many years to come the course he so ably, and with such gratifying results, has followed during the past quarter of a century or more. He and Mrs. Malone are members of the United Brethren church at Mud Pike, and are earnestly interested in all the good works of the neighborhood, very properly being regarded by all as among the leaders in the social development of their community. The Democratic party claims Mr. Malone's allegiance and he takes a thoughtful and intelligent interest in the political questions of the day, his counsels being received with grave consideration by the party managers in his part of the county.

This veteran school teacher is a man whom all delight to honor, and it surely may be said of him that his good works long will live after him in the lives of the children upon whom his warm personality has been impressed and who have been so beneficently influenced by his teachings.

JACOB C. WEAVER.

The gentleman to whom attention is directed in this review has attained pronounced prestige by reason of natural and acquired ability. He takes a deep and abiding interest in everything which pertains to the material advancement of the township, and every enterprise intended to promote the welfare of Daviess county is sure to receive his hearty support. He is rated as one of the progressive citizens of Elmore township and the high respect in which he is held by all classes of people is a deserved compliment to an intelligent, broad-minded and most worthy man.

Jacob C. Weaver was born on July 27, 1868, in Elmore township, Daviess county, Indiana. He is the son of Abraham and Fannie (Barkey) Weaver, the former of whom was born on January 21, 1840, in Mason county, Kentucky, died on July 20, 1908, and the latter born in 1841 in Ontario, Canada, who died on August 14, 1906. Abraham Weaver was the son of Jacob and Charlotta (Kinneman) Weaver, both of whom were natives of Westmoreland county, Pennsylvania. Jacob Weaver was a blacksmith by trade. He and his wife were married in Pennsylvania and later moved to Kentucky. After living in Kentucky for a short time, and when his son Abraham was three years old, they moved to Indiana, settling in Madison township, Daviess county. He worked at his trade in this township during the remainder of his life. Jacob Weaver owned a farm of eighty-five acres. He was a member of the German Lutheran church.

Abraham Weaver, the father of Jacob C., was educated in the subscription schools of Daviess county, but the opportunities for obtaining an education were meager and he attended school only three months before he attained his majority. After that he educated himself largely by home study and was enabled to obtain a license as a school teacher and taught school for about four years. Subsequently he took up farming and building under contract. He did contract building in Greene, Martin and Daviess counties. He owned the farm of two hundred and ninety-five acres where Jacob C. Weaver now lives, which is located in Elmore township, the house on which property was built by Abraham Weaver. He was a Democrat and a member of the United Brethren church, was a charter member of the Mud Pike church, in Elmore township, and a trustee of this church. Abraham and Fanny Weaver were the parents of three children: Jacob C., the subject of this sketch; Christina, who was born in 1870 and who died in 1875, and Levi W., March 9, 1875, married Catherine S. White.

Jacob C. Weaver, the subject of this sketch, was educated in the public schools in Elmore township and in the normal school at Odon. He obtained a good education and, after completing his preparation, began farming in Elmore township. Mr. Weaver at first rented land, but now owns one hundred and forty-five acres, where he is engaged in general farming and stock raising. He has owned a farm since 1908, built a large silo in 1914, and has found this a very great aid in his farm activities. Jacob C. Weaver is a man who believes in both public and private improvements, and is engaged in making repairs and changes on his own farm practically all the time.

On December 24, 1893, Jacob C. Weaver was married to Effie H. Bean. Although they have no children, they have taken a girl, Mary C. Cunningham, to rear.

Mr. Weaver and his family are members of the United Brethren church, and in politics he is an ardent Democrat. He, however, has never been active in political matters.

The paternal grandfather, Christian Barkey, was born on October 2, 1797, and died on August 31, 1878. He married Catherine Strickler, August 7, 1832, who was born on April 10, 1813, and died on September 30, 1895. Christian and Catherine (Strickler) Barkey had twelve children: Anna, born on July 19, 1833; David, January 6, 1835; Barbara, April 15, 1837, died July 10, 1839; Fannie, in 1841; Christina, April 10, 1843; Mary, August 22, 1845; Christian, July 6, 1847; Susannah, March 25, 1849; Magdelina, September 11, 1851; Abraham, January 20, 1854, and Sarah, November 30, 1859. Christian Barkey was a farmer, who lived in Canada. He was a minister in the German Reformed church.

Mr. Weaver has always given liberally of his money to encourage public improvement and worthy public enterprises. He is a man of cheery optimism and for his success in life is always ready to give credit to the beneficent power which rules the universe, reserving for himself the comparatively humble row of proving himself worthy to profit by the beneficence of this power.

CLARENCE POWNALL.

It matters much less where geographically a man comes into the world, than how he comes into this life as a living force for what he does and becomes in it. Heredity and environment have much to do in conditioning his character and power, and fortunate indeed is the individual who has been well born and whose surroundings have made for his best development. The well-known subject of this sketch has been peculiarly blessed in both these respects. He is born of a distinguished father, a resident of Madison township, Daviess county, and was reared under excellent home influences, the result of which is a fine specimen of manhood and citizenship.

Clarence Pownall was born on September 22, 1870, in Madison township, Daviess county, Indiana. He is the son of George W. and Alwilda (Ferguson) Pownall, the former of whom was born in Portage county, Ohio, on September 10, 1841, and the latter born on November 22, 1849. George W. Pownall is referred to elsewhere in this volume. He is the son of Jesse and Nancy (Swift) Pownall, the former of whom was born in Virginia, on April 15, 1815, and died in 1905, and the latter a native of Vermont.

Educated in the public schools of Madison township, Clarence Pownall when a young man worked with his father on the farm. At the age of twenty-one he purchased eighty acres in Madison township, adjoining his father's farm, and lived with his father until he was twenty-five years of age. At the age of twenty-four he started farming for himself and has been farming ever since on the same tract of land, the one which adjoins that of his father. Clarence Pownall now owns three hundred and fifty acres, almost as much as his father, George W. He does general farming and stock raising. Mr. Pownall is an extensive breeder of horses and mules and feeds all kinds of stock. Mr. Pownall erected the buildings that are situated on his farm.

On December 26, 1894, Clarence Pownall married Minnie Mara Woodruff, the daughter of Aaron and Nancy A. (Dillon) Woodruff, and to them has been born one child, Trula, who lives at home.

In political affiliations, Mr. Pownall is a Democrat, while fraternally he is a member of the Knights of Pythias lodge, and Mrs. Pownall is a member of the Tribe of Ben-Hur. Physically, Clarence Pownall is a fine type of American, pleasant and agreeable in his manners and optimistic in his spirit. He is a man who is devoted to public improvement and whose own farm is the best testimonial of his public spirit.

GEORGE W. MEURER.

Among the numerous farmers of German birth in Daviess county, there are few who are better known or more popular than the gentleman whose name is noted above, or to whom the Goddess of Fortune has been more kind. There is something about the German system of farming which gets results. A native tendency to thrift and careful conservation, a trait that has been inbred by centuries of intensive farming in the Fatherland, gives to the farmer of Teutonic extraction in this country an apparent advantage which his Yankee neighbor sometimes is inclined to envy. There is in this apparent advantage no occasion for envy, however. Everything has its reason for being, and if the German farmers have a way of getting ahead, it is because they are more attentive to the lesser details of their work. They operate their farms with a minimum of waste, and, acting on the proper theory that a penny saved is a penny earned, they make the most of everything they have, with the result that in time their thrift makes itself visibly manifest in broad acres and well-kept farms. Such has been the theory of life behind George W. Meurer's efforts, and the secret of his success is not so deep a mystery as to be without solution by the person of careful habits of observation. It may properly be said, in passing, that this secret is one which many would profit by learning.

George W. Meurer was born in Knox county, Indiana, on October 27,

1864, the son of Philip and Margaret (Sanders) Meurer, the former of whom was a native of Germany and the latter of whom was born in Greene county, Indiana.

Philip Meurer came to this country from Germany at the age of thirty-five and settled in Greene county, where he cleared a farm and made a home, in which he lived for many years before moving to his present home in this county. Shortly after coming to this state, Philip Meurer married Margaret Sanders, of Greene county, and to this union there were born nine children, as follow: Henry, who married Mary Miller, lives in Arkansas, where he is engaged in farming; Charles, who married Annie Franch, and lives in Greene county; Thomas, deceased; Anthony, who married Josephine Lankford; George W., the immediate subject of this sketch; Sherman, who married Nora Owens, and lives in Elmore township; Read, who married Laura Wittles and lives in Arkansas, he being married a second time; Elisha, who married Lura Owens and lives in Greene county; Elizabeth, who married Frank Glenn and lives at Terre Haute. These children were brought up in the faith of the Methodist Episcopal church and the father and sons gave their political allegiance to the Democratic party.

George W. Meurer's youth was spent partly in Greene and partly in Daviess county. He received but a limited education in the schools of these counties, but became well grounded in the principles of successful farming, as a young man "working out" on the farms neighboring those of his father's farm, eventually owning a farm of his own. For twenty-four years he lived on Peters Hill in Greene county, and in March, 1908, moved to the farm where he now lives, in Elmore township, where he has been very successful. He began there with a tract of one hundred and sixty acres, which he gradually enlarged until he now owns a fine farm of two hundred and thirty-five acres, all of which is under a high state of cultivation. In addition to his work as a general farmer, Mr. Meurer is also engaged, to a considerable extent, in stock raising, and, in order to keep up the strain of his cattle, keeps a full-blooded Polled Angus bull. Among the recent improvements on this farm is a fine new barn, which Mr. Meurer erected in 1913. The farm is well tiled and everything is done by its owner to insure the greatest possible productivity of the soil.

In the year 1905 George W. Meurer was united in marriage to Lockie L. Roark, the daughter of John and Elizabeth (Vanover) Roark, and to this union has been born one child, a son, Roy, on January 17, 1914.

Mr. Meurer is a Democrat and takes a good citizen's interest in political affairs, being naturally interested in all matters relating to good government, and is much devoted to the best for the community good. He is a man of much native good nature and is deservedly popular in the community in which he has prospered so abundantly and in which he has gladly elected to spend the rest of his days. Mrs. Meurer is a member of the Methodist church.

WILLIAM THIAS.

The rich agricultural section comprised within the bounds of Daviess county, Indiana, is replete with pleasant homes, housing a happy and progressive people. No spot in the great state of Indiana is better favored in this regard than is the county with which this volume particularly treats, and there are few spots more highly favored than is that section of the county comprised within the borders of Elnora township and the picturesque country surrounding the pleasant town of Elnora. Among the farmers in that township there are few who are better known than is William Thias, to a brief biography of whom the reviewer here engages the attention of the reader.

William Thias was born in Jackson county, Indiana, on November 1, 1871, the son of Christian and Sophronia (Burrel) Fraze, to whom also was born a daughter, Sophia, who married John O'Mara, and lives in Jackson county, Indiana.

Owing to differences in the Fraze family which led to the disruption of the home, William, when a very small lad, was brought up by Frederick and Caroline (Hodapp) Thias, neighbors, and grew to manhood in their home, their name being bestowed upon him by adoption. Frederick Thias was a farmer in Jackson county, who retired from active service on the farm in 1908, and is now enjoying the fruits of a long life of industry and toil. On this farm William Thias received a careful training in the rudiments of agriculture and, upon reaching manhood's estate, started farming for himself. In September, 1910, Mr. Thias came to Daviess county and bought a farm of eighty acres, in Elmore township, on which he has since lived and which he has greatly improved since taking possession, at the same time bringing the farm to a high state of cultivation. During the few years he has been a resident of this county, he has made many friends in the community in which he makes his home and is rapidly taking his place among the men of affairs in that neighborhood. He is industrious and energetic and his well-improved acres show the effect of this energy and industry.

On February 24, 1895, William Thias was united in marriage with Bertie Wilkerson, who was born near Cortland, Indiana, the daughter of William and Mary (Stewart) Wilkerson, to whom were born two other children, Thomas, who died in his youth, and Shirley, who married Nettie Peabody and lives at Anderson.

To William and Bertie (Wilkerson) Thias have been born three children: Earl, killed by lightning in 1913, at the age of sixteen; an infant son, and a daughter, Bertha May, who was born on June 26, 1908. Mr. and Mrs. Thias are members of the United Brethren church at Bellview, and are held in the highest regard in that neighborhood, where they are doing well their part in the life of the community. Mr. Thias is a Republican, and is a member of the Modern Woodmen of America and both in politics and in the affairs of his lodge takes a warm interest, as well as in the general affairs of the vicinity in which he elected to make his home a few years ago. He is a modest, unassuming man, who has the respect of all who know him.

MARION M. JOHNSON.

When Dean Swift gave utterance to that immortal passage in his "Gulliver's Travels," reading as follows: "And he gave it for his opinion that whoever could make two ears of corn or two blades of grass to grow where only one grew before, would deserve better of mankind, and do more essential service to his country than the whole race of politicians put together," he gave to the world a terse presentation of a truth that would be difficult to improve on. Agriculturists, in this favored section of the state, if put to the test applied by Dean Swift, would be found doing their part most admirably in the development of the soil's great riches, making two ears of corn grow where one grew before, in the very literal sense indeed. In no phase of man's activities has there been more advance in recent years than in that most important industry relating to the cultivation of the soil, and in this notable advance the farmers of Daviess county have not been found behind those of any other section of the state. Among the prosperous, progressive and up-to-date farmers of the county, there are few who have a wider acquaintance or who are more deservedly popular than Marion M. Johnson, of Elmore township, a brief review of whose life the biographer finds pleasure in here presenting for the information of the readers of this valuable historical and biographical work.

Marion M. Johnson was born near the village of Odon, in Madison township, Daviess county, Indiana, on November 5, 1863, the son of Bryson B. and Lydia (Overton) Johnson, the former of whom was born in Tuscarawas county, Ohio, in 1839, the son of William and Rachael (Vaughn) Johnson, and the latter of whom was born near Odon, the daughter of Moses Overton, a pioneer resident of Madison township.

William Johnson was born in Tuscarawas county, Ohio, and was reared to the life of a farmer and there married Rachael Vaughn, a native of Pennsylvania. About the year 1854 he came to Indiana, locating in Daviess county, buying a farm of one hundred acres in Madison township, about one and one-half miles east of the place on which his grandson, Marion M., now lives. By industry and thrift he was able, with the assistance of his sons, to add to this original tract, until, at the time of his death, he owned about two hundred acres of well-tilled land, comprising one of the best farms in that portion of the county. William Johnson was an excellent citizen and a good neighbor and was regarded as one of the leaders in his section, it being admitted to this day that he exerted a large influence in the development of that section.

To William and Rachael (Vaughn) Johnson were born six children: five sons and one daughter, David, James, Edward, Æsop, Jane and Bryson, the latter of whom was the father of the immediate subject of this biographical sketch.

Bryson Johnson was born in Tuscarawas county, Ohio, and came to this county with his parents upon their migration hither when he was about fifteen years old. He received his early education in the subscription schools of Madison township, in what was known in that day as the Malone school, later attending the Herron school, and upon reaching manhood's estate began farming, his father having reared him in that vocation. He was a farmer all his life and made a pronounced success of his business. He owned one hundred and sixty acres of fine land, one hundred and twenty acres in Madison township, and forty acres in Elmore township. Mr. Johnson married Lydia Overton, and he and his wife were leaders in the social life of their community and did much for the advancement of the best interests of that section.

To Bryson and Lydia (Overton) Johnson were born seven children, as follow: Marion M., the subject of this sketch; Greenville, who married Emma R. Long and lives in Elnora, where he is successfully engaged in the hardware business; Reverend William, who was graduated from DePauw University, married Jennie C. Walls, and is now a resident minister of the

Gospel in St. Paul, Minnesota; Moses, who died in infancy; Levi, who married Margaret Chambers, lives on the old home place in Madison township; Thomas and Rachael, twins, the former of whom married Dora Bowers and lives in New Philadelphia, Ohio, and the latter of whom married Edward Killion, and is now deceased, and Ada, who, after the death of her sister, Rachael, married Edward Killion, her deceased sister's husband. Mr. and Mrs. Johnson reared their family in the faith of the United Brethren church, in the various local beneficences of which they ever took an active part. Mr. Johnson was a Democrat and took a good citizen's part in the political affairs of his county, his influence ever being exerted in behalf of good government.

Marion M. Johnson was educated in the public schools of his home township and was one of the first to be graduated from the common schools of Madison township, under the present system of township high schools. He was reared as a farmer, his father giving him ample instructions in the science of successful agriculture and upon reaching manhood, started farming for himself. In 1887, he bought forty acres of land in Elmore township, and lived there until 1899, in which year he bought his present farm in the same township. His original tract included but forty acres, but by diligence and thrift, he was able to add to this, as the years went by, until now he owns an excellent farm of one hundred and forty-five acres, on which he is successfully engaged in general farming and stock raising. In 1909, he built his present commodious barn, having built in 1890 the barn on his other farm, also building an addition to the house on that place. In all his undertakings, Mr. Johnson has had a most faithful and competent helpmeet in his wife, who, before her marriage on December 3, 1884, was Ida J. Slinkard, the daughter of Moses and Sarah (Smeltzer) Slinkard of Greene county, and he ungrudgingly ascribes much of his present success to her earnest assistance at all times, and particularly during the early days of their struggle to make and maintain for themselves a definite establishment in the prosperous farming community in which they are located. They started their married life with five dollars' worth of furniture besides the cook stove, and by hard work and careful management have accumulated an excellent farm, insuring for themselves a competence in their declining years. As a proper lesson in industry and prudent thrift this is an example which it would be well for many young people of the present day to take to heart.

To Marion M. and Ida J. (Slinkard) Johnson nine children have been born, as follow: Melvin, who married Sina Killion, to which union one child has been born, a son, Kenneth; Jennie May, who died at the age of eight years; Lestie, who married Edwin Winkleplack and has two children, Clifford J. and Bernice; Willis, who died at the age of fourteen months; Helen, at home; Ervilla; Edith; Edison, who died at the age of two years, and Emerson.

Mr. and Mrs. Johnson are faithful and influential members of the United Brethren church, in the faith of which they have reared their children and in the local affairs of which they take a warm interest, ever being found ready to further any cause having as its object the advancement of the best interests of the community, and are very properly regarded as among the leaders in the social life of the neighborhood. Mr. Johnson is a Democrat.

STEPHEN STALCUP.

Among the prominent families of Elmore township, Daviess county, Indiana, few are better known than that of the Stalcups, and certainly none more deservedly entitled to recognition in a historical work of this character, for the family of Mrs. Stephen Stalcup, who was an Elmore before her marriage, enjoyed the distinction of giving to that important division of the county in which they lived the name of Elmore township, and Elmore for many years has been one of the most familiar in the county.

Stephen Stalcup was born on September 17, 1882, on the farm on which he still lives in Elmore township, the old Stalcup homestead, the son of Henry S. and Elizabeth (Feltner) Stalcup, the former of whom was born near Pleasantville, Sullivan county, Indiana, on April 4, 1836, the son of Stephen and Sarah Ann (Smock) Stalcup, the former of whom was born in Tennessee in the year 1794 and died in Sullivan county in 1876.

Stephen Stalcup, grandfather of the subject of this sketch, was for many years one of the best-known and most prominent farmers of Sullivan county, and was known far and wide in that part of the state as a successful dealer in live stock. He was influential in the affairs of his locality, and he and his wife were among the leaders in the good works of that neighborhood. To Stephen and Sarah (Smock) Stalcup were born four children: Henry S., father of the gentleman whose name appears at the top of this biographical narrative; Amos; Lycurgus and Frank.

Reared on the home farm near Pleasantville, Henry S. Stalcup was educated in the schools of that village. As a young man, he started farming for himself, coming to Daviess county and buying a farm of forty acres in

Elmore township at the point at which his son still resides. He was an energetic and enterprising farmer and his affairs prospered largely. He gradually added to his original farm until, at the time of his death, he was the owner of two hundred and twenty-five acres of excellent farm land, the greater part of which was in a high state of cultivation. In addition to his farming, Mr. Stalcup was interested in other enterprises in the neighborhood and was one of the heaviest stockholders in the canning factory at Elnora.

On August 4, 1859, Henry S. Stalcup was united in marriage to Elizabeth Feltner, who was born on January 26, 1841, the daughter of Nicholas and Sophia (Atchley) Feltner, the former of whom was born on March 7, 1817, and who was married, September 3, 1835. To Henry S. and Elizabeth (Feltner) Stalcup there were born seven children, as follow: Laura, deceased, born on January 27, 1861, married John Wadsworth and left two children, Roscoe C. and Lettie I.; Sherman M., December 19, 1865, died in October, 1885; George A., November 19, 1868, died in 1888; Sophia, deceased, died in October, 1887; Emmazilla, died on August 17, 1865; Henry N., July 18, 1876, died in August, 1896, and Stephen, the immediate subject of this sketch. The father of the above children died on May 12, 1908, the mother having predeceased him some years, her death having occurred in October, 1887. Mr. and Mrs. Stalcup reared their children in the faith of the Church of Christ, at Elnora, in the affairs of which congregation they ever took a deep interest and were regarded as among the leaders in all movements designed to promote the best development of that neighborhood. Mr. Stalcup was a Republican and took an active part in the campaigns of his party in this county, ever being counted on the side of good government.

Stephen Stalcup was reared on the home farm, in Elmore township, and received his education in the public schools of that township. Upon reaching manhood's estate, he continued to remain on the home farm, assisting his father in the management of the same, and now owns the old home place, a fine farm of one hundred and forty-five acres, in addition to which he farms another tract near by, the entire amount of land which he has under cultivation being two hundred and fifty acres. In addition to general farming and stock raising, Mr. Stalcup, until a few years ago, was actively interested in the canning factory at Elnora, of which, at one time, he was the heaviest stockholder, having been manager of the same during the years 1912 and 1913, in which latter year he sold his interest in the plant. In 1910, Mr. Stalcup added to the farm buildings which his father had erected on the place, a commodious barn, and, in 1914, erected a silo. He is today recognized as the most extensive grower of alfalfa in Daviess county, and is otherwise regarded as an exceptionally enterprising and energetic young farmer.

On June 7, 1903, Stephen Stalcup was united in marriage with Stella Elmore, who was born in Elmore township, this county, on July 14, 1876, and who is a great-granddaughter of the founder of Elmore township and of the town of Elnora, she being the daughter of Abraham and Lydia (Brintsfield) Stalcup, the former of whom was the son of Stephen Elmore, whose father and brother were the first settlers of that section of the county. They entered the land on which the town of Elnora is situated and the township was given its name in their honor.

Stephen Elmore married Ruth Dillon and to this union were born six children: John, Isaac, Thomas, Dee, Mary and Abraham, the latter of whom was the father of Mrs. Stalcup, who was the sole issue of his marriage with Lydia Brintsfield, a member of another of the old families of that section. Abraham Elmore predeceased his wife and she married, secondly, David Simpkins, to which latter union one child was born, a son, Oscar.

To Stephen and Stella (Elmore) Stalcup one child has been born, a son, Henry Elmore, who was born on April 23, 1904. Mr. and Mrs. Stalcup are members of the Church of Christ at Elnora and are among the most active workers in the various good movements of that organization. Mr. Stalcup is a Republican and gives close attention to the political affairs of the county, being deeply interested in good government. He is a Mason and a Red Man, being much interested in the affairs of those two societies. In other ways he also takes a prominent part in the affairs of the community and is very properly regarded as one of the leading citizens of that part of the county.

JOHN W. WEAVER.

Among the fine farm homes in Elmore township, Daviess county, Indiana, there is one which rarely fails to attract the admiring attention of the casual passerby. This is the home of the gentleman whose name introduces this interesting biographical narrative, one of the best-known and most popular men in the northern part of the county. Mr. Weaver not only has made a most gratifying success of his extensive farming operations, but his work as an auctioneer at stock sales and crier at farm sales, has made his a familiar figure among the people of that entire section, and it is needless to say that he is popular wherever he goes. So well known is he, in fact, and so much a part of the public life of his time has he become in that section, that no history of Daviess county, and particularly in that section of the county in which he resides, would be a proper reflection of the times without due mention of Mr. Weaver and the part he is taking in the development of the county's best interests. The biographer finds pleasure, therefore, in asking the reader's attention to the following brief and modest biographical sketch:

John W. Weaver was born in Elmore township, Daviess county, Indiana, on July 6, 1880, the son of David and Lovina (Haynes) Weaver, the former of whom was born in Madison township, this county, on September 20, 1842, died on September 8, 1908, and the latter of whom was born in Orange county, Indiana, on November 3, 1853, and is still living, an honored member of the household of her son, John W., on the homestead farm in Elmore township.

David Weaver was the son of Jacob and Charlotta (Kinneman) Weaver, the former of whom was born near Adamsburg, in Westmoreland county, Pennsylvania, died in Madison township, Daviess county, in the year 1890, in which township he for many years was one of the most conspicuous figures. In the year 1829, Jacob Weaver migrated from Pennsylvania to Kentucky, locating in Fayette county, in the latter state, where he remained until the year 1841, in which year he moved with his family to Daviess county, locating in Madison township, where he resumed his trade of blacksmith, being a very highly skilled craftsman in that line. He bought a farm in Madison township, which his sons operated while he was engaged in the blacksmith shop, until his retirement was rendered compulsory by blindness overtaking him, and the last fourteen years of his life was spent in darkness. Grandfather Weaver was a man of strong personality and his counsels and advice among his neighbors exerted a large influence in his time.

To Jacob and Charlotta (Kinneman) Weaver were born nine children: William, Jacob, Peter, Abraham, David, Daniel, Susannah, Charlotta and Phoebe. These children were brought up in the rigid faith of the Lutheran church and the sons followed in the political footsteps of their father, all being Democrats and men of influence in the affairs of their community.

David Weaver was reared on the paternal farm in Madison township and received such early education as he was able to acquire in the subscription schools of his time, in that township, his educational facilities, however, being of the meagerst sort. As a young man, he learned the trade of carpenter and followed this much of his life in connection with his work on the farm. He owned and operated a farm of one hundred and eighty-six acres in Elmore township, the same on which his son, John W. now lives. The original tract he bought there was but eighty acres, but as his affairs prospered he enlarged his holdings until, at the time of his death, he possessed the considerable farm above mentioned, all of which was in an excellent state of cultivation. David Weaver was united in marriage to Lovina Haynes, a native of Orange county, Indiana, a member of one of the old families of that section of the state, and to this union there were born but two children, John W., the immediate subject of this sketch, and Elva, the latter of whom was born on July 15, 1885, and died on September 12, 1901. David Weaver was an active worker in the Mission Baptist church, and was a Democrat who took an active part in the political affairs of that community.

Reared on the farm, John W. Weaver received his schooling in what was then known as the Mud Pike school in Elmore township. At the age of eighteen, he started farming in partnership with his father, and has been a farmer all his life, living continuously on the place on which he was born, and which he greatly improved, in 1911, by the erection of his present very comfortable and pleasant home. He adds to this general farming, stock raising on a fairly extensive scale and has had considerable success in this latter line. Mr. Weaver early developed into an unusually successful auctioneer and his services in that direction are in much demand, not only in his own part of the county, but elsewhere in this section of the state, and he cries farm and stock sales for miles and miles in every direction thereabout, being one of the most popular auctioneers in the county.

On September 6, 1903, John W. Weaver was united in marriage to Gertrude Hackler, who was born on July 27, 1885, the daughter of George and Sarah B. (Groves) Hackler, of Elmore township, this county, and to this happy union five children have been born, as follow: Alvin, on June 1, 1904; Imo, January 10, 1906; Willis, December 12, 1908; John D., August 28, 1910, and George, April 23, 1914, a lively set of youngsters who are the delight of their devoted parents' lives and the light of their happy home.

Mr. and Mrs. Weaver are members of the United Brethren church and are bringing up their children in that faith. Mr. Weaver, as were his father and grandfather before him, is a Democrat, and his wide acquaintance throughout the county gives to his connection with that party a peculiar value which the campaign managers in his part of the county are not slow to recognize. He is a member of the Free and Accepted Masons and a member of the Tribe of Ben-Hur, in the affairs of both of which fraternal orders he takes a warm interest. He likewise takes a good citizen's part in all matters of public concern and is generally recognized in his community as one of the leaders of public thought and action. He is a man of large personality, serene temperament and evenly-balanced, well-rounded character, who is liked by all who know him. No one in Daviess county takes a warmer interest in the county's welfare than he and in his home community he is continually to be found "boosting" wherever he goes. It is such citizens as Mr. Weaver that make so strongly for good government and right living and he gives ungrudgingly of his time and talents in promoting all good causes.

GEORGE F. TODD.

No history of Daviess county, and particularly no review of the life of that section of the county comprised in the Elnora neighborhood, in Elmore township, would be complete without proper mention of the Todd family, and of the hale old gentleman whose name appears as the caption of this interesting biographical narrative. Of the true pioneer breed, George F. Todd is one of the interesting survivals which so definitely connect the generation of pioneers in this section with the present generation, and the biographer takes much pleasure in here presenting a brief review of the salient points in his interesting career. No one in his part of the county is better known or more universally popular than Mr. Todd, and it is proper that this sketch should appear in this work in order that the future historian of this section who may turn to these pages for data relating to the present period in the development of Daviess county, may find preserved there information relating to this pioneer family that ought not to be lost in the annals of this quiet neighborhood.

George F. Todd was born in Monroe county, Indiana, on June 7, 1845, the son of John and Elizabeth (Hayes) Todd, the former of whom was born in Bourbon county, Kentucky, and the latter of whom was born in Watauga, North Carolina, on October 15, 1800, and who died in the year 1904, at the age of one hundred and four. John Todd came to Indiana from Kentucky when a young man and settled in Monroe county, where he became one of the best-known and most prominent men in his section. There he met the woman who became his wife, and the two reared their family there, spending all their lives in Monroe county, with the exception of about two years, during which they lived in Missouri, to which state they had moved in 1840. Returning to Monroe county, following their western experience, they again engaged in farming, and, at the time of his death, John Todd was possessed of two hundred and forty acres of land, the larger part of which was in an excellent state of cultivation. He lived to be eighty-six years of age, his health practically unimpaired to within a short time of his death. He was a strong, vigorous man, active and alert, and, at eighty, was able to go to the woods and pick off a squirrel with his trusty old squirrel rifle with as true an aim as in his younger days. He was a man of large influence in his neighborhood and his memory is not forgotten there to this day. Elizabeth (Hayes) Todd, wife of John Todd, who survived him many years, was a remarkable woman and no one in that part of the state was better known or better liked than was she. Elizabeth Hayes, who was a native of North Carolina, was bereft of her mother by death when she was ten years of age, after which she migrated with her father to Tennessee, a little later coming to Indiana, and settling in Monroe county. At that time, the part of the county in which the Hayes family located, was a wilderness, very few white persons having penetrated to that section, and there the future wife of John Todd grew to a vigorous womanhood. When the Monon railway penetrated that part of the state and a station was located near the old Todd home, the station was named Todd, in honor of the little woman who had lived there so many years. Mrs. Todd remained in excellent health until a short time before her death, at the remarkable age of one hundred and four, often being seen riding horse-back over the hills of Monroe county after she had passed her centenary mark. Longevity seemed to be characteristic of her family, her brother, David Hayes, who was a well-known resident of Bloomington, this state, living to be one hundred and two.

To John and Elizabeth (Hayes) Todd were born eight children, as follow: David, who married Eliza Ramsey; Catherine, who married Hezekiah Norman; Eliza, deceased, who married George Helton; Elijah, deceased, who married Mary Anna Sisco; Isaac, who married Eliza Bates; George F., the immediate subject of this sketch; Emily, who married Andrew Piercy, and Alice, who married John Mitchell. The Todds reared their large family in the faith of the Methodist church, in the local beneficences of which they were very active, and were among the leaders in the good works of that community. John Todd was a Democrat and was influential in the councils of that party in his section, his sons following his example in the expressions of their political allegiance.

George F. Todd received his education in the local schools of his neighborhood, and, as a young man, started farming in Monroe county, remaining there until the year 1871, when he moved into Greene county, where he remained one year, living in the vicinity of Gandys Bluff, where Doctor Gandy fell from the bluff and was partly eaten by hogs. He then came into Daviess county and located in Elmore township, where he ever since has made his home, and where he prospered in his farming operations. He owns an excellent farm of one hundred and sixty acres in Elmore township, besides an equal tract of land in Monroe county, the latter being a part of the old Todd home farm. Mr. Todd has been an extensive breeder of live stock, his Percherons and jacks and jennets being widely known throughout this part of the county. He also has been an extensive shipper of stock and has found no small profit in the pursuit of this phase of farming.

In the year 1867, George F. Todd was united in marriage with Amanda E. Sisco, the daughter of Perry and Mary Sisco, of Monroe county, and to this union two children were born: Sheridan, on November 11, 1871, was married on November 22, 1893, to Mary Malone, who was born on March 17, 1877, and to whom was born one child, a daughter, Helen, born on February 1, 1904; and Nora O., December 2, 1881, married a Mr. Goldstone, and lives in New York. The mother of these children died in 1883, since which time Mr. Todd has lived alone on his farm east of Elnora.

Since the year 1868, Mr. Todd has been a Mason, his membership being in the lodge at Newberry, and he takes a warm interest in the affairs of that ancient ritualistic order. He became a Mason at Tunnelton, in June, 1869. As was his father before him, Mr. Todd is an ardent Democrat and takes a good citizen's part in the local campaigns of that party, being much interested in all matters relating to good government. Mr. Todd is a fine, hale and hearty old gentleman, who enjoys the fullest confidence and respect of his neighbors throughout that whole section of the county. Coming of a sturdy stock, he retains the vigor of younger days and takes the liveliest interest in current affairs, keeping fully abreast of the times in all things. As a boy he learned to love the great out-door life, and ascribes much of his present vigor to his life of activity in the open. His father was a great deer hunter, and, as a lad, Mr. Todd learned all the tricks of deer stalking and has many interesting stories to tell of the sport of the early days in this section of the state. His father, at one time, was compelled to defend himself against the desperate charge of a wounded buck, his clothes being torn to shreds by the antlers of the enraged animal before he finally succeeded in cutting the buck's throat. When he was a boy he hunted with his father, and shouldering a pack, would follow the deer in the snow until they came to the crossing, when his father would shoot them.

SILAS M. KETCHEM.

In 1920, only a few years hence, will come the three-hundredth year since the Pilgrim Fathers sailed into Provincetown harbor and later planted their feet on Plymouth Rock. This will be a great event in the history of America and the world, and for the descendants of those who were in the ship "Mayflower," the leader, or in some other ship that came to the shores of the New World with loads of Pilgrim men and women from across the seas between 1620 and 1700. Bancroft declares rightly that "the emigration of the fathers (and mothers) of these twelve commonwealths, with the planting of the principles upon which they rested, was the most momentous event of the seventeenth century. The elements of our country, as she exists today, were already there." In Daviess county there is a no inconsiderable strain of the old Pilgrim breed and among those of that honorable descent here, few families are better known than that of the Ketchems, a brief biography of one of the worthy present-day representatives of which is herewith presented.

Silas M. Ketchem was born in Elmore township, Daviess county, Indiana, on May 19, 1864, the son of Joseph and Charity (Ledgerwood) Ketchem, the former of whom was born in the same township and county, the son of Silas and Mary (Courtney) Ketchem, the latter of whom was born in Greene county, the daughter of David Ledgerwood, a pioneer of that section of the state.

Silas Ketchem was a native of South Carolina, the son of Joseph Ketchem, who also was born in South Carolina, of Pilgrim stock, migrated to Tennessee in the early years of the last century and there married Mary Courtney and, about the year 1830, came to Indiana, selecting Daviess county as a place of residence, and located in Elmore township, early becoming one of the most substantial citizens of this section of the state. He was a man of unusual personality, strong and vigorous, kindly and courteous in demeanor and possessed of extraordinary executive ability, which he exercised so successfully that at the time of his death he was the owner of more than one thousand acres of land in Greene and Daviess counties.

To the union of Silas and Mary (Courtney) Ketchem there were ten children: Marshall, Jane, Joseph, William, Stephen, Caroline, Jacob, James, Nancy and Solomon, the numerous progeny of whom forms today a very important element in the social and industrial life of this section.

Of these children, Joseph, who was born in Elmore township, Daviess county, on November 18, 1828, became one of the leading citizens of his township, having been a farmer in a large way to the time of his death, October 15, 1896. He lived in Elmore township all his life, with the exception of a year or two during which he made his home in Greene county. He was a man of large influence in his community and did very much toward bringing about proper conditions in the social and economic life of that portion of the county. At the time of his death he owned three hundred and thirty acres of land, two hundred acres of which lay in Greene county, the rest in Elmore township, this county.

Joseph Ketchem married Charity Ledgerwood, who was born in Greene county, on February 26, 1830, a member of a pioneer family of that county, and to this union there were born seven children, as follow: David J., on September 3, 1854, died on March 15, 1890; Elizabeth, August 14, 1857, died on August 7, 1876; Mary J., May 3, 1859, died on July 31, 1876; Annetta, December 29, 1862, died on June 24, 1863; Silas M., subject of this sketch; George M., August 5, 1867, married Nettie Vories and lives in Elnora; Stephen E., July 6, 1870, died on July 24, 1876. Joseph Ketchem was a Democrat and took an active part in the political affairs of the county, his counsels receiving much consideration in the deliberations of the party managers in this county. He reared his family in the faith of the Mission Baptist church, and also took a warm interest in all movements for the betterment of conditions in his community, and was much mourned when his death occurred on October 15, 1896. His wife died on January 18, 1890.

Silas M. Ketchem was educated in the district schools of his home township and has lived in Elmore township all his life. He has a fine farm of one hundred and nine acres and is very well circumstanced, his farm showing every evidence of thrift and industry on his part. He is what properly may be called a modern farmer, being content with none but the best and most approved methods in tilling his farm, and, as a consequence, has made a success of his business. He gives considerable attention to stock raising, and also has been quite successful in his venture in that phase of farming. Being a member of one of the oldest and most prominent families in his neighborhood, Mr. Ketchem has a well-established position in the community, and is recognized as among the leaders among the men of affairs thereabout, his interest in all matters relating to the betterment of social and civic conditions in his home township being well known.

On October 1, 1899, Silas M. Ketchem was united in marriage to Emma Miles, who was born on September 29, 1877, the daughter of Patrick and Nancy (Burch) Miles, old residents of Martin county, and to this union five children have been born, as follow: Joseph C., on April 30, 1901; Velma M., August 20, 1902; Mabel May, January 26, 1904; Frederick S., June 27, 1906, and Ruth E., January 31, 1908, bright and lively youngsters who make merry the home of their devoted parents.

Mr. Ketchem is a member of the Baptist church and Mrs. Ketchem is a member of the Methodist church, both being active in the affairs of the congregations to which they are respectively attached. Mr. Ketchem gives his political allegiance to the Democratic party and takes a proper interest in the campaigns of that party in local elections. He and Mrs. Ketchem are active in the social affairs of their neighborhood and are deservedly popular in their large circle of acquaintances.

JOHN EADS.

All progress is continuous; one generation merely gathering the ripe fruit of the labors of its predecessors, each succeeding generation building on the foundation laid by others. Every man is a quotation from all his ancestors. "Rely upon it," declared the great William E. Gladstone, "that the man who does not worthily estimate his own dead forefathers, will himself do very little to add credit or do honor to his country." America has a goodly heritage, which we should endeavor to hand on with value unimpaired to those who shall come after us. Only as we realize our own high duty and responsibility, shall we be able to bequeath to posterity the noble inheritance we, ourselves, have received. There are many old families in Daviess county who cherish most sacredly the traditions which have come down from honorable forbears and who are doing their utmost to hand these traditions on, unsullied by any act of theirs. Among the families which have helped to add luster to the good name of this favored commonwealth, few are better known than that of the gentleman whose name is noted above, the Eads family having been active in the affairs of this county for four generations and have created a stock here which promises to be one of the most persistent and progressive in the community. As a guide to the future historian who may find help in this volume in his work of compiling a story which shall be a fair reflection of the present time, the biographer finds much pleasure in presenting here something of the history of the family of John Eads in this section of the state.

John Eads, one of the most progressive and popular farmers of Elmore township, was born in Washington township, Daviess county, Indiana, on February 11, 1859, the son of John H. and Charity (Wykoff) Eads, the former of whom was born in Dearborn county on February 21, 1821, and the latter born in October, 1820, John H. having been the son of Elijah Eads, one of the pioneers of this portion of the state, who migrated from New Jersey in the early part of the last century, locating first in Dearborn county, this state, later coming to Daviess county when his son, John H., was a small boy. Here Elijah Eads bought the place known as the Storms farm, adding to the same until he had a tract of three hundred and twenty acres, on which he resided for about a quarter of a century, making for himself a distinctive place in the community, having been known as one of the most influential and useful men of his period in this section. He was among the foremost and most honored pioneers of that region. He brought to the then wilderness knowledge and experience which his widely separated neighbors soon learned to rely upon, and it is undoubted that his influence in that community did very much toward bringing about proper conditions of social and economic life in the formative period of the now prosperous and established farming region. He and the woman who was ever at his side, a true pioneer helpmeet, long have been gathered to their fathers, resting well after the stern labors which their hands found to do, and the fifth generation of their descendants in that community finds conditions of living immeasurably easier for their having striven—"blazing the ways."

This pioneer was but a type. Particular reference is made to him here, not as an invidious distinction, but that the present generation may be casually reminded of these honored forefathers of the commonwealth. There were many like him in that community in his day and generation. Of necessity this must have been so—the stalwart men who leveled the forests—and the readers of this volume, will find much of informative interest in these pages as they thoughtfully peruse this valuable collection of family reminiscences, something of the lives of that now long-gone pioneer breed, narrated by those who have not permitted the information wholly to be lost.

Late in life, Elijah Eads moved into the town of Washington, being content to retire from the arduous duties of the farm and there he spent the last few years of his life, his passing causing sincere mourning among a very wide circle of acquaintances. His son, John H., father of the subject of this sketch, was reared on the paternal farm, and, upon reaching manhood, started farming for himself in Washington township, in what is known as Sugarland, where he owned a well-improved place of one hundred acres, and there he remained all the rest of his life, doing, in all things, his full duty by the community, being known as a leader in all movements designed to advance the public welfare. He and his good wife were among the foremost residents of that neighborhood and their helpful counsels have not been forgotten there to this day.

On May 8, 1845, John H. Eads was united in marriage to Charity Wykoff, a member of one of the pioneer families of that neighborhood, and to this union were born seven children, as follow: Eliza Ann, on March 6, 1846, and who married John Jones; Lucy and Hannah, twins, July 16, 1848, the former of whom maried Frank Cross and the latter of whom married R. H. Bell and died on July 30, 1874; Lida, September 10, 1850, died in October of the next year; Sarah, January 10, 1853, died on January 14, 1875, at the age of twenty-two years; and John, the immediate subject of this sketch, who had a twin brother, who died in infancy. John H. Eads was an ardent Republican, taking an active interest in the political affairs of his county, and was a member of and brought up his family in the Mission Baptist church.

John Eads was educated in the public schools of Washington township, and, as a young man, assisted his father on the home farm, continuing to live there, after his father's death, until the year 1900, when he sold the home place and bought his present farm of one hundred and thirty acres in Elmore township, where he is successfully engaged in general farming and stock raising, giving particular attention to the breeding of Shorthorn cattle. He has four strong, healthy boys, whose assistance in the work of the farm their father finds invaluable and who are being brought up to regard the life of the farmer as the most free and independent manner of living, and who give promise in their sturdy young manhood of worthily maintaining the honorable traditions of family life which they so fortunately have inherited. In addition to his home farm, Mr. Eads owns another fine property of one hundred and twenty acres, in Elmore township. On the home farm, he has a splendid home, in which comfort and happiness abound and which is one of the most popular social centers in the community.

Mr. Eads has been twice married. He was first united in marriage to Nettie Muret, daughter of Julius and Eliza Muret, who died on April 30, 1889, to which union three children were born, Eliza, who married Caswell Woodruff, has two children, Lovida M. and Leonard; Bessie, who married Thomas Nugent and has three children, Muret, Thomas and Paul, and

Julius, who died in infancy. In 1893, Mr. Eads married, secondly, Mary E. Tomey, daughter of John and Edith (Ross) Tomey, and to this union four children have been born, Leonard, on September 17, 1894; Floyd, March 29, 1897; Frank, July 2, 1900, and Seth, January 21, 1904, all of whom are at home and who make a lively household for their devoted parents. The family are members of the United Brethren church and are active in all the good works of the community. Mr. Eads is a Republican, and while ever taking a warm interest in local campaigns, being deeply concerned in all matters of good government, has never been included in the office-seeking class, finding his chief pleasure in developing his fine farm lands and in providing for the comfort and happiness of his interesting family.

EDWARD W. BEAN.

It is a well-known fact that success comes as a result of legitimate and well-applied energy, determination and perseverance in a course of action when once decided upon. Success is never known to come to the idler or dreamer, and she never courts the loafer, and only the men who have diligently sought her favor are crowned with her blessings. The man whose name appears at the head of this sketch is one who enjoys a fair portion of success in this community as a result of his strict application and well-directed energies, and has gained for himself the high esteem of his fellowmen.

Edward W. Bean was born on February 19, 1865, in Harrison county, Indiana, and is the son of Charles H. and Nancy A. (Gwartney) Bean, also natives of Harrison county, the former born on March 6, 1842, and the latter on November 7, 1844. The paternal grandfather, Pleasant D. Bean, was born near the town of Knoxville, Tennessee, and came with his parents when fourteen years of age to Corydon, Harrison county, where he received his early education, farmed for a time, and afterward taught school, then later, was county assessor. His wife was Elizabeth Farquar, daughter of William and Elizabeth Farquar, and she gave birth to the following named children: James T.; John; Aaron A.; William; Anna; Charles H., subject's father; George D.; Catherine; Sallie; Milton and Benjamin.

Charles H. Bean was educated in the public schools of Harrison county, but spent very little time in school. At the breaking out of the Civil War, he became anxious to serve his country and enlisted in the year 1861, as a member of Company B, Third Indiana Cavalry, and served until December, 1863, when he was honorably discharged. After serving in the army, he started farming in Harrison county and remained there until 1879, when he went to Greene county and farmed, as a renter, until 1882, and then bought a farm consisting of seventy-one acres, in section 11, of Elmore township, Daviess county, which he farmed for the next five years and then retired from active business. He is residing in Elnora, with his wife, who was a daughter of John B. and Martha Jenkins, and who gave birth to the following children: Edward W., the subject of this sketch; Addie L., who married George Westman, and who have three daughters; Benjamin T., who married Maggie Ward and lives in Montana, and who have one child living and one dead; Effie H., who married Jacob Christopher Weaver; Otto, whose first wife was Lulu Weathers, and who is now married to Flora Williams, who had one child, deceased; Maud, who married Lemuel Gedburg; John W., who married Mary Swayzee, to whom one child was born; Coy, whose first husband was James Swayzee, deceased, and who is now the wife of James Manning, to whom one son was born.

Edward W. Bean, the subject of this sketch, received his education in the public schools of Harrison and Daviess counties, and started farming when quite a young man. In this work he has been successful in raising general crops and live stock. His first land purchase was a forty-acre tract in Elmore township, which he held for about four or five years, then sold it. He next purchased eighty acres in the same township, section 29, and kept this for a period of nine years, then in 1908, bought eighty acres in section 21, known as the east half of the northeast quarter section, and it is on this place that Edward makes his home. Edward W. Bean was married to Delila W. Frets, daughter of Abraham Frets, to which union have been born the following children: Virgil A.; Ray; Carl, deceased infant; Charles; Beulah; Harold; Frank, and Frederick.

Mr. Bean upholds the standards of the Republican party and can be depended upon to render assistance to his party when duty calls him. He is a member of the Modern Woodmen of America, and he is a regular member of the United Brethren church, as is also his wife and family. Personally, Mr. Bean is considered a good-natured, easily approached, straightforward and unassuming gentleman. He commands the respect of all with whom he comes in contact and his friends are in number as his acquaintances.

WILLIAM H. COURTNEY.

America is in the making. The blending of her various peoples into one homogeneous whole to work out the vast problems of civilization both for herself and the entire world, is the immediate task before her. The descendants of the original settlers will be expected to stand foremost among the many in projecting the activities of the future. This is true not only in the wider national sense, but in the more immediate local sense. The burden of obligation rests upon the descendants of those who first made clear the ways hereabout. To the old families of the commonwealth the newcomers naturally look for direction, and this is well and proper. The influence of these old families in the local field, therefore, cannot be estimated too highly. That the present generation of the fine old stock that "blazed the ways" in Daviess county is giving a good account of its worthy heritage, is amply demonstrated in countless local instances, and it does not require the pen of the present reviewer to give proper credit for the noble manner in which the traditions of the past have been maintained by the energetic descendants of those pioneers to whom this section of the state owes so much. It is proper, however, that due attention be paid in a work of this character to the present representatives of those early families and it is a pleasure, therefore, for the biographer here to present a brief and modest review of the gentleman whose name appears at the top of this sketch, a very worthy representative in the present generation of one of Daviess county's best-known and most influential pioneer families.

William H. Courtney was born in Elmore township, Daviess county, on October 6, 1876, the son of James H. and Elizabeth (Crotz) Courtney, both of whom were born in the same township and county, the former being the son of James S. and Frances Ann (Moore) Courtney, pioneers of that neighborhood.

In his day one of the leading men in his part of Daviess county, James S. Courtney was born on September 8, 1811, and his wife, who was Frances Ann Moore, was born on January 29, 1825, she also being of pioneer stock in this county. James S. Courtney was a farmer, and in addition to his work on the farm, he was well known, locally, as a cabinetmaker, he having become a skilled craftsman in that line, and his labors in this connection were much in demand on the part of his neighbors. Many a piece of substantial furniture still in use in that neighborhood, bears conclusive evidence to this day of the thorough character of his work.

To James S. and Frances Ann (Moore) Courtney were born eleven children, as follow: Mary Ann, on August 6, 1842, married Jacob Wesner; William M., October 7, 1843, died in his youth; John A., January 27, 1845, married Mary Treed; James H., father of the immediate subject of this biographical sketch; Thomas J., August 29, 1848, died in his youth; Levi M., October 15, 1849, married Frances Mumaw; Joseph G., March 28, 1852, married Lovina Dillon; Nancy Ann, March 26, 1854, married Frank P. Meyers; Elizabeth S., December 31, 1858, married Thomas D. Slimp; George W., November 23, 1859, married Nancy M. Johnson and has three children, Nellie B., who married Charles Trotter, Ralph and Edna; Sarah F., March 7, 1862, married John Hasting and died on March 10, 1881.

James H. Courtney was born on November 23, 1846. He was reared on the paternal farm in Elmore township, receiving such advantages of schooling as his home township afforded in that day, and, upon his marriage, began farming for himself, early becoming recognized as among the leaders in the social and economic development of that section of the county. He became a man of substance and was active in all the good works of his community, his influence ever being exerted in behalf of all movements having as their object the advancement of the community interest. His death occurred on March 27, 1905, and there was sincere mourning throughout that part of the county at his passing. Mr. Courtney was thrice married. By this union with Magdeline Treed, he had two children, Thomas W., who was born on June 20, 1870, who died on April 16, 1911, and Mary M., on November 26, 1872, who died on April 19, 1880. Upon the death of his first wife, Mr. Courtney married, secondly, on November 8, 1875, Elizabeth Crotz, born on October 11, 1851, who died on October 11, 1876, to which union there was born but one child, a son, William H., with whom this article directly treats. Mr. Courtney's third wife was Mrs. Nancy Grabill, who was born on January 17, 1848, and who died on July 11, 1909. To this union there was no issue.

William H. Courtney was educated in the schools of his native township, was reared to the life of a farmer and has followed that vocation all his life. By diligence and industry he has attained a position in the community well in keeping with that of his forbears and is recognized, as were they, as among the leaders in that part of the county. He has owned his present fine farm, of one hundred and twenty-seven acres, since 1910, during which time he has greatly improved the place, rebuilding the house and barn, erecting additional outbuildings and putting the farm in the best condition as regards fences, drainage, etc. Diligent in his own business, he is not neglectful of the duty which a good citizen owes to society at large and he finds time in connection with the labors of the farm to take part in all movements of a local character designed to improve the common welfare.

On October 16, 1904, William H. Courtney was united in marriage to Rosetta Kinnaman, who was born in this county on July 9, 1882, the daughter of Lafayette and Clara M. (Kepler) Kinnaman, well-known residents of the county, to which union two children have been born, a son and a daughter, Ethel L., and Ross K., lively and engaging youngsters who are the delight of the lives of their devoted parents and the light of their happy home.

Mr. and Mrs. Courtney are members of the United Brethren church at Mud Pike, and are active participants in the various beneficences of that congregation. They are counted as among the leaders in the social affairs of that neighborhood, there being no more popular couple thereabout than they. Mr. Courtney is a Republican and takes an earnest interest in the political issues of the day, the part of all good citizens. He has never been included in the office-seeking class, however, preferring to devote his whole time and energies to the growing interests of a splendid farm, and one of the pleasantest homes in the neighborhood, and he is looked upon in his community as an all-round, good citizen, whom his neighbors delight to honor, even as they honored his father and his grandfather before him.

CLYDE T. AMICK.

The man who devotes his time and energies to the noble work of educating the young, pursues a calling which, in dignity and importance and beneficial results, is second to none. If true to his efforts and earnest to enlarge his sphere of usefulness, he is indeed a benefactor to all his kind, for to him, more than to any other man, are entrusted the future careers of those placed in his charge. Amongst this class of professional men, is the gentleman whose name forms the heading of this sketch, and, who, for many years, has been identified with the people of Daviess county, who hold him high in their esteem on account of his broad human sympathy, honorable methods and constant devotion to his vocation as an instructor.

Clyde T. Amick was born in Scipio, Jennings county, Indiana, on September 5, 1880, and is the son of John D. and Nellie (McCosky) Amick, both of whom were natives of Clark county, Indiana. The father, John D.

Amick, received his early education in the public schools of his native county and afterward learned the trade of blacksmith, which occupied him for the next ten or twelve years in the town of Hartsville, Bartholomew county, this state. He discontinued the blacksmithing business and decided to engage in farming on a tract of land in the neighborhood of Hartsville, which he farmer as a renter, and, at a later date, purchased a farm of eighty-five acres near Scipio. After conducting general farming for a period of about seven years, he sold out and made a trip to Arkansas, where he remained until the following year, when he returned to Indiana and bought ten acres of land near the town of Scipio, Jennings county, where he resides at this time, with his wife, and leads a life of retirement from active business. To them were born the following named children: Elmer, who married Alice Cadby; Rosa, the wife of Albert Amick; Lola, the wife of Charles B. Morgan; Lena, deceased in 1915, and who was the wife of John W. Corya; Samuel, who married Lillie Corya; John P., who married Pearl May; Charles, who married Mabel Gannon; Albert, who married Aura Boston; Clyde, the subject of this sketch. The parents of these children are devout members of the Presbyterian church in Scipio, and in political aspirations, Mr. Amick is an ardent supporter of the Republican ticket.

Clyde T. Amick received his early education in the public schools of Scipio, during which time he resided under the parental roof. After going through the various school grades, he was graduated from the high school, then attended the Normal School in Danville, Indiana, where he remained for a term and then became enrolled in the State Normal School, at Terre Haute, graduating in 1909. He also studied special courses for three summer terms in the State University. Having made up his mind to continue in his chosen profession as a schoolmaster, and having taught for seven years in the Jennings county schools, Mr. Amick made due application and was appointed superintendent of schools in Elnora, Daviess county, and is occupied in that position at the present time.

On September 22, 1907, Professor Amick was married to Lucy Hulse, daughter of Jason and Elvia (Greathouse) Hulse. She was born on November 23, 1879, in Scipio. To their union have been born two children, Elizabeth H., on September 4, 1910, and Frances L., July 10, 1914.

Clyde J. Amick is a Republican and an aggressive advocate of the progressive principles of his party, but does not take any active part in politics. Mr. Amick and wife are firm believers in the Presbyterian faith, to which denomination they lend their support. Personally, Mr. Amick is a man highly esteemed by all who know him and has executed his educational duties in the town of Elnora for the past five years with great credit to himself and the community. Everyone throughout this section speaks well of him as being a man of genial disposition, unassuming, and socially inclined. He has a great many friends and is worthy, in every respect, of the trust reposed in him by his fellow men.

JOHN T. SMITH.

Among the successful self-made men of the past generation in Daviess county, whose efforts and influence have contributed to the material upbuilding of the community, was the late John T. Smith, who occupied a conspicuous place. Being ambitious from the first, but surrounded by none too favorable environment, his early years were not especially promising. Resolutely facing the future, however, he gradually surmounted the difficulties in his way, and, in due course of time, became a prominent farmer in Daviess county, Indiana. Moreover, he won the confidence and esteem of those with whom he came in contact, either in a business or a social way. For years he was regarded as one of the representative farmers of Daviess county. Early in life he realized that there is a purpose in life and that honor, not founded upon work, is futile. His life and labors were noteworthy, because they contributed to a proper understanding of life and its problems. The strongest characters in American history have come from the ranks of self-made men, to whom adversity acts as an impetus for unfaltering effort, and from this class came the lamented John T. Smith.

Mr. Smith was born on the farm where his widow, Mrs. Margaret Smith, now lives, in Harrison township, Daviess county, Indiana, on September 23, 1833. He died on February 29, 1912. John T. Smith was the son of Raphael and Mary Ann (Potts) Smith, the former of whom was born in Kentucky, in 1806, and who died in 1878, and the latter of whom was born in 1821, in Harrison township, Daviess county, and who died in 1892. Raphael Smith, when a young man, came from Kentucky to Daviess county and took up one hundred and twenty acres in Harrison township, at one dollar and twenty-five cents an acre. He lived there until his death. He and his wife were both members of the Catholic church. They had a family of four daughters and four sons.

John T. Smith grew up on his father's farm and bought out the other heirs for the old homestead and lived upon it until his death. John T. Smith came from sturdy Irish stock and was a thrifty farmer. He died of pneumonia, after three days in bed. He was well known in the county and could go to any bank and get money, as he was known to be honest and well-to-do.

The late John T. Smith was married on September 10, 1878, to Margaret (McDonald) McGuire, a widow who was born in Reeve township, Daviess county, on October 12, 1847. Mrs. Smith is the daughter of William and Bridget (Hughes) McDonald, both of whom were natives of Ireland, the former of County Kildare and the latter of County Tyrone. Bridget (Hughes) McDonald came to this country at the age of two years with her parents. They were six weeks in making the voyage from Ireland to New York city. William McDonald came to this country with his parents, who settled in Reeve township, Daviess county. He was killed as the result of a fall from a horse. William and Bridget (Hughes) McDonald had five children, Catherine, John, Margaret, Thomas B. and James, all of whom are now living, and all are more than sixty years of age.

Mrs. Margaret Smith was first married to James McGuire, who died of cholera in 1872. He was a coal miner and received five dollars a day for his services, which was considered enormous wages for that day. By this marriage there were four children born, Matilda Ann, who married William Brewer; William, who lives at Loogootee; John and Mary, who are deceased.

By her second marriage, Mrs. Smith was the mother of five children, Matthew and Leo are deceased; Francis lives in California, where he is a carpenter; Augustine is deceased; Alphonsus lives on the home place with his mother and Francis married Grace Toole. They have had four children, Veronica, Ada, Ernistine and Eleanor.

Alphonsus was married on September 30, 1909, to Lillian Ramsey and lives at Mt. Carmel, Illinois. She was a daughter of James and Frances Greathouse, both natives of Mt. Carmel, Illinois. He was a breeder of registered Poland China hogs, Polled Durham cattle, Barred Plymouth Rock chickens. To them were born two children, Noble E., who married Mary Rigg, who had one son, John Harold. Alphonsus and wife have four children, Frederick, Melvin, and Frances Granella, twins; Marguerette and John A.

The late John T. Smith was married twice. His first wife was Theresa McAtee. There were nine children born to this marriage, but only three of these children are now living, Dan is a carpenter in California; William lives in East St. Louis, and is unmarried, and Sophronia married James Worst and lives in Denver, Colorado.

The late John T. Smith was a splendid specimen of the race from which he sprang. A man of strong convictions and prodigious industry, he did much for the material progress of the community where he lived. He was known far and wide and was respected for definite and positive convictions.

JOSIAH G. ALLEN.

Josiah G. Allen, of the law firm of Hastings, Allen & Hastings, of Washington, this county, was born in Washington township, Daviess county, Indiana, on December 3, 1861, a son of Moses and Ann (Graham) Allen, also natives of this county, who were the parents of four children, of whom Josiah G. was the second in order of birth. Glendora, the eldest child, is the wife of W. C. W. Wright, of Washington township, this county; Decatur D. lives at Shreveport, Louisiana, and William B. lives in Washington, the county seat.

Moses Allen was born and reared in this county, the home farm having been a tract of land near the edge of the town of Washington. Shortly after his marriage he moved to Vigo county and purchased a farm of one hundred and twenty acres, where he reared his family, but later in life returned to Daviess county and spent his last days in a comfortable home at the edge of the city of Washington, his death occurring in February, 1911, he then being seventy-two years of age. His widow still survives and is now seventy-two years old. She is a member of the Baptist church, as was her husband. Moses Allen was the son of William Allen, a native of New Jersey, of English stock, who moved from New Jersey to Harrison, Ohio, coming to Daviess county after his marriage in 1816, and locating on a farm one mile east of Washington. William Allen and his wife, who was an Eads, were the parents of twelve children, William, John, George, Robert, Elijah, Johnson, Firman, James, Moses, Melvin, Jane and Hannah. Moses Allen married Ann Graham, a daughter of the Rev. John Graham, a native of Scotland, who married in Maryland and emigrated to Indiana, becoming a pioneer in Daviess county. He was a Baptist preacher and rode horseback on his circuit. He and his wife located three miles southeast of Washington on a farm and spent the remainder of their lives there, both living to an advanced age. One of their sons, Josiah, was killed during the battle of Chickamauga, while fighting for the cause of the Union.

Josiah G. Allen was reared on his father's farm in Vigo county and in Daviess county. He attended the district schools and the public schools of Washington, and then taught in the district schools for four years. Subsequently he read law for two years in the office of Judge Ogdon, and was admitted to the bar in 1886. Mr. Allen and M. S. Hastings have been in partnership since the former's admission to the bar, a period of nearly thirty years. In 1896 E. E. Hastings was admitted to the firm and since January, 1913, Mr. Allen's son, A. W. Allen, who was graduated from the law department of the University of Michigan at Ann Arbor, has also been a member of this firm.

On March 13, 1888, Josiah G. Allen was married to Sallie A. Wright, a daughter of Roderick and Ann (McJunken) Wright, and to this union three children have been born, Arthur W., Nell and Josiah G., Jr. Arthur W. married Willoughby Stamper. Nell, who was graduated from Franklin College and taught in the Washington high school for two years, married Lyle Constable, and lives on a farm near Goodland, Illinois. Josiah G., Jr., is in charge of a plantation in southern Arkansas. He spent two years in the Texas Agricultural and Mechanical School and two years in the agricultural department of the University of Illinois.

Mrs. Allen was born on a farm in Washington township, this county, her parents, both of whom are now deceased, having also been natives of this county, members of pioneer families. They were the parents of four children, Marion, William C. W., Sallie A. and Laura S., the latter of whom is a missionary in India, where she has been stationed for the past eighteen years. Roderick Wright's father, a North Carolinan, married Sarah Hawkins, also a native of that state, and came to Daviess county in 1808, and lived for a time in the blockhouse near the present town of Maysville. They spent the rest of their lives in that neighborhood, both living to very advanced ages. They were the parents of four children, John, Roderick, Joseph and Nancy. Mrs. Allen's maternal grandfather was Harvey McJunken, a native of Mississippi, a lawyer, who came to Daviess county from Kentucky and died here when about twenty-six years old. His widow, who was a native of North Carolina, lived to an advanced age.

For years Josiah G. Allen has been prominently identified with the Republican party in Indiana. He served as a representative from this district in the Indiana General Assembly, sessions of 1893-95, and occupied the important position of chairman of the committee on ways and means of the House of Representatives. Mr. Allen was a school trustee in Washington for six years, being a member of the board when the contract was let for the erection of the fine new high school building. He is now president of the Hospital Association. Mr. Allen is a member of Pythagorean Lodge No. 118, Knights of Pythias, at Washington, with which he has been prominently associated for the past twenty-eight years. Mr. and Mrs. Allen are members of the First Baptist church at Washington, and he is a trustee of this church and has been superintendent of the Sunday school for more than twenty years.

STEPHEN E. MYERS.

One of the distinctive functions of this publication is to take recognition of those citizens of the commonwealth of Daviess who stand eminently representative of their respective spheres of endeavor, in which connection there is absolute propriety in according to Stephen E. Myers, of the law firm of Mattingly & Myers, recognition for his enviable standing in the legal profession. Mr. Myers is numbered among the leading members of the bar of Daviess county, and has also been influential in the political and civic life of the county of his birth. Like so many young men of the present generation, who are "making good" in the world, Stephen E. Myers was reared on the farm, and there it was that he laid the foundation for a career that has already been marked with a large measure of success.

Stephen E. Myers was born in Bogard township, Daviess county, August 1, 1883, the son of Daniel I. and Ada J. (Williams) Myers, natives of Indiana, who were the parents of six children, namely: Stephen E., of Washington; Alva E., deceased; Pearl, wife of William Lester, of Steele township; Vernie Grace, a school teacher, and Nelson and Earnest, who live at home.

Daniel I. Myers, a well-known farmer of Bogard township, is now serving the people of his community efficiently as township trustee. He was reared in Bogard and Steele townships, and owns a farm of one hundred and fifty acres in Bogard township, where the family was reared. Mr. Myers belongs to the United Brethren church and Mrs. Myers to the Methodist church.

The paternal grandfather of Stephen E. Myers was Elijah Myers, an early settler of Steele township, this county, whose original log cabin stood until about three years ago. He lived to be past eighty years old, but his wife, who was an Eaton, died while still a comparatively young woman. They had several children, Frank P., Daniel I., Elijah W., James, Joseph and Arilda. Elijah Myers was the son of Daniel Myers, whose father was killed in the Revolutionary War. Elijah Myers was twice married, his second wife having been Clarinda Carp, and to this union four children were born, Wilson B., Anna Bush, Stella and Ollie. The maternal grandparents of Mr. Myers were Joseph and Eliza J. (Peachee) Williams, the latter a native of Kentucky and now living at the age of ninety-six years at Alva, Oklahoma. They were the parents of six children, Ada J., Rosa, Rachel, Matilda, Lewis and Stephen, the latter of whom was killed in the Civil War.

Stephen E. Myers was reared on his father's farm in Bogard township, attended the district schools and later was graduated from Washington College. He also attended the Indiana State Normal at Terre Haute for two years, and was two years at the Indiana State University at Bloomington. Meanwhile he had been teaching in the district schools of this county, having begun this important form of public service when sixteen years of age, and taught for six years. He then took up the study of law in Washington and was admitted to the bar in 1905. He practiced alone until 1908, in which year he formed a partnership with Mr. Mattingly, under the firm name of Mattingly & Myers, which firm has continued very successfully since that time, with offices at Washington, the county seat.

On June 2, 1909, Stephen E. Myers was married to Bessie R. Allen, who was born in Washington township, this county, the daughter of Hamlet and Rebecca (Hyatt) Allen, natives of Indiana, the latter of whom is dead, but the former of whom is still living in Washington. They were the parents of two children, both daughters, Bessie Reed and Helen Hyatt. The paternal grandparents of Mrs. Myers were Johnson and Mary J. (Stanford) Allen, natives of Mason county, Kentucky, and pioneers of Daviess county, Indiana. Rebecca Hyatt was the daughter of Thomas Hyatt.

Mr. and Mrs. Myers are members of the Baptist church. Mr. Myers is a Mason and is a member of Washington chapter No. 92, Royal Arch Masons, and of Washington council No. 67, Royal and Select Masters. He also is a member of the Washington Lodge of Odd Fellows and of the Modern Woodmen of America. Politically, he is a Republican. No lawyer in Daviess county has accomplished more in the same length of time than has Stephen E. Myers, and few men are more deserving the confidence and esteem of the public than he.

WILLIAM H. SWINDA.

Clearly defined purpose and consecutive effort in the affairs of life will inevitably result in the attaining of a due measure of success, but in following out the career of one who has attained success by his own efforts there comes into view the intrinsic individuality which made such accomplishment possible, and thus there is granted an objective incentive and inspiration, while at the same time there is enkindled a feeling of respect and admiration. The qualities which have made Mr. Swinda one of the prominent and successful men of Elmore township, Daviess county, have also brought him the esteem of his fellow citizens, for his career has been one of well-directed energy, strong determination and honorable methods.

William H. Swinda was born on September 17, 1863, in Clay county, Indiana, and is the son of Harmon and Barbara (Smith) Swinda, both natives of Germany, but who came to this country with their respective parents at the ages of eighteen and sixteen, respectively. Their first place of settlement was on a farm near Columbus, Ohio; afterward, in 1858, they came to Clay county, where he engaged in the grocery business, in the town of Staunton, and conducted the store until the time of his retirement, twenty years later. He was twice married, the first time to Miss Snore, by whom the following children were born: Henry, who lives in Terre Haute; Mollie, deceased, wife of Christopher Robinstein, of Ohio; the second marriage was to Barbara Smith, and she gave birth to the following named children: W. H., the subject of this sketch; Mamie, the wife of John Shinner, of Riley; Elizabeth, the wife of John Bolin, Cleveland; Anna, wife of Fred Morgan, of Brazil; Catherine, who married Charles Ashburger, of Riley, and John.

William H. Swinda received his education in the public schools in Staunton, Clay county, and began his career as a coal miner in the neighboring coal fields, where he remained in that work for eight years, then, in 1893, he bought forty acres of land, to which he added ninety acres more in Elmore township, Daviess county, and now farms a total of four hundred acres. On his own land he has erected all of the buildings and, in 1903, he built the first barn. In 1908, he erected his home and built a second barn in 1910. These barns are models of their kind and are said to be the finest in this part of the country. Mr. Swinda makes it his business to carry on general farming, but gives particular attention to the breeding of horses, and is the owner of blooded Percheron stock and a high grade of jack stallion. Among his buildings is one used especially for breeding purposes and an American-bred mare that he owns carried off a premium as as champion breeder, and second prize in the open class. Besides horses, he gives considerable attention to Rhode Island Red chickens, and is a large breeder of Poland China hogs.

Mr. Swinda takes a deep interest in progressive farming and is ever studying improved methods for farming and breeding. His farm is in an ideal location and everything is kept up to the best possible advantage around the place, and the casual observer quickly comes to the conclusion that the owner is a man of careful management and successful as an agriculturist and stock raiser.

William H. Swinda was twice married, the first time to Ella Ringo, who died without having given birth to any children; his second wife is Jennie S. Taylor, daughter of Samuel and Mattie (O'Dell) Taylor, farmers in Daviess county. No children have been born to their union, but they are rearing Ethel, an adopted child.

Mr. Swinda is a stanch believer in the principles of the Republican party and has always given his support to that organization. He is a member of the Methodist church. Personally, he is a man of broad sympathies and takes an abiding interest in the welfare of those about him, and, because of his genial disposition and high character, enjoys a large popularity in the community where he has spent so many years.

WILLIAM WESLEY BARNETT.

One of the influential citizens of Washington, this county, William Wesley Barnett, is ranged with the leading business men and representative citizens, a man of excellent endowment and unright character, who has been a valued factor in local affairs for years. Mr. Barnett, a veteran of the Civil War, now proprietor of a livery and automobile garage business, has ever commanded the confidence and esteem of the people of Daviess county, having ever been loyal to the progress of the community, and ever vigilant in his efforts to promote the common interests along material, moral and civic lines.

William W. Barnett was born on July 9, 1842, near Rockport, in Spencer county, Indiana, the son of James M. and Harriet (Myers) Barnett, who lived near Rockport nearly all their lives, James M. Barnett living to be eighty-six years of age and his wife, who survived him, to be eighty-five. Both were active members of the Methodist church. They were the parents of nine children: John F., deceased; William W., of Washington; Walker, deceased; Jacob O'Connell, deceased; George, of near Rockport, Indiana; Sally, the wife of Louis Snyder, who lives on the old homestead near Rockport; Minerva, the widow of John Taylor, of St. Louis, Missouri, and Hannah Belle, who is unmarried and lives in St. Louis. James M. Barnett was the son of John and Sarah (McNealy) Barnett, natives of Virginia and pioneers in Spencer county, Indiana. John Barnett was a farmer and was prominent in the politics of Spencer county, having at one time held an important county office. He died of cholera about 1853, and his widow lived to be eighty-nine years old. They were the parents of eight children, Newton N., James M., Othnell A., Friend, Narcissa, Sallie, Leafy and Nancy Minerva. Mr. Barnett's maternal grandparents were Jacob Myers and wife, early settlers in Spencer county, who were the parents of six children, John, William, Hannah, Christina, Mahala and Harriet.

William W. Barnett was reared on his father's farm in Spencer county and attended the district schools, supplementing this schooling by a course in the college at Rockport, Indiana. In 1861 Mr. Barnett enlisted in Company F, First Indiana Cavalry, for service during the Civil War. This company was assigned to the Twenty-eighth Regiment, and Mr. Barnett served valiantly for three years in the Union army, at the end of which trying service he suffered a physical breakdown. With that he abandoned his intention to study law and began farming. He had saved about six hundred dollars, and this was used to get a start on the farm. He bought a small tract of thirty-six acres, upon which he built a house, and there he lived from 1868 to 1880, in which latter year he sold the place and purchased a livery stable at Rockport, which he operated until 1891, when he came to this county, locating in Washington, where he went into the livery business on Fifth street. He later rented a large barn at the corner of Third and Van Trees streets, which he still operates, in connection with which he also conducts an automobile garage and a transfer line, and has been very successful in business, a success that is not a matter of accident, but which has come to him as a consequence of his industry and good management and unexcelled patience.

On December 19, 1865, William W. Barnett was married to Mary M. Shackleford, daughter of John D. and Elizabeth (Snyder) Shackleford, to which union have been born Harry, Samuel L., George S., Walter S. and Stella C. Harry died at the age of four years. Samuel married Claude Wright and they have two children, Mary Louise and Bernard. George S. married Cora Stull and has three children, Bruce, Verne and Max. Walter

S. married Kate Boltman. Stella C. married Benjamin Clawson and has two children. Mrs. Mary M. Barnett died in 1901, at the age of fifty-four years. She was born in Spencer county, near Rockport. Her father was born at Rising Sun, Indiana, and her mother in Spencer county. They were the parents of three children, Anna, Mary M. and George Washington. The paternal grandparents of Mrs. Barnett were Washington Shackleford and wife, who were the parents of two sons, John and Redman. Her maternal grandparents were Willis Synder and wife, whose children were Enoch, William, Elizabeth, Moravia and Willis.

In July, 1912, William W. Barnett married, secondly, Mrs. Mary A. Cressy, widow of Oscar Cressy and the daughter of Henry and Jennie (Harris) Mosier, who was born in Owen county, Indiana. Her father was a native of North Carolina and her mother a native of Owen county. The latter died in Owen county when her daughter, Mary, was a small child. Henry Mosier died in 1910 at the age of eighty-four years. Mrs. Barnett had two sisters, Emma and Ettie. Henry Mosier was married three times. By the first marriage, there were two sons, Perry and Philander. By the last marriage there was one child, Frecina. To Mrs. Barnett's first marriage there was born a son, Fred Everett, who is a piano tuner at Indianapolis. He married Lilly Grafe and has two children, Ruth Elizabeth and Crystal Thelma.

Mrs. Barnett is a member of the Methodist church. Mr. Barnett is a Republican and a member of Grant post, Grand Army of the Republic, and also of Pythagorean lodge, Knights of Pythias.

DR. ERNEST HOLLINGSWORTH.

Dr. Ernest Hollingsworth, a well-known physician and surgeon of Washington, this county, is fairly entitled to representation among the progressive and enterprising citizens of this county. He is devoted to his profession and takes a warm interest in the general welfare of the community.

Ernest Hollingsworth was born in Edwardsport, Knox county, Indiana, on January 4, 1876, the son of William K. and Sarah L. (Azbell) Hollingsworth, both natives of Indiana, who were the parents of seven children who lived to maturity, namely: Jennie, of Edwardsport; William, of Edwardsport; Kitty, the widow of J. W. Hedrick, of Dugger, Indiana; Charles C., of Indianapolis; Frank a telegrapher; Amy, the wife of John Atkinson, of Dugger, and Ernest, the subject of this sketch.

William K. Hollingsworth was reared in Edwardsport, Indiana, and followed wagon-making in his young manhood. Later he was a merchant in Edwardsport and was trustee of the township for a time. He later followed farming for two years, at the end of which time he resumed the mercantile business, and was thus engaged until he retired, his death occurring in 1908, he then being seventy-four years of age. His widow, now seventy-five years of age, is a member of the Christian church. William K. Hollingsworth was a Mason and was master of the lodge in Edwardsport for more than twenty years. Politically, he was a Democrat. His parents were natives of Georgia. Seven Hollingsworth cousins came to Daviess and Knox counties, Indiana, in an early day, and one of them was killed on White river by an Indian. The father of William K. Hollingsworth located in Knox county and died there at the age of about fifty years. His widow, who was a Keith, lived to be ninety years old and died in this county. They were the parents of two sons and two daughters, William K., Kitty, Jane and Thomas, the latter of whom was a soldier in an Indiana regiment during the Civil War. Sarah L. (Azbell) Hollingsworth was the daughter of William and Mary (Azbell) Azbell, natives of Kentucky and early settlers in Knox county, Indiana, where they died, he at the age of fifty and she at the age of eighty-nine. They were the parents of four children, Sarah C., Charles C., John and Nettie.

Ernest Hollingsworth was reared in Edwardsport and attended the public schools of that place. He later entered the University of Louisville and was graduated from the medical department of that institution in 1898. He began practicing his profession in Edwardsport, and in 1901 came to this county, locating in Washington, and has practiced there since that time.

On November 27, 1902, Dr. Ernest Hollingsworth was married to Ida M. Nimnicht, who was born in Vincennes, Indiana, the daughter of Frank L. and Lucetta (Macy) Nimnicht, to which union one daughter, Lucile E., has been born. Mrs. Hollingsworth's father, who was born in Germany, died in Washington, this county, in March, 1914. His widow is still living. They were the parents of six children, Charles F., Louis H., Ida M., Laura, Christopher and Edward. Frank L. Nimnicht's parents were early settlers in Edwards county, Illinois, where both died well advanced in years. They were the parents of eight children, Frank, Ernestine, Anna, Minnie, Augustus, August, William and Herman. The maternal grandparents of Mrs. Hollingsworth also were natives of Germany and died in Edwards county, Illinois. They were the parents of three children, Lydia, Lucetta and Tillie.

Dr. Ernest Hollingsworth is a member of the Daviess County Medical Society and of the Indiana State Medical Association, and is also secretary of the local board of health. He and his wife are members of the Christian church, and he is a member of Charity Lodge No. 30, Free and Accepted Masons.

GEORGE RIESTER.

The gentleman whose life history is herewith briefly outlined has lived to good purpose and achieved a much greater degree of success than falls to the lot of the ordinary individual. By a straightforward and commendable course he has made his way to a responsible position in the world, winning the esteem of his fellow citizens and earning the reputation of an enterprising man of affairs.

George Riester was born on June 18, 1864, in Dubois county, Indiana, the son of Stephen and Caroline (Ehler) Riester, both natives of Germany, born in 1814 and 1827, respectively. His father's parents lived and died in Germany, but his mother's parents immigrated to this country and settled first in the state of Ohio, later coming to Daviess county, going hence to Dubois county, Indiana, where they spent their last days. Grandfather Ehler was an extensive road contractor and builder and at one time was engaged in the construction of a canal near Sandy Hook, this county. He was the father of seven children, Mary, Reka, Mena, Frederick, Phillip, Theresa and Caroline.

Stephen Riester came to the United States from Germany about the year 1843 and settled in Dubois county, this state, where he married, afterwards going to Louisville, Kentucky, where he remained a year, at the end of which time he returned to Dubois county, where he remained until 1887, in which year he came to this country, and here he spent the rest of his life, his death occurring in 1901. He was a shoemaker by trade but followed farming in Dubois county and met with considerable success in agricultural pursuits. He was a stanch supporter of the Democratic party and a member of the Catholic church. He and his wife (the latter died in 1899) were the parents of the following children: Phillip, Preston (deceased), Stephen (deceased), Henry (deceased), Peter, Andrew, Thomas (deceased), John (deceased), George, William, Barbara (deceased), and Jacob (deceased).

George Riester lived on his father's farm in his youth and received his early education in the parochial schools, also attending the public schools. When about twenty-two years of age he went to Oakland City, in Gibson county, this state, where he remained during a summer season, and in 1886 came to Daviess county, and engaged in the manufacture of brick at Washington. Later, he also engaged in the gravel-road contracting business and is thus now engaged.

On October 10, 1885, George Riester was married to Helen Benget, who was born on August 18, 1865, in Dubois county, this state, a daughter of Xavier and Magdaline (Haas) Benget. Xavier Benget was born in Germany in 1832 and came to this country when quite a young man, first settling in Dubois county, where he married Magdaline Haas, who was born in that county on September 21, 1841. To their union were born, Kate, Phillip, Helen, John and Jacob (deceased). Grandfather Haas was a farmer who lived on his farm in Dubois county for thirty years. He died in Washington, this county, in 1905 and his widow, who still survives him, is living in that city. Mrs. Riester's maternal grandparents were both natives of Germany and immigrated to this country in an early day, settling in Dubois county, where the grandfather died a comparatively young man and his widow survived and lived to the age of ninety-three years.

To George and Helen (Benget) Riester the following children have been born: Barbara, Tillie, Albert, Minnie, Hattie (deceased), Anna, Charles (deceased), Leo and Bernard. Mr. and Mrs. Riester are members of the Catholic church and their children have been reared in that faith.

Phillip Riester, elder brother of the subject of this sketch, was born in Louisville, Kentucky, and received his early education in the public schools there, then, when quite a young man, engaged in the brick business with his brother and is now retired from active business. At one time he was working in the coal mines of southern Indiana. Possessing considerable thrift and industry he began buying real estate in Washington, where he is the owner of several houses and lots. He was married on November 16, 1873, to Frances Shuble, who was born in Dubois county, Indiana, a daughter of Nathan and Columbia (Slettenogden) Shuble, both natives of Germany, who came to this country and they settled in Dubois county, this state, where Nathan Shuble died, his widow dying in Washington, this county. To Phillip Riester and wife were born the following children: Caroline, Hattie, Stephen, Minnie (deceased), Lucy, Frank (deceased), George, Ella,

Oster (deceased), and Bessie. The mother of these children died on August 2, 1913, the husband and father surviving. Phillip Riester is an ardent supporter of the Democratic party and a member of the Catholic church. He has been a resident of Washington since May 10, 1873, and is held in the highest esteem by all who know him.

George Riester has taken time to give particular attention to the welfare of the people of his community, in addition to his regular business, and is a member of the city council. He was first elected to this office, on the Democratic ticket, in 1909, and having been re-elected will continue in office until 1917. Fraternally, he is a member of the Knights of Columbus, the Woodmen of the World, the Modern Woodmen of America, the Fraternal Order of Eagles and the Loyal Order of Moose. He has a large circle of warm friends and is regarded as a man of sterling worth.

RAYMOND ENGELHART.

Enterprise and industry are the essential elements to success in any degree, and these qualities coupled with well-directed energy are bound to produce the desired results. Among the men of Daviess county who have attained to a definite degree of success in agricultural pursuits is the man whose name appears above and whose career has been one of honorable methods. He is worthy of the esteem of his fellow men and deserving of recognition in a work of this character.

Raymond Engelhart was born in Jasper, Dubois county, Indiana, on June 10, 1885, the son of Paul and Margaretta (Behlein) Engelhart. Paul Englehart who was born in 1846, was raised in Dubois county and received his early education in the public schools of Jasper, that county. During his youth he was employed as a farm hand but at a later date purchased one hundred and sixty acres of land, which he owned and farmed until about the year 1894, when he sold the same and moved to Daviess county, where he bought two hundred and forty acres of land, in Steele township, raised his family and spent the remainder of his life there, his death occurring in the year 1911. His wife died some years previously, in the year 1889. She also was a native of Dubois county, having been born near Jasper in that county. To their union were born the following children: Theresa, who is now the wife of Bert Harpstrite; Elizabeth, who married Joseph Wichman; Anthony, who married Anna Wilz, and Raymond, the subject of this review. The family professed belief in the Catholic faith and were regular attendants of St. Mary's church of Washington, Indiana. Politically, the father was a member of the Democratic party. He was well thought of by all who knew him and bore the reputation of being absolutely honest and trustworthy. He was kind and gentle in his nature and thoroughly devoted to his family.

Raymond Englehart remained with his parents in early youth and received his education in the schools of Jasper and also at Washington, this county. In the former town he attended school two years and in the latter about one year. He started farming when quite young, renting until 1911, in which year he acquired possession of the one hundred and sixty acres on which he now resides and continue to farm. In addition to cultivating the soil, Mr. Englehart operates a thrashing outfit in season and by this means has made a great many acquaintances and friends throughout this section. Since moving to the present farm he has made a great many modern improvements, including the erection of a first class silo and which he finds quite profitable for the feeding of stock. The old home has been remodeled and is commodious, comfortable and substantial. Besides giving his attention to general crop raising, Mr. Englehart devotes considerable time to the care of live stock and has had a good deal of success in this line.

On June 13, 1909, Raymond Englehart married Frieda Blessinger, daughter of John and Helen (Eckstein) Blessinger, to which union one child has been born, Harvey H., who was born on June 13, 1910.

Mr. Englehart is a man who does not take much active interest in political affairs, but is recognized as a man of sound judgment and perfectly in accord with progressive principles that tend to the material advancement of mankind in general. He and his wife are members of the Catholic church and are regular attendants of St. Mary's church in Washington. Mr. Englehart is a man who attends strictly to his own affairs and takes a deep interest in his possessions. He is ever watchful for modern methods that prove to be an improvement over older ways, always ready to give thorough consideration to all meritorious inventions intended to promote efficiency on the farm, and possesses the respect and esteem of his fellow men.

FULLNAME INDEX

----, Frances Ann 428 Henry 38 James 93 John 428 John T 167 Melissa 428 Nettie 422 Sam 301 Samuel F 155 Sarah 428 William 428
ABEL, Father 199 Joseph 105 Martha 105-106 William 241
ABELL, C W 304 Father 197 James B 286 John 201
ABRAHAM, G D 267 George D 298
ABRAMS, George D 604 Mr 604
ACHOR, Florence M 296 J M 266 James M 253
ACHORS, J H 266
ACKLEY, Mrs 312 Mrs T A 312
ACKMAN, Cora E 590
ACRE, Sarah J 424 William T 424
ADAMS, 57 Edward 67 274 John 107 Mary Ann 448 Mr 316 Rev 185 Simon 96 Thomas 315
ADAMSON, H H 192
ADE, 62
ADKINS, Christopher 429 John 429 Luke 167 Nancy L 428-429 Nellie 429 Nelson 167 Nelson C 112
AGAN, B 227 D R 112 Fred 227 John P 112 Laura E 233-234 P S 292 Sarah 234 Thomas 197
AIKMAN, 252 Charles A 634 Eleanor 584-585 Ella 506 Ethel 634 George 576 Helen 634 Henry 111 114 259 306 James 69 95 James B 576 John 66 83 93 100 102 108 210 232 246 Josephine 576 L C 437 Margaret 576 Maria 346 Mr 437 Naoma 576 Paul 576 Samuel 69 Thomas 66 69 William M 306
AKESTER, 378
ALBAUGH, Basil 424 Eli 424 Elizabeth 424 Lavina 424 Melinda 424 Peter 424 Samuel 424 Sarah 424 William 424
ALBERTI, Catherine 570 Christian 570 Elizabeth 570 Jennie 570 Louis 570 Louise 570
ALBERTSON, Alice 394 Carrie 394 Eliza 394 George 394 Laura 394 Nathaniel 394 Sarah Deane 393-394
ALBERTY, Alma 581 Anna M 581 Carrie 580 Eugene 581 Harriet 581 Harry 581-582 Harry L 259 Henrietta 580 Henry 580-582 Jesse C 581 Kate 580 Katie 581 Louis 580 Louis Carl 581 Louise 580 Martha E 581 Mary 582 Minnie 580 Mrs Phillip 581 Phillip 580-581 Phillip C 581 Phillipena

ALBERTY (Cont.)
580 Roy 582 Theresa 582 Walter 582
ALBRIGHT, O M 297
ALEXANDER, Asbury D 156 Isaac 154 J A 241 Johanna 349-350 Joseph A 219 R W 192-193 Sallie 505
ALFORD, Barton 282 Betsy 630 Elvira 621 George G 189 George W 113 James 274 281 621 Janie 459 John W 548 Lafayette 154 Lucy Ann 621 Margaret 548-549 Melvina 548 Nancy 629-630 T G 234 T J 621 Wayne 154 194 William 274 630 William J 168
ALLEN, 219 333 349 A W 348 706 Alfred 619 Alkinah 483 Amanda 483 Ann 705 Anna J 337 Arthur 252 Arthur W 706 Asenath 464 Banner B 370 Bessie 338 478 Bessie R 708 Bessie Reed 338 Bessie Reed 708 Charles 367 Clara 435 Clem 434 Clementine 370 Col 337 Cyrus 369 483 Cyrus M 250 Decatur D 705 Elihu 483 Elijah 705 Elijah R 337 Eliza 367 483 Elizabeth 337 483 499 Elkanah 190 483 Ellsworth 370 Emma 237 367 Emma B 619 Esther 366-367 Firman 337 705 Florence 483 George 337 705 Glendora 705 Gordon 483 H H 187 286 Hamlet 142 218 226-228 234-236 312-313 336-338 708 Hannah 705 Hannah A 337 Harriet 619 Heber H 180 Helen 113 338 Helen Hyatt 338 708 Hiram 347 352 482-483 Isabel 483 J G 251 348 J W 296 James 281 367 483 499 650 705 James C 337 Jane 367 650 705 Jennie 489 Jeremiah 106 John 66 101 233 300 337 367 705 John Sr 93 Johnson 337 705 708 Joseph 367 Josiah G 114 348 705-706 Josiah G Jr 706 Katherine 370 Kezia 370 Keziah 347 352 482 Laura 332 377 483 Lauretta 347 351-352 Lodusky H 369 Logan 370 Lucetta 483 Lydia 434 Mahalia 483 Malinda 367 Margaret L 369-370 Mary 352 367 483 499 Mary E 347 Mary J 337 708 Mary Jane 337 471 Maryette 483 Mason 483 Melville W 337 Melvin 705 Milton L 347 352 482-483 Miss 313 586 Moses 337 586 705 Mr 142 482-484 706-707 Mrs 338-339 484 706-707 Mrs William 337 Nell 706 Norma 228 Old Bill 274 Oliver P 370 Oriena 370 Orrin P 483 Ottie L 228 Pearl 397 Polly 483 Professor 336-339 Rachel 337 Rebecca 338 708 Robert 337 705 Ross 483 Roy D 483 S

DAVIESS COUNTY, INDIANA.

ALLEN (Cont.)
C 377 Sallie A 706 Samuel 471 Stancil 367 Susan 367 Susie 483 Tabitha 483 Theresa 370 Tolbert 367 Virginia C 337 W B 397 Walter 483 Willard Robert 370 William 337 705 William B 705 William H 221 298 Willoughby 706
ALLISON, Beula Pearl 509 Charles Ray 509 Dickson 508 Elizabeth 508 Ellen 503 Harriette 508 Isaac 507-509 J C 227 Jane 508 John 275 508 John A 507-508 John Albert 509 Joseph 89 508 Joseph C 109 Laura G 508 Lillie 508-509 Luther M 509 Martha 508 Martha Ann 481 Martha G 508-509 Mary 507-508 Mary Elizabeth 509 Mr 509 Nancy 508 Nora 527 Owen 508-509 Owen C 507 509 Robert 508 Sarah 508 Smith 509 Smith M 508 W H 193 227 William 508 William H 193
AMERMAN, George W 256
AMICK, Albert 702 Alice 702 Aura 702 C T 226 228 Charles 702 Clyde 702 Clyde J 702 Clyde T 238 701-702 Elizabeth H 702 Elmer 702 Frances L 702 John D 701-702 John P 702 Lena 702 Lillie 702 Lola 702 Lucy 702 Mabel 702 Mr 702 Nellie 701 Pearl 702 Professor 702 Rosa 702 Samuel 702
ANDERSON, Elizabeth 360 Francis A 253 J W 255 John 276 Walter L 256 William 360 William B 254
ANDIS, Julianna 611
ANDREWS, 312
ANNEN, Albert F 112
ANSELM, Brother 200
ANTOINETTE, Marie Queen Of France 54
ARBAUGH, D 195
ARFORD, A W 195 227 Catherine 605 Evangeline 605 F 227 Frank 93 Frank B 92 Jacob 605
ARISON, Celina G 453
ARLINGHOUSE, Catherine 403
ARMS, Henry 426 Laura 426
ARMSTRONG, John 42 Lillian 271 William 180
ARNOLD, B B 191 Belle 526
ARRELL, Alice 542-543 Katy 585 Matilda 321
ART, Jabez 210
ARTERBURN, William 228
ARTERMANN, Elsie 442
ARTHUR, Elijah 416 Hamilton M 255 Martin L 255 Nora Maude 255 Sarah D 416
ARVIN, John H 173 Joseph 268 Thomas E 228 Thomas H 110
ASBURY, C E 187
ASHBURGER, Catherine 709 Charles 709

ASHCRAFT, Joshua Curtis 254
ASHLEY, Nettie Francis 616 Robert T 616
ATCHLEY, Sophia 685
ATKINS, Malinda 671
ATKINSON, Amy 713 John 713
ATTERBURN, Samuel P 446 William C 446
AULD, John G 164
AUTERBURN, Alson 446 Anna 446 C Harvey 446-447 Charles 446 Chauncey 446-447 Clay H 446 Constant H 446 Dicie 446 George W 446 Hallie 446 Harry 447 Hattie 447 Isaac Henderson 446 Laura A 445-446 Lowell 446 Martin A 446 Mary Jane 446 Mattie 447 Maud J 446 Maude J 446 Mr 445-446 Nell 446 Norman A 446 Ola 446 Opal 446 Ora 447 Ralph 447 Roy A 446-447 Samuel 447 Samuel P 445-446 Sarah E 446 Sarah S 446 Thelma 446 William C 445-446 William T 446 William Thomas 446
AVERY, Charollete A 555 Nettie 419 William R 254
AVIS, Sarah 599
AXTELL, W F 226 234 313 William F 235
AZBELL, Charles C 713 John 154 713 Mary 713 Nettie 713 Sarah C 713 Sarah L 712-713 William 713
BACH, Caroline 659 Eda 659 Edwin 659 Eliza 659 Elizabeth 659 Emanuel 659 Jesse J 659 Laura 659 Lena 659 Lena B 659 Leroy 659 Louis 659 Mary 659 Rolla E 659 Sadie E 659 William 659 Zula 659
BACKES, Bertha Katherine 513 Henry 183 340 512-513 John Joseph 513 John P 512 Katherine 512 Laura 512 Laversa J 513 Mr 183 512-513 Mrs 513 Richard Paul 513
BACKUS, 172
BACON, Alice Marie 437 Charles 436 Charles D 436 Doris Margaret 437 Edward S 436 Elizabeth A 436 Howard J 436 James 436 Joseph D 436 Lulu 436 Mary Ann 436 Mary Ethel 437 Mary J 436 Mary Jane 436 Mr 436-437 Mrs 437 Mrs Joseph D 436 Ralph Vance 437 Sarah C 436 Theophilus 436 Thomas J 436 W J 421 423 436-437 William Hyatt 437 William J 436-437
BAERLE, Christena 578
BAGNAL, Elizabeth 548
BAILEY, 283 I A 193
BAIR, Ada 238 Benjamin 431 Catharine 431 Esther 431 Esther B 430 457 Jacob 431 John A 111 431 Jonas 431 Kizzie 431 Leah 431 Mary 431
BAIRD, Oliver P 178 Samuel 66
BAKER, Alice 648 Barton 563 Byron 549 Clara B 549 Comfort 413 Conrad 58 441

INDEX. 721

BAKER (Cont.)
Earl 563 Elizabeth 548 562 648 Frances 563 Frances L 562 George 648 Helen 549 Henry 160 Hugh G 549 Isaac 548 562 J W 187 John 249-250 648 Jonas 648 Judge 249 Lilbert 549 Mamie A 549 Margaret I 549 Mary 475 648 Mary Jane 442 Melvina 548 Minnie 548 Mr 71 Rolina 648 Rolla M 549 Shannon 192 Thomas 259 Thomas A 259 Thomas F 88 Uttley 563 William 66 280 William D 548-549 William Franklin 549 William R 296
BALDWIN, Col 153 Emma 227
BALLARD, Dicey 356
BALLOU, William 102
BALLOW, Fleming 69 Mason 94 Thomas 233 William 65-67 83 93 95 100 108 138-139 274 301 William T 213
BALSH, Nancy 444
BALTHUS, John 156
BANCROFT, 692
BANKS, 157
BANTA, A T 193 Abraham 452-453 Abraham T 452 Abram 392 Abram T 391 Betsey 392 Charles 392 Charles A 114 279 294 452-454 Dell 392 Dora 392 Eliza 392 Eliza Ann 391 452 Elizabeth Jane 452 Etta 392 Garnetta B 453 Glen Dora 452-453 Henry 392 453 Henry B 453 Henry D 453 Ida M 453 Jackson 392 John 392 Margaret 392 Martha 392 Martha A 391 Martha Ann 452 Mary B 453 Mr 294 392 452-454 Mrs 453 Mrs Charles A 453 Noah F 453 Phoebe 360 Sarah Etta 453 Susan Dell 452 Thomas 392 Thomas S 453 W G 193 William 392 William W 452
BARBER, A C 260 Aden 541 591 Aden C 541 Adon C 591 Bertha 598 Bertha A 541 591 Charles 591 Cora D 541 591 Cora Dell 505 Edgar 541 591 Eliza Katherine 541 591 Ellis 541 591 Emma J 542 Ethel 521 542 Fern 591 Frank 541 591 George L 541 591 Hattie 591 Hazel 542 Jennie 420 542 Jennie Pearl 541 591 Jessie 542 John N 541 Lester 591 Lew W 505 541-542 591 598 Lillian 542 Mary 505 541-542 590 Mildred 542 Mr 542 591 Mrs 591 Nelson 505 541 590-591 Norman 591 Ottis C 541 591 Robert N 542 Ruth 591 Stanton 272 541 590-591 Thomas Dale 591 Venus 591 Viola G 591 Viola Glenn 590 Virgil 591
BARENS, Katherine 512
BARKER, William 82
BARKEY, Abraham 677 Anna 676 Barbara 677 Catherine 676 Christian 676-677 Christina 677 David 677 Fannie 669 675

BARKEY (Cont.)
677 Magdelina 677 Mary 677 Sarah 677 Susannah 677
BARKLEY, Anna 600 Douglas 602 Emanuel 601 Esther 602 Joseph 600-601 Leland 602 Lena 601 Millie 601 Mr 601-602 Nicholas F 600-601
BARLEY, Bertha Ellen 491 Edward 489 Elias A 490 Flossie 228 Francis P 490 George A 490 Harrison D 490 Jennie 489 John 489 John H 489 Laura J 490 Lavina L 490 Lovina L 490 Malintha 489 Mr 490-491 Mrs 491 Mrs Thomas F 490 Parlina 489 Pauline 489 Plas 489 Rettie 489 Sarah 489 Susan 489 Thomas 489 Thomas F 489-490 William 489 William P 489 William T 490
BARMORE, Pearlie 459
BARNES, Dawson E 254 Eula 357
BARNETT, Bernard 711 Bruce 711 Claude 711 Cora 711 Friend 711 George 711 George S 711 Hannah Belle 711 Harriet 710 Harry 711 Jacob Oconnell 711 James M 710-711 John 711 John F 711 Kate 712 Leafy 711 Mary A 712 Mary Louise 711 Mary M 711-712 Max 711 Minerva 711 Mr 710-712 Mrs 712 Nancy Minerva 711 Narcissa 711 Newton N 711 Othnell A 711 Sallie 711 Sally 711 Samuel 711 Samuel L 711 Sarah 711 Stella C 711-712 Verne 711 Walker 711 Walter S 711-712 William W 710-712 William Wesley 710
BARNHOUSE, C L 345
BARR, Annie L 384 Catherine 317 Eliza 384 Emily H 384 Estella A 384 Florence E 384 Glenn E 384 Hugh 189 274 305 J M 251 James 66 383-384 James W 266 Jane 384 John 383-384 John H 164 Juda 384 Julia 383-384 Mr 190 384-385 O W 384 R J 307 Robert C 384 Robert J 109-111 173 383-384 Susan 384 William 384 William W 384
BARRETT, John J 242
BARROWS, 316 Evangelist 193
BARTL, Florian Jr 296 Tolbert 234
BARTLE, Tol 282
BARTON, C G 253 Doctor 312 Enoch 112 G G 90 113 251 312 M E 227 Mary E 234 Philip 248 258
BASCOM, Mary Ann 233 Nathan 258
BATCHELOR, Abel 376 Catherine 376 Enoch 376 Ernest Henry 536 Etta May 536 Frances 376 Frances E 376 George 376 535 541 590 Indiana 376 John 376 John T 376 Julia 376 Katherine 535 Laura 376 Martha 376 Mary 376 505 541 590 Minerva 376 Mr 535-536 Rachel 376 Sarah 376 Sarah J

BATCHELOR (Cont.)
 376 Stephen H 535-536 Stephen Henry 535
 William 376
BATES, Annetta B 526 Benjamin 434 Caroline
 434 Edward 434 Eliza 690 Jefferson 526
 Mary Ann 434-435 William 434
BAXTER, Sarah M 348
BEAN, Aaron A 697 Addie L 698 Anna 697
 Benjamin 697 Benjamin T 698 Beulah 698
 Carl 698 Catherine 697 Charles 698
 Charles H 697 Coy 698 Delila W 698
 Edward W 697-698 Effie H 676 698
 Elizabeth 697 Flora 698 Frank 698
 Frederick 698 George D 697 Harold 698
 James T 697 John 697 John W 698 Lulu
 698 Maggie 698 Mary 698 Maud 698
 Milton 697 Mr 698 Nancy A 697 Otto 698
 Pleasant D 697 Ray 698 Sallie 697 Virgil A
 698 William 697
BEAR, Eliza 491
BEARD, John R 99
BEARMIN, William 571
BEASLEY, Clara 488 Edwin 382 Elizabeth
 382 John 488 Martha 381-382 Mary 488
 Mr 623 Sarah 503 Thomas 488
BECHTEL, Aaron D 660-661 Abraham 660
 Albert 660 Benjamin F 660 Blanche 660
 Clara 666 Elijah 660 Elizabeth 660 Ellen B
 666 Fay 661 Frank 666 Hannah 661 Harold
 660 Hester 660 Iva 660 Jacob 660 James
 660 Jane 660 John 660 Lizzie 661 Martha
 M 660 Martin 660 Mary 660 Mary Jane
 660 Mr 660-661 Mrs 661 Nancy 660
 Palmer 661 Rachael 660 Russell 661
 Samuel 660 Sarah Ann 660 William 660
 Zula 661
BECK, Christ 345 Mary 345 Nellie 345 Rose
 345 William 345
BECKES, Ann 540 Benjamin 540
BECKET, John 259
BECKETT, Eva 526 J 227 John 259
BEDDLE, Elias 279
BEDDOE, Arthur 304
BEEKER, Anna 474 Anna Grace 474 Clara
 474 Edna Laura 474 Eula May 474
 Florence E 474 Frederick 474 John 474
 Lewis 474 Louda 473-474 Margaret 474
 Mary 474 Matilda 474 Mr 474 Mrs Louda
 474 Ora L 474 Pauline 474 Tessie 474
BEEVER, H H 286 Henry H 286
BEHLEIN, Margaretta 716
BEITMAN, Isadore 260 Jacob 306 L P 260
 Nathan 260
BELDING, Alice 233 Mr 182-183 S 182
 Stephen 182 191 258 301 309 340 Steve
 180

BELL, Charles A 617 Daniel W 255 Elijah 249
 Ethelind L 617 Frances D 490 George W
 490 Hannah 696 Henry 266 J A 195 John
 116 John W 255 R H 176 696 W E 291
BENEFIELD, John 276
BENGET, Helen 715 Jacob 715 John 715 Kate
 715 Magdaline 715 Phillip 715 Xavier 715
BENHAM, Almira 517-518 Charles W 254 Ira
 518 Mary 518
BENN, Agnes L 330 Elbridge 330
BENNEM, Elmira 650 Mary E 650
BENNETT, Ann 623-624 Catherine 624
 Catherine M 624 D H 420 Edward W 241
 Elizabeth 624 James 624 Jennie 420
 Jerome 624 John 624 Margaret 548 Mary
 624 Michael J 623-624 Mr 624 Myrtle 425
 Patrick 623-624 Reason 292 William 624
 William P 248
BENNINGTON, Ann 193 Benjamin 428
 Charles 616 Della 428 Miss 651 Sarah A
 616 Thomas 109
BERENS, Anna 622 Anna Marie 622 Catherine
 622 Charles 622 John 622 Mary 623 Mary
 B 622 Mr 622 Peter 622 Peter Jr 622 Rose
 622 Thomas 622 William 622
BERKSHIRE, Cornelius 248 258 J S 309 John
 S 110 112 William R 112
BERNHART, Elizabeth 570
BERRY, 85-86 106 Amelia 318 Ann Eliza 317
 Arthur 317 Beverly 317 Charles G 177
 Colonel 301 Etta 228 Evaline 317 Frank
 395 Henry 317 James M 233 317 John D
 266 318 Louisa 318 395 Maggie 268 Mary
 Ann 317 Sarah 318 Susan 318 Walter 318
 William C 177 309
BESTE, Mr 128
BEVERIDGE, Ex-Senator 558
BIBLE, Ann 471
BIDDINGER, Almira 343 Andrew 343
 Andrew J 342-344 Caroline 342 Catherine
 343 Deborah A 342 Dora 344 Elizabeth
 343 Frederick 343 George 343 George W
 342-343 Jacob 343 James 343 John W 342
 Jonathan 343 Mary 343 Melinda 343
 Michael 343 Mr 342 344 Mrs 344 Ruth 344
 Solomon 343 Solomon A 342
BIDWELL, John 119
BIES, John 654 Mary 654
BIGGER, Samuel 57-58
BIGGS, William 48
BIGLER, Angeline 458
BILLHEIMER, John C 251
BILLINGS, Abram R 526 Anna 534 Annetta B
 526 Annie A 526 Arthur 527 Belle 526
 Bettie 526 Charles S 526 Dewill 527
 Dorothy 527 Elizabeth 527 Ellen 527 Eva

INDEX.

BILLINGS (Cont.)
  526 Floyd 527 George W 526 Gladys 527
  Harry 527 James 527 Jennie 527 Jesse 525-
  526 534 Jesse Frank 526 John 526 John M
  527 John W 525-527 534 Lessie 527
  Lillian 527 Lillie M 526 Louis S 526
  Lovina 526 Mary 526-527 Mary S 526
  Mary T 527 Mort 193 Morton E 526 Mr
  527 Nellie 527 Nora 527 Oscar 527 Rettie
  526 Sarah 525-526 534 Stewart 527 Turrie
  526 William 526-527
BINGHAM, A W 296 August W 254 Edith 539
  Ezra 539 H S 161 O A 254
BISHOP, John 89
BLACK, Alice 658 Barbara 657 Bertha 658
  Elizabeth 657-658 Emma 658 Frank 658
  George 658 James 118 Lycurgus 658 Mary
  658 Samuel 657-658 W H 326
BLACKBURN, P 112
BLACKFORD, 300 Isaac 82
BLACKWELL, Etta 268 Jennie 527
BLAINE, James G 119
BLAKE, Judge 301 Thomas H 248
BLANC, Father 198 Napoleon 199
BLANKENSHIP, 301
BLEDSOE, Mary Jane 446
BLESSINGER, Frieda 717 Helen 717 John 717
BLEVINS, Hezekiah 107
BLOCK, Henry 166
BLONDINA, Sister 243
BLOUGH, John 168
BOARDMAN, Stephen 158
BOAZ, Mrs S S 268
BODKIN, William A 161-162
BOGARD, 71 73 Cornelius 69 Noah 172 Sarah
  192 W 70 76
BOGART, Elbert 226
BOGLE, Blanche 660
BOGNER, Elizabeth 270-271 Joseph 266
  Lucia 312
BOLAND, Father 243 W V 202
BOLIN, Elizabeth 709 James 166 John 709
BOLTMAN, Kate 712
BOLTON, Nelson 148 Nelson M 155 Sarah T
  62
BOND, Mrs 129 Shadrach 48-49
BONDURANT, O E 260
BONHAM, Alfred N 254 Allen 400 Alma Inez
  401 Amelia 400 C O 401 Clifford 401
  Clifford O 112 401-402 Elizabeth 627
  Fanny May 401 Frankie Maud 401 George
  H 401 Inez 228 Lucretia 271 401 M L 401
  420 Marguerite 401 Maria 400 Martha J
  401 Martin L 401 Martin Luther 400-401
  Mary L 401 Mr 401 Mrs Clifford O 402
  Rhoda 400 Sarah 401 Selana 401

BONHAM (Cont.)
  Washington 400 Z A 401 Zedekiah 400-
  401 Zedekiah A 401
BONNER, George Washington 255
BOOKER, Oscar 228
BOON, Ratliff 58
BOOS, Catherine 531
BOOTH, Elizabeth 608 Mary E 333 Rachel
  358
BOOTHE, Nancy Jane 649
BORDERS, Mary 271 Mary F 270
BOSTON, Aura 702 W L 191
BOTHWELL, Ann 418 Anna 418 David 418
  Hugh 418 Isabelle 418 James 418 John 418
  Margaret 418 Martha 418 Martha A 418
  Mary 418 Nancy 418 Samuel 418 Sarah
  418
BOULTMAN, Edith 271
BOUQUET, Henry 36
BOWEN, William 99
BOWERS, Dora 683 Stephen 187
BOWLBEY, Siren 401
BOWLER, Thomas 242
BOWMAN, Allegra 612 Alpha O 612 Amanda
  611 Arla 612 Cynthia 671 Cynthia A 671
  Doctor 611-613 Edith 672 Elizabeth 611
  Gov 672 Grover 672 Hannah 671 Hazel
  612 Howard 671 Ira E 255 610-612 Isaac
  611 Jacob 611 John 611 671 Julianna 611
  L C 319 Laura 672 Leona 319 Mahala 671
  Malinda 671 Margaret 517 611-612 671
  Martin 671 Mary Jane 611 Michael 671
  Milton 671 Mr 611-612 671-672 Mrs 613
  672 Nancy 516 Nancy Jane 671 Nora 612
  Orin Howard 612 Paul 672 Pearl 612
  Pleasant 611 671 Sally 671 Sally A 672
  Sarah 611 Sarah Alice 671 Sarah Ann 671
  Sidney E 612 Starling E 612 Susannah 671
  Victor V 612 Willard 670-672 William 111
  611 671 William H 517 611-612
BOYD, Elizabeth 339 J M 109 James M 219
  Jane 447 John 339 John Scudder 340
  Joseph M 218 Mary 411 Matilda 270-271
  Millie B 339 Miss 477 Mr 183 339-340
  513 Polly Ruth 340 S B 240 321 513
  Samuel B 182-183 219 223 Samuel Brown
  339 Samuel Jr 340 Tillie 340 Tillie F 321
  William 109 William C 158
BOYDEN, W P 112
BOYLE, Addie 494 Mr 494
BRADBURY, William 156
BRADFIELD, P J 297
BRADFORD, George 301 Joseph 246 Martha
  416 Thomas 95 Thomas H 416
BRADLEY, Capt 161 Catherine 654 Francis P
  250 Maggie 228

BRADY, Mary 320 William 203
BRAGG, 163 Braxton 159
BRAND, Frances 191 Reason W 191
BRANDUS, H 106
BRANN, O H 266 Oliver H 180
BRANNOCK, B B 254
BRASHEARS, Ira C 158
BRATTON, John 69 Nancy 641 Robert 69 641 William 186 300
BRAY, Harry 260 Ida 666 Victor 666
BRAYFIELD, Carl C 182 John 177 Mr 177
BRAZA, James 85
BRECKENRIDGE, 116
BRECKINRIDGE, John C 116
BREDEN, Della 359 John 195 Walter 359
BREEN, John 200 Mr 200
BREEZE, James 106 113
BREMMETT, Julia 595
BRENNAN, Catherine 573 Owen 573 W E 261
BRETT, Alice 540 Anna 540 M L 288 305 Mary 539 Mathew L 114 Matthew L 86 88 110 151 539-540 Mr 539-540 Mrs 540 P M 249 Patrick M 113 233 539
BREWER, John 197 Margaret 228 Matilda Ann 704 William 704
BRICKERT, C W 189
BRIGGS, Joseph W 148
BRIGHT, Margaret A 422
BRINER, William H 267
BRINTSFIELD, Lydia 686
BRITTAIN, Stephen A 254
BROCK, Caleb 67 274
BROOKE, C M 194
BROOKER, Effie 442
BROOKS, 315 Daniel 271 Emily 438-439 Eunice 439 Grace 439 Hannah Eustace 439 Jefferson 439 John 439 Kyle 190 Lewis 439 Lewis C 316 Lucy 439 Seymour Waldo 439 Susan 439 Thomas 439 Thomas Jefferson 439
BROTHER, Edith 228 Helen 228
BROUGHMAN, Angeline 319 Charles 319 Colonel 319 Fremont 319 Mr 319 Sylvester 319
BROWN, Alonson 525 Alonzo B 576 Andrew J 160 Ann 528 Anna 528 Annetta B 524 Annette 576 Benjamin 610 Bessie 228 Charles R 249 Eunice 228 George 259 440 H C 111 H H 166 H K 109 Henry C 180 J F 190 James K 513 Jessie 228 Johanna 440 John 142 Joseph 104 108 111 528 Lou 621 Margaret 525 576 Margaret A 422 Mary 565 Mr 422 Nancy Ellen 528 Polly 460 Scholastica 528 Stella 610 T M 267 Thomas 112 300 W L 224 W T 220 296 621 William 156 164 528 William T 226

BROWNING, Ada May 492 Harrison 267 Joseph T 446 Mary Jane 446
BROYLES, T L 298
BRUCE, Alexander 67 82 84 97 246 301 James 166 Joseph 246 280 Squire 280 William 82-83 97
BRUMFIELD, Nathan 667 Sarah E 667
BRUMMETT, Minerva 661
BRUNER, A B 303 Fannie 269 George 301 Miss 233
BRUTE, Bishop 196
BRUTTON, William 111
BRYAN, 533 W J 119 William Jennings 120
BRYANT, James R 168
BUCHANAN, 278 Agnes L 330 Allen K 332 Anna Maud 330 Bradie 330 C H 194 Charles H 193 329-330 332 Elizabeth Gay 330 George A 330 James 116 329 James W 329 Mary J 329-330 Maud 330 Minnie I 330 Mrs 331 Nancy 597 Rev 330 Victor 597 Victoria R 330 William J 330
BUCKLE, Alfred 330 Anna Maud 330
BUCKNER, Addie 421 Gen 153
BUELL, 153 159 163
BUGHER, Asa 466 Dicie 446 Elizabeth 466 Jennie 466
BUHER, Catherine 376
BULLEY, 312
BULTMANN, Father 204 William 204
BUN, Dennis 266
BUNCH, W H 298
BUNTING, G N 86
BURCH, America 356 Ann 410 Charles 410 Christopher 410 Darius 410 Emily 410 Ernest 228 Eugene 410 George 410 John 276 Lemuel 410 Mary 410 Milletus 410 Nancy 693 Wiley 410
BURDICK, Loron 254
BURGE, George W 157
BURGH, George W 157
BURGHER, Alonzo C 158
BURK, Catherine 433
BURKE, Cornelius 193 Judge 249 M F 203 305 Matthew F 242 262 Michael 233 Michael F 249
BURKHARDT, Father 204 L M S 203
BURKS, D B 193 Nancy 413
BURLINGAME, B F 161
BURNETT, E A 186
BURNS, 125 Anna 651 Francis 405 Hannah 405-406 Michael 405 Rosa 516
BURREL, Sophronia 680
BURRELL, Albert 380 Anna 380 Carl H 380 Carrie 380 Harley 380 Harry 380 Hilbert 380 J A 373 379-380 James A 379 John W 379-381 Mr 379-380 Mrs John W 380-381

BURRELL (Cont.)
Nellie 380 Richard 379-380 Samuel 380 Sarah 379-380 553
BURRESS, Bert D 255 Harriet 619
BURRI, Elizabeth 502
BURRILL, Horace H 254
BURRIS, 221 225 251 A J 384 B J 220 Benjamin J 224 309 C J 261 338 Eleanor Rebecca 338 Harriet 269 Helen 338 Jacob 256 Juda 384 Julia 383-384 Laura 328 Levi 254 Mabel 228 Mahala 384 Mannie 228 Robert 67 384
BURRISS, John 168
BURROUGHS, Leland 236
BURROWS, W B 160
BURTON, Caroline 318 Caswell R 318 Clara 378 Eliza A 318 Eliza Ann 317 George W 318 Hugh F 318 J W 151 250-251 John C 318 Judge 151 Juliette 318 Margaret 318 Mary S 318 Matilda 318 Philip 139 Ransom 318 S H 378 Sarah J 318 Shubil 318 Virginia C 318 William H 318 Zachariah 318
BUSIC, Ella 577 Marvin 577
BUSKIRK, Samuel H 250
BUSSARD, Ada 599 Beulah 599 Christopher 598 Clark 598 Della 598 Edna 599 Elsie 599 Ervin 599 Florence 599 Flossie 599 Hannah 598 Hattie 598 Herbert 599 Ida 598 Letha 599 Mazie 599 Mr 599-600 Nelson 598 Noah 599 Nora 598 Porter 598-599 Thomas 598
BUTCHER, Eleanor 603
BUTLER, Amos 49 Benjamin F 119 Calvin 185 233 Charles 123 Thomas 195
BUTT, Archibald 373
BUZAN, Albert 354 467-469 Bertha S 354 468-469 Edna Pearl 354 Elizabeth 468 Elmer 112 353-354 Elmer H 468 George 468 John 354 John W 468 Lafayette 354 468 Maria 354 468 Maria S 354 Martha 468 Martha F 468 Mattie A 354 Mr 354-355 467-468 Mrs 469 Nettie 468 Norwood 469 Norwood Howard 355 Pearl 469 Ruby Alberta 355 Ruby Elbert 469 Sarah 468 Sarah A 468 Sarah Adaline 354 Theodocia 354 Theodosia 468 William 354 468
BYNUM, Minnie 666 William D 179 303
BYRD, Charles W 42 Charles Willing 42
BYRER, Ava 408-409 Casper 408 Demma 408 Eliza 408 Emily 408 Frederick 408 Gottlieb 408 Henry 408 Hiram 408 John 408 Matilda 408 Noah 408 Phoebe 408 463 Uretta 408 William 408
BYRN, John B 253
BYRNE, John 199 Miss 199

CABEL, 389 524 576 Anna 202 Austin F 283 Elva B 271 Elva Bondurant 270 Joseph 312 Mrs A F 313 Mrs Austin F 312
CABLE, 372 434 Anna 540 Austin F 540 Brett 540 Mr 540 Mrs 540
CACARYN, May 414
CADBY, Alice 702
CADDEN, Agnes 512 Annie 512 Bridget 511 Daniel 511-512 George 512 Harry 512 Martin 511 Mary 512 Mr 511-512 William 511-512
CADOU, Edward Leon 657 Eugene Jepson 657 Felix L 657 Felix L Jr 657 Lucy 657
CAHILL, L P 296 Martin 261 307
CAIN, James W 92-93
CALDWELL, A G 250 John L 248
CALHOUN, J 112 James 105 258 301
CALL, Jacob 248 Judge 301
CALLAHAN, Alva 448 Anna 448 Annias 448 Arla 448 Daisy 448 Elisha B 447 Eveline 447 Fannie 447 Grant 220-221 241 448 Harold 448 Henry 447 Isaac 447 James 448 Jane 447 Joe 194 John T 447 Joseph 448 Lucinda 448 Lula 448 Maggie 448 Margaret 447 Martha 448 Martin 447 Mary 448 Mr 447-448 Mrs 448 Nancy Jane 447 Olva 448 Peter 448 Polly 447 Rebecca Jane 448 S E 447-448 S Y 447-448 Sarah 447 Southey E 447 Stearer Y 447-448 Stella 448 Tabitha 448 William 448
CALLOWAY, Nancy 254
CAMP, Bertha E 558 Charles C 558 Chester 558 Clara A 558 Electa Jane 558 Ella 558 Harriet 558 Harrison 558 Isaac 558 Jesse 558 John B 557 John H 558 John R 558 Lewis 558 Mason H 558 Mr 557-559 Mrs John R 558 Sarilda 557 William C 557-558 William J 558
CAMPBELL, Alexander 192 435 507 Archibald 438 Col 438 E A 187 Elizabeth Gay 330 Emily 438-439 Ethel 440 Eugenia 440 Harlan Anderson 440 Ida 237 440 Isabell 387 James 203 305 James M 160 Jane 438 John C L 254 438 440 John Milton 438 Margaret 438 Mary 240 387 440 Milton 438 Miss 237 Mr 438 Percy W 330 Robert 387 Sarah 203 Susan Brooks 440 William 387
CANADY, J W 566 Sarah 566
CANE, Julia 637
CANFIELD, J S 163 John S 163 168
CANN, Catherine 343 Elizabeth 343
CANTRELL, E A 190
CANWOOD, Smallwood 276
CARESS, Abraham 501 Eldena 518 Eldina 501 Eliza 501 Elizabeth 501 Frances

CARESS (Cont.)
  Margaret 501 Hadden 501 James 501
  Jerome 501 Johanna 501 John 500-501
  Martha 501 Maud May 501 Mr 501-502
  Sarah 500-501 Sarah Isabel 501 Simon
  500-501 Tabitha 501 William H 501
CARITHERS, John 140
CARLAND, Mr 69
CARLETT, Lolie 610
CARLEY, Patrick 148
CARLIN, Daniel E 275
CARLTON, A B 250 Simon B 254
CARMAN, Robert M 113
CARNAHAN, Abram W 154 Aikman 114 227
  266 Clara 268 Eliza 315 Elizabeth 420
  Ellen 520 Florence 420 Hattie 316 Helen
  316 J 227 James 420 James A 168 James R
  266 Jennie 420 John G 520 M J 316
  Magness J 305 315-316 Margaret 316
  Martha J 401 Mary E 420 519-521 May
  420 Minnie 229 Mr 316 Mrs J Blair 233
  Nellie 420 Ramona 316 Rebecca 520
  Robert 315 402 520 Sidney 229
CARNEGIE, Andrew 311 Mr 311
CARNEHAN, John 640 Mary E 640
CARP, Clara 477 Clarinda 708 Wilson 477
CARPENTER, Floyd 229 L L 193-194 Mr 283
  Willard 283-284
CARR, Henry M 163 Homer Frank 255 Mr 301
CARRALL, Joseph 158
CARRINGTON, Gen 56
CARROLL, Benjamin Rufus 391 Dickson 508
  Harriet 391 James 550 John 508 Leutitia
  508 Luetta 550 Mary 507-508 Mary
  Frances 391 Nathaniel 508 Robert 508
  Rufus 508 William 508
CARSON, John 186 Thomas H 249 W R 158
CARTER, Alice 437 David 437 David R 253
  Florence 437 Florence R 437 Mattie 437
  Mr 437 Nancy 568 Sarah 437 W H 167
CASE, Abraham 279 John 67 Joseph 67 280
  Miss 70-71
CASEY, Albert R 370 Clara 370 Delilah 370
  Effie 370 Fred E 370 Herschel D 370
  Homer F 370 Louella 370 Millie 370
  Minnie E 370 Minnie Ellen 370 Mr 370
  Thomas W 157 370 Thomas Walker 370
CASS, Lewis 115
CASSIDY, Capt 165 John 112 John A 157 161
CASTLEMAN, D A 667 Luetta B 667
CASTO, Adelia 313
CATERSON, James P 667 Minnie 667
CATO, J Barton 255
CAVANAUGH, Bridget 388 Charles 389 Clara
  389 Daniel 388 Dennis 389 Elizabeth 388
  George 389 James 388 John 388-389

CAVANAUGH (Cont.)
  John P 262 388-390 Joseph 389 Margaret
  388-389 Mary 389 522 Mr 388-389 Mrs
  389 P J 306 Patrick 388 Richard 388 Sarah
  389 William 389
CAVNES, Agnes 646 Agnes J 646 Sion 646
CAWOOD, John 106
CAYWOOD, Jemimah 355-356
CHAD, Jane 392
CHAFIN, 120-121
CHAMBER, Manda 647
CHAMBERS, Amanda 363 Benjamin 48 Flora
  323 Frank 323 Lakie Janes 363 Margaret
  683 Thomas 363
CHAMPIONER, M 199 Rev 198
CHAMPONIER, Father 198
CHANDLER, Earl 395 Fred 395 Indiana 377
  394 J C 377 John A 394 Lillian 395 Loran
  395 Mabel 395 Marie 395 Martha Glenn
  394-395 Matilda 367 Raleigh 395
CHANNIS, Samuel 246
CHAPMAN, Charles R 166 Eli 76 78 272
  Elijah 113 248 272 Ella 586 Henry O 159
  James 586 James M 158 Josephine 271 L J
  270 L Josephine 270 Mary K 271 Matilda
  586 William 178 272 300
CHAPMEN, J P 259
CHAPPELL, Elliott 109 Eugenia 440 S W 440
CHARTIER, Rev 199
CHASE, Henry 271 Ira J 59 William 233
CHASSE, Father 242 J B 202
CHATARD, Bishop 203-204
CHATTIN, Cleo 505 N H 229
CHEIRS, J B 191
CHENOWETH, Samuel A 440 Susan Brooks
  440
CHESTNUT, A L 229 Hattie 433
CHILDS, Capt 152 161 165 468 Charles 148
  152 165-166 259
CHILES, Margaret 254
CHINN, Hazel A 229
CHIPPS, Sarah 419
CHOWNING, Harriet 254
CHRIST, Emily 440
CHURCH, Joseph 266
CHUTE, Daniel 271 441 Hannah 439 441
  James 271 Professor 441
CLAIRE, F Della 254
CLAPP, 283 Alice Mary 392 Corinne 392 Fred
  S 392 Mary S 191 233
CLARK, A Lawrence 229 563 A M 563-564
  Albert M 280 Alva 296 Ann 338 Belinda
  564 Belle 564 Bethuel 157 Carolina 327
  Charles A 564 Clara 327 Clara Ida 564
  Delphia 564 Dennis 67 246 Doctor 377
  Donald G 564 Edwin 328 Effie 328

INDEX.

CLARK (Cont.)
   Elias 267 Ellenor 564 Emma 296 327-328
   Fred 328 Gen 37-38 George Rogers 37
   Hale 304 Harry Hobbs 564 Howard 241
   327 Ira M 253 J W 260 Jacob G 110 Jacob
   W 253 James 564 John 109 112 327-328
   564 John A 564 John L 327-328 John V
   328 John Y 564 L 227 Laura 233 Lawrence
   563-564 Len L 328 Lenora 241 Lewis 158
   Lillie 564 Lloyd 290 Lyle 328 Marshall
   Lovina 564 Mary 327 564 Mary E 328
   Maud 268 Mr 327-329 563-564 Mrs 329
   Myron 564 Oliver H 564 Ollie 327 Ralph
   Waldo 564 Raymond E 328 Robert 328
   Rosettie 563 Samuel 328 Sarah E 328
   Tabitha Ann 575 Vivian 328 Walter 328
   William 328 338 564 William B 255
CLARKE, Catherine 559 Katherine 559 W H
   193 William 46
CLARY, William D 297
CLAWSON, Benjamin 712 Stella C 712
CLAY, 57 Henry 114
CLAYTON, Quinton 253
CLEAVER, Almira 343 J B 190 R D 343
CLEMENS, Ethel 440 Harvey J 440 Miss 459
CLEMENTS, Leo 229 Lewis 229 R A 90 249
   Richard A 113 Richard A Jr 114 Sarah 634
CLEMMER, C O 256
CLEMONS, Julia 410
CLERRY, William D 297
CLEVELAND, Grover 119
CLIFFORD, Ambrose C 255
CLIFT, Daniel 67 George 67
CLINTON, Flora 229 Hazel 229 Zella 409
CLORE, Edward 401 Frankie Maud 401
CLOSSMAN, Josephine 460
CLOUD, Justice 155 Nancy 318 Thomas David
   256
COAN, Mary J 436 W P 436
COATS, Beulah 599
COCHRAN, C F 305 Charles F 259 G W 268
   Helen 228 Margaret 607
COCKRUM, W M 123 143
COFFEE, 125
COFFEY, W O 254
COFFIN, George 483 Lucetta 483
COFFMAN, 372
COHORN, Charles 652 Delilah 652 Emily 652
   William 652
COLBERT, Abner 171 Abner D 173 Amanda
   229 Charles 111 F B 226 Fielding 111
   Friend B 112 George W 179 J A 306 James
   A 261 John 247 Levi D 295 Susie 229 T E
   229 William F 297
COLE, E P 234 Elizabeth 506 Emily H 384
   Jacob 384 James 506 Laura C 317

COLE (Cont.)
   Margaret 191 Ruth 618 W G 190-191 210
   William G 106 233 244 William H 317
   Willis H 255
COLEMAN, Adda 387 Arilla 495 Bridget 511
   Christopher 272 Daniel 511 Frances 495
   Francis 597 Helen 387 John 94-95 138 597
   John B 245 495 John W 87 Miss 585
COLLICOTT, J G 225
COLLINS, Blanche 229 Dan 192 J W 632
   Maud 632
COLVIN, Elizabeth 624 John 624
COLYER, Frank 260
COMAN, Carolina 327
COMBS, Mary 398
COMER, Daniel 66 96 111 Samuel 67 69 279
COMPTON, Joseph 454 Lodusky H 369
   Margaret 454
CONARD, Lucinda 646 Rebecca 655
CONDO, A B 195
CONETER, Thomas 148
CONKLE, Salina 664
CONLIN, Agnes 573 Anna 573 Catherine 573
   Charles 573 Dorothy 573 Henry 573 James
   572 James M 572-573 Margaret 573
   Marguerite 573 Mary 512 Mary Anne 572
   Mattie 573 Michael 573 Mr 573 Mrs 573
   Rose May 573 Sarah 573 William 573
CONNAUGHTON, Charles 261 E 227 M T
   227
CONNELL, Leonard 218
CONNELLY, Arthur 214
CONNOLLY, A 227
CONSTABLE, Carrie B 327 Lyle 706 Nell 706
COOK, 479 Citizen 152 Harriet E 228-229
   Harry H 292 Keziah 347 352 482 Martha
   562 William 482-483 562
COOMBS, Benjamin 277
COONEY, Christopher J 219
COOPER, Ina 413 Joseph 413 Lowery 550
   Lowry 292 Nancy 413 Peter 118
CORBIN, Mattie 494 Mr 494
CORE, Lew S 110 226 Robert 226 Robert J
   238
CORLETT, B F 193
CORNETT, Samuel 283
CORNING, Alice 270-271 Alice Evans 270
   Mrs J W 312
CORRELL, Beldwin 373 Belinda 564 Charles
   373 Clement 298 372-373 Eleanor 373 G
   W 380 George 172 George W 172 372-374
   H C 267 H N 267 Harvey 373 Ira 373
   Jacob 373 John 158 373 Mary 373 Mr 373
   Nancy 372-373 Rachel 373 Richard 373
   Roberta 373 Walter 373
CORYA, John W 702 Lena 702 Lillie 702

COSBY, 434 Abner 102 Ellen 527 L 227 O 227 Overton 527 Stansel 259 Susan 227
COSTELLO, John M 261
COTTINGHAM, Edith 228
COUCHMAN, Andrew 279
COULTER, Thomas 148
COURJAULT, Rev 199
COURTNEY, Alice C 369 Anna 459 D H 369 Edna 700 Elizabeth 699-700 Elizabeth S 700 Ethel L 701 Frances 641 700 Frances Ann 699-700 George W 700 James 641 James H 699-700 James S 699-700 John A 700 Joseph G 700 Levi M 700 Lovina 700 Magdeline 700 Mary 692 700 Mary Ann 700 Mary M 700 Mr 700-701 Mrs 701 Nancy 700 Nancy Ann 700 Nancy M 700 Nellie B 700 Ralph 700 Rosetta 701 Ross K 701 Sarah 641 Sarah F 700 Thomas J 700 Thomas W 700 William H 699-701 William M 700
COURTRIGHT, Charles Henry 425 Claudia M 425 Edna Alice 425 Guy W 425 Mary Louise 425
COVAL, Delilah 583 John 583 Laura 583
COVALT, Cheinah 634 Cheniah 579 634 Edgar L 579 634 Elizabeth 579 634 Fannie M 579 Ferdinand 579 634 Hoyt 579 634 Lemoa Anna 579 Lillian 579 634 Louisanna 579 634 Mildred 579 634 Mr 579-580 Mrs E L 580 Myrle 579 634 Nellie 580 Ola 579 634
COVENTRY, Mary 387
COVERT, Jacob 155 178-179 181
COVEY, Nancy 617
COWAN, Mary 516
COWARDIN, Mary 233
COX, Ada 476 Elizabeth 487 Emerine 413 Gabriel 413 John 487 John E 476 Laura 413 Madge 626 Margaret 193 Martin 641 Minnie 229 Nancy 641 Sarah E 487-488 William 266-267
CRABB, A W 193
CRABS, David 108 Jacob D 105 108
CRAFT, Henry 160
CRAGER, Anna 435
CRAMER, Mary 418 Sarah 419 Warren A 166
CRANE, J E 389 Mary 610
CRAWFORD, G P 193 J M 291 Lucia 271 Margaret 580
CREAGER, D V 266 John W 266
CRECELIUS, Owen 229
CREMS, David 449 Sarah 449
CRESSY, Crystal Thelma 712 Fred Everett 712 Lilly 712 Mary A 712 Miss 233 Oscar 712 Ruth Elizabeth 712
CRIM, A L 193

CRIST, Nora 476 R J 476
CRITCHLOW, G M 267 G W 267 James 167 Mary 571 William 296
CRITTENDEN, Col 153 Thomas T 153
CRITZLOW, George M 646 Mary Ann 646
CROFOOT, Miss 330
CROOK, Charlotte 514 Cyrus 280 Howard 292
CROOKE, Anna 552-553 Edith 553 Elizabeth 552-553 Fannie 553 Frank 553 H H 298 607 Harry H 114 306 552-553 Harry Jr 553 Hazel 553 Howard 114 239 292 298 380 552-553 J M 298 John B 240 Joseph 553 Lela 553 Lillie 553 Maggie 553 Margaret 553 Margaret L 607 Martha 553 Mason 553 Mr 292 553 Nancy 552 Ned 553 Ollie 552-553 Olly 292 Oren 553 Ozias 294 Sarah 380 553
CROPP, Bernetta 444 James 444
CROSBY, Alice 193 Ella 237 Mary 254
CROSLEY, Alice 193
CROSS, Albert 378 Alfred 378 Carrie 378 Charles 187 233 Florence 599 Frank 696 Glendora 378 Iona 599 Judson 378 Laura 378 Lizzie 378 Lucy 378 696 Merle 599 Robert 599
CROSSON, Ernest A 203 Thomas 242
CROTZ, Elizabeth 699-700
CRUIKSHANK, Mary 401
CRUSE, Henry 99-100 James P 156 Joseph 258 Mrs P 152 Philip 185 Sarah 185 Seth H 285
CULBERTSON, John 69 John W 254 Joseph 69 Josiah 66 69 75 113 279 Samuel 69 75
CULLOM, Amelia 400
CULMER, Fannie 553 George F 254 Stephen O 253 Steven 553
CULNER, Anna 552
CUMMINGS, Angeline 476 Anza M 460 Catherine 460 Charles 546 David 460-461 Delilah 546-547 Eliza 460 Elizabeth A 460 Evaline 460 Grace 628 Jane 460 546-547 Jemimah 460 John 460 John K 460 Joseph 460-461 Levi 460 M 194 Malachi 460 Mary 460 Miss 233 Mr 460 Polly 460 Rebecca 460 Robert 460 Rosanna 460 Sarah 460 Susan 460 Tabitha 460 William 460
CUNNINGHAM, A B 189 Alonzo 168 448 Alvira 448 Andrew 164 Archa 448 G A 229 Goolie 448 John 448 Julia 448 Lewis 448 Lizzie 448 Martha 448 Mary 448 Mary Ann 448 Mary C 676 Mr 189 448 Mrs Nelson 188 Murl 229 Nancy 448 Nelson 188 Ray 228 Robert Wesley 448 Thomas 90 193 W T 166 William Thomas 448
CUPPY, Carter 568 Flora 568 Nancy 568

INDEX.

CURLEY, Patrick 158
CURRENT, J D 195
CURRY, Mr 69
CURTIS, George 84 299
CUSKADEN, Mary 555-556
DAGES, Corrien 229 Omer 229
DAGLEY, E L 254 Elias L 254
DAKIN, Samuel 271
DALE, James A 163 James H 164
DALTON, Effie 328 341 S W 341
DAMEREL, 233
DAMEWOOD, Boston 414 May 414 Susan E 414-415
DANKS, Belle 431 Charles 431 Clara 431 Emma 431 Joseph 431 Lydia 431 Mayme 431 T C 187 Thomas C 431
DANLEY, Carrie B 368 Joseph 368
DANNER, Amelia 458 Emma 458 J F 297 Joel 240 Joseph 458 Rufus J 255 William J 298
DANT, 198 Barbara 556 Catherine 345 Charles 345 Dora 526 Elizabeth 566 Mary S 526 Thomas L 566 William 275
DARBY, J W 175 190
DARKS, Clara 458
DAUGHERTY, Allen 268 Ann 629 Eugene 629 James H 109 John W 109 Joseph 112 Victoria 629
DAVIDSON, Araminta 425 E E 190 John 67
DAVIES, Charity 524 Christian 524 Elias 524 Eliza J 524 Julia 524 Levi 524 Mary A 524
DAVIESS, Capt 83 Joseph H 83
DAVIS, Abner 89 Abner M 113 Alfred 245 Alfred B 305 Alfred P 322 Allie 322 Anna V 321 Bertie 322 Eliza J 523 George 322 Harry 322 Henry S 166 Jacob 166 John 192 John H 266 John O 322 Laura 271 Lina 617 Mary 526 Nathan 69 R C 305 321 Richard C 322 Robert J 210 W M 192 W S 157 William E 157 Wilson S 234
DAVISON, John 94
DAWSON, Hattie 447
DAY, C M 194
DAYTON, Della May 593
DEAL, J A 229
DEAN, Mrs Thomas 203
DEARMIN, Ada P 571 Carl L 571-572 Day 614 Doctor 614 Dott 614 Elbert T 614 Eliza 571 Eliza A 613-614 Etta 269 Eva P 614 Evelyn P 608 George 571 613 Henry 571 James L 571 John 253 292 571 613 Joseph 571 613 Joseph E 571-572 Margaret V 572 Martha F 571 Mary 571 Mary E 613 May 614 Maysel C 615 Miles R 572 Minnie 614 Mr 572 614-615 Mrs 572 Percy 571 Rebecca 571 Rena L 614-615 Robert Mason 615 Russell Paul 615 Susan 614

DEARMIN (Cont.)
Thomas 571 Walter 608 614 Walter Fred 615 Walter T 613-614 William 571-572 613
DEBIENVILLE, Celeron 35
DEBRULER, L Q 250
DEBS, 121 Eugene 120
DECKER, Anna 444
DEER, A C 323 Gussie E 323 J J 323 Margaret L 323 Marshall 323 Martha L 323
DEFFENBALL, William B 255
DEFFENDALL, W B 306
DEKAMP, Rachael 660
DELAHAILANDIERE, Bishop 197 200 Right Reverend Bishop 199
DELANEY, John 197 Michael 197
DELAUNE, J 197 199
DEMOTTE, Albert 360 Calvin 361 Clara 360 Doctor 359-361 Elizabeth 360 Ella 360 Elvis 360 James 359 Jerome 359-361 John 360 Lawrence 360 Olive 361 Pauline 361 Phoebe 360 Russell 361 Sebastian 360
DENNIGEN, William P 252
DENNY, E G 192 J S 194 James C 249
DERMOSLY, Philip 162
DESTPALAIS, Father 197 M 197 199
DEWEY, Charles 250-251 Judge 301
DIBBLE, A E 298
DICKERSON, David 164 Elizabeth 506 Serat 506 Susan 506 Zadock 506 Zeddeck 164
DICKERT, Anderson 158
DICKEY, John M 184-185 Mr 184 Rev 184 Sol C 184
DICKINSON, Harvey H 168 William T 109
DIEFENDORF, Albert 601 Mr 601
DILLARD, Addie 398 Amadeus Byron 399 Dyanthia 399 Estella 399 Fannie 398 Henry 398 Ida 398 J W 260 John W 398 John Warren 399 Mary 398 Miranda E 399 Mr 399-400 Mrs 399 V E 229 236 Vassall Edgar 399 William 398
DILLEY, John A 523 L H 298 Martha D 523
DILLON, Ada 605 Ada E 674 Agnes 605 Albert H 605-606 Arthur B 606 Blanche 606 Clara 606 Dorothy 606 Edith 672 Eliza 605 Evangeline 605 F D 674 Franklin D 605-606 644 Frederick 672 George 672 Harold 606 Inez 606 Inez E 644 Jacob C 109 John C 109 Lovina 700 Mable 672 Margaret 606 Margaretta 605 Mr 606 Mrs 606 Nancy 641 Nancy A 678 Ruth 606 686 Sheldon 672 Walter S 605 Wesley 674 Wesley T 605-606 644 William 605 William J 605
DISBROUGH, Anna 409 Lewis 409
DISSER, John 624 Mary 624 Michael 451

DISSER (Cont.)
  Rose 451
DIVENS, Charles W 254
DIXON, Frank 220 John 259 Solomon 276
DOBBS, Blanche 606
DOBBYN, B 109 Richard B 109
DOBSON, Mary Ann 436
DODAMEL, Abraham 69
DONAHUE, Ella 229
DONALDSON, Margaret 481
DONE, William 297
DONNOLLY, Catherine M 624 Mary 624
  William 624
DOOLEY, Michael M 254
DOOLIN, Bertha May 413 Comfort 413 Diaz
  413 George W 412-413 Hazel A 413 Ina
  413 Irene 413 John S 413 Laura 413
  Martha 413 Martha A 413 Mary Frances
  413 May 413 Mrs 413 Mrs George W 413
  Myrtle 413 Nora E 413 Pearl 413 Robert
  413 Robert E 413 Rozella 413 William 413
DORNAUF, Elizabeth 577
DORSEY, S O 286
DOSCH, John 112 262
DOTY, Jonathan 248 Judge 248 Samuel 104
DOUGHARTY, Alexander H 148
DOUGHERTY, Clay 413 Elbert 229 John T
  259 Leonard 413 Mary Frances 413
DOUGLAS, Stephen A 116-117
DOUGLASS, James A 186
DOVE, Agnes 269
DOVER, Minnie 577
DOW, Neal 118
DOWDEN, John H 249 Sudie P 268
DOWNEY, Catherine 624 John 92-93 304-305
  624 Lewis J 255
DOWNS, Helen 229
DOYLE, Ann 624 Father 197-198 203 John
  220 226 John W 197 202 261-262 Martin
  624 Mayme 243 Michael 203
DREW, Catherine 654 George B 225 John 654
  Maria 654 Mary Catherine 654
DRUM, Philomena 625
DUBOIS, Henry 258 Touissant 66
DUCOUDRAY, Father 199 201
DUFFY, Thomas C 162
DUNCAN, B 76 Robert C 234
DUNKIN, Elizabeth 408
DUNLAP, Clemens 641 Clement 267 Cora 641
  Drusilla 359 Hattie 641 James 359 Martha
  641 Mary Eleanor 358-359 Mary Ellen 359
  Mr 359 R B 167 Ray 358-359 Ruth 358-
  359 Samuel 267 292 359 Sarah 641 Scott
  641
DUNN, 74-75 George G 249 251 Hattie 316
  Joseph 250

DUNNING, Paris C 58 250-251
DUPONTAVICE, H 202
DURBIN, Winfield T 59
DUTTON, Nellie 327
DUVAL, Capt 74
DWYER, James D 229
DYAL, Julia 371
DYE, Kenneth 248
DYER, Charles 194 Claude 413 David H 268
  Elbert 413 Elder 193 George 341 George A
  215-218 226 Irmel 413 M 227 Maria 341
  Mary 442 Mary A 413 Mary Jane 442
  Nancy 387 Pearl 413 Rozella 413 S H 193
  Sarah 340-341 Susan 413 Walter 413
  William 442
DYKE, Agnes 341 Angie 341 Carl 341 Dons
  341 Ebenezer 341 Effie 341 Geneva 341
  George 341 George W 340-341 Gladys 341
  James 340-341 Josephine 341 Mary 341
  Mr 341-342 Norman 341 Sarah 340-341
  William 340-341
EADS, 705 Bessie 696 Charity 695-696 Elijah
  695 Eliza 696 Eliza Ann 696 Elizabeth 337
  Floyd 697 Frank 697 Hannah 696 James B
  337 John 694-696 John H 695-696 Julius
  697 Leonard 697 Lida 696 Lucy 696 Mary
  E 697 Mr 696-697 Nettie 696 Sarah 696
  Seth 697 Thomas L 253
EAGLE, 73 Mr 72 475 Thomas 72 247
EARLE, E E 285
EASTRIDGE, George 462
EATON, 708 Asemeth 477 Benjamin 167
  Frank P 327 Isaac 477 Jane 650 Jefferson
  650 Joseph 477 Joseph Sr 477 Ollie 327
ECHELBARGER, Elizabeth 579 634
ECKLES, Delana R 249
ECKSTEIN, Helen 717
EDGIN, Lillie 553
EDMONDSON, Gilbert W 255 John 268
EDMONSON, Wiley 292
EDWARDS, Anna 409 Augustus 409 Ava 408-
  409 Belle 510 Bettie 510 Dasie 409
  Delphia 409 Edith 347 352 Edna 409
  Elizabeth 408 Emma 409 Florence 409
  Gladys 229 409 Helen 409 Henry 69 95
  409 Isaac 583-584 Jackson 156 Jane 581
  John 69 279 Joseph 407-409 Josie 409
  Lucile 409 Margaret 392 Mr 409 Mrs 409
  Omer 229 Pearl 409 Ruth 409 Sarah Ellen
  409 Thomas 408-409 W K 259 William
  156 Zella 409
EGAN, James J 202
EGGLESTON, 211 George Cary 210
EHLER, Caroline 714 Frederick 714
  Grandfather 714 Mary 714 Mena 714
  Phillip 714 Reka 714 Theresa 714

INDEX.

ELLEGE, Z B 195
ELLEN, Mrs A W 322
ELLIOTT, John 378 Martha A 377 Martin A 378
ELLIS, D V 268 David 69 John 69 Mary 269 Rebecca 468 W P 259-260 266 Widow 69 William 69 William P 304 309
ELMORE, 276 Abraham 686 Bernice 229 Dee 686 Isaac 277 686 John 686 Mary 686 Ruth 686 S W 297 Stella 686 Stephen 686 Thomas 296-297 686
ELROD, Miss 563 Stephen B 255
ELSIVIC, G D 267
EMERLING, Mary 555
EMERY, Foster 621 Sarah 621
EMMERLING, Anthony 587 Austin 588 Bridget 587 Charles 587 Effie 588 Frank 587 George 587-588 Gertrude 588 John 587 Joseph 587 Lena 588 Lester 588 Mary 587 Mr 587-588 Noble 588
EMMICK, Frank 630 Martha Jane 630
ENGELHART, Anna 716 Anthony 716 Elizabeth 716 Margaretta 716 Mr 717 Paul 716 Raymond 716-717 Theresa 716
ENGELING, Rachel 480
ENGLAND, Gallatin 193 Linda 193
ENGLEHART, Elizabeth 403 Frieda 717 Harvey H 717 Mr 717 Paul 716 Raymond 717
ENGLISH, Alexander 105 108 Ernest 413 John 108 Noble Alexander 413 Nora E 413 Thomas E 413
ENNIS, Albert W 509 Lucy M 427 Martha G 508-509 Mary Jane 509
ERWIN, Caleb 656 Elsie E 656
ESKRIDGE, 182 Elijah 303
ESLINGER, Hattie 269
EUBANKS, Melvina 427
EVANS, Ada 229 Ann Eliza 317 Frank A 176 267 Jane 438 John 95 179 John A 298 John L 255 John N 249 Pantha Ann 369 Robert Sr 277 Sarah 371 Walter Ann 404 William L 253
EVERETT, Elizabeth 464
EVERT, Elizabeth 475
EWING, John 113 301
FAITH, Abraham 445 490 Abraham H 254 531 Catherine 531 Dianah 531 Don C 229 659 E C 252 309 Ed 521 Edward C 112 531 658-659 Fannie 490 Frances 531 Frances C 445 Frances D 490 George 521 George A 112 252 531 659 George Alvin 530-532 George Alvin Jr 532 Grant 112 521 531 659 Harold B 659 Harrison 490 Helen Virginia 532 Henry C 531 Hugh G 531 John 531 John Head 532 Laura 490 531

FAITH (Cont.)
Laura A 445-446 Lavina 490 531 Lena 659 Louisa 490 531 Malhaly 641 Matilda J 531 658 Melissa 531 Milton Z 531 Mr 530-531 658-659 Mrs 532 659 Thomas 490 531 Thomas W 531 658 Virginia Hays 532 William 192 641
FANNING, Bridget 566 Frank 566 John 109 Mary B 566 Mr 566
FARIS, W H 159 William H 266
FARLEY, Josiah 154
FARMWALD, Leonard 389
FARQUAR, Elizabeth 697 William 697
FARRELL, August 199 James 297 William D 107
FARRIS, Alvilda 643 Alwilda 643 Belle 269 Caroline 643 Clara 643 Clementine 643 Clifford 277 606 643-644 Ella 643 Grace 644 Gray 644 Helen 644 Inez 606 Inez E 644 John Leonard 643 Leonard 643 Lindsey 643 Lovina 644 Marie 644 Maud 644 Mildred 644 Milton 268 643-644 Mr 643-645 Mrs 643 Nauma 643 Oscar 644 Paul 643 Porter 644 Roland 644 Sanders 643 Sarah 643 Susannah 644 Theodore 643 William E 644
FEAGAN, Ellen 573 Henry 573 Mary Anne 572
FEAGANS, Hazel 229 J 227 M 227 W W 303 William W 416
FEE, Daniel 157 Peter 389
FELIX, Nettie 603 S G 603
FELLER, Anna 600
FELTNER, Elizabeth 684-685 George 641 Nancy 641 Nicholas 685 Sophia 685
FELTS, Charity 524
FERGUSON, Alwilda 664 677 Amy 663 Blackburn 663 Clara 327 Francis 327 John 109 601 664 Kell 229 Millie 601 Nannie 601 Salina 664
FERRELL, Goldie 427
FESLER, George L 157
FICKE, Edna Pearl 354 Glendora 355 William H 355
FICKEY, Pearl 469
FIELDER, A L 666 Cora 666 Martha 666
FIELDS, Bruce W 193
FIETNER, R 167
FILLMORE, 115 Millard 116
FINCH, Edwin M 259
FISH, Blanche 229 Leander C 424 Sabina 424
FISHER, Earl C 324 George 48 Herbert M 324 Lester 324 Mabel C 324 Mary J 324 Nellie 324 William 325 William H 324
FISK, Clinton B 119 Miss 233 Rev Mr 227
FITTS, Mary C 268

FITZGERALD, Benjamin 192 Milton 111
FITZGIBBON, John 253
FITZPATRICK, Alma 522 Bettie 522 Celia 522 Doyle 522 Elizabeth 522 Frank 242 Frank J 522 Helen 521-522 James 522 John 521-522 Mary 521-522 Mr 523 Nicholas 522 Patrick 522 Susanah 522 Ternes 521-522 William 522
FLAGET, Bishop 197 199 201
FLANDERS, Charles H 162
FLANNIGAN, Bridget 566
FLEEMER, Otto Florea 255
FLICK, Edith 229
FLINN, Jacob 267 M E 227 W J 158
FLINT, 139 John 113 Obe 69 272 Obed 72 83 246 Ovid 111 Roy 229 William 66 69
FLORA, David 65-66 84 246 299
FLOWERS, Thomas W 254
FLOYD, Davis 48 J F 190
FLUMMERFELT, Eliza 501
FLYNN, Mollie 203
FOLSON, Benjamin 171
FORD, Capt 148 Dennie 229
FORDEN, J 139 John 69
FORDING, Ann 410
FORE, Elizabeth 487
FORNWALD, F B 397 Frank B 306
FORREST, Gen 162
FORSTER, William 258
FORSYTHE, Andrew J 324 Betsey 324 David 323-324 David P 323-324 Elkanah 324 Ernest 323 Ernest E 309 323-325 Flora 323 Gussie E 323 Harold 324-325 John E 323 Josephine 323 Mabel C 324 Margaret 323-324 Margaret L 323 Martha L 323 Mary L 323 Miss 394 Mr 323 325 Mrs 324-325 Oscar D 323 Paul 324 Sarah 324 Sarah J 323 Thomas T 323
FORYTHE, Ernest E 323
FOSTER, Alice 203 Alice V 421 Department Commander 267 Henry 67 274 John W 165 William 420
FOUST, Anna 415 B L 415 Charles 415 Charles Hastings 415 Cleo 415 D M C 456 Daniel 414 Dialtha M 432-433 Dorothy Ellen 415 Florence 415 Florence Margarite 415 John Donald 415 John N 414-415 Joseph 456 Juanita 415 Lyman 415 Mary Edna 415 Mildred Alzora 415 Mr 415 Mrs 415 Nora 415 Ralph 415 Standley 415 Susan E 414-415 Theodore Claude 415 William Charles 414-415
FOX, Adam 474 Edith 652 Laura 474 Mr 652 Tessie 474
FRANCH, Annie 679
FRANCIS, Brother 200

FRANK, Susan 642
FRANKLIN, Alvin Marshall 533 Charity 533 Cora H 533 Estella 533 Floyd Frederick 533 Jewell Dott 533 John F 109 532-533 545 Joseph D 532-533 Laura 533 Laura J 532 545 Martha M 533 Mary E 533 545 Mr 532-533 Mrs 533 Parlina 489 Pleasant 107 Sarah 659 Susan A 533 W T 297
FRAVEL, Charles 259
FRAZE, Christian 680 Sophia 680 Sophronia 680
FREED, Earl 229 Susannah 673
FREELAN, Aaron 94
FREELAND, Aaron 87 102-103 J 69 Jacob 246 John P 113 Lorraine 354 Rachael 583 Ruth 468
FREEMAN, 576
FREMONT, John C 116-117 278
FRESHLEY, Bessie P 498 Carrie 497 Catherine 497 Doctor 497-498 Flora 497 Frederick 497 Frederick J 255 497-498 George 497 Ida 497 Irma 497 Mary A 497 Mrs 498 Oscar 497-498
FRETS, Abraham 698 Delila W 698 William A 297
FRIEDLY, F A 187
FRISBY, George 439
FRITCH, Louis C 308
FROMME, Albert 561 Anna 561 Charles 561 Christina 561 Frederick 561 Gustina 561 Henry 561 Louis 561 William 561
FROST, David 254 Mr 72
FRY, W T 234
FRYER, John 186
FULKERSON, A O 187 219-220 226 230 237 307 369 Alice C 369 Allen B 369 Alva O 221 225 Alva Otis 368-370 Arthur L 369 Clarence D 369 Clarence Dale 255 Edgar L 369 Effie L 369 Eldon 369 Henry 369 Irene E 369 Isaac 369 Jacob 369 James 369 Margaret L 369 Marion 369 Michael 369 Minnie Ellen 370 Mr 370-371 Mrs 370 Oliver H 288 369 Pantha Ann 369 Superintendent 370 William 369 Z Roy 369 Ziba 369
FULLERTON, Mary E 268
FULTON, Anna 582 Richard 296 Thomas 82
FUNCANNON, Walter 229
FUNKHOUSER, H C 195 Hugh 240
FYFFE, Adaline 637 Anne 637 Benjamin 637 Charles Edward 638 Edgar 638 Edward Perry 637 George Ransom 638 George W 171 638 George Wilson 637 Harry Halcomb 638 James 637 James Austin 638 Julia 637 Lafie 638 Lora Agnes 638 Lulie Bell 638 Marion 637 Martha 637 Mills 637

INDEX.

FYFFE (Cont.)
  Milton Frederick 638 Mr 637-638 Mrs 638
  Nellie L 637 Raymond Earl 638 Rebecca
  637 Rillie Angeline 638 Sarah 637 Sarah
  Ethel 638 Susan Adie 638 Thomas Scott
  638 William A 638
GADBERRY, William 267
GAFFNEY, William 213 William S 214 216
GAINES, William 158
GALLAGHER, M 227
GALLAND, Isaac 84 299
GALOONY, Ann 623 Bernard 624 Ellen 624
  John 624 William 624
GAMBLE, Bertha 229
GANDY, Doctor 691
GANNON, Mabel 702
GANTZ, Daniel 298
GARAGHAN, P T 261
GARD, W M 193
GARDENER, Emma 550
GARDINER, 311 348 Charles G 251 Judge
  251 W P 171 W R 151 161 175 306
  William R 180 251 306-307 312
GARDNER, 177-178
GARFIELD, James A 118
GARRIOTT, T A 195
GARTEN, Bertha J 333 Bertha Jane 358 Bessie
  552 Betsie 551 Capt 239 333 551 Charles
  R 191 Cyrena 551 Delight 358 Eliza 551
  Elizabeth 552 645-646 Frank 552 J E 238 J
  H 167 James 358 551 James E 239 333
  James Edward 358 James H 167 333 551
  James Harvey 357-358 Jane 551 Lillie 564
  Lucinda 358 Lydia 358 551 Mage 552
  Mary Ann 551 Mary E 333 Mary Eleanor
  358 Minnie 551-552 Mr 357-358 Mrs 358-
  359 Nancy B 551 655 Robert 552 Sarah
  551 Sarah E 551 Walter C 292 Walter
  Clarence 551 Z V 167 239 267 292 551
  Zimri 551
GARTON, Nancy 649
GASHIEN, Brother 200
GATES, Emmeline 527 John 528 Nancy Ellen
  528
GATLET, Michael 162
GAUL, Jane 653
GAY, Mary J 329-330
GEDBURG, Lemuel 698 Maud 698
GEE, Samuel 233
GEETING, 219 D M 234 David M 218 222
  George 260 John 178 John A 234
  Superintendent 223
GEIGER, Elizabeth 362 George 362 Isaiah 362
  Wiley 362
GEORGE II, King Of England 35
GEORGE, Thomas Benton 240

GERBER, Major 156
GERISH, John 186
GERS, Henry 113 253 Tillie 243
GEUGELBACK, E E 255
GIBAULT, Father 37-38
GIBBINS, Margaret 324
GIBBS, George L 259
GIBSON, 548 Annie 312 Annie H 312 Grace
  439 John 46 58 P R 439 T M 155
GIDDINGS, Callie 459
GIEGE, Elizabeth 362
GILES, 643
GILIS, Sarah 362
GILL, Albert 379 Carrie 345 379 Carrie B 368
  Charles 345 420 Edward 421 Eli 368 379
  Elizabeth 379 Elizabeth Wilson 379 Frank
  379 Fred 379 Helen 420 Jacob 379 James
  A 419-421 James C 421 Jennie 420 Joseph
  401 420 Joseph H 420 Laura 420 Lucy 379
  Maggie 379 Mary E 420 Mayme G 420-
  421 Mr 401 419-421 Mrs 421 Robert 421
  Ruth 421 Sarah 368 379 William H 421
GILLASPIE, Della 616 Ella 617 Ellen 616
  Fannie 616 Francis 616 Francis C 616
  Georgia 616 Grace 616 J W 229 242 James
  617 James W 615-616 Jesse Omar 616
  John 616 John W 616 Mary A 616 Mr 617-
  618 Mrs 616-617 Mrs Francis 616 Nettie
  Frances 616 Sarah 616 Sarah A 616 Simon
  A 616 William A 616
GILLEY, A O 499 Alvin P 498-499 Crystal
  Juanita 500 Ebenezer P 499 Ebenezer
  Picket 498 Elizabeth 498 Ira 499 J W 195
  James 96 274 James E 229 273 366 498-
  500 James P 281 296 499 James W 268
  John M 499 Levi 499 Margaret 268 Martha
  366 Martha A 500 Mary 499 Mary J 498
  Mr 499-500 Mrs 500 Robert 274 Ulysses G
  499 Wayne 296
GILLIATT, Amanda 449 Catherine 450
  Darinda 449 Harvey 229 449 Hazel 449 J
  H 449 James 449 Leach 449 Lenore 450
  Leona 449 Mandy 449 Maudie 449 Mr
  449-450 Mrs 450 Myrtle 449 Olene 450
  Ollie 412 449-450 Opal 450 Ottis 449
  Samuel 449 Sarah 449
GILLICK, Deenva 435 Edward T 435 Genieve
  435 Mary 435 Melvin 435
GILLOOLY, Bernard 280
GILMORE, Elizabeth 406 William 277
GILTNER, Grant 229
GINNSZ, G M 197-198
GIPSON, Rebecca 255
GIST, Christopher 35
GIVEN, Chairman 151 Noah E 114 Noah S
  150 214

GLADSTONE, William E 694
GLASS, Rachel 373
GLEASON, Ida 398 John J 242 William 398
GLENN, Angie 331 550 Elizabeth 679 Frank 679
GODALL, Amable 66
GODWIN, Aaron 210 Alfred M 366 Benjamin 108 Carrie B 368 Edward 366-367 500 Eliza 384 Emma Jane 366 Esther 366 500 George 111 306 366-368 Helen 367 Jesse 366-367 632 John 367 Keith 367 Martha 366 Martha A 500 Mary 367 Maud 367 Mr 366-368 Neil 367 Ralph 367 Thomas 367 W H 384
GOLD, Mary E 268
GOLDSBERRY, Elizabeth 667
GOLDSTONE, Mr 691 Nora O 691
GOLLIHER, Ada D 610 Amanda 609 Anna 609 Benjamin 610 Catherine 609 Charles B 609 Delight 610 Edward 610 Elizabeth 609 Frederick 609 Henry 609 Ida 610 Jackson 609 James 609 John A 610 John S 609 Lettie 609 Lolie 610 Margaret 609 Marvin 609 Mary E 610 Memory 609 Mr 608-610 Mrs 610 Nora 610 Nora E 610 Paul 193 608-610 Pauline Ann 609 Richard 609 Sallie 609 Sarah 609 Sarah C 610 Stella 610 Stella M 610 William 609-610 William E 610 William Washington 609
GOOD, Mary J 324
GOODMAN, Sharon 13
GOODWIN, Aaron 344 386 Aikman 386 B 111 Benjamin 113 Eliza 650 Elizabeth 517 George 166 Jane 386 Laura 386 Margaret 344 386 Mary A 344 Mary Ann 385-386 Matilda 386 Mr 272 Ruth 386 William 386
GOOKINS, Samuel B 249
GOOTEE, Overton Ethan 255
GOOTIE, Susie 483
GORBY, I I 186 311
GORDON, 157
GORE, Henry 210
GORMAN, Willis A 250
GORSAGE, Nancy 423
GOSHORN, John S 294 Mrs John S 339 N J 227 Noah Jefferson 254
GOSS, Lena 229
GOUGH, Agnes 646 Elias 167 Joshua 158 Mary 594 Rose 594 Scholastica 528
GOULD, James S 619 Jennie 619
GRABILL, Nancy 700
GRACE, Elias 112
GRAFE, Lilly 712
GRAHAM, 244 Ann 705 Ann M 520 Anna M 639 Catherine 638-639 Dossie 674 Elinor 465 Eliza 315 Elizabeth 413 Emerine 413

GRAHAM (Cont.)
Franklin 413 Jennie 541 591 Joe Jr 465 John 190-191 233 520 639 705 John A 413 John C 250 Joseph B 203 465 Josiah 154 706 Katherine 519-520 Margaret 597 Martha 413 413 Mary Ann 597 Mary Lavina 413 Mattie 674 Melissa 413 Miss 437 Mrs Joseph 271 Nathan 413 Nell 465 R 77 227 R N 259 Rebecca 413 Richard C 305 Richard J 161 Robert C 203 Sara Elizabeth 465 Sarah Angeline 413 Stephen 413 Thomas 245 Virginia 465 William 76-77 156 Ziab 445 Ziba F 308
GRANEDIR, Rev 199
GRANGER, John 194-195
GRANNAN, Margaret 229 W A 229
GRANT, 56 163 Gen 117 267 Nancy 408 514 Ulysses S 117 William 408
GRAVES, James M 111 Rebecca 229
GRAY, Catherine 514-515 Isaac P 58-59 249 Lydia 358 551 Sarah 484
GRAYBLE, J P 297
GREATHOUSE, Charles A 225 230 Elvia 702 Frances 704 James 704 John Harold 704 Mary 704 Noble E 704
GREELEY, Horace 118
GREEMAN, Margaret 653
GREEN, Byron 285
GREENWOD, Arthur H 524 Mrs 525
GREENWOOD, Annette B 576 Arthur 260 576 Arthur H 252 523-525 Arthur H Jr 524 Carrie 229 Catherine 524 Charles B 523 Elisha H 524 Eliza J 523 Elizabeth 524 Franklin K 523 Harry P 523 John W 524 Joseph R 524 Lydia 524 Mack 524 Martha 524 Martha D 523 Mr 524-525 Mrs 524 Mrs Arthur H 525 Nettie B 524 R H 111 Richard H 523-524 Rookh 229 Ruth 524 Sarah 524 Sina 524 Theodore 523-524 Theresia 524 William 524
GREGORY, Alford 426 Anna 496 Austine 496 B T 158 Bennett 426 Charles 427 Chris 69 Christopher 279 Clarence E 427 Daniel 66 69 Dora 496 Dora B 427 Dora M 496 Dorothy May 428 Elijah 496 Elsie 427 Ephraim 229 Etta 496 F S 426 Florence 428 Florence M 427 Franklin 427 Franklin S 426-428 George 67 496 George W 426 Goldie 427 Hallie 496 Hamlet 496 Jeremiah 279 John 427 496 John S 160 Julia Ann 426 Laura 426 Lawrence M 427 Letta 635 Lettie 427 Leva 496 Lucy M 427 Lydia 496 Mary 426 Mary A 616 Melinda 426 Melissa E 428 Minnie 428 Minnie E 427 Morton 427 Morton S 427 Mournen 496 Mr 428 Mrs 428 Ona 496 Oral W 427

GREGORY (Cont.)
  Pearl 496 Robert 426-427 496 Robert S
  427 Sanford 427 Thelma Mary 428
  Thomas 158 Walter 496 William 426
  Zilphea 630 Zylpha 426
GREINER, Elizabeth M 544
GRIFFIN, J L 189 J M 178 John 46
GRIFFITH, William C 285
GRIFFITHS, Evan 254
GRIMES, Patrick 261
GRISMORE, Albert 631 George 631
  Grandfather 632 Maria Jane 631
GROOVER, Emma J 494
GROSCUTH, John Henry 256
GROSE, George R 225
GROSS, Caspar 570 Lawrence Charles 569-
  570 Louise 570 Martin 570 Mr 570 Mrs
  570 Mrs Lawrence Charles 570
GROVE, E L 446 Sarah E 446
GROVES, John H 164 Sarah B 688
GROW, Christopher 510 Elmer 193 Sarah 510
GRUBB, Bessie 428 Della 428 Eli 428 Melissa
  E 428 Virgil 428
GUERGUEN, John 197 202
GUTHRIE, Christopher D 111 Elisha 158
  Eulala 229 Grace 494 Mrs 494
GUY, W N 266
GWARTNEY, Nancy A 697
GWATHMEY, Samuel 48
HAAG, Alodia F 296 Andrew 625 Carrie 625
  Charles Andrew 626 George C 625 Hellen
  Phillis 626 Henry 625 Madge 626 Mr 626
  Mrs 626 Philomena 625 William 625
HAAS, Grandfather 715 Magdaline 715
HACK, Mary 556 628 Victoria 557
HACKLEMAN, P H 259
HACKLER, George 688 Gertrude 688 Sarah B
  688
HAGANS, Harvey 296
HAGERTY, John C 306
HAIG, Asa 297 W S 608
HAIR, Dorris 401 Earl 401 Fanny May 401
  John Clifford 401 Marguerite 401
HALBERT, Joel 95 Silas T 113
HALCOLM, Turman 166
HALE, John P 115
HALL, 96 Dovie 399 Dyanthia 399 Elizabeth
  271 Elizabeth F 321 Elizabeth S 270
  Elizabeth Scudder 270 Emma 458 Henry
  94 Henry C Sr 152 Jane 667 Lt 165 Mrs
  321 Rebecca A 399 William 399 Willis 399
HALLER, Isaac S 160
HAM, Al J 653 Albert 652-653 Anna 651-652
  Charles 652 David 652 Delilah 652 Edith
  652 Emily 652 Hannah 652 James 651-652
  Marcellus 653 Margaret 652-653

HAM (Cont.)
  Mary Ann 652 Melissa 652 Mr 652-653
  Mrs 653 Nellie 653 Peter 651 Rose 653
  Sarah 652-653 Talbot 653 Thomas 652-653
  Walter 653 William 651-653 William M
  652
HAMERSLY, L E 306
HAMILTON, Gen 38
HAMMERSLEY, Elizabeth 641
HAMMOND, Abram A 58 Elijah 271
HANCOCK, Caroline 342-343 Charles 343
  Deborah 343 Green 343 John W 343 Julia
  Ann 343 Lloyd 343 Phinx 343 Seneca 343
  Winfield S 118
HANEY, George 518 Mary 518 Mr 519 Oscar
  518-519
HANLEY, J Frank 59
HANNA, Daisy 418 Maud 330 William 158
HANNAH, Vienna 529
HANNERS, Celia 641 Nathan 641
HARARD, Mary 229
HARBERT, Albert 440 Imogene 440 Marion
  440 Susan 440
HARBISON, Lucile 630 Nellie 630 Paris 630
  William 630
HARDIN, Thomas 156
HARDY, Alexander 251 Francis 457 Hannah
  457 Laura 433 Laura F 457
HARGAN, Henry C 255-256
HARGRAVE, William F 254
HARLIN, William 89
HARMAR, Josiah 41
HARMON, George W 111
HARNED, F M 305 Francis M 253 W F 187
HARPER, Lucy 418
HARPOLD, George W 193
HARPOLE, G W 191
HARPSTRITE, Bert 716 Theresa 716
HARRALL, Elizabeth 504 Jane 504 Mildred
  589 Uncle Buck 504 William 504
HARRELL, Belle 621 L 621
HARRIS, 88 Anna A 296 Cora B 503 Della
  583 Doctor 65 E C 291 Edward 503
  Elizabeth 360 502-503 Fred C 503 George
  L 112 114 Isaac 281 Jennie 712 John 176
  John T 179 Joseph A 503 Josiah C 291 L C
  282 Laura 583 Lew 193 502-503 Lewis
  503 Lewis C 502 Lizzie 296 Mary 502-503
  Morton 503 Mr 503 Nathan 502 Otto
  Marion 503 Robert C 238 503 Samuel F
  254 Sarah 503 Thomas 110 266 Wilbur
  Murray 503 William 503 583
HARRISON, 251 375 531 Benjamin 119
  Christopher 82 Gen 55 67 114 119 246
  Gov 39 46-47 55 67 William H 58 585
  William Henry 34 42 44 46 67 177

DAVIESS COUNTY, INDIANA.

HARROD, Dully 229 George M 218
HARSHEY, Lela 359
HARSTINGS, Elmer E 171
HART, A S 418-419 Abraham 419 Cecile 419 Dodge 125 Douglas 255 Elizabeth 392 Emeline 418 Everett 419 Ida 419 Laura 419 Margaret 419 Mary Ada 418-419 Mr 125 Nettie 419 Ora 419 Philip 171 173 266 Sarah 419 Victor 419 Warren 112 125
HARTER, Caroline 578 Charles 578 Christena 578 Ignatius 578 Joseph 578 Lena 578 Mr 578 Mrs 578 Theresa 578
HARTSOCK, A D 286
HARTSONRADER, Carrie 625 Margaret 626 Nicholas 625-626
HASKINS, I K 195
HASLER, Josephine 649
HASTING, John 700 Mary 229 Sarah F 700
HASTINGS, 705 Abbie 515 Ada 641 Addie 672 Alice 641 Anna 641 Bertha J 333 Celia 641 Charles 353 641 Charlotte 347 352 Cora A 352 E E 251 348 706 Edith 347 352-353 Edith L C 348 Edith Laville 348 Eleanor E 333 Elizabeth 347 352 404 641 646 Ellie 415 Elmer E 113 332-333 347 351 Florence 415 Frank H 353 George 641 Hannah Elizabeth 640-641 Harvey 277 641 Hattie 641 674 Henry H 352 Howell 347 352 Isar 641 James 641 Jams 641 Jane 641 Jefferson 641 John 277 292 415 640-641 John A 332 347 351-352 John Arthur 347 John S 333 John T 213 Joseph 218 277 515 640 672 Joshua T 167 Joshua Thomas 347 Judge 349 Laura 332 353 Lauretta 347 351 Levi 641 Lois 348 M S 190 251 332 347-349 706 Malhaly 641 Margaret 641 Mary 351 353 Mary E 347 406 Milton S 259 347-348 351 Milton Simpson 347 Mr 179-180 332-333 347-349 351-353 641 Mrs 333 348 353 Mrs M S 313 Nancy 641 Nellie 641 P A 190 305 Paris 641 Paris A 114 179-180 347 351-353 Paul 353 Ralph G 333 Rebecca 641 Rosa 641 Rufus 347 Sally A 672 Sarah 641 Susannah 640 Thomas 352 William 167 640-641 William Henry 347 Zachariah S 352 Zachariah Simpson 347
HATCHETT, Archibald 440 Jane 440 Mary 440
HATFIELD, E L 189 305 Elisha L 259
HATHAWAY, 71 73 Mr 70 Richard 70
HATRY, Aaron 473 Anna E 473
HATTERY, Aaron 267 Addison Hayes 255 Anna 603
HAVENS, Samuel 160
HAWES, Rev 286

HAWKINS, Benjamin 67 Bertha 569 Catherine 139 Charles 69 Charner 289 Eli 65-66 69 138-139 George 156 Joseph 69 Mary 569 Mr 65 139 Peter 156 Sarah 706 William 65-66 69 77 95 138 William W 569
HAWLEY, R E 186 266 Ransom 185
HAY, John 48
HAYES, 200 Alice 540 Amelia 568 Ann 540 Anna J 337 Beatrice 372 Bertha 569 Carter 568 Charles 372 Cora B 372 Courtland E 568 Daniel W 371-372 David 690 Delilah 627 Dolly 371 Dow 372 Dwight 372 Edwin 568 Edwin A 568 Edwin Jr 568 Elizabeth 689-690 Estella 421 Flora 568 Fred G 371 Gideon 371 Glenn 568 Harold 372 Hayden 187 Helen 421 Jack Edwin 569 John 371-372 Julia 371 M J 337 Margaret 363 372 Mary 371 Mayme G 420-421 Mr 371-372 568-569 Mrs 372 Pauline Elizabeth 569 Robert 372 Rosanna D 371 Rutherford B 118 Sarah 371 Turrie 526 Viola 372 William 540 William M 202 421 Winifred 421
HAYNES, Alice 398 Jackson 277 Lovina 687-688 Robert 114
HAYS, Alexander 69 Deliah 509 George T 193 Joseph 67 104 274 Robert 67 69 280 Sarah 532 T J 193 Thomas J 193 William 94
HEAD, Hallie 532 Hillary 532 Hillory 191 Nellie 532 Sarah 532 Virginia 532 Virginia Hays 532
HEALEY, Sarah 199
HEALY, Catherine 486 James 486
HEATON, Isaac 210 233 William 212
HEAVENRIDGE, M S 187
HECKATHORNE, Della 616
HEDDEN, Isaac 301
HEDRICK, J T 296 J W 712 John T 254 Kitty 712
HEFFERNAN, William 113 252 306 317
HEFRON, David J 113 180 227 249 303 Judge 249 Mr 303
HEGE, D J 255
HEIMER, George 168
HEINBOUGH, Anna 415
HEITHECKER, Albert 229
HELBIG, Alfred 345 Irma 497 Mary 345 Valentine 497
HELM, Eli 267 Leonard 38
HELMS, W S 157
HELPENSTEIN, Thomas J 168
HELPHENSTEIN, Emily 585 Mr 585
HELPHENSTINE, A M 297 John 346 Maria 346 Mary 346 Peter 274 William 259 346
HELPHINSTINE, B N 106 Maud 346 Will H 106

INDEX.

HELTON, Eliza 690 George 690
HEMBREE, Orian 296
HENDERSON, 362 Benjamin S 226 Catherine 450 Seth 450
HENDRICKS, 57 Cora A 352-353 Grace 353 Lora 353 Mary E 353 Milton 353 Myra Jane 353 Orestes H 353 Thomas A 58 Vada 353 William 58
HENLEY, Capt 424
HENNEGAN, Edward A 250
HENRY, Clementine 643 Dora 344 Emma 471 Isaiah 344 James 67 Nancy 344 William 643
HENSHAW, William 404
HERINSHAW, James 158
HERMAN, Harry 229
HERNDON, J F 266
HERR, Henry 255
HERRONDON, G W 158
HESS, Louis 260
HESTER, Craven P 250
HETHINGTON, Elizabeth 528
HETTINGTON, Mary 592
HIBNER, John 548
HIGHTOWER, Lettie 325
HILBURN, E W 255
HILDEBRAND, Maria 254
HILDRETH, William 298 William J 298
HILL, Bennett 427 Henderson 427 Henry 427 John 154 Mournen 496 Thomas W 158 Zylpha 426-427
HILTON, Andrew 247
HINDS, Alexander R 279 Martha 418
HINER, Frederick T 254
HINTON, Alexander 301 Forrest 483 Loueda 483 Susie 483 Wallace 483
HITCHCOCK, Aaron 286 E 259 Harry 286 John 267 Wiley 236 238
HIXON, David 189 193 David M 192 Mr 192
HIXSON, David M 108
HOAR, Lucy 439 Senator 439
HOBBS, Cyrus 564 Melvin 564 Mildred 564 Rosettie 563-564 W P 563-564 William Jr 564 William P 253
HOBSON, J T 194-195
HOCHGESANG, Katie 581 Martin 581
HODAPP, Caroline 680
HODDINOTT, John 114 Willis 261
HODGE, Andy 652 Sarah 652
HOFFMAN, Maud 651 Stella 421 W F 260
HOFFMANN, 235 Mr 312 William F 234 312
HOGSHEAD, David 89 Glendora 355 Hiram 350 L 227 Lizzie 226
HOLCOMB, Anna 437 Jerry 437 John 437 Sarah C 436-437 Timothy 437 William 437
HOLDER, Mary T 527 Union H 112

HOLDER (Cont.)
William H 255
HOLLAND, Doctor 301 Hezekiah 258
HOLLCROFT, Elijah P T 255
HOLLINGSWORTH, Amy 713 Anna 459 Charles C 712 Ernest 255 712-714 Frank 713 Ida M 713 Isaac 274 Jane 713 Jennie 712 Kitty 712-713 Lucile E 713 Mrs 713 Sarah L 712-713 Thomas 713 William 712 William K 712-713
HOLLIS, Rebecca E 268
HOLLOWAY, J C 189 Rev 189
HOLT, Anna 515 Calvin 515 Catherine 514-515 Chrispen 515 Dawswell 515 Drury 515 Elizabeth 515 Emerson 515 Henry 514-516 Henry Jr 515-516 James 515 James H 515 John 515 Malinda 515 Margaret 515 Sally 515 Sarah 515 Susan 514-516 Susannah 611
HOLTZMAN, Francis 266
HOMANN, Frederich J Jr 256
HONEY, G W 158 Peter 109 163
HOOD, 159 162 166-167
HOOPINGARNER, Hazel 229 Hilda 229
HOOVER, Anna 446 Catherine 343
HOPKINS, 146 Bernadette 229 Eldridge 145 Gen 74 Mr 147 Samuel 74 W E 112
HORRAL, E E 260
HORRALL, Albion 111 309 Alfred 350 Anna 350 428 Capt 179 Carrie Belle 350 Cleaver 349 Cleo 417 Cynthia Ann 350 Daniel Cleaver 350 Edith 539 Editor 150 Edwin Ray 349-350 Elizabeth 350 538 Ella 428 Elvira 375 Emmor 539 Ermel Ethel 351 Florence 428 Florence M 427 George 428 George W 160 Glenn Irene 351 Jason 375 Johanna 349-350 John 69 John M 108 375 Joseph 427 L S 110 Lawrie Isaac 350 Leonidas S 350 Leonidas Sexton 349 Lily Jewel 351 Melvina 427 Mildred 374-375 542 Mr 349-351 538-539 Nancy 271 375 Nellie Lissie 351 Pansy 270-271 Polly 375 Roy 351 S F 149 151 159 161 177-178 266 Sarah 428 Spillard F 159 Spillard Fletcher 179 Steward Sexton 351 Thomas 66 69 538 Thomas G 538-539 Thomas Sr 538 Videtta 350 W A 178-179 William 66 69 375 428 William A 254 309
HOSKEN, William P 185-186
HOSLER, Lovey 254
HOUGH, James M 114
HOUGHTON, Aaron 113 Catherine 548 H 108-109 H Q 113 249 Judge 312 Mr 548 Phoebe J 547 William H 108
HOUSTON, Josephine 323 N F 323
HOUTS, Eliza K 541 591

DAVIESS COUNTY, INDIANA.

HOUTS (Cont.)
  Eliza Katherine 541 591 George 541 591 J
  B 374 Jennie 541 591 Matilda 374
HOVEY, Alvin P 59 156 248 Gen 248 Louisa
  491
HOWARD, Ann 451 Anna 574 Baldwin 277
  Daniel 661 Hannah 661 Minerva 661 Sarah
  514 Thomas 210 232 Tilghman A 249 251
  William C 574
HOWE, Mr 233 Mrs 233
HOWELL, Thomas 104
HUBARD, Napoleon 154 T J 298
HUBBARD, Edward 662 Ida A 662 John 267
  William 148 157-158 267 Willis 158
HUFF, James M 113
HUGHEN, Samuel 277
HUGHES, Bridget 704 James 249 251 Thomas
  W 107
HUGHNER, Hiram 663 Louisa 663
HULON, Elias P 166
HULSE, Elvia 702 Jason 702 Lucy 702
HUM, Emily 210
HUMERICKHOUSE, Amanda 604
HUMMER, Catherine 442
HUMPHREYS, Andrew 113 Manoah 166
HUNT, Hannah 656
HUNTER, Aaron 154 Cora 229 Cora B 503 D
  Eckley 234 301 Francis M 503 Harry 229
  Henry S 160 Hiram 210 258 301 Hiram A
  233 Reuben 160 W A 193 Walter M 254
HUNTINGTON, Elisha M 248 250-251
  Nathaniel 248
HURST, Helen 411
HUSKES, Henry 158
HUSTON, Catherine 427 George 427
HUTSON, Nicholas 67
HYATT, 434 Adelaide 382 Alice Rosetta 437
  Alta 383 Ann 382 Charles Winton 437
  Clarence 383 Elisha 180 295 303-304 339
  381-383 585 Elisha Jr 382-383 Elisha Sr
  364 382 Eliza 339 382 437 Elizabeth 381
  Emma B 365-366 Ethel 465 Etta 382
  Evelyn P 383 Evelyn Pearl 255 383
  Florence R 437 George 339 346 437
  George Read 437 H H 260 266 Harry V
  365 465 Helen 339 346 437 Henry H 155
  180 Hiram 304 364-365 381 John 90 112
  114 151 234 303 339 382 585 597 Lucinda
  339 597 Lydia 381 Margaret 339 346 382
  437 Martha 381 Martha E 383 Mary 339
  346 346 382 416 437 Mary Ann 339 Mary
  Ethel 437 Miss 585 Mr 381-383 Mrs 365
  383 Mrs Harry 271 Rebecca 338-339 346
  437 708 Rebecca Ann 346 Richard 382
  Robert 383 Sara Emily 465 Theodore F 381
  Thomas 339 346 381-382 708

HYATT (Cont.)
  William 338-339 346 382 416 437 597
  William A 365 William C 437
HYLAND, P 202
HYSER, Elizabeth 499 Jacob 499 Mary 499
INDIAN, Big File 72 247 Little Turtle 42
  Pontiac 36 Tecumseh 33 55 67 The Prophet
  55
INGRAM, Edward W 254
INMAN, Dean M 238 Eph 113
IRELAND, Bishop 200
IRONS, Miss 585-586
ISENOGLE, Abigail 480 Adam 480 Adeline
  480 Alonzo C 479 Arba 480 Catherine 480
  Cyrus 480 Etta 480 Ettie 480 George E 480
  Gideon 480 Jacob 480 Jane 480 John 479-
  480 Lavina 480 Lawrence Bell 479 Martha
  479 Mr 479-480 Mrs 479-480 Nora Eddie
  479 Rachel 480 Sadie 479 Stephen 480
  Willard 479-480 Willard E 479-480
ISHAM, Elizabeth 254
ITSKIN, Charles 413 Claude 413 Myrtle 413
  Virgil 413
JACKMAN, Addie 348 Beatrice 619 Bernard
  620 Charles S 348 Clara 619-620 Clyde E
  619 Constance B 619 David 618 David S
  274 618-619 Edith L C 348 Edith Laville
  348 Ella 619 Emma B 619 Florain B 619
  Florence V 348 Florida 348 Garnet B 619
  Gertrude 619 Harry E 348 Isaac 618 Isaac
  W 296 618-619 Jennie 619 John M 171
  John W 173 Martha 618 Marvel Mattie 619
  Mary E 348 Minnie 348 Mr 618-620 Mrs
  619 Olive E 619 Robert 619 Ruth 618 620
  Ruth Anna 619 Sarah 269 Sarah M 348
  Spencer 296 Spencer O 619 Wesley 348
JACKS, Beatrice 617 Cora B 617 Ella 617
  Emma R 617 Ethelind L 617 Flora 617
  James Harvey 617 Justina F 617 Lina 617
  Mary A 617 Milton H 617 Mr 617 Mrs 617
  Nancy 617
JACKSON, 57 157 Altha 396 Andrew 594
  Daniel 210 288 John 396 Milton 156 Mrs
  W L 185 Nelson 148 288 Sarah M 233 W
  L 306
JACOBS, Phoebe 642 Tillie 268
JAMES I, King Of England 441
JAMES, Sarah 637
JARVIS, Dimmit 193
JEFFERSON, President 42
JENKINS, John B 698 Martha 698 Zebulon
  277
JENNINGS, 57 Jonathan 49-50 58 82
JENSEN, Nicholas N 255
JEPSON, Elizabeth 657 George 657 Hannah
  656 Hannah Elizabeth 656 Jessie 657

JEPSON (Cont.)
John 656-657 John Samuel 657 Lucy 657
Mr 656-658 Mrs 657-658 N H 180
Nathaniel H 656-657 Nathaniel Hunt 656
658 Samuel L 657
JOACHIM, Brother 200
JOCELYN, George B 259
JOHNSON, 50 A E 175 259 267 Abner 375
Ada 683 Adam 165 Aesop 682 Albert C
166 Alfred 628 Alfred E 141 374-376
Annie R 628 Anson B 374-375 Anthony
155 397 Bryson 682 Bryson B 682 Callie
459 Capt 165 Charles D 537 Christopher
277 David 682 David E 537 Deborah 537
Deborah A 536 Dora 683 Dudley 210 233
Edison 684 Edith 684 Edith L 376 Edith
Llewellyn 376 Edward 276 628 682
Edward H 397 Eli 537 Elijah 141 374-375
542 Elmer K 537 Elva Myrtle 376 Emerson
684 Emma C 537 Emma R 682 Ervilla 684
Ezra 374 Flora 397 Frances E 376 Friend
375 George 375 George Mcclellan 537
Grant 376 Grant C 376 Hazel 229 Helen
684 Hiram M 255 Hugh Clinton 376 Hulda
374 Ida J 683 Isaiah 277 J Wesley 537
James 271 375 537 682 Jane 401 682
Jennie C 682 Jennie May 683 John 48-49
67 John L 317 375 Jonathan 277 Joshua
375 Kenneth 683 L B 286 Lena 376
Lenson 374 Lestie 684 Levi 536 683
Lucian B 537 Luther 397-398 Lydia 682
Malcolm 376 Malina 374 Malina B 542
Margaret 683 Maria 375 Maria J 537 Marie
628 Marion M 681-683 Mary E 317 Mary
Ellen 513 Mary H 537 Mary M 586
Matilda 374 Maud L 376 Melvin 683
Mildred 374 542 Milford D 397 Millie B
339 Miss 424 Mollie 397 Moses 683 Mr
141 374-376 397-398 586 682-684 Mrs
376 397-398 683-684 Nancy 397 Nancy M
700 Nannie 586 Nelson 374 Nettie 398
Norma 376 Norvan 374 Ola 397 Osee 397
Pearl 397 Peter 542 Polly 375 Primmellar
537 Rachael 682-683 Rebecca 375 Reuben
162 375 Robert 397 Sally 375 Sarah 650
Sarah A 536 Sarah N 537 Sina 683 Stella
397 Susan 397 Susan C 537 Thelma 398
Thomas 155 683 W H 226 W Hays 234 W
J 195 240 William 375 682 William H 537
Willis 684
JOHNSTON, G W 248 250 Isaiah 296 James
190 Judge 248
JOLLIF, Della 662
JONES, 177 Allie 322 Ann 410 Anna M 581 C
H 260 E 99 Ebenezer 66 69 75 95 97 102
111 410 Elijah 354 Eliza Ann 696

JONES (Cont.)
Elizabeth 538 566 Ella 354 Elsie 229 Emily
410 Ephraim 100 Eugene 581 Harriet 581
Harry L 581 Henry B 581 Hosea 354 J N
305-306 James G 159 Jane 581 Jesse 75
Jessie C 581 John 90 158 696 John M 254
John Rice 48-49 65 Joseph 279 Laura 426
Lewis 85 89 106 113 186 244 279 Lorraine
354 Mary 65 Mary C 354 Mary Emaline
630 Maude 494 Mr 90 Mrs Thomas 188
Ora 530 Ruth 468 Sarah A 468 Sarah
Adaline 354 Spillman 426 Theodore 354
Theodore T 111-112 Thomas 188 354 468
Thomas M 567 Vance 66 69 94 W H 254
W S 254 Wiley R 69 410 William 250 279
William H 538 William P 160 Z 163
Zachariah 111 Zack 136 180 266
JORDAN, John 242 Sarah 520 638
JOSEPH, Alexander F 254 Brother 200 E Peter
254
JUDAH, Samuel 250
JULIAN, J W 187
JUVENALL, Betsey 392 Eliza A 392 Eliza
Ann 391 Mr 392
KAGGS, Wesley D 107
KANE, William 197
KAUFFMAN, 434 524 576 August 112 George
303 305 Margaret 229
KAUFMAN, W S 190
KAUGGMAN, 389
KEACH, C W 397
KEAGY, Lena 601
KECK, Andrew M 256 Catherine 485 Christian
485 Harriett 485 Lucinda 472 Luranda 603
William 485
KEEN, Maria 400
KEENAN, Bridget 388 J J 388 Mr 388
KEISER, Delilah 370 Miss 435
KEITH, 713 Abbie 390 580 Abierilla 580 Ann
391 Arthur 391 B F 254 Benjamin 391
Bonnie 391 Charles 391 580 Charles
Arthur 530 Charles W 391 529-530 Clara
634 Dicey 391 Dicy 391 Elmer 391 634
Elmer F 391 Elvida 633 Emily 391
Ephraim J 391 Ethel 634 Fannie 580
Fannie M 579 George 67 391 580 636
George Benjamin 530 George H 390-391
George H Sr 579-580 George J 190 306-
307 390-391 393 529 Grant 225 580 Harley
391 James 391 James A 391 James Prime
391 Jane 392 Jarat 636 Jarit 390-391 633
John 580 Lewis H 306 Lewis W 306
Lillian 634 Lily 391 Lola 392 Louis E
634 Louis H 580 Louis W 633-634 Lucinda
391 Lucretia 391 530 Lucretia R 529
Margaret 392 Martha 391-392

KEITH (Cont.)
    Martha A 391 Mary 580 Mary Frances 391
    Mary J 636 Mildred 391 Mr 390-392 530
    633-635 Mrs 390-392 Oscar 391 Oscar H
    391 Prentis S 530 Ray 391 Ray A 391
    Rhoda Jane 390 Ruby 391 Russell 391
    Sarah Jane 579 Shirley 634 William 391
    Wilson 303 391
KEITHLY, Sarah 460
KELENBERGER, P B 266
KELLAMS, John W 173
KELLAR, Clyde B 259 John R 158
KELLE, F W 399
KELLEMS, J W 266
KELLER, Bessie 229 Estella 421 Joseph J 262
KELLEY, George D 242 John 259 M D 307
    Marie H 306 Mr 200
KELLY, John D 242
KELSEY, Mary J 331 Myrtle 458 Sarah 331
    550
KELSO, Emmor 539 Mr 274 Samuel 89 246
    Samuel I 105 Samuel J 93 108 244 300
KELTY, William 258
KEMBLE, Gen 381
KEMP, Miranda C 254
KEMPER, John 526 Lillie M 526
KEMPF, Andrew 254
KENDALL, Edward F 256 Enoch 387 George
    387 George D 164 John 387 John R 275
    Joseph 387 Joseph T 266 Martha 387 Mary
    387 Nancy 387 Sarah 387 W H 165
    William 387
KENIRISTRICK, Sarah 380
KENNEDY, Anna 227 Anna S 234 D H 112
    David H 285 Edward 266 James W 297
    Mrs Edward 268 William 111 113 180 227
    306
KENNEY, Edward 266
KENT, M C 254
KEPLER, Clara M 701
KERCHER, Gottfried 396 Louisa 395-396
KERCHEVAL, Samuel E 180
KERN, Catherine 470 John 470
KERSHER, Louisa 396
KETCHAM, Almira 517-518 Amanda 650
    Betsie Ann 650 Blaine 650 Britta 229
    Britta M 651 Daniel 517 650 Daniel W 518
    Dollie M 651 Eliza 650 Elizabeth 517
    Elmira 650 Eva 674 George 650 Glendora
    R 651 Grace 651 Hettie 650 J M 650 J S
    229 Jane 650 John M 518 650 John S 651
    John W 651 Joseph 650 661 Larinda 650
    Laura A 517-518 Lauranda 650 Lewis 650
    Lucine 650 Malinda 650 Mary 518 650
    Mary E 650 Maud 651 May 650 Minerva
    650 Mr 517 650-651 Mrs 651 Rebecca 650

KETCHAM (Cont.)
    Rosetta 650 S L 267 Sarah 650 661-662
    Seth L 517-518 W Evert 518 William W
    651
KETCHEM, Annetta 693 Caroline 692 Charity
    692-693 David J 693 Elizabeth 693 Emma
    693 Frederick S 694 George M 693 Jacob
    692 James 692 Jane 692 Joseph 692-693
    Joseph C 694 Mabel May 694 Marshall 692
    Mary 594 692 Mary J 693 Mr 693-694 Mrs
    663 694 Nancy 692 Nettie 693 Ruth E 694
    Silas 692 Silas M 692-693 Solomon 692
    Stephen 692 Stephen E 693 Velma M 694
    Vine 655 William 692
KETCHUM, John E 261
KETTERY, Catherine 433 Charles 433 D M C
    456 Dialtha M 432-433 Earl Elsworth 457
    Elizabeth 456 Hattie 433 Jacob 432-433
    456 456 Jane 433 456 John 433 456 Joseph
    433 456 Joseph E 433 456-457 Joseph Sr
    456 Laura 433 Laura F 457 Lizzie D 433
    Lydia 456 Lydia H 433 Mary 432-433 456
    Mary H 433 Mr 456-457 Pearl Angeline
    457 Ruby May 457 Ruth Sunshine 457
KEUTCH, Elizabeth 472 Finley 472
KEYS, Jasper H 178
KEYSER, David B 167
KIDWELL, 198 Barbara 556 Charles A 261-
    262 Ellen 465 John 556 John H 112
    Nicholas 275 Stella 556
KIEFER, 175 Albert 345 Anton 345 Benjamin
    345 Caroline 345 Carrie 345 Catherine 345
    Clarence 345 Emma 345 Gustave 345 John
    C 346 Joseph 345 Joseph P 344 Lawrence
    345 Leonard 345 Mary 345 Maud 346 Mr
    344-346 Mrs 346 Rose 345 Stephen 345
    William 344 William H 110 344-346
    William R 346
KILGORE, Charles 107 Katurak 488 Katy 585
    Kitura 565 Mr 585 Stephen 107 Thomas
    227
KILHON, Ernest 449 Mr 449
KILLGORE, Charles 408 Eva 408 Hiram 408
    514 Ina 408 Katura 514-515 Keturah 408
    Malinda 408 Matilda 408 Nancy 408 514
    Perry 408 Pollie 408 Reuben 408 Rollen
    408 Sallie 408
KILLIAN, Arnold 429 Cecil 429 Mary 193
KILLION, Ada 683 Albert 356 432-433
    Alexander 355-356 432 442 Alfred 356
    Alice 412 Alvin 442 America 356 Anna
    641 Betsie 356 Catherine 442 Clarence 357
    Clarence E 356 Claude E 442 Cora 356
    Cordeli 356 Cordelia 356 David 276 356
    Dicey 356 Earl 442 Edward 683 Effie 442
    Elmer 442 Elsie 442

INDEX. 741

KILLION (Cont.)
 Ernest E 294 356 411-412 Ernest E Jr 412
 Ethel 432 Eula 357 Eva 356 F L 297 Frank
 356 Harley 442 Iva May 442 Ivy May 442
 James 356 Jemimah 355-356 Jesse 442
 Jessie 442 John 154 356 John N 253 Louisa
 442 Martha J 356 612 Mary 356 432-433
 442 Mary Jane 446 Mildred 357 Mr 355-
 357 411-412 432-433 442-443 Mrs 357
 432-433 Nathan 355-356 432 442 Nathan E
 294 355-357 411 Ora 442 R Elmer 294 518
 Rachael 683 Rachel 356 Ralph A 356-357
 Ralph Jr 357 Sallie 356 Sarah J 485 Sina
 683 Susan Almira 518 Thomas 641 Vernon
 432 Virgil 432 Wiley 356 William 356 442
 William A 442 William Alexander 441-442
 William F 109-110 298 Wylie B 253
KIMBALL, Gen 439 Margaretta 605 Nathan
 264 439
KING, Charles W 254 H N 286 Joshua 418
 Lucy 418
KINGSLEY, Calvin 186
KINNAMAN, Clara M 701 Eli 277 Jacob 277
 James S 267 Joseph 292 Lafayette 701
 Rosetta 701 W H 267
KINNEMAN, Charlotta 675 687 Charlotte 669
KINNEY, A C 301 Amory 248 Amory C 249
 Armory 258 Armory C 139 Judge 248
 Lawyer 139
KIRK, Charles 448 Cletus Verne 448 Daisy
 448 Mace 140 Ruth 448
KLEIN, Hilbert P 255
KLINE, William 109
KLINGINGSMITH, G 260
KNAPP, A B 255 George 255
KNOX, Henry 81
KOCHER, Albert M 262 Anthony Jr 261
KOHR, Della 359 Edgar Ray 359 H B 227
 Henry B 218 221 240 292 358-359 Henry
 Booth 358 James 358 Jonas 358 Lela 359
 Mary Eleanor 358-359 Rachel 358 Walter
 Preston 359
KOLLER, Alberdina 577 Elizabeth 577 Frank
 577 Jacob 577 John 577-578 Mary 577 Mr
 578 Peter 577 Theresa 578
KRAMER, Albert 556 Bernard 556 Catherine
 556 Ernest 556 Frank 556-557 628 George
 556 Harold 556 Helen 556 Henry J 556
 Henry Joseph 628-629 John 556 Kate 556
 Louis 556-557 628 Mary 556 628 Mr 556
 629 Mrs 629 Mrs Frank 556 Peter 556-557
 Ralph Joseph 629 Stella 556 Victoria 629
 William 556
KREBS, Malachi 179-180
KRETS, John 401 Mary L 401
KRETSCH, Cass 471 Flora May 471

KRETSCH (Cont.)
 Harry 471 Madge 471 Rachel Minerva 471
 Russell 471
KRIBS, David 185
KRUTSINGER, William 192
KUHLMAN, Christina 561 Elizabeth 402
KUNTZ, Thresa 451
KUTCH, Eleanor 603 Elizabeth 603 Mary 650
 Melkard 603 650
KYLE, Thomas H 213
LABLANC, J 197
LACEY, Spencer 271
LACY, Joseph J 110
LADD, Laura F 234
LAFFERTY, Thomas J 296
LAKE, Sarah 546
LALUMIERE, Father 197 201-202 242 Rev
 198 Rev Mr 196 S P 199 Simon 242 Simon
 P 196 202
LAMB, Catherine 654 Edward 654 Elizabeth
 653 Frank 109 Penanas 166
LAMBERT, James 154
LAND, Edith 552
LANE, A A 194 551 A K 267 Allen K 253 331
 550 Alonza Albert 550 Alonzo A 292 549-
 550 552 Andrew Jackson 255 Angie 331
 550 Arthur W 550 Blanche 331 Bradie
 330-331 Charles 552 Chester A 331
 Cynthian 550 Doctor 331-332 Ellen 550
 Emma 550 Harvey 550 Henry S 58 250-
 251 Jane 331 550 John Albert 550 Luetta
 550 Martin 550 Mary J 331 Maude 331
 Minnie 551-552 Mr 550-552 Nellie 552
 Richard 331 550 Ruphus 550 Sarah 331
 550
LANHAM, Catherine 455 Levi 455
LANKFORD, Josephine 679
LANNUM, Jennie 368 John 368 Lizzie 368
 Mary 367-368 Matilda 367 Perry 368
 Robert 367
LARKIN, Patrick 451
LASALLE, 33-34
LASHBROOK, H W 195
LASHLEY, George 246 James 158
LASHLY, George 270
LAUGHLIN, Amanda 650 Ausman A 363
 Bertha 364 Cleta D 362 Cora 364 Daisy
 Fay 364 Edgar T 113 252 361-362 364
 Elizabeth 362 364 662 Elva Pearl 362
 George 363 J D 267 James B 363 James D
 113 Jane 364 John D 363 John O M 362
 662 John R 363 John Richard 362 Joseph D
 361 363-364 Joseph Dunn 362 Joseph G
 363 Joseph H 363 Lakie J 361 364 Lakie
 Jane 363 Laura 364 Lily 364 Matilda E 363
 Maude 364 Merinda C 363 Minerva 650

DAVIESS COUNTY, INDIANA.

LAUGHLIN (Cont.)
Minerva E 363 Miranda C 662 Mr 362 364 604 Mrs 363 Nancy M 656 Nellie 364 Nora Blanche 362 O R 604 Oliver O 364 Osman 650 Paris 229 Paris M 656 Rufus J 363 Sarah 362 Sarah F 363 U G 650 Ulysses G 363
LAUGHRIDGE, John T 254
LAVELLE, Catherine 654 Elizabeth 653 J C 227 James C 110 James J 654 Jane 653 Louis Joseph 654 Lucile Josephine 654 Mary 654 Mary Catherine 654 Michael 653-654 Mr 654 T J 110 Thomas 227 Thomas J 654 W A 229 William A 653-654 William Andrew 653 William Paul 654
LAVELY, Franklin 164 John 164
LAVERTY, J 227
LAW, John 248 250 Ransom 193
LAWINS, Miss 324
LAWSON, Katrina 574
LAWYER, Abner 444 Anna 444 Austin 444 Bernetta 444 Bishop 444 Charles 444 Flora 444 Frederick 444 Huldah 444 Ida 444 Joe 444 John 444 John A 443-445 Joseph 443-444 646 Laura 444 Leonard 444 Louise 443-444 Maggie 444 Martha 444 Mattie 444 Mckinley 444 Mr 444-445 Mrs 444 Pearl 444 Raleigh 444 Ralph 444 Rebecca 444 Richard 444 Vivia E 646
LAYCOCK, Mrs 188
LAYE, H W 190
LAYTON, Thomas 158
LAYTTON, Amanda 483
LEACH, Amanda 449
LEAP, Jacob 148
LEAVITT, S K 165
LECHNER, Frank 557 Kate 556-557
LEDGERWOOD, Amanda 363-364 Ava 661 Barbara 364 647 Candice 661 Charity 692-693 Charles 107 363-364 647-648 Charles Hays 647 David 692 Edna 648 Eliza 647 Eliza Jane 364 Elizabeth 364 647-648 Hannah 661 Henry 661 Henry H 661 James 364 647 John 229 John W 661 Joseph 363 Laca Jane 647 Lakie J 361 364 Lakie Jane 363-364 Manda 647 Margaret 363-364 647 Mary Jane 647 Milton 364 Milton B 647 647-648 Minerva 661 Mr 647-648 Nathaniel 647 Ralph 648 Raymond 648 Rebecca 647 Ruth 648 Sally 515 Sarah 661 Sarah Jane 647 Susie 649 Thomas 364 647 William 364 William Riley 647
LEE, 157 162 Addie 421 Alice V 421 Allen L 555 Anna 554-555 C 305 Carlton M 555 Charles M 555 Charles W 555 Clement 114 298 David 555 David R 554-555 Eda 554

LEE (Cont.)
Edgar L 555 Gashum 554 Glenn 555 James 421 Jessie 555 John 554-555 John T 555 Lawrence H 555 Lelia L 556 Lester 554 Lester L 555-556 Lewis 554 Lloyd 555 Lodema 554 Lottie A 555 Manuel 554 Mary 555-556 Mr 555-556 Nancy 554 Nellie 429 Orla H 555 Sarah 555 Sarah H 554-555 Stella 421 William 554 Winifred 421
LEMING, John 93 John G 92 111 268 Thomas 258
LEMMON, Abraham 336 Anna 271 Catherine 336 Clay Houston 336 David 336 Edith 271 Elijah 335-336 Elizabeth 336 Isabel 335 J C 229 Jacob 336 Jacob Sr 336 James 336 Jennie 271 John 336 Judith 335-336 Lavina 268 Lavinia 268 Scott 336 Susan 336 William C 214
LEMON, C M 501
LENAHAN, Bridget 389
LENTZ, 280
LEONARD, Bert 419 Laura 419 Margaret 419 Miner 419
LESLIE, Alexander 89
LESTER, Elvida 633 John 108 Julia 391 L H 298 Louisa Ann 391 Pearl 707 Pearl May 478 Rhoda Jane 390-391 William 106 391 478 707 William Harrison 391
LETT, Arilla 495 Artimecy 495 Dora 495 Dora M 496 Eli 495 Ellis 495 Emery 495-496 Ethel 496 Everett 496 Gibson 495 Hamilton 495 Hamlet 496 Hazel 229 Ida 495 James 495 Laura 495 Mr 272 495-496 585 Nancy 495 585 Orris E 112 255
LEVERING, 120 Joshua 119
LEVINGS, 382 C W 304
LEVY, Gus 260
LEWIS, 177-178 E A 161
LILES, Bazzel 109
LILLIE, Andrew 109
LINCOLN, 117 155 Abe 250 Abraham 116 148-149 250 401 439 582 Henry 401 Jane 401 Mary 401 President 55 551 Selana 401 Siren 401
LINDSEY, Polly 375
LINVILLE, Preston T 162
LITTELL, Abraham 405 Absalom 405-406 Absalom Jr 405 Amos 405 Ann 405 Anna M 406 C L 437 Charles A 405-407 415 Edith 407 Elizabeth 406 Ella A 406 Ellie 415 Ethel 229 George C 406 Hannah 405-406 Indiana 406 John G 405-406 415 John Gilmore 406 John T 405 Josiah T 405-406 Lillian 406 Lillian A 407 Lucinda K 406 Margaret 405 Margaret R 406 Mary 405

INDEX.

LITTELL (Cont.)
  Mary Almira 407 Mary J 406 Matilda 406
  Mr 405-407 Mrs 407 T E 193 Thomas 194
  Thomas E 406 Verna Irene 407 W O 193
  406 William 194 William F 406 Wit 193
LITTEN, Susannah 596 Susannah Q 637
LITTLE, Andrew 69
LITTLELL, John G 193
LIVINGSTON, Hugh L 250
LLOYD, Saulsbury 165
LOCHRIDGE, Alma Lenora 435 Harvey 435
  Irene 435 Leo 435 Maxine 435 Robert 435
LOCKWOOD, Aaron 548 Aaron W 547-549
  Anna Laura 548 Bessie 549 Catherine 548
  Charles Aaron 549 Clay 548 Delano 548
  Dottie 548 Enni 548 Eula 548 Eva 549
  Glenn 548 Gordon 549 Greeley 548 Horace
  H 548 Inez E 548 Jesse S 548 John B 549
  Katie 548 Lewis Brooks 548 Minnie 548
  Mr 548-549 Mrs 548-549 Mrs Aaron W
  549 Muriel 549 Odell 548 Ora 548 Phoebe
  548 Phoebe J 547 Seymour B 547-548
LOGAN, Albert 303 Elliot 324 Harvey 324 John
  324 Margaret 324 Mary L 323-324 Nancy
  Eaton 324 Nathan 158 Paulina 324
LONG, Emma R 682 Ida 576 John 641 John K
  277 Malhaly 641 Mary 229 Mrs 129
LORAIGN, Nancy 418
LOUDERMILK, Flora J 428 J G 428
LOUGHMILLER, Clara 422 Clara B 422 Edith
  422 Harry 422 John 422 Joseph C 422
  Lafayette 422 Lida E 422 Maggie 422
  Mary 422 Mr 421-423 Mrs 423 Nettie May
  422 Rachel 422 Sarah 422 Sarah Elizabeth
  422 William E 421-423 437 William
  Russell 423 Willie Ann 422
LOUTHER, Rev 286
LOVE, Carrie 380 Edward 380 Howard 297
  Jane 440
LOVELESS, S 227 Samuel 233
LOWERY, Ellen 550
LOWREY, Ellen 550
LUCAS, Jeremiah 66 69 Ola 579 634
LUKEN, Mary 403 Otto 403
LUTES, Francis G 112 W B 298
LUTZ, I W 397 May 420
LYCAN, Anna 271
LYLE, Elnore 663 John 663
LYNCH, Jake 100 Mary 641 William 641
LYNDALL, W H 164
LYNN, Francis 186
LYONS, Maud 435
LYTTON, Hosea 483 Tabitha 483
MACKEL, James F 560
MACKELL, Anna 559 Catherine 559 Henry
  560 James 559 James F 559-560

MACKELL (Cont.)
  John 559-560 Katherine 559-560 Mr 560
MACKINNEY, Griffin 392 Lola M 392 Mary
  Anna 392
MACKLIN, Anna 402 George 402
MACY, Lucetta 713-714 Lydia 714 Tillie 714
MADDEN, Bridget 587 Michael T 112
MAHAM, Catherine 661 James 661 Minerva
  661
MAHER, Alice 202 James E 261 Laura 512
  Lawrence 242
MAHONEY, J 227
MAHONY, Catherine 522 Ellen 522 Helen
  521-522 James 522 John 522 Julia 522
  Mary 522 Michael 522
MAJOR, 62 George 197
MALLET, Demia 463-464 Phoebe 463 Rettie
  489 W W 463
MALLETT, Versie 467
MALLORY, James 157
MALONE, Ada 605 Ada E 674 Albert 229 237
  605 672-674 Amy 673 Catherine 673 Day
  B 674 Dossie 674 Elias 673-674 Ellis 229
  641 674 Eva 674 Frederick 673-674
  George 674 Grover C 674 Hattie 641 674
  Henry 673 Jacob 673 John 673 Leonard
  674 Lyman 674 Martha C Leon 673-674
  Mary 673-674 691 Mattie 674 Mr 674-675
  Mrs 675 Ruth 674 Samuel 673 Susannah
  673 William 673
MALONEY, Stephen 261
MALOTT, Judge 249 Newton F 249
MALOY, Elizabeth 388
MANGIN, Anna 574 Barbara 574 Catherine
  574 Catherine M 574 Frances 574 Frank
  574 Katrina 574 Margaret 574 Mary 574
  Mr 574-575 Nicholas 575 Rose 575
  Rosemary 574 Vincent 574
MANLEY, Sarah 641
MANN, Andrew 271
MANNING, Coy 698 Harvey 237 267 James
  698 Joshua 277
MARIEN, Brother 200
MARKLE, Clifford 260
MARKLIN, Louisa 631 Margaret 632 William
  632
MARKS, H E 604
MARLATT, Lafayette 193 Lucy 193
MARLEY, Benjamin B 426 Elizabeth 425
  Manley 425 Mary 426 Mary E 425 Melissa
  426 Susan 426 Walter T 426 William 426
MARLOW, John W 254
MARMADUKE, W W 260
MARR, Martha 670
MARSHALL, Elizabeth 515 James B 113
  Thomas R 59 William 515

MARTIN, Ambrose S 667 Andrew 88 111 B L 192 C C 291 Colvin 667 Doctor 667-668 Elizabeth 667 Ella 667 Ethel 667 Eva 667 Ezra J 667 J C 186 James 112 271 Jane 331 550 667 John H 667 Joseph 667 Lucinda 667 Luetta B 667 Lulu 667 Minerva 667 Minnie 667 Nancy 667 Nora 668 Peter J 189 Phoebe J 667 Rev 301 Richard 667 Sarah E 667 Sarah J 667 Simeon 173 667 Simon 667 William 180 667
MARTS, James J 177
MASON, Arnold 608 Dott 608 Ethel 608 Eva P 614 Evelyn P 607 George 69 Gilbert 607 J M 177 Jennie 607 Jennie M 608 John 607 Maggie 553 Margaret 607-608 Margaret L 607 Martha 607 614 Mary Alma 608 Mr 177 608 Nancy 607 Plesy 608 Plesy W 608 Rankin 607 Robert 607-608 Robert W 607-608 614 668 Ruth 608 Sarah 607 Walker 607 William 607-608 614
MASSEY, Catherine 609
MASTERS, Mollie Ann 455
MASTON, Sarah 478 Stephen 104
MATHERS, Louise 443-444 Nathan 444
MATHES, John 189
MATHEW, J P 260
MATHEWS, A H 259
MATHIS, James 192 John 192 194 Mary G 386
MATTHEWS, Claude 59 Father 244 Gov 340 W B 158
MATTINGLY, 707 Albert G 317 Augustine 317 C E 189 Caroline 317 Catherine 317 Edward J 317 Elisha 317 Elizabeth 530 Ezra 113 175 240 252 307 311-313 316-317 George E 317 Henry 69 Jack 182 James 317 James W 259 317 John 317 401 Laura C 317 Martha 317 Mary 229 Mary Ann 317 Mary E 317 Mr 175 316-318 401 708 Mrs Ezra 318 Samuel 317 Sylvester 317 Tillie 317
MAXWELL, Elizabeth 418 Nancy 418 Thomas 418
MAY, Bessie P 498 Grace 616 John 498 Leututia 508 Mamie 498 Pearl 702 Vance 255
MAYFIELD, 242 Arthur 241
MCARTOR, Peter 109
MCATEE, Daniel 581 John 581 Lizzie 581 Lucy 581 Marce 581 Martha 581 Martha E 581 Mary 581 Phillip 581 Theresa 704 Vina 581
MCAVOY, Margaret 486
MCBARRON, William 267
MCBRIDE, George 489 Ida May 446 James 489 630-631 Kaiser 489 Lydia 630

MCBRIDE (Cont.)
Malintha 489 Martha 489 Mary 489 Nell 446 Sarah 489 Wiley 446
MCCAFFERTY, 219 Benton 154 Earl 261 Ermel 229 F L 220 George W 111 Grace 229 Green 279 Henderson 218 Jack 182 James H 160 John 279 John C 399 Stella 229 270-271 T R 229 Thomas 279
MCCAIN, C 186 Martha M 533 Rev 233
MCCALL, Alexander 481 Andrew 481-482 Edward 482 Elizabeth 481 Ellen 481 Etta 480 Ettie 480 Eva 482 Everett 482 George W 480 John 481 John Austin 482 Lula 482 Margaret 481 Martha 481 Martha A 480 Mary C 481 Mr 481-482 Mrs 482 Mrs Andrew 481 Rose 482 Sarah 481 William A 481
MCCAN, J F 187
MCCAREY, John 90
MCCARTER, Ada G 649 662 Catherine 662 Clenton 662 D L 267 Daniel L 662 Della 662 Delphia C 646 Densel 662 Dewey R 646 Edna 662 Elizabeth 662 George 662 Glen 662 Ida A 662 J K 220 Jane 662 John 662 John K 662 Joseph 661-662 Minerva E 662 Miranda C 662 Moses 661-662 Mr 662 Nancy 662 Paul T 646 R D 649 Rufus D 278 662 Sarah 661-662 Thadius 662 Viola B 646 W H 109 Walter 662 William 662 William C 109 William H 646 661-662
MCCARTY, Eli 159 Elizabeth 290 J W 309 James 290 John 160 303 John W 171 175 262 304 311-313 Mr 290 Patrick 290 Patrick H 114 W W 261 Walter 182
MCCHESNEY, P B 259
MCCLEARY, Mary 593
MCCLELLAN, George B 117 Theresa 510 534
MCCLESKY, Joseph 214
MCCLOSKEY, Joseph H 106
MCCLURE, 139-140 John 246 300 Lucinda 630 Margaret 339 Nellie 630 William 311 630
MCCLUSKEY, John D 108 William 77
MCCONNELL, F M 220 226 241 James 114
MCCOOK, 153
MCCORD, Ella 619 Frank 619 J A 296 Jabez A 111 Joseph A 218 281 M H 619 Mason 296 Morton M 255 Ruth Anna 619 W J 306
MCCORMACK, I W 159 Isaac W 111 159 Lt 165
MCCORMICK, 86 Andrew 404 641 Cecil 411 Clay 260 Clyde 411 Cyrus 210 233 Ed 193 Elizabeth 404 641 Gordon 411 John 106 Nancy 641 Nellie 411 Rachel 404 Roscoe 411 S R 266 W L 229 William 76 109 258
MCCORY, John 109

INDEX. 745

MCCOSKY, Nellie 701
MCCOWAN, C C 254
MCCOWN, Charles C 112 Ruth 229
MCCOY, Ann 334 Anna 554-555 Clarence 229
  D P 195 Eliza 233 Elizabeth 380 608 Hugh
  292 380 608 J A 292 James 381 John 380
  O P 229 Plesy 608 Plesy W 608 Ruth 380
  Sarah 379-380
MCCRACKEN, Betsey 392 Charles 160
  George 422 Henry H 112 Mary 422
  Matthew 296 Nora 631 O M 229 Richard
  Wood 255 Thomas 109 William 631
MCCRAY, Nancy 667
MCCRISAKEN, Edward 151
MCCUEN, Ann 623
MCCULLOCH, Elliott 417 Fannie T 417
MCCULLOUGH, Elliott 304 Margaret 344
  386 Mary 518 Mr 304
MCCULLY, Sadie 479
MCCUTCHEON, 62
MCDANIEL, Marguerite 401
MCDERMOTT, John 202
MCDONALD, Asenath 464 Bridget 704
  Catherine 704 Daniel 85 David 113 233
  248-249 251 Eleanor 464 Francis 464-465
  Francis I 465 G 163 Green 163 180 464 J H
  112 James 704 John 66 289 704 Lily 391
  Louisa 191 Lucretia 344 Margaret 704
  Richard 110 173 Thomas B 704 William
  704
MCFADDEN, Margaret V 572
MCFARLAND, B F 267
MCFERREN, Margaret 339
MCGANNON, Darby 271
MCGAUGHEY, Alonzo C 168 Helen 421 J P
  108 James P 107-108
MCGAUHY, A J 255
MCGAWHEY, James P 113
MCGEE, Hazel 612
MCGEEHER, Richard 160
MCGEHEE, Frank 259 Lucy 229
MCGHEE, W H 255
MCGILL, Sarah 643
MCGOWEN, 73 Mr 68 William 68
MCGRAYEL, Julius P 261-262
MCGUIRE, Anna C 234 H L 186 James 704
  John 704 Margaret 704 Mary 704 Matilda
  Ann 704 Nauma 643 William 704
MCHENRY, Philander 220-221 224 226 Van
  453
MCINTIRE, John 227
MCINTOSH, J P 113 William 66
MCINTYRE, Charles 233 Jane 504
MCJUNKEN, Ann 706 Harvey 706
MCJUNKIN, E H 309 Erasmus 113 Erasmus H
  248-249 Mr 248

MCKEE, O M 186
MCKEOWN, John 254
MCKERNAN, Ella C Peek 270 Hugh 109 173
  181 203 Mary 271
MCKINLEY, President 56 471 501 William
  119-120
MCKINNEY, Archibald 392 Catherine 392
  Griffin 392 Margaret 392 Robert 392
MCKITTRICK, Henry C 256 Mrs Lou 193 O
  H 193 297 Oliver H 114 253 Ora K 112
MCKLIN, Sarah 595
MCKOWN, Bertha E 590
MCLAUGHLIN, J Z 259 Thomas 203
MCLIN, Anna 520 Ellen 520 George 520
MCLUIN, Joshua 154
MCMAHON, William 308
MCMASTERS, Allen 599 Bessie 599 Blanche
  599 Carl 599 Leta 599 Letha 599 Mary 599
  Raymond 599
MCMULLEN, Archie 593-594 Charles 226
  238 594 Donald 594 F A 593-594 Francis
  A 297 Frank A 593-594 Gerald 594 James
  202 John 593-594 Laura 593-594 Lewis
  594 Lois 594 Lola 594 Mary 593-594 Mr
  593-594 Mrs 594 Rose 594
MCNEALY, Sarah 711
MCNEIL, Roberta 228
MCNUTT, William 191
MCPHEETERS, Doctor 331 James 331
MCPHERSON, Doctor 451 S L 291 Solomon
  L 114 254 T R 305
MCRAE, W B 298
MCREYNOLDS, James 616 Mary A 616
MCTEGART, William Jr 203 William Sr 203
MCWILLIAMS, Carl 229 236 Charles 298
  Dello 229 George B 111
MEADE, Alfred D 627 Alfred Davis 626-628
  Annie A 526 Annie R 628 Charles E 628
  Delilah 627 E E 229 Edward E 628 Edwin
  E 110 Emanuel 627 Frank S 628 Giles W
  628 Grace 628 James 526 James B 628
  Joseph 627 Lucile 628 Martin L 628 Mary
  E 627 Milton 628 Minnie 628 Mr 627 Mrs
  627-628 Ruso 627 Sarah 627 Sarah E 628
  Sentony 627 William 627 William A 628
MEADS, Alfred 510 Alfred D 510 Anna 510
  534 Belle 510 Bettie 510 Charles 510
  Christopher 510 Claudia 510 Deliah 509
  Elwood 510 Emanuel 510 Gertrude 510
  Harry 510 James 534 James H 534 James
  M 110 510 534 John 283 510 John M 173
  Joseph 193 510 Joseph H 509-510 534
  Lillian 510 Mr 511 535 Rousseau 510
  Sarah 510 Sentna 510 Theresa 510 534
  William 510 William C 509
MEARS, Charles M 113 252

DAVIESS COUNTY, INDIANA.

MELSHEIMER, Earl 327 Ella 327
MENARD, Pierre 48
MENEFEE, Delphia 564
MEREDITH, B F 112 E F 251 Ed F 136
  Edward F 180 R W 162 Richard W 152 S
  259 Thomas 186 247 Thomas C 266 W R
  305
MERIDETH, Mr 247
MERIDITH, Ed F 306 William R 306
MERRIL, Catherine 139 Mr 139
MERRILL, Samuel 54
MERRIMAN, Angeline 319 Basil 319 Cyril
  319 Douglas 319 Elizabeth 236 320
  Eugene D 234 318-320 Forrest 319 George
  319 Hixon 319 Hortense 319 Jacob 319
  Leona 319 May 319 Merrill V 320 Micajah
  319 Mr 320 Mrs 320 Newton 319 Professor
  318-320 Superintendent 320 Wayland 319
MESSER, George 156
MESSERSMITH, Minerva 667 Peter 667
MEURER, Annie 679 Anthony 679 Charles
  679 Elisha 679 Elizabeth 679 George W
  678-679 Henry 679 Josephine 679 Laura
  679 Lockie L 679 Lura 679 Margaret 679
  Mary 679 Mr 679 Mrs 680 Nora 679 Philip
  679 Read 679 Roy 679 Sherman 679
  Thomas 679
MEYER, Edward W 256 William Henry 255
MEYERS, Frank P 700 Nancy Ann 700
MICHELS, Joseph F 255
MIKELS, Rosa M R 228
MILBURN, Richard 113
MILES, Celia 633 Emma 693 Nancy 693
  Patrick 693 William W 633
MILHITE, Franklin 106
MILLER, 312 Charles Everett 429 Doris 429
  Elizabeth 339 Ivan 429 J G 89 266 John
  526 Joseph 246 275 Laura E 462 Lola A
  429 Lt Col 74 Mary 243 679 Mary A 497
  Michael 497 Minerva E 662 Philip 662
  Samuel 186 301 Sarah 525-526 534
  Susannah 526
MILLIS, Burton J 318 Caroline 318 Edward D
  253 317-318 Eliza Ann 317 John 318
  Nancy 318 Tillie 317-318 William E 318
MILLS, Clara E 633 J C 195
MITCHELL, Alice 690 Ambrose 378 Belle
  377 Charles 378 Charles S 377 Clara 378
  Clare 378 Claude 378 Doctor 378-379
  Edwin S 377 Elizabeth Wilson 379 Ella
  566 Emily 378 Emma A 377 Indiana 377
  394 John 690 John C 256 John S 253 377-
  378 Laura 377 Leonidas S 377 Lucy 378
  Martha A 377 Mehitable 378 Milton M 566
  Mrs 379 R S 211 254 378 Ringgold S 255
  377 379 Ringgold Scott 377-378

MITCHELL (Cont.)
  Solomon 378
MITCHELTREE, George 94
MOATS, Gabriel 148
MODE, John 166
MOFFITT, W B 259
MOLEY, William 162
MONTGOMERY, 195 Ada 647 Addie 458
  Ambrose 451 Ann 451 Cletus 451 Corinne
  451 E W 458 Emery W 647 Frank 451
  Frank W 451 Harriett 450 Henry 451 James
  67 275 451 James C 290 297 James W 451
  John 156 451 John D 450-451 John R 652
  Josephine L 451 Mary 451 Mary Ann 652
  Mary E 451 Mr 198 450 452 Rose 451
  Rose Ann 451 Sadie 451 Sadie F 451
  Thresa 451 Valentine 290 Valentine B 290
  450-451 William 451
MOODY, Zachariah 168
MOONEY, William J 261
MOORE, Charles C 255 Frances 641 Frances
  Ann 699-700 G R H 250 H 632 Huldah
  May 632 J H 192 J L 266 Jackson L 157
  253 John W 166 Melissa 663 Thomas C
  113 William 277 663 William H 297
MOORMAN, L H 236
MOOTS, Anthony 282 503 Gabriel 166 Martha
  503
MORAN, George W 266
MORGAN, 127 597 Anna 402 486 520 709
  Catherine 471 486 Charles B 702 Charles
  D 106-108 Coleman 69 D H 227 David K
  422 525 Della 525 Elizabeth 290 525 Ethel
  328 Frank 328 Fred 709 Gen 56 George
  192 Hattie 328 Hugh 229 486 Hugh Jr 486-
  487 Hugh Sr 486-487 J 227 James 290 328
  486 James S 245 Jesse 67 John 328 422
  486 525 John D 111 Jonathan 67 Laura 328
  Lida 422 Lida E 422 Lizzie 422 Lola 702
  Lucinda 328 Lucretia 328 Lydia 525
  Margaret 486 525 Margaret A 422 Martha
  328 Mary 328 486 Mary E 328 Moses 272
  Mr 487 525 Mr Sr 487 Patrick 486 Richard
  422 525 Sarah 328 422 525 Thomas 104
  328 Valentine E 422 Volney 525 W T 112
  William 328 422 525
MORIN, G W 227 George W 227 234 Rollie
  229
MORRIS, Gen 153 Martha Glenn 394 Robert
  394 W B 194
MORRISON, John L 168 William 66
MORSE, Anna H 228
MORTON, Gov 55-56 127 249 264 492 Oliver
  P 58
MOSIER, Emma 712 Ettie 712 Frecina 712
  Henry 712 Jennie 712 Mary 712

INDEX. 747

MOSIER(Cont.)
 Mary A 712 Perry 712 Philander 712
MOSS, Daniel 259
MOTTE, Jerome D 255
MOUGIN, John 197
MOULDEN, Mr 378
MOUNT, C L 194 James A 59
MOVEROD, J R 259
MULHOLLAND, Ellen 465 S H 165 Samuel H 165 180 218 465 Sarah 465
MULLEN, John 652 Melissa 652
MUMAW, Frances 700
MUNHOLLAND, Samuel 468
MUNSON, Contractor 126 Doo 125
MURET, Eliza 696 Julius 696 Nettie 696
MURPHY, 195 Amanda 506 D J 171 Father 197 Harriett 203 John 85 301 306 309 Michael 248 301 309 Mike 110 Nancy 397 P J R 197
MURRAY, Ellen 503 J A 227 Joseph A 192 Martha 503 Mary 502-503 Samuel 503
MYERS, A 195 Absalom 423 Ada J 707 Ada Jane 478 Alfred C 428-429 Alva E 478 707 Andrew T 92-93 347 351 Anna Bush 708 Anna Elizabeth 423 Anna K 477 Arilda 708 Arla 612 Arnold W 428 Asemeth 477 Bessie 338 478 Bessie R 708 C Will 229 Carrie 229 Cecil 429 Charles H 428-429 Christina 429 711 Clara 477 Clarinda 708 Daniel 477 708 Daniel A 477 Daniel I 477-478 707-708 Della 428 Dollie 407 E H 229 Earnest 707 Effie G 429 Elias 276 429 Elijah 477 707-708 Elijah H 477-478 Elijah N 477 Elijah W 708 Elizabeth 429 Emma 428 Ernest L 478 Fannie 490 Flora J 428-429 Frances 531 Francis A 219 Frank 227 477 Frank P 180 423 Frank P 477 708 Frederic 141 George W 429 Grace 229 Grant 423 Hannah 711 Harriet 710-711 Harry 619 Henry 558 Isabella 477 Jacob 711 James 477 708 John 558 711 John F 283 Joseph 276 429 708 Joseph M 428-429 Josiah 477 Lewis 612 Lola A 429 Mahala 711 Martha J 612 Mary 351 356 429 477 Mary E 347 Mary S 477 May 477 Mr 428-430 477-479 707-708 Mrs 429-430 478-479 707-708 Mrs Thomas C 430 Nancy 423 Nancy L 428 Nelson 707 Nelson L 478 Olive 477 Olive E 619 Oliver E 428 Ollie 708 Pearl 612 707 Pearl May 478 Roscoe 229 Roy F 293 S E 252 477 Sarilda 557-558 Stella 477 708 Stephen 478 Stephen E 317 338 478 707-708 Susan 558 Tempa 477 Thomas 477 Thomas C 428-430 Verna 478 Verna Grace 478 Vernie Grace 707 William 429 477 711

MYERS (Cont.)
 William A 159 Wilson B 708 Wilson C 477
MYRES, Elizabeth 466 Frances C 445
NASH, Carroll 168 Enoch 157 Michael 111
NEAL, 182 Alexander 582-583 Anna 582 Asa 582 Charles 582 Della 583 James 161 165 582 Jane 582 John T 260 Margaret 582 Maria 582 Mary 582 Mr 583-584 Mrs 584 Robert 582 Sarah 582 William H 582-583
NEELY, Joseph 271
NEENIMER, W R 292
NEIGHBOR, Lena 588 William 588
NELLIS, Ozias 253
NELSON, Agnes 605
NEUMANN, John W 666
NEW, W 268
NEWBERRY, A R 160
NEWLAND, Mahalia 483
NEWTON, Charles 621 John 620 Lena 621 Mary Ann 620-621 Miss 585
NIBLACK, Judge 249 Sanford 439 Susan 439 William E 113 248 250
NICHOLAS, Simon 66 69
NICHOLS, G J 306 J 227
NICHOLSON, 62 G E 229 Mayme 229
NIMNICHT, Anna 713 August 713 Augustus 713 Charles F 713 Christopher 713 Edward 713 Ernestine 713 Frank 713 Frank L 713 Herman 713 Ida M 713 Laura 713 Louis H 713 Lucetta 713 Minnie 713 William 713
NIONINGER, Hannah 598
NIXON, Clara 383 David 188 Elisha 383 Eliza 383 Elizabeth 383 Emma 268 Etta 382-383 M 382 Mr 383 Mrs 383 Myrtle 383 O B 297 Ruth 383
NOBLE, Noah 57-58
NOBLET, Alice 641 William 641
NOFSKER, Susannah 643
NORMAN, Catherine 690 Gladys 229 Hezekiah 690
NORRIS, Mary 405
NOYES, 192
NUGENT, Bessie 696 Cora 229 Milton B 238 Muret 696 Paul 696 Thomas 110 112 696
OBERST, Oia 397 Otto 397
OBRIAN, Arlie 229 Mrs 451
OBRIEN, Eugene 261 William F 296
OBRYAN, Ann 410 Elva 411 Eugene 410 Geraldine 411 Helen 411 James 410-411 John W 411 John Wesley 410 Joseph 410 Julia 410 Mable 411 Mary 411 Merle 411 Mr 409-410 Mrs 410 Nellie 410-411 Pearl 411 Sarah 409-411 Sylvester 409 Thomas 409-411 William 410-411
OCALLAHAN, Anna 622 Mary 410

OCONNOR, Anna 565 Edmond 566 Edward F 565 Edward T 565-566 Elizabeth 565 Estella 566 Francis Fanning 566 Joanna 229 John 229 565 Marguerite Marie 566 Mary 565 Mary B 566 Mary K 565 Mary Kitura 566 Michael 515 565 Mr 565-566 Mrs Edward T 566 Nancy 515 Nora 229 565-566 Vincent Edward 566
OCONOR, Charles 118
ODELL, Alex 292 298 Alexander 240 C E 298 C R 380 Caleb 218 240 292 Edgar A 241 Elizabeth Jane 484-485 Elva Pearl 362 Emsley 484 Famie 229 Jacob L 255 John 267 John W 362 Lizzie 200 Mattie 710 Nellie 380 Sarah 484
ODONAGHUE, Dennis 203 Maggie 229
ODONALD, Beryl 229 Owen 109 Stella 229 William T 298
ODONNELL, 316
OGDEN, Autumn 646 Dawson B 646 Helen 646 Helvia 646 Leota E 646 Margaret 646 Miss 95 Pauline 646 Phoebe B 646 Rebecca Josephine 646 Vella J 646
OGDON, J W 567 James W 249 304-306 Judge 706
OKAVANAUGH, Mary A 243
OLIVER, Mary 458 Robert 244
OMABEY, Lizzie 193
OMARA, John 680 Sophia 680
OMARRY, William 166
OMELVENA, James 186
ONEAL, Henry 107 Hugh 251 J H 303 James 229 James M 107 John H 114 312 M G 251 306 Miles G 306 Mr 312
ONEALL, John H 234 John Henry 180
OPPEER, E A 254
ORENDER, Mattie 447 Ola 446
ORMSBY, John 307 Robert 162
ORR, Miss 483
ORSBORN, Orpha E 646
OSBORN, Daniel 664 James 672 Jane 672 Laura 672 Lovina 526 Teletha 664
OSBORNE, Cynthia A 671
OSGOOD, Sarah A 233
OSMAN, Charles 168 444 Margaret 444 Martha 444
OSMON, Ada 476 Alice 476 Austin 460 475 Austin B 475-476 Benson 476 Bessie 476 Bonnie 476 Charles 475-476 Clotie 476 Cordelia 475-476 David 475 Dyer 475 Elizabeth 475-476 Ellen 476 Everett 476 F F 229 George 476 George W 475-476 Homer 476 Isaac 475-476 Jabez 280 Jabus 475-476 John 475 Lorie 476 Margaret 475 Martha 476 Mary 475 Maud 460 476 Mr 476-477 Mrs 477 Mrs Austin B 476

OSMON (Cont.)
Mrs Charles 476 Nora 476 Pauline 476 Philip 475 Robert 476 Roena 476 Sarah 475 Thomas 475 Wesley 475
OSTERHAGE, Architect 191
OSULLIVAN, Martha C Leon 673-674 Mary 673 Robert 673
OVERTON, Anderson 469 Clementine 469 Enola 488 Frank 304 J A 601 Lydia 682 Moses 682 Mr 601 William 488
OWANIGEN, Oscar 160
OWEN, George W 166
OWENS, Lura 679 Nora 679
PACE, Mr 287
PACKARD, Eunice W 191
PADDOCK, William 276
PADGETT, 251 A J 261 Alvin 113 Arnold J 262 Margaret 269
PAGAN, Henry 254
PAGETT, Edna 599
PAGUE, Martha 501
PAHMEIER, John W 255
PAINTER, Henrietta 544
PALMAR, Martin 94 William 94
PALMER, 120 140 Charles 154 Col 182 H W 261 Helen 229 Hiram 107-108 J A 159 John F 635 John M 119 Joshua 635 Joshua A 159 Lydia 635 Mary 504 635 Mason 635 Mason R 635 Mrs T R 234 Parmenes 97 Parmenius 272 Permenus Allen 635 Perminus 589 Rachel 635 Rev 191 Richard 65 69 77 111 139 300 T R 182 191 Uncle Dick 301 Winnie 537 589
PARK, Richard 228
PARKE, Benjamin 48-49 52
PARKER, Alton B 120 533
PARKS, 178 James F 112 114 253 R M 191
PARR, George L 255
PARRET, Francois 199
PARROT, Miss 493
PARROTT, Anthony 202
PARSONS, Austin R 530 Benjamin 529 C P 233 Dovie L 530 Elizabeth 381 498 530 Ervin A 530 Hattie 494 530 I M 381 L B 250 Lola 229 Lucretia 391 530 Lucretia R 529 Mary 530 Mr 79 Ora 530 Samuel Holden 42 Vienna 529 William A 530
PATE, Agnes 229 Alice 229 Dovey 494 John 494 Louis 229 Minnie 614 Noah 614 Randa E 664-665 William 665
PATERSON, Clara Ida 564
PATRICK, William 268
PATTEN, Thomas 67
PATTERSON, 191 Capt 71 Mary 327 Sanford 114 220 W H 327 William 67
PATTON, 312

INDEX. 749

PAUL, Sallie 609 Thomas 609 William 609
PAULEY, Grace 644
PAULSON, May 614 Paul 614
PAYNE, James 267 John 249 Thomas 285
  Thomas J 109 285
PAYTON, Patsy 514
PEABODY, Nettie 681
PEACHEE, Alfred 481 Benjamin 481 Eliza
  478 481 Eliza J 708 Harrison 159 Hiram
  481 Isaiah 481 James 481 John 481 Martha
  A 481 Martha Ann 481 Mary C 481
  Matilda J 481 Mirrah 481 Nathaniel 193
  Osiah 481 Rebecca 481 Retha 481 Sarah
  481 Sophia 481 William 481
PEACHY, Betsey 392
PEARCE, Amanda 555 Charollete A 555
  Herman A 555 Mary F 555 Sarah H 554-
  555 Thornton C 168 William M 555
  William W 555
PEARCY, Rebecca 571
PECK, Barton 85 106 Harvey 156 Joseph 151
  Josiah 233 Samuel W 90 161 253
PEEK, Bertha E 590 Cager 589 Callie Eveline
  590 Carrie B 537 Carrie Belle 590 Charles
  E 266 537 588-591 Cora E 590 Ella 271
  586 Ethel K 521 John 537 589 John E 590
  John M 584-586 Joseph 586 Julia A 537
  589-590 Levi 584 586-587 Louise 586
  Mary 586 Melina Opha 590 Mildred 589
  Mr 586 588-590 Mrs 590 Oren 521 Richard
  586 Sallie 584 Sarah 586 Thomas J 590
  Viola G 591 Viola Glenn 590 William E
  590 Winnie 537 589
PENNINGTON, Stephen 197
PENROD, Sarah 469 William K 207 212 220
  298
PENSENNEAU, George 345 Rose 345
PERCY, William 69
PERINE, Mildred 391
PERKINS, Abbie 390 Abierilla 580 Abraham
  111 Albert 491 Alfred 468 Asbury 430 Ben
  278 Eleanor 429-430 Emma Jane 366 John
  101 John A 430 Louisa 491 Lucy Ann 621
  M 227 May 471 Rebecca 468 Reuben A
  366 Sarah 253 468 Sarah J 491 William A
  298
PERRY, Mr 68-69
PERSHING, Albert 229 Arla 448 Calvin 448 E
  S 227 Homer 448 J E 297 Lora 229
  Magdaline 614 Raymond 448 Solomon 614
  Susan 614 Susannah 644
PERSING, Albert 494 Hazel 494
PETER, Uncle 141-142
PETERSON, 280
PEYTHIEU, Hugo 202-203
PHILIPS, J R 191
PHILLIPPE, Hester T 255

PHILLIPS, John R 215-217 234 William 69
PHIPPS, John B 267
PICKEL, J M 255
PICKELL, James Augustus 255
PICKETT, C A 194 Edna 229
PIERCE, Anna 404 E R 191 Father 244
  Franklin 115 485 Joseph 266
PIERCY, Andrew 690 Emily 690
PIERS, B 198 Barthol 199 Father 199 244
PIERSON, C L 292 298
PIPER, Emma 606
PIPHER, Rev 301
PLEISS, Mamie 498
PLUMMER, Katie 254 Thomas K 254
POINDEXTER, Ainley 604 Amelia 472 Anna
  603 Anna E 473 Christian 472-473 603
  Clara E 604 Clay 492 Dimple 604 Early W
  603 Effie 604 Elizabeth 472 603 Elmer 492
  Emelia 603 Flossie May 473 Freely 492
  604 George 603 Harriett 485 Henry 472-
  473 Huette 112 602-604 Ida 472 Irwin 473
  Ives T 604 John 473 John S 603 Leotie 604
  Lorinda 472 Lucinda 472 Luranda 603
  Lurinda 603 Mary 492 Mr 472-473 603-
  604 Mrs 473 603-604 Nettie 603 Paris E
  604 Paton 472-473 Patten 603 Roy W 604
  Rufus 473 Rufus M 603 Samuel 473
  Tillman 473 Tillman H 603 Veecher 604
  Verlin L 604 Whitton 472-473 Wiley 473
  603 William 473 603 Zela Irene 604
POLK, James K 114
POLKE, William 113
POOR, Hannah 439 John 439 Susan 439
POORE, Joseph 271
POPE, R D 255 Ransom 286
PORTER, A W 254 Albert G 58 Alvilda 643
  Alwilda 643 Ann 334 Artie 336 Bessie 336
  Calvin 335 Charles A 256 Clara 336 619
  Claudia 510 Elizabeth 335 Eva 336 F T
  193 George 335 Gertrude 619 J C 227
  James 109 113 173 334-335 James Sr 335
  John 335 John R 248-249 Joseph 335 619
  Joseph M 220 Judith 335 Laura G 365
  Margaret 335 Marion 335 Mc G 255 Mr
  335-336 Mrs 336 Nathan 643 Robert 335-
  336 S M 619 Senator 334-336 Steward 335
  Susannah 643 Thelma 336 William 335
POSEY, 145 Doctor 144 146-147 John W 140
  144 Thomas 58
POTER, Eleanor 373
POTTS, Glenn 555 Henry 653 Jane 392 Luther
  229 Mary Ann 703 Nellie 492 Rose 653
  Samuel 384 Susan 384 William 168
POUCHER, John 464
POWELL, Emerald 413 Leon 413 Leonard 413
  Mr 413 Pearl 413

POWNALL, Alwilda 664 677 Amy 663 Byron 663 Clarence 664 677-678 Elnore 663 Florence 664 Geneva 665 George W 663-665 677-678 George Washington 663 Georgia A 665 Hallet C 665 Herschel D 665 Jesse 663 665 677 John 663 Louisa 663 Melissa 663 Minnie 664 Minnie Mara 678 Mr 663-665 678 Mrs 678 Nancy 663 665 677 Randa E 664-665 Teletha 664 Theodore C 664-665 Theodore Clemens 664 Trula 678
PRATER, Frank 384 Jane 384
PRATHER, Lt-Col 153
PRENTICE, John 366
PRENTISS, John 366 Laura 322 393 Laura G 365 Thomas Green 365
PREWITT, James P C 165
PRICE, 162 Gen 531 Maud 644
PRIDE, E W 160 Hubbard 160 J T 160
PRINCE, Judge 246 William 246 248
PRINGLE, Ida 419 T T 234
PRITCHARD, James A 218 Margaret 323
PRITCHERT, Henry 189
PRITCHETT, Basil B 306
PROFFIT, George 250 George H 251
PUGH, Frank 660 Glenn 660 Herford 660 Lester 660 Nancy 660 Neva 660
PURCELL, Benjamin 376 Charlotte 376 Elijah 66 Hiram 376 Indiana 376 James 376 Jennie 435 Jesse 66 87 102-103 376 Prudence 376 Rachel 376 William 376
QUEEN, Mason 409 Sarah 409-410 Thomas Jr 296
QUICK, Charles W 387 Edith 387 John 513 Laversa J 513 Mary Ellen 513 Mr 513 William G 250
QUIGLEY, Hugh M 242 William 102-103 258
QUILLIAM, Anna Elizabeth 423 Bernard 423 Clara 422-423 Ellen 423 Frank 423 James 423 Jane 423 John 423 John J 423 Lillian 423 Richard 423 Roy 423 William 423
QUILLIAMS, James 530 Mary 530
QUIRK, Lillian 423
RADER, W S 187
RADSPINNER, Harriet 271
RAGDILL, Hezekiah 111
RAGLE, Addie 494 Alma 411 Alva 411 Bertha 411 Charles A 494 Claude 422 Dovey 494 Edith 422 Emma J 494 Flossie 494 Grace 494 Harley 494 Hattie 494 Hazel 411 494 Jacob 411 James 493 Jerome 494 Jesse 494 John 408 493 Margaret 492 494 Martha 494 Mattie 494 Maude 494 Mr 493-495 Myrtle 494 Paul 494 Pearl 494 Peter 492-495 Peter Jr 493-495 Peter Sr 493-494 Sarah 411 Sarah R 494 Thomas 411

RAGLES, Hattie 530
RAGSDALE, G 69 Hezekiah 66 508 James 188 John 69 Laura J 532 545 Lyda 356 Mark H 254 Mary 508 Mrs James 188 P H 171 173
RAINEY, Eliza 571 Elizabeth 514 George 277 Reuben 277
RALSTON, Samuel R 59
RAMSEY, Eliza 268 690 J W 266-267 Lillian 704 Post Commander 267
RANDOLPH, 50 Thomas 49
RANEY, Charles A 259
RANG, Arthur A 255
RANKIN, David 298 Parnetta 193 Thomas B 255
RANKLE, Barbara 574 George 574
RAPER, Robert 111
RASER, Sally 671
RASLER, Mary 371
RATCLIFF, Sarah Elizabeth 422 Thomas 422
RATTAN, Samuel 160
RAY, Bessie 428 James B 58 Rev 301 Thomas G 254
REA, M D 254
READ, Cleo 417 Doctor 128-129 Effie 604 Fannie T 417 George C 339 416 J G 99 James 300 James G 83-84 96-97 99 101 246 248 258 James J 309 Louis I 305 417 Lydia 416 Martha 339 416 Mary 339 416 Mary A 416 Mildred 417 Miriam 339 416 Mr 300 416-417 Mrs 417 Mrs Nathan G 417 N G 110-111 305 Nathan 339 416 Nathan G 218 339 416-417 R N 110 Rebecca 338-339 Rebecca Ann 346 Richard H 417 Richard N 86 339 416 Robert Roy 417 Sarah 339 Sarah D 416
REASON, Eleazar 277 Stephen 277 Thomas 277
RECTOR, Ann 489 Cynthia Ann 514
REDDICK, Seth 309
REDFORD, Pearl 271 Pearle Horrall 270
REED, Ada May 492 Albert 492 Albert Laverne 492 Carlton 492 Charles 491-492 Clara 492 Cleo 271 Eliza 491 Elizabeth 491 Francis 491 James G 113 300 John 492 Mary 492 Mr 492 Nellie 492 Sarah 491 Sarah J 491 Stella 492 Wallace 491 William A 491 William W 491-492
REEDER, Jacob 67 274 Mary 571
REESE, William 190
REEVE, Alice 412 Ethel 236 Joseph F 254 Joshua 274 Mr 274 S T 412
REEVES, George E 260 Joshua 69 95 Levi 219 227
REID, Samuel 187
REILEY, C M 298

INDEX.

REINEY, Mary E 613
REISTER, 191
RELEFORD, Leva 496
RESLER, Arla 666 Barbara 665 Clara 666 Cora 666 David 665-666 Dorothy Eunice 667 Ellen B 666 Ethel 667 Florence 667 Frank 666 Fred S 667 Harvey 666 Ida 666 Isaac 666 Isaac J 665 Jacob 666 Jennine 666 Jessie 666 John 665 John Henry 666 Martha 666 Mary 666 Minnie 666 Mr 666 Phoebe 666 Roy 666 Suda 666 Susannah 665 Thomas E 665-668
RETTGER, Louis J 225
REVERE, Paul 439
REYNOLDS, 315 Caleb 166 Mary Jane 446 Miles 239
RHOADS, Eunice 642 John 642 Susan 642
RHODES, C C 236 Delilah 546-547 Henry 156
RICE, 155
RICHARDS, 88 John 191
RICHARDSON, Edna 662 Ora 662 W A 195
RICHISON, Lizzie 661
RICKARD, John E 623 Mary 623 Mrs 623
RICKS, Hattie 591
RIESTER, Albert 715 Andrew 714 Anna 715 Barbara 715 Bernard 715 Bessie 716 Caroline 714-715 Charles 715 Ella 715 Frances 715 Frank 715 George 714-716 Hattie 715 Helen 715 Henry 714 Jacob 715 John 715 Leo 715 Lucy 715 Minnie 715 Mr 715 Mrs 715 Oster 716 Peter 714 Phillip 714 716 Preston 714 Stephen 714-715 Thomas 714 Tillie 715 William 715
RIGDON, Rebecca 481
RIGG, Mary 704
RIGGINS, Elisha A 219 253 Emma 488 Harvey 488 Lula 448
RILEY, 62 Anthony 389 Bridget 389 J 195 John 389 Julia 243 Mary 389 Michael 389 Terrence 389 William 389
RINDINGER, Rettie 526
RINGO, Ella 710
RINK, Charles J 447 Chauncey 447 J C 447 James 453 Joe Merel 447
RINKS, Delight 610
RISLEY, Harrison 160 Mary 426 Perry 426
RITCHEY, Elam 165
RITTER, Benjamin 229 Benjamin H 466-467 Clay 467 Elizabeth 466 Jacob 466 James 466 Jennie 466 Mary 466 Minnie 467 Mr 467 Ola 467 Olive 467 Roscoe 467 Versie 467 W H 466 Walter J 467
RITTERSKAMP, Altha 396 Amelia 396 Amelia H 396 Carl 396 David 396 Ella 396 Emil 395 Ernest G 395-396 Fred 395-396 Harriet 396 Louisa 395 Mollie 396 Mr 396

RITTERSKAMP (Cont.)
Mrs 396 Oscar 396 Otto 395-396 Viola 396 Walter 296 William 396
ROACH, Edith 406 William 107
ROARK, Elizabeth 679 John 679 Lockie L 679
ROARTY, Catherine 573
ROBB, David 82 H 259 Hamilton 178 191
ROBBINS, Charles W 617 Emma R 617
ROBERSON, Mattie 268
ROBERTS, Arla 666 Clara E 633 Flora Nevada 632 Huldah May 632 J F 631 John F 631 John Franklin 631-632 Louisa 631 Lovina 644 Maria Jane 631 Maud 632 Mr 631-633 Mrs Rett 633 Rett 633 Rett A 226 229 631-633 Robert Austin 632 William 631
ROBERTSON, Charles 189 Clara 642 James 642 Phoebe 642
ROBESON, James 104 Michael 103
ROBINSON, Andrew 255 Elijah 496 Elizabeth A 460 Etta 496 Flossie 494 Francis 405 Frank E 256 G 227 G M 253 James 277 John W 296-297 Lucretia 496 May 228 May E 229 236 Otis T 256 T N 191
ROBINSTEIN, Christopher 709 Mollie 709
ROBISON, Martha 641
RODARMEL, Grace 271 John A 179-180 Mr 179 O F 151 153 Oscar F 152 S A 309 Samuel A 112
RODDICK, George 85 111 George W 157 Ophelia 227 Ophelia H 234
RODERICK, Mrs 192
RODICK, Seth 300
ROGERS, 252 Alexander 277 Amos 66 69 104 Clayton 66 Elizabeth 527 Emma 428 Hugh 382 John 428 Lydia 382 Thomas 277
ROOSEVELT, Col 558 Theodore 120-121
ROOT, W H 112
ROSE, Miss 451 Senator 451
ROSECRANS, 159 163
ROSENBERRY, Sarah 489
ROSENBURG, Joseph 666 Mary 666
ROSENBURY, Arnold 470 Bertha 469 Clementine 469 Edith 470 Emma 469 George W 469-470 George William 469-470 Harry 470 Harry Belden 469 Irene 470 Joseph E 469 Josiah 469 Mary 469 Minnie 469 Myrtle 470 Sallie 469 Sarah 469 Wallace 470 Wirtsel 469-470 Wirtsel V 469-470
ROSS, Charles 286 Edith 697 Mary 478 Philip 158
ROSSEAU, 153
ROUSSEAU, Lovell H 249-250 Richard H 249
ROUTT, George H 104-105 Jephtha 244 Lester 190 William H 83 113 246 248 258

ROWAN, Father 201 P 199
ROWE, G Halleck 193
ROWER, Patrick 203
ROWLAND, Calvin L 255
RUBLE, Henry 82-83 Peter 97
RUCKER, Pascal 277
RUDOLPH, John W 291
RUGGLES, Aaron 583 Delilah 583 Elizabeth 583 Jacob 583 Mary 583 Nancy 583 Rachael 583 Thomas 65 583
RUMINER, John 276
RUPORT, Michael 258
RUSSELL, Elizabeth A 436 Elmer 436 G W 260 George W 256 John 160 171 173 Maria 341 Robert 92 110 304
RUST, Andrew 642 Charles 642 Clara 642 Eunice 642 Grace 236 642 Henry 642 James Rhoads 642 James W 642 John Henry 642 Lillie 642 Lottie 642 Mary Millicent 642 Mr 642-643
RUTHERFORD, Anthony 592 Elizabeth 592 Etta May 536 Harriette A 592-593
RUTLEDGE, W J 263
RYAN, L 227
SABIN, A L 254
SAINTCLAIR, Arthur 41-42 58 81 Arthur Jr 44 Gen 34 Gov 42 44
SAINTJOHN, John P 119
SAMPLES, John 148 Mary Jane 509 William 148
SANDERS, Margaret 679 William 148
SANFORD, 178 Ann 328 338 525 Eliza 338 Elizabeth 338 Eula 229 George 181 George L 180 182 Graham 180-182 Hamilton 575 Hamlet 89 108 338 John C 338 Josephine 229 Leigh 182 Lucinda 338 Lucretia 338 496 Mary J 337 Mary Jane 338 Miriam 416 Mr 304 Pauline 229 Pierce 338 Reuben 338 Tabitha 338 575-576 Tabitha Ann 575 Virginia 338 William 111 220 304 338 416
SARGENT, Winthrop 42 81
SASS, H A 229 236
SASSEL, Father 203 243 John P 203
SATTERFIELD, Dove 458 Eliza 605 John 241 S W 241 Solomon W 220
SAUSE, James T 110 173 Julia 522
SAWYER, Samuel 178
SCALER, Thomas 69
SCALES, Grant 229 Philip 268
SCANLON, Michael 253
SCARLETT, Katherine 535
SCHNEIDER, Elizabeth 466 J J 356
SCHOONOVER, L L 195
SCHRUM, Mark 255
SCHUCK, Catherine 570 Henry 570 Lena 570 Louis 570 Louise 570 Mary 570

SCHUCK (Cont.)
Peter 570 Philip 570
SCHULER, Kate 557 Mary 557 Miles 557
SCHULTE, Amelia H 396 Christ 396 Clara 396 Emma 396 Fred 396 Louisa 396 Lydia 396 Mollie 396 William 396
SCHULTZ, Jacob 479 Martha 479
SCHURZ, Hattie 268
SCHWINDLER, Laura 420 Russell L 420
SCOBLE, Claire 465 Marguerite 431 Roy 465
SCOTT, A C 195 Dollie M 651 Frances D 490 George T 184 H B 186 J Thomas 254 James 490 John 271 Joseph 490 Joseph G 154 Laura E 655 Lovina L 490 Lucinda 490 Malintha 490 Miss 531 Mrs 490 Nona 651 Rawley 248 258 Reason 490 Samuel 651 Samuel A 655 William 490 Winfield 115
SCOVILLE, Charles R 194
SCUDDER, Alice 542-543 Anna V 321 Carrie 543 Charles 253 321 Charles P 112 253 260 320-322 David A 321 David Fenwick 322 Doctor 321-323 Elizabeth 322 Elizabeth F 321 Ellen 543 Emma 321 Helen 321 Helen S 365 Jacob F 543 Jacob S 321 James 321 John 114 321 542-543 John A 253 266 321-322 340 394 543 John Anderson 271 Kenneth 543 Laura G 321 Louise J 322 Lydia 543 Margaret E 271 Margaret Ellen 270 Matilda 270 321 Mr 542-543 Mrs 322-323 Nathaniel 271 321 Thomas 322 Tillie 340 Tillie F 321 William C 542-544 William G 173 William W 322
SEAL, 252 F A 251 Flavian A 113 William S 256
SEALS, Julian L 256 William 109
SEARS, Andrew 447 B R 267 Barton 253 Bessie 331 Betsie 551 Blanche 331 Dale 331 David 166 Evaline 460 F M 254 Hobart 331 John 460 John M 166 John T 331 Lettie 331 Lola 594 Lucinda 358 Luther 594 Margaret 331 447 Maude 331 Paul 194 331 Ripple 331 S P 229 T M 252 285 Thomas M 254 Verna 331
SEFRIT, C G 352 Charles 464 Charles G 178-181 257 464-465 Charles Green 464 Claire 465 Eleanor 464 Ethel 465 Frank I 180 182 309 465 George 464 H H 109 Henry H 109 Louis B 182 Moses L B 180 464 Mr 179-180 257 315 464-465 Mrs 465 Nell 465 Ruth 465 Sarah 465
SEIFERD, Margaret 444
SEIFRIT, Charles 475 Elizabeth 475 Margaret 475 Mrs Charles 271
SELFRIDGE, William T 255

INDEX. 753

SELLMAN, John P 255
SENEFF, Amanda 604 Clara E 604 John H 255
    Joseph H 604
SEXTON, Marshall 259
SEYMOUR, Horatio 117
SHACKLEFORD, Anna 712 Elizabeth 711
    George Washington 712 John 712 John D
    711 Mary M 711-712 Redman 712
    Washington 712
SHAFFER, Clara 229 John G 474 Matilda 474
SHAFFFER, Andrew 218
SHAKE, Newton 285 S J 286
SHALEY, John 164
SHALTZ, Frederick 95
SHAMFFELBERGER, Sam 286
SHANK, Margaret 474 Peter 474
SHANKS, 375 Anna 520 639 Anna Martha
    453 Bertha 521 640 Catherine 638-639
    Celina G 453 Clifford J 521 640 E J 453
    Edward J 453-454 Emma Jane 453 Ethel
    521 640 Ethel K 521 Frank C 521 H N 454
    Ida M 453 Ida May 453 J G 109 John 519-
    520 638-639 John Frank 640 John Franklin
    453 John G 109 519-521 638-640
    Katherine 519-520 Laura Belle 453 Mary E
    519-521 640 Mary Elizabeth 453 Mr 521
    639-640 Mrs 640 Mrs John G 520-521
    Russell 521 Russell C 640 Sarah 519-520
    638 Sarah Catherine 453 Sarah E 520 639
    Sarah Jordan 454 William 112 519-520
    638-639 William J 112 519-521 640
SHANOWER, Susannah 665
SHARPLESS, Absalom 671 Rosa 641 Sarah
    Alice 671
SHATTUCK, Asa 271
SHAW, Henry M 113 Piney 627 Sarah 627
SHEKELL, O M 226 229
SHELTON, John W 255
SHEPARD, Francis A 156 John 275 W D 233
SHEPHERD, Ellen 616 Ralph C 256 W D 210
    W F 256
SHEPPARD, Mary 460
SHERIDAN, W F 187
SHERMAN, 56 162 164 166 425 444 468 614
    627 646 B C 189 Gen 159 480
SHERWOOD, H I 255
SHIELDS, J H 256
SHINEFELT, Sarah 577
SHINNER, John 709 Mamie 709
SHIRCLIFF, John 104
SHIREMAN, Emeline 418-419 Maxwell 419
    Sarah 419
SHIREY, Addie 425 Araminta 425 Charles V
    425 Claudia 425 Dora 425 Frank M 425
    Merlin D 425 Michael 425 Siegel 425
SHIRKLIFF, Alex 594 John 594

SHIRKLIFF (Cont.)
    Laura 593 Mary 594 Rose 594
SHIRLEY, Emily 440 Herman Vincent 440
    James L 440 Jasper 440 Johanna 440 John
    440 Laura E 440 Mary 271 440 Mary C
    229 270 313 439-440 Mary Campbell 438
    440-441 Mary Lois 440 Mrs 441 Robert P
    440 Susan 440
SHIVELEY, Elizabeth 517 Leotie 604 Walter
    604 Willet 517
SHIVELY, Elizabeth 499 Henry 499 Mary J
    498 Sanford 499
SHOCKLEY, Georgia 616 Sanford 616
SHOLTZ, Frederick 96 113
SHOTWELL, A J 282
SHRADER, John 186
SHROY, John 373 Nancy 372-373 Rachel 373
SHUBLE, Columbia 715 Frances 715 Nathan
    715
SHUFFLEBARGER, Samuel 286
SHULL, Clara B 422 John 422
SHUTT, Lewis C 255
SHUTTS, G M 193
SIFRIT, Mary 429
SIMMONS, Miss 424
SIMMS, Cornelius 138
SIMPKINS, David 686 Oscar 686
SIMPSON, Hiram 297 Mazie 599
SIMS, Abbey 488 Abbie 515 Ada 641 Addie
    672 Adolphus 518 Alden J 488 Alfred 488
    513-518 Alva 641 Anna 517 565 Asbury
    280 294 487-488 514-515 565 Bonnie 641
    Charlotte 514 Clara 488 Clarence 488
    Cynthia Ann 514 Doras 641 Edward 488
    515 Effie 517 Eldena 518 Elizabeth 514-
    515 517 Emma 488 Enola 488 Firman C
    518 Francis 516 Harvey 517 641 Hiram
    488 515 James 517 Janet 518 John 514 516
    641 671 John A 487-488 Julia 641 Katura
    514-515 Katurak 488 Kitura 565 Laura A
    517-518 Laura Bernice 518 Lloyd 641
    Louisa 641 Luava 518 Madge 518 Malinda
    488 515 Margaret 517 611-612 Mary 488
    515-516 Mr 487-488 514 517-518 Mrs
    Asbury 514 Mrs John A 488 Mrs Starlin
    515 Mrs Zachariah 488 Nancy 488 515-516
    Nancy Jane 671 Nellie 641 Nicholas 514
    Noah 488 515 Patsy 514 Polly 488 Rosa
    516 Roscoe 488 Russell 488 Sallie 488
    Samuel K 518 Sara Cathleen 518 Sarah
    514-515 Sarah A 516 Sarah E 487-488 Seth
    D 518 Starlin 488 514-517 Starlin Jr 514
    Starlin Sr 514 Starling 167 611 Susan 488
    514 516 Susan Almira 518 Susannah 611
    Valda 488 William 514 516 Zachariah 487-
    488 514-515

SIMUEL, Shellie 229
SINCLAIR, James 176
SINGLETON, Bertha 598 Cordeli 356
 Cordelia 356 Delilah 597 Dennie 597
 George 356 Hulda 374 Hunley 597 James
 W 597 John V 597 Laura 597 Lucinda 597
 Lyda 356 Maude Glenn 597 Mr 596-598
 Mrs 598 Nancy 597 Nellie 597 Perry 597
 Thomas 597-598 Thomas C 112 596-598
 William 374 597
SINKS, Charles 69 Mr 70 Samuel 69
SINNOTT, John A 261
SIPES, Claude 661 Henry 229 Zula 661
SISCO, Amanda E 691 Mary 691 Mary Anna
 690 Perry 691
SKAGGS, Nancy 484-485 Wesley 210
SKAGS, Nancy 493
SKOMP, Albert 641 Charles 641 George 641
 Hannah Elizabeth 641 Jane 641 John 641
 Mary 641 Samuel 641
SLATER, W C 112
SLAUGHTER, Louvinia 607
SLAVE, Ann 138 Buck 138 David 138 Dish
 139 Henry 138 Isaac 138-139 Jake 138-139
 Judy 139 Mary 138 Peggy 138 Ralph 138
 Sam 138-140
SLAVEN, Nimrod 229
SLAVENS, Ida 610 Theodore 610
SLAYBACK, C S 260
SLETTENOGDEN, Columbia 715
SLICER, T A 114
SLIMP, 311 Edith Elizabeth 348 Elizabeth 641
 Elizabeth S 700 Lois 348 Oliver F 348
 Susannah 640 T D 189-190 Thomas D 114
 252 700 Thomas G 110 William 268
 William J 267
SLINKARD, Ida J 683 Margaret 641 Moses
 683 Rebecca 641 Sarah 683
SLOCUM, Gen 164
SLOVEN, Elizabeth 413
SMALL, Ann 328 525 Annetta B 524 Annette
 576 Annette B 576 Benjamin 328 525 575-
 576 Ella 525 577 Helen 328 525 576 Ida
 576 Jennie 525 John 328 525 John W 576
 Joseph 328 575-577 Joseph W 524-525 576
 Lucretia 328 525 576 Mary 328 525 575
 Mary Jane 576 Minnie 577 Mr 576-577
 Mrs 525 Naoma 576 Naomi 525 Nettie 525
 Nettie B 524 Reuben 328 525 576 Sarah
 525 576-577 Sarah E 328 Tabitha 328 575-
 576 Tabitha Ann 576 Tabitha C 525
 Theresa 576 Thomas 328 525 Thomas
 Jefferson 577 Thomas R 576 Virginia 328
 576 William 525 575-576 William H 328
 576
SMELSER, John C 166

SMELTZER, Anna Belle 229 Sarah 683
 William 286
SMILEY, A J 112 Abner 431 Abner G 430-431
 457-458 Ada 647 Addie 458 Andrew J 431
 Angeline 458 B D 292 Charles 431 Clara
 431 458 Curtis 458 Doctor 187 430-431
 Dove 458 Elizabeth 431 Emma 458 Esther
 431 Esther B 430 457 Eva 458 Flossy 229
 George 457 Harvey 431 Irwin 458 Jane 431
 John 292 Karl 431 Lafayette 431 Margaret
 553 Marguerite 431 Martha 431 Mary 458
 Mr 458 458-459 Mrs 459 Mrs R M 431
 Myrtle 458 Nancy 431 Paul 431 Payson
 458 Payson A 430 R M 187 430-432 R P
 458 Raleigh 458 Reisin P 430 Roland M
 256 430-431 Roy 432 Roy D 256 430-431
 Royland 458 Sarah 458 T J 112 Thomas J
 112 W S 457-458 W Seward 458 W T 167
 Wallace 430 458 William 431 Wilson S
 430 457-458
SMITH, 177 A W 227 Ada 704 Ainley 604
 Alma Lenora 435 Alphonsus 704 Alta 383
 Alvin 434 Anna 435 Augustine 704 Ballard
 249 Barbara 709 Beatrice 617 Blanche 462
 Catherine 461 551 Cecil 229 461 Cecil S
 461-462 Charles 435 Clara 435 Dan 654
 704 Daniel J 253 551 Deenva 435 Denva
 435 Duncan 180 182 Edda 435 Edward 330
 Edward B 433-434 Eleanor 704 Elisha 434
 Eliza 461 Eliza A 613-614 Elizabeth 435
 506 577 657 Emanuel 166 Ernistine 704
 Frances Granella 704 Francis 704 Frank
 435 Franklin 158 Fred 435 Frederick 704
 George 435 George W 92-93 Grace 704
 Green Clay 118 Gussie 435 Harry S 657
 Herbert 435 Howard 614 Ida I 461 Ira 434
 J V 298 James 461 Jane 435 Jennie 435
 Jessie 657 John 68-69 435 John A 704 John
 R 255 John T 703-705 John V 292 461-462
 Joseph B 111 Julius 168 Laura E 462 Laura
 Fay 462 Lavern 435 Leavitt 435 Leo 704
 Leon V 462 Lillian 704 Louis M 461
 Lovina T 435 Lydia 434 Mahala 435
 Margaret 438 461 703-704 Marguerette
 704 Martha 461 Mary 577 Mary Ann 434
 703 Mary J 462 Matthew 704 Mattie C 268
 Maud 435 Melvin 704 Minnie I 330
 Mortimer 434 Mr 434-435 461-462 657
 703 Mrs 435 657 704 Nancy B 461 Peter
 577 R D 109 Ralph E 462 Raphael 703
 Redmond R 462 S M 155-156 Samuel 104
 Samuel M 155 Samuel W 259 Sarah 551
 Sarah E 551 Sophronia 705 Theresa 704
 Thomas 435 Veronica 704 Walter 435
 William 68 148 614 704 William M 617
 William S 461 Z M 228

INDEX. 755

SMOCK, Sarah 684 Sarah Ann 684
SMOOT, D Brooks 255 William P 112
SMOTHERS, Mr 73 William 73
SMYDTH, Samuel Howe 249
SMYTH, Samuel H 113
SNELL, F 233
SNIDER, David 168 Franklin L 112 George W 173 266 Sarah 255
SNORE, Miss 709
SNYDER, Abraham 276 Elizabeth 711 Frederick 371 Louis 711 Rosanna D 371 Sally 711 Sevilla 371 W E 195
SOLOMON, Alanson 152-154 David 109 James 112 Stella 397 William 397
SOMMERS, Martha 229
SORIN, E 199 Father 199-201 Rev Father 200
SOURS, Sarah 401
SPALDING, Archbishop 451 Bernard L 367 Carl 367 Catherine 451 Ceda 450 Helen 367 John 214 L B 297 Maud 367 Nathaniel 196 Rose 450
SPARKS, Daniel S 158 Hannah 457 Mary E 353
SPAULDING, B L 291 George L 254 John B 111 Mary 581 Thomas 254
SPEAR, Anna 609 Hiram 609
SPEARS, Albert H 255 Alfred 166 Friend 69 141 300-301 John 435 Mary Ann 435 Rosetta 435 Sylvester 435
SPENCER, Elizabeth 566 Ella 566 Essie 630 Jennie 566 John G 567 John H 252 304 566-567 Louis 630 Mr 566-567 Sarah 566 Tillie 566 William M 566-567
SPINK, 195 J C 112 303 James 288 Philip A 234 T F 255
SPITZ, Estella 229 Irene 229
SPRAGGINS, Joshua 250
SPRINGER, William H 266
SPROATT, Catherine 461 Reason R 461
SPROUL, Victoria R 330 Walter 330
SROUT, Sarah 616
STACEY, Fred 319 May 319
STAFFORD, Jacob 69 John 69 Thrice 67 69 Trice 274
STALCUP, A R 285 297 Abraham 686 Amos 684 Elizabeth 684-685 Emmazilla 685 Frank 684 George A 685 Henry Elmore 686 Henry N 685 Henry S 684-685 Laura 685 Lycurgus 684 Lydia 686 Mr 685-686 Mrs 685-686 Mrs Stephen 684 Sarah 684 Sarah Ann 684 Sherman M 685 Sophia 685 Stella 686 Stephen 684-686
STALEY, Llewellyn B 254
STAMPER, Bertie 322 Elwood 322 John 322 Louise J 322 Ruth 322 William W 322 Willoughby 706

STANDIFORD, A L 462-463 Aquilla 463 Aquilla L 463-464 Bessie 464 Cornelius 463 Demia 463-464 Eliza 463 Elizabeth 463 Eugene 464 James 463 Katurah 463 Mamie 464 Martha 463 Mary 610 Meriton 610 Mr 463-464 Nathan 463 Omer 464 Pearl 464 Ruth 464 Sarah C 610 Tabitha 463 William 610 William C 463
STANDLEY, Ann 489 George 489 Lewis A 253 Malintha 489 Minnie 229 Nora 415
STANFORD, Mary J 708
STANLEY, I H 259 William 168
STANSBERRY, Deborah 343
STANSIL, Celia 190 Mr 191 William 190-191
STARR, James A 617 Justina F 617
STEELE, Ninien 184
STEEN, Benjamin W 218 J C 109 James 69 James R 109 426 John 69 Melinda 426 Richard 66 69 Samuel 69
STEFFY, J P 254
STELL, James 177
STEPHENS, Eliza Ann 452 John 210 Lewis 113 Robert 301
STEPHENSON, Alexander 67 69 B F 263 Doctor 263 Mr 142-143 Peter 140-142 546 Sarah 546 Stephen 546 Talitha 546
STERRITT, A 186
STEVENS, Alexander 69 James 157 John 112
STEVENSON, Miss 585
STEWART, Mary 681 T J 254
STICKLES, Sherman 229
STILLWATER, Sarah 422
STILLWELL, Anna 595 Charles 595 Gardener 595 Jacob 595-596 Jacob C 595 John 595 Julia 595 Mary 595 Mr 596 Perry 596 Richard 595 Sarah 595 Susannah T 596 Theodore A 596 Thomas 595
STIVERS, Everett 192
STONE, Barton W 192 Charles W 256 Elias 67 280 Elizabeth 504
STORM, Betsie Ann 650 Isaac 650 Lowery 650 Rebecca 650
STORMONT, David 140
STORMS, Julia 365
STOTT, John B 183
STOTTS, J W 240 John B 612 Nora 612
STOUT, Elizabeth 320 Ella 320 George W 158 Jennie 320 Job C 320 John 267 Mary 320 Mattie 320 Nettie 320 William 320
STOY, W L 292
STRANGE, Elizabeth 531 John Joseph 531 John M 210 John S 531 Lewis 531 Lucinda 531 Margaret 531 Martha 531 Matilda 531 Matilda J 531 658 Melinda E 531 Sarah 531 Susan 531 Thomas 531
STRASSER, B F 183 340 Benjamin F 337

STRASSER (Cont.)
  Virginia C 337
STRATTON-PORTER, 62
STRAUSS, Magdalena 254
STREET, James 300
STREETER, A J 119 Joseph S 266
STRICKLAND, Ella 643 William R 169
STRICKLER, Catherine 676
STRINGER, John 69 246
STROPES, Adam 659 Jeremiah 659 Laura 659 Sarah 659 Serinda 659 William 659
STROUSE, William H H 253
STUBBLEFIELD, J G 159 Joseph 194-195 M 227
STUCKEY, Carrie B 537 Charles L 536-537 Charles S 537 Deborah A 536 Donald J 537 Edward 537 Eliza Ellen 537 Elizabeth J 537 Elmer L 537 Elsworth 537 Elva P 537 Emma Grace 537 Frances C 537 George L 537 George P 536-537 Jacob A 537 Jessie 537 Lawson H 537 Lemmon 537 Leonard N 537 Mary B 537 Mr 537-538 Myrtle 537 Noah P 537 Permelia 536-537 Polly H 537 Ray 229 Russell D 537 Samuel Ray 537 Sarah A 536 Simon D 537 W L 220 William S 536-537 Willison L 537
STUCKY, Carrie Belle 590 John 144
STULL, Cora 711
STUREON, Martha 614
STURGEON, Abrigle M 607 Alford 607 Alford W 607 Frances L 607 Louvinia 607 Martha 607 Martha E 607 Mary L 607 Mary M 607 Paulina 324 Robert L 607 Sarah L 607
SUDDITH, Elizabeth 527 Mary 527 William 527
SULLIVAN, George R C 246 248 John 266 296 Mrs Hugh 268 Susan 558 William 160
SULSOR, Mahala 671 Michael 671
SUM, Alberdina 577 Aloysius 403 Elizabeth 403
SUMMERS, Charles 653 Harriet 268 Joseph 276 Margaret 653 Sarah 653 Sarepta 269 271
SUMMERVILLE, Isabel 335 Lola 649 Thomas 649
SUPLEE, Solomon 99
SUTHERLAND, David Campbell 592 Della May 593 Dorothy Belle 593 Ernest T 592 George 592 Harriette A 592-593 James P 592-593 Laura Levina 592 Lucy Jane 592 Margaret 592 Mary 592 Mr 592 Sarah Elizabeth 592 William 592 William Berton 593 William M 592-593
SUTTON, Ellen 573 R B 111 Rowland 114

SWALLOW, 120
SWANN, Cleo 505 Clifford 505 Cora Dell 505 Ellen 505 Ettie 505 Frank 505 Jane 504 Jesse 505 Joseph 504 Joseph M 504-505 Lewis 504 Mary 504 Mrs 505 Nelson 505 Sallie 505 Samuel 505 Silvester 504-505 Thomas 504 William 504-505
SWARTZ, Caroden L 254 John 666
SWAYZEE, Coy 698 James 698 Mary 698
SWEENEY, 86
SWICKARD, Alexander C 112
SWICKMOND, Alexander 621 Alice 621
SWIFT, Dean 681 Edgar James 228 Nancy 663 665 677
SWIM, Martha 463
SWINDA, Anna 709 Barbara 709 Catherine 709 Elizabeth 709 Ella 710 Ethel 710 Harmon 709 Henry 709 Jennie S 710 John 709 Mamie 709 Mollie 709 Mr 709-710 W H 709 William H 709-710
SWOPE, Ruth 322
SWORDS, Agnes 512 Joshua 512 Mary 512
SWYHART, Elizabeth 431
SYMMES, John Cleves 42
SYNDER, Elizabeth 712 Enoch 712 Moravia 712 William 712 Willis 712
TABB, Moses 250
TAFT, 375 President 373 William H 121 William Howard 120
TALBOTT, Estella 399
TALCOTT, E B 250
TANNER, Josiah 271
TARKINGTON, 62
TARR, Alfred M 571 Martha F 571
TATE, Terry 277
TAYLOR, 57 215 348 A 186 Agnes J 646 Almeda 646 Angeline 105 Ann 645 Anna 545 655 Blanche 545 Cemantha 105 Cyrus 105 Cyrus D 254 D H 297 David 297 Elizabeth 545 645-646 Elizabeth M 544 Elsie E 656 Erwin Bowman 656 Fred 545 Gamaliel 259 Gen 115 H 165 Harvey 114 165 253 297 Henrietta 544-545 Henry 108 645 649-650 655 660 Howard 444 J G 655 J P 267 J S 254 Jacob Frederick 544 James 197 James G 655-656 James P 267 645-647 James Russell 650 Jane 645 655 Jennie S 710 John 545 645-646 655 711 John Alvin 650 John F S 254 John Henry 655 John M 544-545 Joseph 276 Joseph M 66 Laura E 655 Leota E 646 Louis G 544-545 Louis Grant 544-545 Lucile 545 Lucinda 646 Lucine 650 Lydia 646 Mary Ann 646 Mary E 533 545 Mary Jane 660 Matthew S 645 Mattie 710 Michael 544 Minerva 711 Mr 544-545 645-647 655-656

INDEX. 757

TAYLOR (Cont.)
　Mrs 545 646-647 N H 106 Nancy 344 649
　Nancy B 655 Nancy M 655 Oliver 259 655
　Oliver A 655-656 Orpha E 646 Pearl 229
　545 Rebecca 444 655 Richard 545 Robert
　645 655 S 186 S H 305 Sam 180 Samuel
　645-646 655 710 Samuel A 655 Samuel C
　105 Samuel H 114 179 214 251 Samuel S
　655 Sarah E 649 655 Vine 655 Viola B 646
　Vivia E 646 W H 167 Waller 49 William
　545 655 William H 646 Zachary 73 115
　Zimri M 646
TEAZ, Elizabeth 592
TEEGARDEN, Matilda 318
TEMPLE, David J 162
TEMPLIN, Lucy 460
TENEY, Fannie T 417 John 417 Mary 417
TERHUNE, Sarah J 323 W D 323
TERRY, 177 E S 249 Elias S 113
THAIR, Rolina 648
THARP, C K 251 304 307 Robert W 252
THAYER, Marion N 255
THIAS, Bertha May 681 Bertie 681 Caroline
　680 Earl 681 Frederick 680 Mr 680-681
　Mrs 681 William 680-681
THOMAS, B M 250 Bettie 526 Charles 597
　Charles W 136 Daisy 418 David 589
　Delilah 597 E M 157 Emma J 542 Ephraim
　194-195 George A 255 Hannah S 188
　Harrison 418 Harry 418 Harry Jr 418 Jesse
　B 48-49 Jessie 418 John 417-419 542 589-
　590 John Sr 418 Julia S 537 589-590 Lucy
　418 Malina 374 Malina B 542 Martha A
　418 Mary 418 Mary Ada 418 Mattie 188
　Mr 417 419 Mrs 419 Mrs John 419 Nancy
　418 Peter 418 Sarah 418 Vina 542 589 W J
　254 William 418 597 William R 374 542
　William W 590 William Wright 537 589
THOMPSON, 62 Arthur D 606 Ephraim 102
　Emma 606 Ephraim 69 83 93 97 102 108
　139 248 G W 190 J 77 J E 303 J Earl 171
　252 James 79 John 65 69 111 141 Joseph G
　86 Margaret 606 Melissa 387 Mr 65 Rhoda
　400 Richard W 249 251 William 79 179
　William E 303
THOMSON, Amos D 490 Jessie H 490
　Lawrence D 490 Lovina L 490
THORNBURGH, J N 157 J W 157 John W
　157
TILBURN, E O 190 Jacob T 168
TILDEN, Samuel J 118
TILSTON, Gertie 268
TIPTON, William 240
TISDAL, James 156
TODD, Alice 690 Amanda E 691 Catherine
　690 David 690 Elijah 690

TODD (Cont.)
　Eliza 690 Elizabeth 689-690 Emily 690
　George F 689-691 Helen 691 Isaac 285 690
　John 689-690 L T 195 Mary 674 691 Mary
　Anna 690 Mr 689 691 Mrs 690 Nora O 691
　S Z 194 Sheridan 674 691
TOLAN, Brentwood 88
TOLBERT, John 187 Nancy 597 Rev 187
TOLIVER, Milton P 285
TOLLIVER, Henry C 256 Milton P 112 254
　William J 255
TOLSON, Benjamin 267 Benjamin J 173
TOMEY, Alma 407 Armistead 407 Caroline
　407 Della 407 Dollie 407 Dollie L 406
　Edith 406 697 Elias P 407 Elijah H 110
　Elizabeth 407 Frederick B 407 Ida K 406
　John 697 John J 406-407 Joseph A 407
　Lillian 406-407 Lillian A 407 Margaret M
　407 Martha 406-407 Martin 407 Mary E
　406-407 697 Mary J 407 Ortho 407 Oscar
　407 William A 407 William P 406-407
TOMLINSON, J 193
TOMMY, Dicey 391
TOMY, Jane 489 Malintha 489 Patrick 489
TOOLE, Grace 704
TOON, Susan 488
TORBECK, Father 204 Francis 513 Rev 204
TOWNSEND, Doctor 292 J 292 Melvina 584-
　585 Miss 506
TRAINOR, C E 255 Chauncey E 112
TRANSPER, Henry 610 Nora 610
TRANTER, John 67 William Sr 303
TRAUTER, Deborah A 342 William F 342
TRAYLOR, Jane 504 Permelia 536-537
TREED, Magdeline 700 Mary 700
TREMOR, J D 112
TREON, Laura 474
TRIMBLE, E C 186 218 222 Emma 234
TRIPPET, Margaret 316
TROTTER, Charles 700 Nellie B 700
TROWBRIDGE, 177
TRUEBLOOD, Arthur 650 Arthur H 173 Dove
　458 Eunice 439 Grace 651 H C 439 Harvey
　440 Hervey 316 Imogene 440 J C 254 Jesse
　218 Jesse A 494 Mark 458 Martha 494
　Mary J 651 May 650 Ralph H 651 Roger K
　650-651 Sarah 458
TRUELOVE, Celia 633 Hilary C 111 Vina 269
TRUSTY, A C 194 Mary A 617 Thomas 617
TUBBS, George Riley 255
TUCKER, H L 296
TUNING, Thomas 301
TURNER, Aaron 187 John M 259 N V 254 W
　S 113 William S 285
TURNEY, H A 194
TWITTY, J M 306 John M 306

TWOMEY, Austin A 634 Clara 634 Wilma 634
TYLER, John 114 W M 305
TYRE, Susannah 526
TYRON, Margaret 632
ULRICH, Ada 561 Adolph 561 Anna 561 Augusta 561 Bertha 561 Carl 561 Cora 561 Erustine 561 Fredricka 561 Henrietta 561 Louis 561 Maud 561 Mr 561 William 561 William E 560-561
UNDERWOOD, Corinne 392 Emma 253 Lola M 392 Lucile 392 Lucille 392 Marshall 392 Marshall K 392 W 254 Walter 187
UNVERSAW, Cecile 419
URQUHART, Alexander 186
USHER, Nathaniel P 250
UTTLEY, Elizabeth 562
VALENTINE, Ada 599 Noah 599 Sarah 599
VANBUREN, Martin 114-115
VANCAMP, Mr 300
VANCE, Campbell 636 Campbell A 635 Cora 636 Elizabeth 635 Emma I 636 Etta 636 Ezra J 636 George C 635 George Campbell 635 Harriet 635 Hattie 636 Isaac 635 J M 220-221 226 John 635 John M 636 Letta 635 Lydia 635 Martha 635 Mary J 636 Mattie J 636 Mr 635-636 O M 109 261 Oliver Mason 635-636 Oliver Mckinley 636 Perry W 636 Sarah 635 T 193
VANDERBURGH, Henry 46
VANDEVER, Amelia 458
VANMATRE, Joseph B 106 277
VANMETER, Hannah 459
VANNUYS, T B 255
VANOSDOL, Loree E 256
VANOVER, Elizabeth 679
VANTREES, Ann Eliza 394 C P 266 C R 161 169 Charity 533 Charles R 152 254 365 394 Col 365 Emanuel 66 83-84 93 97 99 103 110-111 185 233 246 299-301 365 Emma B 365 394 G L 95 H E 153 Harry 393 Harry P 112 Helen 321 394 Helen S 365 Henry 394 Henry E 153 365 John 85 106 110 150 179 250 258 322 365 393-394 John M 251 394 Julia 365 Laura 322 393-394 Laura G 365 Lida 365 Lydia G 394 Martha Glenn 394 Mr 393-395 Mrs 394-395 Mrs Thomas P 393 Samuel 102 Sarah Deane 393-394 T P 112 Thomas Jr 393 Thomas P 393-394 Warren 322 393-394 Warren Jr 394 William 394 William L 365
VARNUM, James Mitchell 42
VAUGHN, Darrell 661 Gladys 661 John 661 Rachael 682 Sarah 661
VEALE, Ada 506 Alonzo 506 Amanda 506 Anderson 92-93 586 Daniel 585

VEALE (Cont.)
Eleanor 584-586 Elizabeth 506 586 Ella 506 Elsie 585 Emily 585 George W 586 George W Jr 586 George W Sr 586 James 272 506 James A 585 James Aikman 507 James C 76 108 138 210 584 597 James C Jr 506 585 James C Sr 506 584-585 597 John M 585 John T 585 Julia 586 Katy 585 Laura 506 Mary M 586 Melvina 584-585 Mr 507 Mrs 506 Nancy 495 585 Nannie 586 Sallie 584 Sarah 586 Susan 506 Walter J 586 Walter Johnson 586 Watis 585 William 258 William T 585 William Thomas 506-507 Willis 506 Zadock 506 Zadock D 505-507
VEELE, James C 94 James Jr 94 William 94
VEST, A J 361 Olive 361
VICKERY, A L 297 William J 234
VIEHE, F W 305
VINCENT, Brother 200 Lawrence Brother 200
VIZE, Paul E 256
VOLLMER, H F 306
VORIES, Nettie 693
VOURMS, Catherine 574
WADE, Thomas 227
WADSWORTH, 220 Alonzo 493 Bloomer 485 Catherine 485 Clotie 476 David 493 Elizabeth Jane 484-485 Elsie 229 Emsley 485 Forest K 485 Forrest 229 Heilman Curtis 255 Hubert 485 J R 297 Jacob 493 James 485 John 111 485 493 685 Joseph 485 Laura 685 Lee 237 285 Lettie I 685 Margaret 485 492-493 Martha 485 Mary 485 493 Mr 484-485 Mrs 485 Nancy 484 493 Nathan S 493 Peter 485 493 Peter R 113 219 Peter Ragle 223 R W 237 Rhoda 493 Robert 493 Roscoe C 685 S A 161 Sarah J 485 Silas 485 Susan 493 Thomas 167 267 484-485 493 Thomas G 484-486 Thomas Jr 484 William 485
WAGGONER, W Winston 255
WAGLEY, Pierson 158
WAGONER, Fay E 268
WAGY, W H 380
WAKEFIELD, Mrs 312 Mrs J M 312
WALDREN, W P 189
WALKER, Anna 455 B F 160 Catherine 455 Charles 387 E W T 166 Ella 387 F M 218 227 242 Frank 199 G W 253 Ignatius 454 Isabella 455 J W 387 James Henry 255 Jennie 455 John 246 Joseph D 454 Joseph E 455 Lewis 455 Margaret 454-455 Martha 618 Mollie Ann 455 Mr 454-455 Oliver 291 454-455 R 106 Robert S 160 Thomas R 262 Wallace 259 William 387 Zachariah 113

INDEX. 759

WALL, Charles T 255 Mary 343 Rev 185-186
WALLACE, 62 D C 160 David 58 Elsie 585
 Gov 123 J P 160 John 66 69 271 299 Josiah
 69 Matilda 586 Mr 585 Nicholas F 160
 Superintendent 224 Thomas 272 W A 226
 Walter 261 Wesley 69 Widow 69 William
 108 113 113 299 William A 110 219-220
 William Alfred 223 William T 89
WALLER, Adda 387 Anna E 344 Charles 387
 Edith 268 387 Edward 386 Edward F 344
 Elizabeth 386 468 Ella 387 George 188 344
 386 George A 85 111 258 George Allen
 105 Hannah 386 Ione 387 Isabell 387
 James 344 387 Jane 386 John 271 344 386
 John M 112 344 John W 111 385-387 John
 W Sr 386 Louis 584 Lucretia 344 Margaret
 344 Mary 271 344 387 Mary A 344 Mary
 Ann 385 Mary E 313 Mary G 386 Melissa
 387 Mr 386-387 Mrs 387 Nancy Mary 386
 Nellie 386 Odell 387 Patsey 386 Richard
 344 Ruth 344 W S 155 171 William H 266
 William S 173 259 344 385-387
WALLICK, Ada G 649 662 Ella 649 Gleason
 650 Harvey 649 Henry 649 Jen 649
 Josephine 649 Larinda 650 Lauranda 650
 Lola 649 Michael 267 373 649 Mr 648-649
 651 Mrs 650-651 Nancy Jane 649 Neva
 650 Oscar 650 Oscar M 648-650 Rachael
 649 Rachel 373 Ray 649 Sarah 649 Sarah E
 649 Susie 649 William H 649
WALLS, Alice 621 Belle 621 Cony 621 Elvira
 621 F M 621 George B 621 Jennie C 682
 John 187 John W 620-621 Lena 621 Lou
 621 Mary Ann 620-621 Mr 621 Mrs 621
 Sarah 621 William 620 William B 253 296
 William Barnett 620-621
WALSH, 252 J M 251 Thomas P 262
WALTER, Henry 136 303 William P 306
WALTERS, G W 161 George 110 Reuben 140
WARD, Claude 229 Cora B 372 Cyril J 262
 Dolly 371 Francis A 111 Jeannette 229
 Maggie 698 Margaret 372 Philip S 372
 Sina 254 Viola 372 William 297
WARNER, Elizabeth 420 Joseph 89 250 258
 300 Robert 154 W 349
WARNOCK, James 246
WARREN, Joseph 258 O L 228
WASHINGTON, George 38 271 John 405
 Sabina Ann 254
WATERS, J 69
WATHAM, Emery 653 Nellie 653
WATHAN, Anna 522 Celia 522 Mary 522
 Raphael 522 Rose 522 Sarah K 522
 Thomas 522
WATHEN, Harriett 450 Mrs Raphael 243
WATSON, 120 Alson 447 Isaac 166

WATSON (Cont.)
 James S 446 Laura 447 Lyle 447 Maude J
 446 Pearl 447 Rex 447
WATT, Mr 493
WATTS, Elizabeth 335 John S 249 Joseph H
 335 William 297
WAY, John W 255
WAYMAN, Julia 391
WAYNE, Anthony 34 41 Gen 42
WEATHERS, Lulu 698 Martha A 418 Richard
 418
WEAVER, Abraham 669 675-676 687 Alvin
 688 Catherine S 669 676 Charlotta 675 687
 Charlotte 669 Christina 669 676 Daniel 687
 David 687-688 Effie H 676 698 Elva 688
 Fannie 669 675 Fanny 676 George 688
 Gertrude 688 Grandfather 687 Imo 688
 Jacob 669 675-676 687 Jacob C 669 675-
 676 Jacob Christopher 698 James B 118-
 119 John D 688 John W 686-688 Jonathan
 194 Levi 669 Levi W 668-670 676 Lovina
 687-688 Mary 339 Mary A 416 Mr 668-
 670 676-677 686-689 Mrs 688 Peter 687
 Phoebe 687 Richard 301 Robert Donovan
 669 Susannah 687 William 687 Willis 688
WEBBER, Alfred 268 Elsie 427 Helen 427
 Millard 427 Reba L 427
WEBER, Delight 233 John 158
WEBSTER, James 298 Taylor W 259 William
 277
WECHSLER, H 255
WEDDELL, Benjamin 399 Claybourn 399
 Columbus 399 David 399 Dora 399 Ella
 399 Gabriel 399 Gabriel L 399 Hamilton
 399 Jasper 399 John A 399 Lavina 399
 Maria 399 Martha 399 Mary 399 Mirand E
 399 Miranda E 399 Nancy 399 Newton 399
 Rebecca A 399 Sarah 399 Sheridan 399
 Sherman 399 Stephen 399 Warren 399
 Willis 399
WEDDING, John R 109
WEIMER, D L 297 Lawrence 297
WEIS, D K 250
WELCH, Frank M 256 W H H 256
WELLS, Anna Donita 203 Charles F 104 245 J
 B 255 L 227 W E 160 W H 108-109
WESMILLAN, Jane 641
WESNER, Jacob 700 Mary Ann 700
WEST, Carl R 256 Elizabeth 425
WESTHAFER, A P 229 J S 226 237 J Sherman
 237 Joseph R 555 Lottie 229 Lottie A 555
WESTMAN, Addie L 698 George 698
WEY, 172 Minnie 428 Ray 428
WHALLON, John 258
WHARTON, Laura E 440 W G 440

WHAYNE, Alice 398 Eunice 398 Lucile 398 Nathan 398 Nettie 398
WHEELER, Huldah 444 Laura 444 444 Lemuel 444 Marion 444 Nancy 444 Samuel 444 William 195
WHIPPLE, Bishop 479 495
WHISMAN, Carrie B 327 Ella 327 George 325-326 Harondon L 326 Harry 327 Joseph 327 Lettie 325 Lucy 327 Mary 327 Mr 325-327 Nellie 327 Nicey 326 Oma 327 Richard 327 Sylvester A 325-326 William 327 William G 326
WHITCOMB, Gov 55 James 58
WHITE, Albert S 250-251 Bert 229 Catherine S 669-670 676 Charles L 229 Elizabeth 627 Emma L 670 Essie 630 Flora V 670 Florian 631 Florian B 629-630 Garett 670 Garett W 670 George A F J 254 Gilbert 629-631 Jacob 426 James M 669-670 John 629-630 Joseph 627 Julia Ann 426 Lillian 670 Lydia 630 Martha 670 Martha Jane 630 Mary 569 Mary E 627 Mary Emaline 630 Mary J 669-670 Mr 629-630 Mrs 400 Myrtle 631 Nancy 629-630 Nellie 630 Nora 631 Phoebe 631 Quill 90 Ray 631 Ruth 358-359 380 Sarah 380 Susan 367 631 Thomas 359 380 Walter 229 William 69 William T 670 Zilphea 630
WHITED, T S 187
WHITEHEAD, 86 106 James 85 88 105 258
WHITELEY, Martin 616 Mary A 616
WHITMAN, Jasper 285
WHITNEY, Joseph 247
WHITTEMORE, Franklin J 254
WHITTEN, A M 304 Doctor 304
WHITTON, Doctor 586 Elizabeth 586
WICHMAN, Angela 402-403 Anton 402 Anton Jr 402-403 Catherine 402-403 Elizabeth 402-403 716 Henry 403 John 402-403 Joseph 402-403 716 Mary 402-403 Mr 403 Rosie 402-403
WIDNER, Elias F 182 Mr 182
WIER, Frank P 667 Sarah J 667
WIGGINS, Q K Juniper 179
WIGMORE, Capt 161
WILCOX, Lt Col 74
WILDER, Col 424 Gen 424
WILEY, Michael 300
WILHITE, F 111
WILKERSON, Bertie 681 Mary 681 Nettie 681 Shirley 681 Thomas 681 William 681
WILKINS, 299 James 178 Peter 83 93 185 246 300
WILLARD, A P 249 Ashbel P 58
WILLEFORD, George W 253 Ralph M 255 W C 253 William C 254 297

WILLEMAN, Hiram 580 Margaret 580 Sarah Jane 579
WILLEY, Bertha 547 Carrie 547 Charles 546 546 Cora 547 Hosea 546 Jane 546-547 John R 547 Joseph 545-547 547 Mary Alice 547 Mr 546-547 Mrs 547 Sarah 256 547 Talitha 546-547
WILLIAM, Elizabeth 271
WILLIAMS, A G 112 Aaron 515 Ada 478 Ada J 707-708 Ada Jane 478 Ada Palmer 459 Adolphus G 459-461 476 Alfred 478 Alma 460 Andrew 448 Angeline 476 Ann 528 Anna 448 459 528 651-652 Anna Mary 529 Anza M 460 Archibald 246 478 Augusta Bradfoot 459 Bert 460 Bertha 460 Billy 275-276 Bridget Louisa 529 Callie 459 Carl 563 Cassie 529 Charles 241 459 Charles C 562 Clarence Lee 459 Debby 478 Edna 460 Effie 517 Eliza 478 Eliza J 708 Elizabeth 392 527-528 660 Elwood 510 Emma 327 Emmeline 527 Ephraim 422 Ernest 529 Eugene 459 F A 436 Fenton B 238 Flora 698 Floy 650 Frances Helen 529 Frances L 562 Francis 280 Fred 650 Gertrude 510 H 227 Hannah 459 Henrietta 459 Hiram 1 237 Howard 226-227 233 286 Ira 448 Isabella 459 James 193 424 478 James D 58 113 James R 187 James T 327 Janie 459 John 459 478 528 562 John B 267 650 John J 158 John Leo 529 John Robert 527-528 John W 528-529 John Willis 527-528 Joseph 193 460 478 708 Josephine 460 Lemoa Anna 579 Lewis 478 708 Lewis Vitus 529 Louisa 459 Louisanna 634 Louisianna 579 Lucy 460 Lula 460 Lulu 436 Martha 478 562 Mary 460 478 Mary Anna 392 Mary C 424 Matilda 478 708 Maud 460 476 Miss 501 Missouri 459 Mr 460 527-529 562-563 Mrs 460 Mrs Adolphus G 460 Mrs William H 563 Nettie May 422 Oma 327 Palmer 650 Pearlie 459 Presley 478 Rachel 193 478 708 Richard 460 Richard M 276 Rosa 708 Rosetta 650 Rosie 478 Sarah 404 478 500-501 515 634 Sarah Ann 459 Solomon 112 166 459 634 Stephen 478 708 Stephen H 160 Thomas 651 Vincent 392 W J 305 Walter 460 William 67 275 478 527 William H 562-563 Z T 404
WILLIAMSON, Elizabeth 383 Margaret 652 William 652
WILLIS, Purnell C 254
WILSON, Andrew J 429-430 Andrew Jackson 637 Angeline 637 Anna 350 Clarinda 240 Cordelia 475-476 Cordella 352 David Mcdonald 188 Decie 637 Dicy 391

INDEX.

WILSON (Cont.)
  Edward 604 Eleanor 429 Elizabeth 506
  Emily Jane 637 Flora J 429 George 271
  352 George W 109 Jacob Michael 637
  James 430 James H 189 596 637 James
  William 637 Jennie M 608 John 352 Joseph
  110 180 304 637 Katharine 243 Katherine
  229 Keziah 352 475 L 227 Lillie 509 M A
  608 M H 352 Martha Samantha 637 Mary
  430 637 Milton H 637 Mrs David
  Mcdonald 188 Nellie L 637 S G 506 S L
  256 Susan Tabitha 637 Susan V 506
  Susannah 596 Susannah Q 637 Susannah T
  596 Thomas Theodore 637 W H 158
  Walter J 256 William 350 352 William A
  475-476 William H 154 Woodrow 121
WILTSMAN, James 193
WILZ, Anna 716
WINGFIELD, Sarah 524
WINKELPLECK, Flossie 292 J M 292
WINKLEPLACK, Bernice 684 Clifford J 684
  Edwin 684 Lestie 684
WINKLEPLECK, E O 229 Florence 664 Harry
  229 J 227 Jonas M 664 Myrtle 286 Roland
  D 237
WINN, William 169
WINSTON, Dorothy 229 John L 321 Laura G
  321
WINTERBOTTOM, Jesse 112 Maud L 376
WINTON, Charles Franklin 254
WIRT, Rebecca 234
WIRTS, John B 168 William 266 William F
  167
WISE, A C 226 261 305 Alanson C 220 Alfred
  397 Della 397 Edward 218 221 234 Frank
  266 Henry 397 John 397 Lewis 166
  Lucinda 397 Mary Ann 397 Osa 397 Osee
  397 Weston 227 William 397
WITSETT, A H 571 Ada P 571
WITSMAN, Anna 404 Clara 404 Goldie 404
  James 403-405 James M 404 James Oliver
  404 Lewis Norvell 404 Morris Trimble 404
  Mr 404-405 Mrs 404 Oliver 404 Owen
  Homer 404 Rachel 404 Sadie Pearl 404
  Sarah Jane 404 Walter Ann 404 Walter
  Lyle 404 William H 404
WITTLES, Laura 679
WIZARD, William 297
WOLF, George I 378 Hamilton 254 Mehitable
  378
WOLFORD, 576
WOOD, Edith 229 236 James B 107 John 186
  Lucretia 270 401 Mary J 669 Melina Opha
  590 Miles 286
WOODLING, Amos 471 Andrew 470-471
  Andrew A 471 Andrew Jr 470-471

WOODLING (Cont.)
  Andrew Sr 470 Bernard 471 Calvin 472
  Catherine 470-471 Daniel 471 Edgar Evans
  471 Emma 471 Flora May 471 Frank 471
  Frank Haman 471 Haman 114 173 470-472
  Julia Ann 471 Mable 471 Mary B 471
  Mary Jane 471 May 471 Mr 471-472
  Norman 471 Rachel 471 Rachel Minerva
  471 Ray 471 Simon P 471 Simon Peter 471
  Viola 471 William Oscar 471
WOODRUFF, Aaron 678 Anna 515 Caswell
  696 Eliza 696 Leonard 696 Lilburn 650
  Lovida M 696 Malinda 650 Minnie 664
  Minnie Mara 678 Nancy A 678
WOODY, Catherine 551
WOOLRIDGE, John 65 67 Professor 66
WOOLLEY, John G 120
WORRELL, Jesse 164
WORST, James 705 Sophronia 705
WRAPE, Ann 471 Catherine 471 Henry 471
  Henry Sr 471 John 471 Robert 471
WRIGHT, Ann 706 Claude 711 E R 376 Elva
  Myrtle 376 Glendora 705 J C 298 Jacob
  189 John 706 Joseph 706 Joseph A 58
  Laura S 706 Marion 706 Mary 229 236
  Nancy 706 Primmellar 537 Roderick 706 S
  D 303 Sallie A 706 Sarah 706 Stephen D
  109 W C W 705 William C W 706
WYKOFF, Charity 695-696 James 171 James
  W 173 Rachel 337
YEAGER, E J 260
YENNE, Anna 424 Catherine 424 Charles 424
  Charles H 255 259 424 Charles Henry 423-
  426 Claudia M 425 Doctor 424-426 Dora
  425 Edna 425 Eli P 424-425 Elizabeth 424
  George 424 Harlan S 425 Henry 424 John
  George 424 John Oliver 425 John W 424
  Joseph 424 Joseph A 424 Leah 425 Madge
  229 236 Madge Janet 425 Mary C 424
  Mary E 425 May 425 Mr 424 Mrs 425-426
  Myrtle 425 Ralph 425 Ralph V 425 Robert
  425 Sabina 424 Samuel P 424 Sarah 424
  Sarah Elizabeth 425 Sarah J 424 Sheldon
  425 Susan 424
YOND, Catherine 485
YORK, Almeda 646 Dora 229 Elmer 229 John
  P 646
YOUNG, Charles C 255 Emma 431 Georgia
  616 Jeremiah 177 Luke 229 M H 255 Mary
  403 Melvin H 255 W M 306 William 226
  William L 254
YOUNT, Peter 287
YUELL, Claris 193
ZIMMERMAN, Ernest 229
ZINKAN, Jacob 203
ZINKANS, Francis 109

www.ingramcontent.com/pod-product-compliance
Lightning Source LLC
Chambersburg PA
CBHW071212290426
44108CB00013B/1163